W9-AWZ-563

The AMERICAN POLITY

THE PEOPLE

AND THEIR GOVERNMENT

FIFTH EDITION

The

AMERICAN POLITY

THE PEOPLE

AND THEIR GOVERNMENT

FIFTH EDITION

Everett Carll Ladd

UNIVERSITY OF CONNECTICUT

THE ROPER CENTER FOR PUBLIC OPINION RESEARCH

W · W · NORTON & COMPANY · *New York London*

Copyright © 1993, 1991, 1989, 1987, 1985 by W. W. Norton & Company, Inc.

All rights reserved.

Printed in the United States of America.

Cover photograph by Hiroji Kubota/courtesy of Magnum Photos, Inc.

Acknowledgments and copyrights appear on pages B17–B18, which constitute an extension of the copyright page.

The text of this book is composed in Linotype Walbaum,
with the display set in Egmont Medium and Liberty.
Composition by The Maple-Vail Book Manufacturing Group.
Manufacturing by Courier/Westford.
Book design by Antonina Krass

Library of Congress Cataloging-in-Publication Data
Ladd, Everett Carll.
The American polity : the people and their government / Everett
Carll Ladd.—5th ed.
p.   cm.
Includes bibliographical references and index.
1. United States—Politics and government.   I. Title.
JK274.L23   1993
320.973—dc20   92-40519

ISBN 0-393-96351-9
W. W. Norton & Company, Inc., 500 Fifth Avenue, New York, N.Y. 10110
W. W. Norton & Company Ltd., 10 Coptic Street, London WC1A 1PU

2 3 4 5 6 7 8 9 0

For Ryan

The childhood shews the man,
As morning shews the day. . . .
—JOHN MILTON
Paradise Regained

CONTENTS

PART 2   THE POLITICAL IDEAS

PART 3   GOVERNANCE

PART 4 PARTICIPATION

PART 5 PUBLIC POLICY

CASES IN CONTEXT

PREFACE

Writing a text on American government, and then revising it every two years for new editions, provides about as good a crash course on the scope and pace of political change as anyone could ever get. While I was working on the fourth edition of *The American Polity* two years ago, for example, the world was in the midst of a great surge of revolutionary change—change that brought political independence and far greater freedom to the peoples of eastern Europe, that culminated in the collapse of Soviet communism and of the Soviet Union itself, and that left the United States to operate in a transformed international environment.

This past year, as I completed revisions for the fifth edition, the attention of Americans had shifted; it had turned inward to our domestic problems, especially those involving the economy. Great changes were still occurring internationally: The civil war in the once-united Yugoslavia was taking a terrible human toll; a number of African nations, among them Zaire, Angola, and Somalia, were suffering from oppression, civil war, and starvation; the immense task of transforming Russia and the other countries of the former Soviet Union was only at its beginning, and the outcome remained very much in doubt. The United States itself was grappling with a host of new international challenges, including those of an increasingly interdependent global economy.

Nonetheless, many Americans were preoccupied with domestic problems throughout 1992. The presidential contest—which became a three way affair, with President George Bush challenged by Democrat Bill Clinton and by independent H. Ross Perot as well—was dominated by the widespread demand for action to strengthen the U.S. economy. The Clinton victory on November 3, 1992, owed much to this sense that it was "time for a change."

CHANGES IN THE FIFTH EDITION

As I have with each of the four previous editions, I have revised the text extensively throughout. As always, the charts and tables now include the most recent data, and new and more timely case studies replace earlier, now less relevant ones. But the biggest change made in the fifth edition reflects the desire of American government instructors for a briefer textbook. Toward this end, I have reduced the number of chapters from eighteen to sixteen and the overall page length to just over 500 pages, down from nearly 600 pages. This was achieved by what are, I believe, judicious deletions throughout the book and through a complete reworking to consolidate four chapters into just two. In place of the fourth edition chapters on "Voting and Elections" and on "Political Parties," there is a single fifth edition chapter entitled "Political Parties and Elections." The change is far from cosmetic: The new chapter is entirely revised, focusing now on the more stable and enduring features of the system of American parties and elections—rather than on the most recent presidential campaign and election outcome, which is treated instead in the new appendix chapter (see below).

Similarly, I have recast the fourth edition chapters "Political Economy" and "Public Welfare" into a new chapter entitled "The Economy and Public Welfare," which provides all the essential information more succinctly. The consolidation of these chapters is based on the premise that developments in the U.S. economy—including rates of growth, employment, unemployment, and the like—bear directly on the country's capacity to fashion policy that fosters the welfare of all its citizens.

Among the larger changes in this fifth edition of *The American Polity*, the last chapter on U.S. foreign policy has been extensively revised, reflecting the exceptional upheaval in this area. It's new title, "America in the World," reflects the essential fact of post–cold war global interdependence.

With all of these deletions and condensings, I allowed myself one addition—an appendix chapter entitled "The 1992 Election and the Clinton Administration." I am now at work on it, even as the instructor's version of the book goes to press. In it, I plan to follow the 1992 campaign from its earliest stages to its final outcome, analyzing various data on the electorate's decision, examining changes in the parties' appeals and in the make-up of their coalitions, and assessing the extraordinary innovations that are taking place in our campaign and election processes. I will also look at the new Clinton administration, especially the shifts in the direction of policy it is likely to bring about. [Publisher's Note: Instructors will receive this new chapter as a pamphlet in March 1993; students using the text in fall 1993 will have this new chapter bound into their books.]

APPROACHING THE STUDY OF AMERICAN GOVERNMENT

Like its predecessors, the fifth edition of *The American Polity* responds to the problems, events, and acts of political leaders, and the demands and judgments of the people that make America's political parade march along so rapidly, in such fascinating rhythm. But students need more than fresh, up-to-date information on our government and politics; they need to see how all the parts of our system fit together, how and why it works as it does. What hasn't changed over the five editions of this text is my basic approach to giving students the depth of understanding they must have of the fundamental properties of the American system. This depth is achieved by providing as backdrops three different perspectives: cross national, societal, and historical.

Cross-national Perspective. We are more attentive now to political change around the world, given the magnitude of the change since the collapse of the Soviet Union. Still, *The American Polity* has always applied a cross-national comparative perspective. Some of the responses the United States has given to enduring problems of policy and governance closely resemble those made by Great Britain, France, Germany, and other major industrial democracies. But the American system also reflects its own distinctive institutional arrangements and policy choices. By providing cross-national comparison throughout, I have tried to present our own system in a rounder, more complete, and more accurate way.

Societal Perspective. Social science has carved up the study of social experience into discrete segments, divided among disciplines like political science, economics, and sociology. This is unavoidable, but society is not so compartmentalized. Those parts of American society that we label "government" influence and in turn are influenced by all the other parts—components involving the economy; systems of social and cultural values; education and technology; the ethnic, racial, and religious composition of the population; and many others. The first sec-

tion of the text looks closely at aspects of American society that are especially important in defining the environment for the country's government, politics, and public policy. In the remaining chapters I keep returning to the many concrete links between the polity and the larger society of which it is a part.

Historical Perspective. With so much to discuss about the practice of American government today, the influence of the past can easily be shortchanged. Historical perspective is essential, for two somewhat different reasons. First, contemporary institutions and practices did not suddenly emerge full grown. We understand them better—whether it is the presidency, political parties, or welfare policy—by seeing the course they have taken. To ignore the past is to deprive ourselves of an immense amount of comparative experience.

Second, there have been powerful continuities in American political experience. With the drafting of the U.S. Constitution in 1787 and its ratification a year later, a set of political institutions consistent with the country's political beliefs was put in place (see chapters 3 and 4). The persistence of the primary political institutions—the Constitution, the presidency, Congress, the judiciary, the sharing of power by the federal and state governments—over the last two centuries is an extraordinary feature of American political experience. In the text I frequently draw examples from earlier eras in American life to make more concrete the fact that important continuities are everywhere evident in our political system, even in the face of great social and economic change.

THE PLAN OF THE BOOK

As we have seen, the fifth edition contains many changes, but the basic organization of the book remains intact. The first two parts of

The American Polity survey the setting for American political life. Part 1 examines the social setting, including the country's social origins and development, present-day economic trends, and such diverse social attributes of the populace as their ethnic backgrounds and educational attainments. Part 2 looks at the central beliefs and values of Americans: the country's ideological tradition, derived from classical liberalism; and the expression of this ideology in the basic law, the Constitution.

We move in Part 3 to a detailed consideration of the principal governmental institutions. Part 3 now opens with a chapter on America's unique type of democratic governance built around separation of powers, checks and balances, and federalism. We then look closely, in the four succeeding chapters, at the Congress, the presidency, the executive branch, and the federal courts.

From the organization of government in Part 3 we turn in Part 4 to public opinion, interest groups, political parties and elections, and the communications media—the means by which groups participate in politics and government. For political participation does not occur in a vacuum, but in and through the setting that governmental institutions establish. The American system of dispersed power, accruing from separation of powers and federalism, gives interest groups many diverse points of governmental access through which to advance their goals.

Part 5, the last section of the text, is devoted to American public policy in three major sectors: civil liberties and civil rights, the political economy and public welfare, and global policy. Like every other political system, the American polity ultimately expresses itself in the character of the policy choices it makes.

I call this text *The American Polity*. With the same Greek root as the word politics, polity is a more succinct way of saying "political system," and the two expressions are used inter-changeably throughout this book. But there are reasons beyond stylistic convenience for calling this an inquiry into the American polity. The greatest writer on politics in all of antiquity, and one of the most profound theorists of all time, was the Athenian philosopher Aristotle (384–322 B.C.). The first to write systematically on democracy as a system of government, Aristotle distinguished between two basic forms of democracy: One involved direct rule by the people, which he thought carried with it great threats to personal liberty and minority rights; the other was based on constitutionalism and the guarantee of individual rights, which he thought held promise of being the best of all government. Aristotle called the latter πολιτεια, or *politeia*, translated as "polity" or "constitutional government."[1]

The American system of government is a polity in Aristotle's sense of the term: a particular type of democracy established on the principles of constitutionalism and representation, with safeguards for minority rights. It deserves to be studied as a whole, as something more than a collection of separate institutions and processes. It is in the meshing of diverse political activities and the interplay of people and their government that we most clearly see what is distinctive about our polity.

THE LADD REPORTS

Daily newspapers like the *New York Times*, the *Los Angeles Times*, and the *Christian Science Monitor*, the broadcast networks, and weekly magazines of governmental affairs such as *Congressional Quarterly* and *National Journal* help us follow the ever-changing course of political events. But the perspective of a politi-

---

[1] *The Politics of Aristotle*, H. Rackham, trans. (Cambridge, Mass.: Harvard University Press, 1977), pp. 206–7.

cal science text, going beyond the headlines and analyzing the dynamics of American society and government, is also important. So for the fifth edition I will continue to write *The Ladd Reports,* and the publisher will continue to make *The Ladd Reports* available without charge to all students by request of instructors who are using *The American Polity* in their classrooms.

CASES AND STUDY GUIDE, THE INSTRUCTOR'S MANUAL, AND THE TEST-ITEM FILE

The *Cases and Study Guide,* prepared by Ann G. Serow (Kingswood-Oxford School), is really two books in one. First, the "Cases" section is a collection of brief readings, each of them selected to accompany a chapter in the text. These readings or cases offer students an inside look at America's political institutions and people. The cases range from glimpses into the young lives of leaders like Thomas Jefferson, Bill Clinton, and Jesse Jackson, to the behind-the-scenes politicking of Lyndon Johnson, Ann Richards, and Dianne Feinstein. Other cases highlight downwardly mobile American families, the homeless in New York City, and Washington, D.C., janitors fighting for better pay. Students will discover what it's like to be a "Hill rat" for Congress and how Alaska's teleconferencing network brings democracy to its citizens. Throughout the cases, there are cartoons ("Critic's Corners") that use humor to focus attention on enduring political issues. All the readings and cartoons are followed by questions for class discussion.

The "Study Guide" portion of the *Cases and Study Guide* is for use by students who seek a firm grasp of the textbook. Each chapter takes students through the book, pointing out key ideas, explaining difficult concepts, and clarifying broad themes. No two chapters use the same format in presenting the material, so students do not get bored by a repetitive approach. At the end of each chapter, students can test their command of the material with multiple-choice, true-false, and essay questions.

The *Instructor's Manual* and *Test-Item File,* now two separate books, have once again been thoroughly revised to reflect the many changes in my text, as well as to guide instructors in choosing new audio/visual and computer-simulation materials. The *Test-Item File,* prepared by Ann Serow, is virtually brand new. It is available in booklet form and on diskette.

THE AMERICAN POLITY READER

Published in 1993, *The American Polity Reader,* Second Edition, is a valuable supplement to my text. Edited by my colleagues Ann Serow and W. Wayne Shannon, and myself, the *Reader* includes 106 selections, carefully edited for the student from key works on American government and politics, together with introductory essays on each group of readings.

ACKNOWLEDGMENTS

Like its predecessor, the fifth edition of *The American Polity* benefited from use by teachers and students at numerous universities, colleges, and community colleges—a broad and representative proving ground for a basic American government text. I particularly thank Ryan J. Barilleaux of Miami University (Ohio) for his thoughts on shortening the text, as well as Cliff Hirst of Temple University and Pamela

Rendeiro of Southern Connecticut State University for their comments. Fellow teachers of introductory American government classes who have used *The American Polity* have provided me with helpful suggestions that I have done my best to follow. My own classes of Political Science 173 at the University of Connecticut have continued to be a wonderful source for what works and what doesn't work, in introducing students to American government and politics.

I also want to add a special note of thanks to Ann Serow for her fine work on the *Cases and Study Guide* and the all new *Test-Item File*.

Burns W. Roper, chairman of the Roper Organization, and Richard J. Cattani, editor of the *Christian Science Monitor*, have been sources of guidance and inspiration in a great many personal and professional regards. The friendship and counsel of Karlyn H. Keene, the editor of *The American Enterprise* (and before that, of *Public Opinion* magazine) means more to me than I can ever express.

My colleagues at the University of Connecticut have been kind, helpful, and forbearing. Special thanks are due my Roper Center colleagues: Donald Ferree, Wayne Shannon, Ronald Milavsky, John Barry, Anne-Marie Mercure, John Benson, Lois Timms-Ferrara, and Marc Maynard.

Marianne Simonoff, my research assistant since 1982, has again made major contributions to the revision. I am delighted to be able to acknowledge once more the unique contribution of Lynn A. Zayachkiwsky, my administrative assistant at the Institute for Social Inquiry

and the Roper Center since 1982. I know of no one able to handle such diverse responsibilities as well. She has kept our many projects, of which this text is but one, on track.

Donald S. Lamm, president of W. W. Norton, has been a valued friend, editor, and all-purpose advisor since I first met him over twenty-five years ago. He has given strong support and guidance to all of my books for Norton, none more so than *The American Polity*. Donald Fusting has been the editor of *The American Polity* throughout its five editions. Working with him has been a great pleasure; I am privileged to have a fine editor who is also a good friend. Manuscript editor Jane Carter, new to this edition, brought fresh eyes and intelligence to a manuscript, which is now greatly improved by her efforts. With the completed manuscript, an elegant design by Antonina Krass, judiciously selected photos by Bonnie Hall, and layouts by Roberta Flechner, production editor Ruth Dworkin produced with efficiency and speed this fifth edition. Working with the Norton team continues to be a delight.

First things last: *The American Polity* is dedicated to the memory of my father, Everett C. Ladd, Sr., and of my mother, Agnes Macmillan Ladd; to my wife Cynthia and our children Benjamin, Melissa, Corina, and Carll; to Melissa's husband Paul Edward Teed; to Carll's wife, Elizabeth Lovejoy Ladd, and their son, Ryan Carll.

E.C.L.
Storrs, Connecticut
November 16, 1992

The
AMERICAN
POLITY

THE PEOPLE

AND THEIR GOVERNMENT

FIFTH EDITION

Part 1

AMERICAN SOCIETY

Keith Meyers/NYT Pictures

Chapter 1

SOCIAL CHANGE AND POLITICAL RESPONSE

On May 9, 1831, a twenty-six-year-old French aristocrat arrived in the United States to study closely the new American experiment in democracy. Alexis Charles Henri Clerel de Tocqueville had come ostensibly to study American prisons in order to advise his government on penal reform. But Tocqueville's real intention was to examine "in detail and as scientifically as possible, all the mechanisms of that vast American society which everyone talks of and no one knows." On February 20, 1832, having crisscrossed the United States and interviewed hundreds of Americans—including President Andrew Jackson—Tocqueville sailed for home. It was not until a year and a half later, in the fall of 1833, that Tocqueville began in earnest to write his book. Working quickly, he finished one volume of his study in just a year. In January 1835, that first volume of *De la Democratie en Amérique (Democracy in America)* was published in Paris. It was immediately acclaimed a masterpiece not only in France but also in Great Britain and the United States. Now, more than 150 years later, it still lays fair claim to being considered the best book ever written about American society and politics.

Tocqueville set out to accomplish two objectives that relate to the study of

American government in our own time: to see the system as a whole and to see where it was headed and why. He largely succeeded.

To See the System as a Whole. Tocqueville believed that one could not understand a country's government by looking just at its governmental institutions, for there is a strong interaction among (1) the beliefs and values of a people, (2) their social institutions, and (3) their political system. He thought, for example, that the religious beliefs and institutions the Puritans had brought with them to New England contributed much to the vigorous democratic practice that took root long before independence was achieved from the British Crown. The Puritans thought that every individual should have a knowledge of Scripture, which meant that everyone should be able to read—

Alexis de Tocqueville. Lithograph by Chasseriau.

so they pioneered in establishing a compulsory system of public education. This helped make citizens more aware and better able to involve themselves in community life. Believing that each individual was equal in the eyes of God, the Puritans proposed rules, compacts, and institutions that gave each person a voice in affairs such as government. Such beliefs were "not merely a religious doctrine, but . . . corresponded in many points with the most absolute democratic and republican theories," Tocqueville wrote. In New England "a democracy more perfect than antiquity had dared to dream of started in full size and panoply from the midst of an ancient feudal society."[1]

This was just one of many linkages involving beliefs, social institutions, and governmental arrangements that Tocqueville described in *Democracy in America*. We cannot understand today's American government and politics unless we recognize that ideas and values, economic perspectives and institutions, the social makeup of the population as defined by ethnicity, education, income, and all such dimensions of American society constantly impinge upon the country's political life.

To See Where We Are Headed and Why. Today, we are in the midst of enormous political change around the world. Tocqueville lived at a time when Western society was caught up in extraordinary change. The old order based on the principle of aristocracy—in which social position was determined by birth, and a small hereditary elite enjoyed a great disproportion of wealth, social status, and political power—was coming under attack and being replaced, with varying rates of speed from one country to another. The newly ascendant principles were: (1) individualism, (2) social equality, and (3) political democracy. Individualism involves the

[1] Alexis de Tocqueville, *Democracy in America* (New York: Vintage Books, 1958), vol. 1, p. 37.

idea that society is built around the individual and is obliged to provide him with such rights as life, liberty, and a full chance to pursue happiness. It also carries with it an emphasis on individual responsibility, and the belief that society advances best by encouraging individual achievement. Tocqueville saw the tide of individualism rising throughout the West.

Tocqueville also believed that the increase of *social equality* was irresistible. The aristocracy to which he belonged in France had been humbled by the cry of *egalité* (equality) during the French Revolution which began in 1789; similar currents were sweeping through Europe. "The gradual development of the principle of equality is, therefore, a providential fact. It has all the chief characteristics of such a fact: it is universal, it is lasting, it constantly eludes all human interference, and all events as well as all men contribute to its progress."[2] Social arrangements rooted in the idea that some groups have a permanent claim to superior status, which was the basis of aristocratic society, were collapsing and would never be reestablished. *Political democracy* followed naturally from individualism and social equality. If societies were giving greater recognition to the claims of individuals who had equal rights and deserved an equal chance to work and achieve, political institutions providing for popular sovereignty or rule by the people would have to be devised and extended.

The world Tocqueville knew was beset by changes that forced societies to come to terms with the great ideas of individualism, equality, and democracy. It was a revolutionary era. Where would it end? The young Frenchman felt that "there is a country in the world where the great social revolution which I am speaking of seems to have nearly reached its natural limits." He meant America. So he came here

in order to discern its natural consequences and to find out, if possible, the means of rendering it profitable to mankind. I confess that in America I sought more than America; I sought there the image of democracy itself, with its inclinations, it character, its prejudices, and its passions, in order to learn what we have to fear or to hope from its progress.[3]

CONTINUITY

The political ideals that dominated American life in Tocqueville's day remain ascendant in our own time. They continue to shape the approach of many of the most important political and social movements.

INDIVIDUALISM

The United States is still distinguished by strong currents of individualism. Over the years, the precise claims that individuals make have changed, and so have our views concerning whose rights are insufficiently recognized. Today, for example, the movement for women's rights is far stronger than in the past. The women's movement is wide ranging, with a variety of different goals, but underlying it is the basic idea that women are individuals whose claims to the opportunity to achieve personal fulfillment and happiness are the equal of men's. Individualism frames, too, the terms or boundaries of many of the sharpest political disputes in the contemporary United States. What are the rights of individuals accused of crimes, and what measures must law enforcement officials and courts take to ensure them? How are these rights to be balanced against the rights and interests of the rest of the population? Or, in

---

[2] Ibid., p. 6.

[3] Ibid., p. 15.

American women are succeeding in occupations that were formerly the domain of men. Here, astronaut Sally Ride and construction worker.

another area, to what extent should abortion be a matter of individual choice, rather than proscribed by law? No polity has done more than that of the United States to put the individual at the forefront—or argued more about which individual rights deserve greater emphasis.

EQUALITY

In the same way, the egalitarianism that Tocqueville found in early America will continue to distinguish the United States in the twenty-first century. The public's ideal of equality has consistently asserted that each individual must be given an opportunity to strive and to achieve according to his or her efforts and ability, without regard to the individual's social background. It is an ideal that insists on equality of opportunity—although not on equality of result. If some individuals work harder or are more able, they should, in the American sense of

equality, be permitted to enjoy their rewards. During the Great Depression in the 1930s, public opinion pollsters asked a sample of the populace whether they thought government should impose limits on how much money people could earn. Even with economic hardship widespread and tensions high, the majority of the populace rejected the idea of income limits. Even the poorest Americans said no to it. This same response is given by Americans today.

Equality of opportunity for everyone is, even with the greatest effort, impossible to achieve fully. And the United States at times has not even made the effort. The denial of equality of opportunity to black Americans is the most flagrant instance where we have mocked our ideal. But if it has been denied far more than we like to acknowledge, the goal of equal opportunity is nonetheless a powerful force in our national experience. It underlies the many laws national and state governments have enacted to bar discrimination by race, religion, sex, and other such attributes extraneous to individual effort and performance. And it helps account for the enormous positive commitment the United States has made to education, including bringing higher education within the reach of a larger proportion of the population than in any other country. For we see the provision of educational opportunity as the primary means by which individuals of diverse backgrounds are enabled to compete effectively in social and economic life.

DEMOCRACY

The third principle that Tocqueville saw shaping the American political system also remains in place: Government should rest on the foundation of majority rule. Over the years, the precise machinery through which citizens choose their political leaders and control democratic governmental functions has changed in a number of ways, some far from inconsequential. But the commitment to political democracy has remained vital. One aspect of this vitality is a general recognition that the democratic ideal is never fully or finally realized. Throughout U.S. history, there have been recurring movements committed to "political reform," which in virtually all instances has meant trying to make the democratic system operate in closer accord with certain ideals.

As we will see in the chapters that follow, debate continues today about what steps should be taken to increase the rate of voter turnout in American elections. Issues of campaign finance—including the increasing cost of electioneering, where the money now comes from and where it should come from—are lively ones. Reforming the political parties so that they can better perform their representative functions is under continuous debate, especially with regard to the presidential nomination process. Congressional reform—involving

such matters as the organization and powers of committees and subcommittees, and the influence of interest groups in the legislative process—is seen by many to be critical. The role of the Supreme Court and the rest of the federal judiciary in making public policy prompts heated debate about the proper distribution of power and responsibility among the three branches of government.

The fact that the ideas and ideals of individualism, equality, and democracy still form the underpinnings of the American system and frame the terms of the political debate imparts an extraordinary continuity to our political life. As historian Henry Steele Commager remarked, "Circumstances change profoundly, but the character of the American people has not changed greatly or the nature of the principles of conduct, public and private, to which they subscribe."[4]

SOCIAL CHANGE DRIVES POLITICAL CHANGE

For all the persistence of governmental institutions and underlying values, American society has been far from static. Evolving from a small farming nation settled on the eastern edge of the North American continent to a highly developed nation spanning the continent and exerting great influence on world affairs, the United States has packed into its two hundred years since independence massive changes in technology, economic life, demographic makeup, and more. With these changes, every American political institution has grown and evolved. Not every piece of social change has had a major impact on government and politics, of course, but the accumulated changes

[4]Henry Steele Commager, *Living Ideas in America* (New York: Harper and Brothers, 1951), p. xviii.

have. The components of a social setting are subject to many new developments starting at different times and proceeding at different rates; these changes finally merge to produce a new setting distinct from the preceding one. The idea of a **sociopolitical period** refers to the persistence of underlying social and economic relationships, and their accompanying demands on government, over time. The United States has seen four great sociopolitical periods, each defined not by the passing of years but by the changing of society (Table 1.1). We are mainly interested here in the last of these, the period in which we are living, but we can better understand the present by seeing the process of change through which American society and government have arrived at it.[5]

THE RURAL REPUBLIC

During the first great social and political period, from the time the Constitution was drafted and ratified in the late 1780s to just before the beginning of the Civil War, the United States was a preindustrial society: Land-owning farmers were the dominant group, economically and politically. In 1800 more than four out of every five Americans who worked were farmers, and fifty years later farmers still comprised about two-thirds of the labor force. In 1839, agriculture accounted for nearly 70 percent of the total value of the commodity output of the U.S. economy. Since most people worked in jobs that required little formal or theoretical training, education could be limited to what was required for literacy. Besides, this preindustrial society could not afford to sustain any substantial portion of its productive-age population in "nonproductive" schooling. The U.S.

educational system was a primary-school system: Of the 3.5 million pupils enrolled in 1850, only 20,000 were in grades nine and above; less than 1 percent of the population were high-school graduates; and the degrees awarded by all institutions of higher education numbered fewer than 3,000.

The economic activities we identify as "business"—banking, trade, manufacturing—were limited. Big business simply did not exist; the idea of global businesses stretching across the world was not even imagined. The Northeast was the center of the country's nascent commerce and manufacturing. In 1850 it accounted for three-fourths of the United States's manufacturing employment, concentrated in industries such as cotton and woolen goods, men's clothing, and shoes.[6] The West of this first period was the "Old West," what we now know as the North Central states. Its economy was mostly agricultural, and wheat and corn were the most important crops.

The American South underwent major social and economic changes in the first half of the nineteenth century. In 1800 it was a land of small farmers. Their egalitarianism was much more characteristic of the South than was the privileged life of the great planters and their slave-based agriculture in areas like tidewater Virginia. But in the early nineteenth century the South's cotton culture became a highly prosperous and expanding enterprise, and slavery an entrenched institution. The most important causes of this transformation were Eli Whitney's invention of the cotton gin, a machine for cleaning cotton; the opening up of extremely rich soil perfectly suited for the cotton culture in Georgia, Alabama, and Mississippi; and, with the peace and renewal of trade that fol-

---

[5] These developments are discussed at length in Everett C. Ladd, *American Political Parties: Social Change and Political Response* (New York: Norton, 1970).

[6] Douglass C. North, *The Economic Growth of the United States, 1790–1860* (New York: Norton, 1966), pp. 115–60.

lowed the Napoleonic wars in Europe, an enormous market for raw cotton to be used in textile manufacturing. The South produced only 73,000 bales of cotton in 1800, but more than 525,000 bales in 1825, 2.1 million in 1850, and 4.4 million in 1861.[7] The extension of the plantation system made southern society much more highly stratified and increased inequalities of income. Power came to rest with the planter class. The net effect of these changes was to set the South further apart from the rest of the country; differences in political culture, modest at the turn of the century, had become a chasm on the eve of the Civil War.

In 1790, 95 percent of all Americans lived on farms or in small villages; the biggest city, Philadelphia, had less than 50,000 inhabitants. Even by 1850, 85 Americans in every 100 were still rural dwellers. This population was scattered over an area that grew through annexations from just under one million square miles in 1790 to 3 million at mid-century. People and goods moved through this vast expanse by waterways, and on land by animal and on foot. There were no railroads until 1830 and in 1850 only the beginnings of the vast railroad network soon to be developed. In communications the first telegraph service (between Baltimore and Washington) did not begin until 1844. There was no integrated national economy, no national media of communication; Maine and South Carolina were separated by weeks of arduous travel.

In this highly localized society, "states' rights" had a basic legitimacy that most of us cannot easily recognize now. A large federal government just was not needed in this independent farming society. Federal spending averaged only two dollars per capita each year from the turn

[7]U.S. Bureau of the Census, *Historical Statistics of the United States: Colonial Times to 1970* (Washington, D.C.: Government Printing Office, 1975), p. 518.

of the century through the 1850s. Most governing occurred at the state and local level.

THE INDUSTRIALIZING NATION

In the years from the end of the Civil War in 1865 up to the 1920s, the United States became the leading industrial nation, with about one-third of the world's total manufacturing capacity. In the 1860s a clear majority of American workers were in agriculture; but the agricultural labor force began a precipitous relative decline as manufacturing and commerce expanded. By 1920 only about one out of every four workers were engaged in farming, while between 1870 and 1920, the number of workers in trade and finance jumped from 830,000 to 8.5 million, in transportation and other public utilities from 640,000 to 4.2 million, and in manufacturing from 2.3 million to 10.9 million.

The population of the United States tripled between 1870 and 1920, reaching 106 million. During this period the great cities we know today were built. By 1900, New York City's population had climbed to over 3 million, and New York had taken its place as one of the world's great metropolises. In place of small family farms producing food only for local areas, big corporations drew resources from throughout the country and the world, and serviced national markets. This was the half-century in which all the major electronic media except television developed. Telephones first came into use in the 1870s, and by 1920 13.3 million of them were in use in the country. A new transportation network was established, centered on the railroad and the motor car, and the physical mobility of the population was vastly extended. The productive capacities of the economy were enormously expanded by industrialization. Between 1870 and 1920 the gross national product (GNP) of the United States—measur-

TABLE 1.1   ERAS IN AMERICAN SOCIAL AND POLITICAL DEVELOPMENT

Sociopolitical period	Approximate time span	Sociopolitical period	Approximate time span
Rural republic	1780s–1850s	Industrializing nation	1860s–1910s

A rural and localized society; land-owning farmers are the dominant economic group; government's role is highly limited and centered at the state and local levels.

An urbanizing society of increasing scale; there is rapid growth of industry and commerce, leading to the ascendancy of corporate business; government's role involves the promotion of industrialization and, subsequently, its regulation.

ing the value of all goods and services produced—increased in real terms by roughly 800 percent.[8]

The increases of scale and interdependence that took place in the second period spurred the expansion of government. Regulation for working conditions had made little sense when most Americans were independent farmers; it

was a different matter when millions entered the ranks of factory labor. Pure food and drug legislation did not seem imperative when most people lived on farms and consumed what they produced; the call for such regulation became increasingly insistent with the impersonality of big cities and big business corporations. The industrializing society required much higher investments in education than its agricultural predecessor had; total public expenditures for education grew from just $90 million in 1875 to $558 million in 1913 and $2.2 billion in 1927. The expansion of government services took place mostly at the state and local level; federal expenditures were only moderately

[8]These data are from *Historical Statistics of the United States*, p. 231. Describing the increase as 800 percent in real terms means controlling for the effects of price changes. In this case, the purchasing power of the dollar in 1929 was used as the base for recalculating the GNP for each year in the span between 1869 and 1931.

TABLE 1.1 (CONTINUED) ERAS IN AMERICAN SOCIAL AND POLITICAL DEVELOPMENT

Sociopolitical period	Approximate time span	Sociopolitical period	Approximate time span
Industrial state	1920s–1950s	Postindustrial society	1960s–present

A mature urban, industrial society; complex, integrated industrial economy requiring central management; organized labor becomes a major economic and political interest group, power shifts to the national government, and government's role is greatly expanded.

A society of advanced technology, built on a heavy commitment to science and education; the service sector of the economy expands greatly, while manufacturing proportionally declines; older economic interests, including organized labor, lose influence; the proper management of government's role in the political economy becomes the primary domestic issue.

higher in the 1870–1920 period (apart from World War I) than they had been before the Civil War, and what increase did take place was largely accounted for by defense, veterans' pensions, and interest on the debt.

THE INDUSTRIAL STATE

The Great Depression, which began in 1929, did not so much create as abruptly signal the emergence of a new sociopolitical setting, the third decisive period in American history. It shifted national attention from one set of concerns to another with unaccustomed speed. Long before the Depression there had been

recognition that the further industrial development proceeded and the bigger and more integrated the economy became, the more central economic management and regulation the country would require and the more governmental protection individuals would need. Overall, though, in 1929 the response in American political thought and governmental institutions lagged behind the requirements of the new setting.

Political power in the United States was redistributed after 1929. In the half-century of rapid industrialization, businessmen had acquired enormous political influence. They had come to be seen as the architects of pros-

President Franklin D. Roosevelt signing the social security bill into law.

perity. The country was engaged in a great enterprise, and they were the instruments for its betterment. Then, almost overnight with the Depression, there were boos and catcalls instead of cheers. Instead of being the custodians of American prosperity, the builders of the American dream, America's business leaders were presiding over an economic system in unparalleled collapse; they appeared powerless to effect a remedy.

Organized labor was one of the principal new claimants for power and recognition in the industrial state. Industrialization had created a large urban working class, but for it to assume real political power it needed effective organization. This was achieved in the ten years after 1935. In the early 1930s just over 10 percent of the nonagricultural work force belonged to labor unions. The general encouragement to unionization given by the administration of Franklin D. Roosevelt, legislation enacted by Congress, and the vigorous initiatives of a new generation

of labor leaders produced a surge in membership, which brought it to about 35 percent of the nonagricultural labor force just after World War II. As a result, labor leaders acquired much more economic and political influence than they ever had before.

Prompted by the economic collapse of the 1930s, and more generally by the increased number of demands made by an urban and industrial society, government took on a growing number of responsibilities. In 1913 total spending by the national, state, and local governments had been about $33 per person. That figure jumped to $130 per person in 1936, $375 in 1948, and $837 in 1960. Inflation accounted for some of this increase, but much of it was real and reflected government's assumption of a big role in public welfare and economic management. And, responding to the greater integration and interdependence of the society and the national character of many of its problems, the federal government's share of public spending rose above the combined total of the states and municipalities after World War II, the first time this had occurred when the country was at peace. Federal spending has exceeded state and local spending every year since.

POSTINDUSTRIAL SOCIETY

Today we read about how American politics is changing. By the late 1960s and 1970s, a great variety of changes had come together to define yet another social era, the fourth in the country's history: the postindustrial society. Since American society now differs significantly from that of the New Deal industrial era, the polity could scarcely have remained static.

In the next chapter we review the key transformations that have ushered in the new postindustrial setting and shaped it. And throughout this text we discuss government and politics against the backdrop of the contemporary society—its needs and resources, its group composition and interests, and its social organization.

FOR FURTHER STUDY

Ladd, Everett C. *American Political Parties: Social Change and Political Response.* New York: Norton, 1970. Analyzes changes in American political parties and politics against the backdrop of basic changes occurring in American society.

Lipset, Seymour Martin. *The First New Nation.* New York: Doubleday, 1963. A classic study of the social origins and development of the United States by a distinguished political sociologist.

Rossiter, Clinton. *Seedtime of the Republic.* New York: Harcourt, Brace, Jovanovich, 1953. A thoughtful, highly readable history of American social and political experience in the colonial and revolutionary periods, stressing the development of American political thought.

Tocqueville, Alexis de. *Democracy in America.* 2 vols. New York: Vintage Books, 1959. A brilliant interpretation of the underlying dynamics of American society and government, written and first published in the 1830s by Tocqueville, a young French aristocrat who had toured the United States during Andrew Jackson's presidency.

U.S. Bureau of the Census. *Historical Statistics of the United States: Colonial Times to 1970, Parts 1 and 2.* Washington, D.C.: Government Printing Office, 1975. An extremely useful historical reference work in two volumes, containing comprehensive census data on diverse aspects of American life dating back to the first census of 1790.

Chapter 2

POSTINDUSTRIAL SOCIETY

Many times over the past century, observers have been struck by the pace of social and political change. Never before, though, has this feeling been stronger than it is today. The sweeping political shifts in many countries, especially in Eastern Europe and the newly independent republics of the former Soviet Union, contribute to the vivid sense of a world on the move. But all across American society, too, the new is coming with exceptional speed—sometimes welcome, sometimes daunting.

Consider communications. This author remembers when his parents purchased their first television set and how the family would sit before it, straining to see the faint outlines of Uncle Miltie (comedian Milton Berle) and his variety-show guests. Today U.S. television viewers flick by remote control through the scores of channels available on most cable systems. In June 1980, the new Cable News Network (CNN) was established to report just news, twenty-four hours a day. At the end of 1991, CNN was received by 58 million households in the United States and 100 million worldwide. And beyond the elaboration of television technology in our own country and the vast expansion of the media's political role, the entire planet has in fact become, through

Support group and some of the technology behind a Cable News Network (CNN) broadcast.

TV, what media theorist Marshall McLuhan called "the global village."[1] For instance, the entire world could tune in to see the videotaped beating of motorist Rodney King in 1991 by officers of the Los Angeles Police Department and the news footage of the 1992 riots following the jury's acquittal of the officers involved. Similarly, viewers in the United States can now watch leading Russian news programs over the cable network C-SPAN, while viewers in France can tune in "The CBS Evening News with Dan Rather."

[1] Marshall McLuhan and Bruce R. Powers, *The Global Village: Transformations in World Life and Media in the 21st Century* (New York: Oxford University Press, 1989). Also by McLuhan: *Understanding Media: The Extensions of Man* (New York: New American Library, 1964). McLuhan argued that human nature was being rapidly translated into electronic information systems that produce great *global sensitivity and no secrets.*

American society itself is changing in ways large and small. At the time the 1990 census was conducted—the twenty-first decennial population census in U.S. history—the *New York Times* editorialized on how technology was reshaping social experience (Table 2.1). Over the past half-century, the *Times* noted,

TABLE 2.1 HOW HAS AMERICA CHANGED IN FIFTY YEARS?

	1940	*1990*
Telephones	41,100,000	151,000,000
Radio stations	862	8,942
Motor vehicles sold	4,472,200	14,100,000
Magazines	460	2,160
Federal civil cases	34,734	233,293
Divorces	250,000	1,190,000

Source: "America Doubled," editorial, *New York Times*, April 1, 1990; *Statistical Abstract of the United States, 1991*, p. 608. *Survey of Current Business*, Nov. 1990, p. 27.

the proportion of Americans living on farms had declined from 23 percent in 1940 to just 2 percent—reflecting in large part the enormous advances in agricultural technology that enable far fewer farm workers to grow enough for the entire population. In 1940, the biggest day of the year on the New York Stock Exchange saw 4 million shares change hands. Today the number often exceeds 200 million shares, thanks to computers and other electronics. The number of magazines, excluding trade publications, has more than quadrupled over the last 50 years—reflecting in part advances in publishing technology that permit entire magazines to be produced right in the offices of even small organizations. The *Times* concluded: "Just since

the 1940 census, America has doubled [in population], all right. It has also been transformed."[2] The overall growth has, incidentally, not occurred evenly across the country. Figure 2.1 shows, for example, that in the 1980s, four states and the District of Columbia actually lost population, while six others—New Hampshire, Florida, Nevada, Arizona, California, and Alaska—grew by more than 20 percent.

This chapter is about us—our society, our makeup as things stand today—and about the social changes that have brought us to our present status.

[2]"America, Doubled," editorial, *New York Times*, April 1, 1990.

FIGURE 2.1   SHIFTING POPULATION: WHAT THE 1990 U.S. CENSUS FOUND (% CHANGE BETWEEN 1980 AND 1990)

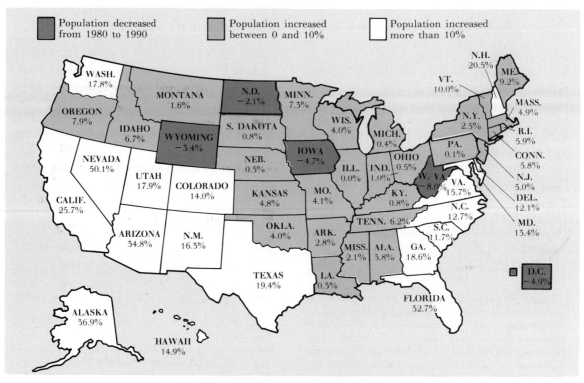

Source: U.S. Bureau of the Census, as published in *Congressional Quarterly*, May 18, 1991, pp. 1309–12.

Products of two eras: for the industrial age it was heavy industry, here, steel; for the postindustrial era it is the computer industry.

CONTEMPORARY AMERICA: A POSTINDUSTRIAL SOCIETY

Some of the most important changes of recent years—changes that have great implications for all aspects of how we live, including our politics—come together to create what social scientists sometimes describe as the postindustrial era. The term *postindustrial society* was first introduced by sociologist Daniel Bell.[3] He contrasted this era with the preceding one, writing that while "industrial society is the coordination of machines and men for the production of goods," postindustrial society is "organized around knowledge."[4] The key developments defining the postindustrial era are "the exponential growth and branching of science, the rise of a new intellectual technology, the creation of systematic research through R & D [research and development] budgets, and . . . the codification of theoretical knowledge."[5]

Throughout this book, *postindustrial society* refers specifically to the cumulative result of five key developments or sources of social change.

[3] Bell has noted that the term actually appeared earlier than his first use of it, with quite a different meaning, in an essay that David Riesman wrote on "Leisure and Work in Postindustrial Society," printed in the compendium *Mass Leisure* (Glencoe, Ill.: Free Press, 1958). Bell's most important treatment of postindustrialism may be found in his book *The Coming of Postindustrial Society* (New York: Basic Books, 1973).

[4] Bell, *Coming of Postindustrial Society*, p. 20.

[5] Ibid., p. 44.

(1) Advanced Technology. Postindustrial America is a society built upon advanced technology. Technology itself is not a recent phenomenon, but technology built primarily upon abstract and theoretical knowledge is new.

(2) The Knowledge Base. This technology requires an unprecedented commitment to science and education. And it permits an unprecedentedly large proportion of the populace to engage in intellectual rather than manual labor.

(3) Occupations: The Service Economy. The occupational makeup of the work force in the postindustrial setting differs from that of the industrial era and earlier times. The white-collar and service sectors grow. Bureaucracy becomes the distinctive work setting.

(4) Mass Affluence. Postindustrial America is an affluent society, one where the increase in national wealth, built on technological innovation, has been so substantial as to move a large proportion, though by no means all, of the populace beyond active concern with matters of subsistence.

(5) New Class Relationships. The character of social classes and their relationships in the postindustrial era are very different from previous eras. Increased wealth and education, together with a new occupational mix, produce a new class structure.

Let's look more closely at each of these components to understand better recent changes that have altered not just the economy and social relations but also the setting for American political life.

ADVANCED TECHNOLOGY

Technology is commonly defined as the application of knowledge for practical ends. In this general sense the United States has made serious use of technology from its very inception. In the nineteenth century, knowledge about electricity and steam engines was applied with an extraordinary practical impact in manufacturing, transportation, and communication. The country was crisscrossed with rail, telephone, and telegraph lines, and heavy industries like coal and steel were developed. All this contributed to exceptionally large increases in industrial productivity. Manufacturing output climbed by about 1200 percent in the half-century following the Civil War.[6]

Almost all of the major industries that grew up in the nineteenth and early twentieth centuries—including steel, electric power, the automobile, and the telephone—were "mainly the creation of inventors, inspired and talented tinkerers who were indifferent to science and the fundamental laws underlying their investigations."[7] William Darrah Kelley and Sir Henry Bessemer developed the oxidation process that made it possible to mass-produce steel—even though they were unaware of the emerging science of metallurgy. Thomas Alva Edison did his major work on something he vaguely referred to as "etheric sparks," which resulted in the electric light and otherwise sparked the first electronic revolution—even though he was not sympathetic to the theoretical research being done on electromagnetism.

What distinguishes the technology of postindustrial society is a change in the character of innovation: the sustained application of theoretical knowledge for practical ends. Most of the worlds that lay before the "talented tinkerers" have been conquered. Since World War II

[6] Based on an index of manufacturing production developed by Edwin Frickey, *Production in the United States, 1860–1914* (Cambridge, Mass.: Harvard University Press, 1947). The index is reprinted in U.S. Bureau of the Census, *Historical Statistics of the United States: Colonial Times to 1970, Part 2*, p. 667.

[7] Bell, *Coming of Postindustrial Society*, p. 20.

technological progress has been based directly and explicitly on theoretical knowledge—and thus on the work of the scientific community. From chemicals to computers, from military hardware to agriculture, from genetic engineering to superconductors, the dependence on science is now generally acknowledged.

Some aspects of advanced technology are intensely debated. A prime example involves the use of nuclear power to generate electricity. Is it safe enough? In recent years, protests over the Shoreham nuclear power plant on Long Island, New York, and the Seabrook plant in New Hampshire have been intense. Table 2.2 shows that the United States is about midway among industrial nations in the proportion of its total electricity needs satisfied by nuclear power.

SCIENCE COMES OF AGE

One indication of society's dependence on science is the extent to which business corporations have tied themselves to science and higher education. New industrial complexes have grown up around leading research universities. The development of the computer industry in the Silicon Valley near Stanford University in California, and on Route 128 near the Massachusetts Institute of Technology (MIT), are the most dramatic instances. Many of the leading corporations have become major employers of scientific talent. International Business Machines (IBM), the largest computer manufacturer, employed about 2,500 Ph.D.s in 1984. Bell Laboratories, a unit of American Telephone and Telegraph (AT&T), employed over 2,600 in 1985; and DuPont, the chemical giant, had over 3,400 men and women with doctorates on its payroll in the United States alone in 1989—a larger number than that employed at most research universities.

There has been a vast increase in the economic resources committed to **research and development** (R&D). The age of the great inventors like Alexander Graham Bell and Thomas Alva Edison, and the gifted implementors of technology like Henry Ford, is in many ways an attractive, even romantic one, involving as it did the solitary individual working with very modest resources in his own garage or tiny laboratory. The practice in postindustrial America contrasts greatly with James Conant's recollection that during World War I, as president of the American Chemical Society, he offered the services of the society to Newton D. Baker (then Secretary of War) only to be told that those services would not be needed because the War Department already had a

TABLE 2.2 TOTAL AND NUCLEAR ELECTRICITY GENERATION IN VARIOUS INDUSTRIAL COUNTRIES, 1988 (IN TERRAWATT HOURS*)

Country	From all sources	From nuclear	Percent produced from nuclear
Australia	132.0	0.0	0.0
Belgium	61.9	40.9	66.1
Canada	487.0	78.2	16.1
Denmark	29.8	0.0	0.0
Finland	51.3	18.4	35.9
France	372.4	260.2	69.9
Germany	402.5	137.8	34.2
Italy	196.8	0.0	0.0
Japan	641.8	174.8	27.2
Netherlands	67.2	3.4	5.1
Norway	110.3	0.0	0.0
Spain	133.3	48.3	36.2
Sweden	141.4	66.4	47.0
Switzerland	57.5	21.5	37.4
United Kingdom	282.9	53.3	18.8
United States	2,701.0	527.0	19.5
OECD total	**6,075.9**	**1,430.2**	**23.5**

*One terawatt-hour equals one thousand billion watt-hours.
Source: OECD Nuclear Energy Data 1989, NEA/OECD, 1989.

chemist! Conant also described a board headed by Edison, created to help the Navy during World War I, on which Edison placed one physicist because, as he told President Woodrow Wilson, "we ought to have one mathematician fellow in case we have to calculate something out."[8]

However romantic that earlier industrial era seems, it is gone forever. Technological innovation now requires large commitments of resources. Economist John Kenneth Galbraith notes that it cost just $28,500 to produce the first Ford in 1903, compared to $60 million to engineer and tool up for the production of the first Mustang in 1964. And two decades later, it cost Ford $3 billion to produce the first Taurus.

It is widely recognized that in this advanced technological age of ours huge investments must be made in R&D if economic growth is to be

[8] James Bryant Conant, *Modern Science and Modern Man* (New York: Columbia University Press, 1952), pp. 8–9.

achieved and competitiveness maintained. A lively and important debate is going on as to whether the United States is making a big enough commitment in this area. As is so often the case, the main focus is on the effort of the United States as compared to that of Japan. Economists with the National Science Foundation say Japan is still way behind the United States in total spending on R&D. But some private-sector economists say otherwise—that Japan now spends as much or even more, at least with regard to product development. Which analysis is correct is hard to say: The statistical picture is really quite complex.

We do know for certain that R&D expenditures in the United States increased enormously during World War II and have continued to grow in real—i.e. inflation-controlled—terms. While government spending for research and development has been quite flat (controlling for inflation) since 1960, spending by private industry has increased sharply (Figure 2.2).

FIGURE 2.2   FEDERAL GOVERMENT AND INDUSTRY SPENDING ON RESEARCH AND DEVELOPMENT

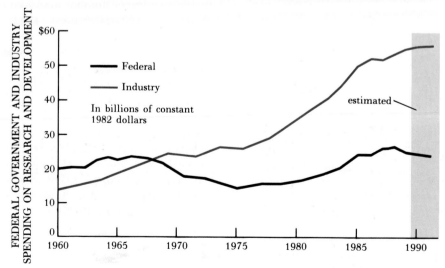

Source: National Science Board, "Science & Engineering Indicators, 1991" as published in *National Journal,* April 4, 1992, p. 806.

THE KNOWLEDGE BASE

Advanced technology, derived from theoretical knowledge, requires a large cadre of scientists and engineers for its continuation and a highly trained and educated labor force for its use. At the same time, by developing machinery to do work once assigned to manual labor and by increasing productivity and national wealth so massively, it has permitted an unprecedented proportion of the population to engage in educational and other intellectual activities.

THE AMERICAN EDUCATION EXPLOSION

We see the essential character of the knowledge society in the United States's commitment to education since World War II. In 1940 just 5 percent of the population age 25 and older

had graduated from college. But by 1989 the proportion was over 21 percent. As Figure 2.3 shows, in the last two decades alone the level of formal education attained by the American population has increased dramatically. In 1970, about 28 percent of those 25 years and older had only elementary school training; in 1989, that proportion had been more than cut in half, dropping to just under 12 percent. The proportion with at least some college training climbed from about 21 percent to about 38 percent.

Not only are these figures extraordinary by comparison to earlier periods in U.S. history, but they are also impressive when compared to other countries—even the most advanced nations. In 1987–88, when 13 million Americans attended institutions of higher education, only 1.6 million West German, 1.1 million British, and 1.3 million French citizens were enrolled in comparable schools in their respective countries. Those nations have much smaller

FIGURE 2.3 EDUCATIONAL ATTAINMENT IN AMERICA, 1970 and 1989 (PERCENTAGES ARE OF THOSE 25 YEARS OF AGE AND OLDER)

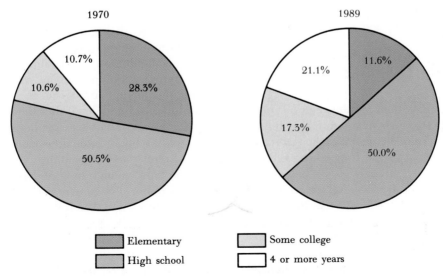

Source: U.S. Bureau of the Census, *Statistical Abstract of the United States*, 1991, p. 138.

FIGURE 2.4   LEVELS OF HIGHER EDUCATION IN LEADING INDUSTRIAL NATIONS

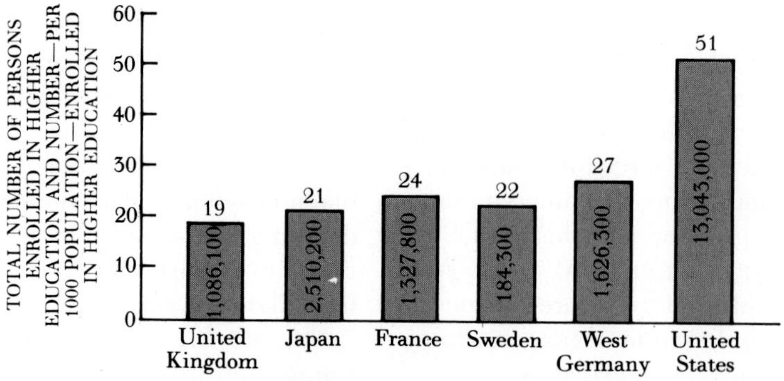

Source: OECD, *Education in OECD Countries, 1987–88* (Paris: OECD, 1990), p. 104; *OECD in Figures, 1991,* pp. 48–49.

total populations than the United States, of course, but as Figure 2.4 shows, controlling for population differences, the United States enrolls a much higher proportion of its population than do other countries. Data compiled by the Organization for Economic Cooperation and Development (OECD) show, for 1987–88, 51 Americans per 1,000 population enrolled as college and university students. The ratios were just 27 per 1,000 population in West Germany (before reunification), 24 per 1,000 in France, and 21 students per 1,000 people in Japan.

SOARING EXPENDITURES FOR EDUCATION

America's commitment to education has been costly. In 1930, we spent roughly $3.4 billion for education, from elementary school through college, public and private. Expenditures climbed only modestly through 1950—but at this point they took off. By 1990, as shown in Figure 2.5, spending for education in the United States had reached $358 billion—$143 billion for higher education and $215 billion for elementary and secondary training.

Americans have borne these heavy financial obligations to education with little complaint.

In 1990, the General Social Survey (GSS) conducted by the National Opinion Research Center (NORC) asked a cross-section of the public whether they thought we were, as a nation, spending too much, too little, or about the right amount on education. Seventy-one percent said we were not spending enough—this at a time when national expenditures for education were almost $358 billion a year! Only 7 percent responded that too much was being expended, while 23 percent said expenditures were at approximately the right level.

Vigorous arguments continue on important issues facing the American educational system: For example, are educational standards high enough? Should parents be given vouchers, paid for with tax dollars, that they can use to pay for private as well as public primary and secondary schooling for their children? Some critics argue that at present the nation's schools are not doing enough to teach basic skills, nor are they doing enough to prepare young people for tomorrow's jobs. But if the search for excellence and equity in American education is complicated and unending, there seems to be no doubt that the public recognizes education's immense role in our postindustrial society and is prepared to support it.

FIGURE 2.5 EXPENDITURES ON EDUCATION IN THE UNITED STATES, 1960–1990 (IN CONSTANT 1989–1990 DOLLARS)

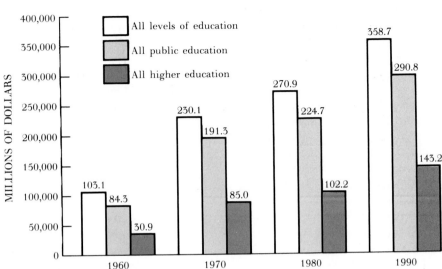

Source: U.S. Bureau of the Census, *Statistical Abstract of the United States,* 1991, p. 134.

OCCUPATIONS: THE SERVICE ECONOMY

In 1790, the first American decennial census found 95 percent of the total work force engaged in agricultural pursuits. As late as 1860, on the eve of the Civil War, roughly three-fifths of the work force was still in agriculture—compared to about one-fifth in non-farm manual labor jobs and one-fifth in various white-collar and service positions. The rapid industrialization of the late nineteenth and early twentieth centuries changed this ratio dramatically. Millions of Americans left farms and rural areas for factories and the cities. Between 1860 and 1920, the number of Americans engaged in non-farm blue-collar jobs jumped from 2 million to 17 million and neared what was to be its all-time high as a proportion of the total labor force.

After World War II, with the further introduction of machinery into agriculture, the pro-portion of farmers in the labor force continued to drop—but so did the proportion of blue-collar workers. Between 1950 and 1988, the American labor force increased by about 59 million—again entirely accounted for by the white-collar and service sector. The rapid expansion in the blue-collar and manufacturing work force had been a prime indicator of the growth of the industrial society. The explosion in the number of white-collar and service workers is a distinctive sign of postindustrialism. When in 1956 the number of white-collar workers outnumbered blue-collar workers, it was the first time in the United States or anywhere in the world that the balance had thus shifted.

SERVICES, SERVICES

One problem in referring to the growth in the number of "white-collar and service" workers is that the category covers so much ground. It includes those who work as household servants; persons in other personal services such as the operators of beauty salons and retail stores; those in business services like banking and real estate; individuals employed in transportation, communication, and utilities; and those in health, education, research, and government.

One way to bring the current mix of occupations into sharper focus is to classify all jobs by the industrial sector into which each falls. The U.S. Bureau of Labor Statistics (BLS) identifies nine such sectors. Four of them might be thought of as "things-producing": agriculture, mining, construction, and manufacturing. The shares of the total labor force employed by two of these sectors—agriculture and manufacturing—have continued to get smaller, in large part as a result of enormous increases in workers' productivity. The proportion in agriculture dropped from 4.4 to 2.7 percent from 1970 to 1989, while the proportion in manufacturing declined from 26.4 to 18.5 percent.

The other five sectors that BLS identifies are all in some sense "services-producing," but the range of services is extremely broad, including: communication and transportation; wholesale and retail trade; finance, insurance, and real estate; public administration; and a large residual category of other services including computer and data processing, entertainment and recreation, health and education. As Figure 2.6 shows, over 72 percent of all American workers were in one or another of these service industries.

PROFESSIONAL AND
TECHNICAL EMPLOYMENT

The ranks of those employed in professional and technical jobs (teachers, scientists, computer programmers, engineers, etc.) have expanded twice as fast as the entire work force. In 1950 about 4.5 million people held professional and technical service positions; by 1980 the total had climbed to almost 16 million—a gain of more than 350 percent. The number of engineers rose from 363,000 to 1.4 million over these three decades; lawyers from 182,000 to

FIGURE 2.6 EMPLOYMENT BY INDUSTRY SECTOR, 1989 (IN PERCENT)

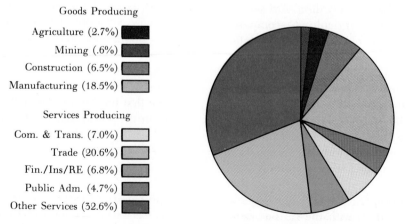

Goods Producing
Agriculture (2.7%)
Mining (.6%)
Construction (6.5%)
Manufacturing (18.5%)

Services Producing
Com. & Trans. (7.0%)
Trade (20.6%)
Fin./Ins/RE (6.8%)
Public Adm. (4.7%)
Other Services (32.6%)

Source: U.S. Bureau of the Census, *Statistical Abstract of the United States,* 1991, p. 400.

502,000 (most of this since 1970); teachers from 1.1 million to 4.3 million. Along with this overall growth have come significant shifts in the sex of those practicing in the professions. Only 6,000 women were lawyers in 1950 (3 percent of the total in this profession), and only 12,000 women were physicians (6 percent). By 1988 about 140,000 women were lawyers (just under 20 percent), and over 100,000 women were physicians (20 percent).

BUREAUCRACY

The field a farmer plowed typified the work setting of the agricultural society. The factory assembly line was the distinctive setting for the industrial society. Bureaucracy is the predominant work setting for the postindustrial era. The term *bureaucracy* has long had unfavorable connotations, suggesting large, unresponsive, cumbersome administrative units that deal impersonally with those who turn to them for services. "I tried to get action, but that bureaucracy just won't move." "You have to file six copies of everything, and wait at least six months for an answer." But bureaucracy as originally conceived meant something very different. The influential German sociologist Max Weber (1864–1920) identified it with "rationalized administration."[9] The management of organizations was advanced, Weber argued, by introducing knowledge of administrative techniques and practice, by striving for impartiality in the administration of services, and by the general recourse to rationality (rather than subjectivity or personal whim) in organizational manage-

[9]See, for example, Max Weber, *Economy and Society*, Guenther Roth and Claus Wittich, eds. (New York: Bedminster Press, 1968). Weber's work was composed between 1913 and 1914.

ment. In this sense, bureaucracy was a great advance over earlier forms of administration.

Today, the principles of rationalized administration have been applied across most large institutions in the United States, from governmental agencies to large business corporations. The tremendous growth of these bureaucracies has made them, for better or worse, the occupational homes of millions of American workers.

DEVELOPMENTS IN THE ECONOMY

Throughout human history, people have had to struggle for subsistence: taking in enough calories to sustain life, having clothing warm enough to protect against the elements, acquiring basic housing or shelter. Even in more fortunate times and countries where most of the population did not face actual hunger or starvation, the margin over subsistence was always worryingly thin. There might be enough food today, but one could not forget that, as a result of natural disasters, crop failures, or illness, there might not be enough food tomorrow.

Set against this historic experience of extreme scarcity, the economic position of the United States and other postindustrial countries today is very fortunate. Of course, we usually don't think in those historic terms. In comparison with our own past or with most other countries now, the United States is an affluent society. But when we think about our own needs and problems, we realize that our affluent society is not one where everyone is wealthy and poverty has been abolished. Millions of Americans—just how many is hard to estimate—experience some economic deprivation, such as inadequacy of diet or substandard housing. Government statistical data for 1990 show that between

27 and 34 million people live below the poverty line, depending on how the value of various forms of government assistance, such as Medicare and Medicaid, are calculated. That's between 11 percent and 13.5 percent of the population.[10]

Furthermore, poverty is not an absolute condition: An important meaning of being poor is having considerably less than most other people. We think of ourselves as deprived when our standard of living is well below the level that has been established as the norm for the society—even if our diet is good, we have enough clothing, and our needs for shelter are met. Of course our economic expectations rise with what we see around us. Poverty is in part a relative condition.

The relative prosperity of the United States and other postindustrial countries stands out, compared to the rest of the world. And, as is of great concern to many observers, the gap is *growing*. One reason is the huge increases in population that many nations in Africa, Central America, and South Asia are having to absorb and provide for. It has been estimated that every fifteen minutes over 2,000 more individuals join the human population, now estimated at more than 5 billion. *Christian Science Monitor* writer Timothy Aeppel observed that "each week we add the equivalent of another Houston; each year, another Mexico."[11] Consider the plight of Nigeria, stuck in a "demographic trap" where population growth, estimated to increase five-fold in the next half-century, will render efforts to advance the nation economically virtually futile. Even though one United Nations study suggests that world population will stabilize at around 10 billion in the next century, the environmental impact of such numbers will be enormous. Overpopulation is not a problem in the United States today, and among a number of the advanced industrial nations of Europe, extremely *low* birthrates are even viewed with some alarm.

ECONOMIC GROWTH

Between 1947 and 1973, median family income in the United States doubled in real (inflation-controlled) terms. More individual family purchasing power was acquired in this quarter of a century than in all preceding years of American history combined. When we remember, too, that at the close of World War II the United States was already a wealthy country by any historical or cross-national standard, the extent of this revolutionary economic change is more sharply etched.

This big jump in wealth permitted Americans to become huge consumers. Since World War II we have consumed twice as much fossil fuel (mostly oil and gasoline) as we had in all of the preceding years of the nation's existence (a fact that clearly attests to major changes in lifestyle, just as it helps explain why an energy crisis developed in the 1970s). The increase of 6 million in college and university enrollment between 1947 and 1973 is four times the total enrollment in 1940. Expenditures for toys climbed 500 percent in this quarter-century, those for cosmetics by 550 percent. Personal spending for recreation increased 500 percent.

A big argument has been going on about the economic developments of the last two decades. Some argue, for instance, that the United States has been losing its competitive edge. Certainly competition is fierce in today's global economy. Still, the available data suggest that the overall growth of the American economy in the 1970s

[10] U.S. Bureau of the Census, *Measuring the Effect of Benefits and Taxes on Income and Poverty: 1990*, Series P-60, No. 176, August 1991, p. 11.

[11] Timothy Aeppel, "Five Billion and Counting," *Christian Science Monitor*, July 6, 1987, p. 16.

FIGURE 2.7   GROWTH IN REAL PER CAPITA GROSS NATIONAL PRODUCT, 1890–1990

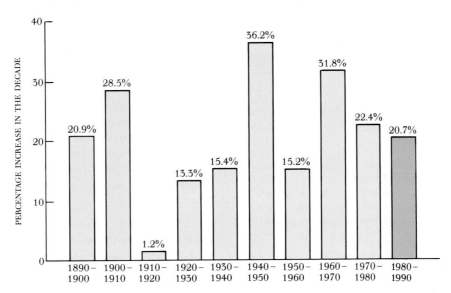

Source: U.S. Bureau of the Census, *Historical Statistics of the United States, Colonial Times to 1970*, p. 224; Council of Economic Advisers, *Economic Indicators*, November 1981, p. 2, and June 1990, p. 2.

and 1980s was close to the historic average (Figure 2.7). The three decades best for growth were 1900–10 (29 percent), 1940–50 (36 percent), and 1960–70 (32 percent). Next best is the span since 1970. Real per capita GNP climbed by 22 percent in the 1970s and by an additional 21 percent in the 1980s. The decade of the 1990s began with a recession. Analysts will be charting the course of the recovery carefully to determine how much strength, in terms of economic growth, is regained.

INCOME IN THE UNITED STATES AND ABROAD

Much attention has been paid to the comparative economic position of the United States and Japan, the country that has become our leading economic rival. There has been so much hype in the reporting of this competition that getting a clear view of what has been happening is difficult. Fortunately, staff economists for the Organization for Economic Cooperation and Development, an outstanding statistics-gathering agency based in Paris, have provided a helpful measure of economic growth in the United States, Japan, and the other advanced industrial countries. Table 2.3 shows the relative positions of these countries in 1970, 1980, and 1990, in terms of Gross Domestic Product (GDP), adjusted on a per capita basis. From this we can see that Japan's economy has indeed grown at a faster rate than ours over the last two decades, but that the United States still has a substantial lead. In fact, our closest competitor in per capita GDP isn't Japan, but Canada, followed by what was West Germany.

TABLE 2.3 NATIONAL INCOME COMPARISONS, 1970–1990 (PER CAPITA GROSS DOMESTIC PRODUCT, EXPRESSED IN PURCHASING POWER PARITIES)

	1970	1980	1990
United States	4,919	11,794	21,449
West Germany	3,884	10,170	18,291
Japan	2,932	8,225	17,634
France	3,696	9,740	17,431
Denmark	3,724	9,085	16,765
Austria	3,158	9,081	16,620
Belgium	3,310	9,076	16,405
Italy	3,123	9,610	16,020
Netherlands	3,699	9,233	15,766
United Kingdom	3,399	8,259	15,720
Spain	2,366	6,126	11,792
Ireland	1,853	5,190	10,659
Portugal	1,545	4,511	8,389
Greece	1,507	4,426	7,349

Source: OECD, *National Accounts*, vol. 1, Main Aggregates, 1960–90 (Paris: OECD, 1992), pp. 146–47. The methodology used by the OECD in deriving the above data involves valuing the goods and services sold in different countries in a common set of international prices. The OECD calls this "purchasing power parities (PPP)." PPPs are international price indexes linking the price levels of different countries. They show how many units of currency are needed in one country to buy the same amount of goods and services that one unit of currency will buy in the other country: for example, how many French francs are needed to buy in France what one U.S. dollar will buy within the United States.

CLASS RELATIONSHIPS

The concept of **social class** denotes status deriving from the amount of income received as well as the sources of this income: interest earnings from inherited wealth, ownership of a farm, a factory job, and so on. The concept also refers to the social and cultural perspective that results from income status. For Karl Marx, capitalists were a social class not just because they had relatively large amounts of wealth, but also because of how they derived their money—from their ownership of private industry—and because they shared common interests and a common worldview.

America's class divisions historically have been relatively weak. Social norms and interests commonly described as middle class have been the common property of many disparate economic groups. In particular, the American working class has never had the coherence and self-consciousness found historically in Europe. And socialism, which developed as a working-class ideology, has always been weak in America (see chapter 3).

WORKING-CLASS CONSCIOUSNESS

Still, the United States has not been totally without a politically self-conscious and organized working class. The industrial era—especially during Franklin Roosevelt's presidency (1933–45)—stands as its high-water mark. Under the new or greatly expanded government programs of the Roosevelt administration, known as the New Deal, working-class Americans received important recognition and support: national legislation guaranteeing the right to organize and bargain collectively; minimum-wage legislation; social security benefits; various guarantees of occupational health and safety, and of the general humaneness of working conditions. Legislation securing these benefits was not directed exclusively toward urban factory workers, but this group was a principal claimant and beneficiary.

During the New Deal the labor union movement gained strength. The political climate that followed the outbreak of the Great Depression in 1929—including the general encouragement of unionism given by the Roosevelt administration, new supportive legislation, and the vigorous initiatives of a new generation of labor leaders—produced a surge

The United Auto Workers, 1937: General Motors workers stage a daring strike to force GM to recognize the UAW.

in union membership, from 3.5 million in 1931 to 10 million on the eve of World War II, to more than 14 million when the war ended. This was the heroic age of American labor.

In the late 1940s and 1950s, however, union membership as a proportion of the nonagricultural labor force leveled out, and since 1960, it has steadily declined. In 1955, 33 percent of all workers in nonagricultural pursuits were unionized. Today, it is just half that. Not only has the American labor movement come to represent a declining proportion of workers, but the sectors where it holds the greatest promise of expansion lie outside the traditional industrial, blue-collar sector. Government employees and teachers have been big growth areas in recent years. Between 1968 and 1988 the membership of the American Federation of State, County, and Municipal Employees (AFSCME) grew from about 360,000 to 1.1 million. The American Federation of Teachers (AFT) quadrupled in this time span—from 165,000 to 665,000 members.

ECONOMIC GAINS

If the traditional working class—urban, blue-collar, and trade union—has lost ground numerically, it has also become an established class in contrast to its new claimant status of the New Deal era. Most of the urban working class of the 1930s were economic have-nots; if not poor, they were right on the margin. As such, they supported government-directed efforts to change the economic order. The trade union movement organized the working class and pushed effectively for its economic betterment and security.

The United Auto Workers, 1992: Union members picket the Caterpillar plant in Mossville, Illinois.

Over the ensuing decades, unions have achieved many of their objectives through collective bargaining, aided greatly by the overall growth of the American economy. The unionized labor force has moved up the socioeconomic ladder. In 1989, according to data from seven national surveys taken by the Gallup Organization, over 76 percent of union families—those in which at least one of the principal wage-earners belonged to a labor union—owned their home rather than rented it. Home ownership has long been considered one indicator, even if only a rough one, of middle-class status. Only about 4 percent of union members had less than a high-school education, and 19 percent were college graduates. Just 5 percent of these union families reported incomes of under $10,000 compared to 16 percent of non-union families. At the same time, 58 percent of union households, compared to 38 percent of nonunion households, had incomes of $30,000 a year or more. Both relatively and absolutely, the unionized work force has dramatically improved its economic position since the 1950s—just as its position in the 1950s represented a big gain over that of the Depression years.[12]

[12] The data presented here are derived from Gallup surveys taken nationally between February and August 1989. Combining a number of surveys gives a larger composite sample size—here, about 15,000 cases—which in turn makes possible a more reliable picture of the economic positions of union and nonunion families. Survey data have to be used because no comparable census information is available.

MIDDLE CLASS, EVEN CONSERVATIVE

The political consequences of drawing a large portion of the working class—especially that represented by labor unions—into what is for all practical purposes lower-middle-class status have been noted for some time now. "The fire has gone out in labor's belly," suggested journalist Stewart Alsop in 1967, because trade unions were no longer representing have-nots. Alsop recalled Franklin Roosevelt's packing Cadillac Square in Detroit with a half-million cheering workers in an October 1936 rally. He contrasted this to the mere 30,000 who turned out for Democratic President Lyndon Johnson in 1964, when Johnson was at his most popular and his Republican opponent, Barry Goldwater, gave labor its clearest target in many moons. Why then the poor turnout? "The workers who crowded shoulder to shoulder into Cadillac Square to hear Franklin Roosevelt regarded themselves as 'little guys' or 'working stiffs.' . . . The poor, and those who regarded themselves as poor, were in those days a clear majority of the population."[13] Alsop went on to point out that the typical trade unionist in 1964 was simply much better off, absolutely and relatively, than his counterpart had been twenty-five or thirty years earlier. He was more inclined to go boating or camping than to participate in solidarity rallies; and he no longer sustained the drive for social change.

George Meany, president of the AFL-CIO from 1952 until his death in 1980, spoke insightfully of the transformation of labor's place in the postindustrial era. In a 1969 interview with the *New York Times*, Meany appeared willing to accept both "middle class" and "conservative" as descriptions of the membership of the labor movement:

Labor, to some extent, has become middle class. When you have no property, you don't have anything, you have nothing to lose by these radical actions. But when you become a person who has a home and has property, to some extent you become conservative. And I would say to that extent, labor has become conservative.[14]

A working class that in many ways is middle class and conservative is a distinctive feature of postindustrialism.

NEW CLASS GROUPINGS

Another key development affecting class structure has emerged from the extraordinary expansion of higher education since World War II. Most people in the burgeoning college stratum don't fit into the traditional class groupings. They are hardly in working-class jobs: Only 10 percent hold manual-labor positions of any sort. But neither are they, for the most part, business men and women. Just 24 percent of them are managers or administrators of any kind. Nearly 60 percent of college graduates hold professional and technical jobs.[15] Such positions can be classified as middle class, but it is hard to fit them into traditional theories of class and politics. The vast expansion of the college-trained population has fueled a broad transformation of the upper middle class in the United States, from a business-defined and inclined posture to one shaped by intellectual experiences and values. Some observers see large elements of the college-trained population taking on the properties of an intelligent-

[13] Stewart Alsop, "Can Anyone Beat LBJ?" *Saturday Evening Post*, May 1967, p. 28.

[14] "Excerpts from Interview with Meany on Status of Labor Movement," *New York Times*, August 31, 1969, p. A9.

[15] These data are derived from two large surveys of the American public conducted in 1988 and 1989 by the National Opinion Research Center of the University of Chicago (NORC). This ongoing series is known as the *General Social Survey*.

sia: a social class whose occupational roles, status, and outlook all spring from its involvement in the application of trained intelligence.

ETHNOCULTURAL MAKEUP OF THE UNITED STATES

As throughout its history, the United States today is highly diverse ethnically and religiously. This diversity has continually exerted great influence on national life. It has, for example, been the source of social conflict. Securing full citizenship and rights for all the ethnocultural groups that form the American nation was a real challenge a century ago and still is in our own day.

The United States is a nation built on immigration. Between 1820 and 1980, more than 50 million immigrants decided to make the United States their home. The greatest wave of immigration took place between 1900 and 1924, when 17.3 million people moved to America—by far the largest migration in any quarter-century in human history. Over the last decade the United States has again experienced large-scale immigration. Many have come from Latin American countries, especially Mexico, but immigration from Asia is also substantial. In 1980 there were 3.8 million Asian Americans. By 1988, there were 6.5 million, a 70 percent increase in just eight years. People of Asian ancestry now make up about 3 percent of the U.S. population—a proportion expected to grow to 5 percent by 2010. The story of American ethnic diversity is still being written.

While people of English, Scottish, and Welsh background remain the largest ethnic group in the United States, they are now a distinct minority of the population. About 83 percent of Americans are whites, 12 percent blacks, and 5 percent of other backgrounds. Hispanic Americans—8 percent of the population, or

FIGURE 2.8   MOVING TO AMERICA: IMMIGRANTS TO THE UNITED STATES, 1981–1990 (BY AREA FROM WHICH THEY EMIGRATED)

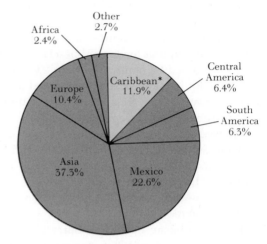

*Antigua-Barbuda, The Bahamas, Barbados, Cuba, Dominica, Dominican Republic, Grenada, Haiti, Jamaica, St. Kitts and Nevis, St. Lucia, St. Vincent and Grenadines, and Trinidad and Tobago.
Source: Center for Immigration Studies, *1990 Immigration and Naturalization Service Yearbook,* as reported in *The New York Times,* May 6, 1992.

about 20 million people—are not a racial group; a majority classify themselves as whites in Census surveys, but a large minority now describe themselves as "other" (not blacks or whites) when asked their racial identity.

Figure 2.8 shows the recent growth in the U.S. population through immigration from Central and South America, and Asia. Between 1981 and 1990, about 47 percent of all immigrants came from Latin America, 37 percent from Asia. Just 10 percent of the immigrants who came to the United States in the last decade came from Europe.

RELIGION

The American populace is now roughly 63 percent Protestant, 25 percent Catholic, and 2 percent Jewish, with 10 percent falling into the category of "other" or "no" religious preference (see Figure 2.9). Among Protestants, Baptists are by far the largest group, making up about 19 percent of the entire population.

Religious beliefs and values remain important to Americans. It used to be thought that when countries become highly developed economically, when large proportions of their populations are college-trained—when they enter their postindustrial eras—the forces of secularization strengthen and religious commitments weaken. The present-day United States confounds this view. There has been some decline in church attendance, but Americans still show strong religious attachments. The proportion of the public stating that their religious beliefs are important to them is much higher in the United States than in any other of the highly developed countries.

SOCIOECONOMIC
DIFFERENCES

Many Americans take pride in the ethnic and religious diversity of their country. But they also want a unity in the diversity, part of which involves equality of group access to income,

education, and jobs. What is the present performance in this regard?

Within white America, historic ethnic-group differences in socioeconomic standing have been greatly reduced in recent years. Surveys taken by the University of Chicago's National Opinion Research Center (NORC) show that groups such as Irish Catholics—who in the past were widely subject to discrimination—have advanced greatly in the post–World War II years. The fabled melting pot has eliminated many of the old ethnic differences in socioeconomic status.

Blacks and Hispanics, however, are still in inferior economic positions. The median income for all white families in 1990 was about $37,000, but only $21,400 for black families and $23,400 for Hispanics. Even here, though, some movement is occurring. Among married-couple families where both spouses work, the median income for whites was $47,000 in 1990, for blacks $40,000, and for Hispanics $34,800—significant differences, but markedly smaller than what had prevailed in the past.[16]

[16]The median income of a group of families is the income exactly in the middle of the range: half of all families earn more, half less.

FIGURE 2.9   RELIGIOUS AFFILIATION (PERCENT OF POPULACE)

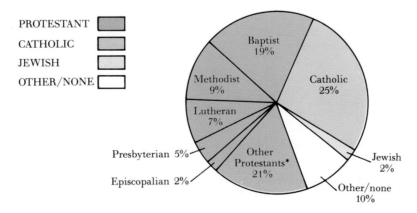

* "Other Protestants" includes other, no denomination given, or a nondenominational church.
Source: Surveys by the National Opinion Research Center, 1989, 1990, and 1991 combined.

REGIONALISM

The major geographic areas of the United States have been fed by different streams of immigration, have experienced contrasting economic development, have had differing needs, and frequently have been at odds politically. For every generation of Americans up through the 1950s, the Northeast was the "establishment" region. It was seen as the great center of industrial wealth—and was attacked by populist movements in the South and West. By the 1970s, however, some said that things had been turned around. We no longer had the

imperial Northeast; the region was described as a troubled Frostbelt, in a state of decline as it lost people, jobs, and political influence. The South was no longer victimized; it had been redefined as the buoyant Sunbelt. Seemingly, winter-time temperatures had become the decisive feature of American regionalism.

This trendy interpretation, however, had the story somewhat twisted. The main economic development was not Frostbelt decline. In fact, the New England and Middle Atlantic states had the highest per capita incomes in 1990. As Figure 2.10 shows, the various sections of the United States were vastly unequal at the turn of the century—hardly a desirable situation in

FIGURE 2.10   COMPARING INCOME LEVELS IN THE UNITED STATES BY REGION, 1900–1990

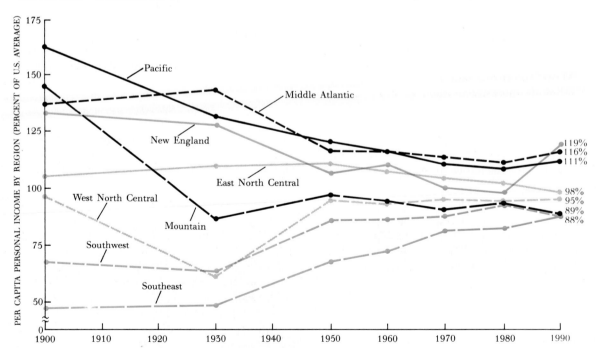

Note: New England: CT, ME, MA, NH, RI, VT; Middle Atlantic: DE, DC, MD, NJ, NY, PA; East North Central: IL, IN, MI, OH, WI; West North Central: IA, KS, MN, MO, NE, ND, SD; Southeast: AL, AR, FL, GA, KY, LA, MS, NC, SC, TN, VA, WV; Southwest: AZ, NM, OK, TX; Mountain: CO, ID, MT, UT, WY; Pacific: CA, NV, OR, WA, AK, HI.
Source: Advisory Commission on Intergovernmental Relations, *Regional Growth: Historical Perspective*, June 1980, p. 11; idem, *Significant Features of Fiscal Federalism*, Vol. II, October 1991, pp. 32–33.

PARTY IDENTIFICATION, 1940 and 1990

| DEMOCRAT | REPUBLICAN | INDEPENDENT |

| 1940 | | 1990 |

New England	East South Central	Mountain

1940			Region	1990		
29%	36%	35%	New England	31%	26%	43%
39%	42%	19%	Middle Atlantic	37%	39%	24%
35%	41%	24%	East North Central	34%	34%	32%
41%	44%	15%	West North Central	32%	36%	32%
66%	25%	10%	South Atlantic	39%	35%	26%
78%	14%	8%	East South Central	39%	33%	27%
79%	11%	10%	West South Central	45%	30%	25%
46%	33%	21%	Mountain	31%	40%	29%
40%	42%	18%	Pacific	43%	33%	24%

Question: In politics, do you consider yourself a Republican, Socialist, Independent, or Democrat?
Note: "Other" category which included Socialist calculated out for comparison purposes.
Source: Survey by the Gallup Organization, July 21–28, 1940.
Question: Regardless of how you voted today, in politics today do you consider yourself a Democrat, Republican, Independent or something else?
Source: Voter Research and Surveys, November 6, 1990.

terms of national unity. Over the last half-century in the United States, though, per capita income by region has become much more uniform. The Sunbelt states of the South have improved their position vis-à-vis the Northeast and Midwest, but this improvement must be understood as a reduction of the South's historic economic lag. The southern Sunbelt is still the least affluent part of the country and its population has the nation's lowest education levels.

SOCIAL AND POLITICAL
REGIONALISM

In social and political terms, America's regions have also come closer together. Racial attitudes in the southern states still differ from those elsewhere in the country, but not nearly as much as they did three and four decades ago. Sectional differences in party loyalties are also much smaller now than they used to be. The trend in political attitudes is toward regional convergence (Figure 2.11 and 2.12). Regional variations are not going to disappear. On such social questions as abortion, sexual norms, and the role of women, and in aspects of race relations, they remain especially striking. Note in the data presented in Figure 2.13 a general bicoastal liberalism, with New England, the Middle Atlantic, and the Pacific states the most socially liberal, and the South and Midwest more conservative. Overall, though, American regionalism has lost a lot of its historic divisiveness, as the regions have become more alike socially, economically, and politically.

FIGURE 2.12   RACIAL ATTITUDES IN THE SOUTH: DIFFERENCES WITH NATION DIMINISH

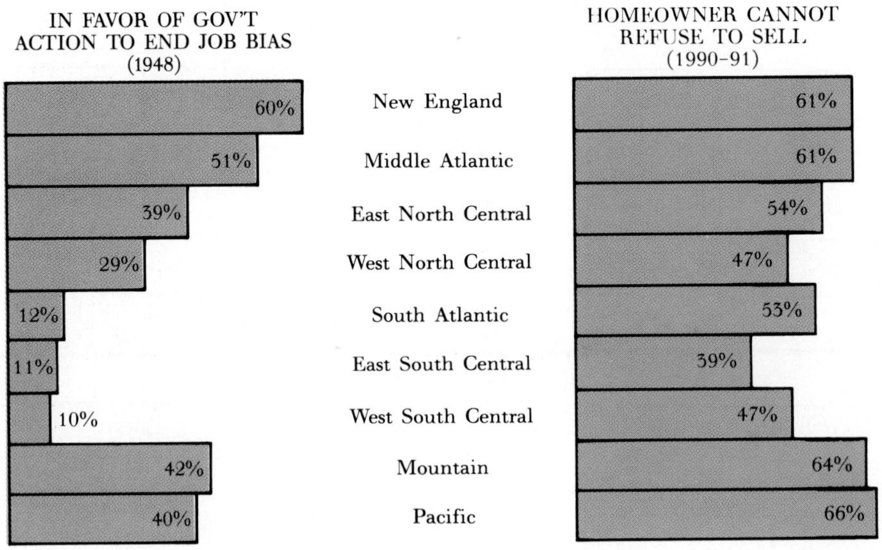

IN FAVOR OF GOV'T
ACTION TO END JOB BIAS
(1948)

HOMEOWNER CANNOT
REFUSE TO SELL
(1990–91)

60%	New England	61%
51%	Middle Atlantic	61%
39%	East North Central	54%
29%	West North Central	47%
12%	South Atlantic	53%
11%	East South Central	39%
10%	West South Central	47%
42%	Mountain	64%
40%	Pacific	66%

Question: One of Truman's proposals concerns employment practices. How far do you yourself think the federal government should go in requiring employers to hire people without regard to their race, religion, color, or nationality? The percentages shown here are responses for federal government going all the way to end job bias.
Source: Survey by the Gallup Organization, March 5–10, 1948.
Question: Suppose there is a community-wide vote on the general housing issue. There are two possible laws to vote on: One law says that a homeowner can decide for himself whom to sell his house to, even if he prefers not to sell to Blacks. The second law says that a homeowner cannot refuse to sell to someone because of their race or color. Which law would you vote for? (White response, 1990–91).
Source: Surveys by the National Opinion Research Center, 1990 and 1991.

OPPORTUNITY AND MOBILITY

The sense that the United States has extended opportunities for individual advancement has figured prominently in the nation's experience. Millions of immigrants moved here seeking a better life. The idea that any person can work his or her way up in wealth and status is central to the country's self-image or conception. Table 2.4 (on page 38) tells us that many Americans in all social groups still believe that they have the opportunity to get ahead if they make the effort. NORC asked respondents in a series of

surveys whether "people get ahead by their own hard work," or whether "lucky breaks or help from other people are more important." This question addresses two related matters central to the American ideology: First, does the United States offer to the many real opportunity for advancement? Is hard work in fact broadly rewarded? Second, do Americans accept the normative claim that they should rely heavily on their own efforts?

Two-thirds of the U.S. public agree that one's own effort determines success or failure. That's an impressive affirmation of individualism. Even more impressive, 60 percent of black Americans accept this standard. In the combined

FIGURE 2.13   BICOASTAL LIBERALISM

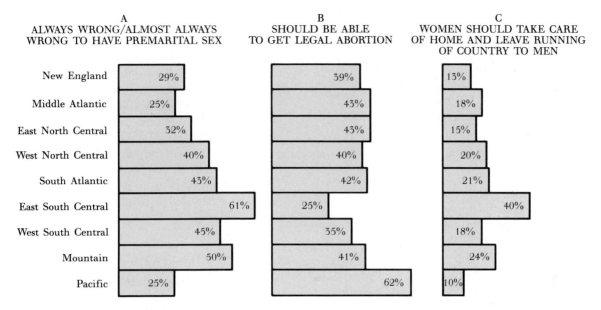

	A ALWAYS WRONG/ALMOST ALWAYS WRONG TO HAVE PREMARITAL SEX	B SHOULD BE ABLE TO GET LEGAL ABORTION	C WOMEN SHOULD TAKE CARE OF HOME AND LEAVE RUNNING OF COUNTRY TO MEN
New England	29%	39%	13%
Middle Atlantic	25%	43%	18%
East North Central	32%	43%	15%
West North Central	40%	40%	20%
South Atlantic	43%	42%	21%
East South Central	61%	25%	40%
West South Central	45%	35%	18%
Mountain	50%	41%	24%
Pacific	25%	62%	10%

A. *Question:* There's been a lot of discussion about the way morals and attitudes about sex are changing in this country. If a man and a woman have sex relations before marriage, do you think it is always wrong, almost always wrong, wrong only sometimes, or not wrong at all?
Source: Surveys by the National Opinion Research Center, 1990 and 1991.
B. *Question:* Please tell me whether or not *you* think it should be possible for pregnant woman to obtain a *legal* abortion if . . . the woman wants it for any reason?
Source: Surveys by the National Opinion Research Center, 1990 and 1991.
C. *Question:* Do you agree or disagree with this statement: Women should take care of running their homes and leave running the country up to men?
Source: Surveys by the National Opinion Research Center, 1990 and 1991.

NORC surveys of 1985 and 1987–91, 69 percent of Hispanic Americans agreed. So did 63 percent of those earning less than $12,500 a year.

"THE RELUCTANT BRIDE"

Because they believe they have substantial opportunity to improve their positions and are individually responsible for doing so, Americans have been less inclined than citizens of most other industrial nations to turn to government for the kinds of programs and assistance

often referred to as "the welfare state." The United States has been, in the words of University of Chicago social scientist Tom W. Smith, "the reluctant bride of the welfare state, instituting national programs later than most countries . . . and spending a lower share of its national income on social welfare than most. . . ."[17] Drawing on data from the United States and a number of European countries collected

[17] Tom W. Smith, "The Polls: The Welfare State in Cross-National Perspective," *Public Opinion Quarterly*, Fall 1987, p. 406.

TABLE 2.4 THE OPPORTUNITY TO GET AHEAD: WHAT AMERICANS FROM VARIOUS SOCIAL GROUPS THINK ABOUT IT

Group	Percentage saying hard work more important than luck
National	66%
White	67
Black	60
Hispanic	69
Protestant Irish	72
Catholic Irish	68
English/Scottish/Welsh	68
Protestant German/Austrian	68
Catholic German/Austrian	71
Scandinavian	70
Italian	61
Eastern European	60
American Indian	71
Protestant	68
Catholic	65
Jewish	57
Unaffiliated	59
Age 18–29	68
Age 30–44	66
Age 45–59	64
Age 60+	65
Less than $12,500	63
$12,500–24,999	69
$25,000–$49,999	67
$50,000 or more	66

Question: Some people say that people get ahead by their own hard work; others say that lucky breaks or help from other people are more important. Which do you think is most important?
Source: Surveys by the National Opinion Research Center, 1985, 1987–1991, combined.

under the International Social Survey Program (ISSP), Smith shows how different Americans are in their attitudes toward individual versus governmental responsibility. Only 36 percent of Americans said they considered it government's responsibility to "reduce income differences between the rich and poor," compared to 72 percent of Austrians, 63 percent of West Germans, 81 percent of Italians, and 70 percent of the British. Thirty-three percent in the United States maintained that it was government's responsibility to "provide a job for everyone who wants one," as against 81 percent in Austria, 80 percent in Germany, 88 percent in Italy, and 69 percent in Great Britain.[18] We examine the consequences of such attitudinal differences in chapter 15, which provides a detailed assessment of American welfare policies.

SOCIAL MOBILITY

Another way to approach the question of individual opportunity is to examine objective data on social mobility. Mobility may be measured by comparing a person's present income, or educational or occupational position with that of his or her parents. Individuals are upwardly mobile when their status is higher than that of their parents.

Throughout much of history, social mobility was limited. In most democratic societies, as a rule, people stayed in the social and economic rank to which they were born, and they worked in the same jobs as their parents. Economic and technological developments of the last two centuries have, though, greatly extended opportunities for upward mobility in countries around the world. Mobility has been especially pronounced in the United States.

In Table 2.5 individuals are located first by the amount of education they have received

[18]The ISSP surveys cited here were conducted in each of the countries mentioned in 1985, except for the Austrian survey, which was done in 1986.

TABLE 2.5 EDUCATIONAL MOBILITY (ROW PERCENTAGES)

Respondent's education	Father's education			
	Less than high school graduate	High school graduate	Some college	College graduate
Less than high school graduate	83	12	3	3
High school graduate	57	32	6	6
Some college	38	32	12	18
College graduate	27	26	13	34

Note: Respondents were asked 2 questions: 1. How much schooling did they have: a. less than high school graduate? b. high school graduate? c. some college? d. college graduate? 2. How much schooling did their fathers have: a.? b.? c.? d.?

Of the respondents who said that they themselves had had less than high school graduate training, 83 percent had fathers (read across) who had less than high school graduate training; 12 percent had fathers who were high school graduates; 3 percent had fathers with some college; and only 3 percent had fathers who were college graduates. Of the respondents who said they were high school graduates, 57 percent had fathers (read across) with less than a high school education; 32 percent had fathers who were high school graduates; 6 percent had fathers with some college; and 6 percent had fathers who graduated from college.

Source: Surveys by the National Opinion Research Center, 1987, 1988, and 1989, combined.

and then by the educational experience of their fathers. An exceptionally large proportion has been upwardly mobile educationally. Among those who today are college graduates, only 34 percent come from families where the father was a college graduate. Two-thirds have more education than their fathers. Of high school graduates, only 12 percent come from families where the father had more than a high school education, while 57 percent are from families where he had less schooling. These data reflect the fact that for each succeeding generation in this century, and especially since World War II, the amount of available education has risen sharply.

A similar relationship can be seen when individuals' current occupational status is compared to that of their fathers. Parents' social position certainly has some influence on what positions their children come to hold. Many people, though, achieve positions different from those of their parents, and often they manage to move up the ladder. Thus the objective data seem to square with people's perceptions that they have a good chance to advance through their own initiatives.

INEQUALITY

Still, if mobility and opportunity are real, they coexist with a great deal of income inequality. The gap between winners and losers in America's mobility race remains a wide one. In 1990 the 20 percent of families with the highest incomes received 44 percent of all earnings, while the lowest-paid 20 percent received only 5 percent of national income. Together, the top 40 percent of all families gained over two-thirds of earnings, while the bottom 40 percent

FIGURE 2.14   INCOME DISTRIBUTION SINCE 1929 (PERCENT OF ALL MONEY INCOME RECEIVED BY LOWEST 40 PERCENT AND HIGHEST 20 PERCENT OF AMERICAN FAMILIES)

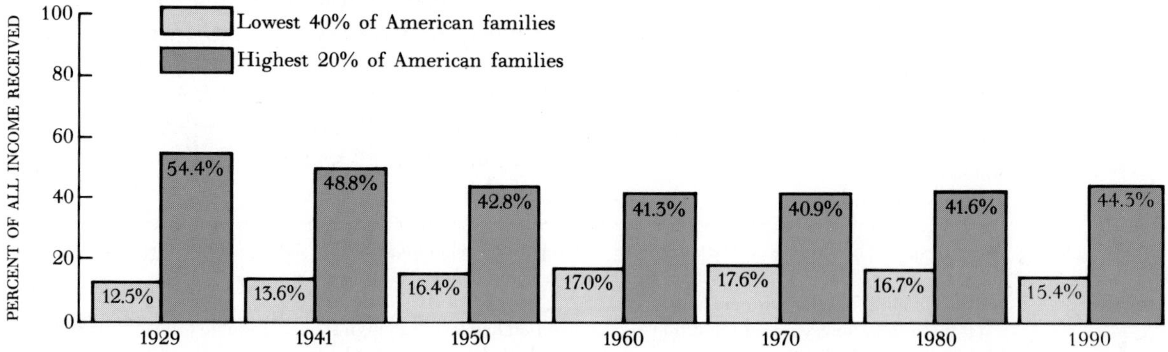

Source: 1929–41: U.S. Bureau of the Census, *Historical Statistics of the U.S.: Colonial Times to 1957*, p. 166; 1950–70: idem, *Historical Statistics of the U.S.: Colonial Times to 1970*, p. 293; 1980–1990: idem, *Current Population Reports*, Series P-60, No. 174, August 1991, p.202.

received under one-sixth of national income (see Figure 2.14).

The degree of income inequality seems to have diminished from the 1930s through the 1960s, even as the amount of income available overall greatly expanded. In 1929, the richest 20 percent of families received 54 percent of all income; the proportion subsequently declined significantly, reaching a low of 41 percent in 1965–70. Various social welfare programs, described in chapter 15, contributed to this income redistribution. Recent data suggest, however, that income inequality increased in the 1970s and 1980s. It should be noted that income distribution is a complex matter that is not easily measured. Chapter 15, provides further interpretation of what has been happening.

SOCIOECONOMIC DETERMINISM?

Among diet-conscious Americans one sometimes hears, "You are what you eat." Nutrition certainly affects our health and well-being. We know, however, that many other things help make us what we are. The setting for politics is formed partly by key economic and demographic characteristics. Even so, American political life is not simply a product of such factors. They are only one part of our political environment. In the next section our focus shifts to another part: the political beliefs of Americans and the ways these beliefs have been expressed in the nation's governmental institutions.

SUMMARY

Postindustrialism is a term, first introduced by sociologist Daniel Bell, that is now commonly used to describe central features of recent social change in the United States and other developed countries. The United States has gradually emerged into its postindustrial era over the last quarter-century.

The postindustrial setting is distinguished by five interrelated developments.

1. It displays extraordinary technological advances which, for the first time, accrue primarily from the systematic applications of science.

2. It requires great commitments to the knowledge base. This is especially evident in the rising proportion of the population receiving college training and the big outlays for education at all levels.

3. Postindustrialism is characterized by the predominant place of the service sector, compared to agriculture and manufacturing. In the United States and other advanced countries, white-collar positions have come to far outnumber blue-collar positions.

4. The achievements of science and technology have produced a level of national wealth in the United States that surpasses that of the earlier industrial era as dramatically as the industrial era surpassed the economic attainments of the agricultural setting.

5. Finally, social class composition and political behavior in postindustrial America differ from what they were in the preceding period. In particular, the working-class base for trade union activity has eroded, and union members have become more conservative politically. The growing college-trained population scrambles earlier assumptions about class makeup and interests.

Many social and political changes occurred as the United States entered the postindustrial era. Nonetheless, in other important regards, contemporary American society is distinguished by the persistence of familiar features.

For example, the ethnic and religious diversity of the United States is an old story. Key to the American political experience has been the task of building a new national identity out of many disparate traditions. Inevitably, ethnic conflict has been prominent in the United States, as the country has moved from one ethnic frontier to another. The split between Protestants and Catholics was once a deep one, but it has long since lost its force. The groups making up white America have become more alike in socioeconomic position and political outlook. In our own time, the oldest of the ethnic cleavages in the country—between whites and blacks—has defined the frontier of ethnic change.

Regional interests and culture have been important parts of the setting for American politics. The greatest political division in U.S. history involved the drastically different sectional interests of North and South. Today, regional differences are still substantial in our society. In economic position and social outlook, though, the regions are less dissimilar now than ever before in U.S. history—this despite the hype about the Frostbelt and the Sunbelt.

American social makeup has been influenced by the amount of social mobility that has occurred. Many people experience movement up and down the social ladder. Class lines are fluid, not fixed. The belief is widely held in the United States that opportunity to move ahead is present, if one makes the effort, and this belief is shared by those with low as well as high incomes. The legitimacy of the political system is thus enhanced.

FOR FURTHER STUDY

Bell, Daniel. *The Coming of Postindustrial Society*. New York: Basic Books, 1973. The most comprehensive account of the social and economic changes encompassed by the concept of postindustrialism, written by a distinguished political sociologist.

Galbraith, John Kenneth. *The New Industrial State*, 4th rev. ed. Boston: Houghton-Mifflin, 1985. A leading interpreter of American economic experience discusses changes in the composition and mode of operation of large institutions, governmental and private sector alike, in the United States.

Morgan, James W. et al., eds. *Five Thousand American Families: Patterns of Economic Progress*. Ann Arbor, Mich.: Institute for Social Research, 1988, vol. 21. A massive, ongoing, multivolume study of the economic experience of Americans.

Organization for Economic Cooperation and Development (OECD). *National Accounts, Volume I: Main Aggregates, 1960–1990* Paris: OECD, 1992. An annual aggregation of economic statistics for twenty-five countries, covering a span of over two decades. An excellent reference for cross-national comparisons.

Riesman, David, Nathan Glaser, and Ruel Denny. *The Lonely Crowd*. New Haven, Conn.: Yale University Press, 1950. An early, classic interpretation of changes in social relationships, centering especially on individualism, in the United States after World War II.

U.S. Bureau of the Census. *Statistical Abstract of the United States*. Washington, D.C.: Government Printing Office, published annually. Like *Historical Statistics*, this publication (latest edition, 1992) is a superb reference work; it contains current and recent historical information on such topics as population, vital statistics, education, geography and the environment, elections, federal, state, and local finances and employment, national defense, social insurance and human services, employment, income, banking, agriculture, manufacturing, and commerce.

OPTIONAL COMPUTER EXERCISES

for *The Ladd Election ANALYZER*

ARE AMERICANS BETTER OFF NOW?

As we saw in this chapter (pp. 25–28), the United States continues to be in a fortunate economic position compared to other nations, but were American voters happy with their lot in 1992? With the *ANALYZER* up and running, press [Enter] at "Analysis 92," again at "Select question to analyze," and again at "Policy view question." Finally, press [Enter] at "Family better off than 1988," the question for analysis. First, run the analysis for all respondents by choosing "Analyze" and then "Perform analysis." After you've gotten the data for all voters, consider looking at various groups: From the "Demographics" menu (under "Include respondent characteristics") select an income level and a region, then "Analyze." Next, delete income and select an educational level, then "Analyze." Do the responses differ? What patterns can you read?

RACE AND VOTING

Asians voted predominantly for George Bush and blacks for Bill Clinton in the 1992 election. Confirm this by selecting the "1992 Vote" from the "Vote questions" menu under "Select question to analyze." Can this difference in candidate preference be attributed to income differences? Did low-income Asians also vote for Bush? Did high-income blacks also vote for Clinton? Analyze the Hispanic vote across income, as well.

INCOME AND VOTING

Overall, did those with low-incomes vote for Clinton and those with high-incomes for Bush? Was this affected by each groups' perceptions of the economy? Also, did those with low incomes who thought the economy was doing well and those with high incomes who thought the economy was doing badly vote like others in their income cohort?

Part 2

THE
POLITICAL
IDEAS

Chapter 3

THE AMERICAN IDEOLOGY

The late 1980s and early 1990s have witnessed perhaps more concentrated global political change than any other comparable period in human history. The revolutionary developments that have toppled regimes and are transforming social, economic, and political life have taken somewhat different form in each country thus involved—from the Soviet Union to Yugoslavia, Poland to Romania, South Africa to Nicaragua. But it is evident that a strong common element runs through all this diverse national experience: the assertion of claims for more individual liberty and for political institutions based on individual choice. Not everyone wants them, of course, and not everyone understands them in the same way, but freedom and democracy are in a fundamental sense the shared objectives.

The revolutionary change that is dominating world politics today is rooted, then, in political ideas. Political revolutions, though spurred by material conditions—economic performance, for instance, and the desire of people caught in poverty for a better life—are in essense the culmination of great ideological battles, involving competing notions of how peoples should be governed.

Today's sweeping transformation is part of a continuous stream of political change reaching back into the seventeenth century and including, in the eighteenth century, the American and French revolutions. Philosophically, what happened in America in 1776 and 1787—establishing the United States as a new nation on new principles of governance—is closely linked to what is occurring now in Eastern Europe. At the same time, the *way* the United States experienced its revolution, and the course other countries have followed, are often vastly different. For one thing, ours came much earlier and in the distinct political and economic environment of that era. For another, it was completed relatively quickly, and the country thus escaped deep-seated, continuing conflict. America shares with many countries the experience of desiring democracy and laboring to become democratic—which is first and foremost a revolution in political ideas. But our revolution followed a different course than other countries, and the consequences of our distinct course remain much in evidence today. As we examine the American ideology in this chapter, we need to be aware both of its kinship to philosophical shifts around the world, including those today in Eastern Europe and what was the Soviet Union, and of its own unique properties.

PHILOSOPHIC ORIGINS: CLASSICAL LIBERALISM

John Adams, later to become the country's second president, did more than anyone else, with the possible exception of Washington, to advance the cause of American independence. Adams understood that the "real" American revolution came about long before 1776. "The Revolution," he wrote in 1818 in a letter to Hezekiah Niles, "was effected before the war [with England] commenced. [It] was in the minds and hearts of the people." This revolu-

John Adams.

tion involved a powerful ideological transformation in what Adams called "the principles, opinions, sentiments, and affections" of the inhabitants of the thirteen colonies. A new American nation, rejecting aristocratic institutions and values, and replacing them with an egalitarian and individualistic order, had emerged bit by bit over the century and a half following the first settlements in Massachusetts and Virginia. The Declaration of 1776 proclaimed an independence that had already been gained philosophically.

This revolution "in the minds and hearts of the people" drew heavily on developments that were taking place in Europe. American political ideology has its roots in a body of political ideas that developed in Europe in the seventeenth and eighteenth centuries—the time when the American colonies were being settled. The European "parent" ideology was known as **liberalism.** It has subsequently often been called

classical liberalism to distinguish it from narrower usages of the terms liberal and conservative in everyday discussion (such as "I am liberal on the question of abortion, but conservative on government spending."). Elements of classical liberalism were brought to the United States by the early settlers and through books by European liberal theorists (such as the seventeenth-century English philosopher John Locke), which were well known in the colonies. Liberalism found fertile soil in America.

Six interrelated beliefs or commitments form the core of this ideological system. (1) **Individualism** is the idea that societies and polities exist to fulfill the right of each individual to "Life, Liberty and the pursuit of Happiness." (2) In order to realize their rights fully, individuals must have **freedom,** the opportunity to make their own choices with a minimum of restraint. (3) Systems of hereditary privilege are rejected by classical liberalism, in the name of **equality.** The intrinsic worth of each person should be seen as equal. (4) One set of goods that all individuals must be permitted to hold is defined by the term **private property.** By acquiring private property, people fulfill deep needs. Private property is a primary way individuals define themselves, protect themselves, and locate their own niche in society. (5) Governments should reflect some measure of **popular choice,** rather than be dominated by a hereditary ruling class, the aristocracy. (6) The reach of governmental power must also be tightly circumscribed. For individuals to be strong and their rights protected, **limited government** must be achieved.

EUROPEAN ORIGINS

We can better understand classical liberalism by exploring briefly how it emerged in Europe in the seventeenth and eighteenth centuries. Liberalism developed as a protest against the then-dominant values, institutions, and class arrangements of aristocratic society. Aristocratic values defended legal and social inequality, special rights, privileges, and obligations of social classes, and arbitrary government as the proper and unalterable nature of things. Each social class had a fixed place in society and had duties and obligations that it had to meet for the well-being of the whole. In the corporeal analogies so common to ideological defenses of monarchy and aristocracy in Europe, the relationship of the nobility and the peasantry was likened by theorists to that of head and limb. What nonsense it would be to speak of the equality of the two! They were naturally different in their abilities, and each had its proper place and function. As the head decides for the human body, so the monarchy and the aristocracy did for the society. Political ideology in every aristocratic society justified permanent subordinate status for most of the populace and their complete exclusion from decision making.

The ascending middle classes, whose numbers and influence were greatly expanded by the commercial and scientific development that began in seventeenth-century Europe, challenged the aristocratic system. Central to their challenge was a wide-ranging attack on the moral and intellectual foundation of aristocracy. New conceptions developed, for example, of how the human mind functions. The brain was seen as a machine—much like that conceived in the scientific thought of the great seventeenth-century English theorist Sir Isaac Newton. Ideas come from the senses. The job of the brain is to organize the many impressions brought to it. If the brain's input (the sensations from the individual's environment) can be controlled, then the output (the way a person thinks and acts, the type of person he is) can be determined.

Philosophers then took the argument one step further. The human brain, as a type of Newtonian machine, is approximately the same for all people. The outputs are different only because the inputs vary. John Locke described the brain at birth as an "empty cabinet," a "white paper . . . void of all characters, without any ideas."[1] This is heady stuff. People are approximately equal in natural capabilities; they differ in performance only because the environments of some are less good. How, then, can the permanent privilege of the monarchy and the nobility be justified? Aristocrats are simply people blessed with better environments. The intellectual basis of individualism emerged in part from a view of humanity that attributed performance to environment.

The great economic expansion made possible by the commercial revolution of the sixteenth and seventeenth centuries and, a century later, by the industrial revolution, also encouraged individualism. It did so by creating material output great enough to offer people the promise that life could be something more than a struggle for survival. When most people had no prospect of living beyond bare subsistence, no matter how available resources were distributed, they acquiesced to extensive privileges for the few, from which they and their children were formally and permanently excluded. In societies of great scarcity, if any culture is to flourish, it is only by arbitrarily granting privilege to a few. Let the pie dramatically expand—precisely what economic and technological developments began to achieve in the seventeenth and eighteenth centuries—and people outside the hereditary privileged classes will step forward to claim their share. They will come to feel that life here and now owes them something more than perpetual wretchedness.

There was a continuing interaction between events and ideas. The economic stirring of trade, banking, and industry in the seventeenth and

eighteenth centuries created new expectations. Masses of people came to believe that they could change the way they lived, and they channeled their energies into improving their day-to-day existence. Society became more secularized, and people came to view themselves as sovereign beings with rights, not merely duties.

Society became more heterogeneous as economic development produced new social groups. An entrepreneurial middle class existed before the seventeenth century, but now there was a tremendous expansion of this middle class and a proliferation of specialized professional groups. Having arrived at positions of economic importance in the new order, operating from new centers of power that the economy had generated, confident in their ability to understand the world and participate in it, told by the new ideology that there was no tenable basis for the continuing privilege of the old hereditary ruling class, the middle classes launched their demands for sweeping changes in the character and makeup of the society.

ENTER AMERICA

The United States was born at the juncture of the revolutionary changes in economic life, science, and political thinking that nurtured liberalism and its sweeping innovations. Liberalism was not made in America; it developed in Europe and was brought to America by the colonists. But once here, liberalism was quickly and quite profoundly modified by American conditions.

In Europe, the aristocratic social structure had been long in existence and was not easily eradicated. For example, those who made the French Revolution in 1789 and the years following never won a complete victory. They succeeded in greatly weakening the aristocracy's grip, but much of the old society survived. Liberalism took root—but as the ideology

[1] John Locke, *Essay Concerning Human Understanding* (Oxford: Oxford University Press, 1894), p. 129; (first published, 1689).

of one class, the middle class, within a larger society. In the United States, however, the middle class was able to develop without the class awareness and conflict thrust upon its counterparts in Europe. America was formed as what historian Louis Hartz called a "fragment society": a piece of seventeenth- and eighteenth-century Europe was broken off and transplanted here. The middle-class fragment, separate from the motherland, flourished in the New World without having to confront its natural ideological and class enemies. "A part detaches itself from the whole, the whole fails to renew itself, and the part develops without inhibition."[2]

In contrast to the European experience, liberal political ideas and values were not seen in America as the distinct property of one class—an entrepreneurial middle class—but rather as the common property of all citizens. Classical liberalism was thus transformed. It became simply "Americanism," the American ideology. Louis Hartz has described this development nicely:

> There has never been a "liberal movement" or a real "liberal party" in America: We have only had the American Way of Life, a national articulation of John Locke which usually does not know that Locke himself is involved. . . . Ironically, "liberalism" is a stranger in the land of its greatest realization and fulfillment.[3]

As liberal political ideals were recast as a national ideology, they necessarily were subject to a whole host of additional changes. Both classical liberalism and the American ideology stress the importance of private property and individuals' property rights. But the ideal of a private-property–based economy seems very different when it is added that all citizens should have the opportunity to acquire property and

[2] Louis Hartz, *The Founding of New Societies* (New York: Harcourt, Brace, 1964), p. 9; idem., *The Liberal Tradition in America* (New York: Harcourt, Brace, 1955) p. 23.

[3] Hartz, *The Liberal Tradition in America*, p. 11.

otherwise advance economically, than when it is claimed that property rights are the perquisite of one social class. Leon Samson had this in mind when he insisted that "the idea that everybody can become a capitalist is an American conception of capitalism."[4]

Building a Nation on an Ideology. There were political disagreements aplenty among those who created the new American government in the late eighteenth century. But those disagreements were within tight boundaries, because of the breadth of the agreement across the young country in the central political values we have been describing. Indeed, it was the broad popular commitment to this ideology that created among the mostly British settlers in eighteenth-century America a sense of being members of a new American nation. Subsequently, adherence to the ideology constituted a bond of common identity and citizenship among the diverse peoples who emigrated to the United States in the nineteenth and in our own century.

Many nations are established on a common ethnic heritage. But the United States is a nation of immigrants, coming from many ethnic traditions. For it to have developed its own unity and identity some other type of cement was needed. Ideology provided it. G. K. Chesterton, a distinguished writer and English visitor to the United States in the 1920s, noted that much of the great American experiment

> of a democracy of diverse races, ... has been compared to a melting pot. But even that metaphor implies that the pot itself is of a certain shape and a certain substance; a pretty solid substance. The melting pot must not melt. *America is the only nation in the world that is founded on a creed.* That creed is set forth with dogmatic and even theological lucidity in the Declaration of Independence; perhaps the only piece of practical politics that is also theoretical politics and also great literature.[5]

AMERICA'S REVOLUTION ... AND OTHERS'

The American Revolution was but one of two great bursts of political and ideological change in the eighteenth century. The other was the French Revolution, which began in 1789. Alexis de Tocqueville, the great French interpreter of both revolutions, understood how different the two were, for all that they had in common. One difference he saw involved the progress of individualism, equality, and democracy in the two countries. The advance of these ideas in America came swiftly and was relatively free of conflict. The revolutionary impact of the ideas occurred

> with ease and simplicity; say rather that this country is reaping the fruits of the democratic revolution which we [in Europe] are undergoing, without having had the revolution itself. The emigrants who colonized the shores of America in the beginning of the seventeenth century somehow separated the democratic principle from all the principles which it had to contend with in the old communities of Europe, and transplanted it alone to the New World.[6]

France's was in many ways a "textbook" revolution. It entailed the abrupt overthrow of the old established ruling class and its many

---

[4] Leon Samson, "Americanism as Surrogate Socialism," in John H. M. Laslett and Seymour Martin Lipset, eds., *Failure of a Dream?* (Garden City, N.Y.: Anchor Press/Doubleday, 1974), p. 429. Taken from a chapter in Samson's *Toward a United Front* (New York: Farrar and Rinehart, 1935).

[5] Gilbert K. Chesterton, *What I Saw in America* (New York: Dodd, Mead, 1922), pp. 7–8.

[6] Tocqueville, *Democracy in America* (New York: Vintage Books, 1958), vol. 1, p. 14.

institutions and values. America's, too, rejected aristocratic society, but it did so gradually and nonviolently. The French Revolution was a dramatic event, fixed at a precise moment in time. The American revolution cannot be precisely located.

The French Revolution was anything but easy, and it certainly did not reach its "natural limits" in 1789. Whereas America's revolution was concluded in the eighteenth century, France's was ongoing throughout the nineteenth century and well into the twentieth. The old aristocratic order never again achieved the ascendancy it had enjoyed prior to 1789, but it remained a potent part of French society, battling with the new social institutions and political ideas.

Because its revolution was for so long incomplete and continuing, France's governmental institutions were highly unstable for a considerable length of time. In the two-hundred-plus years since George Washington's inauguration on April 30, 1789, the United States has been governed under a single constitution. In this same time span, France has had ten distinct constitutional systems, including five republics, the latest of which came into being just three decades ago.

Interestingly enough, the Fifth French Republic (established in 1958 and initially expected to be short-lived, perhaps not surviving beyond the life of its principal architect, Charles de Gaulle) may well be the regime that marks the end of France's long political instability. The process of ideological change and institutional groping that began in 1789 seems finally to have run its course. France is now a relatively tranquil place politically. In 1989 France celebrated the bicentennial of a revolution that, at last, belongs to the past.

TOCQUEVILLE ON "HISTORICAL INEVITABILITY"

Tocqueville described the values America and France sought in their respective revolutions by a number of different names—as the principle of "*egalité*," or of "equality of condition," or sometimes simply as "democracy." As we have seen, the literature of social science has commonly referred to these values as classical liberalism. Today we might be most precise, though, in naming them *liberal individualism*—a body of ideas that places the sovereign individual at the epicenter of society. According to this philosophy, no government or movement can be deemed legitimate unless and until it respects individual rights: of expression, choosing leaders, gaining and disposing of property, defining one's own future.

Tocqueville did not state it precisely this way, but he clearly understood that only two large philosophical systems had for a millennium shown enduring legitimacy: *aristocracy*, or the ascriptive class principle, which posited a col-

lectivist society based on inherited privileges and duties; and *liberal individualism,* which began stirring when deep underlying changes in the economy, religion, science, and politics began to topple the ancient aristocratic order. Aristocracy had long prevailed. In most countries the collapse of so comprehensive a system would entail painfully chaotic transitions, where all manner of charlatans might win out before the new order finally prevailed.

Here is Tocqueville on the historic inevitability of individualism's victory: "The gradual development of the principle of equality is, therefore, a Providential fact. It has all the chief characteristics of such a fact: it is universal, it is lasting, it constantly eludes all human interference, and all events as well as all men contribute to its progress."[7]

The young Frenchman explained in 1835 that he had come to America because it was there that liberal individualism had found its first full historical expression. "There is one country in the world," he wrote, "where the great social revolution that I am speaking of seems to have nearly reached its natural limits."[8]

In time, Tocqueville explained, this individual-centered view of man and society would reach out and triumph everywhere: "It appears to me beyond a doubt that, sooner or later, we shall arrive, like the Americans, at an almost complete equality of condition."[9] It should be noted that he saw society based on thoroughgoing individualism as something far from perfect. But it was inevitable and far preferable to the transitional regimes, and it should be prepared for.

To someone imprisoned in Joseph Stalin's prisons in 1935, or arrested in the Hungarian revolt of 1956, talk of Soviet communism as a "transitional system," carrying in its rejection of individual rights the seeds of its own destruction, might have seemed unbearably naive and callous. But the developments we see today across Eastern Europe and the former Soviet Union are indeed part of the process that Tocqueville saw a century and a half ago as inevitable and that, over the ensuing years, has in fact continued to work its way.

THE LEGACY OF THE AMERICAN IDEOLOGY

The ideas of liberal individualism—with their emphasis on the rights of individuals to political freedom, limited government and self-government, private property, and social and economic opportunity—are set forth in the great documents of American political life: the Dec-

"But enough about my unique brand of Americanism. Tell me about your unique brand of Americanism."

Drawing by Richter; © 1984 The New Yorker Magazine, Inc.

[7] Ibid., p. 6.
[8] Ibid., p. 14.
[9] Ibid.

laration of Independence, the Constitution, and such speeches as Lincoln's Gettysburg and Second Inaugural addresses. How much have these ideas really shaped American social and political behavior?

In all societies, ideas taken most seriously have sometimes been ignored or flouted. This is not to make excuses for American shortcomings. We can hardly forget that a number of the men who signed the Declaration of Independence, with its bold insistence that all people are created equal, were themselves owners of slaves. Slavery is, of course, a powerful denial of the ideal of individual rights and equality. Yet it survived and even expanded its hold, until it was finally ended by the Civil War (1861–65). Still, pervasive racial discrimination was permitted long after slavery as such was abolished.

It is one thing to recognize that the United States has at times fallen far short of the highest ideals professed by its ideology, something else to insist that these shortcomings make the ideology's claims mere sham. If one insists that a set of beliefs always be adhered to before we should take its claims seriously, one ends up dismissing every one of them. Where is the Christian nation that has lived up to the religion's highest claims? America's ideological commitments, including the emphasis on individual rights, have had great impact on the nation's social and political life, even though the dictates of these ideas have sometimes been ignored.

AMERICAN IDEOLOGICAL BLINDSPOTS

In many ways the deficiencies of American ideology are outgrowths of its strength. The ideology stresses the equality of individuals and the legitimacy of their respective claims for a chance at the good life. Throughout U.S. history, deprived groups—ethnic and religious

minorities and women, among them—have effectively used these values in their fight for equality and recognition. The strength of the ideology, together with the extent to which American national identity has been built around it, has provided a means of entry into full citizenship for millions of immigrants. American political values have often opened rather than closed doors to those previously on the outside.

A Certain Intolerance. The very strength and unity of the ideology, however, carries with it the basis for a special American form of intolerance. Historian Garry Wills has observed that if there is an American idea, to really be an American "one must adopt this idea wholeheartedly, proclaim it, prove one's devotion to it." There has never been a legislative committee on "un-French activities," or one on "un-English affairs." But the strength of the American creed has allowed the formation of the House of Representatives Committee on Un-American Activities and this committee's general intolerance in the 1940s and 1950s of dissenting ideas.[10] "Now a creed," G. K. Chesterton observed, "is at once the broadest and the narrowest thing in the world."[11] The American creed, on which national identity was established, has attracted and been open to people from all over the globe. It is at the same time narrow in its insistence that citizenship must be based upon adherence to certain political values.

American Insularity. "Can a people 'born equal,'" Louis Hartz asked at the close of his study of the American liberal tradition, "ever understand peoples elsewhere that have to become so? . . . Can it ever understand itself?"[12]

[10] Garry Wills, *Inventing America* (New York: Vintage Books, 1978), p. xxii.
[11] Chesterton, *What I Saw in America*, p. 7.
[12] Hartz, *The Liberal Tradition in America*, p. 309.

In the 1950s, the extreme anti-communist campaign waged by Senator Joseph McCarthy during the House Un-American Activities hearings showed a disregard for human decency and civil liberties.

The American ideological world has been insular. At the outset, it was cut off from the conflicts of European countries. Over the last two centuries, when countries around the world have been struggling to overthrow aristocratic institutions and traditions, the United States has been sympathetic—yet removed from their experiences and problems. One result of this is the common tendency of American conservatives and liberals alike to moralize about the shortcomings of other countries or governments. We often seem to feel a bit self-righteous: "We were able to overcome these problems; why can't they?"

A POSITIVE LEGACY: THE CASE OF FORD

Every enduring ideological system has strengths and weaknesses. The American ideology is no exception. It has its narrowness and insularity, its cases where emphasis on individualism seems excessive—a prescription for greed or hedon-

ism. But it also has shown the capacity to encourage behavior that honors its claims to equality and opportunity. The case of Henry Ford and "five dollars a day minimum pay" is revealing.

On Sunday morning, January 4, 1914, American automaker Henry Ford sat in his office in Highland Park, Michigan, with three other Ford Motor Company executives. Ford had called the meeting to discuss employee wages for the coming year. His company's minimum wage was then $2 a day, an amount in line with what American industry was paying. This rate was much lower than present wages, but not as much lower as it appears, because a dollar bought so much more then— a loaf of bread, a bar of Ivory soap, and a pound of sugar each cost about 8 cents, a bed sheet 35 cents, a pair of women's shoes $3.35, and a nine-day all-expense-paid cruise to Bermuda just $46.

Henry Ford told his colleagues that he wanted to raise the minimum wage significantly; he had various calculations of what the company could afford posted on an old blackboard in the office. Charles Sorensen was one executive present with Ford that cold January morning, and years later he wrote a detailed account of the meeting:

> Mr. Ford . . . had me transfer figures from the profits column to labor costs—two million, three million, four million dollars. With that daily wage figures rose from a minimum of $2 to $2.50 and $3. Ed Martin [another executive present] protested. . . . While I stood at the blackboard, John Lee [the fourth Ford executive in the office] commented upon every entry and soon became pretty nasty. It was plain he wasn't trying to understand the idea and thought he might sabotage it by ridiculing it. This didn't sit well with Mr. Ford, who kept telling me to put more figures down—$3.50, $3.75, $4.00, $4.25, and a quarter of a dollar more, then another quarter.

At the end of about four hours, Mr. Ford stepped up to the blackboard. "Stop!" he said. "Stop it, Charlie; it's all settled. Five dollars a day minimum pay and at once."[13]

Real wages at Ford increased 150 percent companywide that day. Henry Ford took perhaps the most dramatic step in the entire history of American industry without any pressure from workers; the company was not even unionized. He made his decision over the protests of his fellow Ford executives, who thought it would bankrupt the company. And after word of the pay raise had reverberated across the country and around the world, Ford was denounced by many other business leaders, who believed massive harm would result to all of American business from this "dangerous

[13] Charles E. Sorenson, *My Forty Years with Ford* (New York: Norton, 1956), p. 139.

A 1913 Ford assembly line in Dearborn, Michigan.

precedent." Even more startling, as Ford raised wages, he lowered the price of his car, the Model T. Priced at $850 in 1908, the Model T sold at steadily reduced rates until, in 1926, it cost just $295. Why did Ford do it?

Henry Ford offered his own explanation.

> It ought to be the employer's ambition, as leader, to pay better wages than any similar line of business. . . . The best wages that have up to date ever been paid are not nearly as high as they ought to be. . . . We made the change [the $5 day] not merely because we wanted to pay higher wages and thought we could pay them. We wanted to pay these wages so that the business would be on a lasting foundation. We were not distributing anything—we were building for the future.[14]

CAPITALISM, DEMOCRACY, AND THE AMERICAN IDEOLOGY

What Ford did proved to be good business. As prices dropped and wages rose—together with dramatic productivity increases through innovative assembly-line procedures—American workers were able to buy many more cars, Ford cars included. But the $5 day was not just an imaginative economic calculation. Ford took his dramatic step on January 4, 1914, because he believed that it was the responsibility of American business to "abolish poverty."

In implementing the $5 day, Ford was acting out—with unusual force and insight—an ideology that he shared with millions of his countrymen. He believed in the idea of **democratic capitalism.** America's private-property–based economy existed for something more than making businessmen rich; it existed to make

possible an ever-higher standard of living for the general population. It was capitalism committed to democratic and egalitarian ends.

"The idea that everybody can become a capitalist," wrote Leon Samson, a brilliant young American socialist, in 1935, "is an American conception of capitalism. It is [also] a socialist conception of capitalism. Capitalism is, in theory, and in Europe, for the capitalists. . . ." In America, though, it has highly democratic and egalitarian elements, Samson argued.

> Nowhere is capitalism so well advanced [as in the United States]. But one must be careful to distinguish between the development of American capitalism and the development of the American as capitalist. For, if one were to examine the underlying aspirations of the American, his real sentiments and moods, it would not be difficult to discover in him trends of the soul that, far from being the traditionally capitalistic trends, are on the contrary tinged with every variety of socialism. Thus, for example, so unmistakable an American as [former President Herbert] Hoover from time to time unburdens himself of the belief that it is the destiny of the American system to abolish poverty. Now, Hoover may not know it but when he talks this way he is simply talking socialism. To "abolish poverty" is a time-honored socialist aim. Who has ever heard a responsible spokesman of European capitalism announce that it is the aim of, let us say, the French or the English "system" to "abolish poverty"?[15]

Henry Ford's decision to raise his company's minimum wage from $2 to $5, without any immediate pressure to do so, was unusual, even heretical, in the general context of capitalist beliefs and behavior. It was consistent, however, with democratic capitalism—and more generally with the political ideology on which the United States was built.

[14] Henry Ford, in collaboration with Samuel Crowther, *My Life and Work* (Garden City, N.Y.: Doubleday, 1923), pp. 117–30, *passim.*

[15] Samson, "Americanism as Surrogate Socialism," p. 437.

One challenge to national unity: Violence broke out in Los Angeles in May 1992 following an all-white jury's acquittal of four white Los Angeles police officers accused of using excessive force in the arrest of black motorist Rodney King. Here, firefighters struggle against arsonists' blazes.

CHALLENGES TO NATIONAL UNITY

As a nation built not on a common ancestry, but rather on the uniting of people from diverse ethnic, linguistic, and cultural backgrounds, the United States has often seen itself as uncomfortably vulnerable to centrifugal pressures. Is our cohesiveness, we have wondered periodically, being eroded by too much immigration from different traditions? Is national unity threatened by assertions of particularistic ethnic and linguistic claims? Is what Chesterton called "the great American experiment . . . of a democracy of diverse races" somehow being put in jeopardy?

Such doubts are again front and center. The "two nations—black and white" argument seems to many to have been reinforced by an all-white jury's acquittal of officers of the Los Angeles Police Department in the beating of a black man, Rodney King, and by the violence and protests in L.A. and other U.S. cities that followed. And concerns about national unity are broader than this. For example, in a recent book the distinguished historian Arthur Schlesinger, Jr., examines critically efforts that would, he believes, reverse our historic progression from *pluribus* to *unum*. Schlesinger writes that, in recent years, "ethnic ideologues" have opposed "the old American ideal of assimilation," and called on the country "to think

in terms not of individual but of group indentity. . . ."[16]

However, even as he expresses concern about challenges to national unity, Schlesinger stresses the enormous strength and staying power of America as a nation, made one by a widely shared set of social and political ideals. He concludes that "the campaign against the idea of common ideals and a single society will fail. . . . A historian's guess is that the resources of the [American] Creed have not been exhausted."[17] What Schlesinger calls "the resources of the Creed" is, of course, the attraction American ideals and promise have had for millions who have migrated here and the strong sense of nationhood they have made possible among these peoples through shared ideological adherence.

Today the United States faces enormous tensions in race relations. It has, of course, been beset by ethnic and other social-group tensions throughout its history. The potential for conflict has always been enormous in a country as diverse as ours. But will the nation's historic philosophic commitments be sufficient to mitigate the current conflict? Will the integrative capacities of shared values be sufficient to stop that conflict from intensifying?

Survey data suggest strongly that the answer to both these question is yes. On the broad principles on which the United States was founded, in fundamental attachment to the country, and in respect for its symbols as expressions of national unity, surveys reveal strong agreement across group lines. Centrifugal pressures are surely present, but if they are gaining strength, the available data emphatically do not show it.[18]

---

[16] Arthur Schlesinger, Jr., *The Disuniting of America* (New York: W. W. Norton, 1992), p. 130.

[17] Ibid, p. 131.

[18] For a review of the data, see "The American Ideology: An Exploration of the Origins, Meaning, and Role of American Values." A preliminary version was presented at a conference, "The New Global Popular Culture," sponsored by the American Enterprise Institute for Public Policy Research, Washington, D.C. March 10, 1992. See, too, "American Values in Comparative Perspective," *The Public Perspective*, November/December 1991, pp. 5–8.

THE ROLE OF IDEOLOGY

American politics is sometimes described as nonideological. In only one sense is this valid: conflict among competing ideological traditions has been rare in the United States, for reasons we have just described. But American politics is highly ideological in other regards. Most importantly, it is shaped and informed, even dominated, by a distinctive set of political beliefs.

An ideology may be defined as a set of political beliefs and values that are *constrained*, or tied together. Like a quilt, an ideology is more than the sum of its patches; it is the patches bound together in a specified and ordered arrangement. An ideology isn't just a random collection of beliefs but rather a coherent view of the world. It provides answers to such questions as how government should be organized and power distributed, and what goals the society should try to realize.

POLITICAL SOCIALIZATION

As we grow up, participate in assessing the nation's history and politics in school and with our families, listen to news programs on television, and read books, we are introduced to the underlying political beliefs and values of our society. This is called **political socialization.** Through it, we absorb bits and pieces of the political ideology.

Many citizens do not spend a lot of time examining political ideas. Political scientist Philip Converse showed over two decades ago that most people absorb only portions of formal ideologies. Their beliefs and preferences are organized loosely, sometimes even illogically.[19]

Similarly, in his study of the political beliefs of a group of working-class Americans, Robert E. Lane noted that their views were characterized by "loosely structured and unreflective statements."[20]

There is a big difference between the formal coherence of American ideology, as it gets set forth in books, and the more disjointed political outlook of the average citizen. But even so the links are there. People often do not know precisely where their underlying values come from, so general is the process by which they are introduced to these views. But they are, nonetheless, guided and oriented by the prevailing political ideology. It seeps in through all sorts of openings and informs the way they view the world.

THE IDEOLOGICAL FOUNDATION OF AMERICAN INSTITUTIONS

The ascendancy of liberal individualism in the United States has had a profound influence on American politics. This influence has been strongest in molding the country's political institutions and providing their rationale and legitimacy.

We will develop this point in the next chapter, in discussing the origins of the U.S. Constitution, its longevity, and the type of democracy it ordains. Our political system owes its strength in large part to the faithfulness with which it articulates a dominating national ideology. That ideology and the governmental order go hand in hand; the latter institutionalizes the central assumptions of the former.

[19] Philip Converse, "The Nature of Belief Systems in Mass Publics," in David Apter, ed., *Ideology and Discontent* (New York: Free Press, 1964), pp. 206–61.

[20] Robert E. Lane, *Political Ideology: Why the American Common Man Believes What He Does* (New York: Free Press, 1962), p. 11.

SUMMARY

Americans have strong feelings of national identity and unity. In contrast to other countries, whose sense of ethnic identity is highly developed, this sense of national unity has been achieved in the United States without ethnic commonality.

The American nation has been built on a system of political beliefs or ideology. This ideology had its origins in the social frustrations and political interests of the rising middle classes of seventeenth- and eighteenth-century Europe. Known as *classical liberalism*, the ideas were brought to the New World by the middle-class fragment that settled here. They were enlarged and transformed by American social conditions. They are perhaps most precisely described today as *liberal individualism*.

As it has developed in the United States, liberal individualism stresses an individualistic rather than a collectivist view of society: individual rights, including political freedom and private property rights; equality of opportunity; and limited, democratic government. It has been espoused by groups across the social spectrum, rather than remaining the outlook of one social class. Individuals have at times argued that America has denied them their rights under the liberal creed, but few have attacked the legitimacy of the creed itself. Institutions established under the American ideology, such as the Constitution and a private-property–based economy, have drawn strength from its dominant hold on national thought.

FOR FURTHER STUDY

Bellah, Robert N., et al. *Habits of the Heart: Individualism and Commitment in American Life.* Berkeley, Calif.: University of California Press, 1985. An important new examination of American individualism that is highly critical of recent developments within it.

Chesterton, Gilbert K. *What I Saw in America.* New York: Dodd, Mead, 1922. An insightful interpretation of American political ideology, written by a distinguished British writer and intellectual.

Hartz, Louis. *The Liberal Tradition in America.* New York: Harcourt, Brace and Co., 1955. The most important interpretation by an American political scientist of how the conditions under which the United States was founded have continued to shape American political thought.

Locke, John. "Second Treatise of Civil Government: An Essay Concerning the True Original Extent, and End of Civil Government" in Peter Laslett, ed. *Two Treatises of Government.* New York: New American Library, 1965; essay originally published, 1690. An essay by a major figure in the development of liberal thought in the seventeenth century that influenced the conceptions of government of the American founders.

Schlesinger, Arthur, Jr. *The Disuniting of America.* New York: W. W. Norton, 1992.

Chapter 4

THE CONSTITUTION AND AMERICAN DEMOCRACY

The main articles of the U.S. Constitution were drafted in the spring and summer of 1787. And when, four years later, the first ten amendments, known as the Bill of Rights, were added, the formal acts of American constitution making were largely finished. As a result, constitutional scholars Robert Goldwin and Art Kaufman observe, "Americans are accustomed to thinking of constitution writing as something done hundreds of years ago by bewigged gentlemen wearing frock coats, knee breeches, and white stockings."[1]

In fact, though, most constitution writing around the world is of very recent vintage. "The Constitution of the United States is now more than 200 years old, but most of the other constitutions in the world," Goldwin and Kaufman point out, "are less than fifteen years old. That is, of the 160 or so national written constitutions in the world, more than half have been written since 1974."

[1] Robert A. Goldwin and Art Kaufman, eds., *Constitution Makers on Constitution Making: The Experience of Eight Nations* (Washington, D.C.: American Enterprise Institute, 1988), p. 14.

THE STAYING POWER OF AMERICA'S CONSTITUTION

The U.S. Constitution was not the first written constitution. In the years immediately preceding 1787, each of the American states (with the qualified exceptions of Rhode Island and Connecticut) had drafted and put into operation a written constitution. And the Constitution of 1787 was not the first national constitution of the United States. The Articles of Confederation and Perpetual Union was agreed to in November 1777, by delegates of the thirteen states, just a little over a year after the signing of the Declaration of Independence. Still, as political theorist Walter Berns points out, those who drafted the Constitution in Philadelphia in 1787 "knew very well indeed [that] they were engaged in what was still a novel enterprise, an experiment, and one for which history provided little guidance."[2]

The founders also were keenly aware of the importance of their new venture as an example for other peoples around the world. In the first of *The Federalist Papers*—85 essays, justly deemed classics, written in defense of the new Constitution in the fall of 1787 and the winter of 1788—Alexander Hamilton observed that

> it has been frequently remarked that it seems to have been reserved to the people of this country, by their conduct and example, to decide the important question whether societies of men are really capable or not of establishing good government from *reflection and choice*, or whether they are forever destined to depend for their political institutions on *accident and force*. If there be any truth in the remark, the crisis at

which we are arrived may with propriety be regarded as the era in which that decision is to be made; and a wrong election on the part we shall act may, in this view, deserve to be considered as the general misfortune of mankind.[3]

This sense that theirs was a great opportunity, and a formidable responsibility, clearly guided the constitution making in Philadelphia in 1787, as it did so much of the work of America's early leaders. John Adams, who was to become the country's first vice president and second president, had closed his influential pamphlet, *Thoughts on Government*, with this extraordinary vision:

> You and I, my friend, have been sent into life at a time when the greatest lawgivers of antiquity would have wished to live. How few of the human race have ever enjoyed an opportunity of making an election [that is, choice] of government, more than of air, soil, or climate, for themselves or their children! When, before the present epocha, had three millions of people full power and a fair opportunity to establish the wisest and happiest government that human wisdom can contrive?[4]

James Madison, who was to become the fourth president, told the constitutional convention on June 26, 1787: "We ... decide forever the fate of Republican government."

It is still doubtful, even given their lofty expectations and sense of responsibility, that the founders could have dreamed their handiwork would survive and prosper as it has for over two hundred years now. In unbroken succession, the United States has been governed under a single basic law since 1787. In the same span of time France has been gov-

---

[2]Walter Berns, "The Writing of the Constitution of the United States," in Goldwin and Kaufman, eds., *Constitution Makers on Constitution Making*, p. 119.

[3]Alexander Hamilton, *Federalist Paper* No. 1, in Clinton Rossiter, ed., *The Federalist Papers* (New York: New American Library, 1961), p. 33. Emphasis added.

[4]John Adams, *Thoughts on Government* (Philadelphia, 1776), p. 27.

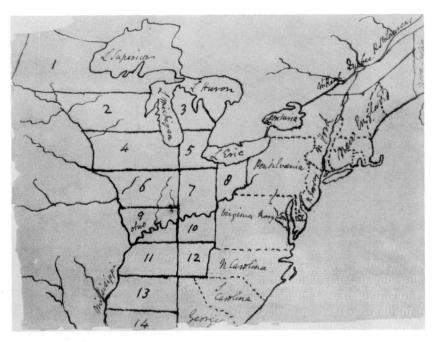

A map of the young nation including the original states and some proposals for new states drawn by Thomas Jefferson.

erned by ten separate and distinct constitutional orders, including five different republics, two empires, one monarchy, one plebiscitary dictatorship, and one puppet dictatorship installed at Vichy during World War II. The United States has had but one constitution and, created under it, one set of governing institutions. Built on America's ideological foundation, the Constitution owes its remarkable staying power to the continuing dominance of liberal ideas.

But it is not just the basic constitutional form that has survived. So, too, has the spirit, the animating assumptions. The American Constitution of the 1990s is in all essential regards the Constitution of 1787. American democracy today bears the deep imprint of the founders' design.

The founders believed that concentrated governmental power was a prime threat to individual liberty, so they dispersed power across a number of separate and independent governmental institutions—at the national level: Congress, the presidency, and the federal courts. They gave each of these institutions the means of checking and balancing the others. Today, some wonder if the founders did too good a job in this regard. They worry that separation of powers, especially involving the executive and the legislature, leaves our national government unable to act coherently on a number of pressing national problems. We will look at these issues in detail in the chapters ahead, especially in chapter 5.

The debate over what our democracy requires is as lively as ever. If Americans have learned anything in their two hundred years of experience with democratic government, it is that democracy is wonderfully rewarding, always demanding, and at times frustratingly difficult to achieve satisfactorily. The great British prime minister Winston Churchill once remarked that "democracy is the worst form of government . . . except for all the others." This backhand defense of democracy may well be the most profound defense. Presumably, much of the current push for democracy around the world stems from just this sense—that, not perfect, it is far preferable to the alternatives.

Preference for limited, democratic government is, as we noted in chapter 3, a key part of the American ideology; and the U.S. Constitution has provided a set of such democratic institutions. For many Americans, then, for more than two centuries the question of whether democracy is the best form of government involves little debate. Nonetheless, some observers insist that the government of the United States is flawed, by democratic standards. Behind the latter argument lies a basic question: What does democracy as a political theory really encompass? Since the idea of democratic government goes back 2,400 years, to the Greek city-state of Athens, we might think that the question of democracy's meaning would have long since been resolved to everyone's satisfaction. It has not, however. Later in this chapter we will take a close look at various conceptions of democracy, especially those common in the United States. We will trace the concept from its Greek origins, through the thinking of the framers of the U.S. Constitution, to present-day perspectives on what democratic government means or requires, and we will discuss different views on the quality of America's democratic performance.

We begin, though, by looking closely at the origins of the document that underlies and animates our democratic system: the Constitution. Three related questions need to be answered if we are to understand American constitutional experience and assess properly its legacy. How did the Constitution come to be written, approved, and implemented in the form we know today? Who were the men most

responsible for the Constitution and what were their primary political objectives? What are the essential characteristics of the type of government that the Constitution establishes?

THE FIRST STIRRINGS

On July 2, 1776, the Continental Congress—representing thirteen North American colonies—approved a motion that had been introduced by Richard Henry Lee of Virginia about a month earlier: "That these united colonies

Thomas Jefferson's draft of the Declaration of Independence.

John Trumbull's painting of the signing of the Declaration of Independence.

are, and of right ought to be free and independent states." Assisted by Benjamin Franklin and John Adams, Thomas Jefferson expanded the resolution into the famous Declaration of Independence that was adopted on July 4. The Declaration powerfully affirmed the liberal ideal of individual rights made familiar by John Locke and advanced by a century and a half of American experience. (The text of the Declaration of Independence is reprinted in the Appendix to this book.)

The War for Independence, which began in 1775, was not decided until October 19, 1781, when the British General Charles Cornwallis surrendered his army to General George Washington. With their military band playing "The World Turned Upside Down," 7,000 British troops marched out of Yorktown, Virginia, and laid down their arms. Preliminary articles of peace were signed a year later, on November 30, 1782, and the final treaties were signed in Paris on September 3, 1783. America's ideological independence had been achieved long before 1783, however, and was framed around a national commitment to liberal and individualistic values.

THE ARTICLES OF CONFEDERATION

On July 12, 1776, a committee of the Continental Congress brought in a draft of a proposed constitution. After more than a year of arguing about such questions as how war expenses should be apportioned and voting power allocated among the states, the Congress finally approved the document on November 17, 1777, and submitted it to the thirteen state legislatures for consideration. **The Articles of Confederation,** as this first national constitution was called, were approved by all thirteen states except Maryland by 1779; Maryland ratified in 1781.

The Articles faithfully reflected American political values of the time. They provided for a national government founded on republican principles—the idea that governmental institutions should be responsive to the will of the people—and distinguished by a commitment to individual liberty achieved through dispersed and limited governmental power. But in some basic structural regards, the government of the Articles of Confederation was flawed.

The main deficiency stemmed from the states' position as fully sovereign entities that merely ceded certain limited powers to the national government. The sovereign character and equality of the thirteen states was reflected in the manner of their representation in the Continental Congress. Each state, whatever its size, had only one vote; this was cast by delegates appointed by the state legislature. The states were supposed to contribute to the common expenses of the nation—for example, the costs of maintaining a national army—according to the value of their lands. But the national government lacked any means to compel state compliance, and it was always teetering on the brink of bankruptcy.

The impotence of the Continental Congress left the United States singularly ill-equipped to protect its own national interests in dealing with other countries. For instance, the Congress had printed paper money to meet the costs of the war with England. Near the war's end, this currency had become virtually worthless in the absence of a national taxing power. The Congress was forced to beg money and supplies from France. After the war, the Congress had to borrow money from bankers in Holland. When it turned to the states for funds

as provided in the Articles, or when it sought the power to levy a 5 percent tariff on imports, the states turned this "beggar nation" down. In order to impose a tariff, the unanimous approval of the states was required; in 1781 and again in 1783 at least one state refused.

Since the Congress did not have the power to levy taxes and could not force the states to use their authority to tax as provided in Article VIII, it was unable to raise enough money for the common defense or general welfare of the United States. Even Revolutionary War debts could not be paid, including salaries owed for military service. Army officers encamped themselves at Newburg, New York, in 1783 and threatened mutiny to force the Congress to pay their long-overdue wages. This financial weakness also contributed to the Congress's inability to protect the trans-Alleghany wilderness region. It could not support troops to defend settlers from Indian attacks, nor could it prevent the British and Spanish governments from establishing settlements in these lands.

Along with its own financial weakness, the Congress had to contend with states issuing their own currencies. Article IX granted the Congress "sole and exclusive right and power of regulating the alloy and value of coin struck by their own authority or by that of the respective states. . . ." But this did not stop states from issuing money. Debtor and creditor factions in various states engaged in bitter struggles. Some states passed laws forcing acceptance of devalued paper currency at its face value; others deferred the collection of debts and prohibited courts from issuing judgments for debts. A former Army captain, Daniel Shays, led a group of armed Massachusetts farmers in an insurrection in 1786, attempting to prevent the county courts from sitting in judgment on debts. The whole system of monetary exchange was in chaos.

Under the Articles of Confederation, the national government was little more than an aspiration. The claim of Article II, that "each state retain its sovereignty, freedom, and independence," was the reality. The provision of Article III that the states "hereby severally enter in a firm league of friendship with each other" fairly described the governmental order.

THE MOVE TO A STRONG NATIONAL GOVERNMENT

As a statement of republican principles embodying an ideal of popular government, the Articles of Confederation were admirable. As a constitution for a workable national government, they were a failure. Dissatisfaction with the Articles was not distributed evenly across the populace. American nationalists such as George Washington and Alexander Hamilton were the most profoundly troubled. Merchants in seaport towns felt the weakness of the Articles more acutely than did farmers in the heartlands. Not surprisingly, then, those philosophically committed to the idea of a strong, unified nation, encouraged by mercantile interests, took the lead in efforts to modify the Articles to provide for a stronger national government.

Still, most Americans shared a sense of nation, built around their common political values. Thomas Paine was reflecting this general sentiment when he wrote in his first publication after the peace with Great Britain had been secured, "I ever feel myself hurt when I hear the Union, the great palladium of our liberty and safety, the least irreverently spoken of. . . . Our citizenship in the United States is our national character. Our citizenship in any particular state is only our local distinction."[5] Such views strengthened the hand of the most advanced nationalists, like Washington and

Hamilton, who at the time were often called "Continentalists."

The biggest barrier to constitutional change grew out of the country's philosophy of liberal individualism. Americans were suspicious of anything that suggested concentrated governmental power. The Articles of Confederation, whatever their deficiencies, did not create a tyrannical government. Those favoring a new constitutional arrangement had to convince a majority of their fellow citizens that the new government would not be too strong.

COMPLETING THE REVOLUTION: THE CONSTITUTION OF 1787

While many people contributed to the new Constitution, three men played the leading roles: George Washington and James Madison of Virginia, and Alexander Hamilton of New York. Of the three, Washington's involvement was the least intensive and direct, but perhaps the most important. His prestige, as the general who led the fight for independence, was enormous, and his character inspired confidence. The most decisive single factor in the implementation of the Constitution of 1787 was George Washington's total commitment to it. Washington gave essential legitimacy to the effort.

Madison and Hamilton furnished much of the energy and practical political imagination needed for constitutional reform. As early as September 3, 1780, from Washington's camp at Liberty Pole (now Englewood), New Jersey, Hamilton penned a long letter to James Duane (a member of the New York delegation in the Continental Congress, which included delegates from all the states) indicting the Confederation as "neither fit for war or peace." He

[5]Thomas Paine, *Thoughts on the Peace, and the Probable Advantages Thereof, Common Sense*, Philadelphia, April 19, 1783; in William M. Vander Weyde, ed., *The Life and Works of Thomas Paine* (New Rochelle, N.Y.: Thomas Paine National Historical Association, 1925), p. 245.

Alexander Hamilton, James Madison, and George Washington.

proposed correcting the "want of method and energy in administration" by instituting departments with single heads and giving the Congress "complete sovereignty in all that relates to war, peace, trade, finance, and to the management of foreign affairs."[6] Note the urgency of the call sounded by this twenty-four-year-old statesman:

> The Convention [to reform the national government] should assemble the first of November next. The sooner the better. Our disorders are too violent to admit of a common or lingering remedy.... I require them to be vested with plenipotentiary authority that the business may suffer no delay in the execution and may in reality come into effect.

Hamilton pressed his case over the next seven years. So did James Madison. The two worked in concert in 1782–83 when both were delegates to the Continental Congress. In 1786, they again joined talents and energies at the Annapolis convention, called to discuss the economic difficulties of the states and to "consider how far a uniform system in their commercial regulations may be necessary to their common interest and their permanent harmony." The convention in turn delivered a call to the Congress to appoint delegates "to meet at Philadelphia on the second Monday in May next [1787] to take into Consideration the situation of the United States; to devise such further Provisions as shall appear to them necessary to render the Constitution of the Federal Government adequate to exigencies of the Union; and to report such an Act for that purpose to the United States in Congress Assembled...."[7] The Annapolis convention was a joint triumph for Hamilton and Madison.

[6] Harold C. Syrett and Jacob E. Cooke, eds., *The Papers of Alexander Hamilton*, vol. 2. (New York: Columbia University Press, 1961), p. 407.

[7] Max Farrand, *The Framers of the Constitution of the United States* (New Haven, Conn.: Yale University Press, 1913), p. 10.

PHILADELPHIA, 1787

On May 25, 1787, with 29 men from nine states having arrived at the State House in Philadelphia, the constitutional convention officially opened. By unanimous vote, George Washington was chosen as its president. When it adjourned four months later, the convention had drafted the Constitution of the United States as we know it today.

The assigned task of the convention was to revise the Articles of Confederation. But the delegates quickly decided to go beyond their instructions. They would establish an entirely new constitution. On May 30 they voted that "a national Government ought to be established," and they proceeded to work out its details.

The delegates agreed at the outset that there should be a federal system, composed of state governments and a national government with limited but constitutionally secure powers. While they differed in their assessment of democracy, they agreed that ordinary citizens should play a large role in choosing those who would administer their affairs. The delegates believed that ordinary people were capable of actions both sublime and dangerous. A proper constitution should create a setting that would blunt the latter and encourage the former. The delegates shared the liberal distrust of concentrated power, and they created a constitution that would prevent such concentration and thus avoid tyranny.

Alexander Hamilton was a delegate, but his role in the convention's deliberations was relatively modest. The contributions of Oliver Ellsworth and Roger Sherman of Connecticut, Benjamin Franklin and James Wilson of Pennsylvania, and George Washington as the convention's presiding officer and unquestioned moral leader were much greater.

The decisive intellectual work was done by James Madison. His influence and arguments were everywhere: in the convention debates, in the compromises struck, in the very language of the Constitution. Referring strictly to the work of the Philadelphia convention—rather than to activities leading up to it or those that followed in securing ratification and implementation—James Madison must be seen as the father of the Constitution.

The critical question of what powers should be granted to the central government prompted little argument. The national government should be able to levy taxes and regulate both interstate and foreign commerce. It should be able to raise and maintain an army and a navy. Concurrently, the states must be stripped of their powers to issue money, make treaties, and tax imports. Power had to be shifted from the states to the central government.

Over who should control the new government the delegates argued fiercely. The larger states pushed for representation in the national legislature based on population; the smaller states, understandably, wanted to maintain the old system of equal state representation. The *Virginia Plan*, proposed by the larger states, was drafted by Madison and presented to the convention by Edmund Randolph, Virginia's governor. The small states backed the *New Jersey Plan*, written by William Paterson, a former New Jersey attorney general. In mid-July the delegates reached what is known as the *Great Compromise*. Seats in the lower house of the legislature—the House of Representatives—were allocated according to population and filled by popular vote; seats in the upper house—the Senate—were allocated two to each state regardless of size, and filled by vote of the state legislature.

Slavery posed another important argument over control and representation. Southern delegates favored including slaves in the population base that would determine representation in the House of Representatives (although they had no thought of permitting the slaves to vote). In the three-fifths compromise, the delegates agreed that "three-fifths of all other Persons" (slaves) would be counted for taxation and representation. Final resolution of the slave trade issue was put off for two decades by the constitutional clause (Article I, section 9) that prevented Congress from outlawing the slave trade until 1808.

Having struck these compromises, the delegates easily resolved their remaining differences. And on September 17, 1787, they assembled to affix their signatures to the new Constitution. They had provided for a national government with a bicameral or two-house legislature, an executive branch headed by a president with broad powers, and a national judiciary consisting of a Supreme Court and such "inferior courts" as Congress might decide to create.

KEY PROVISIONS

The most distinctive feature of the document crafted in Philadelphia is its unremitting attention to the problem of power. The Constitution established a federal system in which authority would be divided between the national and state governments. The formal responsibilities of each would be extensive. Power was then further divided among the three branches of the national government; each was given its own base of authority. An elaborate system of **checks and balances** was established, giving each branch the means to restrain the other two.

Separation of powers had long been provided for in aristocratic societies among the monarchy, nobility, clergy, and "the commons"— the latter including the rural gentry and urban middle classes. In eighteenth-century England the king had powers distinct and separate from the rest of the nobility—which was represented in the upper chamber of Parliament, the House of Lords—and from the middle classes, which had a base through representation in the lower chamber, the House of Commons.

In this aristocratic model, separation of powers reflected the divergent claims of the several power centers of the society. But in America after independence, there was no monarchy or aristocracy; here was a middle-class society where "the commons" was very nearly the

Thomas Rossiter's painting of George Washington presiding over the signing of the Constitution.

whole of the social order. The classical liberal commitment to **separation of powers** expressed itself in a system of independent branches of government, each intended to represent the interests of the general public. The president was expected to serve this common interest; so was Congress. The power of "the commons" itself was to be divided, lest any popular impulse or greedy faction threaten individual claims and minority rights.

In the American Constitution, every basic grant of authority is carefully limited. The president is commander-in-chief of the armed forces, but it is Congress's power to declare war and "to raise and support armies." The president has broad appointive powers, but his appointments require "the advice and consent" of the Senate. Congress has the sole constitutional responsibility for enacting all legislation, but the president has a veto over such acts, a veto that can be overridden only by a two-thirds vote of each house. All legislation must be approved in identical form by both houses of the legislature. Never before or since has so sustained an effort been made to provide for governmental authority at once vigorous and checked. The new government would be strong enough to establish a setting where individual initiatives could flourish and checked enough so that individual rights would not be violated. The Constitution of the United States is the crowning political testament to these claims of the liberal creed.

James Madison expounded on the liberal theory of power in *Federalist Papers* Nos. 10 and 51, written in late 1787.[8] (See the Appen-

dix for *Federalist Papers* Nos. 10 and 51.) As Madison saw it, special interests necessarily abound in free societies. He called them **factions.** "Liberty is to faction," he wrote, "what air is to fire. . . ." To abolish liberty because it permits the expression of narrow, selfish interests would be as great a folly as "to wish the annihilation of air, which is essential to animal life, because it imparts to fire its destructive agency."

The answer to this dilemma, Madison insisted, was to prevent any individual or interest, or governmental institution, from gaining too much power. In *Federalist Paper* No. 51, Madison gave the classic liberal answer—the American constitutional power—to the problem of power.

> But the great security against a gradual concentration [of power] . . . consists in giving to those who administer each department the necessary constitutional means and personal motives to resist encroachment of the others. . . . Ambition must be made to counteract ambition. The interest of the man must be connected with the constitutional rights of the place. It may be a reflection on human nature that such devices should be necessary to control the abuses of government. But what is government itself but the greatest of all reflections on human nature? If men were angels, no government would be necessary. If angels were to govern men, neither external nor internal controls on government would be necessary. In framing the government which is to be administered by men over men, the great difficulty lies in this: You must first enable the government to control the governed; and in the next place oblige it to control itself.[9]

RATIFICATION

The framers of the Constitution required their handiwork to be ratified by special state conventions. They may have been motivated in this by a desire to bypass the state legislatures,

[8] *The Federalist Papers* is a series of 85 papers written in late 1787 by Madison, Hamilton, and John Jay, a colleague of Hamilton's from New York, who was to become the first chief justice of the Supreme Court. Their purpose was to help persuade New York to ratify the Constitution. A very convenient edition of *The Federalist Papers* is that edited by Clinton Rossiter (New York: New American Library, 1961). All references following to *The Federalist Papers* are to this edition. *Federalist Papers* Nos. 10 and 51 are reprinted in the Appendix to this book (pp. A21–A28).

[9] Ibid., p. 322.

where many members might resent the reductions being made in state authority. But the legislatures could still have blocked ratification by refusing to call for state conventions. Only Rhode Island did so.

The summoning of state ratification conventions prompted a vigorous national debate between those who favored the Constitution—called Federalists since they were endorsing a strong federal union—and their opponents known as anti-Federalists. The anti-Federalists feared that the new national government would prove too strong and would endanger the country's hard-earned liberty. Ultimately, they charged, America would become a single consolidated governmental unit. Article VI of the Constitution, which provided that "this Constitution, and the laws of the United States which shall be made in pursuance thereof . . . shall be the supreme law of the land, . . ." seemed to many anti-Federalists to make inevitable the submergence of the state legislatures and the supremacy of the Congress. Not too much should be made of this split. A leading expert on this subject, Cecelia M. Kenyon, concluded that

> the factors that united the Federalists and Anti-federalists were stronger than those that divided them. . . . There was a general agreement that liberty and certain other related rights and interests of the individual were the proper ends of government; that consent was the only legitimate source of political authority; that the only form of government proper and feasible for Americans was republican; that republican governments . . . should be limited in the exercise of their powers, and by written fundamental laws or constitutions; that there should be some kind and degree of union among the separate states.[10]

[10] Cecelia M. Kenyon, ed., *The Antifederalists* (Indianapolis, Ind.: Bobbs-Merrill, 1966), pp. xcvii–xcviii. This quotation is from Kenyon's long introductory essay to this collection of anti-Federalist writings.

In most states the Federalists won easily—remarkable, considering the magnitude of the constitutional change being proposed. Delaware acted first, ratifying the Constitution unanimously on December 7, 1787. A few days later, Pennsylvania followed suit by a two-to-one majority. New Jersey gave unanimous approval on December 18, as did Georgia on January 2, 1788. The vote in Connecticut on January 9, 1788, was 128 to 40 in favor of the Constitution. The Massachusetts vote was the first close one. Delegates approved the Constitution by just 187 to 168 in early February 1788. Maryland endorsed the Constitution overwhelmingly in April, as did South Carolina in May. When New Hampshire ratified on June 21, by a close vote of 57 to 47, the Constitution had received the requisite endorsement of nine of the thirteen states. Virginia followed, also by a close vote, approving the Constitution on June 25.

Three states remained outside the new national union, but only one—New York—was of critical importance, for it was one of the big states, and it separated New England from the states to the South. Opposition in that pivotal state was strong and well-organized, and the anti-Federalist faction won 46 of the 65 seats of its convention. Alexander Hamilton was a member of the Federalist minority, however, and his energies on behalf of the Constitution give us a fascinating example of how much effective leadership can mean. Hamilton pleaded, cajoled, and compromised; and more importantly, he offered an intellectually imposing defense of the Federalist position. Through his labors, and aided by the fact that New York looked like a person standing on the pier while the schooner—here, the new government—was sailing away, the New York convention finally voted in favor of ratification on July 26, 1788, by a vote of 30 to 27. The new government was launched—though North Carolina did not ratify until November 1789 and Rhode Island

Box 4.1
The 1992 Ratification of the Twenty-Seventh Amendment

The latest of the twenty-seven amendments, deemed ratified in 1992, is among the least consequential but certainly has the most unusual history. It provides that "No law varying the compensation for the services of the Senators and Representatives, shall take effect, until an election of Representatives shall have intervened." That is, if Congress votes itself a pay raise, the raise can't take effect until after the next election—presumably so that voters unhappy with the action would have a chance to vote the rascals out before they profited from their venture.

Most of the forty states that had approved the amendment as of May 1992—with thirty-eight required for ratification—did so in the course of the last decade, as a response to public dissatisfaction with congressional performance (a topic we will be discussing in chapter 6). It was a way, more symbolic than anything else, of giving the national legislature its comeuppance.

What makes the amendment's history unique is that it was first proposed in 1789—yes, almost 203 years prior to its ratification! James Madison had introduced it along with eleven others in the first Congress. Ten of these amendments were promptly ratified, and we know them as the Bill of Rights. One of the proposed amendments has never gone anywhere. The other remaining one has finally made it. Six states—three short of the nine that were then needed for ratification—had approved the amendment by 1791. But no other state approved it until Ohio did so in 1873. Another century went by before Wyoming added its approval in 1978. Then, in the 1980s, states began ratifying the amendment in large numbers.

These days whenever Congress proposes an amendment it puts a time limit on ratification. But the first Congress put no such limit. Still, many observers believe that the 203 year journey of the Twenty-Seventh Amendment violates the constitutional tradition of a contemporaneous amendment process. But there the amendment is, for what it's worth, part of the nation's fundamental law.

withheld consent to the Constitution until May 1790.[11]

PUTTING THE NEW INSTITUTIONS IN PLACE

Legislative elections were held in January and February, 1789. By early April enough congressmen had completed the journey to New York, the temporary capital, for the govern-

[11] The story of Hamilton's momentous role in the New York ratifying convention is ably told in Rossiter's *Alexander Hamilton and the Constitution* (New York: Harcourt, Brace and World, 1964), pp. 50–70.

ment to commence operation. The ballots of the presidential electors were counted in the Senate on April 6. George Washington was the unanimous choice for president and, receiving 34 electoral votes, John Adams became vice president. Washington took his oath of office in Federal Hall in New York on April 30, 1789. Fewer than twenty-four months had elapsed between the convening of the convention in Philadelphia and Washington's inauguration as president under the new Constitution. It had been an extraordinary march along the road of nation building, and the pace did not slow over the next three years. The task of implementing the new system was as demanding as its writing and ratification had been.

By the end of 1792, though, the new government had been firmly established. The American Constitution continues to be a living, evolving instrument that receives definition from precedent and practice; at least twenty-seven constitutional amendments now exist (see Box 4.1). But the decisive steps of constitutional nation building had been taken and implemented, and the major articles of the Constitution are as strongly in force today as in the last years of the eighteenth century.

GEORGE WASHINGTON AND AMERICAN DEMOCRACY

Of those involved in the many decisions that helped the infant United States get started successfully, no one rivals George Washington, the man who commanded the country's armies in the war for independence and then became the first president. Yet, ironically, almost everyone who has written about him complains that the "real" Washington has vanished in the legends (see Box 4.2). Garry Wills, who gave a fine portrait of him in his *Cincinnatus*, feels that "Washington eludes us, even in the city named for him."[12] Marcus Cunliffe, the twentieth-century historian who has come closest to finding Washington and what he meant, thinks discerning "the actual man behind the huge, impersonal, evergrowing legend" is an almost hopeless task.[13] More than a century ago, Henry Cabot Lodge, his greatest nineteenth-century biographer, complained that "Washington is

still not understood—as a man he is unfamiliar to the posterity that reveres his memory."[14]

Part of the biographers' frustration is that this living, flesh-and-blood person, who did so much and about whom so much is known, has been lost in a vast mythology that has left Washington a paragon of bloodlessly insipid virtue. But the disappearance of the man is nothing compared to the vanquishing of the political leader. In his handling of leadership, Washington has no equal in the history of democratic statecraft. The world still has much to learn from his performance, and it needs to be uncovered.

Washington's primary task, as he saw it, was to establish democratic norms. Talleyrand, Napoleon's foreign minister, delivered an extraordinary tribute following Washington's death, in which he described him as "the man who . . . first dared believe that he could inspire degenerate nations with the courage to rise to the level of republican virtues. . . ."[15] Washington was the first great teacher of democracy's essential style and substance.

LEADERSHIP AND THE USE OF POWER

"The eyes of Argos are upon me," Washington once complained—referring to the one-hundred-eyed guardian of Io, ancestor of the people of Argos, Greece—"and no slip will pass unnoticed." Like many others among the founders, he saw the American experiment as rich with promise but fragile, and he began to recognize early on—certainly during the war for independence—that his high standing meant that his example might well determine the success of the entire experiment.

---

[12] Garry Wills, *Cincinnatus* (Garden City, N.Y.: Doubleday, 1984), p. xix.

[13] Marcus Cunliffe, *George Washington* (New York: New American Library, 1958) p. 2

[14] Henry Cabot Lodge, *George Washington* (Boston: Houghton Mifflin, 1889), p. 8.

[15] "Report of Talleyrand, Minister of Foreign Affairs, on the occasion of the death of George Washington," vol. 1, nos. 172, 173, in the manuscript series *ETAT-UNIS*, 1799, 1800.

Box 4.2
George Washington Is Inaugurated as the Country's First President:
A Contemporary Account

The first president of the United States of America, George Washington, took his oath of office, as provided by the new Constitution, on April 30, 1789. The following account of Washington's arrival in New York (the first capital) for his inauguration, from the *Connecticut Courant* of May 4, 1789, gives us a sense of just how momentous the event was for many Americans of that time:

[NEW YORK, April 25.] Thursday last, between 2 and 3 o'clock p.m. the Most Illustrious PRESIDENT of the UNITED STATES arrived in this city. . . .

It is impossible to do justice in an attempt to describe the Scene exhibited on his Excellency's approach to the city. Innumerable multitudes thronged the shores, the wharves and the shipping—waiting with pleasing anticipation his arrival. His Catholic Majesty's Sloop of War, the *Calviston*—the ship *North Carolina,* (Mr. Dohrman's) and other vessels, were dressed, manned, and highly decorated. His Excellency's Barge was accompanied by Several other Barges, in one of which were the Hon. the Board of Treasury—the Minister of Foreign Affairs—and the Secretary of War—besides a long train of vessels and boats from New-Jersey and New-York. As he passed the *Calviston* they fired a salute of 13 guns—The Ship *North Carolina,* and the *Battery,* also welcomed his approach with the same number. . . .

The Procession moved through Queen Street to the House prepared for the reception of the President—from whence he was conducted, without form, to the Governor's where his Excellency dined.

This great occasion arrested the publick attention beyond all powers of description— the hand of industry was suspended—and the various pleasures of the capital were concentered to a single enjoyment—All ranks and professions expressed their feelings, in loud acclamations, and with rapture hailed the arrival of the FATHER OF HIS COUNTRY. . . .

The Scene on Thursday last was sublimely great—beyond any descriptive powers of the pen to do justice to—How universal—and how laudable the curiosity—How *sincere*—and, how *expressive* the sentiments of respect and veneration!—All Ranks appeared to feel the force of an expression, that was reiterated among the crowd . . . "WELL, HE DESERVES IT ALL!"

The spontaneous essations of gratitude to the illustrious WASHINGTON, exhibited by all ranks of people, in a thousand various indications of the sublime principle, are the highest reward that virtue enjoys, next to a conscious approbation which always precedes such undissembled testimonials of publick affection.

Many persons who were in the crowd, on Thursday, were heard to say, that they should now die contented—nothing being wanted to complete their happiness, previous to this auspicious period, but the sight of the Saviour of his Country.

Some persons, advanced in years, who hardly expected to see the illustrious President of the States, till they should meet him in Heaven, were in the concourse on Thursday, and could hardly restrain their impatience at being in a measure deprived of the high gratification, by the eagerness of the multitudes of children and young people, who probably might long enjoy the blessings.

Such a view of one's role can become an unappealing exercise of ego or an enervating burden. But it can also become the source of exceptional discipline. Such was the case with Washington. No other modern political leader has thought so long or so keenly on what examples were needed for the public's political education and how these should be presented.

Much of his teaching dealt in one way or another with the problem of power. Washington provided a type of leadership that Max Weber, the great German sociologist of the early twentieth century, called charismatic. By this Weber meant that legitimacy, the right to lead, is conferred by the leader's personal qualities and actions. Yet Washington looks wildly out of place in the general roster of such leaders, from Napoleon Bonaparte, his contemporary, to Mao Zedong. Charismatic leaders

cultivate personal authority in their efforts to replace the old order, but the intensely personal base of their power typically detracts from the legitimacy of the institutions they leave behind. And bent on using personal power for what they believe are essential ends, they are often exceedingly sloppy in thinking about just what it is that institutions require in order to succeed.

George Washington was the great exception—a charismatic leader who cultivated immense personal authority to nurture new institutions. Consider his wartime commitment to civilian control of the armed forces. At every stage during the Revolutionary War, Washington deferred to Congress. He pleaded with its members for the material support his often ragged army badly needed, but he never hinted at a challenge to their authority—although the

George Washington (tallest figure) and his men at Valley Forge. Le Marquis de LaFayette is on Washington's right. Engraving by H. B. Hall after the painting by Chappel.

frustrations of running an army amid such fractured authority were enormous. And when, early in 1783, talk of mutiny grew among the officers of his army encamped in Newburg, New York, Washington not only skillfully headed off revolt, but he also then sought to remove any sense that his officers had even contemplated a retreat from the standard of a "patriot army" that knew its proper place.

Washington was an unusual blend of the revolutionary and the conservative. The former is evident in his dogged determination to establish representative democracy, for the first time anywhere in the world. But this was done with such unremitting attention to institutional forms and proprieties that the new almost at once seemed established and Washington more the instrument of preservation than change.

Washington's most elaborate examples were designed to domesticate political power. He taught that the most glorious use of power comes in relegating it to a subordinate place in a larger scheme of values. He manifested the republican ideal of the limited state, not only by backing an elaborate constitutional system of checks and balances, but also by abandoning his own positions of power as soon as duty permitted: he resigned as a commander in chief of the Army of the United States in December 1783, *immediately* after the departure of the last British troops from New York. Later he made much of his desire to relinquish the presidency quickly—asking Hamilton and Madison to prepare drafts of what was to be his farewell address in his first term, five years before it was actually delivered. He often remarked of his love for Mount Vernon and his longing to return there as soon as his responsibilities allowed. The most successful public figure in modern history, Washington endlessly celebrated private life.

Washington and his principal allies were nationalists, called Continentalists, who believed that realization of the American idea required

vigorous national authority. They sought a seemingly unstable combination: government marked not only by its limits but also by its energy. Building public confidence that it would not be abused was necessary if national power were to be there for essential purposes and to be transferred peacefully from one governing party to the next.

WASHINGTON'S ACHIEVEMENTS

The greatest barrier to seeing Washington as a democratic leader of outstanding skill and judgment is the implicit sense that it would all have worked out all right anyway. Even the most secular contemporary minds, who reject the Puritan view of America as divinely inspired, seem to see its extraordinary institutional successes—including a constitutional order now in its 203d year—as somehow predetermined. Surely it is true that in the philosophic unity of the people and its fortunate physical setting, the United States began with impressive resources. And Washington was hardly the country's only able leader.

The question of what difference he made cannot, of course, be answered precisely. We do know that democracy had never been attained in a large nation state, and that the infant institutions of American democracy were delicate, untested, and groping for legitimacy. In this setting of uncertain promise, George Washington stood at the center of every major development—from managing the war for independence, to enacting the Constitution, to launching the new institutions—teaching through brilliantly contrived example what constitutional democracy requires of its leaders and its people. The "textbook" he thus wrote can be read profitably in today's new nations now striving to establish democratic institutions that are stable and legitimate.

THE CONSTITUTION AND DEMOCRACY

Political scientist Martin Diamond has discussed the two central values that occupied the revolutionary generation—liberty and democracy—and how they were treated in the two great documents of the revolutionary era, the Declaration of Independence and the Constitution. The Declaration, Diamond argued, was a bold statement of a principle. It set forth the primacy of liberty as the comprehensive good, the objective against which all political administrations and activity had to be measured.[16] The Constitution set forth the means for the attainment of liberty, a form of government that "had to prove itself adequately instrumental to the securing of liberty." In this pursuit, the Constitution "opted for democracy . . . embodying the bold and unprecedented decision to achieve, in so large a country as this, a free society under the democratic form of government."[17]

Democracy derives from two Greek roots: *demos*, meaning the people, and *kratis*, meaning authority. During the fifth century B.C., the Greeks, particularly the Athenians, used the term to refer to government by the many, as contrasted to government by the few (oligarchy) or by one person (monarchy). In his famous "Funeral Oration," the Athenian statesman Pericles (495–429 B.C.) declared that "our [Athens's] constitution is named a democracy, because it is in the hands not of the few, but of the many." This idea that ultimate political authority should rest with the general public remains central to all conceptions of democracy.

Within this general understanding, however, a number of different conceptions of democracy can be found. The term itself has been used with sharply different meanings—which naturally poses problems for students seeking to learn about the subject. We need to locate the American conception of democracy in the broader historical context.

ARISTOTLE'S IDEA OF DEMOCRACY

The first great political theorist to treat democracy coherently as a system of government was the Athenian philosopher Aristotle (384–322 B.C.). He argued that there were three general forms of government—kingship, aristocracy, and constitutional government or "polity"—and three others that were corruptions of the three proper forms: "tyranny corresponding to kingship, oligarchy to aristocracy, and democracy to constitutional government. . . . Tyranny is monarchy ruling in the interest of the monarch, oligarchy government in the interest of the rich, democracy government in the interest of the poor, and none of these forms governs with regard to the profit of the community."[18] In Aristotle's view there were broad interests to be served (what we would call national or public interests). Any regime was degraded when it ignored these interests and instead advanced the selfish claims of one segment of society.

Especially important to our study is the distinction Aristotle made between "democracy" and "constitutional government"; he defined democracy as the perverted form. He was not opposed to popular sovereignty, to regimes based on the consent and participation of the many. He objected only to extreme direct democracy,

[16] Martin Diamond, "The Declaration and the Constitution: Liberty, Democracy and the Founders," *The Public Interest* Fall 1975, pp. 46–47.

[17] Ibid.

[18] *Aristotle in Twenty-Three Volumes, XXI Politics*, H. Rackham, trans. (London: Heinemann, 1977), Book III, p. 207.

Aristotle.

democracy and oligarchy of the most unbridled kind. . . ."[19] Either the few will be successful in preserving their extreme privilege, by resorting to tyrannical rule, or the resentful many will deny minority rights in advancing their claims. What is necessary for constitutional democracy is a large middle class and a fairly even distribution of property. "It is clear therefore that the political community administered by the middle class is the best, and that it is possible for those states to be well governed that are of the kind in which the middle class is numerous . . . for by throwing in its weight it sways the balance and prevents the opposite extremes from coming into existence."[20]

AN IDEA A LONG TIME COMING

Aristotle's assessment of democracy in the *Politics* has remarkable range and prescience. And like the experience of his native Athens with a limited form of democratic government, Aristotle's thinking was far in advance of the historical period in which it occurred. One would have to wait two thousand years—until Europe and America in the late seventeenth and eighteenth centuries—to find sustained philosophic inquiry that advanced beyond Aristotle's contribution and the first successful implementation of democratic ideals.

As we saw in chapter 3, social and economic changes that began in seventeenth-century Europe nurtured a new set of political ideas and a new view of people and their rights that we know as classical liberalism. The keystone of liberalism is the high value it places on the rights and freedoms of the individual. Democratic government is the natural political expression of liberal individualism, for only

which lacked a legal structure for protecting minority rights and interests. In short, he defended what we today know as constitutional democracy: majority rule tempered by basic laws that uphold the ideal of the public interest and protect individual and minority rights.

Aristotle anticipated a question that has occupied many contemporary students of government: What social conditions are necessary for constitutional democracy to flourish? Such a government simply is not possible, he felt, in most social settings. It is impossible when a small elite has great economic privilege while the vast majority has virtually nothing. "Where some own a very great deal of property and others none . . . there comes about either an extreme democracy or an unmixed oligarchy, or a tyranny may result from both of the two extremes, for tyranny springs from both

[19] Ibid., p. 331.
[20] Ibid.

democracy gives individuals the power to govern themselves. Once social conditions were such that individualism would flourish, democracy became a practical possibility.

The United States had no monopoly on such social conditions—and no monopoly on governments giving recognition to the claims of individuals. In Great Britain limits were increasingly placed on the powers of the monarchy and aristocracy in the eighteenth and nineteenth centuries, while at the same time the powers of representatives in Parliament grew. But the requisite social conditions emerged faster and more fully in eighteenth-century America, and so in response did democratic government.

MADISON'S IDEA OF DEMOCRACY

The work of the founders of the new American government of 1787 was a major step in both the theory and practice of democracy. The unique opportunity to establish a national government based on democratic principles in an environment so generally supportive of the enterprise, but with so little precedent in the experience of other countries, forced the founders to confront fundamental issues of democratic theory. In prior examinations of democratic theory, from Aristotle to John Locke to French philosopher Jean-Jacques Rousseau (1712–1788), one critical element had been missing: close attention to the practical governmental mechanisms through which constitutional democracy could protect minority rights and achieve social balance. In 1787 the idea of constitutional democracy was a familiar one, but the actual articulation of the institutions of representative democracy was still in its infancy. The plan for representative institutions developed in *The Federalist Papers* is an important advance in democratic theory.

Madison and Hamilton carried over the basic Aristotelian distinction between democracy and polity, though they referred to the latter as "republicanism." Like Aristotle, the authors of *The Federalist Papers* professed fear of democracy and understood the term to mean unrestrained government prone to mob rule, disrespectful of minority rights, and incapable of realizing the national interest.

The Federalist Papers argues the case for **republicanism:** as James Madison wrote in *Federalist Paper* No. 10, "a government in which the scheme of representation takes place. . . ." The people are sovereign, but they cannot and should not govern directly. Representative institutions like legislatures need to be established within a governmental structure of clearly defined and dispersed powers. Through separation of powers and checks and balances, minority rights receive protection, and narrow interests opposed to the general public good are curbed. The framers thought, for example, that some majority passion might sweep through the legislature a law contrary to the basic rights and interests of some minority. But they felt that such checks on the legislative power as the president's veto and the judiciary's power to review and interpret the laws in light of constitutional requirements lessened the chance that minority rights would actually be abused. Through this elaborate process of checks and balances, the public would still remain the ultimate source of all political authority.

The representative democracy that the framers of the Constitution sought gave equal weight to popular sovereignty and individual rights. Popular sovereignty required the selection of political leaders through regularly-held free elections. Individual rights required mechanisms to stop anyone, even popular majorities, from infringing upon certain rights of citizenship such as those set forth in the **Bill of Rights.** (See Box 4.3.)

MAJORITY RULE VERSUS MINORITY RIGHTS

The American idea of democracy is a system of government equally committed to majority rule and the protection of minority rights. In many instances these two different commitments do not conflict with one another. But sometimes they do. For example, school segregation as practiced before *Brown v. Board of Education of Topeka*—the landmark desegregation decision handed down by the U.S. Supreme Court in 1954—seems often to have had majority backing. If we conclude that such segregation denied the claims of American democracy, it is because we believe that majority rule itself is undemocratic when it opposes essential individual rights.

But which rights are so essential as to be off-limits even to majority will? American constitutional law, as it has developed in decisions of the Supreme Court, addresses this question, and we will examine what the Court has said in chapters 9 and 14. But there has never been full agreement among experts in constitutional law, or the public at large, on where the democratic requirement of majority rule must be suspended because the democratic requirement of respect for individual rights requires it.

PRAYER IN PUBLIC SCHOOLS

The often heated argument over school prayer is a good case in point. Various individuals and groups long opposed what was the common practice of opening the school day with the recitation of a prayer. They argued that it violated the right to full religious freedom guaranteed by the First Amendment to the Constitution. Some students were not in sympathy with the particular religious beliefs expressed by the prayer, and the government

(in the form of public school officials) was abridging their freedom of religious choice.

In 1962 the Supreme Court agreed with the challenge to the constitutionality of prayer in public schools, in the case of *Engel v. Vitale.* The New York State Board of Regents had recommended to school districts that they adopt a specific nondenominational prayer, to be repeated voluntarily by students at the beginning of each school day. The prayer read: "Almighty God, we acknowledge our dependence upon Thee, and we beg Thy blessings upon us, our parents, our teachers, and our country." The school board of the New York community of New Hyde Park adopted this prayer, but it was challenged by the parents of ten pupils in the district. These parents claimed that the prayer was contrary to their religious beliefs and ran counter to the "establishment" clause of the First Amendment: "Congress [and, by application, the states] shall make no law respecting an establishment of religion. . . ."

Writing for the Supreme Court's majority, Justice Hugo Black ruled that the "constitutional prohibition against laws respecting an establishment of religion must at least mean that in this country it is no part of the business of government to compose official prayers for any group of American people to recite as a part of a religious program carried on by the government." The majority had violated a constitutional guarantee of individual religious freedom. In subsequent cases the Court extended its ruling—for example, by prohibiting the recitation of the Lord's Prayer or other verses from the Bible.

These Court decisions generated strong opposition. Critics argued that the constitutional ban on laws "respecting an establishment of religion" was not meant and should not now be construed to prevent citizens in various communities from deciding that they would like to have a brief prayer at the start of

Box 4.3
The Bill of Rights

In 1991, the United States celebrated another bicentennial—the 200th anniversary of the ratification of the first ten amendments of the Constitution, popularly known as The Bill of Rights.

Submitted for ratification to the thirteen states by the first Congress of the United States on September 25, 1789, these first ten amendments, crafted by James Madison of Virginia, were designed to allay public fears that the just-ratified U.S. Constitution contained insufficient safeguards against encroachments on civil liberties by the federal government. By June 1790, when nine states had ratified, approval by only one more state was needed to meet the three-fourths requirement for passage. But that one final vote for ratification was not gained until eighteen months later, when Virginia finally added its consent. The Bill of Rights was thus brought into force on December 15, 1791.

In reading the full text of those ten amendments (Appendix, pp. A13–A15), note that the amendments are in fact in original design less a statement of rights than of prohibitions: For the most part they list things that Congress (i.e., the federal government) cannot do. Thus the first amendment begins: "Congress shall make no law respecting an abridgment of religion. . . ."

While it would be inaccurate to dismiss any part of the Bill of Rights as unimportant, the following provisions have been especially consequential in American law throughout the country's history.

AMENDMENT 1

Congress shall make no law respecting an establishment of religion, or prohibiting the free exercise thereof; or abridging the freedom of speech, or of the press; or the right of the people peaceably to assemble, and to petition the Government for a redress of grievances.

---

the school day, in which anyone who wanted could choose not to participate. They insisted that school prayer did not abridge a basic constitutional right, and hence the preferences of the majority should be followed.

Public opinion surveys have consistently shown decisive majorities in favor of prayer in schools and in favor of an amendment to the Constitution to overturn the Court's rulings. About three-fifths of the public regularly tell opinion pollsters that they oppose the Supreme Court's 1962 ruling "that no state or local government may require the reading of the Lord's Prayer or Bible verses in public schools." According to an NBC News / *Wall Street Journal* survey of December 1991, 61 percent favored amending the Constitution to allow school prayer. Seventy-eight percent of those interviewed by Yankelovich Clancy Shulman for *Time* magazine in October 1991 said they favored "allowing school children to say prayers in public schools."[21]

[21] *The Public Perspective*, November / December 1991, pp. 5–8; and "The Uniting of America," *The Public Perspective*, May / June 1992, pp. 3–11.

Amendment 4

The right of the people to be secure in their persons, houses, papers and effects, against unreasonable searches and seizures, shall not be violated, and no Warrants shall issue, but upon probable cause, supported by Oath or affirmation, and particularly describing the place to be searched, and the persons or things to be seized.

Amendment 5

No person shall . . . be subject for the same offence to be twice put in jeopardy of life or limb; nor shall be compelled in any criminal case to be a witness against himself, nor be deprived of life, liberty, or property, without due process of law. . . .

Amendment 6

In all criminal prosecutions, the accused shall enjoy the right to a speedy and public trial, by an impartial jury of the State and district wherein the crime shall have been committed . . . and to be informed of the nature and cause of the accusation; to be confronted with the witnesses against him; to have compulsory process for obtaining witnesses in his favor, and to have the Assistance of Counsel for his defence.

Amendment 8

Excessive bail shall not be required, nor excessive fines imposed, nor cruel and unusual punishments inflicted.

The efforts to amend the Constitution to permit school prayer first came to a vote in 1966. A majority of U.S. senators voted for such an amendment—but not the two-thirds required. Article V of the Constitution contains this provision designed to make it hard for a majority to make changes in the country's basic law; Congress can propose amendments to the Constitution only by two-thirds majorities of both houses; the amendments must then be ratified by at least three-fourths of the states before taking effect. In 1984 another attempt was made to enact a school prayer amendment, and again the major battle was fought in the Senate. The proposed amendment read:

> Nothing in this Constitution shall be construed to prohibit individual or group prayer in public schools or other public institutions. No persons shall be required by the United States or any state to participate in prayer. Neither the United States nor any state shall compose the words or any prayer to be said in public schools. (Senate Joint Resolution 73)

Once again, the effort to enact the amendment failed. Fifty-six senators voted for it—11 votes

The school classroom has been a battleground for those who debate the constitutionality of issues ranging from allowing prayer in public schools and the requiring of the reciting of the Pledge of Allegiance in public schools to the allocating of public funds for religious-based private schools.

short of the two-thirds the Constitution requires for constitutional change.

The next chapter in the argument over school prayer was written by the U.S. Supreme Court. In *Wallace v. Jaffree* (1985), the Court struck down as unconstitutional, by a three vote margin, an Alabama statute authorizing a one-minute period of silence in all public schools for "meditation or voluntary prayer." Writing for the majority, Justice John Paul Stevens ruled that Alabama's "endorsement . . . of prayer activities at the beginning of each school day is

not consistent with the established principle that the government must pursue a course of complete neutrality toward religion." But in his sharp dissenting opinion, Warren Burger (chief justice from 1969 to 1986) insisted that "to suggest that a moment-of-silence statute that includes the word "prayer" unconstitutionally endorses religion . . . manifests not neutrality but hostility toward religion."

In 1992, the Court issued an important new school prayer ruling in *Lee v. Weisman*, a case that posed the immediate issue of whether the First Amendment prohibits prayer at public school graduation cermonies. Writing for a 5–4 majority, Justice Anthony Kennedy reaffirmed the general line of interpretation that has been the Court's since *Engel* thirty years ago. In the case in question a Rhode Island junior high school invited a clergyman—in this case a rabbi—to deliver two nondenominational prayers at a graduation exercise. The majority decided that this was just as much government action, Kennedy wrote, "as if a state statute decreed that the prayers must occur." It is beyond dispute, he maintained, that "the Constitution guarantees that government may not coerce anyone to support or participte in religion or its exercise. . . . The States involvement in the school prayers challenged today violates these central principles."

The Court's majority rejected Rhode Island's argument that no pupil was compelled to attend the graduation or in any way to participate in the prayer and, thus, that no one was being coerced. "What to most believers may seem nothing more than a reasonable request that the nonbeliever respect their religious practices," Kennedy went on, "in a school context may appear to the nonbeliever or dissenter to be an attempt to employ the machinery of the State to enforce a religious orthodoxy." In the present case, the school district's control of the graduation ceremony "places public pressure, as well as peer pressure, on attending students to stand as a group or, at least, maintain respectful silence during the Invocation and Benediction." Young school children may not be constitutionally so compelled, whatever majority preferences on the matter may be.

Four justices—Chief Justice William Rehnquist, Antonin Scalia, Byron White, and Clarence Thomas—saw things very differently. In his dissenting opinion, Justice Scalia stressed the interests of the community at large. He wrote that the case involved "a community's celebration of one of the milestones in its young citizens' lives, and it is a bold step for this Court to seek to banish from that occasion, and from thousands of similar celebrations throughout this land, the expression of gratitude to God that a majority of the community wishes to make."

DIRECT DEMOCRACY VERSUS REPRESENTATIVE DEMOCRACY

Though the framers opted for representative democracy, aspects of the idea of direct democracy have continued to find support in the United States. In the contemporary context, those who advocate more direct democracy want the people to vote or otherwise express themselves directly on major questions of government and policy. Many Americans believe that an extension of direct participation makes the country's democracy purer or more complete. Responding to these views, the United States government has incorporated some of the institutions and practices of direct democracy.

TOWARD PURER DEMOCRACY: THE DIRECT PRIMARY

In the early twentieth century, a new political movement known as **progressivism** gained great

strength in many parts of the United States and advanced an ambitious program of political change. The Progressives included in their ranks men and women from all classes and sections of the country, but they were especially strong among the growing professional middle classes of the urban Northeast and Midwest. The latter believed that the big-city political party "machines" of the day were often corrupt, beholden to special interests, unenlightened. To purify this "boss-dominated" system, Progressives argued that the people must be given more power to rule directly.

One key reform urged by the Progressives was the **direct primary,** whereby the choice of party nominees is made by rank-and-file party supporters in primary elections, not by party leaders through party conventions and caucuses. The Progressives enjoyed great success

Progressive Hiram Johnson campaigning in 1922.

in this effort; direct primaries became the dominant instrument for choosing candidates in most parts of the country.

THE REFERENDUM AND THE INITIATIVE

The Progressives also criticized the legislatures of their day as dominated by special interests—railroads, big corporations, and construction companies wanting contracts for roads and public buildings. They urged that the general public be permitted to vote directly on legislation through referenda and initiatives. In a **referendum,** a legislative body certifies a question for presentation to the public in a general ballot; in an **initiative** the public, through petitions signed by requisite numbers of voters, requires that policies be put to popular vote. Under the aegis of the Progressives, the referendum and the **initiative** were widely adopted. South Dakota (in 1898) was the first state to provide for the initiative.

At the local level, referendum democracy flourishes; several thousand measures are presented each year to the voters in school districts, cities, and counties. The public votes directly on appropriations for school buildings, fluoridation of community water supplies, and the siting of waste disposal facilities. In the November 1988 elections, political scientist Austin Ranney found that "forty-one states had at least one initiative or referendum on their ballots, and in all 23 propositions were voted on. . . ."[22] A measure that would permit the governor and lieutenant governor to run as a team passed easily in Iowa. Arkansas voted to bar the use of public funds for abortion, while Colorado rejected a similar proposition. South Dakota voters rejected a measure that would have limited property tax to 2.5 percent of the

1984 true value. Massachusetts voters refused to stop electric-power generation by nuclear power plants that produce waste. And, in the referendum that created the biggest furor of all in 1988, Californians voted narrowly to require rate reductions of at least 20 percent for all property and casualty insurance sold in the state.

There is no simple answer to the question of whether the United States now strikes a proper balance between the direct and representative dimensions of democracy. Yet many agree that democracy in a complex society makes heavy demands on such intermediary institutions as political parties and legislatures, and on their leadership. Such institutions cannot be bypassed too frequently and still have the capacity to perform the functions we expect of them as vital intermediaries. While democracy cannot exist if the wishes of the general public are not freely and fully expressed and ultimately followed, succumbing too frequently to temptations to bypass representative institutions—bypass parties through direct primaries, for example, and legislatures through the initiative—may weaken these institutions to the point where they can no longer work effectively. In chapter 12 we discuss this point with specific reference to the American party system.

HOW DEMOCRATIC IS AMERICAN DEMOCRACY?

A debate goes on today over just how democratic American democracy actually is. A book appeared in 1913 that for a time greatly influenced many people's thinking about the Constitution. It was Charles A. Beard's *An Economic Interpretation of the Constitution of the United States.* Beard argued that, rather than a document written by public-spirited men for the protection of "life, liberty, and the pursuit of

---

[22] Austin Ranney, "Election '88: Referendums," *Public Opinion,* January / February 1989, p. 15.

happiness," the Constitution represented the assertion of economic interests of banking, manufacturing, and commerce. Furthermore, he maintained that, instead of extending democracy, the Constitution was imposed to rein in the majority. The Constitution was depicted as the product of a cabal of self-serving "plutocrats" who were fearful of the democratic impulses unleashed after the Revolutionary War. It had to be made to serve popular ends later on under the democratic leadership of leaders like Andrew Jackson, who was president from 1829 to 1837.

Was this view of the Constitution's founders justified? Beard's interpretation has been strongly criticized and largely discredited recently, especially by the work of historians R. E. Brown and Forrest MacDonald.[23] Most scholars now hold a view similar to the prevailing view of nineteenth-century America: While the framers were not above self-interest, they were by no means a narrow, undemocratic economic elite. As historian John Garraty concluded, "the closest thing to a general spirit at Philadelphia was a public spirit. To call men like Washington, Franklin, and Madison self-seeking would be utterly absurd."[24]

For a nation to be called a democracy, ordinary citizens must have real political power. Not only must they be able to vote, but they must be able to exercise ultimate authority over the big decisions of their country's political life. What are these big decisions? How can we know whether the people ultimately make them or whether political elites—individuals and groups with disproportionate political resources—manage to assume the decisive

decision-making roles? The concept of power is one of the most complex that political science contends with. Yet for all the analytic difficulties the concept poses, how power is distributed is a matter of great importance to democratic government. At some point power becomes so concentrated in the hands of political elites as to make a mockery of any claim to popular sovereignty. Some observers argue that this has happened in the United States. Others, while denying that this point has been reached, still see extensive power in the hands of elites as a serious problem in American democracy.

CONCENTRATION OF RESOURCES

Various developments over the last century and a half have produced major concentrations of resources. There were no great fortunes in the United States a hundred and fifty years ago, but now there are enormous accumulations of wealth. Economic units—whether farms, banks, or factories—were generally very small in the 1830s; in the 1980s we have huge national and multinational corporations. The great consolidation of newspapers and magazines into large units that has occurred over the last century had not even begun in the 1830s, and the age of concentrated electronic communication had not even been imagined.

In the 1830s the primary political unit was the local government; now it is the national government. The hundreds to few thousands of citizens in a typical town a century and a half ago had a measure of direct control over government that is simply unattainable in today's far more complex and centralized nation-state.

How have these developments affected political power? Consider the case of an individual who has acquired millions of dollars in personal property as well as the presidency of a big business corporation. If he chooses, he may

[23] See R. E. Brown, *Charles Beard and the Constitution* (Princeton, N.J.: Princeton University Press, 1956); and Forrest MacDonald, *We the People: The Economic Origins of the Constitution* (Chicago: University of Chicago Press, 1976).

[24] John A. Garraty, *The American Nation*, 4th ed. (New York: Harper and Row, 1979), p. 123.

Today's advanced communications technology makes more immediate the debate over the power and influence of television networks. Vic de Lucia / NYT Pictures

precedent. Political leaders in Congress, the executive office, and state capitals around the country are certainly aware of his or her capacity to take political messages into millions of households. How likely is it that the anchorperson's influence in American political life is roughly equivalent to that of the average citizen?

Many others enjoy disproportionate resources. A president of a big university has more resources than the average student at his or her institution. The head of a major labor union has resources dwarfing those of the typical unionist. The point seems beyond dispute: Politically relevant resources are unevenly distributed; and the economic and technological developments discussed in chapters 1 and 2 have on balance led to greater concentrations.

What are the implications for democracy of such inequalities? As political scientist Robert Dahl has asked, "In a political system where nearly every adult may vote but where knowledge, wealth, social position, access to officials and other resources are unequally distributed, who actually governs?"[25]

contribute large sums of money to candidates for elective office. His wealth, and the economic power derived from his position in business, give him a measure of access to political leaders far beyond that of most citizens. A telephone call to a politician from this wealthy corporate leader is likely to have a much greater impact on policy deliberations than one from the average voter.

But there are many types of politically important resources other than great wealth. Consider the position of an anchorperson for one of the network's evening news programs. He or she is seen nightly by an audience in the range of 20 to 30 million persons, and thus has communications resources beyond any historic

POWER ELITES

No mature theory of American politics questions that there are elites: groups of people who possess disproportionately large amounts of scarce resources and hence power. The fact of disproportionate resources in the hands of special-interest groups requires the constant attention of all who are committed to democratic government. President Dwight Eisenhower, a conservative Republican who had been commander-in-chief of allied forces in Europe during World War II—and who was hardly

[25] Robert Dahl, *Who Governs?* (New Haven, Conn.: Yale University Press, 1961), p. 1.

unfriendly to either business or the military—in 1961 warned his fellow citizens to be vigilant against "unwarranted influence . . . by the military-industrial complex."[26] After World War II, a high level of defense spending became a permanent part of American national government, and interests such as defense contractors and military officials became active and influential lobbyists for their special concerns. Eisenhower saw the dangers this collection of strong, well-organized interests posed for democratic decision making in the vital area of defense and foreign policy.

Some commentators go well beyond these widely shared concerns and perceptions, however, to the highly debated conclusion that the concentration of power in the hands of elites precludes real democracy in the United States. An extreme case is the argument of contemporary Marxist theorists. Their starting point is the proposition Karl Marx advanced in much of his work in the last century: Power in any society is derived from economic arrangements, and in any capitalist society like the United States the government "is nothing more than a committee for the administration of the consolidated affairs of the bourgeois class as a whole."[27] Building on this perspective, political scientist Michael Parenti states that

> our government represents the privileged few rather than the needy many and . . . elections, political parties and the right to speak out are seldom effective measures against the influence of corporate wealth. The laws of our polity operate chiefly with undemocratic effect . . . because they are written principally to protect the haves against the claims of the have-nots. . . . Democracy for the few . . . is not a product of the venality of office holders as such but a reflection

of how the resources of power are distributed within the entire politico-economic system.[28]

This view is not confined to Marxist scholars. In *The Power Elite*, sociologist C. Wright Mills maintains that America is run by a narrow group of people drawn from three central institutions: leaders of major private business corporations, the heads of the armed services and the defense establishment, and the political leadership of the executive branch of government.[29] For most of American history these units were relatively small and feeble, but after World War II they grew enormously. By the late 1950s, Mills asserted, there was no longer

> on the one hand, an economy, and on the other hand, a political order containing a military establishment unimportant to politics and to moneymaking. There is a political economy linked in a thousand ways with military institutions and decisions. . . . If there is government intervention in the corporate economy, so is there corporate intervention in the governmental process. In the structural sense, this triangle of power is the source of the interlocking directorate that is most important for the historical structure of the present.[30]

Mills's power elite is composed not of isolated groups and individuals but rather of people who have common interests and act together coherently to dominate policy on the major issues of national life.

THE LIBERAL DEMOCRATIC REBUTTAL

Is there a coherent, interactive elite that makes most of the big decisions in the United States,

---

[26] Eisenhower's "Farewell Address," January 17, 1961.

[27] D. Ryazanoff, ed., *The Communist Manifesto of Karl Marx and Friedrich Engels* (New York: Russell and Russell, 1963), p. 28.

[28] Michael Parenti, *Democracy for the Few* (New York: St. Martin's Press, 1974), p. 2.

[29] C. Wright Mills, *The Power Elite* (New York: Oxford University Press, 1959).

[30] Ibid., pp. 7–8.

leaving popular sovereignty but an aspiration? Most political scientists don't think so; neither does the general public. The liberal rebuttal to the charge of elite rule must begin with the work of the Constitution's framers, because that work has defined the American system. Those who drafted the Constitution assumed that some interests would inevitably be stronger than others. The task of a properly arranged constitutional democracy, James Madison argued in *Federalist Papers* Nos. 10 and 51, was to put limits on what these interests could achieve. He believed that he and his fellow constitution makers had provided sufficient barriers to any power elite: a large, diverse nation of many contending interests, with government power divided first between the national and state units, and then further divided between legislature, executive, and judiciary. Behind all of this were the people, able to choose their leaders in free elections and thereby to set the general course of public policy.

THE PLURALIST POSITION

Most contemporary political observers in the United States think that Madison has been proved right. Political power in the United States is highly fragmented, as interest groups contend within a government structure of dispersed authority. Public policy is the outcome of a highly involved pattern of political bargaining among constantly shifting interest alignments. Sometimes this perspective is called *pluralist*, because it identifies a plurality of competing power centers. The predominant perspective among political scientists is that power is so dispersed at the national level, among the many committees and subcommittees of Congress, federal executive agencies, interest groups, and others, that overall public policy suffers a serious lack of coherence.[31] The

current preoccupation with the fragmentation of the policy process runs almost diametrically against the idea of a coherent power elite able to control public policy.

To see this argument in action, consider the area of military spending, which was one of Mills's prime examples of a power elite. Big defense contractors certainly interact closely with Defense Department officials and influential congressman. Typically, though, they do not cooperate but instead fight it out with one another to secure contracts—as when United Technologies Corporation and General Electric battle for contracts to build new jet engines for Air Force planes.

None of this should be construed as a contention that American democracy does not confront continuing problems stemming from the presence of large concentrations of resources in a few hands. The whole area of money in politics involves one set of such problems. Various individuals and organizations—including businessmen and large corporations—have extensive financial resources; they also have strong interests in the decisions legislatures and executive agencies make. They try to advance their interests by lobbying and by making contributions to the campaigns of candidates who support their views or who are in key positions to decide future questions. Through the vehicle of political action committees (PACs), millions of dollars of interest-group money are contributed to campaigns each election year. In chapters 11 and 12 we discuss the role of PACs, the legislation regulating them, and the larger issue of how American elections are, and should be, financed.

The United States in the early nineteenth century abounded in what we might call "natural equalities." Great fortunes, for the most part, had not yet been built. The size of audience that one could reach by a speech was limited to how far the unamplified human voice could carry. Big bureaucracies, big military

---

[31] Chapters 5–8 develop these arguments.

Free elections—the cornerstone of democracy.

establishments, big corporations, simply did not exist. We shouldn't romanticize this era as a time without problems; there were many, some that dwarf those of our own day. But the fact is that the idea of democracy was somewhat easier to envision and implement in that age before bigness, concentration, and scale. Today we have to work harder to maintain the ideal of popular choice or rule that is far-reaching and robust. But we still have important resources for doing so.

SUMMARY

The Articles of Confederation were the first constitution of the new American nation. Ratified in 1779, the Articles were consistent with the prevailing American belief in limited, popular government. But the central government they established was so weak that it could not meet economic or foreign-policy needs, or fulfill the emerging sense of nation.

George Washington, James Madison, and Alexander Hamilton gave leadership to the forces seeking to strengthen, or replace, the Articles of Confederation. Their efforts and those of other like-minded politicians culminated in the constitutional convention that met at Philadelphia in the spring and summer of 1787 and drafted a new Constitution for the United States. Ratification was completed in 1788 when New York, the last big state to approve, narrowly voted its endorsement.

The Constitution reflected the basic impulses of the American ideology. Government was to be at once vigorous and restrained. It was to create a climate where individual initiative could flourish and national identity could be expressed, while being so checked and balanced that it could not threaten individual rights.

Authority was divided between national and state governments; and within the former, among the executive, legislative, and judicial branches, which were at once independent and mutually dependent. Ambition, as Madison put it in *Federalist Paper* No. 51, was made to counteract ambition.

The first conception of democracy arose in Athens in the fifth century B.C.: government by the many rather than by the few. Aristotle enlarged this concept by combining two distinct elements: popular sovereignty and minority rights. Aristotle chose to call a system that successfully combined these elements a constitutional government or polity. Democracy meant an unrestrained direct democracy or mob rule. The framers of the American Constitution incorporated much of Aristotle's thinking. But they went even further in their specification of a system of carefully engineered representative institutions. What we now call a constitutional or representative democracy the framers called a republic.

Democracy in America is sometimes called liberal democracy. It places equal emphasis on realizing popular sovereignty and protecting individual and minority rights. These two objectives are sometimes in conflict, when majorities take actions that minorities think violate certain of their essential rights as citizens.

The American constitutional tradition holds that majority rule must be superseded in cases where majority actions infringe essential rights of citizenship, such as those articulated in the Bill of Rights. But as the country's experience in the area of civil rights shows, the most fundamental of minority rights have sometimes been denied. And thoughtful people necessarily disagree on just which rights or interests are

so essential as to be off-limits to majority choice or action.

One criticism of American democracy holds that power is so concentrated in the hands of certain elites as to make impossible the meaningful exercise of popular sovereignty. Defenders of American liberal democratic performance contend, in rebuttal, that the Madisonian system has generally succeeded in preventing great concentrations of power. They agree that some individuals and groups have more of such politically important resources as money, but they argue that the common pattern finds these elites in competition with each other for general public support.

FOR FURTHER STUDY

Aristotle's Politics. Book 3, Vol. XXI of *Aristotle in Twenty-Three Volumes.* H. Rackham, trans. London: Heinemann, 1977. A brilliant interpretation of political institutions and experience, including the first systematic writing on democracy, by perhaps the greatest of all political philosophers.

Barker, Ernest. *Reflections on Government.* New York: Oxford University Press, 1958; first published, 1942. A rich, subtle defense of democracy by a distinguished British theorist, written during the profound totalitarian challenge to democracy that culminated in World War II.

Dahl, Robert A. *Dilemmas of Pluralist Democracy.* New Haven, Conn.: Yale University Press, 1983. The latest interpretation of the problems of pluralism by a distinguished American political scientist and theorist.

Diamond, Martin. "The Declaration and the Constitution: Liberty, Democracy and the Founders," *The Public Interest*, Fall 1975, pp. 39–55. A brilliant essay by a political theorist explaining the relationship between the Declaration of Independence and the Constitution, and the ideals and approaches they articulate.

Downs, Anthony. *An Economic Theory of Democracy.* New York: Harper and Row, 1957. A major interpretation of democracy drawing upon economic models and exchanges.

Hamilton, Alexander, James Madison, and John Jay. *The Federalist Papers.* Clinton Rossiter, ed. New York: New American Library, 1961; first published, 1787–88 in New York newspapers. Perhaps the most important work ever written on the nature of the American governmental system and the ideas underlying it; authored by three leading proponents of the Constitution in the ratification debate in New York.

Mills, G. Wright. *The Power Elite.* New York: Oxford University Press, 1959. Perhaps still the best known and most provocative statement of the view that a unified "power elite" makes the key decisions in the United States.

Rossiter, Clinton. *Alexander Hamilton and the Constitution.* New York: Harcourt, Brace, 1964. A description of the immense role Alexander Hamilton played in the events leading up to and following the ratification of the Constitution of the United States.

Wills, Garry. *Explaining America: The Federalist.* Garden City, N.Y.: Doubleday, 1981. A useful analysis of the central ideas expressed in *The Federalist Papers* and the objectives of their authors.

Part 3

GOVERNANCE

Chapter 5

THE AMERICAN SYSTEM
OF DIVIDED GOVERNMENT

The most distinctive, and consequential, feature of governance in the United States is its elaborate machinery for dispersing authority. American ideology has insisted that for individuals to be strong and their rights protected, government must be sharply restrained. This restraint is achieved through a system that assigns power to competing branches, each with its own independent constitutional base, and requires that they bargain and compromise with each other in order for anything to get done. In our **federal system,** both the national government and the states have their own constitutionally guaranteed positions and responsibilities. The national government is our main concern in this text, but the states also have large spheres of action and influence. At the national level, the Constitution divides power among three independent branches: executive, legislative, and judicial. We call this division the **separation of powers.** Separation of powers and federalism are, then, the two main components of a larger system—inspired by American ideology and set forth in the Constitution—of divided government.

One manifestation of this system of divided authority is that the United States has government, plenty of it, but not "the government," in the sense one speaks of it in other countries. For example, think of the sentence, "The government has decided to raise taxes." In Great Britain, people refer to the prime minister and the cabinet as "the government," for the very proper reason that the prime minister and the cabinet hold the preponderance of real governmental authority. They could in fact decide to raise taxes—and make that decision stick. In the United States, the president, his key political advisers, cabinet secretaries, and others clearly have broad powers and responsibilities, but they are not "the government." One is more likely to call them "the administration." This seemingly innocent distinction in terms reflects a profound reality: The president and his team are not the entire government because they share essential, central governmental authority with an independent, co-equal legislature. For all practical purposes, we don't get a tax increase until and unless the president and Congress agree to it. With Bill Clinton's election in November 1992, both "halves" of the government of the United States—the presidency and the Congress—are now controlled by one party for the first time since 1980.

Many countries in the former Soviet Union and Eastern Europe are experimenting with new democratic institutions. It will be interesting to see how many will adopt the essential feature of the system of the United States, the world's oldest democracy, how many will install machinery designed to prevent government from becoming too strong, not just by providing "bills of rights" and other guarantees of individual liberty, but by dispersing authority among a number of competing units. We know that in the past most democracies around the world— with the notable exception of some in Latin America—have felt the U.S. system divides power far too much for them. They have seen it as unwieldy, confusing. How does anything get done?

The U.S. system can be enormously frustrating, as we will see in this and the chapters that follow. It is hard to make big government work without having "the government" empowered to act coherently. Still, the American system of divided government has served the country well for over two centuries. We need to understand why.

James Madison provided the classic statement of the American system in *Federalist Paper No. 51*, which he wrote just months after he played the leading role designing it in Philadelphia. He argued that the Constitution had solved the problem of power through the mechanism of a "compound republic." In it, "the power surrendered by the people is first divided between two distinct governments"— national and state—"and then the portion alloted to each [is] subdivided among distinct and separate departments." Those who administer each unit have been given "the necessary constitutional means and personal motives to resist encroachments of the others. . . . Ambition must be made to counteract ambition." If men were angels, Madison argued, no government would be needed, while "if angels were to govern men, neither external nor internal controls on government would be necessary." But, human nature being what it is, an elaborate system of checks is essential, lest power get concentrated and abused.

Federalism is the term we now use to describe what Madison referred to as the division of power "between two distinct governments." And **separation of powers** is the phrase we use for what he had in mind when he wrote of both national and state governmental authority being "subdivided among distinct and separate departments." At the national level, these are the legislative branch or department (Congress), the executive (the presidency), and the judicial (the Supreme Court and the other federal courts).

SEPARATION OF POWERS IN ACTION

Madison argued in *Federalist Paper* No. 47 that "no political truth is certainly of greater intrinsic value . . . [than that] the accumulation of all powers, legislative, executive, and judiciary, in the same hands, whether of one, a few, or many, and whether hereditary, self-appointed, or elective, *may justly be pronounced the very definition of tyranny*" (emphasis added). The Constitution that he and his colleagues had finished drafting in Philadelphia only months before went to great lengths to preclude any such "accumulation."

First, it made the three branches formally separate and distinct. The tenure in office of the officials of each cannot be determined by the others. The president is elected by the people of the fifty states and serves out his four-year term without any intervention by another branch—except in the highly unlikely event of his being formally impeached by the House of Representatives and then convicted by the Senate for "high crimes and misdemeanors." Congress is also separately elected by the people: House members serve two-year terms and senators six-year terms that cannot be altered either by the president or the courts. Federal court judges—including justices of the U.S. Supreme Court—are appointed by the president with the "advice and consent" of the Senate for life terms, and removal is possible only through the rarely used procedure of impeachment and conviction by both houses of Congress.

Second, president and Congress share power in virtually every sphere of national government action; the federal courts are also important participants. Article I of the Constitution gives Congress the authority to pass all laws, but the president may veto them. If the presi-

The Capitol building in Washington, D.C., where Congress initiates and debates bills, reacts to the president's legislative initiatives, and contemplates being overruled by the U.S. Supreme Court.

dent vetoes a bill, it must be passed again by two-thirds in both the House and Senate to take effect. The president and his executive-branch subordinates administer the laws, but they in turn are subject to legislative "oversight" (see chapter 6, pp. 168–69). Disagreement over the meaning of legislation and how it should be applied may be brought to the courts for their resolution; the Supreme Court has the final power to strike down acts of Congress and state legislatures, if it finds them in violation of the Constitution.

The president is commander-in-chief of the U.S. armed forces, but Congress has the power to declare war and, much more important in giving it a loud voice on defense issues, has the responsibility for appropriating every cent of the money spent by the armed forces for personnel and weapons. The president has the constitutional authority to negotiate treaties with foreign governments, but these treaties do not take effect until the Senate gives its approval by at least two-thirds.

PRESIDENT AND CONGRESS SQUARE OFF OVER CHINA

Interbranch divisions are as natural in the American system as the sun's rising each morning. Examples are everywhere, in foreign and domestic policy alike. The division that developed in 1989–90 between the Bush administration and Congress over China policy illustrates a number of aspects of the separation of powers in action.

After the Chinese government surpressed its country's pro-democracy forces in June 1989, a debate began in the United States over how this country should respond. The debate quickly evolved into a test of wills between president and Congress. George Bush and his foreign policy advisers took the position that, repugnant though the Chinese regime's actions were, the United States needed to temper its response to the crackdown. First, Bush believed that if U.S. ties to China, and our efforts to persuade its leaders to accept the pro-democracy movement rather than repress it, have failed to achieve what we want, our involvement nonetheless aids the long-term cause of liberalization in the world's largest country. Second, the administration argued, the current, aging Chinese leadership is unlikely to hold power much longer. The United States should maintain

working relations with China, including economic ties, so as to be in the best possible position to encourage future reform. Finally, the administration maintained, China is an important country, and the United States has interests that are served by working with it. The argument for developing U.S. links with China over the 1970s and 1980s never assumed we condoned the Communist regime's continuing repressiveness.

So, after criticizing the Chinese regime for the crackdown, Bush moved quickly to restore the United States's relationships with it. His actions included sending a secret delegation to China in July, just over a month after the massacre of hundreds of Chinese civilians in Tiananmen Square on June 3 and 4, 1989. The secret mission was followed by a public visit in December by national security adviser Brent Scowcroft. On December 19, Bush lifted a ban he had imposed on exporting three communications satellites to China.

Many Americans disagreed with these actions and argued that whatever its intent the administration appeared to be condoning the Chinese repression. Criticism was strong in Congress and was by no means confined to the opposition Democrats. One expression of the feeling that the administration wasn't being tough enough was the introduction of legislation that would defer indefinitely the deportation of Chinese students in the United States whose visas expire and waive for students on "J" visas a requirement that they return home for two years before applying for permanent U.S. residence. The bill (HR2712) sailed through the House with virtually no opposition and, after some dickering, the Senate accepted most of the House's language. (See Figure 5.1.)

On November 30, 1989, the president vetoed the Chinese Immigration Relief bill. "I share the objectives of the overwhelming majority in the Congress who passed this legislation," Bush

FIGURE 5.1   MAKING FOREIGN POLICY: THE CASE OF THE CHINESE STUDENTS

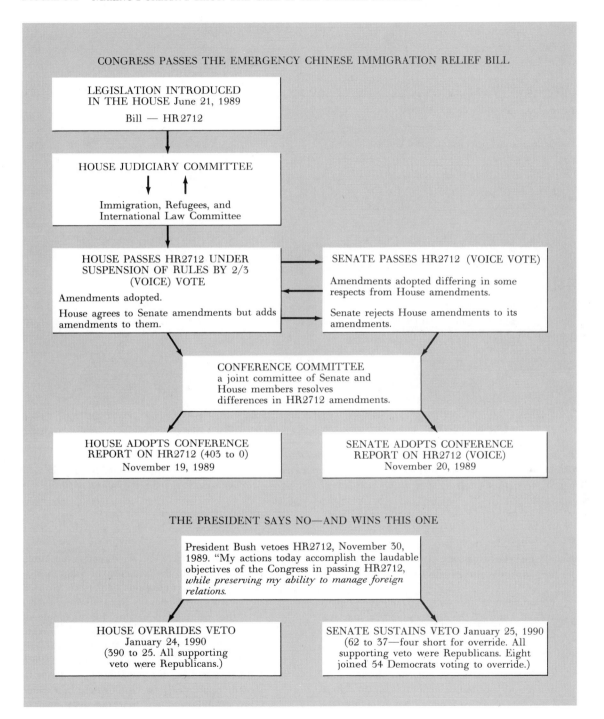

CONGRESS PASSES THE EMERGENCY CHINESE IMMIGRATION RELIEF BILL

LEGISLATION INTRODUCED
IN THE HOUSE June 21, 1989

Bill — HR2712

HOUSE JUDICIARY COMMITTEE

Immigration, Refugees, and
International Law Committee

HOUSE PASSES HR2712 UNDER
SUSPENSION OF RULES BY 2/3
(VOICE) VOTE

Amendments adopted.

House agrees to Senate amendments but adds
amendments to them.

SENATE PASSES HR2712 (VOICE VOTE)

Amendments adopted differing in some
respects from House amendments.

Senate rejects House amendments to its
amendments.

CONFERENCE COMMITTEE
a joint committee of Senate and
House members resolves
differences in HR2712 amendments.

HOUSE ADOPTS CONFERENCE
REPORT ON HR2712 (403 to 0)
November 19, 1989

SENATE ADOPTS CONFERENCE
REPORT ON HR2712 (VOICE)
November 20, 1989

THE PRESIDENT SAYS NO—AND WINS THIS ONE

President Bush vetoes HR2712, November 30,
1989. "My actions today accomplish the laudable
objectives of the Congress in passing HR2712,
*while preserving my ability to manage foreign
relations.*

HOUSE OVERRIDES VETO
January 24, 1990
(390 to 25. All supporting
veto were Republicans.)

SENATE SUSTAINS VETO January 25, 1990
(62 to 37—four short for override. All
supporting veto were Republicans. Eight
joined 54 Democrats voting to override.)

The democracy movement in China and its violent aftermath became subjects of heated debate between two branches of government—the legislative and the executive—concerning the status of Chinese students studying in the U.S. Here, pro-democracy students and workers protest in Tiananmen Square, Beijing, the capital of China.

said in his veto message, but he insisted that the measure was not needed.

> Within hours of the events of Tiananmen Square in June, I ordered the Attorney General to ensure that no nationals from the People's Republic of China be deported against their will, and no such nationals have been deported. Since June, my Administration has taken numerous additional and substantive actions to further guarantee this objective. Today I am extending and broadening these measures to provide the same protections as HR2712. I am directing the Attorney General and the Secretary of State to provide additional protections to persons covered by the Attorney General's June 6th order deferring the enforced departure for nationals of China.... These further actions will provide effectively the same protection as would HR 2712 as presented to me on November 21, 1989. Indeed, last June I exercised my authority to provide opportunity for employment to a wider class of Chinese aliens than the statute would have required. My action today provides com-

plete assurance that the United States will provide to Chinese nationals here the protection they deserve.

Handling U.S. foreign policy in this area is my job, the president was saying. In effect, Congress—stay out of my hair. He actually put it a bit more politely: "My actions today accomplish the laudable objectives of the Congress in passing HR2712 while preserving my ability to manage foreign relations."

When a bill passed by Congress is vetoed, it is dead unless both houses again approve it, this time by at least two-thirds. The House of Representatives got the requisite number and then some, voting to override on January 24, 1990, by 390 to 25. This vote was, in effect, set in terms of Congress versus the president, rather than along party lines. All 25 of those voting with the president were Republicans, but most Republicans opposed their president. This development is common in the American system. Competing party interests are almost always present, but contending institutional interests and perspectives often come into play as well. Congress does not agree that making foreign policy is really the president's business.

In the Senate, though, Bush won. That chamber voted 62–37 to override, 4 votes short of the two-thirds needed. He won by convincing Republican senators that the "us and them" in the conflict should be seen as "us Republicans" versus "them Democrats," not "us senators" versus "those guys in the executive branch." Many of the 37 Republican senators who voted with the president had reservations about the overall direction of his China policy, but in this case they were persuaded that HR2712 was more than anything else a Democratic effort to embarrass a Republican president. Congress versus the executive, and Republican versus Democrat are both almost always present in separation of powers contests.

SEPARATION OF POWERS IN FLUX: NEW WINE IN AN OLD BOTTLE

From formal constitutional provisions through which the three branches of the national government are given independent grants of authority and checks over one another, an elaborate, informal system of interactions has emerged that has given full meaning to the separation of powers. Again and again throughout American history, the branches have clashed as they have been forced to share power and responsibility in the same policy areas. Clashes between president and Congress have been especially common, because their interaction is so extensive.

In 1789, for example, just days after the new administration was sworn in, Congress was ready to challenge the claim that the president—even a president as prestigious as George Washington—should have the sole right to *remove* from office persons appointed by him with the Senate's consent. George Washington won that key battle—but only by the narrowest of margins after he and House Speaker Madison had lobbied vigorously. During the Civil War, Abraham Lincoln and a Senate majority battled without respite to determine which branch would shape policy on conduct of the war, abolition, and future reconstruction. After World War I, Woodrow Wilson and Republican leaders in the Senate fought it out over whether the constitutional requirement that the Senate give its "advice and consent" to treaties meant that it could, through "reservations," modify the terms of U.S. membership in the League of Nations negotiated by the president. Early in his second term, Franklin Roosevelt found his initiatives repeatedly blocked by Congress, even though he had just won an overwhelming mandate and his party commanded huge majorities in both houses.

Pervasive interbranch conflict is an enduring result of the separation of powers. But some elements of the conflict have been altered in the modern period, as the United States has found itself in a period of change and experimentation in the operation of its national governmental institutions. Adding divided party control onto the traditional executive / legislative separation set forth in the Constitution has been, perhaps, the most notable feature of this change.

Separation of powers puts constitutionally independent branches in a state of perpetual rivalry—each strong enough to check the others. For most of U.S. history, however, this *institutional competition* was curbed by the practical *political cooperation* encouraged by unified party control. Indeed, from 1789 to 1955, the same party or faction held the presidency and majorities in both houses of Congress for all but 38 years—and 30 of these were "natural" transitions to new administrations. That is, in 15 presidencies—from John Quincy Adams's in the 1820s to Herbert Hoover's at the start of the 1930s—the party of the soon-to-be-out-going chief executive lost control of at least one house of Congress for his last two years in office.

In recent decades things have been different much of the time. Through the 102d Congress (1991–93), a Republican president faced a Democratic legislative majority for 26 of the preceding 38 years. Even triumphant presidents were not immune. In 1984, when Ronald Reagan won by 17 million votes, Democrats gained a 70-seat advantage in the House. In 1988, when George Bush's margin surpassed 8 million, the Democrats took an 85-seat majority in the House and a 10-seat edge in the Senate. Americans are less bound by party loyalties now than they used to be, so they find it easier to split their vote for president and members of Congress. And the public's ambivalent feelings as to how much government it wants may incline it in the long run to seek different things from the executive and legislative branches—and thus entrust them to different parties. Divided partisan control of the two branches persisted so long—for all but 4 years, from 1969 to 1992—that both parties began looking at it as part of a new natural order.

It wasn't until the November 1992 elections that Americans again installed unified party control over the executive and legislative branches. Bill Clinton won the presidency—only the second Democrat to do so since LBJ's victory in 1964—and his party maintained its lock on Congress. Divided party control may prove to have been merely a historical accident. But only time will tell whether unified party control will be reestablished as the norm.

THE ''USE-OF-FORCE'' RESOLUTION IN THE GULF WAR

The Democratic Congress and the Republican White House have repeatedly clashed over foreign policy in recent years. Again, it needs to be pointed out that the U.S. system of separation of powers makes some such conflict inevitable—two independent branches are intimately involved every day in the development of American foreign policy. But having two different parties in charge, one of Congress, the other of the presidency, has certainly exacerbated the constitutional split.

A major constitutional confrontation was barely avoided during the Persian Gulf War, which resulted when Iraqi forces under the leadership of Saddam Hussein invaded and then occupied Kuwait in August 1990. By December, the Republican Bush administration and congressional Democrats appeared on a collision course. The latter counseled waiting longer to give economic sanctions a chance to work, before U.S. forces were employed to expel the Iraqis. The Bush administration, on the other hand, insisted on immediate action to achieve the U.S.–driven objective of United Nations Security Council Resolution 678—which called for Iraq's unconditional withdrawal from all Kuwaiti territory. President Bush claimed that his position as commander-in-chief (Article 2, Section 2) gave him the authority he needed to commit U.S. forces, whether Congress authorized their use or not. Congressional Democrats maintained, on the contrary, that a declaration of war was exclusively the province of Congress—as set forth in Article 1, Section 8 (see Box 5.1).

While asserting his independent authority to act, the president nonetheless asked, in a letter of January 8, 1991, that "the House of Representatives and the Senate adopt a Resolution stating that Congress supports the use of all necessary means to implement U.N. Security Council Resolution 678. . . . "I am determined," Bush concluded, "to do whatever is necessary to protect America's security. I ask Congress to join with me in this task."

In the end, Congress did support the president's intended action, but the margin in the Senate was narrow. Fifty-two senators voted for the use-of-force resolution, while 47 voted against it. The resolution was in fact a declaration of war on Iraq, even though those exact

---

Box 5.1
Who Has the Authority?:
President or Congress

The long-running debate between presidents and Congress over the authority to wage war is rooted in these passages from the Constitution:

"The Congress shall have power . . . to declare War, grant Letters of Marque and Reprisal, and make Rules concerning Captures on Land and Water; to raise and support Armies, but no Appropriation of Money to that Use shall be for a longer Term than two Years; to provide and maintain a Navy; to make Rules for the Government and Regulation of the land and naval Forces; to provide for calling forth the Militia to execute the Laws of the Union, suppress Insurrections, and repel Invasions. . . ."

—Article I, Section 8

"The President shall be Commander in Chief of the Army and Navy of the United States, and of the Militia of the several States, when called into actual Service of the United States. . . .

—Article II, Section 2

Headlines on January 17, 1991, proclaim the bombing of Iraq by allied forces initiating the Persian Gulf War. Terrence McCarthy/NYT Pictures

THE BATTLE OVER THE FEDERAL COURTS

Article II, Section 2 of the Constitution gives the president the power to "nominate . . . Judges of the supreme Court and all other officers of the United States, whose Appointments are not herein otherwise provided for. . . ." But the same clause requires the "Advice and *Consent*" (emphasis added) of the Senate before the nomination becomes an actual appointment.

Again, in an age where divided party control is common, division of authority has been an open invitation to prolonged interbranch conflict over judicial nominations. The enormously bitter split over President Bush's choice of Clarence Thomas for a seat on the Supreme Court in the fall of 1991 is the latest (as of the time this was written in the fall of 1992) in a string of contentious, highly partisan battles over the composition of the federal courts. We discuss the Thomas nomination—ultimately confirmed by the Senate by a 52–48 vote—in chapter 9, pp. 269–70.

Another result of this split partisan control was long delays in confirming federal judges. That is hardly surprising. Many Senate Democrats have had very different ideas from those of the Republican administration of what judicial policies are desirable. When a Republican president nominated people with views similar to his own, the Democratically controlled Senate Judiciary Committee often dragged its feet on the nominations. As of May 1992, 66 Bush nominees to the federal courts (out of roughly 825 district-court and circuit-court judgeships) were awaiting Senate action.

Party members in Congress are often themselves divided; sometimes enough Democrats vote with the minority Republicans to give the Republican administration the support it needs on a piece of legislation. Moreover, compromises of all sorts are struck between the president and the congressional Democratic major-

words were not used. What if Congress had voted against the resolution? Almost certainly, the president would have committed U.S. forces nonetheless. At a minimum, there would have been constitutional scars and interbranch recriminations lasting well beyond the Gulf War itself.

ity, so conflict and stalemate are hardly the only dimension to their relationship. It is the case, nonetheless, that for all but four years, from 1969 to 1993, the United States was governed under a novel and conflict-exacerbating arrangement in which one party has dominated Capitol Hill and the other, at the opposite end of Pennsylvania Avenue, the White House.

SEPARATION OF POWERS: NEED FOR REFORM?

Developing public policy in the United States is a messy process, thanks to separation of powers. It is almost always frustrating: Many independent actors have a piece of the action. But the framers *intended* it to be frustrating for president and Congress—each of whom wants things its own way but is forced by separation of powers to share and compromise.

For the last one hundred years, some have argued that the end product of separation of powers is sufficiently flawed as to make necessary basic constitutional reform. One early critic put it this way:

> As at present constituted, the federal government lacks strength because its powers are divided, lacks promptness because its authorities are multiplied, lacks wieldiness because its processes are roundabout, lacks efficiency because its responsibility is indistinct and its actions without competent direction. It is a government in which every officer may talk about every other officer's duty without having to render strict account for not doing his own, and in which the masters are held in check and offered contradiction by the servants. . . . Talk is not sobered by any necessity imposed upon those who utter it to suit their actions to their words. There is no day of reckoning for words spoken.

The speakers of a congressional majority may, without risk of incurring ridicule or discredit, condemn what their own committees are doing; and the spokesmen of a minority may urge what contrary courses they please with a well-grounded assurance that what they say will be forgotten before they can be called upon to put it into practice. Nobody stands sponsor for the policy of the government. A dozen men originate it; a dozen compromises twist and alter it; a dozen offices whose names are scarcely known outside of Washington put it into execution.[1]

These searing criticisms, all centering about separation of powers, were made by a young political scientist, Woodrow Wilson, who was to go on to become president of Princeton University, governor of New Jersey, and president of the United States (1913–21). If the style with which Wilson expressed his criticisms has a nineteenth-century ring to it, the substance of the criticisms seems to us distinctly contemporary. Wilson's intellectual successors now make many of the same charges.

Today's critics of separation of powers argue that it does awful damage to political accountability. Who is to be held responsible for policy when so many different officials, each independent of the other, in Congress and in the executive branch, have some hand in the action, yet no one has a controlling hand? Our huge federal deficits are a case in point. The president says he is distressed by their size, congressional Democrats and Republicans similarly proclaim their opposition to big deficits and their determination to bring them under control. In fact, almost no one anywhere in the executive or legislative branches defends the sustained high deficits of the 1980s and 1990s. Still, they have persisted.

[1] Woodrow Wilson, *Congressional Government: A Study in American Politics* (Baltimore, Md: Johns Hopkins University Press, 1981; first published, 1885), pp. 206–7.

Congressional Democrats have blamed executive branch Republicans for the deficits, arguing that their refusal to accept sufficient tax increases and their support for defense spending are responsible. Republicans in turn have blamed the Democrats in particular and Congress in general for being too inclined to respond favorably to interest-group demands for spending programs, without regard to the fact that such programs must ultimately be paid for. To some considerable extent, everyone is right: Congress and the president share responsibility for the high deficits. And, critics would argue, the system is also responsible: It permits many different officials to influence the shape of the budget without giving any one official formal authority such that he or she can be held accountable for the end product.

The second major criticism of separation of powers is that it hamstrings the chief executive. He may win a huge majority in the presidential balloting but he is not really given the means to form a government. He always has to go hat in hand to Congress—a Congress that about half the time since World War II has been controlled by the opposition party. Lloyd Cutler, who was counselor to President Jimmy Carter, notes that in 1979 the British Conservative party won a majority of some 30 to 40 seats in Parliament, and Conservative Leader Margaret Thatcher thus became prime minister. Thatcher had, Cutler observed, "a very radical program, one that [could] make fundamental changes in the economy, social fabric, and foreign policy of the United Kingdom." Though there was reason for real doubt about whether this program could in fact achieve its objectives,

there is not the slightest doubt that she will be able to legislate her entire program, including any modifications she makes to meet new problems. In a parliamentary system, it is the duty of

each majority member of the legislature to vote for each element of the government's program, and the government possesses the means to punish members if they do not. In a very real sense, each member's political and electoral future is tied to the fate of the government his majority has formed. Politically speaking, he lives or dies by whether that government lives or dies.[2]

As a high-ranking Carter aide, Lloyd Cutler looked upon the British prime minister's position with more than a little envy.

President Carter's party has a much larger majority in both houses of Congress than [does] . . . Prime Minister Thatcher. But this comfortable majority does not even begin to assure that President Carter or any other president can rely on that majority to vote for each element of his program. No member of that majority has the constitutional duty or the practical political need to vote for each element of the president's program. Neither the president nor the leaders of the legislative majority have the means to punish him if he does not. In the famous phrase of Joe Jacobs, the fight manager, "it's every man for theirself."[3]

The third criticism of separation of powers is that it makes it virtually impossible for American government to frame the kind of coherent, integrated approaches to complex policies that the modern era demands. The policy incoherence bred of separation of powers was one thing in 1793, when the federal government did very little and could take a long time to do what it did—something quite different today when the national government spends over a trillion dollars a year and operates a variety of programs that influence the course of the

[2]Lloyd N. Cutler, "To Form a Government," *Foreign Affairs*, Spring 1980, p. 129.
[3]Ibid., pp. 129–30.

national economy, affect every citizen, and have a real responsibility for international peace and security. Critics insist that we now need to be able to form a government that can come up with coherent programs, see these through into law, and be held fully accountable politically for their success or failure.

PROPOSALS FOR CHANGE

From the young Woodrow Wilson to present-day commentators, critics of separation of powers have looked longingly at parliamentary government, especially the form of parliamentarianism that evolved in Great Britain. An election is held and one party wins the majority of legislative seats. That party's leadership becomes the government. The prime minister is hardly a dictator; her authority is entirely dependent upon her party's legislative majority, and a new election must be held within five years. Moreover, she shares governmental power with the other leaders of her party. Nonetheless, the prime minister and cabinet, assured of a legislative majority, and generally possessing the means of disciplining recalcitrant members into supporting party programs, can develop policies while being assured that they will actually become law. Critics of separation of powers might not want to see the United States emulate Great Britain in many ways, but for the most part they would like to see it emulate British parliamentarianism.

No one argues, however, that the United States should abolish its present constitutional system and replace it with a full-fledged parliamentary system. Simple political realism accounts for much of the reluctance to urge so momentous a shift. Since the chances of it happening are literally zero, what would be gained by urging it, even if it seemed desirable? But more than this is involved. Like other analysts, critics of separation of powers in the United States recognize that our system has been in place for two hundred years and thus is an integral part of the national political tradition. No successful reform can ignore the traditions of the country for which it is being prescribed. Consequently, those who would like to see separation of powers changed have sought some means of doing so that don't make too dramatic a break from the existing system.

In reviewing various proposals for reform, Lloyd Cutler has argued that "the most one can hope for is a set of modest changes that would make our structure work somewhat more in the manner of a parliamentary system, with somewhat less separation between the executive and the legislature than now exists."[4] One proposal calls for a constitutional amendment providing that, in presidential years, voters in each congressional district would be required to elect a trio of candidates as a team: president, vice president, and member of the House of Representatives. The idea here is to tie together the political fortunes of each party's presidential and congressional candidates. By constitutional necessity, were this proposal enacted, they would all stand or fall together.

A second proposal would amend the Constitution to permit (or require) the president to choose 50 percent of his cabinet from among his party's members in the House and Senate. These appointees would retain their congressional seats while in the cabinet. Article I, section 6, of the Constitution states that "no person holding an office under the United States shall be a member of either house [of Congress] during his continuance in office." This would have to be repealed. The idea behind this proposed change is to create a greater sense of cooperation and intimacy between the executive and the legislature and add to their sense of shared responsibility for policy.

A third proposal would amend the Constitution to give the president power to dissolve

[4]Ibid., p. 139.

Congress and call for new congressional elections. The president could exercise this only once in his term—to avoid any possibility that a president's dissatisfaction with congressional performance would lead him to send it back to the voters again and again, producing serious instability. The objective of this proposal would be to add a new means of breaking serious impasses between president and Congress; the president could make the case that he needs a Congress more supportive of his policies and let the voters decide whether they want to choose new representatives.

A fourth proposal has called for constitutional change permitting an extraordinary majority (perhaps two-thirds) of both houses of Congress to declare "no confidence" in the president and call for new presidential elections.

There are problems with many of these reform proposals. Consider, for example, the last one cited, that Congress be able to declare "no confidence" in the president. This would graft a common parliamentary device onto a system that would remain essentially nonparliamentary. The vote of no confidence is a standard means in parliamentary systems for bringing down a government. A vote on a particular bill is declared one that represents a formal test of whether the government continues to enjoy majority support. If the government (which is to say, the cabinet) loses the vote, it must resign. This is entirely natural and appropriate in the parliamentary tradition—where the very legitimacy of the executive is defined in terms of its enjoying majority support in the legislature. But in the American tradition, the strength and legitimacy of the executive is dependent not on its enjoying a congressional majority, but on its having been elected by popular vote expressed through a majority in the electoral college, and thereby entrusted with "the executive Power" of the United States.

SUPPORT FOR SEPARATION OF POWERS

A famous flap occurred in 1937 over President Franklin D. Roosevelt's attempt to curb the independence of a recalcitrant Supreme Court. The Court had invalidated a number of key New Deal measures, and Roosevelt, just off a huge victory in the 1936 elections, decided he had a mandate to change things. He proposed that the president be given power to appoint a new Supreme Court justice, up to a total of five, for every sitting justice who reached 70 years of age and didn't retire. This would increase the efficiency of the Court, the president argued, adding younger justices to pick up the workload. Everyone knew, of course, that Roosevelt's real intent was to get five additional appointments immediately; he would certainly have used these openings to "pack" the Court with judges who would agree with him on the basic constitutional propriety of New Deal actions.

Congress refused to go along with the president's proposal. The proposal was decisively beaten in a Senate controlled by the Democrats by a huge margin of 76 to 16 over the Republicans. Even without his court-packing plan, the president soon attained his judicial objectives, in part through shifts in the "swing votes" of two sitting justices and in part through the normal processes of retirements and new appointments. Today, most students of the Court, including those strongly supportive of Roosevelt's New Deal, think the president was wrong in trying to use his huge electoral margin to change the constitutional balance. That a president as popular as FDR would lose on this issue in the spring and summer of 1937 is impressive testimony to the strength of the American commitment to separation of powers, a commitment based in part on the view

that even very popular and able officials can at times be wrong.

Historian Arthur Schlesinger, Jr., has argued that the key problem facing modern public policy in the United States isn't that we have in hand a set of wonderful solutions that we can't enact because of the fracturings produced by separation of powers.

> Our problem—let's face it—is that we do not know what to do. . . . If we don't know what ought to be done, efficient management of a poor program is a dubious accomplishment—as the experience of 1981 demonstrates. [Schlesinger was critical of various economic proposals that the Reagan administration urged and that Congress did in fact enact.] What is the great advantage of acting with decision and dispatch when you don't know what you're doing?[5]

[5] Arthur Schlesinger, Jr., "Leave the Constitution Alone," in Donald L. Robinson, ed., *Reforming American Government* (New York: Norton, 1980), p. 53.

Schlesinger goes on to argue that

> when the country is not sure what ought to be done, it may be that delay, debate, and further consideration are not a bad idea. And if our leadership is sure what to do, it must in our democracy educate the rest—and that is not a bad idea either. . . . I believe that in the main our Constitution has worked pretty well. It has insured discussion when we have lacked consensus and has permitted action when a majority can be convinced that the action is right.

Many would make the same general point a little more softly: Granted, there are cases where the net effect of separation of powers is to make it harder—not impossible—to implement sensible programs; there are also a great many other cases where separation of powers has helped block action that would have been unwise—unwise in part because it lacked a popular mandate. At a minimum, it is far from clear that, overall, the United States has been badly served by the division of authority, the sharing of responsibility, and the slowing of action that separation of powers encourages.

THE HISTORICAL RECORD

The picture that constitutional reformers paint of American government as a helpless giant, unable to act coherently in the face of severe challenges, is itself highly questionable. Over the last half-century the United States Congress has passed, and the president has signed into law, an enormous amount of legislation dealing with public problems. It is very hard to accept the argument that our government has been persistently unable to act. When it hasn't acted very coherently, as with the deficit, the failure may reflect less the impact of separation of powers than lack of agreement in either party on what should be done, given the variety of contending economic and political objectives. Reformers seem to overstate the incapacities for action in the American system—and the coherence of policy and programs that results from the working of parliamentary democracies like West Germany, Italy, and Great Britain.

THE AMERICAN AND BRITISH SYSTEMS COMPARED

Even with separation of powers, the American president is hardly a feeble chief executive. He does find it relatively hard to move Congress in desired directions—compared to political chief executives and their parliaments in other democracies. But his standing as the repository, alone, of the executive power of the United States gives him extraordinary visibility and legitimacy that are counterbalancing assets. Winston Churchill made this point to Franklin Roosevelt in a wartime conversation. "You, Mr. President," Churchill remarked, "are concerned to what extent you can act without the approval of Congress. You don't worry about your cabinet. On the other hand, I never worry about Parliament, but I continuously have to consult and have the support of my cabinet."[6] The president is far more the master of his cabinet departments, whose heads are clearly subordinate to him constitutionally, than the British prime minister is of his government, where cabinet secretaries are party leaders occupying positions whose constitutional status is similar to, not subordinate to, that of the prime minister.

Interestingly, while in the United States some observers criticize the American system for dispersing power too much, making coherent action difficult, in Great Britain more voices are now being heard criticizing the British system for concentrating power too much in the hands of the prime minister and cabinet, making government insufficiently responsive to popular wishes. Commenting on this growing debate, *New York Times* correspondent Craig R. Whitney wrote that some are even asking, "Is Britain really a democracy?" At first the question might seem silly—given Britain's record of party competition, free elections, and a vigorous free press. But, Whitney noted, the argument is being made that "democracy in Britain begins and ends with national elections to the House of Commons every few years. After that, a government with a healthy majority, like those enjoyed by Prime Minister Margaret Thatcher since 1979, can do just about what it wants, with few formal checks or controls."[7]

For a century some American scholars have looked fondly across the Atlantic at British government and argued that we should try to

---

[6] Winston Churchill, as quoted by Schlesinger in ibid., p. 51.

[7] Craig R. Whitney, "Where All-Powerful Central Government Lives On," *New York Times*, May 6, 1990, E-3. Mrs. Thatcher was replaced as prime minister in November 1990 by fellow Conservative, John Major.

emulate the coherence with which it acts. Now, troubled by various policies that have been pushed through, which they believe were inadequately scrutinized and unresponsive to popular wishes, some British scholars and politicians are looking fondly at the design of U.S. government. A system of more dispersed, decentralized authority looks attractive to them. The lesson here is that no set of arrangements can realize all objectives. America's divided government is in fact a system with both strengths and weaknesses.

PRESIDENT AND CONGRESS: LOOKING FOR THE PROPER BALANCE

At various points in U.S. history, alarms have been sounded that one branch or another is getting too strong. While there has been some criticism of the courts in this regard, most of the concern has been directed at either president or Congress. In the late 1960s and early 1970s, prompted by widespread dissatisfaction with the use of presidential power in the Vietnam War and abuse of power in the Watergate affair (discussed in chapter 7, pp. 163–64), many observers argued that the presidency had gotten too strong. The phrase "the imperial presidency"—the title of a book by Arthur Schlesinger, Jr.—captured this concern.

A counterreaction in Congress resulted. In a spurt Congress passed the War Powers Resolution over President Richard Nixon's veto in 1973. In 1974, it enacted the Congressional Budget and Impoundment Control Act, which expanded Congress's budget-making role and limited the president's role. These and many other assertions of congressional authority are discussed in detail in the next two chapters, pp. 164–68 and 199–201.

By the 1980s, as a result of these congressional actions, concern shifted. Instead of an "imperial presidency," criticism mounted of an overassertive Congress seen intruding excessively on the executive's turf. Now in the early 1990s, the Bush administration is attempting to redress the balance in the executive branch's favor.

With regard to foreign policy, George Bush had argued in 1987, when he was vice president, that

> over the last twenty years we have witnessed a departure from the way we have conducted foreign policy for nearly centuries. Congress has asserted an increasingly influential role in the micromanagement of foreign policy—foreign operations, if you will—and at the same time Congress, through the use of laws . . . ushered courts and lawyers into an uncomfortable but very visible role in the development of our foreign policy.[8]

As president, Bush acted on these concerns. In November 1989 he expressed "profound constitutional concerns" about an effort by Congress to forbid the administration from making its employees sign agreements that they would not divulge certain information. In signing a big appropriations bill that contained this prohibition, Bush said that he would ignore it. He insisted that his role as commander in chief includes the duty "to ensure the secrecy of information whose disclosure would threaten our national security." Not surprisingly, many in Congress cried foul. The chief legal adviser to the House maintained that "the president has no authority whatsoever to determine what duly enacted statutes shall constitute the law of the land."[9]

Early in his presidency, George Bush indicated an interest in testing the theory, advanced

[8] George Bush, address to the Federalist Society, January 1987.
[9] Chuck Alston, "Bush Crusades on Many Fronts to Retake President's Turf," *Congressional Quarterly*, February 3, 1990, pp. 291–95.

by some constitutional scholars, that the line-item veto power is in fact inherent in the existing constitutional grant of veto authority (Article I, section 7). This test would presumably mean that the president would proceed to veto specific spending items in some bill. Congress would, presumably, object, and a case challenging the president's action would be taken to the Supreme Court to settle the issue.[10] By mid-1990, however, the administration had backed away from making this test. Bush and his advisers presumably concluded that, even if they won, it would be too costly in terms of all future dealings with Congress.

This skirmishing over the precise boundaries of presidential and congressional authority is ongoing. Both branches have great resources to use in protecting their basic constitutional positions. Still, the early 1990s are likely to be a time of further presidential efforts to swing the balance a bit back the executive's way.

FEDERALISM

The American commitment to limited, divided government has sustained a dispersion of national governmental authority that has few parallels elsewhere in the world. The same commitment is evident in our country's federal system, in which the power to govern is consti-

tutionally assigned both to the central government and to the governments of the fifty states. Within a complex and continually evolving set of constraints, the national and state governments share some functions and exercise others independently. Sorting out where the proper responsibilities of the national level leave off and where those of the state level begin, and keeping intergovernmental relations reasonably smooth and productive, have always been demanding tasks in the American federal system, and "boundary disputes" have been common.

The future of American federalism has sometimes seemed bleak. At the time of the Civil War, the question was whether a national federal union could and would endure. More recently the question has been whether the states can or should play an important role in the American governmental scene. Commenting on what many thought was the states' poor performance in responding to the economic crisis that beset the country during the Great Depression, political scientist Luther Gulick asserted that "the American state is finished. I do not predict that the states will go, but affirm that they have gone."[11] Today, some argue that the dispersion of power and decentralization inherent in federalism are anachronistic, given the interdependence of the society and the national character of so many of its problems in the postindustrial era.

Each time it has been counted out, however, the federal system has recovered and shown its strength and resiliency. It remains one of America's most striking political inventions. Political scientist Samuel Beer noted that "at Philadelphia in 1787, it is generally recognized, the Americans invented federalism. . . ."[12]

---

[10] Article I, section 7, states in part: "Every Bill which shall have passed the House of Representatives and the Senate shall, before it becomes a Law, be presented to the President of the United States; If he approve he shall sign it, but if not he shall return it, with his Objections to that House in which it shall have originated, who shall enter the Objections at large on their Journal, and proceed to reconsider it. If after such Reconsideration two thirds of that House shall agree to pass the Bill, it shall be sent, together with the Objections, to the other House, by which it shall likewise be reconsidered, and if approved by two thirds of that House, it shall become a Law."

[11] Luther H. Gulick, "Reorganization of the State," *Civil Engineering*, August 1983, p. 420.

[12] Samuel H. Beer, "Federalism, Nationalism, and Democracy in America," *American Political Science Review* 72 (1978), p. 11.

Martin Diamond called it "the most important contribution made by the American founders to the art of government. . . ."[13] And in an eloquent opinion penned in 1971, Supreme Court Justice Hugo Black asserted that " 'our federalism' occupies a highly important place in our nation's history and its future. . . ."[14]

THE CONSTITUTIONAL BASE OF AMERICAN FEDERALISM

In developing federalism, the American framers could draw on some earlier political thought. In the seventeenth century, German theorists who dealt with questions of law and government were especially interested in arrangements through which the territories making up the German empire could retain their separate existence while the empire would be able to perform its appropriate central functions. But this German thought and governmental practice were so remote from the American experience of the eighteenth century that it is doubtful they actually exerted much influence. English and French schools of political philosophy, on which the framers drew so heavily, wholly ignored issues of federalism. A new governmental form really was invented at Philadelphia in 1787, in response to two inescapable elements of American political thought of the time: There should be a strong national union under a government with substantial authority, and the states should continue to have major political roles and power. American federalism has since proved attractive to other nations and their constitution makers. Today, approximately twenty countries have federal systems.[15]

American federalism has been highly dynamic and changing. But the Constitution clearly spells out its basic structure. Constitutional provisions on federalism can be usefully divided into five categories: those relating to the powers of the states, the powers of the national government, restrictions on states, federal guarantees to states, and interstate relations.

POWERS OF THE STATES

Article I, section 3, of the Constitution establishes the upper house of the national legislature, the Senate, as the federal chamber. Seats are apportioned to represent the states as equal units. Each has two U.S. senators (California with 24.7 million residents in 1982 and Alaska with just 438,000). Today this is the only instance in American legislative representation where districts of unequal size are still sanctioned, as constitutionally they must be. Article II, section 1, delineates a state role in the selection of the president. Each state chooses, in a manner determined by its legislature, a number of presidential electors equal to the number of senators and representatives the state has in the U.S. Congress.

Article V provides for a formal state role in amending the Constitution, by establishing two different procedures, both of which involve state governments directly. In the first, after Congress by a two-thirds vote has proposed amendments to the Constitution, the amendments are submitted to the state legislatures; at least three-fourths of the legislatures must ratify them before they can take effect. In the second, which has never been tried but often discussed,

[13] Martin Diamond, "The Federalist on Federalism: 'Neither a National Nor a Federal Constitution, But a Composition of Both,' " *Yale Law Journal* 86, 6 (May 1977), p. 1273.

[14] *Younger v. Harris,* 401 U.S. 37 (1971).

[15] According to Daniel Elazar, in 1982 18 countries had federal forms of government: Argentina, Australia, Austria, Brazil, Canada, Czechoslovakia, the Federal Republic of Germany, India, Malaysia, Mexico, Nigeria, Pakistan, Switzerland, the United States, the Soviet Union, the United Arab Emirates, Venezuela, and Yugoslavia. See Daniel Elazar, "State Constitutional Design in the United States and Other Federal Systems," *Publius: The Journal of Federalism* 12 (Winter 1982), p. 8.

legislatures of two-thirds of the states may call for a convention to propose amendments. As in the first procedure, the amendments would still have to be ratified by three-fourths of the state legislatures (or state conventions) before becoming law.

Probably the most discussed constitutional provision relating to the powers of the states is in the Tenth Amendment: "The powers not delegated to the United States by the Constitution, nor prohibited by it to the States, are reserved to the States respectively, or to the people." The Supreme Court has given different constructions to these words at different times in U.S. history. For much of the nineteenth and into the early twentieth century, the Court interpreted the amendment as an important statement of states' rights and residual powers. From the 1930s through the 1960s, however, the Court generally backed assertions of national authority and gave the Tenth Amendment little weight. For example, in the landmark case of *United States v. Darby* (1941), it broadly construed Congress's powers under the commerce clause of Article I and dismissed the Tenth Amendment as but stating "a truism that all is retained which has not been surrendered." Over the last decade the Court has seemed unsure how much weight it wanted to place on the Tenth Amendment. Its most dramatic ruling came in *National League of Cities v. Usery* (1976), when it struck down the amendments to the Fair Labor Standards Act that Congress had enacted two years earlier. These amendments extended to state and local government employees federal minimum-wage and maximum-hour requirements that previously had been applied only to employees engaged in interstate commerce. In the majority opinion, Justice William Rehnquist argued that "this Court has never doubted that there are limits upon the power of Congress to override state sovereignty. . . . One undoubted attribute of state sovereignty is the states' power

to determine the wages which shall be paid to those whom they employ to carry out their governmental functions."

Just nine years later, however, a closely divided Court (5–4) overruled its *Usery* decision, in *Garcia v. San Antonio Metropolitan Transit Authority* (1985). At immediate issue in this case was whether the San Antonio transit authority, a governmental entity of the state of Texas, was bound to pay its employees according to federal minimum-wage and maximum-hour legislation. In the majority opinion overturning *Usery*, Justice Harry Blackmun argued in effect that the courts should be extremely reluctant to intervene in a political argument between the states and Congress over the extent of the latter's legislative powers. Dissenting, Justice Lewis Powell, Jr., criticized the majority for promulgating a new doctrine, that federal officials "are the sole judges of the limits of their own power." *Usery* went one way; *Garcia* went the other way: Both decisions were 5–4, decided differently because one justice (Blackmun) switched sides. The issue of what the Tenth Amendment requires is still far from settled.

POWERS OF THE NATIONAL GOVERNMENT

The most formidable statement of the powers of the national government comes in Article I, section 8. After a long enumeration of what Congress can do—borrow money, raise armies, declare war, regulate commerce, advance science and the arts—section 8 declares that "the Congress shall have power . . . to make all laws which shall be necessary and proper for carrying into execution the foregoing powers, and all other powers vested by this Constitution in the government of the United States, or in any department or officer thereof." This sweeping grant has supported a generally expanding set of federal government functions and responsibilities. Article VI establishes the Constitution and the laws made under it as "the supreme law of the land," and requires state judges to uphold these provisions, "anything in the Constitution or Laws of any State to the Contrary notwithstanding."

RESTRICTIONS ON STATES

The Constitution in a number of instances tells the states things they cannot do. The biggest set of prohibitions comes in Article I, section 10. No state can make treaties with foreign countries, issue currency, grant titles of nobility, or pass any "bill of attainder," "ex post facto law," or any law "impairing the obligation of contracts"; and without the consent of Congress no state can tax imports or exports or keep military forces in time of peace.

Five amendments to the Constitution, all enacted after the Civil War, add other important prohibitions on state action. The Thirteenth Amendment was directed against the southern states and forbade slavery. Coming on its heels and also passed with the South in mind, but with language that has had much broader applicability, the Fourteenth Amendment asserts that no state "shall abridge the privileges or immunities of citizens of the United States; nor shall any State deprive any person of life, liberty, or property, without due process of law; nor deny to any person within its jurisdiction the equal protection of the laws." As we will see in chapter 9, a stream of important Supreme Court cases have arisen under these expansive terms.

The Fifteenth Amendment requires that no state deny to its citizens the right to vote "on account of race, color, or previous condition of servitude." In the Nineteenth Amendment, ratified in 1920, states were prohibited from denying the vote on the basis of sex. And the Twenty-sixth Amendment, which became law in 1971, brought the legal voting age down to eighteen all across the country by stipulating that the right of citizens who are eighteen years or older to vote shall not be denied by any state "on account of age."

FEDERAL GUARANTEES TO STATES

States are given a number of guarantees under the Constitution. According to Article I, section 8, all taxes that Congress levies must be uniform in their rates and other provisions for all states; no state may be taxed discriminatorily. Article IV, section 3, provides that no new state shall be brought into the Union from territory of one or more existing states without the express consent of the concerned state legislatures as well as the approval of Congress. In Article IV, section 4, the national government guarantees each state a republican form of government, protection against invasion, and, when the state requests it, federal assistance against domestic violence. Presidents have mobilized the National Guard and even used regular army troops to maintain calm and order in the states. Article V stipulates that the Constitution cannot be amended to deprive states of equal representation in the U.S. Senate.

INTERSTATE RELATIONS

The last of the constitutional provisions on federalism bears on the relations of one state to another. Article IV, section 1, stipulates that "full faith and credit" shall be given by every state to the laws and actions of every other state. The next section of this article provides that a state is bound to apprehend and extradite a person formally accused or convicted of violating the felony laws (those covering more serious crimes) of another state. It also asserts that each state shall grant the "privileges and immunities" given its own citizens to those of every other state—a provision presumably inserted to ensure that a resident of, say, Virginia would not be discriminated against by the police or other governmental officials when traveling or doing business in New York or South Carolina. This may seem quaint today, but it was a natural enough concern in 1787.

This is the federal framework that the Constitution establishes. Both the national government and those of the states are given expansive governmental mandates. Both are told there are things they cannot do. The national government is pledged to assure the states some basic protections, and the states in turn are pledged to honor each other's laws. This structure has been broad enough to permit a great deal of change in federal-state relations, but precise enough to maintain federalism over two centuries of extraordinary social and political transformations.

EVOLUTION OF AMERICAN FEDERALISM

We can safely say that the founders would not be at all surprised by the operation of separation of powers today. The national government does much more at present than it did two hundred years ago, of course, and all three branches now play larger roles. But the relationship of the three branches, the way they must share power, has changed very little.

This is not so with federalism. The relationship of the national and state governments has shifted dramatically at various points in U.S. history. The constitutional form of federalism is unchanged, but its practice has been transformed.

THE EARLY YEARS OF STATES' RIGHTS

Most of what was done by American government in the country's early years was accom-

plished at the state and local level. Education was exclusively a local affair, and law enforcement very nearly so. The federal government played a significant role in national defense, of course. In domestic affairs it promoted such internal improvements as building roads and canals needed to move people and goods around the nation. But that was about all. Before the Civil War the states were clearly the dominant actors in most domestic affairs.

States were understandably jealous of their prerogatives, and elaborate formulations of states' rights flourished. One example is the doctrine of **nullification,** whose main proponent was South Carolinian John C. Calhoun. Calhoun held that the Union was composed of sovereign states that did not surrender sovereignty upon entering it. As a condition of its sovereignty, a state retained the right to review the actions and laws of the central government and, if need be, to declare them "null and void." The ultimate extension of the idea of state sovereignty, of course, was the assertion of the right of secession.

If a state believed the demands of the Union were incompatible with its own interests and sovereignty, according to those who advocated the right of secession, it could pull out of the Union altogether. In 1861, eleven southern states exercised what they saw as their right to secede, and the American Civil War began.

In an environment where state's rights had broad appeal, one of the most consistent advocates of a broader national role was John Marshall, chief justice of the Supreme Court from 1801 to 1835. Marshall managed to win some victories for his nationalist perspective; his ruling in *McCulloch v. Maryland* (1819) is the most celebrated.

In 1791 Congress created the Bank of the United States to hold and dispense federal funds and perform other monetary functions. Though the Constitution says nothing explicitly about Congress's power to create corpora-

President Jefferson Davis (seated facing) General Robert E. Lee, and the Cabinet of the Confederate States of America.

tions like the bank, the bank's constitutionality was not contested in the courts before its charter expired in 1811. A second bank was chartered in 1816, but it proved politically unpopular, partly because it competed with state banks. Maryland passed legislation imposing a heavy tax on bank notes issued by the Bank of the United States. McCulloch, a cashier of the bank's Baltimore branch, issued notes without paying the required tax, thus setting the case in motion.

In the opinion of the Court, the Constitution and the laws enacted under it by the government of the United States form the supreme law of the land and cannot be infringed or countermanded by any state. Among the pow-

ers enumerated in Article I, section 8, there was no mention of establishing a bank or creating any other corporation. But neither was there anything prohibiting such action. The Constitution, Marshall insisted, clearly provided for a variety of actions not expressly mentioned when it stipulated at the end of section 8 that Congress shall be able to enact "all laws which shall be necessary and proper for carrying into execution the foregoing powers...." Establishing a national bank was a legitimate congressional act under the "necessary and proper" clause.

We admit, as all must admit, that the powers of the government are limited, and that its limits are not to be transcended. But we think the sound construction of the Constitution must allow to the national legislature that discretion, with respect to the means by which the powers it confers are to be carried into execution, which will enable that body to perform the high duties assigned to it. . . . Let the end be legitimate, let it be within the scope of the Constitution, and all means are appropriate, which are plainly adapted to that end, which are not prohibited, but consist with the letter and spirit of the Constitution, are constitutional. . . .[16]

Despite such ringing language, however, Judge Henry Friendly noted, "the use made of these powers through the first century of our history under the Constitution was restrained."[17]

POWER AND RESPONSIBILITIES SHIFT TO THE NATIONAL GOVERNMENT

In stages beginning with the Civil War, the role of the national government—"Washington," as it's often referred to today—has grown at the expense of the states. Extensive changes took place in the New Deal years. Under President Franklin D. Roosevelt after 1933, the managerial and welfare functions of the national government were greatly extended. New regulatory bodies such as the Securities and Exchange Commission (SEC) were established to watch over sectors of the economy—in the case of the SEC, to protect investors and the stock market through orderly procedures in securities exchange. The national government also intervened on behalf of groups that found it hard to compete without assistance. For example, the National Labor Relations Act (the Wagner Act) was passed in 1935 to aid trade unions by making it unlawful for an employer

to interfere with workers' rights to organize and bargain collectively.

The national government also assumed welfare functions previously handled informally through private channels, by state and local agencies, or not at all. In 1934 Roosevelt told Congress that the American people demanded "some safeguard against misfortunes which cannot be wholly eliminated in this man-made world of ours." And in 1935 the Social Security Act was passed. Two of the most important new national programs encompassed by the Social Security legislation were unemployment compensation and retirement benefits. More generally, the national government declared that henceforth it would be responsible for smoothing out business cycles, preventing excessive unemployment, promoting economic growth—in short, for maintaining and extending prosperity.

In response to all these new functions, federal expenditures again increased sharply. Between 1925 and 1941, federal per capita spending jumped 400 percent. And, reflecting a pronounced tilt toward the national government, combined state and local spending dropped below federal spending during World War II and stayed below it when peace returned—for the first time in American history.

FEDERALISM IN THE POSTINDUSTRIAL ERA

Throughout American history, technological development has brought society closer together, making its members more interdependent; thus government has had to play a bigger role. In the postindustrial era, as we noted in chapter 1, advances in communications, particularly television, have made it possible for Americans in northern Maine, in the industrial heartland

---

[16] *McCulloch v. Maryland,* 17 U.S. 316 (1819).
[17] Henry J. Friendly, "Federalism: A Forward," *Yale Law Journal* 86 (May 1977), p. 1020.

of the Midwest, in the rural South, and in the suburban sprawl of southern California, to hear the same news, watch the same entertainment programs, see the same products advertised, and in general share in a remarkably national cultural life. Further integration of the economy has exerted similar centralizing pressures. In response, studies of public opinion and popular culture have shown that state and regional variations in outlook have diminished and a more uniform national pattern has emerged.

NATIONAL RIGHTS

Another factor affecting American federalism has been an enlarged sense of national rights and responsibilities. Beginning in the 1950s, strong assertions of the rights and claims of national citizenship successfully challenged the racial discrimination that was the South's his-

torical legacy. By the 1960s national opinion had moved to the point where major changes in race relations were required. Of course, the traditions and institutions that had consigned black Americans to second-class citizenship throughout the southern states were not produced by federalism. But the nature of a federal system, which gives considerable latitude to the states in policy choice, permitted discriminatory racial practices to be perpetuated with the force of state law. The attack on segregation became, in a sense, an attack on federalism. When southern governors like Orval Faubus in Arkansas and George Wallace in Alabama proclaimed their states' rights to continue to discriminate against blacks, they helped undermine the claim to legitimacy of the larger concept of states' rights that underlies federalism itself. Writing about federalism in 1975, William Riker observed that in the century

In 1963, Governor George Wallace defied the federal government's ruling that blacks must be allowed to enroll in state universities and blocked entrance to the University of Alabama.

after the Civil War "the main beneficiaries have undoubtedly been southern whites, who could use their power to control state governments to make policy on blacks that negated the national policy. . . . Clearly . . . in the United States, the main effect of federalism since the Civil War has been to perpetuate racism."[18]

STATES' RIGHTS UNDER ATTACK

If Riker erred in so sweeping an indictment, the lessons of the 1950s and 1960s seemed to be that the people talking the loudest about the importance of states' rights were those who took issue with the basic American value of equality. Surely this validated the expansion of national governmental authority and initiative not just in race relations but across the broad spectrum of public policy. As the claims of national citizenship have grown stronger, and the practical role of the national government has been greatly enlarged, the states have been left in an awkward position. Just what is their role and legitimacy? If the states are not sovereign but simply administrative units of the national government with changing roles in an evolving political process, why should one worry about pushing them aside if national approaches seem more productive? "Federalism came to be seen as a passing phase in the developmental process. . . ."[19] The governmental enterprises of the fifty states, with their 14.5 million employees (in 1988) and myriad departments and functions could scarcely be ignored. But prevailing theory could and did accord them a fairly feeble, largely administrative status.

[18] William Riker, "Federalism," in *Handbook of Political Science*, vol. 5, Fred I. Greenstein and Nelson W. Polsby, eds. (Reading, Mass.: Addison-Wesley, 1975), p. 154.
[19] David R. Beam, Timothy J. Conlin, and David B. Walker, "Government in Three Dimensions: Implications of a Changing Federalism for Political Science," paper presented at the 1982 annual meeting of the American Political Science Association, Denver, Colo., September 2–5, 1982.

A TIDE OF NATIONAL LEGISLATION

The volume of new national legislation testified to the erosion of the states' position. One big thrust came in civil rights, but change was by no means confined to this area. Extensive new federal legislation was enacted on behalf of public safety and well-being, utilizing the "commerce" power. Protection of borrowers and consumers was extended. The national government was placed firmly behind efforts to protect the environment. The list goes on and on in almost every sector of public policy. The change was not incremental; it was a massive increase that qualitatively altered the national government's role. Let the end be legitimate, Congress was saying, and legislation on almost any conceivable subject is permitted, even required.

Growth of national power was further enhanced by various Supreme Court decisions—in their own way as consequential as the new legislation. In a long series of cases, the Court selectively incorporated key provisions of the first eight amendments to the Constitution within the due process clause of the Fourteenth Amendment, thus making them applicable to the states. (See chapter 14 for a full discussion of *selective incorporation*.)

GRANTS-IN-AID

In some cases the national government addresses problems by authorizing its agencies to spend money directly to deal with them. In many instances, however, reflecting the large presence of the states and municipalities in the American governing system, federal funds are given to states and municipalities in the form of federal **grants-in-aid,** with various stipulations on how they are to be spent.

Before the Great Depression, Congress made grant funds available to the states for only a few clearly national functions such as building "post roads"—so called because the original rationale for a roadway system connecting all parts of the country was to service a national postal service mandated by the Constitution. During the Depression, a variety of new grant programs were added to cover additional services including welfare, employment assistance, public health care, public housing, and school lunches. From the end of World War II until the 1960s, still other programs were established providing grants for airports, hospitals, urban renewal, and library services. When John F. Kennedy took office in 1961, some forty-four federal grant programs were in place.

Extensive new grant programs were enacted in the 1960s and 1970s. Congress passed legislation through which revenues raised nationally were made available to states and cities to clean up the environment, provide health benefits for the elderly poor, make loans and grants to college students, establish or enlarge urban transportation systems, combat crime, get rid of slums, and extend a host of other services. Some authorities conclude that about 500 federal grant programs were providing aid to state and local governments when Ronald Reagan took office in January 1981; others put the total even higher.

In 1955, federal grants totaled approximately $3.2 billion and provided about 10 percent of the total amount expended by state and local governments. A decade later, these grants had risen to $11 billion and accounted for 15 percent of state and local expenditures. By 1980, federal grants to state and local governments had reached $91 billion and were providing 26 percent of all funds spent by states and municipalities. In the twenty years between 1957 and 1977, grants-in-aid doubled in real terms—that is, controlling for inflation—every five years and increased overall by an extraordinary 700 percent.[20]

FIGURE 5.2   TRENDS IN FEDERAL GRANTS-IN-AID (FEDERAL GRANTS AS A PERCENTAGE OF STATE AND LOCAL EXPENDITURES)

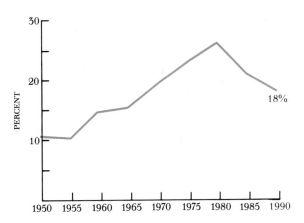

Source: Office of Management and Budget, *Budget of the United States Government, FY 1985, Special Analyses,* p. H-16; idem, *Budget of the United States Government, FY 1992,* p. 2–166.

THE REAGAN REVERSAL

The steady growth of federal grants to the states over the late 1950s, 1960s, and 1970s was halted by the Reagan administration in the 1980s. Seeking curbs on domestic spending, the administration cut back on what it considered unnecessary grants-in-aid. Major programs—revenue sharing, Urban Development Action Grants, the CETA job-training program—were killed. Others were consolidated. Total spending under federal grants leveled out in terms of actual dollars and fell substantially both as a percentage of the gross national product and as a proportion of all state and local government spending. (See Figure 5.2.) In 1978 26.8 percent of state and local expenditures were supported by federal grants; by 1990 the

[20] G. R. Stephens and G. W. Olsen, *Pass-Through Federal Aid and Interlevel Finance in the American Federal System,* *1957–1977,* vol. 1, a report prepared for the National Science Foundation, Washington, D.C., August 1979.

"IT'S FROM THE WHITE HOUSE... THEY'VE RUN OUT OF ROOM!."

A cartoonist's view of the Reagan administration's efforts to shift some social programs to the states.

proportion had dropped almost 9 points to 18 percent. Outside of the major entitlement programs of health and income security, such as Medicaid and Aid to Families with Dependent Children (AFDC), federal grants to state and local governments fell far more precipitously, from $68 billion in 1980 to $43 billion in 1990—measured in dollars of constant 1982 purchasing power.

Many state officials have had a decidedly mixed reaction to these cuts. "There's a schizophrenia out there," said Raymond Scheppach, director of the National Governors' Association. "Some governors would like the federal government out of things. But that depends on whether they have to raise taxes to compensate."[21] In other words, the flow of federal grants has been a vehicle for increased federal control; many state officials are happy to see the source of this control reduced. At the same time, they liked one feature of the federal support—that it came to them without any need to raise taxes.

THE FUTURE OF FEDERALISM

The states still play an imposing role in American governmental relations, one bequeathed them by the Constitution and reinforced by centuries of practical governmental experience. The place of the states is enhanced, too, by their considerable political muscle. As Samuel Beer noted, in a country with 80,000 governments embracing 500,000 elected persons, there is a powerful built-in intergovernmental lobby on behalf of federalism.[22] Thousands of state and local government officials have an active interest in keeping their units of government active and viable.

[21] Quoted in "Deficit Limits Reagan's Options in 1989 Budget," *Congressional Quarterly*, February 20, 1988, pp. 328–29.

[22] Samuel H. Beer, "The Adoption of General Revenue Sharing: A Case Study in Public Sector Politics," *Public Policy* 24 (Spring 1976):129.

At the same time, as we have seen, the role of the states, and their *de facto* constitutional position, has diminished significantly over the past half-century. The end result has been that a host of "boundary disputes" have gone against the states. When a disagreement has arisen on whether a decision should be made by the national government or by the states, the trend has been toward the national government. A couple of examples make this development clearer. Neither may seem very momentous individually—but they become important as part of a larger pattern. The first involves the setting of speed limits on the nation's highways; the second is the federal government's ability to regulate voter registration.

THE 55 MILE PER HOUR BATTLE

Automobiles didn't exist in 1789, of course; they didn't appear on the scene until over a hundred years later. Early Americans did, however, confront many situations where public order, health, and safety required the use of the government's policing authority. Who would exercise this authority—the states or the national government? In the American federal system, the answer was the states and their local administrative units, towns and counties. These functions were not seen requiring national action—in the way, say, that coining money, declaring war, and regulating commerce with other countries were considered national functions.

When autos did appear in large numbers early in the twentieth century, and laws regulating their use on the country's roads became necessary to protect the general well-being of drivers of autos as well as horse-drawn carriages, pedestrians, and property, the laws were enacted by the states under their well-established police powers. No one even thought of it being otherwise. This continues in our own time. The terms under which we get and main-

tain our driver's licenses, register our motor vehicles, and operate these vehicles on the highways are determined by state law and vary from state to state. When we are arrested for exceeding posted speed limits, it is by state police, county sheriffs, or municipal police, not by law enforcement officials of the federal government. And we are required to appear in state or municipal courts, not in federal courts. Setting speed limits is a state function.

As in so many areas of American federalism, however, the states' position here has been eroded. Might there be occasions when highway speed limits would have some national purpose and be subject to congressional action? In 1973 and 1974 just such an occasion appeared. Amid the first round of big price increases and fuel shortages caused by the Arab oil embargo—a cutoff of oil to the United States to punish America for its support of Israel—Congress passed legislation to lower the maximum highway speed limit to 55 miles per hour—in the national interest of encouraging fuel conservation, as 55 mph was considered the most fuel-efficient driving speed.

Even at that time, when the nation saw energy problems at near-crisis proportions, some members of Congress objected to the national government's intruding into what was basically a state responsibility. Senator Carl T. Curtis (R-Nebraska) argued: "The states are irritated now about all the requirements placed on them, and if they do not comply their federal funds are in jeopardy. That sort of coercion is not the right way to do it."[23] This and other such arguments were brushed aside. The mood in Congress and among the general public was: Do something. We have a serious national problem.

The vehicle for congressional action is interesting. Congress did not believe it could pass a

[23] Quoted in "Senate Approves Heavier Trucks, Lower Speeds," *Congressional Quarterly*, September 14, 1974, p. 2451.

law directly setting highway speeds in Vermont, Minnesota, Arizona, and the other forty-seven states; passing such a law was the clearly established province of the states. What Congress did was mandate that the states themselves pass the new speed limit. What if the states refused? In 1973 each state was receiving a substantial portion of its highway construction and maintenance funds from federal grants, money for which came partly from distribution of federal gasoline tax revenue. Congress said to the states, "Setting highway speed limits is your business, but if you don't reduce the limit to 55 miles per hour on all roads we will cut your federal highway grant funds." The states complied. Here again is a key element in the evolution of federal-state relations in the twentieth century: the use of federal leverage to impose uniform responses to what are seen as national problems.

By 1986, conditions relating to energy were very different from the time of the Arab oil embargo. OPEC's clout had diminished as an oil surplus replaced the earlier shortage. Oil prices were falling and energy conservation no longer seemed the compelling national need that it did in 1973. It was generally recognized that the 55 mph limit had reduced highway fatalities, but the public was less convinced of the necessity of the limit. Monitoring of highway speeds showed more and more of the driving public exceeding 55 mph—and more and more states weakly enforcing their official limits. In Montana, for instance, a driver cited for traveling 70 mph on an interstate highway during daylight hours could expect to be punished by nothing more than a fine of $5. Throughout the west a *de facto* state rebellion against the 55 mile speed limit was in progress.

Facing this political pressure, Congress in effect struck a deal with the states. In 1987 it permitted them, if they chose, to raise the speed limit to 65 mph on rural interstate highways—those outside congested areas. Later in the year Congress also allowed the states to raise the speed limit to 65 mph on rural highways, primarily state turnpikes, that met the same design standards as interstate highways. It's important to note, however, that while the states finally got most of what they wanted, Congress is now firmly established as the arbiter of highway speed limits. The states had to petition Congress to permit them to raise the speed limit— even on what are purely state roads, out of the federal interstate system.

REGULATION OF
VOTER REGISTRATION

We can get a good sense of the pressures to extend the national government's role at the expense of the states by looking at legislation introduced in Congress in 1990 to provide broad new federal regulation of voter registration. Historically, most of the rules governing voter registration and the conduct of elections have been made by state governments. But legislation proposed in 1990 would establish uniform, nationwide voter registration procedures. An application for a driver's license, or its renewal, would serve as an automatic application to register to vote—hence the designation as the "National Motor-Voter Registration Act." Applications would also be made available at libraries, unemployment and public assistance offices, schools, and other locations. The bill also included address-verification procedures designed to prevent voter fraud, which would be made a federal crime. In 1992, "motor-voter" passed both Houses, but Congress failed to override the president's veto.

The goals are commendable. But, critics charge, voter registration has been the purview of the states, not the federal government. If, whenever there is a worthwhile end to be served, national action is taken overriding the role of the states, federalism will lose much of its vitality.

To respond to the national crisis brought on by fuel shortages during the 1973 Arab oil embargo, the federal government, through Congress, set the speed limit at 55 miles per hour. Though the setting of speed limits was the province of the states, the federal government used as leverage the funds given to states to build and maintain highways.

THE CASE FOR A
VITAL FEDERALISM

Adapting American federalism to the social and political requirements of the approaching twenty-first century will present a continuing challenge. There is a compelling case for national responses to problems that are increasingly national, if not global. There is also an impressive case for maintaining federalism's vitality.

The link between federalism and the maintenance of freedom can be traced back to *The Federalist Papers*. We have seen that Madison and Hamilton integrated the principle of separation of powers with the idea of federalism to produce what they believed would be a watertight defense of freedom. Other countries such as Great Britain have achieved high levels of political and social freedom without such dispersion of governmental authority. But many Americans still hold to the classical liberal belief that divided power as promoted by federalism

helps guard against any unit of the government becoming too strong.

A related defense of federalism is the idea that the diverse needs of a heterogeneous population scattered over a big territory can best be served by a multilevel government. While various public opinion studies of recent years have shown that many citizens have a greater awareness of national officials and programs than of the state and local counterparts, the public still finds the system of semi-autonomous states useful to articulate local needs and interests. Even the strongest proponents of national citizenship agree that there are some areas where local choice should prevail. Few voices are heard, for example, on behalf of a national school system.

There seems to be merit in a governmental system that gives states room to experiment with programs reflecting their contrasting needs and interests. Many states pioneered social programs long before the national government acted on them. The state of New York introduced minimum-wage, maximum-hour, and child-labor legislation decades before it was achieved nationally. If describing them as "laboratories of federalism" seems extravagant, the states have in fact experimented productively with many programs and policies. "It is one of the happy incidents of the federal system," Supreme Court Justice Louis Brandeis wrote in 1932, "that a single courageous state may, if its citizens choose, serve as a laboratory, and try novel experiments without risk to the rest of the country."[24]

SUMMARY

The American constitutional system differs from that of most other democracies by providing for an elaborate division of governmental power. It does this principally through separation of powers and federalism. In a parliamentary system like Great Britain's, no separation of executive and legislature exists: The government or cabinet, which performs executive functions, is made up of the leaders of the party (or coalition) that has a majority in the legislature. The government holds office only so long as it can command a legislative majority and can secure legislative approval for all of its major programs.

The principal effect of American separation of powers is a great expansion of the number of officials with formal roles in all policy decisions. The very size and independence of this group—which includes the president and other executive branch officials, Republican and Democratic leaders of the House and Senate, majorities on various committees in both chambers, and often each individual member

of Congress—ensures that the policy-making process will be fractured, decentralized, and dominated by a continuing need for compromise.

Various critics have long urged constitutional change to limit separation of powers. A century ago, Woodrow Wilson criticized the system as unacceptably dispersing power and responsibility across the executive and legislative branches. Today's reformers, including former Carter aide Lloyd Cutler, make the same charges. They also stress what they consider to be the special problems that separation of powers poses in an age of big government and complex, fast-moving problems.

Opponents of the proposed reforms deny that any major constitutional change is the answer. They defend separation of powers as providing constitutional means of blocking unwise and precipitate action. They stress that the view of the U.S. government as hamstrung and unable to act coherently is overdone. And they insist that separation of powers has contributed notably to maintaining Congress as a powerful and responsive representative institution.

Federalism was invented by the framers of the U.S. Constitution in 1787 to meet two contrasting objectives to which many Americans were committed: achieving a strong national union and preserving the states as important political units. Federalism is a system of government in which formal authority is shared by the national and the state governments. Today, about twenty countries have some form of federal system.

Federalism has a detailed and explicit base in provisions of the U.S. Constitution. Various articles and amendments specify the powers of the states and of the national government, impose restrictions and extend guarantees to the states, and treat interstate relations.

At the end of the 1980s, the states retain important roles in the America system of divided government. Their dependence upon Wash-

---

[24] *New State Ice Co. v. Liebmann*, 285 U.S. 262, 311 (1932), Justice Brandeis dissenting.

ington for funding has actually declined over the past decade, as the federal budget deficit and Reagan administration pressure brought about reductions in grants-in-aid. Still, the federal government now enjoys an ascendancy in American constitutional theory that would have been unthinkable in earlier periods of the country's history.

Over the last half-century "boundary disputes" between the federal government and the states have been settled mostly in the former's favor. Today it's the intellectual case for independent spheres of state action, not the case for broad spheres of national government responsibility, that needs careful tending.

FOR FURTHER STUDY

Bryce, James. *The American Commonwealth.* 2 vols. New York: Macmillan, 1916. The classic account of American institutions, including the separation of powers, written by a distinguished English theorist.

Diamond, Martin. "The Federalist on Federalism: Neither a National Nor a Federal Constitution, But a Composition of Both," *Yale Law Journal* 86 (1977) pp. 1273–85. A classic essay on the nature of American federalism by a theorist profoundly sympathetic to it.

Elazar, Daniel J. *American Federalism: A View from the States,* 3rd ed. New York: Harper and Row, 1984. Perhaps the best general treatment of the historical development and present operations of the American federal system.

Friendly, Henry J. "Federalism: A Foreward," *Yale Law Journal* 86 (1977), pp. 1019–34. A brilliant review of developments in American law affecting the operations of the federal system.

Grodzins, Morton. *The American System.* New Brunswick, N.J.: Transaction Books, 1983; edition revised by Daniel J. Elazar. An updating of Grodzins's classic analysis of American federalism.

Robinson, Donald L. *To the Best of My Ability.* New York: W. W. Norton, 1986. A lucid account of the historical development of separation of powers and a penetrating criticism of contemporary problems derived therefrom.

Wilson, Woodrow. *Congressional Government: A Study in American Politics.* Baltimore, Md.: Johns Hopkins University Press, 1981; first published, 1885. A classical account of American national government in the late nineteenth century, lamenting the dispersion of power and the lack of political accountability.

OPTIONAL COMPUTER EXERCISES

for *The Ladd Election ANALYZER*

WHO VOTED FOR DIVIDED GOVERNMENT IN 1992?

In 1992, for the first time since the 1970s, Americans gave one party, the Democrats, control of both the presidency and the two houses of Congress. This ended twelve years of divided government. Still, some Americans voted to continue the split by supporting one party's nominee for president and another party's nominee for the House of Representatives (see p. 104). Using the 1992 data in the *ANALYZER,* find out what proportion of the electorate split their tickets in this manner.

A few advanced analyses. What can we say about the voters who did split their tickets? Again select "1992 Vote" and "For which representative voted" (under "Vote variables"). First, determine how these voters look in terms of age, in terms of education, in terms of where they live. Next, compare the three groups of ticket splitters: (1) Those who voted for Clinton for president but for a Republican House candidate, (2) those who voted for Bush for president but for a Democratic House candidate, and (3) those who voted for Perot for president and for either a Republican or Democratic House candidate. Which group was the most numerous?

Chapter 6

CONGRESS

It was not by chance that the framers devoted the first article of the U.S. Constitution to Congress. They expected the legislature to be the strongest branch of the new government. They also considered it the most important branch, because representative democracy simply could not exist in the absence of an autonomous legislature able to enact laws and be accountable ultimately to the people. Much has happened over the past two centuries to alter the operations of Congress and its place in the American governmental system. Today few would consider it dominant; the role of the president and the executive branch has become too great for that. But Congress is still in the middle of policy making in the United States.

In this chapter we will be examining the distinctive features of Congress as our national legislature—in particular, how it organizes itself to conduct legislative business and its continuing rivalry with the executive branch in the complex system of policy and politics established by the separation of powers. To illustrate this, we will follow one important piece of legislation along its eighteen-month journey through Congress and one presidential veto, to its subsequent reenactment in revised form and its being signed into law.

The U.S. Capitol building in Washington, D.C.—Senate chamber on left, House chamber on right.

Before turning to these matters of organization and process, however, let's examine the political controversy that surrounds Congress over how satisfactorily it is performing its essential role in American democracy.

CONGRESSIONAL PERFORMANCE: INCUMBENCY AND INCREASED DISSATISFACTION

Two areas have been receiving special scrutiny. One involves the advantages of **incumbency**—a position that has enabled members of both parties, especially in the House of Representatives, to win reelection over challengers in record proportions and by typically overwhelming margins—and what this erosion of competition means for Congress as a *representative* body.

The other concern involves **ethics,** including the relationship of members to powerful interests that are directly affected by Congress's actions and that lobby actively and spend freely to influence those actions. Ethical issues also center around members' abuse of privileges, evident in the House of Representatives' bank scandal that so roiled the political waters in 1992. The House ethics committee released on April 15, 1992, the names of 252 current and 51 former representatives who were permitted, without penalty, to overdraw their House bank checking accounts. Some did so in such amounts and with such frequency that they were being given, in effect, large interest-free loans. "I can't do that at my bank; why should they?" was the common public response. By itself not the most serious of abuses, some members' milking of the House bank seemed to many to symbolize the fact that legislators are moving further and further away from those they represent.

INCUMBENCY

American voters have in recent years been routinely reelecting House incumbents from both political parties. What's more, they have done this by overwhelming margins, even though they are dissatisfied with Congress's performance as an institution. This is in part because specific House votes are substantially divorced from judgments about parties and policies in general. Much the same thing seems to be happening in state legislatures, for the same basic reasons.

It was more than a decade and a half ago that political scientist David Mayhew called attention to the "vanishing marginals"—House seats where the winner's margin was small enough that the contest could be seen as competitive.[1] In 1960, when most observers thought

both parties had too many safe seats, 203 of the 435 contests (47 percent) were at least marginally competitive, with the winner held to less than 60 percent of the vote. Two decades later, the low competitiveness of 1960 suddenly seemed robust. In 1980, only 140 House seats (32 percent) saw the winner's margin under 60 percent. In 1988, the number had plunged to 65 seats, though in 1990 it was up somewhat to 121, 28 percent of the total.

In 1986, only 7 House incumbents who sought reelection were defeated. In 1988, only 6, and in 1990, 15. Not only have we been seeing return rates for incumbents of 96 to 98 percent, but most of these incumbents are winning by margins that can't be explained by the mix of party loyalties and policy preferences in their districts. House voting is the least competitive it has ever been in U.S. history. In 1988, winners were either unopposed or beat their opponents by 40 percentage points or more in 242 of the 435 districts, by 20 to 40 points in 128 districts, and by 10 to 20 points in another 36.

[1] David R. Mayhew, "Congressional Elections: The Case of the Vanishing Marginals," *Polity* 6 (Spring 1974), pp. 295–317.

In only 29 districts—7 percent of the total—did the loser come within what might properly be considered striking distance, trailing by 10 points or less.

DISSATISFACTION

In the 1990 House elections, the winner's popular vote margin was 20 percentage points or greater—often much greater—than the loser's in 314 of the 435 districts. Once again, that is, the vast preponderance of House races were entirely uncompetitive. This doesn't mean, however, that most voters were happy with what they saw of the national legislature's performance. The public's criticism of Congress rose sharply in 1990.

It has continued to climb. At present the level of expressed dissatisfaction is perhaps higher than ever before. For example, a national survey taken in April 1992 by American Viewpoint found just 17 percent saying they approved of the way Congress is doing its job; 75 percent disapproved, 51 percent calling their disapproval strong. This judgment cuts across party lines: 79 percent of Republicans, 75 percent of independents, and 72 percent of Democrats came down on the negative side.

Figure 6.1 uses polls taken by CBS News and the *New York Times* to show just how sharply public approval of Congress's performance has declined in recent years. The institution's ratings show a good deal of variation in the short term, but a downward trend over-

FIGURE 6.1   INCREASING PUBLIC DISAPPROVAL OF CONGRESS—BUT MY REPRESENTATIVE IS NOT TOO BAD

Question: Do you approve or disapprove of the way Congress is handling its job? How about the representative in Congress from your district? Do you approve or disapprove of the way your representative is handling his or her job?

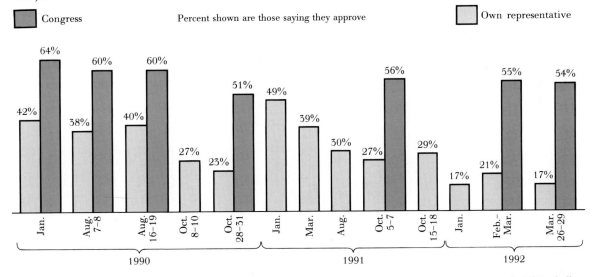

Note: Of those who said in the March 1992 survey that they disapprove of the way Congress is handling its job (75% of all respondents), 76% said they mainly disapprove of both the Democrats and the Republicans in Congress; 13% said mainly the Democrats and 8% said mainly the Republicans.
Source: Surveys by CBS News / *New York Times*, latest that of March 26–29, 1992.

all. Note, though, that many people continue to distinguish between the performance of the legislature in general and that of their own representative. "Congress is all messed up, but my representative seems nice enough." The latter is often true, but making this distinction as they do makes it difficult for voters to bring about overall change in the legislature—which they plainly want.

When its standing is compared to that of a variety of other institutions, we see the extent of the public's dissatisfaction with Congress even more strikingly. For example, Gallup asks its respondents whether they have "a great deal, quite a lot, some, or very little" confidence in the military, banks, Supreme Court, and so on. Congress is consistently near the end of the pack. It always lags well behind churches, the military, public schools, and the Supreme Court. Similarly low-rated institutions are organized labor, television, and big business. In February 1992, when 50 percent said they had a great deal or quite a lot of confidence in the military, only 10 percent held Congress in such esteem. (See Figure 6.2.)

A battery of questions about Congress

FIGURE 6.2   CONFIDENCE IN INSTITUTIONS: CONGRESS FAR BACK IN THE PACK

Question: As far as people in charge of running . . . are concerned, would you say you have a great deal of confidence, only some confidence, or hardly any confidence at all in them?

Have a great deal of confidence
in the people in charge of running . . .

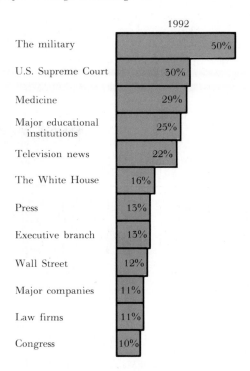

Source: Survey by Louis Harris and Associates, February 19–26, 1992.

included in a May 1989 ABC News / *Washington Post* survey illustrates the general tone of public assessment of Congress in recent years, (See Figure 6.3.) Seventy-one percent agreed that most congressional candidates will make promises they have no intention of fulfilling in order to win elections, 76 percent that most members will lie if they think it expedient, 75 percent that most members "care more about special interests than they care about people like you." However, such testimony should not be read literally. The public often takes advantage of specific poll questions to convey a general message—here, that it's somehow dis-satisfied with the performance of its national legislature.

Professed dissatisfaction was not nearly as high in the past. No single question has been asked over the entire span covered by polling—the late 1930s to the present—but a great many readings similar to those of recent years were taken in earlier periods. For example, a Gallup poll of August 20–25, 1958, asked whether Congress was doing a "good job" or a "poor job." It found only 12 percent saying poor. Another Gallup study, this one in September 1964, asked how much "trust and confidence you have" in Congress. "The top of the ladder

FIGURE 6.3 CONGRESS: GENERAL PUBLIC DISSATISFACTION

Question: I'm going to read a few statements. For each, can you please tell me if you tend to agree or disagree with it, or if, perhaps, you have no opinion about that statement? Most members of Congress . . .

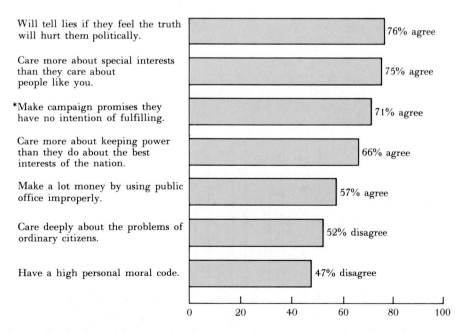

*The question wording for this is the same as the others, except the last sentence reads: "To win elections, most candidates for Congress. . . ."

Source: Survey by ABC News / *Washington Post*, May 19–23, 1989.

in this case means the greatest possible confidence, the bottom no confidence at all." There were eleven rungs, numbered 0 through 10. Only 2 percent placed themselves on one of the lowest three, 46 percent on the highest three. The median was between rungs 6 and 7.

As late as 1970, Americans were still rating Congress quite positively. In June 1970, Gallup showed its respondents a card on which there were ten boxes, numbered from +5 (for institutions "you like very much") down to −5 (for those "you dislike very much"). Only 3 percent assigned Congress to the −4 or −5 boxes, while 36 percent put it either in +4 or +5. Only 10 percent gave Congress a negative score of any sort. It was during the 1970s that Congress's standing took its biggest plunge. Despite some short-term movement over the past twenty years, public confidence in the national legislature has remained low.

In the span when competitiveness in House races has been greatly diminished, dissatisfaction with Congress's operation—vague and unfocused but substantial nonetheless—has become a more prominent part of public attitudes. We certainly should not attribute all of the dissatisfaction to the growing incumbency advantages and the resultant weakening of practical public control, but it is clear that something about Congress—rather than simply about government in general—now troubles many Americans. Part of it seems to be that

FIGURE 6.4   WALKING AWAY FROM WASHINGTON

☐ House members not running for reelection because they are running for another office

◼ House members retiring from elective office (as distinguished from those who left to run for another office—breakdown not available before 1958)

In addition to the 67 House members retiring or running for higher office in 1992, 19 had already lost in primary elections by September 15.

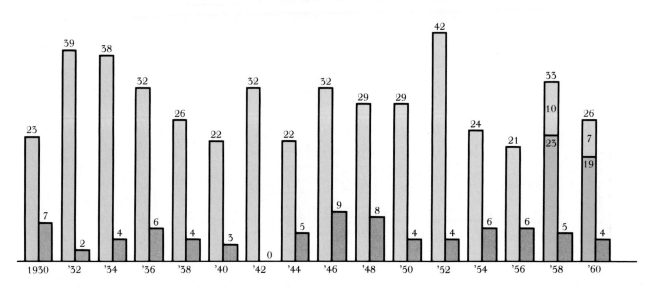

Source: Congressional Quarterly. Figures before 1946 were compiled by *Congressional Quarterly* from Congressional Research Service data, as published in the *New York Times,* May 17, 1992.

congressional incumbents are seen to behave as a kind of permanent government that continues on its way, somehow impervious to concerns over its performance. Ethics violations, especially those attributable to abuses of privilege and congressional incumbents' being heavy recipients of campaign money contributed by groups seeking to influence government action, adds to the general public unease.

FRUSTRATION BOILS OVER

By 1992 the dissatisfaction was having an effect. The number of senators and representatives deciding not to seek reelection, or being defeated

in nomination contests, was unusually large.

Every election year finds some choosing to retire for various personal reasons. And every ten years, the census reveals changes in population that require legislative reapportionment and, as a result, the redrawing of many House district lines. This might mean that two incumbents are forced to run against each other in a redrawn House district that includes parts of both their original districts.

This said, turnover was much greater than usual in 1992, as voters expressed their dissatisfaction and some legislators decided they just didn't want to serve in the current environment (Figure 6.4). As of May 1992, seven senators had announced their retirement—two of them

FIGURE 6.4 (CONTINUED)

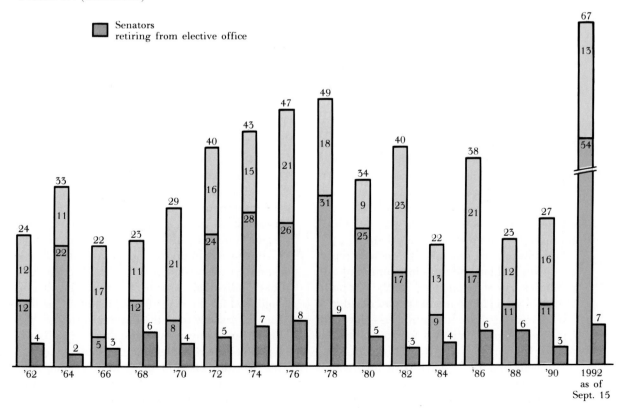

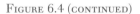 Senators
retiring from elective office

forced to by personal scandals. Fifty-four House members said they would not seek reelection—some of them had been caught up in the check-kiting scandal or another ethics problem, and others were simply discouraged by the way things were going. Matthew F. McHugh (D-NY), who was acting chairman of the House ethics committee (officially, the Committee on Standards of Official Conduct), was among the latter. "I'm saying I may not be able to accomplish enough," McHugh stated, "to justify, after eighteen years, continuing to put my family through this. Not just my family—me."

In addition, one senator and nineteen representatives had lost their parties nominations in primaries (as of September 1992). An additional thirteen House members had decided to run for another office in November—eleven for U.S. Senate seats and two for governorships. Adding in turnover due to the death of an incumbent and races where two incumbents had to face each other in a redrawn district—there were certain to be one hundred new members in the 103d Congress, even before the November results were in.

Nonetheless, we shouldn't conclude that the pronounced advantages to incumbents, so decisive in recent elections, have been removed. They are still very much in place.

One is the huge advantage incumbents typically enjoy in resources for promoting their candidacies. Staff provided to House members tripled in the 1960s and 1970s (see pp. 152–53), and members have put many of their new assistants to work in their home districts. Staff expansion was justified by the argument that Congress would thus be better able to do battle with the expert-laden executive branch and that individual members would be better equipped for their legislative business. The former is certainly true; the latter may not be true at all. But in any case, the augmented staffs are a potent year-round electoral resource—servicing constituents and in general keeping the member's name before district voters in a way virtually no challenger can rival.

Incumbents also enjoy big leads in campaign contributions. Knowing that current office holders are likely to be reelected and that they will have to be dealt with in advancing certain legislative goals, the formidable array of organized interests that envelops the national government today backs incumbents heavily, through the contributions of their political action committees, known as PACs. (Discussed in detail in chapter 12, pp. 367–73, PACs are arms of business corporations, trade associations, labor unions, and other organizations authorized under current law to raise funds and dispense them as political contributions.) The $94 million that PACs contributed to House campaigns in 1987–88 in contests where an incumbent was running for reelection, went to incumbents over challengers by slightly more than 8 to 1. The almost $80 million given by political action committees in such races in 1989–90, through October 17, 1990, went to incumbents by an even greater margin: $74.7 million to $4.7 million, or roughly 16 to 1. PACs gave about $58 million to Democrats, but just $28 million to Republicans—reflecting the reality of longstanding Democratic control of Congress.

An analysis of contributions data by the *Washington Post's* Richard Morin and Charles Babcock noted that "not surprisingly, much of the PAC money went to members of committees with jurisdiction over the PAC's industries and unions."[2] For example, PACs for the maritime industry—both unions and shipping companies—were big donors to members of the House Merchant Marine and Fisheries Committee and the Senate Commerce, Science, and Transportation Committee. David A. Keene, a spokesman for the Marine Engineers Beneficial Association union, noted that poli-

cies crafted by those committees "will dictate the health or growth of the domestic maritime industry. Therefore you would obviously expect everyone in the industry to be working with and supporting members of those committees."

In races for state governor and U.S. senator—as well as that for president—many voters know a substantial amount about the candidates' records. In these contests, even well-funded incumbents who are better known than their opponents may readily be defeated when the electorate is in a mood for policy change. But House members simply don't have governors' and senators' visibility. Their stands and performance are largely unknown to most of the electorate. But voters are more likely to have a vaguely favorable image of the incumbent than of his resource-poor challenger.

Political party ties are the one thing that could upset this dynamic. A voter might not know anything consequential about a member's record but still vote against him or her in favor of a less well known challenger, because the voter preferred the challenger's party. That is in fact exactly what happened historically. But over the last quarter-century, as incumbents have accumulated election resources far greater than before, the proportion of the electorate bound by strong party ties has declined precipitously. Better educated and drawing their political information largely from the communications media, American voters feel they need parties less than did their counterparts of times past. In many ways they may be right in this inclination to dispense with parties and focus on the candidates alone—but not in the case of House candidates where voters typically won't exert themselves to learn enough to form a coherent independent judgment.

In highly visible races like those for president, senator, and governor, voters do often acquire enough information to make up for the decline of the guidance that party ties long provided. At the other end of the spectrum, in

[2] Richard Morin and Charles R. Babcock, "Keep That PAC Money Rolling," *Washington Post*, Weekly Edition, May 14–20, 1990, p. 15.

elections for school-board members, aldermen, and other positions, voters often have enough close, personal knowledge to reach reasonably informed judgments. House races and other "intermediate" contests are a problem. Here, party voting is no longer decisive, but substantive knowledge of the candidates' records is insufficient to furnish a substitute base. Enjoying huge advantages in resources for self-promotion, incumbents are still hard to challenge, even after the strong public protest of the early 1990s, so long as they avoid public scandal.[3]

ORGANIZATION OF CONGRESS

The American Congress is charged with representing the public in making laws. In this it resembles other national legislatures, such as the British Parliament, the French National Assembly, and the German Federal Parliament. It differs from them, though, in its constitutional independence from the executive. As discussed in chapter 5, separation of powers distinguishes all of American government, including the relations of Congress and president.

[3] Incumbency advantages are clearly substantial, but some observers caution against overstating the case. For example, Congressman Mickey Edwards (R-Oklahoma) points out that "there is not, as some people charge, a permanent Congress. Approximately two-thirds of the people who were serving in the Congress a dozen years ago have been replaced. . . . The Congress is, in fact, a constantly changing body, with a much higher rate of turnover than is found in business, academia, or most significant institutions." "A Conservative Defense of Congress," *The Public Interest*, Special Issue, Summer 1990, p. 83. See, too, in the same issue, political scientist Norman Ornstein's careful review of congressional incumbency effects and other factors that shape the political control of Congress, "The Permanent Democratic Congress," pp. 24–44.

A majority of the world's democratic governments are parliamentary in form, where executive authority is derived from the legislature. In such countries as Australia, Canada, Great Britain, Sweden, Germany, India, and Japan, the chief executive official—variously called the prime minister, premier, or chancellor—holds a seat in the national legislature. So do the heads of the principal executive departments, called, together with the prime minister, the cabinet, council of ministers, or simply the government. They hold the reins of power in the government because they are the leaders of the legislative majority and are voted into office by the majority coalition. In the American scheme, however, the legislature and the executive are separately chosen and constitutionally distinct. The main result of this—and as we saw in chapter 5, since the 1950s, the common actual experience—is the possibility of one party controlling the executive branch, the other the legislative. Divided control cannot happen in parliamentary systems such as those in Canada and Italy.

BICAMERALISM

Within Congress, the idea that power should be divided expresses itself through **bicameralism.** Legislative authority is assigned to two coequal chambers, the Senate and the House of Representatives. Although two-house legislatures are not uncommon, the U.S. arrangement, where the two chambers share power equally, is rare. In parliamentary systems like Great Britain, West Germany, and Japan, one house has much more authority than the other. The British House of Commons, for example, elects the government and plays the major role in shaping legislation, while the House of Lords has come to have a distinctly inferior role.

In the United States, the framers provided for two chambers different in size, constituency, and term of office of their members. The

House of Representatives, with a membership based on population, was (and is) the larger of the two bodies. In the first and second Congresses it had 65 members, compared to the Senate's 26. Since 1910 House membership has been fixed at 435. Composed of two senators from each state, the Senate had 96 members from 1910 until the late 1950s; when Hawaii and Alaska entered the Union, the total reached the present 100.

The Constitution stipulates that the House of Representatives must be chosen through direct popular election; members are voted into office from districts of roughly equal population. In contrast, reflecting the federal character of the American union, the Constitution provides equal representation in the Senate for each state, regardless of state populations. Until ratification of the Seventeenth Amendment in 1913, the commitment to different constituencies for the Senate and House also included different election procedures: House members through direct popular ballot, senators by their state legislatures. The Seventeenth Amendment changed the latter provision by requiring direct popular election for the Senate. Regarding term of office, all House members are elected every two years. Senators serve six-year terms, with one-third of them up for election every biennium.

The framers also believed that each chamber should possess its own distinctive legislative character. The House was to be what Madison called "the grand repository of the democratic principle of government."[4] With its short terms and popular election, it was expected to be sensitive to public opinion. At the same time, the House was thought likely to display certain weaknesses common to large, popularly elected legislatures: instability, impulsiveness, unpre-

dictability, inclination to change decisions, and "a short-run view of good public policy." The Senate would be a counterbalance. It would be the source of "a more deliberate, more knowledgeable, longer-run view of good public policy."[5]

This sense of contrasting legislative styles is illustrated in a revealing anecdote about the two chambers. Thomas Jefferson had been in France during the Constitutional Convention. Upon returning to the United States, he asked his fellow Virginian George Washington why the latter had agreed to a second chamber, rather than providing for a single-house legislature responsible to the people. "Why," asked Washington, "did you pour that coffee into your saucer?" "To cool it," Jefferson allegedly replied. "Even so," Washington responded, "we pour legislation into the senatorial saucer to cool it." Not all of the framers' expectations have been fulfilled. The Senate is quite capable of acting precipitately, and the House coolly and deliberately. All in all, though, the requirement that both chambers must consider and approve a piece of legislation before it becomes law has remained an important practical element of American legislative practice. As political scientist Richard Fenno observes, while "the framers did not . . . create one precipitate chamber and one stabilizing chamber . . . they did force decision-making to move across two separate chambers, however those chambers might be constituted."[6]

Such characteristics of the Senate and House as the former's smaller size, larger constituencies, and less frequent elections have also led the two chambers to operate somewhat differently. For example, Fenno concludes that senators' six-year terms do insulate them a bit

[4] James Madison, *Notes of Debates in the Federal Convention of 1787,* available in a recent reissue (Athens, Ohio: Ohio University Press, 1976), p. 39.

[5] Richard F. Fenno, Jr., *The United States Senate: A Bicameral Perspective* (Washington, D.C.: American Enterprise Institute for Public Policy Research, 1982), p. 3.
[6] Ibid., p. 5.

from the fluctuating currents of public opinion. Some senators acknowledge the "statesman" proposition: Their longer terms make it easier for them to do what they think is right. One senator interviewed by Fenno in the first year of his term observed candidly that "I wouldn't have voted against [a piece of legislation] . . . as I did last Saturday if I had to run in a year. The six-year term gives you insurance. Well, not exactly—it gives you a cushion. It gives you some squirming room." Reflecting upon the Senate's 1978 passage of the controversial Panama Canal Treaty, which would cede sovereignty of the Canal back to Panama by the year 2000, another senator doubted that "you would have ever gotten [it] through the House. Not with the election coming up and the mail coming in so heavily against it. The [private] sentiment in the House might not have been any different from what it was in the Senate. But you could never have passed it."[7]

HOUSE AND SENATE RULES

Like other democratic legislatures, Congress has developed various rules and procedures governing the way it handles the flow of legislative business. While the impetus for them has typically been nothing more than the need to establish orderly and expeditious procedures, the rules have sometimes become highly consequential politically, as members have learned how to manipulate them for their own particular legislative objectives.

[7]Quoted in ibid., p. 37. For an insightful study of self-perceived constituency pressures on members of the House of Representatives, see idem, *Home Style: House Members in Their Districts* (Boston: Little, Brown, 1978).

EXTENDED DEBATE AND FILIBUSTER

Because it is much smaller than the House, the Senate is able to operate much more informally. Senate rules afford members greater freedom in floor debate. Senators are permitted to speak as long as they see fit on bills and other legislative issues, whereas the time for House debate is strictly rationed. Frequently, however, senators in the minority on a bill use the extended-debate provision not to air their views fully but to block a vote they know they would lose. The **filibuster** is simply a legislative talkathon, an effort by a minority to hold the floor so long that the majority gives up its effort to secure passage of a bill—because of the press of other business—or at least makes concessions. Senate history is full of instances where determined senators have literally talked bills

True story of Bill, a senator's child.

The filibuster has kept more than a few congressmen in their Capitol chamber overnight

to death. Southern senators' use of the filibuster to block civil rights legislation in the 1940s and 1950s is the most notable instance, but many different Senate blocs have filibustered for many legislative ends.

CLOTURE AND UNANIMOUS CONSENT AGREEMENTS

Senators are jealous of their individual prerogatives and unwilling to eliminate the extended-debate provision. They have recognized, however, the need to cut off debate in some instances where it was being abused to thwart the majority. The **cloture** rule was first adopted in 1917. In its present form, it permits stopping debate upon the vote of three-fifths of the entire Senate membership—sixty votes. When cloture is invoked, the bill must be brought up for final action without more than thirty hours of additional debate.

In order to expedite work on legislation, the Senate often dispenses with its time-consuming formal rules and follows privately negotiated agreements submitted to the full chamber for its unanimous approval. These agreements specify the time and procedures of debate on a bill, what parts of it are open to amendment, and, sometimes, when the vote on final passage is to take place. **Unanimous consent** means just what it says; such agreements do not come into force if even one senator objects.

HOUSE RULES AND THE RULES COMMITTEE

With 435 members, the House of Representatives has to be more structured and less individualistic than the Senate. If, for example, it gave its members the right of extended debate, it would literally be paralyzed. One of the ways the House has responded to its need for more formal and restrictive rules of operation has been to empower a committee on procedure.

Before any bill is placed on the calendar for House action, it must receive a rule governing the terms of amendment and debate. Issuing these special orders is the task of a committee of the House, the Rules Committee. The rules specify such matters as how long a bill may be debated and how the time for debate is to be apportioned, and what kinds of amendments can be offered. In recent years, rules have become especially complex, requiring in some cases prior notice in the *Congressional Record* (the official report of congressional proceedings) of any amendment to be introduced, the authorization of only certain members to introduce amendments, and so on.

As might be expected, the Rules Committee has often used its procedural control over House business for policy ends—in particular, to block legislation that the committee opposes. For a long period, roughly from the end of World War I until 1970, its independence from House majority leadership made the Rules Committee a potent obstructive force. While in theory the House could always discharge the Committee and bring a bill directly to the floor, it was reluctant to do so, in part because members were not much inclined to cross so influential a body. Over the past two decades, however, the obstructiveness of the Rules Committee has been largely removed. Still firmly in the role of traffic cop, it has been made to function in a manner responsive to the majority party leadership.

SUSPENSION PROCEDURES

For speedy handling of noncontroversial legislation—such as measures to provide special assistance following some natural disaster—the House has adopted a procedure whereby every Monday and Tuesday members may vote to suspend the rules and consider minor bills— provided that no amendments (provisions added to a bill after it has been introduced) are offered, debate is limited to 40 minutes, and two-thirds approval is required for passage (rather than the usual simple majority). Concerned that some important legislation might slip through even given these restrictions, the Democratic caucus—which is the assembly of all House Democrats—has directed the Speaker

to remove from consideration any bills requiring the expenditure of more than $100 million in one year. The Speaker is the chief presiding officer of the House. He is also the leader of the majority party and is elected by that majority to his post.

DISCHARGE PETITIONS

To dislodge a bill stalled in a House committee for more than 30 days following referral, the discharge rule allows the House to remove the committee from jurisdiction upon the petition of at least 218 members—a House majority. The petition is then placed on the discharge calendar; if the discharge petition is supported by a majority when it is called for a vote, the bill being discharged is brought to the floor for immediate consideration.

THE COMMITTEE SYSTEM

An army, the old adage has it, moves on its stomach. Its food supply determines its capacity to advance. In much the same way, it may be said that Congress moves on its committees. The legislative process in Congress is very much a committee process. Congressional committees play such an important role in large part because of congressional workload. American government does much more today than it did in the nineteenth century. More complicated pieces of legislation must be conceived, drafted, debated, and enacted. The number of bills introduced and laws enacted tell part of the story. Just 207 bills were introduced in the 8th Congress, which sat between 1803 and 1805; 111 were passed. By contrast, 6,534 bills and joint resolutions were introduced in the 101st Congress (1989–91), and approximately 242 measures were enacted into law. Total federal spending provided for by Congress in 1803 was less than $8 million; in 1992, federal spending stood at $1.4 trillion.

One congressional response to these increasing demands has been longer sessions. In the early nineteenth century, Congress met for only short periods each year: after fall harvesting and before spring planting. Many members were farmers, and their needs had to be accommodated. Even as late as World War I, Congress was in session only nine months out of every twenty-four. Today, however, the national legislature is in nearly continuous session, punctuated by fairly short recesses for vacation, campaigns, and district work. A more important response to the growth of legislative business has been to do most of the work in committees. A chamber of 435 representatives, or 100 senators, operating as a committee of the whole for the consideration of legislation, cannot begin to cope with the volume and variety of the contemporary legislative agenda.

The dominant role of committees in the American legislative process cannot be explained solely by the amount of work to be done, however. The British Parliament also enacts a lot of complex legislation, but it has fewer committees than Congress, and more importantly, it relies on them much less for the conduct of its affairs. The reason for this is the tight party discipline that prevails in Parliament, leaving no room for strong autonomous committees. The government, consisting of the majority-party leadership, dominates the legislative process. It certainly does not want, and has not permitted, strong legislative committees to develop; the latter would only undermine the government's control.[8]

As a general rule, the stronger the political parties are in a legislature, and the tighter the control they maintain, the weaker committees

are. In the U.S. Congress, party discipline and control are weak, and the committees are very strong.

TYPES OF COMMITTEES

Congress has four principal types of committees: 1) standing, 2) select or special, 3) joint, and 4) conference. Together with their many subcommittees, the **standing committees** of Congress are where most of the work of legislating takes place. They are called "standing" because they are permanent units with continuing membership and staff. Among the sixteen standing committees of the Senate are Agriculture, Nutrition, and Forestry; Appropriations; Armed Services; Energy and Natural Resources; Finance; Foreign Relations; and Judiciary. House standing committees (of which there are twenty-two) include Appropriations; Armed Services; Banking, Finance, and Urban Affairs; Budget; Education and Labor; Public Works and Transportation; Rules; and Ways and Means. Every bill introduced into either house is referred to a standing committee responsible for the policy area in which it falls. The committee and its relevant subcommittee have the power to amend the measure as they see fit and to delay action or speed it on its way. The committees sift through the immense volume of legislation introduced each session, work out compromises, and try to hammer out workable legislation.

Select and special committees are of two main varieties: those established for the purpose of investigating problems and reporting on them to the parent chamber, as in the case of the House Select Committee on Aging and the Senate Select Committee on Intelligence; and those with membership from one party only, set up to perform party functions. Among the latter are the National Republican Senatorial Committee, which dispenses campaign funds to Republican Senate candidates, and the House Democratic Steering and Policy Committee, which acts as a kind of executive committee of the Democratic caucus and nominates Democrats for election by the caucus to the various standing committees when vacancies occur. In the 102d Congress (1991–93), there were eleven select and special committees in the House of Representatives, nine in the Senate.

Joint committees serve as coordinating vehicles within the bicameral legislature, drawing their membership from both the House and Senate. In recent decades, they have been used largely for congressional oversight (discussed later in this chapter) and policy exploration. Joint committees have functioned in such areas as atomic energy, defense production, and the reduction of federal expenditures. There were four joint committees in the 101st Congress, the most important of which were the Joint Committee on Taxation and the Joint Economic Committee.

Conference committees grow out of the requirement that every bill must pass the House and Senate in exactly the same form before it can become law. Conference committees adjust differences between the two chambers. They are set up to deal only with specific pieces of legislation; they have no life beyond the measures for which they were convened. When the House and Senate conferees agree upon a report, they submit it for approval to the full chambers, and it must be accepted or rejected without amendment. When both houses accept a conference report, the measure is passed and sent to the president for signing. If either chamber rejects a conference report, however, the bill is returned to the same or to a newly constituted conference committee. Conferees are supposed to consider only those portions of bills on which the two chambers disagree; and when the differences are modest, the conferees' discretion is in fact quite limited. But when the House and Senate versions differ more drastically, conference committees have much greater discretion and sometimes produce legislation at variance from what either chamber had envisioned. To curb runaway conference committees, the Legislative Reorganization Act of 1970 required them to supply the full chambers with statements on the reasoning behind their recommendations and the policy effects. This act also stipulated that conference committee reports could not be officially considered until at least three days after they were presented—when, hopefully, some members had found time to review the reports.

THE AGE OF SUBCOMMITTEES

House and Senate committees have long had subcommittees, for the same reason that the parent chambers themselves first established committees: to break the business of legislating into units of manageable size. Given the increasing volume and complexity of legislation, recourse to specialized subcommittees was unavoidable. For example, the House Appropriations Committee—charged with reporting spending bills for every area of federal activity—has thirteen subcommittees. Each subcommittee handles appropriations in one relatively manageable sector: agriculture, defense, transportation, and so on. (Figure 6.5 shows the place of subcommittees in the legislative process.)

This graphic shows the most typical way in which proposed legislation is enacted into law. There are more complicated, as well as simpler, routes, and most bills never become law. Bills must be passed by both houses in identical form before they can be sent to the president. The path of a House bill is traced by a solid line, that of a Senate bill by a broken line. In practice most bills are introduced at roughly the same time in both chambers, though usually in somewhat different form.

Source: Congressional Quarterly Guide to Current American Government, Spring 1986 (Washington, D.C.: Congressional Quarterly, Inc., 1986), p. 145.

Figure 6.5   How a Bill Becomes Law

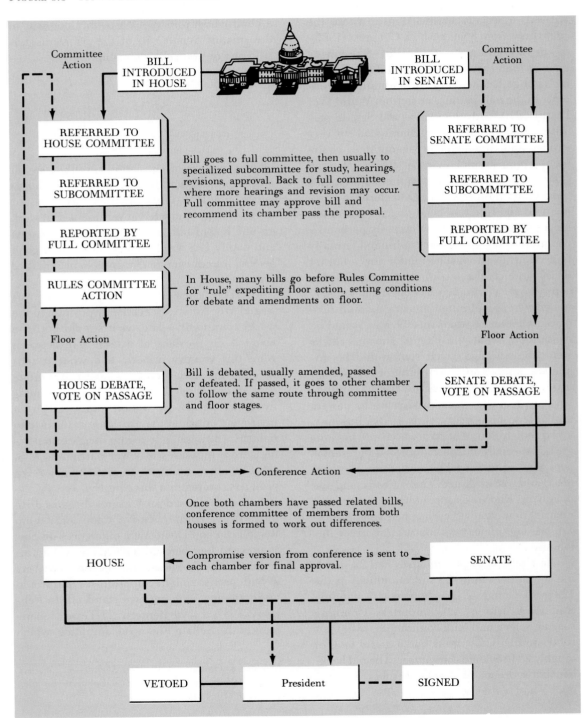

Committee Action

BILL INTRODUCED IN HOUSE

BILL INTRODUCED IN SENATE

Committee Action

REFERRED TO HOUSE COMMITTEE

REFERRED TO SUBCOMMITTEE

REPORTED BY FULL COMMITTEE

Bill goes to full committee, then usually to specialized subcommittee for study, hearings, revisions, approval. Back to full committee where more hearings and revision may occur. Full committee may approve bill and recommend its chamber pass the proposal.

REFERRED TO SENATE COMMITTEE

REFERRED TO SUBCOMMITTEE

REPORTED BY FULL COMMITTEE

RULES COMMITTEE ACTION

In House, many bills go before Rules Committee for "rule" expediting floor action, setting conditions for debate and amendments on floor.

Floor Action

Floor Action

HOUSE DEBATE, VOTE ON PASSAGE

Bill is debated, usually amended, passed or defeated. If passed, it goes to other chamber to follow the same route through committee and floor stages.

SENATE DEBATE, VOTE ON PASSAGE

Conference Action

Once both chambers have passed related bills, conference committee of members from both houses is formed to work out differences.

HOUSE

Compromise version from conference is sent to each chamber for final approval.

SENATE

VETOED

President

SIGNED

While the number of subcommittees has increased, especially in the House, where the count grew from 83 in the 84th Congress (1955–57) to 135 during the 102d (1991–93), having gone as high as 151 in the 94th (1975–77), the big change has come in subcommittee autonomy. In the half-century or so from World War I until 1970, both the House and Senate permitted their affairs to be dominated by very strong and independent committee chairmen—congressional "barons" they were often called. These chairmen acquired and maintained their positions through **seniority:** a time-honored and rarely violated practice where the most senior member of the majority party on a committee was appointed chairman. Virtually impervious to removal no matter how arbitrary their conduct, the chairmen exercised broad control over committee business. They determined when committee meetings would take place, whether or when specific bills would be considered, what jurisdiction subcommittees would be assigned, what staff would be appointed, and so on. Subcommittees were then firmly under the thumb of any parent committee chairman who chose to exercise the powers available to him. In the early 1970s, however, a vast redistribution of power occurred in Congress, especially in the House of Representatives. Authority was taken away from the "barons" and redistributed among rank-and-file members. Known as **spreading the action,** this internal democratization has had wide ramifications; one major result is subcommittee autonomy.

The House of Representatives had 22 standing committees and 135 subcommittees in the 1991–93 Congress; the Senate, 16 standing committees with 87 subcommittees. Counting special, select, and joint committees, with their subcommittees, Congress had a grand total of roughly 284 separate committees. The old backbencher's dream of "every member a chairman" had come remarkably close to being realized. Over half of all House Democrats had a chairmanship in the 1991–93 Congress; in the smaller Senate, 50 of the 56 Democrats held one or more chairmanship.[9]

THE 1988 TRADE BILL: CONGRESS IN ACTION

No single piece of legislation can illustrate all of the complex workings of our national legislature and how the legislature fits into our larger system of divided government. But work on one recent bill, a massive effort to change and codify U.S. trade policy, gives us a good general introduction to Congress in action. (See Figure 6.6.)

In recent years a wide-ranging debate has waged over America's economic position in the world community—and what should be done about it. In the face of a large gap between what this country imports and what it sells abroad—the trade deficit—global *competitiveness* emerged as a prime Washington buzzword. Proposals for action have run from improving education to providing assistance to industries struggling to regain their world position, from measures to lower barriers to U.S. sales in other countries to restricting foreign products coming into this country.

Against this backdrop, Congress began a drive in 1987 for comprehensive trade legislation. Republican and Democratic differences on how to proceed had blocked legislation in the preceding (99th) Congress, and this time members in both parties sought compromises that would avoid another such partisan stand-off. In February 1987, Lloyd Bentsen (D-Texas), chairman of the Senate Finance Committee, which

[9]Norman J. Ornstein, et al., *Vital Statistics on Congress, 1991–92* (Washington, D.C.: American Enterprise Institute, 1992), pp. 110–115.

FIGURE 6.6   THE 1988 TRADE BILL

Here is the route that the 1988 trade bill took from its original introduction in the House and Senate, February 5, 1987, to final passage on August 23, 1988, after sustaining one presidential veto.

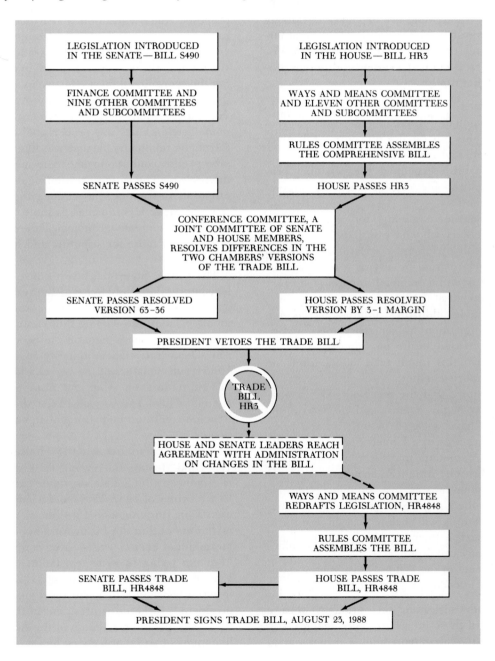

has jurisdiction over key elements of trade legislation, introduced a bill with strong bipartisan
support. The bill Bentsen introduced was cos-
ponsored by fifty-six senators—thirty-one
Democrats and twenty five Republicans—among
them majority leader Robert Byrd (D-West Virginia) and minority leader Robert Dole (R-
Kansas). It contained a variety of different provisions that would:

- extend the president's authority to
  negotiate international trade agreements but require him to consult more
  with Congress on these matters;
- establish expedited congressional procedures for considering trade agreements;
- increase eligibility for assistance to
  workers who have lost their jobs as a
  result of foreign competition and fund
  this program by levying a new customs
  duty on commercial imports of up to 1
  percent of their value;
- enable industries injured by foreign
  competition to get relief more easily.
  Increased tariffs on imports were one
  form this might take, quota limits on
  imports another;
- require that the president take retaliatory action against nations determined
  to have engaged in unfair trade practices with the United States, unless he
  can stipulate that the retaliation would
  harm the American economy;
- tighten laws against "dumping": the sale
  in the United States by foreign producers of goods below cost in efforts to
  increase their market share and harm
  American producers;
- create in the White House a new council to coordinate U.S. trade policy.

The administration was unhappy with a
number of these provisions, even though they
had substantial support among congressional

Republicans. Part of its unhappiness involved
the ongoing "turf" battles between the executive and legislative branches. The administration didn't like Congress telling it in the
proposed trade legislation that it had to take
retaliatory action against unfair competition; it
argued that the president and his trade advisers
should have the discretion to move in the manner they considered most effective in situations
that are often of great complexity. Apart from
this, the president insisted that freer trade, not
more barriers, was the proper goal and that
relying on retaliatory barriers was likely only to
prompt other countries to take more such actions
themselves. The administration sent its own
proposals to Capitol Hill—among them measures to make U.S. businesses more competitive and to stimulate technological development
by spending more for scientific and high-tech
research.

The United States has a two-house national
legislature. Both the House of Representatives
and the Senate must pass trade measures—and
all other measures—before they can be sent to
the president for his signature to become law.
The Democrats had a majority in both the
House and Senate, but the two chambers had
different ideas on what the final trade bill
should be like. And, as we will see, the administration's position had stronger support in the
Senate.

The key committee on the House side is
Ways and Means—the revenue committee, just
as Finance is the Senate's revenue committee.
In the winter of 1987, Ways and Means chairman Dan Rostenkowski (D-Illinois) began to
unveil the outlines of his own trade proposals.
He said that he, too, was seeking compromise.
"I'm not trying to write legislation to please
Lane Kirkland," Rostenkowski said. "I'm trying
to write legislation that will be signed by the
president." Kirkland is president of the country's principal labor federation, the AFL-CIO;
like many other labor leaders, he was advocat-

ing strong restrictions on imports—a position diametrically opposed to the administration's strong free-trade stance. Still, Rostenkowski supported the goals of an amendment to the previous year's trade bill that had been pushed by Congressman Richard A. Gephardt (D-Missouri). The Gephardt amendment would require the reduction of imports from countries that do not act decisively to reduce their large trade surpluses with the United States. Japan was one prime target, South Korea another. "We can amend the Gephardt language," Rostenkowski said, "but we cannot compromise the principle involved."[10]

In fact, the Ways and Means Trade subcommittee did compromise the principle somewhat in the trade package that it sent along to the full committee. Specifically, it eliminated the mandatory percentage cut in foreign countries' trade surpluses with the United States that was a prime feature of the Gephardt amendment. The subcommittee bill still was more protectionist than the Senate Finance Committee bill—and much more so than the administration found acceptable. In a letter to Ways and Means Committee members, the U.S. trade representative outlined administration objections to the emerging House bill. "If the [objectionable] provisions are not either eliminated or substantially improved," he wrote in his detailed nine-page letter, "I would find it exceedingly difficult to recommend that the president sign any trade bill including them. . . ."[11] On the Senate side, the trade bill the Finance Committee approved in May 1987 followed very closely the outlines of Senator Bentsen's February proposals.

Finance and Ways and Means were the key committees responsible for developing trade legislation. The package was so broad, however, that a number of other committees in both the House and Senate were involved in its content. The Senate Judiciary Committee worked on a measure that would for the first time protect U.S. firms from foreign manufacturers who use patented processes without paying royalties. The Senate Commerce Committee worked on an amendment that would allow the Secretary of Commerce to investigate the national security or "essential commerce" effects of a foreign firm's proposed merger, joint venture with, or acquisition of a U.S. company. In all, nine Senate committees contributed to the trade bill.[12] In the House, eleven committees were involved in the trade legislation package—including the Rules Committee which, with its legislative management responsibilities, combined separate bills coming out of a number of the other committees into a single comprehensive measure to be acted on by the full House.

The House passed its trade bill—known formally as the Trade and International Economic Policy Reform Act of 1987—in April 1987. After four weeks of vigorous debate, the Senate passed its bill in July—known officially as the Omnibus Trade and Competitiveness Act of 1987. The margins of passage in both chambers were about two to one. As is almost always the case with complex legislation, the House and Senate trade bills differed; the next step was the convening of a conference committee. The House-Senate conference committee first convened in August. The committee grew to an enormous size of nearly 200 members, 155 from the House and 44 from the Senate. The bills that were being reconciled were highly detailed packages, each covering about 1,000 pages.

---

[10] John Cranford, "Trade Bill: Options Aired, Markup Postponed," *Congressional Quarterly*, March 7, 1987, p. 433.

[11] John Cranford, "Conflicts Sharpen as House Trade Bill Advances," *Congressional Quarterly*, March 21, 1987, p. 519.

[12] Drew Douglas and David Rapp, "Foreign Relations, Judiciary, Labor Add to Trade Measure," *Congressional Quarterly*, June 6, 1987, pp. 1181–83.

Other political players were intimately involved in the continuing deliberations on the trade bill, even though they weren't formally represented on the conference committee. The administration actively negotiated with House and Senate members to try to obtain a final version more to its liking. If the administration was satisfied, Congress would avoid a presidential veto. In addition, a great variety of business and labor organizations continued to lobby actively for specific provisions dear to their hearts. The elaborate search for compromises went on for months. By early April 1988, House and Senate conferees had finally narrowed differences down to a few issues. The toughest of these was a requirement that any U.S. corporation with 100 or more workers notify employees sixty days in advance if it were going to close a plant—to move it somewhere else, to consolidate factories to get greater efficiency, or any other reason. Business groups strongly opposed this measure; labor strongly backed it. The administration opposed the measure.

Congressional leaders wouldn't budge. Legislation worked out by the conferees—including the plant-closing provision—was reported back to the two chambers. It passed the House by a huge three-to-one margin, which meant that many Republicans (68 in fact) joined Democrats in supporting it. This tally meant that on the House side the bill was essentially veto-proof. A two-to-one margin is all that is required to override a presidential veto. The Senate was a different matter. Though the bill passed, the margin was 63 to 36, three votes short of the 66 that would be needed to override. The president vetoed the trade bill. The House then overrode the veto by 308 to 113. But as expected, the Senate sustained the president: Only 61 senators voted to overturn his veto.

This particular trade bill was dead—but not any trade bill. The president probably would

have preferred having no bill at all, but many Republicans in Congress felt the folks back home expected them to take some action. They pushed the president to limit his objections to just a few provisions, so that these items could be stripped from the original bill and the measure then passed. He agreed. Finally, on August 3, 1988, over eighteen months after Senator Bentsen offered his initial proposals, after intense lobbying, countless committee meetings, and endless compromises, an omnibus trade bill that the president could accept passed the Senate, having passed the House three weeks earlier. The president signed it into law on August 23.

No one has gotten all or even most of what he or she wanted. Many, including the administration, had managed to block provisions they most opposed. The final law was less protectionist than labor had hoped, more protectionist than free traders wanted.

STAFFING CONGRESS

Over the past quarter-century, congressional staff has greatly expanded. Like the increase in subcommittees, the staff explosion has come in part as a response to greater demands of legislative business. The big staff expansion also reflects a successful search for independence. Analyst Allen Schick notes that staff is the currency permitting congressmen to gain greater expertise and hence independence for the legislature from the executive branch, and for rank-and-file members from committee chairmen and other congressional leaders.[13]

The greatest expansion has occurred among aides employed in the service of individual congressmen. Members' staff more than tri-

[13] Allen Schick, "The Staff of Independence: Why Congress Employs More But Legislates Less," paper presented at the White Burkett Miller Center for Public Affairs, University of Virginia, October 1980, p. 13.

pled between the 1950s and the 1980s in both the House and Senate. Congressmen have put many of their new assistants to work back in their legislative districts. At present about 3,000 are so assigned—almost seven per congressman. As noted at the beginning of this chapter, members have found this useful in serving their constituents' needs for help in dealing with government and useful as a little electoral machine made available to them year-round at public expense, as well.

The number of assistants assigned to committees also grew over the 1960s and 1970s. Between 1979 and 1983, however, House committee staff growth leveled off, and Senate committee staffs were reduced by almost one-sixth. The cut on the Senate side occurred as the Republicans took control of the Senate in 1981 for the first time in a quarter-century and proceeded to fulfill their pledge to scale back committee staffing. But in the mid-1980s both House and Senate committee staffs again began to expand.

No other national legislature staffs itself so lavishly. The Canadian Parliament comes closest, and it employs only about one-tenth as many assistants as Congress.[14] The contrast between Congress and Great Britain's Parliament is even more striking. House of Commons committees are very lightly staffed. In 1987, each member of Parliament (MP) received a personal allowance for secretarial and research assistance of (in dollar equivalents) about $36,500—one-eleventh of what was provided at that time to a member of the U.S. House of Representatives.[15]

Each member of the U.S. House of Representatives in 1991 received a personal allow-ance of $475,000 for staff support and $135,000 to $317,000 for "official expenses," depending on certain contingencies such as the distance of his or her district from Washington. Each senator received between $754,000 and $1,760,000 for staff salaries, the precise amount determined by the size of the state represented. In addition he or she was given extensive allowances for postage, travel, telephone, office furnishings, and the rental of office space in his or her home state. Whereas the total cost of operating Congress in 1955 was about $70 million, the price tag had climbed to $2.3 billion in 1991.[16]

PARTY ORGANIZATION

Those members of Congress who are Democrats, and those who are Republicans, vote as solid blocs against each other on all issues involving the partisan organization of the House and Senate. For example, majority-party members in the House always vote together and elect their leader to the office of Speaker—the chief presiding officer. Whichever party has a majority in each house names the chairmen of all the standing committees and subcommittees, and allocates to itself a majority of committee seats. Republicans and Democrats in both houses also establish their own party leadership bodies, shown in Figure 6.7.

Partisan discipline and coherence does not, however, extend beyond the divvying up of "the spoils of office." On the substance of policy, the Democratic and Republican parties in Congress cannot hold together. The obser-

---

[14] Michael Malbin, *Unelected Representatives: Congressional Staff and the Future of Representative Government* (New York: Basic Books, 1980), p. 10.
[15] British Consulate General, New York, N.Y., unpublished 1988 data.

[16] These data are from *Vital Statistics on Congress, 1991–92 Edition* (Washington, D.C.: American Enterprise Institute, 1992), pp. 140–43, passim; and Executive Office of the President, OMB, *Budget of the United States Government, FY 1993*, pp. A1–23.

FIGURE 6.7   PARTY ORGANIZATION IN THE 101ST CONGRESS

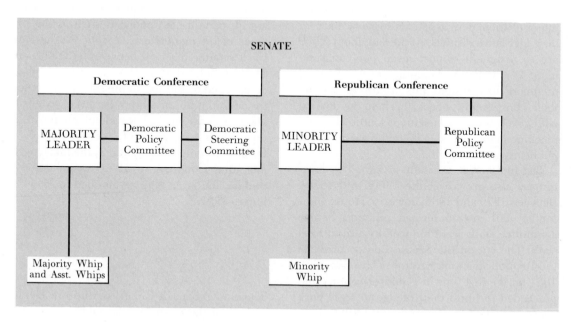

vation of political scientist E. E. Schattschneider, made nearly fifty years ago, remains a valid description of the lack of party cohesion in Congress:

> The roll calls in the House and Senate show that party votes are relatively rare. On difficult questions, usually the most important questions, party lines are apt to break badly, and a straight party vote, aligning one party against the other, is the exception rather than the rule. . . . Often both parties split into approximately equal halves. . . . At other times one party votes as a unit but is joined by a substantial fraction of the other. Finally, a predominant portion of one party may be opposed by a predominant portion of the other party, while minorities, more or less numerous, on each side cross party lines to join their opponents. . . . [Overall] the roll calls demonstrate that the parties are unable to hold their lines in a controversial public issue when the pressure is on.[17]

[17]E. E. Schattschneider, *Party Government* (New York: Rinehart, 1942), pp. 130–32.

As Figure 6.8 shows, in recent Congresses about half of all recorded votes have been what *Congressional Quarterly (CQ)* calls "party unity" votes. And *CQ*'s usual standards for such votes reflect the general lack of cohesion in the congressional parties. A "party unity" vote is one where at least a bare majority of Democrats oppose a bare majority of Republicans.

American political parties are relatively undisciplined, a subject we discuss further in chapter 12. In most democracies the government—the prime minister and the cabinet—are members of the legislature and are voted into their executive posts by the legislative majority. Were Conservative MPs in the British House of Commons to cross party lines and vote with the opposition Labor party, they would, in the parliamentary tradition, be declaring "no confidence" in the Conservative government and would remove it from office. The very structure of legislative-executive relations in a parliamentary system strongly encourages party discipline and unity. But the opposite

FIGURE 6.7   (CONTINUED)

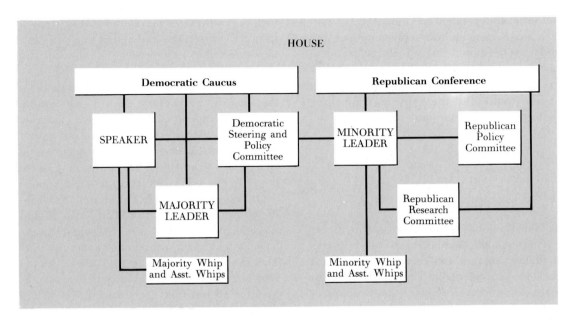

FIGURE 6.8   "PARTY UNITY" VOTING IN CONGRESS

Percentage of recorded votes in which the parties are on opposite sides—a majority of Democrats opposing a majority of Republicans.

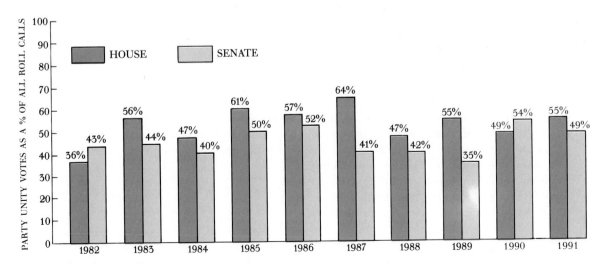

Source: Congressional Quarterly, December 28, 1991, p. 3789.

applies in the American system, given separation of powers. The president holds office for a fixed term, independent of Congress. His tenure is unaffected by how representatives and senators vote (though his success as president depends on it). Party leaders try to exert pressure, of course, and they can appeal to feelings of party loyalty. But there are no compelling structural incentives for party unity voting.

THE COMPOSITION OF CONGRESS

The Constitution sets only three requirements for congressional membership: 1) Before taking office, senators and representatives must have been citizens of the United States for at least nine and seven years, respectively; 2) a senator must be at least 30 years of age and a representative at least 25 years; and 3) each member must be an inhabitant of that state in which he or she shall be chosen. Not surprisingly, though, the membership of Congress has a much more distinctive cast than these general and nonrestrictive standards dictate.

PARTY MEMBERSHIP

Partisan ties are surely the most important entrance requirements. Although political party organizations are relatively weak in the United States compared to other democracies, and many Americans now hold their party loyalties very lightly, one still does not, with rare exception, gain election to Congress without a strong party connection—and, specifically, without ties to either the Democratic or the Republican party. The largest group of senators and representatives to come to office in the past half-century unattached to either of the two major parties were the 17 elected in 1936 from minor parties that temporarily gained strength in

response to the Great Depression. No Congress since World War II has had more than three members who were not Democrats or Republicans. Every senator and all but one representative elected in 1990 belongs to one of the two major parties.

Since the New Deal realignment made them the majority party more than a half-century ago, the Democrats have dominated Congress with a consistency unequaled by any other party in American history. Of the last twenty-nine Congresses (from the 73d chosen in 1932 to the 102d elected in 1990) only two had Republican majorities in both House and Senate—the 80th, elected just after World War II, and the 82d, which came in with Dwight Eisenhower's first-term presidential victory in 1952. The Democrats have had majorities, usually very large ones, in the House of Representatives for all but four years since 1930. When the GOP ("Grand Old Party," as the Republicans came to be called in the late nineteenth century) gained control of the Senate in Ronald Reagan's big 1980 victory, and retained it in 1982 and 1984, these were only their third, fourth, and fifth upper-chamber successes since 1932. The box score for the last 30 Congresses shows a lopsided electoral game: 25 Congresses with the Democrats controlling both houses, two with the Republicans controlling both, and three with split-party control. The 1980s are the closest the Republicans have come to a "congressional era" since the Great Depression. Their Senate majorities from 1981 through 1986 represent the only time in fifty years that they have controlled either house of the national legislature for consecutive terms.

SOCIAL AND RELIGIOUS BACKGROUND

Members of Congress generally look like they belong to a national political elite. They are more highly educated than the public at large,

"I propose legislation. I do my best to aid in the process of government. And I try like hell to keep my name out of 'Doonesbury.'"

Drawing by Ziegler; © 1985 The New Yorker Magazine, Inc.

come disproportionately from a few prestigious occupations, and are far above average in wealth. Virtually every senator and representative has a college degree. A majority have done some form of graduate work, with law school training by far the most common. Law, business, politics itself, and teaching are the occupational backgrounds most frequently encountered in today's Congress. Early in the twentieth century, the Senate acquired a reputation as a club for millionaires. Its present composition does little to dispute that status. About a third of all senators are millionaires—a position they did not derive from their relatively modest senatorial salaries of $98,400 in 1989. House members are generally of upper-middle-class standing; only 30 or so are millionaires.[18]

The religious makeup of members of Congress differs significantly from that of the general public. But this is not unusual for a group of national leaders, for certain denominations are generally stronger among high-status groups. Of all senators and representatives in 1991, 26 percent were Catholics, roughly the proportion of Catholics in the general populace. But Episcopalians and Presbyterians—small denominations in the country, with members of notably high social status—had large numbers of congressional adherents; while the biggest Protestant denomination nationally, the Baptists, had relatively few adherents in Congress. Eleven percent of the members of both houses in 1991 listed themselves as Episcopalians, 10 percent as Presbyterians, and only 11 percent as Baptists. Eight percent were Jewish.[19] Every Congress in American history has been composed disproportionately of white males. In recent years, though, the number of

---

[18] *Vital Statistics on Congress, 1991–92 Edition*, pp. 22, 28.

[19] Ibid., p. 35.

TABLE 6.1 WOMEN AND BLACKS IN CONGRESS SINCE 1917

Congress	Women		Blacks	
	D	R	D	R
65th (1917)	–	1	–	–
70th (1927)	2	3	–	–
75th (1937)	6	1	1	–
80th (1947)	3	5	2	–
85th (1957)	9	7	3	–
90th (1967)	5	6	6	1
95th (1977)	13	5	16	1
100th (1987)	13	12	22	–
101st (1989)	15	12	23	–
102d (1991)	20	10	25	1

Source: Vital Statistics on Congress, 1991–92, pp. 38–39.

women and blacks has been moving upward. In the 1990 elections, 26 blacks won election to the House of Representatives; all but one were Democrats. The 28 women elected to House seats in 1990, together with the two senators who were women, surpassed by three the total of 27 elected in 1988. Women made further gains in 1992. They are disproportionately Democratic (see Table 6.1).

THE CHANGING CONGRESS

Today's Congress is the product of two centuries of evolution and change. While its formal position in the American constitutional scheme is essentially the same now as it was in 1789, its role in the dynamic process of policy making is very different. Congressional-presidential relations have seen important shifts, and Congress's internal distribution of power has changed as well.

EARLY LEGISLATIVE PREDOMINANCE

Through much of the first century after independence, Congress was the dominant branch of U.S. government. This status was in accord with the preferences of most Americans at the time. Their experience with the British Crown and governors of the colonies had engendered among them a strong mistrust of executive authority. The new constitution drafted in 1787 was a highly conscious effort to end government-by-the-legislature and provide for a coherent, active, countervailing executive authority. Yet even the Constitution's framers expected Congress to dominate the new governmental system. And following the first fifteen years or so under the Constitution—when the great Federalist leaders in George Washington's cabinet, and subsequently Thomas Jefferson and his aides, provided relatively strong executive leadership—Congress did in fact become the governmental fulcrum.

The Civil War changed the legislative-executive balance temporarily by putting a premium on presidential leadership. But with the end of the war and the assassination of Abraham Lincoln in 1865, the era of congressional ascendancy resumed with a passion. A young political scientist, Woodrow Wilson, voiced this reality in the title of his classic work, *Congressional Government*, published in 1885. Wilson noted that "the business of the President, occasionally great, is usually not much above routine. Most of the time it is mere administration, mere obedience to directions from the masters of policy, the Standing Committees [of Congress]."[20]

---

[20] Woodrow Wilson, *Congressional Government* (New York: Houghton-Mifflin, 1913; first published, 1885), pp. 253–54.

PARTY GOVERNMENT

Over the 1880s and 1890s, power shifted within Congress as strong party leadership developed in both House and Senate. This gave the country its only era of legislature-based party government. There were two stages to this development. In the first, the Speaker of the House managed to accumulate an impressive array of prerogatives. By the time Thomas B. Reed held the post in 1889–91 and 1895–99, the office had assumed such authority that Reed was likened to a prime minister. This ascendancy was short-lived. Even in their heyday, strong Speakers like Reed and his successor, Joseph Cannon, were burdened with such nicknames as "Boss" and "Czar." Reformers in both parties had a potent weapon with which to attack them: appeal to a populace inclined to view strong party leadership as undemocratic. In 1910, a House revolt against Cannon greatly weakened the Speaker's authority.

There was one final attempt at disciplined party government, this time with the caucus of

Joseph Cannon, Speaker of the House early in this century.

SPEAKER REED KNOWS HIS BUSINESS.
From the *World* (New York).

House Democrats as the instrument of control. In 1911, the caucus directed Democrats on various committees not to report any legislation other than that submitted by the leadership "unless hereafter directed by this Caucus."[21] Two years before, the caucus had adopted a rule whereby a two-thirds vote in caucus would subsequently bind all party members. When a bill came up for a vote, members were expected to vote as the party caucus instructed them. Violation resulted in the loss of such party entitlements as committee assignments. A similar rule applied in the Senate.

[21] Wilder H. Haines, "The Congressional Caucus of Today," *American Political Science Review* 9 (November 1915), p. 697.

The outcry against government-by-caucus built up quickly. Republicans were outraged because the domination of the Democratic caucus left them with little influence. Reformers thought "King Caucus" was as objectionable as the Speaker's control had been. The secretary to the National Voters' League, established in 1913 by prominent proponents of congressional reform, charged that the Democrats had not abolished "Cannonism"—referring to the regime of Speaker Joseph Cannon—but only disguised it. A minority still ran Congress, now through the caucus rather than the office of Speaker.[22]

Democrats fought back in defense of the caucus with some of the most coherent arguments for party government ever heard in the American legislature. Democratic Speaker Champ Clark of Missouri argued that "responsibility rests upon the majority, and we shrink not from acknowledging our responsibility to the country and of acting accordingly. . . . We intend to place our ideas upon the statute books on the great questions now pressing for solution. . . . We must have organization in order to enact the will of the people into law, and we have got it. . . ."[23]

But soon even Democrats joined in the attack on the caucus system. For a party member to be required by a binding caucus vote to back a bill that he disagreed with was unworthy of the Congress of the United States, Senator Gilbert Hitchcock of Nebraska argued in 1913. "Like all caucuses, I believe the fact to be that our Democratic caucus degenerated into a political machine."[24] Outside Congress the attack was even stronger. "King Caucus" was dethroned, never to be restored.

LEADERSHIP SHIFTS TO THE PRESIDENCY

By 1915 the brief American experiment with congressional party government had been abandoned. In the absence of central party leadership, power flowed back to the committees and to the chairmen, who dominated committee action. At the same time an equally momentous shift was propelling policy initiative away from the legislature altogether and to the presidency. Whereas government-by-the-legislature prevailed throughout most of the nineteenth century, government-by-the-president has been the rule in much of the twentieth century.

One factor in this shift was the growth of an industrial economy, which required an expansion of federal regulation and management. Theodore Roosevelt, Republican president from 1901 to 1909, was the first to recognize and articulate the growing public feeling that stronger presidential leadership was needed to handle the greater demands on government. He argued that "it was not only his [the president's] right but his duty to do anything that the needs of the nation demanded unless such action was forbidden by the Constitution or by the laws. . . ."[25]

Although the Republican presidents of the 1920s were less assertive than either Theodore Roosevelt or Democrat Woodrow Wilson, they could not escape responsibility when things went sour. Herbert Hoover, rather than Congress, received most of the blame for the Great Depression and for the perceived inadequacy of the government's response to it. And the subsequent success of Franklin Roosevelt in providing vigorous leadership to combat problems of the Depression solidified the public's inclination to look to the presidency rather

[22] Lynn Haines, *Your Congress* (National Voters' League, 1915), pp. 67, 76–77.
[23] *Congressional Record*, September 24, 1913, pp. 51, 57–59.
[24] Ibid., August 29, 1913, pp. 38, 58–59.

[25] Theodore Roosevelt, *An Autobiography* (New York: Scribners, 1925; first published, 1913), p. 357.

President Theodore Roosevelt, rugged individualist, strong president.

than to the legislature. In the three decades or so after 1935, a mythology developed around the presidency. The president came to be seen as the great engine of democracy, "a kind of magnificent lion who can roam widely and do great deeds."[26]

THE CONTEMPORARY CONGRESS

By 1965, Americans had for several decades been given a picture by the press and other commentary of the presidency as the repository

[26] Clinton Rossiter, *The American Presidency*, rev. ed. (New York: New American Library, 1960), p. 84.

of boldness and vision, and Congress of recalcitrance and conservatism. There was enough truth to these assertions to give them credibility, but there were also enough flaws in them to invite a powerful rebuttal in subsequent years. Four developments in 1965–75 changed presidential-congressional relations and the prevailing view of them. First, Congress was gripped by a new surge of political individualism. It has always been an institution where the individual member has been given much power and independence. But in the 1960s it experienced new demands by members that changed its internal operation and made it far more assertive vis-à-vis the president. Second, the idea that a strong president was good for the nation was shaken by a stream of events that came in rapid succession, especially the Vietnam War. Third, belief that presidential initiative was synonymous with liberal-progressive government was upset as the United States entered an era of aggressively conservative presidents. Suddenly, Congress became the progressive branch. And fourth, there was Watergate. The Watergate scandal gave the cult of the virtuous presidency a hard kick in its solar plexus and for a time knocked most of the air out of it. The temporary weakening of the presidency—with Richard Nixon forced to resign from office, Gerald Ford left to pick up the pieces, and Jimmy Carter desperate to project a new model of presidential comportment—gave Congress an extraordinary opportunity to reassert itself.

CONGRESSIONAL INDIVIDUALISM IN THE POSTINDUSTRIAL AGE

Political individualism—the antithesis of party regularity and cohesion—has been both a cause and an effect of the weakness of political party organizations in the United States. The new wave of political individualism of the 1960s

President Lyndon B. Johnson working on a major address to the nation on his Vietnam strategy. His Southeast Asian policy eventually caused him to decide not to run for a second full term as president.

was heightened by the communications media. Television, a personality-emphasizing institution, became the dominant medium of mass communication in the 1950s and 1960s. From this and other structural changes a new type of legislator gradually emerged: more assertive and less inclined to defer to leadership, whether in Congress or the executive branch.[27]

[27] In discussing "the forces fueling the individualistic tone of the present-day Congress," Thomas E. Mann puts the case bluntly: "As far as elections are concerned, senators and representatives are in business for themselves. . . . They are political entrepreneurs . . . seizing opportunities, generating resources, responding to pressures. . . ." Thomas E. Mann, "Elections and Change in Congress," in Thomas E. Mann and Norman J. Ornstein, eds., *The New Congress* (Washington, D.C.: American Enterprise Institute, 1981), p. 53.

In the 1960s, many younger Democrats pushed for shifts in the balance of power in Congress itself, especially in the House of Representatives, by spreading the action widely among all Democratic members. From roughly the end of World War I until the late 1960s, the majority party member who had served longest on a committee automatically became its chairman and was virtually assured of retaining that post as long as he or she remained in Congress. But in the late 1960s and early 1970s the seniority system was modified, with the provision that the Democratic caucus could displace chairpeople who proved insufficiently responsive to the membership. As noted earlier, the power and autonomy of the subcommittees was greatly extended and the number of subcommittees increased. The staff available to individual members and to legislative committees was also greatly expanded. Through these and other means, power was distributed more widely among the rank-and-file of the majority party and, to a much lesser degree, among the minority party as well.

SOME EFFECTS OF STRONG PRESIDENTS

America's involvement in Vietnam was a political watershed for the country. The loss of life which the war exacted, its staggering material cost, the domestic protests it engendered, and the government's seeming inability to achieve a satisfactory resolution shook and divided the nation. For liberal Democrats, this was especially painful, since it was an activist liberal Democratic president, Lyndon Johnson, who led the country into heavy involvement in the fighting in Vietnam. Many Democrats changed their thinking about the virtues of bold executive leadership.

If Vietnam attested to the fact that strong presidents could serve ends that many deemed ill-advised, conservative activists like Richard Nixon and Ronald Reagan taught many liberals that the "great engine of democracy" could be a strong force against their policy interests. In 1965 liberals could look back on thirty-two years of a presidency dominated by liberal Democrats, with Dwight Eisenhower's eight years merely a "breath-catching" interlude. In 1992, though, they look back on the forty years since Eisenhower's election as a period when Republicans have dominated the presidency— a hold broken only by the eight years of the Kennedy and Johnson administrations and the four years of Jimmy Carter.

THE WATERGATE SCANDAL

The errors of judgment and the betrayal of responsibility by a president and many of his closest aides—what Watergate has come to mean for many—capped off widespread disil-

The late Senator Sam Ervin of North Carolina (center) headed the Senate Watergate Committee hearings that eventually brought an end to the Nixon presidency in 1974.

lusionment with presidential power, which had been growing since the mid-1960s. While most Americans still esteemed the office and looked to it for leadership, the presidency was stripped of the sometimes uncritical reverence that had enveloped it since the 1930s. On August 9, 1974, the day Richard Nixon resigned, few Americans would describe the president as "a kind of magnificent lion who can roam widely and do great deeds." The lion was drummed out of office. Suddenly, separation of powers was looking a lot better than it had a decade earlier.

LEGISLATIVE RESURGENCE

Picture a legislature composed of ever more assertive and individualistic politicians, who concluded with increasing frustration that they had relinquished too much authority and initiative to the executive. Then picture them occupying a branch of government constitutionally independent of the executive and co-equal to it. Finally, picture them suddenly liberated from the myth that their executive-branch rivals had a corner on political wisdom and virtue. "I seen my opportunities and I took 'em," the eminent Democratic politician from New York, "Boss" George Washington Plunkett of Tammany Hall, offered as his political epitaph earlier in this century.[28] Watergate

---

[28] See William Riordan, *Plunkett of Tammany Hall* (New York: E. P. Dutton, 1963), p. 3. The Society of Tammany, known as Tammany Hall, was a fraternal organization that controlled the New York Democratic party from roughly the middle of the nineteenth century until the middle of this century.

presented Congress with such an opportunity. The result was congressional resurgence. Three areas where Congress reasserted itself are especially important. One involves the power of the purse, especially the congressional efforts to develop a national budget more coherently. A second is the expansion of legislative oversight over the departments and agencies of the executive branch. The third, related to oversight, involved expanded congressional use of the legislative veto as part of an effort to ensure that executive-agency actions conform to legislative wishes. As we will see, the legislative veto ran into a constitutional challenge in the 1980s.

THE BUDGET PROCESS

One important aim of Congress in its resurgence of the 1970s was to recapture its **power of the purse**—which for all practical purposes was in the hands of the executive branch. The president—especially through his Office of Management and Budget (OMB), discussed in chapter 7 on p. 194—had all the budget experts; Congress was not staffed to deal with the complexity of the budget process. To add to the problem, Congress's budget functions were scattered among too many—mostly uncoordinated—committees. As things stood then, the president would present the taxing and spending halves of the budget program to Congress. The budget proposals would then be divided and assigned to different committees in both the House and Senate, which would act on them independently. On the spending side, a number of separate appropriations bills (bills allocating funding for programs and agencies) were enacted each session, each handled by a different appropriations subcommittee and considered by Congress independently of one another. Many in Congress felt there was no coherence to *their* approach to the budget process. Beyond this, a growing proportion of governmental expenditures were outside the control of the appropriations committees altogether, having been mandated by "backdoor spending" provisions included in legislation written by various standing committees. "Backdoor spending" refers to expenditures beyond the control of the appropriations committees, such as social security payments, farm price support payments, and pensions paid to retired government employees. How could priorities be determined and the overall impact of individual spending decisions on the total budget be properly assessed and controlled? The United States didn't have a fiscal policy, one commentator noted, only "a fiscal result."[29]

Congress acted to remedy this situation and passed the Congressional Budget and Impoundment Control Act in June 1974. This legislation imposed a new organization on congressional budget making, one which was to operate with little formal change from the mid-1970s through 1990. Then in October 1990, as part of a complex budget agreement reached between Congress and the Bush administration, the budget process was again substantially changed. We will first review how things worked from 1975 to 1990, and then consider the 1990 revisions.

THE PROVISIONS OF THE 1974 LAW

Under this statute, a budget committee in each house, together with staff of the Congressional Budget Office (CBO), arrived at recommendations on the basic outlines of fiscal policy. The budget committees and the CBO were supposed to consider such questions as how large a deficit was desirable or permissible given the state of the economy, and what taxing and spending measures were consistent with this target. Then, according to the plan, they specified spending levels for all major programs—national defense, agriculture, health, and welfare—taking into account recommendations from the standing committees that consider legislation in each of these areas. The budget committee recommendations were reviewed by House and Senate and, as modified, went into the first annual budget resolution in May. The resolution recommended overall federal spending levels and set financial guidelines. Each substantive committee, whether Agriculture, Education and Labor, or Foreign Affairs, was given an expenditures target that it was supposed to observe as it took up the bills that came to it.

In September, the House and Senate budget committees reported a second resolution that reflected the May commitments along with new judgments on national economic needs. If the spending decisions Congress made during the spring and summer exceeded the total provided by the September resolution, budgetary discipline could be imposed through a reconciliation process. Under reconciliation, Congress could direct the standing committees to report bills that either raised revenues or cut spending.[30] In effect, the budget committees emerged in the role of fiscal watchdogs within Congress.

---

[29] Edwin L. Dale, Jr., *New York Times*, June 15, 1975.

[30] A detailed account of this budget process can be found in Allen Schick, *Congress and Money* (Washington, D.C.: The Urban Institute, 1980). See also James P. Pfiffner, *The President, the Budget, and Congress: Impoundment and the 1974 Budget Act* (Boulder, Colo.: Westview Press, 1979); and Roger H. Davidson and Walter J. Oleszek, *Congress and Its Members* (Washington, D.C.: Congressional Quarterly Press, 1985), chap. 12.

CONGRESS AND THE DEFICIT: THE SAGA OF GRAMM-RUDMAN-HOLLINGS

Frustrated by its inability to reduce the huge federal deficit and prodded by the Reagan administration to take action, Congress passed in December 1985 the Balanced Budget and Emergency Deficit Control Act of 1985, better known by the names of its three principal Senate sponsors, Phil Gramm (R-Texas), Warren Rudman (R-New Hampshire), and Ernest Hollings (D-South Carolina). The president signed the Gramm-Rudman-Hollings bill into law on December 12, 1985. It required that the federal budget not be in deficit by more than $171.9 billion in fiscal year (FY) 1986, $144 billion in FY 1987, $108 billion in FY 1988, $72 billion in FY 1989, $36 billion in FY 1990, and that the budget be balanced in FY 1991. To achieve these budget goals, the measure required across-the-board cuts of nonexempt programs by a uniform percentage to meet the deficit targets, if regular budget and appropriations actions failed to reach the goals.

Gramm-Rudman-Hollings had very limited implications for federal welfare spending. A great many welfare programs were excluded from automatic cuts. Among the programs exempted: Social Security, veterans' compensation and pensions, Medicaid, Aid to Families with Dependent Children, Supplemental Security Income, food stamps, and child nutrition. In addition the cuts were limited in five health programs including Medicare.

The Gramm-Rudman-Hollings law's approach to controlling the deficit was controversial. Even those convinced of Gramm-Rudman-Hollings' utility readily admitted that the record of Congress and the president on the deficit was pretty bad. For one thing, the reduction targets were gotten around in a number of ways. When the first enacted set of annual targets set in 1985 proved too hard to

"WELL, THAT DOES IT... I'M GOING TO HAVE TO MOVE THIS FENCE BACK!"

meet, Congress and the president simply agreed to new ones that were easier—that reduced the deficit more slowly, over a longer period. Even these revised targets were skirted. The Office of Management and Budget used optimistic forecasts of tax revenues and expenditures—which helps explain why each year the *actual* deficit exceeded the one *projected*.

THE 1990 BUDGET PROCESS CHANGES

In the prolonged 1990 budget negotiations between the Bush administration and Congress, public attention focused on what cuts would be made in federal programs and what taxes would be raised. The tax issue, in particular, generated intense controversy—between Republicans and Democrats, and within the GOP between the administration and a large bloc of House members led by Minority Whip Newt Gingrich. Somewhat overlooked in all the partisan wrangling were the major changes made in the very structure of the budget process.

Five-year Budgeting. Budget resolutions and reconciliation bills will now be required to make projections as to spending, revenue, and deficits for five-year periods, not just one year.

Shifting the Emphasis Away from the Size of the Overall Annual Deficit. Instead of being geared, as they had been under the Gramm-Rudman procedure, to meeting a target for the permissible total deficit, appropriations bills will now be required to stay within specific caps that have been set, separately, for defense, foreign aid, and so-called "discretionary" domestic spending. Basically, the latter excludes spending for entitlement programs such as Social Security and assistance for the needy.

The New Sequestration Rules. The old Gramm-Rudman procedure of an initial automatic spending cut (known as a sequester), that would take place in October if the deficit target was projected as not being met, is gone. The new rules envision a different type of sequestration. It would offset appropriations in any of the three areas that, for the coming fiscal year, exceeded the cap limits noted above. There would have to be an across-the-board cut *in the spending category*—say, in defense—rather than in overall discretionary spending, that would bring outlays down to the cap target. If Congress enacts a supplemental appropriations bill for the current year—increasing foreign aid, for example—the cap for that category for the *next fiscal year* would have to be reduced by the amount of the excess appropriation.

A Bigger Role for OMB. Under the old law, OMB's task involved monitoring the size of the overall deficit. Under the new, its responsibilities become, at least potentially, much broader. Some in Congress think this change entails an actual shift in budget power from Congress to the executive branch. Now OMB has continuing authority to monitor all tax and spending bills as they move through the legislative process—something done previously by the CBO. OMB's scoring of the implication of these bills—whether they fall within cap targets, for example—has been made binding on Congress. How OMB tallies the costs of the various annual appropriations bills will determine whether the appropriations committees stayed within their spending limits, and hence whether sequestration will be invoked. The Congressional Budget Office protested this shift of authority to OMB.

A Reduced Role for the Budget Committees. Observers see the new rules strengthening the role of the appropriations committees in Congress and diminishing the budget committees'

MICHAEL RAMIREZ
© Baker Communications

responsibilities. With a five-year agreement on spending targets in place, there doesn't seem to be much left for the budget committees to do. As long as they work within the overall spending ceilings that have been specified for the next five years, the appropriations committees can be confident that their allocations for various programs will not be altered.

The New Calendar. Changes have been made in the dates for various budget-related actions. Now Congress is supposed to complete action on its budget resolution by April 15, rather than in May. Fifteen days after Congress adjourns in the fall, OMB is to issue its final sequester report; and on the basis of this the president would order spending cuts, if needed to meet the targets.

Do the new rules sound complicated? They should—because they are. What is clear is that the 1990 negotiations between the White House and Congress culminated in a set of compromises that change importantly the way budgets are made. And it appears that the changes somewhat strengthened the president's hand, by enhancing the role of his Office of Management and Budget.

LEGISLATIVE OVERSIGHT

Legislative oversight involves efforts by Congress to supervise the vast executive establishment set up to administer laws it has enacted. Prior to the 1930s, when the national government was small, oversight was a fairly easy matter. Today, government is so large and does so much that effective oversight is difficult to manage.

During the 1970s, Congress began placing much more emphasis on its oversight function.

It broadened the spending oversight of the General Accounting Office (GAO). More importantly, it extended the number and independence of its subcommittees and greatly expanded their staffs. One result was more time for oversight hearings and related meetings. In addition, Congress began routinely adding onto legislation the requirement that executive agencies notify the appropriate committee(s) before promulgating program changes, so that the committees could call hearings if they chose and bring their influence to bear, perhaps taking steps to reverse the agency actions. Such legislative stipulations typically provide for a waiting period of 30 to 60 days between the time the agency notifies the committee(s) and the time its administrative action is due to take effect.

Congress also began asserting a near-absolute right to information as part of its oversight function. As this took place, presidents and their executive department subordinates came to feel that congressional oversight had expanded beyond reasonable limits. And more neutral observers agree that at times the new congressional demands are burdensome. Cabinet officers and other agency officials now spend enormous amounts of time testifying before one subcommittee or another. And "Give us all your records on [some agency activity]" can require a huge amount of staff work. Oversight has become a key element in Congress's ongoing power struggle with the presidency.

THE LEGISLATIVE VETO

The **legislative** or **congressional veto** provision was first employed in a 1932 law. President Herbert Hoover was authorized to reorganize agencies by executive order, but it was further required that each such order be transmitted to Congress, where it could be disapproved by either house within 60 days. This provision turned the usual legislative-executive relationship upside down: The president was allowed to write the equivalent of law, but Congress could subsequently veto (reject) what he had written.

In the 1960s and 1970s, Congress turned increasingly to the legislative veto, because it found the provision useful in meeting two somewhat contrary objectives: giving the president and executive agencies the authority to act and keeping Congress very much in the picture, able to overturn executive actions. By 1980, 200 laws containing more than 250 legislative veto provisions were on the books. One-third of these were enacted after 1975.

It isn't surprising that presidents didn't like Congress's increasing recourse to the legislative veto, even though they recognized in many instances that Congress would not have given them authority to act at all unless it retained a ready means of blocking the action. President Jimmy Carter reflected general presidential sentiment when he argued in 1978 that legislative vetoes were "intrusive devices that infringe on the Executive's constitutional duty to faithfully execute the laws."[31] Heavy use of the veto involved Congress in the day-to-day practice of rule making, properly the domain of executive agencies.

With the argument between president and Congress over the legislative veto unresolved, the U.S. Supreme Court entered the dispute, through its ruling in the case of *Naturalization Service v. Chadha* (1983). This case began back in 1974 when Jagdish Rai Chadha, a Kenyan East Indian who had overstayed his student visa, won a verdict from the Immigration and Naturalization Service (INS) suspending his deportation. A year later, though, the House of

---

[31] Jimmy Carter, "Message to the Congress," June 1978, in *Public Papers of the Presidents of the United States—Jimmy Carter, 1978* (Washington, D.C.: Office of the Federal Register, National Archives and Records Service, 1979), book 1, p. 1147.

Representatives exercised the one-house veto that had been written into an immigration act and overturned the INS action. Under the veto, Chadha had to be deported after all, even though INS had decided he could stay in the United States. Chadha appealed to INS and to the federal courts, in a complicated legal battle.

The Court ruled that Congress had stepped unconstitutionally into the executive branch's domain and had skirted the requirements of bicameralism. Writing for the majority, Chief Justice Burger concluded: "To accomplish what has been attempted by one House of Congress in this case requires action in conformity with the express procedures of the Constitution's prescription for legislative action: passage by a majority of both Houses and presentment to the President."[32]

In the wake of the Chadha decision, all of the legislative veto provisions on the books were undoubtedly unconstitutional and hence unenforceable. Political scientist Barbara Craig points out that Congress moved quickly to find replacements for the veto.[33] In many cases it is now required to pass a joint resolution either of approval or disapproval. All joint resolutions must be presented to the president for his signature or veto, but the difference between these two forms is substantial. The joint **resolution of disapproval** is now used most commonly. As an example, in July 1985 Congress passed a Federal Trade Commission (FTC) authorization that would allow it to reject proposed regulations issued by the FTC. The regulations would be overturned if a resolution disapproving them were passed by both houses of Congress and signed by the president. If Congress did not act, the FTC rules would take effect ninety days after being submitted to Congress. If Con-

gress acted and the president vetoed the joint resolution, Congress would have to repass it by two-thirds majorities before its rejection of the FTC rules would take effect.

In a few areas, including some arms sales, Congress has wanted to impose a tougher restriction on the president. In a **resolution of approval,** the specific arms sale (or other executive action) must be approved by both houses of Congress and signed by the president before it can be implemented.

THE TWO CONGRESSES

Congress performs two very different functions: as lawmaker and as representative assembly.[34] As lawmaker it is charged with passing the legislation that the United States requires to address its various public problems. As representative assembly it responds to very different needs. Composed of 535 senators and representatives, each with his or her own electoral interests, Congress must hear and respond to the claims of diverse constituencies—among them, organized interests. And the sum total of these claims may not always be consistent with the requirements of sound public policy for the nation.

Recognition of these different, sometimes opposing, legislative functions came a long time ago, in the early days of legislatures in Europe. In 1774, the great British politician and philosopher Edmund Burke described the constituent-oriented British Parliament as "a congress of ambassadors from different and hostile interests, which interests each must maintain, as an agent and advocate, against other agents and advocates." Then Burke set forth the idea of the same Parliament as lawmaker for the nation, "a deliberative assembly of one nation,

[32]*Immigration and Naturalization Service v. Jagdish Rai Chadha et al., United States Law Week,* June 21, 1983, p. 4918.
[33]Barbara H. Craig, *Chadha: The Story of an Epic Constitutional Struggle* (New York: Oxford University Press, 1988), pp. 235–37.

[34]Davidson and Oleszek, "Introduction: The Two Congresses," in *Congress and Its Members,* pp. 7–12.

with one interest, that of the whole—where not local purposes, not local prejudices, ought to guide, but the general good, resulting from the general reason of the whole."[35]

Are there problems with the way Congress is now organized, in terms of its capacity to advance "the general good"? Many observers worry about the extent to which power is now fragmented, with individual members strong and central leadership weak. In this setting, interest groups are able to take their cases directly to individual legislators, without any party mediation, and establish close working ties with the subcommittee(s) in their areas of interest. Politically active interest groups are a necessary and proper part of a free society. Given the far-flung activities of modern government, it was unavoidable that there would be a proliferation of organized special interests. But in the current era, these special interests have been permitted to operate upon a highly individualistic, fractured Congress—giving them excessive influence.

Changes needed to correct this problem have been hard to achieve and almost certainly will continue to be so. To function better as a lawmaking body, Congress needs more discipline, a defined hierarchy, and leaders who can bargain with the executive branch and with interest groups, and then commit Congress to the best overall mix of programmatic responses. Yet while the fragmentation of power in Congress is widely deplored, even among many members themselves, it generally serves individual members' electoral and representational needs. Why should members who have their own subcommittee and large staff, which can be employed to help their electoral fortunes and to advance legislation that they or their constituents favor, surrender these resources?

We began this chapter by looking at incumbency advantages and ethics violations as prob-

lems in the operations of the contemporary Congress. They are related to each other, and both in turn have a link to the problem of interest group influence. Finding ways to reduce incumbents' advantages over challengers would mean more electoral competition—which would help upset the all-too-cozy ties that now exist between entrenched members and established, well-heeled interests. Were this to occur, the climate for congressional ethics would surely not deteriorate and might be substantially improved.

To ignore problems is short-sighted. At the same time, focusing on them too much can be distorting. For all its institutional problems, Congress is the strongest legislative body in the world. In an age when real authority has swung in most democracies to the executive, Congress retains a genuinely independent voice in policy making. Its vigilence in asserting its constitutional prerogatives has kept separation of powers alive and well. There is much, then, in which to take satisfaction.

SUMMARY

Congress differs from other democratic legislatures in two important regards. One involves separation of powers. In the American scheme—though not in the more common parliamentary arrangement—the legislature and the executive are separate institutions. It is possible, and common, for the two to be controlled by different parties. The two branches must work together if American government is to function, but the Constitution makes them coequal and independent.

Also setting Congress apart is the extent to which power is dispersed within it. Committees and subcommittees are strong; central party leadership is weak. Nowhere in the democratic world is the individual legislator so independent—and so powerful.

[35] Edmund Burke, "Speech to Electors at Bristol," in *Burke's Politics*, Ross J. S. Hoffman and Paul Levack, eds. (New York: Knopf, 1949), p. 116.

For a brief time in the late nineteenth and early twentieth centuries, Congress experienced strong party organization and discipline; this was gone by 1915. Over the last two decades, power has been even more widely dispersed among the membership, as the prerogatives of the once-dominant committee chairmen have been cut back, the number of subcommittees expanded and their independence buttressed, members' staff increased, and more.

In the 1970s, Congress began asserting itself more vigorously. It passed important new legislation dealing with national budget making. It applied its oversight powers so extensively that even some neutral observers thought it sometimes overreached its constitutional boundaries. It took a little-used provision, the legislative veto, and applied it routinely as a convenient means of blocking executive-agency actions that it disagreed with—even matters like a ruling of the Immigration and Naturalization Service to suspend deportation of Jagdish Rai Chadha. In many cases Congress is now required to resort to joint resolutions of disapproval, which must be passed by both houses and are subject to the president's veto.

Over the last quarter-century, a series of circumstances have come together to give congressional incumbents, especially in the House of Representatives, unparalled advantages over their challengers, with the result that they rarely lose and usually win by overwhelming margins. This decline of competition weakens popular control. There are indications that the public senses something is wrong; but thus far its dissatisfactions are unfocused.

FOR FURTHER STUDY

Barone, Michael, and Grant Ujifusa. *The Almanac of American Politics, 1992.* Washington, D.C.: National Journal, 1992. Published every two years, the almanac provides comprehensive descriptions of every congressional district, the voting records of members of Congress on major issues, interest-group ratings of

congressional voting on liberalism-conservatism continuums, and more.

Congressional Directory, 1991–92. Washington, D.C.: Government Printing Office, 1991. Published for each Congress, the directory contains biographies of all members of Congress, provides listings of the members of all committees and subcommittees, gives addresses and telephone numbers for congressional offices, indicates principal staff assistants, and more.

Congressional Quarterly, Weekly Report and Annual Almanac. Washington, D.C.: Congressional Quarterly. The most comprehensive regular reporting of developments on Capitol Hill, including reviews of all major bills introduced into Congress and complete records of all roll-call votes.

Ornstein, Norman J. et al. *Vital Statistics on Congress, 1991–92 Edition.* Washington, D.C.: American Enterprise Institute, 1992. An extremely valuable reference for statistics on Congress, including political, educational, religious background of senators and representatives; election and campaign finance data; congressional committees, staff size, and operating expenses; workload; budget; voting alignments.

OPTIONAL COMPUTER EXERCISES

for *The Ladd Election ANALYZER*

VOTER FRUSTRATION OVER CONGRESS'S PERFORMANCE

Using the ANALYZER, you can get a sense of how voters who were dissatisfied with government performance expressed their desire for change (see pp. 137–38). One way was to vote for an outsider for president. Another was to vote for a change in Congress by backing the out-of-power party (the Republicans) in House races. Take a look at Perot's voters. How did they vote in the House elections? Were they more inclined to vote Republican or Democratic? What about independents? Did they vent their frustration by giving out-of-power Republican candidates a larger share of their vote in House races? Did independents vote differently for members of Congress in 1992 than they did in 1988?

Chapter 7

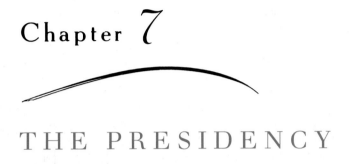

THE PRESIDENCY

A few days before his assassination in November 1963, President John F. Kennedy penned a personal note to political historian Clinton Rossiter, commenting on Rossiter's book on the presidency. Rossiter had introduced his study with a quotation from Shakespeare's *Macbeth*. The Scottish general, about to seize his country's throne, relates to his "first lady" a dream in which "Me thought I heard a voice cry 'Sleep no more!' " Rossiter felt this a fitting commentary on a prime feature of the American presidency: the enormous demands placed on the office.[1]

Kennedy wrote that, while that quotation was apt, he believed there was an even better one in Shakespeare's *King Henry IV, Part 1*. Glendower boasts that "I can call spirits from the vasty deep." Hostpur replies: "Why, so can I, or so can any man; but will they come when you do call for them?" For Kennedy, it was the gap between the calling and the coming, between the large amount a president seeks to accomplish and the little he can accomplish, that best characterizes the position of this democratic chief executive.

The American presidency is a peculiar office. A president has great visibility and great practical importance in our scheme of government. But he also

---

[1]Clinton Rossiter, *The American Presidency*, rev. ed. (New York: New American Library, 1960). The *Macbeth* quotation is from Act II, scene ii.

Reuters / Bettmann

Jose R. Lopez / NYT Pictures

President Bill Clinton, Vice President Al Gore, and former President George Bush.

experiences, even at the height of his popularity and power, great limitations on his capacity to carry the country in the direction he intends. He is in one regard the symbol of America's sense of nationhood and the repository of political leadership and legitimacy. In another sense, though, he is a checked and balanced political executive, sharing the power of American national government not only with a constitutionally independent and politically independent-minded Congress, but with a potent federal judiciary and with other units in the executive branch that are in varying degrees independent of his authority. This pervasive mix of power and limits, political majesty and modesty, led the distinguished British political scientist Harold J. Laski to describe the American president as "both more and less than a king, more and less than a prime minister."[2]

[2]Harold J. Laski, *The American Presidency: An Interpretation* (New York: Harper and Brothers, 1940), p. 11.

PRESIDENTIAL LEADERSHIP STYLES

As we have seen, the Constitution confers legislative authority on the Congress, whose ranks today number 535 senators and representatives. In contrast, Article II stipulates that "the executive Power shall be vested in a President of the United States of America"—not, in other words, among a group of officials, but in one person. The executive branch is a huge, complex array of departments and agencies, run by an army of officials, of course, so the president is far from alone in discharging executive responsibilities. Still, the Constitution's vast assignment of executive authority to the president gives each occupant of that office singular ascendancy in executive affairs and as a symbol of the nation. Whereas Congress is many, the president is one.

This singularity of executive power in the

American scheme means, in effect, that the presidency gets redesigned every time a new individual takes up the office. The constitutional environment in which he operates is largely unchanging, and successive presidents find themselves having to grapple with many of the same basic problems. But each occupant brings his own distinct background, skills, strengths, and weaknesses to the job, thus transforming it. How does the presidency operate? To a very considerable extent it operates according to the personality, values, and leadership style each president brings to it.

THE BUSH PRESIDENCY: FROM TRIUMPH TO DEFEAT

Given the range of problems, foreign and domestic, they are expected to help solve and the many diverse political and managerial skills they are expected to possess, modern presidents often have trouble measuring up, and they see their popular standing plunge. Still, no president has seen a sharper reversal in his fortunes than did George Bush. At the conclusion of the Gulf War in early March of 1991, a Gallup poll recorded Bush's public approval at an extraordinarily high 89 percent. That is, 89 percent of Americans said they approved of the way he was handling his job as president; only 8 percent said they disapproved. Twenty months later, however, Bush's approval stood at around 35 percent. A survey taken by CBS News over October 16 and 17, 1992, two weeks before the election, found just 36 percent of respondents approving Bush's overall performance as president, while 59 percent disapproved. Presidents whose leadership gets approval scores in the thirties are bound to have trouble winning reelection. George Bush's defeat on November 3 at the hands of Democrat Bill Clinton followed the long erosion of his popular standing, which occurred over the last six months of 1991 and much of 1992.

The steep decline in popular support that ended the Bush presidency has been attributed in large part to the weakness in the U.S. economy. Presidents have limited powers and resources to influence the economy's direction, but they are often held responsible when economic difficulties develop. In the survey taken by CBS News over October 16 and 17, 1992, just 1 percent of respondents said they thought the economy was very good and only 17 percent described it as fairly good. In contrast, 38 percent found the economy fairly bad and an extraordinarily high 43 percent called it very bad. One can question the accuracy of these perceptions, but the fact that so many people saw the economy in deep trouble obviously contributed to the "time for a change" sentiment that propelled Clinton's victory. [The 1992 presidential election and the start of the Clinton administration are discussed in depth in a special chapter printed as the fourth appendix to this text.]

However, it is instructive to review the other possible sources of President Bush's decline in popularity, sources that originated in the leadership style he brought to the highest office in the land. Studying the approach George Bush brought to the presidency is also instructive not only in explaining why defeat came after such high marks earlier in his term, but in illuminating problems in presidential leadership generally. No one wins the office without having considerable abilities and strengths. But every president has his weaknesses too. As was the case with George Bush, the strengths and weaknesses often stem from the same basic approach to handling the office—an approach that may work well in some circumstances and poorly in others.

Bush got generally good marks in personal terms. "Sinister" was not an adjective that was often applied to him, as it was, for example, to Richard Nixon, who was elected president in

1968 and again in 1972, but who was forced to resign during the Watergate scandal. In a survey taken February 5–7, 1992, by ABC News and the *Washington Post*, 82 percent of those polled said Bush was well described as "decent"; 71 percent said "moral" was well applied; 65 percent said "honest" was appropriate. And this survey was taken at a time when his overall rating as president had already fallen sharply, and he had the approval of less than half the populace.

No one accused Bush of failing to bring sufficient energy to his conduct of the presidency, either. Indeed, he was so much on the move throughout his four years in office that some worried about his health; his collapse at a state dinner in Japan in December 1991, while apparently not a serious matter, heightened these concerns.

But if many aspects of Bush the man have been readily understood and in large measure noted approvingly, his policies and, beyond that, his animating vision for the country prompted uncertainty and often criticism. One continual argument involves where Bush belonged on the American political spectrum. Was he really a conservative or, in fact, a pragmatist, one who lacks a fixed policy, adopting instead whatever works? Was he a leader who, lacking a coherent political philosophy, was vulnerable, at least in domestic policy, to being influenced unduly by his advisors or to being tossed to and fro in shifting political winds? Was his presidency driven too much by an often belated response to events? Or is there an underlying unity of philosophy and direction in Bush's style of presidential leadership?

A Conciliatory Approach. One of the reasons George Bush's presidential leadership proved to be such a puzzle is that it combined two approaches that are often thought to be contradictory. On the one hand, he espoused many of the tenets of contemporary mainstream Republicanism. Like many in his party, and like his predecessor Ronald Reagan, Bush believed that government has grown excessively in recent decades and that its growth needs to be curbed. Like many in his party, he also thought that greater emphasis should be placed on the individual's exercise of responsibility through family and community life.

This approach is one that Kerry Mullins and Aaron Wildavsky call *individualist*. They write that "Bush's individualist sympathies are particularly evident in the economic realm. Rather than taking a paternalistic attitude toward social welfare issues, he appears to prefer free market solutions and freedom of choice. Free-enterprise zones [where government encourages private investment through tax concessions and the like] are offered as a remedy for economically distressed areas of the country. [And Bush] took a strong stance against a large increase in the minimum wage, emphasizing employer choice over worker protection."[3]

At the same time, though, Bush's ideals and goals are inclusionist. As president, he sought "to integrate all elements of the American polity (classes, races, regions, interests, even political opponents) into a cohesive whole. . . ."[4] This commitment seems rooted deep in Bush's personality. In all of his dealings he was inclined to conciliation. "We need compromise," he said in his inaugural address; "we've had dissention. We need harmony; we've had a chorus of discordant voices." Speaking of tensions

[3] Kerry Mullins and Aaron Wildavsky, "The Procedural Presidency of George Bush," *Political Science Quarterly* 107, 1 (1992), p. 32. (See, too, by Mullins and Wildavsky, *The Beleaguered Presidency* [New Brunswick, N.J.: Transaction Books, 1992].)

[4] Ibid, p. 32.

between the executive branch and Congress, he lamented that "we have seen the hard looks and heard the statements in which not each other's ideas are challenged, but each other's motives."

Often, Bush was pulled one way by his conservative individualism, another by his commitment to compromise as proper due process in intergovernmental affairs or by his commitment to inclusionism in dealing with the groups making up the populace. One of the most politically costly decisions of his presidency came, for example, in the fall of 1990, in the wrangle with Congress over the federal budget. Bush had run in 1988 on a promise of "no new taxes"—a pledge consistent with his party's belief that government had grown too large. In the fall 1990 budget battle, though, Bush was pulled in the opposite direction by his preference for compromise (here with the Democratic leadership of the Congress) over confrontation and by his belief that interbranch give and take is not only unavoidable where one party controls the executive, the other the legislative, but that such compromise accords with due process. But when he compromised on his "no new taxes" pledge and backed tax hikes, Bush seemed to waffle. Clinton hit Bush hard in the 1992 election on breaking the "no new taxes" pledge.

Similarly, his insistence on less governmental and more individual responsibility pushed Bush in one direction when dealing with the country's racial problems, while his desire to see black Americans better integrated into the national community pushed him in another. This conflict led to waffling. But it seemed to originate less in indecisiveness than in a profound tension between two conflicting sets of values, each deeply and genuinely held.

Personal Popularity. Thus, it isn't surprising that Bush has gotten decidedly different marks

from much of the U.S. public, depending on how his approach was faring, given the demands of events. When he was Ronald Reagan's vice president (1981–1989), Bush's inclination to conciliation and accommodation often made him appear weak. He was ridiculed by his opponents in the first half of the 1988 presidential campaign for being a "wimp." But early in his presidency, his emphasis on conciliation was often welcomed, after the greater confrontationism of the Reagan years. Few political figures in modern times had more of a roller-coaster ride politically than he had.

October 1990 saw the beginning of a big downward slide in the Bush presidency (see Figure 7.1). The U.S. economy had slowed and prices at the gas pumps had soared: News coverage became a recession watch. With the United States in the midst of a tax revolt, Bush went on national television on October 2 and completed his reversal on "no new taxes" by insisting that big tax hikes were needed as part of a budget deal. In response, his standing dropped sharply from the high point it had reached following Iraq's August 2 invasion of Kuwait. Surveys by ABC News and the *Washington Post* found the proportion of the public saying they approved Bush's handling of the presidency falling from 75 percent in September to 56 percent in mid-October.

In his Gulf War leadership, Bush's political impulses all led him in a single, consistent direction; he acted decisively, and his popularity soared to some of the highest levels ever recorded in the sixty years public opinion polls have been conducted in the United States. But with the war over and the nation's attention refocused on domestic problems, especially economic ones, in late 1991 and into the 1992 election year, Bush's ambivalence again often left him sounding an uncertain note. As a result both of this uncertainty and the dissatisfactions bred of the recession itself, the president's popular standing fell sharply. The standing of other political leaders and institutions suffered too, as the data on Congress's standing, shown in Figure 7.2, attest.

ASSESSING CLINTON'S LEADERSHIP

The start of the Clinton administration is discussed in a new chapter, which is printed in the fourth appendix to this text. Here, in material written just after the November 1992 election and before Bill Clinton was inaugurated as the nation's forty-second president,[5] we must

confine ourselves to a few brief comments concerning the leadership he is likely to display in office.

Forty-six years old at the time of his election,

[5]Clinton is in fact only the forty-first person to hold the office of president since 1789, when George Washington was sworn in. The statistical oddity through which Clinton is the forty-first man to be president, but the forty-second president, is accounted for by the way Grover Cleveland's tenure is treated officially. Cleveland was elected in 1884 and served from March 1885 through March 1889 as the twenty-second president. He was defeated in the 1888 election, but ran again four years later and won—serving a second term from 1893 to 1897. According to a ruling of the U.S. State Department, Cleveland is both the twenty-second and twenty-fourth president, because his two terms were not consecutive.

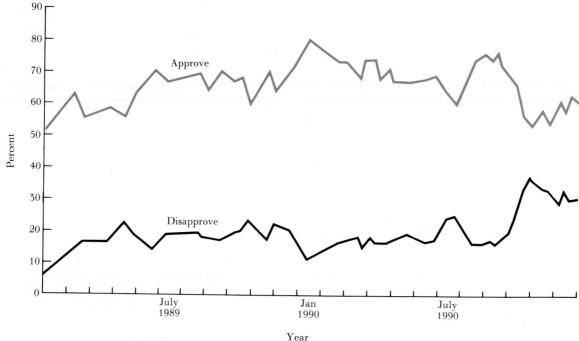

FIGURE 7.1 CHARTING GEORGE BUSH'S POPULAR STANDING, 1989–1992: DECLINE OF A PRESIDENCY

Question: Do you approve or disapprove of the way George Bush is handling his job as president?
Source: Surveys by the Gallup Organization, latest that of September 10–11, 1992.

Bullshit

Clinton is the first U.S. president born after World War II and the youngest since John F. Kennedy. He showed great skill, energy, and determination during his long campaign for the presidency. He is certain to be an aggressive and energetic president.

As governor of Arkansas, a conservative southern state, and in his presidential campaign as well, Bill Clinton has shown himself very much inclined—his critics say far too inclined—to the art of political compromise. He has been reluctant to take a stance on a major policy issue opposed by a large bloc of the electorate. This search for compromise, and a blurring of the edges on various issues and policy commitments, helped Clinton unify the Democratic party behind him in the 1992 campaign to a degree that it had not been unified since the early years of Lyndon Johnson's administration. But it has also gotten Clinton in trouble, as when he fudged things on his effort with regard to the draft in the 1960s, apparently to avoid being seen as having taken a stand that, he felt, a large bloc of the electorate opposed. In fact, though, it was the later fudging, far more than the original action, that brought widespread questioning of his character.

This concern over his character is among the biggest challenges that Bill Clinton faces early in his presidency. He won because many voters turned against George Bush, deciding it was

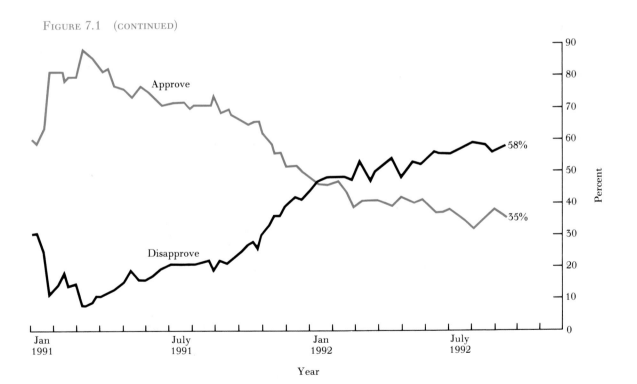

FIGURE 7.1 (CONTINUED)

58%

35%

Percent

Approve

Disapprove

Jan
1991

July
1991

Jan
1992

July
1992

Year

time for a change, not because he had inspired confidence in himself across the broad electorate. Whether in office he wins that confidence will play a big part in determining the success or failure of the Clinton presidency.

In the next section of this chapter, we examine the key structural features of the American presidency—including the extent and limits of the formal powers. Then we turn to a description of what a modern president does, of the many different demands upon this office. The president plays many roles, from party leader to formulator of legislative programs, from commander in chief of the armed forces to administrator in chief of the executive branch. It is not easy to find someone who can do

all of this well. We review the institutional presidency, the collection of aides and offices that now comprise the Executive Office of the President. We conclude the chapter with a discussion of what Americans think about the presidency as an office and how they and scholars assess the performance of recent presidents.

In their constitutional definition of the essential powers and character of the presidency, the framers were breaking new ground. Nowhere in 1787 was there a prototype for the national executive they had in mind. During the nearly two centuries since Article II of the Constitution was drafted, the American presidency has remained a unique office, one where executive

FIGURE 7.2   CHARTING CONGRESS'S POPULAR STANDING, 1989–1992

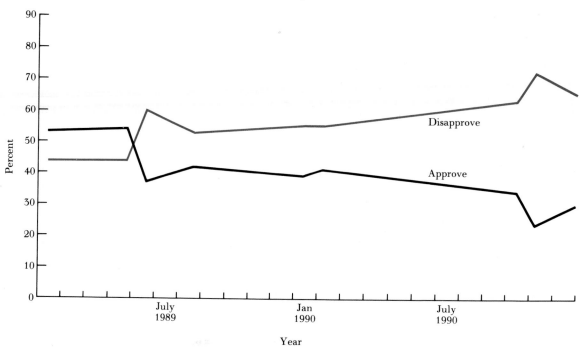

Question: Do you approve or disapprove of the way Congress is doing its job?
Source: Surveys by ABC News and the *Washington Post*, latest that of June 3–7, 1992. *Likely voters.

authority has been organized and articulated differently from any of America's sister democracies.

A REPUBLICAN EXECUTIVE

We saw in chapters 4 and 5 that the political ideals guiding the Constitution's framers, derived from European political thought of the seventeenth and eighteenth centuries, were called "republican"—emphasizing both popular sovereignty and individual liberty. This meant in part that political institutions would no longer have a class and hereditary base but would instead gain their legitimacy from their reliance on the popular will. The American presidency was set up to be consistent with the enlightened expectations of the times. The president would not resemble a king—not even a limited monarch favored by so many European thinkers of that time. He would be elected for a fixed term of four years, with reelection possible; any native-born citizen (or citizen at the time of the Constitution's adoption) of at least thirty-five years of age would be eligible to stand for office. These provisions represented a monumental break from the hereditary, aristocratic practice that still prevailed in Europe.

FIGURE 7.2 (CONTINUED)

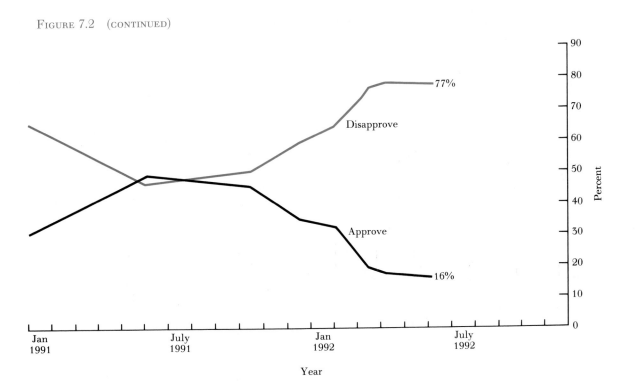

At the same time, the framers were fearful of unrestrained majority rule and the possibility that the American chief executive might be too inclined to appeal to popular passions in ways harmful to minority rights. They sought to insulate the office by having the public participate in presidential selection only indirectly. Their chosen mechanism was the **electoral college.** Article II provided that each state should appoint, "in such Manner as the Legislature thereof may direct, a Number of Electors, equal to the whole number of Senators and Representatives to which the state may be entitled in the Congress. . . ." These electors would meet in their respective states on a day designated by Congress and cast their votes for president. Any eligible person receiving an absolute majority of the votes cast would be declared president. If no one received a majority, the House of Representatives—with each state delegation having a single vote—would select the president from among the (up to) five contenders with the highest number of electoral votes. In 1804 the Twelfth Amendment to the Constitution was ratified, modifying the formal operation of the electoral college to specify that the electors would choose the president and vice president on separate ballots and having the House pick the president from among the three (rather than five) highest vote-getters if no one had a majority. Since 1804, no further *constitutional* changes have been made in the mechanism.

Major *political* changes over the first several decades did, however, transform the practical operation of the electoral college from what the framers intended. The emerging political parties in effect took over the electoral college procedures and *converted them into a means for ratifying popular preferences for president.* Part of this development came about as early as 1796, as selection of presidential electors in the state legislatures became a party contest between the Federalists and the Democratic-Republicans. The people voted one party or the other into majority status in the respective state assemblies, and these legislative majorities then picked electors pledged to vote for their parties' presidential nominees.

Three decades later, states began changing their procedures for picking presidential electors. Instead of being selected by state legislatures, they would henceforth be chosen by direct popular ballot. More and more states made this changeover in the 1820s and 1830s. By 1832, when Democrat Andrew Jackson won reelection over Henry Clay, candidate of the opposition National Republicans, presidential elections had been transformed into the contest we know today: Eligible voters in each state went to the polls on election day and cast ballots for their choice for president by picking a slate of electors publicly pledged to him. This democratization of the presidency strengthened the office. James Sterling Young has observed that

> nomination and election by popular acclaim [gave] the presidency the stature of popular spokesmanship and an independent electoral strength which was convertible, on occasion, to bargaining advantages over Congress. . . . In a nation pervasively mistrustful of government, democracy, and democracy alone, [converted] a figure of authority into a personage of national influence.[6]

AN INDEPENDENT EXECUTIVE

The framers, influenced by their classical liberal preference for dispersed power, provided for an executive branch separate from the legislature and independent of it for its tenure in

[6] James Sterling Young, *The Washington Community, 1800–1828* (New York: Harcourt, Brace, 1966), p. 253.

The office of the presidency is as much enshrined as the individual president in such monuments as the Lincoln Memorial, Washington, D.C. Preserving the Union was Lincoln's goal, the Civil War his burden.

office. To ensure its independence, the executive had to have powers conferred directly by the Constitution, not by another branch of government. Section 2 of Article II made the president commander-in-chief of the armed forces, and established his power to make treaties and to appoint ambassadors, federal court judges, and "all other Officers of the United States." Other constitutional provisions gave the president an explicit legislative role through the veto power (Article I, section 7) and conferred upon him sweeping administrative responsibilities in that "he shall take Care that the Laws be faithfully executed" (Article II, section 3).

A CHECKED AND BALANCED EXECUTIVE

But if the president was to be constitutionally independent of the other branches, especially

the legislature, he was to be subject to restraints by them lest he get too strong. We saw in chapter 5 that every basic constitutional grant of authority to the president is constitutionally limited. The president is commander-in-chief of the armed forces, but it is within Congress's power to declare war and "to raise and support Armies." He has broad appointive powers, but his appointments require "the Advice and Consent" of the Senate. He has the power, in the conduct of foreign affairs, to make treaties, but the Senate's consent is required before the treaties come into force. The president stands at the helm of the ship of state and supervises the execution of all the laws of the United States—a formidable grant of authority, made even more formidable in the modern era by vast increases in the scope of legislation—but Congress determines what these laws shall provide and may repeal them at any time.

IMPEACHMENT

The ultimate congressional check on the chief executive is removing him from office. We have seen that the framers wanted the president to be independent of Congress for his election and tenure in office. But they envisioned the need, in an extreme case, for cashiering an executive who grossly violated his oath. They provided in section 4 of Article II that the president (and other "civil Officers of the United States") shall be dismissed if impeached and convicted of "Treason, Bribery, and other High Crimes and Misdemeanors." Such removal has not been undertaken lightly. Impeachment proceedings have been advanced in Congress against only two presidents: Andrew Johnson in 1868 and Richard Nixon in 1974. The process has two stages. The House of Representatives formally brings charges—which is what **impeachment** means. If it votes to impeach, the president (or other officer) is then tried by the Senate. "When the President of the United

States is tried," Article I, section 3, stipulates, "the Chief Justice [of the U.S. Supreme Court] shall preside: And no person shall be convicted without the concurrence of two thirds of the Members present."

The impeachment of Andrew Johnson. Only one president has ever been formally impeached by the House and tried by the Senate. Andrew Johnson of Tennessee succeeded Abraham Lincoln as president in 1865, upon the latter's assassination, and almost immediately got into deep political trouble. Johnson had been put on the ticket in 1864 as part of the effort to reach out in reconciliation to the South; Johnson was a southerner who opposed secession. But he was not a Republican—instead, he was a (pro-) "War Democrat"—so he began his presidency on the wrong foot with the Republican majority in Congress. Passions ran very high following the long and costly Civil War. Any president, even Lincoln, would have been hard pressed to control these passions as he charted policies for postwar Reconstruction. Johnson lacked the necessary skills, and his rupture with congressional Republicans deepened. Most historians do not believe that Johnson was in fact guilty of "High Crimes and Misdemeanors"—bad policy choices and inept political management would seem the harshest charges that could be sustained—but he was impeached by the House on February 24, 1868.

With Chief Justice Salmon P. Chase presiding, Johnson's Senate trial opened in March 1868. After about two months of often bitter argument, votes were taken on May 16 and 26. A majority voted to convict, but not the two-thirds majority required by the Constitution. By the narrowest of margins (35 for conviction, 19 against) Andrew Johnson was left to serve out the remainder of his term.

Richard Nixon and the Watergate scandal. The only other president subjected to impeachment proceedings, Richard Nixon was never actually impeached—and hence never tried in the Senate. But he was forced by these constitutional provisions to resign from office. When it was clear that he had lost the public backing needed to govern, and that the House would impeach him, Nixon resigned on August 9, 1974.

The events leading to Nixon's resignation are now referred to by the single word "Watergate." But the scandal that forced him from office grew from a complex of developments.[7] The actual Watergate incident was the June 17, 1972, break-in at the offices of the Democratic National Committee (DNC), located in a Washington commercial and residential complex known as the Watergate. Notwithstanding denial by the president himself, the burglary—undertaken for political espionage—was subsequently linked to Nixon's campaign organization, the Committee to Re-elect the President, and to White House aides. Although the incident did not materially affect the outcome of the 1972 elections (Nixon won by a 23 percentage point margin), the subsequent disclosures of a conspiracy to cover up the crime implicated the president and many of his staff and campaign officials. The final blow was the discovery of tape recordings, made on Nixon's initiative, of conversations in his office that showed his knowledge of the cover-up efforts. This revelation of presidential obstruction of justice led to a storm of public protest that culminated in Nixon's resignation.

Watergate was more than a break-in and cover-up. It was a product of the intense passions and protests of the Vietnam War period and the feeling among administration officials that they were under siege politically. It reflected, too, a decade of presidential aggrandizement,

[7] *Congressional Quarterly*'s two-volume account, *Watergate: Chronology of a Crisis* (Washington, D.C.: Congressional Quarterly, 1973 and 1974) is especially helpful because it brings together all of the basic events, testimony, etc.

Military personnel roll up the carpet as a helicopter readies to escort President Richard M. Nixon from the White House lawn after his resignation speech, August 9, 1974.

where the traditional sense of presidential restraint was violated by increasingly assertive—one might say arrogant—behavior. The framers had decided against any ceremonial titles for the president; the occupant would simply be addressed as "Mr. President." But in the 1960s and early 1970s that sense of democratic proportion had been lost. Painful though the process was, Watergate and congressional resurgence helped bring it back.

A VIGOROUS ONE-PERSON EXECUTIVE

Popular feeling in the 1780s and 1790s that the presidency must not in any way resemble the British monarchy was strong and emotional. After all, a war had been fought and won to free the colonies from the absolute tyranny of a king. For most Americans, King George III was the model of a strong executive—and this model was not a comforting one

when the new Constitution proposed to build up the executive power. The framers were acutely sensitive to this climate and did not want to advance anything that resembled monarchy. But the framers were convinced that the country needed more vigorous executive leadership than it had under the Articles of Confederation. The resolution of this tension in favor of a powerful but checked executive was a tribute to George Washington, who was almost universally expected to be the first occupant of the office. Washington favored a strong executive and worked hard to gain approval for it.

DUTIES OF THE PRESIDENT

Presidents and their aides sometimes unburden themselves on how demanding the job of president really is. This always seems a bit curious, since they have worked so hard to get the chance to assume the burden. It is indeed true, though, that the responsibilities of a modern president are so numerous and diverse that it has become virtually certain that no occupant of the office will ever perform all of them well. Box 7.1 shows some of the principal dimensions of the president's job as it has evolved over two centuries of American political experience.

RESPONSIBILITIES

All the president's roles continue to be very real and very demanding. As the only government official elected from a national constituency, the president commands media attention in articulating broad public wants and needs. Since the New Deal, Americans have believed that the president plays the largest part in the national government's prime responsibility to intervene in the economy to restore, maintain, or extend economic well-being. The president not only serves as the head of government, but also as chief of state: the ceremonial head of the nation. (While prime ministers are the head of government in parliamentary democracies, officials who do not bear significant governmental responsibilities, such as the British monarch, are chief of state.)

Box 7.1
Presidential Responsibilities

Chief of State: The president is the ceremonial head of the American government.

Chief Executive: To the president falls the constitutional charge to "take care that the laws be faithfully executed."

Commander in Chief: He controls and directs the American armed forces.

Chief Diplomat: He has prime responsibility for the conduct of U.S. foreign policy.

Chief Legislator: The president is expected to play a large role "guiding Congress in much of its law-making activity."

Chief of Party: He has a partisan role as the leader of his political party.

Voice of the People: He is "the leading formulator and expounder of public opinion in the United States."

Protector of Peace: In the face of challenges, domestic as much as foreign, the president is expected to promote national security and tranquility.

Manager of Prosperity: The president is now expected "to foster and promote free competitive enterprise, to avoid economic fluctuations . . . and to maintain employment, production, and purchasing power," in the words of the Employment Act of 1946.

World Leader: More than just chief diplomat of the U.S., he has broad responsibilities for the Western alliance and for international affairs globally.

Source: Rossiter, *American Presidency*, pp. 16–40, *passim.*

As commander in chief, President Bush sent more than 400,000 U.S. servicemen and women to the Persian Gulf area in late 1990 and successfully ended Iraq's occupation of Kuwait.

The president is head of the U.S. military establishment—a force currently consisting of almost 2.2 million men and women on active duty and a vast array of advanced weapons. Given the economic, technological, and military strength of the United States, the president's utterances and actions in foreign policy greatly affect the world community. The president is responsible for the security of the country. When a serious crisis threatens American lives and interests—whether the disabling aftermath of a hurricane on the Gulf Coast or the prospect of war in the Middle East—he is expected to take calming or restorative action. Rather than sitting back in the Oval Office waiting for Congress to act, the president must formulate programs, present them to Congress, and lobby for their enactment. In many of his leadership roles he is expected to transcend narrow partisanship—yet both his allies and his opponents expect him to uphold the philosophy and electoral interests of the political party on whose platform he was elected.

PUBLIC RELATIONS

Just as the president has an extraordinary array of responsibilities, so he needs an extraordinary array of skills. First and foremost, he must have the **external political skills** required to win the nomination of a major political party and ultimately a national election. As a candidate, he must be able to move among his fellow citizens and convince them to support him over other able and ambitious politicians. He must be able to speak effectively to small groups of businessmen to whom he turns for campaign contributions, to public rallies, and to national audiences linked by the crucial medium of television. He must have the stamina and the will to crisscross the country in the extended campaigns that have come to distinguish American presidential politics. The pressures on presidents and would-be presidents as campaigners are enormous. In office, a president uses appearances at conventions of various interest groups, press conferences, and televised speeches to maintain his popular standing and advance his programs.

WORKING WITH OTHER POLITICIANS

Internal political skills are no less vital to presidential success. The president is the most important member of the political leadership community in the United States. He must interact daily with other leaders—senators, governors, heads of labor unions and major business corporations, and others—to try to persuade them to follow his lead. Political scientist Richard Neustadt has noted that any president's success in advancing his programs and interests depends in large measure upon "the residual impressions of tenacity and skill" that he conveys to the leadership community. Even a president whose popular standing is high will have trouble leading effectively if his professional reputation is low.[8]

Dwight Eisenhower, fresh from his decisive victory in 1956, backslid and equivocated, convincing a large proportion of political Washington that he lacked the skill and determination to set a coherent course for either his party or

[8] Richard E. Neustadt, *Presidential Power* (New York: Wiley, 1980), pp. 47–48.

the country in domestic affairs. "Ike's" general popularity was high but his professional reputation was low. Two years later, Neustadt argues, the situation was reversed. The Democrats had scored big gains in the recession-dominated congressional elections of 1958, and Eisenhower's popularity with the public had dropped. But through skillful and determined action on behalf of his programs, the president in 1959 greatly improved his professional reputation.

The internal political skills required to impress the political community are sometimes quite different from the external skills needed to move the public at large. Strength, determination, steadfastness, the capacity to fight hard for one's policies without personalizing the disagreements, and the sense of when and how to compromise to achieve the largest possible portion of one's program objectives are especially

Presidential duties are many; expectations are even more numerous, and when not met, presidents hear about it (or see it) on the editorial pages of newspapers nationwide.

valued by politicians. They are critical to a president.

ADMINISTRATIVE SKILLS

The president is a politician, but he is also an executive—and his leadership is likely to suffer seriously if he does not possess a high measure of administrative skill. The executive branch is a huge enterprise: Over 3 million civilian employees were involved in the expenditure of almost $1.2 trillion in 1990. The president need have, and can have, little to do with the day-to-day running of the executive branch, but he is ultimately accountable for overseeing and guiding a business so large that it dwarfs corporate giants like General Motors, Exxon, and IBM.

Managing complex organizations has long been thought to involve special abilities and training. Schools of business administration each year turn out thousands of graduates with advanced training in corporate management. Yet little thought seems to be given to the skills needed to manage the most challenging of all executive positions, the American presidency. It is almost as if we are confident that the necessary skills will automatically materialize. Of course the president has no shortage of experts ready to advise him on the proper organization and operation of the executive branch. And his personal staff—the White House Office—includes hundreds of aides. But it's misleading to insist that a president does not need to be a skilled manager because he can hire outstanding managerial talent. Even choosing compatible, responsible, and able subordinates demands administrative skill.

POLICY SKILLS

In our chief executive we expect a composite leader: the president as CEO and the president as politician. Yet even this demanding mix is insufficient without the crucial skill of policy judgment. The president must not only do "it" well but must determine what "it" is that needs to be done. He establishes the policy objectives for which his political and managerial talents are employed. He does not need to be expert in every program area—he has a large staff to assist in this—but he must choose wisely in the substance and politics of policy if his administration is to succeed.

We remember Franklin D. Roosevelt as a great president in large part because his New Deal policies were an effective response to national needs in the 1930s. Though some individual programs were flawed, the overall policy direction that FDR imposed looks good even in the 20/20 hindsight of history. This is what we hope for in the policies of every president—that when the immediate emotions, partisan and otherwise, are past, his approach will have addressed ably the country's pressing needs.

LEADERSHIP: THE WHOLE IS MORE THAN THE SUM OF ITS PARTS

In geometry the whole is precisely equal to the sum of its parts. In social experience, though, it is usually much more or much less. At its best, presidential leadership moves the nation as far as possible in the directions the public favors, by means that are acceptable given prevailing values and institutional requirements. While a successful synthesis is easily perceived, how to attain it through individual leadership is not readily understood or achieved. (See Box 7.2.)

Sometimes, even those close to a leader before he became president hadn't seen in him the special mix of qualities that were to come together under the demands and opportunities of the office to make his presidential leadership successful. The consensus today is that Frank-

Box 7.2
*One Political Scientist's Tongue-in-Cheek "Job Advertisement"
for a Modern-Day President*

Wanted—Chief Executive for Large, Troubled Public Enterprise

Must be dignified and capable of personifying the aspirations of all elements in a diverse and extremely heterogeneous organization. Must be a successful manager, capable of supervising several million employees, most of whom cannot be directly rewarded or punished. All employees except personal staff will also work for a rival employer. Must be skilled in diplomacy and have good knowledge of world affairs. Should be up on military matters as well. Must be capable of program development for entire enterprise. Job performance will be reviewed after four years, at which time applicant's record will be compared with the promises of numerous aspirants for his position. Applicant must be skilled in economics. A premium will be placed on ability to deal with complex fiscal, monetary, and regulatory matters. Should be good at maintaining alliances with other large public enterprises who do not always share common purposes. Applicant must have power drive but pleasant personality, a good sense of humor, and must be flexible and open to criticism. Must be trustworthy but shrewd. Must be a good speaker and skilled at press relations. Boundless energy is a must. . . . There is no certain deadline [for applicant], but early application is helpful, since the board will have to be convinced that the above qualifications are met.

Source: W. Wayne Shannon, "As If Politics Were About Government: Presidential Selection from a Governance Perspective," paper presented to the New England Political Science Association, March 1980.

lin D. Roosevelt wielded presidential power with unusual effectiveness, but many of FDR's friends and associates were frankly startled to find out just how good he was.

And what was it that made him good? This is how historian Arthur Schlesinger saw it, describing FDR's actions in the early days of his presidency, with the United States in the middle of the Great Depression. "Somehow Roosevelt kept all the reins in his hand," Schlesinger wrote. "He seemed to *thrive on*

crisis. . . . Roosevelt had moved into the White House as if he were repossessing a family estate. He now spoke for and to the nation with dignity and ease and evident enjoyment. . . . The combination of power and delight was irresistible to people . . . ; it gave Americans new confidence in themselves." Their results are easily seen, but such intangibles of successful leadership as Schlesinger describes are often *not detected in advance*. We know what works in a presidency when we see it work—the special link of a particular type of leadership with the special demands of a time.[9]

THE INSTITUTIONAL PRESIDENCY

"The president needs help." This was the conclusion of the Committee on Administrative Management, appointed by President Franklin Roosevelt in 1936. The scope of presidential responsibility had become such, the committee felt, that it was necessary to enlarge and formalize the president's staff support. Acting on the committee's recommendations, Roosevelt in 1939 established the Executive Office of the President (EOP). The key units in the EOP were the White House Office, comprising the president's immediate staff, and the Bureau of the Budget (now the Office of Management and Budget—OMB), the executive's agency for budget making and review created by Congress in 1921.

This was the beginning of the *institutional presidency*, built around an elaborate staff structure. The total of White House assistants to President Herbert Hoover had been just 26 in 1930, and annual expenditures for this staff were under $1 million. Even figuring in other executive branch help, such as the Bureau of the Budget, Hoover's assistants numbered under 100. Of course, it wasn't until 1857 that public funds were appropriated by Congress to pay even the salary of a private secretary to the president. The size of Herbert Hoover's staff still seems extremely modest against the backdrop of the vast increases of the past half-century. EOP personnel in the years immediately after FDR's 1939 executive order totaled

roughly 300; by the time of Dwight Eisenhower's presidency in the 1950s it had climbed to 600. In 1970, with Richard Nixon in the White House, EOP personnel had increased to some 2,000, when a leveling-out and then an actual reduction finally occurred. In the Bush administration, the EOP has roughly 1,800 employees.

THE WHITE HOUSE OFFICE

It's as true today as it was in 1937 that the president needs help. It's not at all clear, however, just how that help is best provided or what changes would be most useful. In the 1930s, more help meant more people. But the corps of advisers and assistants has become so large that more people are no longer the answer to how to provide the president with the help he needs. In fact, some experts believe that the White House staff should be reduced further.[10]

Organizing the White House staff. How well any group of staff members actually serve their executive is determined, of course, by the intelligence, experience, personal characteristics, and energy they bring to their jobs. But when staff size increases beyond a handful, organization comes into play. How his White House Office is organized to perform the tasks placed upon it helps determine the success any president enjoys.

Some presidents want to interact regularly with many different aides. They resist rigid hierarchy in their staff. Stephen Hess refers to this style of staff organization as "circular."[11] As practiced by Franklin Roosevelt, Lyndon Johnson, and Jimmy Carter, the circular mode

[9]Arthur Schlesinger, Jr., *The Coming of the New Deal* (Boston: Houghton Mifflin, 1959), pp. 15–16, 21–22. Emphasis added.

[10]*A Presidency for the 1980s*, a report by a panel of the National Academy of Public Administration (Washington, D.C.: National Academy of Public Administration, 1980), p. 17.
[11]Stephen Hess, *Organizing the Presidency* (Washington, D.C.: Brookings Institution, 1976), p. 3.

has a number of senior assistants reporting directly to the president. Other presidents, such as Dwight Eisenhower and Richard Nixon, have been comfortable with a more hierarchical arrangement that places larger coordinating and integrating responsibilities upon a chief of staff. H. R. Haldeman, Nixon's chief of staff until the Watergate scandal forced his resignation, was often criticized for using an authoritarian approach in running the White House and barring the door to the president. But two senior Nixon aides, speechwriter (now *New York Times* columnist) William Safire and national security adviser (later secretary of state) Henry Kissinger, have reported that Haldeman was only performing—quite ably—the role Nixon set for him. The president wanted time for solitary contemplation and he wanted to be shielded from staff intrusions.[12]

Demands on staff. There are some enduring demands on staff organization. Because presidential time is a scarce commodity, staff arrangements must be such that items needing the president's attention get it—in the best form for his action—while other items are carefully kept away. Staff must permit the president to work most efficiently, leave him accessible to officials who need to see him (and whom he needs to see) but not let him be overwhelmed by intrusions, bring him the questions he must decide but not every question he could decide. Then, when the president has chosen a course, an effective staff must help him sail it with as little expenditure of his time as possible.

Naturally, all this is easier said than done. For, while staff are supposed to serve the president's interests, they inevitably also have and serve their own. Every presidency suffers because key White House aides become absorbed in individual pursuits of power and recognition. "No conceivable staffing arrangements will meet all his needs," wrote presidential scholar Hugh Heclo, "and yet every arrangement carries the potential of submerging his interests into those of his helpers and their machinery."[13] The rarefied atmosphere of the White House poses problems for the proper functioning and, in a sense, mental health of the staff who dwell therein. The West Wing of the White House—where the Oval Office and facilities for senior presidential aides are located—is the physical center of the American political universe. Even an occasional visitor to the West Wing cannot fail to detect the air of restrained excitement. It's easy for staff to let this go to their heads or to succumb to the pressure-cooker atmosphere.

Power, especially the ultimate singularity of power, gives the White House its distinctive atmosphere and style. In Congress, formal constitutional authority always rests in many hands; in the White House, it rests in one pair of hands. George Reedy, who was a long-time aide to Lyndon Johnson, notes: "In the Senate no course stands the remotest chance of adoption unless a minimum of fifty-one egotistical men are persuaded of its wisdom. . . ." At the other end of Pennsylvania Avenue, a course carries the day when, and only when, it has the approval of one man. "The life of the White House," says Reedy, "is the life of a court."[14] There is, then, great pressure on staff members to behave like courtiers, to curry the favor of

[12]William Safire, *Before the Fall* (Garden City, N.Y.: Doubleday, 1975); Henry Kissinger, *The White House Years* (Boston: Little, Brown, 1979).

[13]Hugh Heclo, "The Changing Presidential Office," in Arnold J. Miltsner, ed., *Politics and the Oval Office* (San Francisco: Institute for Contemporary Studies, 1981), p. 163.

[14]George E. Reedy, *The Twilight of the Presidency* (New York: New American Library, 1970), pp. xi, 17–18.

the president as the source of whatever power staff members possess. Any aide known to have the president's support or approval is strong; any aide denied access or approbation is weak. In such a setting it takes unusual strength of character to tell a president he is wrong. Having staff mature enough and confident enough to do this is important for the well-being of the nation.

Staffing the Bush White House. George Bush was comfortable with the details of public policy. He delegated much less to his White House staff than did his predecessor, Ronald Reagan. Still, the presidency is so immense a job, with such far-flung responsibilities, that Bush, like any other president, depended heavily on his staff. In the early Bush White House, authority was concentrated in the hands of a strong chief of staff, John Sununu. A former engineering professor at Tufts University and governor of New Hampshire, Sununu won George Bush's confidence during the 1988 campaign.

As Sununu became familiar with the demands of his post, he became more involved in policy making. He worked closely with another key White House aide, budget director Richard Darman. The two established the practice of meeting at the start of every business day. The Washington political community learned that the Sununu-Darman axis was an important one. With the president plainly more interested in foreign affairs than in domestic policy—and at times, as after Iraq's invasion of Kuwait in August 1990, preoccupied with the international scene—his advisers were given more discretion on such domestic issues as the federal deficit.

Still, even a strong-willed chief of staff like John Sununu had no more authority than the president chose to give him. He wasn't deputy president, only the main deputy to the president. The intermittent press suggestions that Sununu was somehow shaping programs against

the president's intentions were just plain silly. There was ample indication that Bush was using Sununu as a lightening rod for unpopular decisions—often referred to as the "bad cop" role, as against the president's "good cop" pose. That is one of the roles of a chief of staff. But when the president's popularity slipped sharply in the fall of 1991, Sununu came increasingly under attack. Many of the enemies he made in his "bad cop" role naturally found it easier to lay blame at the chief of staff's doorstep when things weren't going well politically than when the president's standing was in the stratosphere. Apart from this, John Sununu made his own share of mistakes, some of which resulted from his short temper and prickly personality.

Demands for Sununu's ouster grew stronger, and he was forced to resign on December 3, 1991. For his replacement, Bush turned to Samuel V. Skinner, who had gotten high marks for his work in the administration as secretary of transportation. A good manager, and far less abrasive than John Sununu, Sam Skinner in many ways seemed a good choice. In other ways, however, some analysts argued that Skinner was too much like the president himself. Every chief executive has weaknesses. The job of the chief of staff is to help compensate for them. "A good manager," argues Morris Aderman, a professor of organizational psychology at the Illinois Institute of Technology, "brings in people who can compensate for his shortcomings." George Bush, ambivalent on domestic policy, needed a chief of staff with a sharper and more focused domestic vision.[15] Skinner lasted less than nine months before being replaced by Secretary of State and longtime Bush confidant, James Baker, for the stretch of the 1992 campaign.

---

[15] See Burt Solomon, "Send in the Clones," *National Journal,* March 21, 1992, pp. 678–83.

Staffing the Clinton White House. A new management team moved into the west wing of the White House in January 1993, as Democrat Bill Clinton assumed the presidency. The new president is strong on the details of policy, and he will be an aggressive, "hands-on" administrator. The kind of assistance the Clinton presidency may need most from its White House chief of staff and other key assistants may well involve providing a longer-term perspective to guide day-to-day decision making. In the special chapter on the 1992 election and the start of the new administration, found in the appendix to this text, Clinton's main staff appointments and organization are reviewed.

THE EXECUTIVE OFFICE OF THE PRESIDENT

The personal staff of the White House are the most visible part of the institutional presidency. They are, however, only one unit out of ten in a presidential staff structure—the Executive Office of the President (EOP)—that employs about 1,800 people and cost $190 million to operate in 1991. Figure 7.3 shows the various units of the EOP, when each was formally established, and the number of staff within it. All EOP agencies report directly to the president, and the top officers of each are appointed by him. But, unlike senior staff of the White House Office, the heads of a number of other EOP units must receive Senate confirmation—including the three members of the Council of Economic Advisers, the director of the Office of Management and Budget, and the special representative for trade negotiation. And, while the president has considerable discretion in reorganizing the EOP, many of its units outside the White House operate under the speci-

fications of statutes enacted by Congress. The Council of Economic Advisers, for example, functions under the terms of the Employment Act of 1946; and the National Security Council (NSC), under the National Security Act of 1947.

NATIONAL SECURITY COUNCIL

The National Security Council (NSC) has four statutory members: the president, the vice president, the secretary of state, and the secretary of defense. In addition, the director of the Central Intelligence Agency and the chairman of the Joint Chiefs of Staff are statutory advisers. NSC staff are under the direction of the assistant to the president for national security affairs. The role of the council and its staff was intended to be purely advisory—the president calling upon them as he saw fit to get the balanced information he needed in making foreign policy. The head of the National Security Council in the Bush administration, Brent Scowcroft, operated very much as the original legislation had intended—as a staff coordinator, not a policy maker.

OFFICE OF MANAGEMENT AND BUDGET

The OMB is the largest agency in the Executive Office of the President, successor to the Bureau of the Budget established in 1921. Its roughly 600 staff members help the president accomplish his political objectives in formulating and administering the budget, reviewing the organizational structure and management procedures of the entire executive branch, developing regulatory reform proposals, and assessing program objectives. When a president is trying to achieve major governmental change, he is likely to lean even more upon the staff resources of the OMB.

FIGURE 7.3　THE EXECUTIVE OFFICE OF THE PRESIDENT

Year in parenthesis represents date when office received formal statutory recognition. Omitted from staff figures are approximately 100 employees performing household management and similar tasks. Staff size figures are for 1991.

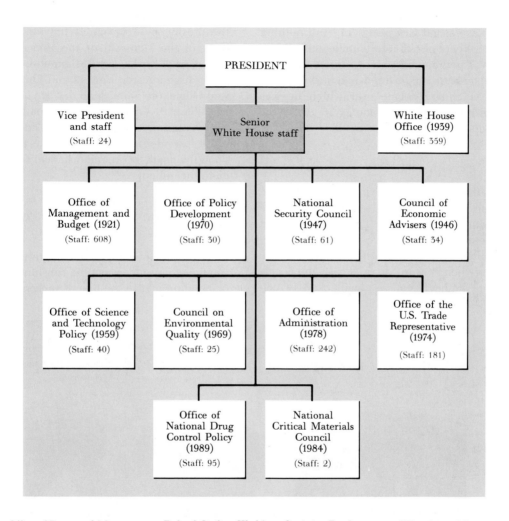

Source: Office of Personnel Management, *Federal Civilian Workforce Statistics, Employment and Trends as of January, 1992,* p. 35.

THE VICE PRESIDENT

It is doubtful that any political office in the United States has been the subject of as many jokes as the vice presidency. Benjamin Franklin did not like the idea of a vice presidency to begin with, and he suggested that the holder of the office should be addressed as "His Superfluous Majesty." In declining a vice-presidential nomination by the Whig party in the middle of the nineteenth century, Senator Daniel Webster of Massachusetts said that "he did not propose to be buried until he was already dead." Thomas Marshall, who served for eight years as Woodrow Wilson's vice president, gave us the classic vice-presidential joke: "Once there were two brothers. One ran away to sea; the other was elected vice president. And nothing was ever heard of either of them again." (Marshall was perhaps best known for his wit. He created another classic line when he whispered during a Senate debate over which he was presiding that "what the country really needs is a good five-cent cigar.")

SUCCESSION

It was the country's first vice president, John Adams, who provided the most perceptive summation of the office: "I am nothing, but I may be everything." A vice president's constitutional powers are feeble: he presides over the Senate (when he wants to) and casts the deciding vote if the Senate is deadlocked (which rarely happens); that is all. But he is, in the constitutional sense, "a heartbeat away from the presidency." Article II provides that "in Case of the Removal of the President from Office, or of his Death, Resignation, or Inability to discharge the Powers and Duties of the said Office, the Same shall devolve on the Vice President. . . ." Thirteen of the nation's forty presidents first served as vice presidents; nine of the presidents succeeded to the presidency upon the death or (in one instance) resignation of an incumbent.

ASSISTANT TO THE PRESIDENT

Since the vice president has no significant constitutional powers, except the constitutional role of standing first in the line of succession, he is

With President Kennedy's widow, Jacqueline, at his side, Vice President Lyndon B. Johnson is sworn in as president on November 22, 1963.

wholly dependent upon the president for his assignments. Historically such assignments have been extremely modest. No vice president through Alben Barkley (who served under Harry Truman from 1949 to 1953) was given major governmental or political responsibilities. The reasons for this are clear. Vice-presidential candidates have often been chosen for political and geographic balance on a ticket. As we saw, Lincoln picked Andrew Johnson of Tennessee as his running mate in 1864 because he wanted a pro-union southern Democrat to strengthen a broad unionist appeal. New York liberal Franklin Roosevelt wanted Texas conservative John Nance Garner for ticket balance in the 1932 presidential race. Thus chosen, vice presidents rarely became friends and confidants of their presidents, and they lost out to more trusted assistants in contests for the president's ear.

But over the last three decades the picture of vice-presidential weakness has substantially altered. Without any single dramatic development, a new consensus has taken form. The enormity of presidential responsibilities, together with the substantial possibility that a vice president will succeed to them, requires that individuals not be chosen as vice-presidential candidates unless they are presidential material. It follows that presidents should not toss their vice presidents into ceremonial oblivion, but should assign them real responsibilities so that they will be prepared to take on presidential duties if necessary. As presidents have begun to act on this strong, if informal, consensus, they have come to find that active, well-informed vice presidents are handy to have around.

The first notable departure occurred with Eisenhower and Nixon in the 1950s. The two men were not close, personally or politically; they were far apart in age and experience. Eisenhower had decidedly ambivalent feelings about his vice president and seriously considered dropping him from the ticket in both

President Eisenhower and Vice President Nixon being nominated for a second term during the 1956 Republican National Convention in San Francisco. Unlike previous vice presidents, a young Richard Nixon took on major responsibilities during his terms of office with Eisenhower.

1952 and 1956. Despite this, the president's strong inclination to delegate responsibility and his lack of interest in Republican party affairs led him to assign his vice president major political tasks. Nixon was also picked to represent the United States on highly visible and important foreign trips. Richard Nixon entered the vice presidency in 1953 as a quite junior Republican politician from California; he left in 1961 as the most prominent Republican (after the retiring Eisenhower) and a man who had come within a whisker of winning election in his own right against Democrat John F. Kennedy in November 1960. Kennedy's choice of Lyndon Johnson as his vice-presidential running mate in 1960, and Gerald Ford's designation of Nelson Rockefeller as vice president in 1974, were also important steps in the rise of the office. Johnson and Rockefeller were powerful, strong-willed figures. Their willingness to accept the vice presidency was symbolically important. Kennedy never really trusted Johnson politically, and Ford could not make the use of Rockefeller that he wanted to because Republican conservatives so disliked the former New York governor. But no office that held political forces like Lyndon Johnson and Nelson Rockefeller could really be described as "His Superfluous Majesty."

THE VICE PRESIDENCY TODAY

Jimmy Carter and Ronald Reagan completed an elevation of vice-presidential responsibilities. Both made their vice presidents—Walter Mondale and George Bush, respectively—close associates and confidants, movers in the inner circles of administration affairs, even though neither president–vice president team had been close prior to their election. Against this backdrop of modern experience and expectations, the vice presidency of Bush's choice for the office, Dan Quayle, elicited much commentary and criticism. Quayle was a young U.S. senator from Indiana when Bush picked him as his 1988 running mate.[16] Even his opponents conceded, though, that Quayle served the Bush administration ably over its four-year term.

For his 1992 running mate, Bill Clinton chose Albert Gore, Jr., of Tennessee. A U.S. Senator since 1984 and the son of a prominent senator, Al Gore, became part of the youngest presi-dent–vice president team in modern American politics. He had himself been a candidate for Democratic presidential nomination in 1988 and was considered a leading contender in 1992 before he decided against seeking that office. This is being written just as the 1992 election has ended, so his precise role in the Clinton administration is unknown as yet. But what has become the tradition in recent decades of vice presidents being active and visible members of their administrations seems certain to continue in Gore's term of office.

PRESIDENTIAL POWER

Richard Neustadt, a former presidential assistant, argues that the power of the presidency gets depicted too much in terms of formal authority and not enough in terms of persuasion.[17] A president is strong or weak, succeeds or fails in his governing tasks, on the basis of whether he can convince the many political groups and offices with whom he must deal "that what the White House wants of them is what they ought to do for their sake and on their authority." In part Neustadt is describing political life under separation of powers. A president's entire legislative program lies beyond his formal powers of command. He has resources to persuade Congress to enact his policies, but he has few means to force legislators to enact them. Democracy limits cases of command and stresses the need for consent. In the extreme case where the consent of the governed is lost totally, a president's constitutional powers of command become an empty shell. As we saw in the months just before the Watergate scandal forced his resignation, Richard Nixon retained the formal authority of the presidency but he was without the capacity to persuade. His most basic, practical power had slipped away.

---

[16] For a valuable study of Quayle's performance and abilities as U.S. senator, see Richard F. Fenno, Jr., *The Making of a Senator: Dan Quayle* (Washington, D.C.: Congressional Quarterly Press, 1989).

[17] Neustadt, *Presidential Power*, pp. 26–43.

President Kennedy at his inaugural ball, January 20, 1961.

The constitutional powers of command of an American president are not very great when placed against his diverse responsibilities and the nation's high expectations of his performance. If a president cannot secure broad approval for his initiatives among the public at large and the political leadership community—especially in Congress—his position is weak. Whenever the country has had effective presidential "rulership," James Young observes, it has received it "within a constitutional framework [that was] deliberately designed to make rulership difficult."[18] We saw in chapter 5 that critics of the separation of powers find the United States too dependent on having a president able to move by persuasion. They grant

that at those times when a politically adroit president enjoys high popularity, the system responds effectively. But too often the president's persuasive resources are insufficient to overcome the fragmentation inherent in the separation of powers.[19]

CHANGING VIEWS OF PRESIDENTIAL POWER

There is reason to be skeptical about such judgments. Any time political institutions manage to sustain strong popular support over a span of two hundred years, the presumption

[18] Young, *Washington Community*, p. 252.

[19] James L. Sundquist, *Constitutional Reform and Effective Government* (Washington, D.C.: Brookings Institution, 1986). See, too, Donald L. Robinson, ed., *Reforming American Government* (Boulder, Co.: Westview Press, 1986).

should be that they are doing something right, at least in the thinking of those governed by them. The American public has shown little dissatisfaction with the constitutional limits on the presidency. And there is no agreement among experts as to whether the United States has a problem with regard to presidential power and, if so, what it is. The presidency of John F. Kennedy in the beginning of the 1960s was hailed by many experts as "Camelot." The vigorous young executive had an office through which he could make good things happen. Arthur Schlesinger, Jr., noted in 1965 that Kennedy's presidency was based on the belief that "the Chief Executive . . . must be 'the vital

center of action in our whole scheme of government.' The nature of the office demanded that the President place himself in the very thick of the fight . . . [that he] be prepared to exercise the fullest powers of his office—all that are specified and some that are not."[20] The presidency was strong, and it was good that it was strong.

Following Kennedy's assassination, however, the activist president who was his successor used his office to lead the United States into a war that saw an American army of half a million men engaged in a small Asian country. The Vietnam War lasted twice as long as any previous military conflict in which the United States had been involved, it claimed more American lives than any conflict other than the Civil War and World War II, and it prompted massive dissent at home. Vietnam dominated Lyndon Johnson's administration and that of his successor, Richard Nixon. The Watergate scandal followed almost immediately upon Vietnam. Many of the same commentators who had proclaimed and endorsed a strong presidency now denounced the presidency as bloated in its powers, imperial in its bearing and style, and dangerously open to personal abuses of power. The presidency was strong—but there was trouble in its strength.[21]

Enter Jimmy Carter. He banished the ceremonial "Hail to the Chief" as the president's song and donned his cardigan for low-key chats with the public. In matters of far greater substance, especially the conduct of U.S. foreign policy, he wanted a more restricted role for the president and for the nation. Quickly, though, events such as the seizure of the U.S. embassy in Iran and the holding of its staff as hostages for fourteen months came to be seen as dra-

The Vietnam War—the burden of both President Johnson and President Nixon.

[20] Arthur M. Schlesinger, Jr., *A Thousand Days* (Boston: Houghton Mifflin, 1965), p. 120.

[21] Idem., *The Imperial Presidency* (New York: Popular Library, 1973), p. 359.

matic signs of the Carter administration's weakness and the decline of American power. The presidency was now weak—and it was bad that it was weak.

These oscillations must have had an impact on the people who saw them, even on presidents. Having seen the glorifications of a strong presidency, might not Lyndon Johnson and Richard Nixon have been encouraged to think that greater assertiveness on their part was really in the national interest? Having been warned repeatedly of the dangers of an "imperial" presidency, might not Jimmy Carter have drawn back more than he should and otherwise would have from the assertion of executive leadership? After Reagan succeeded Carter, however, the situation seemed almost immediately to change. The new administration won support, even in the Democratic-controlled House of Representatives, for substantial portions of its foreign, defense, and domestic programs. The new president seemed amply able to set the tone and direction for American national government. Indeed, discussion shifted to whether a Reagan revolution was altering basic governmental commitments developed over the preceding decades. In Reagan's second term there was talk of his becoming a "lame duck"—a president who could not again seek reelection and whose political clout was thus diminished. For the most part, though, the idea of a weak presidency found little currency in the Reagan years.

The presidency is an office of which much is expected in the American governmental system. It has fairly modest and much-checked formal powers, but great resources for political leadership by persuasion. Different presidents have employed the power of persuasion for contrasting ends, in constantly shifting political circumstances. There is as yet no consensus as to whether the president's powers and institutional position should be changed, much less as to a particular set of changes to be obtained.

ASSESSING PRESIDENTS

Presidents' reputations have undergone some startling changes. No president is all good or bad, of course; each reveals a mix of positive and negative attributes. At any given time, one facet of a president's performance is emphasized; later it may be a quite different facet. Assessments of Herbert Hoover, the country's thirtieth president, reflect this pattern of sharp interpretive shifts over time. Until the Great

Candidate Herbert Hoover campaigning for the presidency, New Jersey, 1928. Hoover's burden began less than a year after his inauguration as president with the stock market crash—the start of the Great Depression.

Depression, Hoover was widely considered a humanitarian, an outstanding organizer and doer, and a progressive Republican. His work in organizing relief to avert starvation in Belgium after World War I earned him international acclaim on both organizational and humanitarian grounds. The election of 1928 was not, at the time, viewed as a contest between a Republican conservative (Hoover) and a Democratic liberal (New York Governor Alfred E. Smith), but rather as one between two moderate progressives; many observers thought Hoover's credentials as a progressive were better than Smith's.

Then came the economic disaster brought on by the Great Depression and President Hoover's responses to it. A new picture of Hoover emerged: of a very conservative, insensitive man who was a failure at managing the great economic crisis. Over the last fifteen to twenty years, however, the picture has again changed. Students of Hoover's presidency have adopted a far more complimentary view of his political commitments and performance. One study published in 1975 declares Hoover to be a "forgotten progressive." "There is a good deal of talk today about a 'new' Hoover. Disparate political groups ranging from the far right to the far left think they are rediscovering him, because his progressive philosophy contained ideas whose time has finally arrived."[22]

Both the positive and the negative judgments of Hoover were correct in part. He was a progressive man of great managerial talent. His administration's response to the Great Depression was by no means only short-sighted and conservative. But Hoover did find it hard to recognize the immense impact of the Depression on the thinking of his fellow citizens, and his response to criticism was to "hunker down" and to emphasize less humanitarian aspects of his political approach. Not surprisingly, as Joan

Hoff Wilson points out, the prevailing judgment during the Depression and its immediate aftermath filtered out the positive dimensions of Hoover's work, while interpretations since the 1960s have seen it through a different, less critical filter.

Dwight Eisenhower's presidency has also prompted striking shifts of interpretation. General Eisenhower came to the presidency a hero of the American effort in World War II. As president, however, his lack of a bold domestic policy and his view that the presidency was to be used sparingly rather than vigorously invited criticism, especially from those who expected the president to be a doer of great deeds along the model of Franklin Roosevelt, in his New Deal and World War II leadership. But recently, Eisenhower's strengths are again being emphasized in something of an "Eisenhower revival." His refusal to be pushed into military action in Vietnam appears far more commendable after the sad experience of that war.[23] His modest judgments on the possibilities of governmental action appear sounder after a long spell of governmental activism than they did before. That Eisenhower had a coherent sense of leadership—which, while very different from FDR's, is impressive in its own right—has come to be better appreciated by leading students of his presidency:

> On reexamination, Eisenhower's approach to presidential leadership emerges as distinctive and consciously thought-out, rather than an unfortunate example of airless drift. . . . When carefully explicated, this approach promises to add significantly to the repertoire of assumptions about how the expanded modern presidency can be conducted.[24]

[22] Joan Hoff Wilson, *Herbert Hoover: Forgotten Progressive* (Boston: Little, Brown, 1975), p. 269.

[23] See Louis W. Koenig, *The Chief Executive*, 4th ed. (New York: Harcourt Brace, 1981), p. 349.

[24] Fred I. Greenstein, "Eisenhower as an Activist President: A Look at New Evidence," *Political Science Quarterly* (Winter 1979–80), p. 596; idem., *The Hidden-Hand Presidency: Eisenhower as Leader* (New York: Basic Books, 1982).

General Eisenhower in England with his men on D-Day, June 9, 1944, prior to their massive invasion into continental Europe. Their mission, to push back the Nazi German forces, led to the end of World War II.

Even Richard Nixon's presidency is already being reinterpreted. When he was forced to resign his office in disgrace, on August 9, 1974, following the Watergate scandal, it seemed unlikely that Nixon would soon see any substantial political rehabilitation. But by the mid-1980s, just such was occurring. *Newsweek* exemplified the changing view of the press, when in a cover story on the former president in 1986, it observed that "the premise of his rehabilitation is that—Watergate aside—Nixon left a legacy of solid achievement, especially in foreign affairs."[25] When the Nixon Library was dedicated in July 1990, the *New York Times*'s R. W. Apple, Jr., characterized the event as "a high point in a long, slow process of political rehabilitation."[26]

All this is a good reminder that it is especially hard to determine how a president's performance will be judged after time has passed and the passions he stirred while in the Oval Office have cooled. We need more time to get history's verdict on Ronald Reagan, George Bush, and, of course, Bill Clinton, whose presidency is just taking shape.

THE PUBLIC'S RATINGS

Americans are not reluctant to criticize presidents for inadequate performance in office, but

[25] "The Road Back," *Newsweek* (May 19, 1986), p. 27.

[26] R. W. Apple, Jr., "Another Nixon Summit, at his Library," *New York Times*, July 20, 1990, p. 1.

How will historians assess the five living presidents who gathered for the dedication of the Ronald Wilson Reagan Presidential Library in November 1991?

at the same time they recognize that the job has been extremely demanding. By large margins, the public thinks that Congress has become more difficult to deal with, that the communications media are more critical of presidents than they used to be, that the problems presidents are expected to solve have become increasingly complicated, and that the public itself may now be too demanding (see Figure 7.4). People want their presidents to set high standards, but they do not expect them to be persons without faults or immune to the problems that affect others.

Americans are sophisticated critics of their presidents. Louis Harris and Associates conducted a poll in 1988 in which people were queried: "I'd like to ask you about the last nine presidents of the United States. Please keep in mind Roosevelt, Truman, Eisenhower, Kennedy, Johnson, Nixon, Ford, Carter, and Rea-

gan. If you had to choose one, which president do you think . . . was best on domestic affairs?" Respondents were then asked to rate presidents in this and other areas. They answered that Roosevelt and Kennedy were best on domestic matters, Nixon and Reagan best on foreign affairs; that Kennedy most inspired confidence; that Nixon set the lowest moral standards; and that Carter was least able to get things done (Table 7.1). The survey shows a public that makes complex judgments about presidents, rather than assigning them to two bins labeled "good" and "bad."

PRESIDENTIAL CHARACTER

Not only do conclusions about the merits of a particular presidency change over time; so do judgments about what we should look for in a

FIGURE 7.4   PUBLIC SEES A TOUGH JOB GETTING TOUGHER

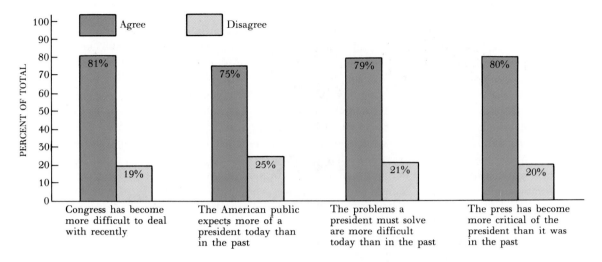

Source: "Attitudes Toward the Presidency," a survey conducted in December 1979 by the Gallup Organization for the Corporation for Public Broadcasting. Respondents were asked whether they agreed or disagreed with a series of statements (above) about the presidency.

prospective president. In the 1930s, 1940s, and 1950s, little emphasis was placed on the requisite personality traits of a potential president. If pressed, one would have conceded that certain types of personalities were better suited to the office, more likely to give the country the performance it wanted. But personality did not seem a critical factor. Neither Roosevelt, Truman, nor Eisenhower—the three men who occupied the presidency between 1933 and 1961—made us anxious by apparent deficiencies in their personalities.

TABLE 7.1   AMERICANS RATE THEIR PRESIDENTS (IN PERCENT)

	FDR	HST	DDE	JFK	LBJ	RMN	GRF	JEC	RWR
Best on domestic affairs	22	6	4	24	6	3	2	7	17
Best in foreign affairs	8	4	5	16	1	26	2	4	23
Least able to get things done	1	2	3	2	6	13	15	46	6
Most inspired confidence	19	7	7	34	1	2	1	2	21
Set the lowest moral standards	1	2	1	9	6	48	2	13	8
Likely to be viewed by history as best over all	27	11	5	28	1	2	1	1	17

Question: "I'd like to ask you about the last nine presidents of the United States. Please keep in mind Roosevelt, Truman, Eisenhower, Kennedy, Johnson, Nixon, Ford, Carter, and Reagan. If you had to choose one, which president do you think [read each item] . . . was best on domestic affairs . . . was best in foreign affairs . . . was least able to get things done . . . most inspired confidence in the White House. . . ." Sample size was 1,252.

Source: Survey by Louis Harris and Associates, November 11–24, 1988.

In succession during the 1960s and early 1970s, however, the United States had two presidents whose personalities raised concern among many people. Lyndon Johnson and Richard Nixon seemed too driven, too aggressive, too inclined to view as hostile the political world with which they had to deal. Personality emerged as a more important variable than it had been for assessing potential presidents. Political scientist James David Barber gave more systematic emphasis to these general concerns. Barber described Johnson and Nixon as "active-negative" personality types. The active-negative "seems ambitious, striving upward, power-seeking. His stance toward the environment is aggressive and he has a persistent problem in managing his aggressive feelings. . . . Life is a hard struggle to achieve and hold power, hampered by the condemnations of a perfectionist conscience."[27] Barber argued that "active-negatives" can be identified before they get to the presidency and that it is important to do so because their presidencies are likely to be deeply troubling for the nation. Others are less confident that we know enough to practice political psychology successfully, except in extreme cases.

SUMMARY

The framers had contrasting objectives in mind when they designed the presidency. They wanted to end the extreme executive weakness that distinguished the government under the Articles of Confederation. But they also wanted the president so checked and balanced that he could not rule arbitrarily.

As the contemporary presidency attests, they succeeded to a large degree in these pursuits.

[27]James David Barber, *The Presidential Character: Predicting Performance in the White House*, 3rd ed. (Englewood Cliffs, N.J.: Prentice-Hall, 1985), p. 9.

The singularity of the office—the Constitution vests "the executive power of the United States" in one individual, the president—adds greatly to its visibility and persuasive force. But the president remains subject to great constitutional restraints, the most basic one being separation of powers: Every law the executive administers, every dollar it spends, requires the action of a separate and very independent branch of government, the Congress.

Many different types of responsibilities have been put on American presidents by the Constitution and modern political necessity. The president is at once party leader and ceremonial chief of state, manager of domestic prosperity and leader of the Western alliance, administrator in chief, commander in chief, and legislator in chief. Sometimes his plate seems to get a little too full. To accomplish all the different things expected of him, a president would have to possess a truly amazing collection of skills. He would have to be a great communicator and campaigner, an adroit politician among politicians, a consummate administrator, a great conceptualizer of policy—and, comprising all these and more, a great democratic leader. Perhaps it isn't too surprising that we don't always get everything in one individual

Of course, the president gets a lot of help. Formalized in 1939, the Executive Office of the President (EOP) is composed of a series of staff agencies. At the center is the White House Office, consisting of senior presidential assistants and other staff. The Office of Management and Budget and the National Security Council are two other pivotal units of the EOP.

No one argues that presidential staffs suffer from any lack of numbers. But getting them to function coherently and efficiently on behalf of presidential objectives is always hard. Often derided in the past as mere standby equipment, the vice presidency seems to have emerged as the source of high-level presidential assistance.

Some observers worry that the formal powers and institutional resources of the presidency are insufficient, when set against the demands placed on the office. Policy stalemate or incoherence, resulting from the executive-legislative separation, is the greatest concern. But over the last quarter-century, assessments of presidential power have undergone great fluctuations, under changing political circumstances and types of presidential leadership. There is now nothing approaching general agreement on any type of institutional change.

Assessments of presidents, by experts and the public, have undergone quite striking shifts over time. Performance that looks deficient by standards elevated by the experience of one generation, often looks better against the backdrop of another generation's problems. The things we worry about or look for most in potential presidents also change, although a president's personality or character is an enduring concern.

FOR FURTHER STUDY

Barber, James David. *The Presidential Character: Predicting Performance in the White House*, 3rd ed. Englewood Cliffs, N.J.: Prentice-Hall, 1985. An analysis of presidential behavior based on an effort to categorize key features of presidents' personalities.

Corwin, Edward S. *The President: Office and Powers, History and Analysis of Practice and Opinion*. New York: New York University Press, 1940. This work—which also appears in a fifth edition by Bland, Randall W., et al., eds. *The President: Office and Powers, 1787–1984*. New York: New York University Press, 1984—is a comprehensive description of the presidency by one of its leading students.

Cronin, Thomas E. *The State of the Presidency*, 2nd ed. Boston: Little, Brown, 1980. A text that provides an especially comprehensive and balanced account of the office.

Neustadt, Richard E. *Presidential Power: The Politics of Leadership from FDR to Carter*. New York: John Wiley, 1980; first published, 1960. One of the most insightful accounts ever written of the nature of presidential power, the limitations on it, and the resources available for its exercise.

Rockman, Bert A. *The Leadership Question: The Presidency and the American System*. New York: Praeger, 1984. A thoughtful, contemporary discussion of the position of the president in the American governing system.

Rossiter, Clinton. *The American Presidency*, 2nd rev. ed. New York: New American Library, 1960; first published, 1956. A short, highly readable description of the American presidency, including a discussion of the many different roles the president is required to perform and the various skills needed for these.

OPTIONAL COMPUTER EXERCISES

for *The Ladd Election ANALYZER*

VOTERS' PERCEPTIONS OF THE ECONOMY AND THE PRESIDENTIAL VOTE

We noted in this chapter (p. 175) that economic concerns appeared to have contributed significantly to George Bush's defeat in the 1992 election. Looking at the category "Condition of nation's economy" on the "Policy views" menu, how did voters perceive the national economy overall? How did Bush voters compare to Clinton or Perot voters in their perceptions of the economy?

A few advanced analyses. How did people identifying themselves as Democrats, who said the condition of the economy was good to excellent, vote in the 1992 presidential race? How did people identifying themselves as Republicans, who said the economy was not doing very well or was doing badly, vote? Go to the "Vote questions" menu and select "Usual party affiliation" to identify Republicans and Democrats.

Chapter 8

THE EXECUTIVE BRANCH

The executive branch of the federal government includes the president, his key aides and cabinet officials—and *more than 3 million* other civilian employees. The total is itself enough to remind us that the administration of modern government has become a huge undertaking, a far cry from what it was two centuries ago. In 1790 the entire federal executive establishment encompassed about 2,000 people, and most of them operated post offices. The federal government is far and away the country's largest employer. Not only does it have to struggle to manage federal programs and policies; it confronts major problems in managing itself.

Every four years Americans elect a president who is vested constitutionally with "the executive Power . . . of the United States of America." Yet if this grant seems unambiguous, the president's relationships with the many departments and agencies that comprise the executive branch—and in particular the extent of his authority over them—are in fact varied and complex. Later in this chapter we look specifically at the different units that make up the federal executive and how they are organized. At the outset, though, we need to get a sense of the extent to which the separation of powers shapes the management and control of the various executive-branch agencies.

The scope of the executive branch's activity is enormous. It ranges from NASA's space explorations to the Department of Agriculture's pesticide battle against the timber-destroying Asian gypsy moth, to the administration of federal emergency funds for Chicago after its 1992 flood (the cause humorously depicted by cartoonist Gary Larson).

Doug Wilson / NYT Pictures

THE FAR SIDE   By GARY LARSON

In a tunnel under the Chicago River, a descendent of Mrs. O'Leary's cow follows her calling.

CONTROLLING THE EXECUTIVE BRANCH

Both president and Congress want to increase their own control over the vast executive-branch machinery—and both have ample constitutional powers and political resources to see that their claims are not ignored. For his part, the president uses his **appointment power** to put in place a team of political executives—including the secretaries who head each executive department (State, Defense, Health and Human Services, Transportation, Education, etc.) and their principal assistants. He also draws on the broad constitutional grant noted above, which vests in him the executive power, to issue **executive orders** and other directives bearing on agency operations. For its part, Congress employs its immense **legislative power** to enact statutes dealing with how executive agencies operate and what programs they administer. It draws on its **appropriations power** to determine how much money each agency has to spend—a source of broad political influence over agency actions, as well as direct budgetary control. In appropriations and all other legislative actions, of course, Congress's formal authority is limited by the president's **veto power,** but it is still vast.

The constitutional power struggle between president and Congress over control of the federal bureaucracy goes on in many areas. One area of intense controversy over the last decade involves control over the form and content of regulations issued by executive departments and agencies. A starting point for this battle was a 1980 statute, the Paperwork Reduction Act, the main objective of which was something everyone applauded: cutting by 25 percent the paperwork and reporting burdens imposed by the federal government on businesses and individual citizens.

To implement the 1980 law, the Office of Information and Regulatory Affairs (OIRA) was set up within the Office of Management and Budget (OMB), which is part of the Executive Office of the President, described in chapter 7, 194. OIRA's job was to review requests for information made by federal agencies and to make sure that the information was really necessary, that it could not be found elsewhere, and that it was collected efficiently. OIRA decided that paperwork includes tests, measurements, and inspections, labeling and disclosure requirements, questionnaires and census forms, applications and tax forms.

The Reagan and Bush administrations used this mechanism for reviewing and limiting government-required paperwork to reduce the scope of federal regulations generally. As Republican Congressman Frank Horton of New York, an administration supporter who helped draft the 1980 law, put it, this was appropriate because "regulations are paperwork."[1] But many congressional Democrats disagreed. They saw the administration's actions as an effort to assert more direction over the sprawling executive branch at Congress's expense and in particular as a means of curbing federal regulations that Congress wanted but Reagan opposed. Both sides were right, of course; they simply had opposing objectives. Under separation of powers, with the GOP holding the presidency and the Democrats strong in Congress, an ongoing battle was unavoidable.

Reagan further asserted the goal of deregulation and used OMB as the vehicle for achieving it by issuing two executive orders. One, in February 1981, required federal agencies to submit both proposals and final regulations to

---

[1] Quoted in Kitty Dumas, "Congress or the White House: Who Controls the Agencies?" *Congressional Quarterly*, April 14, 1990, p. 1130.

FIGURE 8.1 CONTROLLING FEDERAL AGENCY REGULATIONS: THE CENTRAL ROLE OF OMB

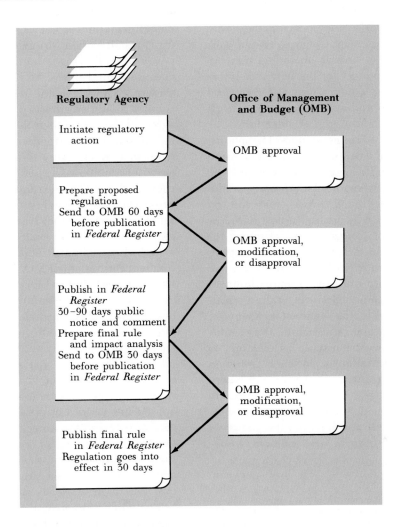

Source: *Congressional Quarterly*, April 14, 1990, p. 1133.

OMB for review—and possible modification or rejection. When George Bush came to the presidency in 1989, he left the OMB review procedures—shown in Figure 8.1—in place. In its first three years, however, the Bush administration pushed much less for deregulation, and in fact in two key areas—involving people with disabilities and environmental protection—it backed legislation that significantly expanded the federal regulatory reach. Only in 1992, under criticism from business and conservatives that regulation was curbing economic growth, did Bush give deregulation renewed emphasis.

The other executive order in January 1985 gave OMB the authority to review an agency's goals and policies as they bear on the entire regulatory environment. Congress fought back with a number of actions, including denying Reagan's 1987 budget for the Office of Information and Regulatory Affairs. On several occasions, compromises have been struck between OMB and congressional leaders.

A number of congressional Democrats, including House Energy Committee chairman John Dingell of Michigan, insisted that the executive orders were unconstitutional—on the grounds they constituted "quasi-legislating" by the president.[2] Not surprisingly, most Republicans disagreed. Congressman Horton, for example, maintained that the Constitution gives the president authority to control executive agencies through executive orders. Political scientist James Sundquist, who chaired a special panel set up by the National Academy of Public Administration to examine the regulatory process, sees the dispute as endemic to modern-day separation of powers. "Congress hasn't arrived at any understanding of where their authority leaves off and OMB's authority begins," he argued. "The thing that complicates the matter so much is that the Congress and executive branch are political opponents"—that is, controlled by opposite parties.[3]

ONGOING CONFLICT WITHIN
THE EXECUTIVE BRANCH:
THE JACK KEMP CASE STUDY

The American system of separation of powers makes it inevitable that conflict will continue between the president and Congress over the direction of executive-branch agencies. But conflict doesn't stop here. In every administra-tion, members of the president's own political and executive family—the heads of the various departments and agencies, and key administration staff—often struggle over policy and power as well. This is hardly surprising. Just because administrative staff share loyalty to the same party and general ideas about how the country should be governed doesn't mean they agree all the time. Often they are at odds over the administration's approach to national problems. In addition, every administration is composed of ambitious women and men with big egos, and personalities and styles that clash. Presidents can't avoid such political family squabbles; how well they handle them is another important test of their leadership.

In the Bush administration, some of the most frequent clashes pitted Jack Kemp, secretary of Housing and Urban Development (HUD), against various other staff members, including budget director Richard Darman. These splits often involved straightforward policy differences. Kemp is a conservative who yields to no one in his insistence that government should be scaled down. But he is also an activist who wants to see implemented creative new approaches to solving public problems in the area of race and the inner cities. This led him to advocate spending for social problems other than those favored by the administration. In addition, he disagreed strongly with Darman over how high a priority should be placed on bringing down the federal deficit. Kemp advocated help for the inner cities, even though such a policy would likely add to the deficit. Darman supported quite the opposite, putting a higher priority on curbing the deficit.

There were also personality clashes. Kemp is a high-profile, high-energy politician. He was clearly too "rah-rah" for some Bush aides and, probably, for the president himself. As a result, Kemp often found himself going before the Democratic Congress with less than full backing from his own administration. Still, he

[2] Ibid., p. 1135.
[3] Ibid.

achieved some important successes. Long a strong advocate of programs to help tenants of public housing become homeowners, he struck a deal with Congress that led to its passing his HOPE plan—Homeownership and Opportunity for People Everywhere—as part of the 1990 Housing Act. That legislation marked the first enactment in more than a decade of new and redesigned programs to expand low-income housing.

In the wake of the violence in Los Angeles following the May 1992 acquittal of the police charged in the Rodney King beating, Jack Kemp suddenly found his political position within the administration greatly strengthened. Most Americans were appalled by the destruction and the unresolved problems underlying the Los Angeles rioting. They hadn't been paying much attention, perhaps, but now they were. Politically, the president needed a vigorous urban program. Kemp's was the only one around in the administration. So on May 8, 1992, Bush declared that he'd push aggressively for an emergency program to help the inner-city poor. And he sided with Kemp against other of his advisors. "Look," he told his aides privately, "Jack Kemp is saying the right things. He understands what we need to be doing."[4] Almost at once, reporter Fred Barnes observed, "The Kemp-bashing [within the administration] stopped. When Bush announced on May 12 his six emergency 'initiatives for strengthening urban areas,' three (enterprise zones, welfare reform, tenant ownership of public housing) were straight from Kemp's playbook."[5]

As the vicissitudes faced by HUD secretary Jack Kemp attest, some of the most important policy battles go on not just between the parties, but among the political officials of a single administration as well.

[4] As quoted by Fred Barnes, "UnKempt," *The New Republic*, June 1, 1992, p. 11
[5] Ibid.

FORMAL EXECUTIVE AUTHORITY

Many of the key administrative units of the executive branch are supposed, of course, to respond in substantial measure to the direction of the president. This is certainly true of departments such as State and Defense. Since carrying out American foreign policy and seeing to the national defense are major undertakings, the departments established to attend to these matters have had to grow to be able to meet their diverse responsibilities. Although reductions are coming, with about 1.1 million civilian employees and more than 2 million men and women on active duty in 1992, Defense was easily the largest department in the executive branch. Still, even State, a very small executive department, employs over 26,000. To suggest that departments such as these, with their layers of policy-making units and staffs, simply respond to what the president wants done would be silly. Still, a determined president has the means of seeing that, in the broad outlines of policy, State and Defense do his bidding.

The president alone decides who will be the chief executive of each department. His choices for secretary of state and secretary of defense require Senate approval, but in the American constitutional tradition the Senate grants the president very wide latitude to pick the people he wants in such posts. If the president is dissatisfied with any aspect of a secretary's performance, he can remove him. Individuals appointed to these high-ranking positions are often strong willed, with ideas of their own about what policies are required. And they often have their own bases of support such that a president must expend some scarce political capital if he chooses to dismiss them before they want to go. Nonetheless, they recognize the president's constitutional and political primacy in the fields of foreign and defense policy. They are his agents.

Other agencies in the executive branch were established with different notions of their proper responsiveness to presidential direction. Sometimes it has been deemed desirable for an executive agency to be insulated from political pressures, in which case the agency would need to be constituted in such a way as to remove it from a president's control. Just such an agency is the Federal Reserve, the central bank of the United States and an executive-branch organization that has enormous responsibilities in the area of U.S. monetary policy. (The Federal Reserve is described in detail in chapter 15.)

At the apex of the Federal Reserve system is its Board of Governors. The seven governors are appointed by the president and must be confirmed by the Senate, but to insulate them from political pressure they are appointed for unusually long terms of fourteen years. Terms of board members are also arranged so that one expires every two years, making it harder for a president to appoint a majority. The idea is that management of the country's money supply shouldn't reside with an official who might be tempted to manipulate it to help his party win in the next election to the long-run detriment of the country. As we will see in chapter 15, the Federal Reserve needs the president's support for its monetary policies to be successful; the president in turn needs the Fed's cooperation if his economic programs are to be properly advanced. The two have strong incentives to work together. But the president does not control the Fed and its policies in the way he determines U.S. foreign policy. The Fed's chairman and the other six governors know that they have been appointed to an agency designed to operate independently of the president and regular political pressures—and often, though not always, they act accordingly.

EVOLUTION OF THE EXECUTIVE BRANCH

For all the present scale of the executive branch of the national government, the constitutional foundations for it are modest. Article II states that the president "shall nominate, and by and with the Advice and Consent of the Senate, shall appoint Ambassadors, other public Ministers and Consuls, Judges of the Supreme Court, and all other officers of the United States, whose Appointments . . . shall be established by Law. . . ." It further stipulates that Congress may "vest the Appointment of such inferior Officers, as they think proper, in the President alone . . . or in the Heads of Departments." Every federal department and agency has come into existence through simple legislation enacted by Congress, and each may be reorganized or eliminated at any time in the same way.

When the first Congress convened in 1789, its members agreed that several executive departments should be established and that each should be headed by a single official—appointed, as the Constitution required, by the president with the Senate's advice and consent. The departments of State, Treasury, and War (the latter renamed and reorganized in 1947 as the Department of Defense) were set up in 1789, as was the office of Attorney General (now the Justice Department). The Post Office Department was also created in 1789, but its present-day successor, the U.S. Postal Service, is no longer a department of cabinet rank.

Only four of the present fourteen executive-branch departments—State, Treasury, Defense, and Justice—trace their lineage all the way back to George Washington's presidency. Four others—Interior, Agriculture, Labor, and Commerce—were established in the late nineteenth and early twentieth centuries. The remaining six have been established since 1950: Health,

Education, and Welfare (HEW) in 1953; Housing and Urban Development (HUD) in 1965; Transportation in 1966; Energy in 1977; Education in 1979; and Veterans Affairs in 1989.

EARLY EXECUTIVE-BRANCH ACTIVITY

The earliest executive offices were restricted to the minimum number of areas—finance, foreign policy, defense, postal service, and law. They also had very limited duties and needed few employees. For example, the State Department at the outset had only nine staff members besides the secretary! A quarter-century after the Constitution was ratified, federal employees numbered just over 4,800. Of these, only 500 or so worked in Washington; most were scattered in towns around the country providing the one service that required many workers—delivering the mail. By 1816 there were over 3,200 U.S. post offices; as the country grew, so did the number of post offices, reaching about 30,000 in 1871. Total federal employment climbed gradually from about 4,800 in 1816 to 51,000 in 1871, and most of this growth was accounted for by the postal service (Table 8.1).

In our own time the largest executive department—indeed, the largest single employer in the country—is the Department of Defense (DOD). DOD employed well over three million Americans in 1992. Compared to this, the American armed services were tiny throughout most of the country's history. Total military personnel numbered just 7,000 in 1801, 21,000 in 1840, 28,000 on the eve of the Civil War, and 42,000 in 1871 (when postwar demobilization had been completed).[6]

---

[6] Students interested in more detailed information on the size of the national government and of the military branches, over the country's history are referred to two publications of

TABLE 8.1 CIVILIAN EMPLOYEES OF THE FEDERAL GOVERNMENT, 1816–1991

Year	Total number of employees	Number employed in the Washington, D.C. area
1816	4,837	535
1821	6,914	603
1831	11,491	666
1841	18,038	1,014
1851	26,274	1,533
1861	36,672	2,199
1871	51,020	6,222
1881	100,020	13,124
1891	157,442	20,834
1901	239,476	28,044
1911	395,905	39,782
1921	561,142	82,416
1931	609,746	76,303
1941	1,437,682	190,588
1951	2,482,666	265,980
1961	2,435,804	246,266
1971	2,874,166	322,969
1981	2,858,742	350,516
1991	3,108,899	374,187

Source: United States Bureau of the Census, *Historical Statistics of the United States, Colonial Times to 1970,* Part 2; pp. 1102–03; U.S. Office of Personnel Management, *Federal Civilian Workforce Statistics: Employment and Trends as of July 1989;* idem, *Employment and Trends as of January 1992.*

GOVERNMENT AS A PROMOTER OF INTERESTS

After the Civil War new federal agencies and programs were established with the intent of promoting the special interests of various segments of the population. Lawrence Dodd and Richard Schott have noted that

---

the U.S. Bureau of the Census: *Historical Statistics of the United States: Colonial Times to 1970,* bicentennial ed., 2 vols. (Washington, D.C.: Government Printing Office, 1975); and *Statistical Abstract of the United States,* published annually by the Government Printing Office. The growth of the American armed services each year from 1789 to 1970 is shown on pages 1141–43, part 2, of *Historical Statistics.*

whereas the original departments had been built around specific federal functions—the War Department for national defense, State for the conduct of foreign relations, and so on—the latter half of the nineteenth century witnessed the creation of certain offices, bureaus, and departments of the federal government around group interests. Farming, the largest occupation in its day, secured recognition with the establishment of a Department of Agriculture that gained full cabinet status in 1889. Education interests got a foothold with the creation of a Bureau of Education (1869) in the Interior Department, forerunner of the Office of Education. The emergence of organized labor, whose ranks were swelled by the industrial revolution, led to the creation of the Department of Labor in 1888. Not far behind were small business and commercial interests that helped secure the establishment of a Department of Commerce in 1903 (actually a joint Department of Commerce and Labor until 1913).[7]

These clientele-oriented departments for the most part were originally intended not to subsidize or regulate but to promote—for example, by collecting and disseminating relevant statistical information and supporting research.

One of the new agencies was, however, a major provider of cash benefits. After the Civil War, the leading veterans' organization, the Grand Army of the Republic (GAR), was fabulously successful in persuading Congress to establish and then liberalize veterans' pensions; the Pension Office (within the Department of the Interior) administered these benefits. In 1891 the Commissioner of Pensions could claim that his was "the largest executive bureau in the world." It had over 6,000 staff members, supplemented by thousands of local physicians paid on a fee basis. Over 40 percent of the entire national government budget in the early 1890s was devoted to veterans' pensions and

other benefits. Political scientist James Q. Wilson notes that in the Pension Office

> the pattern of bureaucratic clientelism was set in a way later to become a familiar feature of the governmental landscape—a subsidy was initially provided . . . to a group that was powerfully benefited and had fewer disorganized opponents; the beneficiaries were organized to supervise the administration and ensure the funding of the program; the law authorizing the program, first passed because it seemed the right thing to do, was left intact or even expanded because politically it became the only thing to do.[8]

GOVERNMENTAL REGULATION

Another important group of federal agencies and commissions involved in economic regulation began to evolve in the late nineteenth century, many of them outside the major cabinet-level departments. While the United States has had less governmental ownership of economic enterprises than most other democratic countries and has attempted less central economic planning, it has extended governmental regulation of the economy further than most democracies. The government tries to realize various public objectives in the economic arena by regulating what private businesses do.

The first major federal regulatory commission was the Interstate Commerce Commission (ICC), set up under the Interstate Commerce Act of 1887. The ICC was given responsibility for regulating carriers—initially railroads and shipping lines—that transported products crosscountry. Other important regulatory legislation followed: the Sherman Anti-Trust Act (1890), the Food and Drug Act (1906), the Federal Trade Commission Act (1914), and the Clay-

---

[7]Lawrence C. Dodd and Richard L. Schott, *Congress and the Administrative State* (New York: Wiley, 1979), p. 27.

[8]James Q. Wilson, "The Rise of the Bureaucratic State," in Francis E. Rourke, ed., *Bureaucratic Power in National Politics*, 3rd ed. (Boston: Little, Brown, 1978), p. 64.

ton Act (1914) which, like the Sherman Act before it, was an antitrust law. There was another burst of regulatory legislation in the 1930s, which included the Communications Act (1934), the Securities Exchange Act (1934), the National Labor Relations Act (1935), and the Civil Aeronautics Act (1938). The latest round came in the late 1960s and early 1970s with passage of consumer protection and environmental legislation, including the Truth-in-Lending Act (1968), the Clean Air Act (1970), and the Clean Water Act (1972). A great variety of agencies and commissions have been created to administer these laws, such as the Federal Trade Commission (1914), the Federal Communications Commission (1934), the National Labor Relations Board (1935), and the Environmental Protection Agency (1970).

GROWTH OF THE EXECUTIVE BRANCH

The departments and agencies of the federal executive have expanded in every era of U.S. history as the business of government has in some way been enlarged. By any measure, however, the greatest growth has occurred over the last half-century. If the measure is the number of government employees, the time of maximum growth was the 1930s and 1940s. During these decades, total federal personnel increased by more than 400 percent—from about 600,000 when Franklin Roosevelt took office in 1933 to roughly 2.5 million in 1953 when Republican Dwight Eisenhower ended the Democrats' twenty-year control of the executive. On the other hand, if the measure of federal growth is expenditures, the time of greatest increase has been the last twenty-seven years. Federal expenditures climbed from $118 billion in 1965 to almost $1.5 trillion in 1992.

Today, we see as one end product of this expansion the prominent presence of governmental agencies, especially federal agencies,

among the largest organizations in the country. Ranked by their expenditures (in the case of government) or by their sales (for business corporations), the three largest organizations in the United States are all executive-branch agencies: the Departments of Health and Human Services, Defense, and Treasury (Figure 8.2). Economically troubled, General Motors still surpassed all other private corporations, but its total sales in 1991 were only about 26 percent as great as the expenditures of HHS. Expenditures by the largest state government, California, were comparable to the sales of the largest companies. Comparing the number of employees, one comes to the same conclusion. The Defense Department still employs over 250,000 more civilian workers than does General Motors, the largest private employer.

THE FEDERAL EXECUTIVE TODAY

The principal departments and agencies of the federal executive branch are shown in Figure 8.3. Fourteen of them—the executive departments—are shown to outrank all other agencies. This position reflects an interesting mix of status, historical experience, and practical political reality.

CABINET RANK

The heads of these fourteen departments, who with one exception, the Attorney General, hold the title of secretary, collectively form the president's **cabinet,** and their departments are described as "of cabinet rank."[9] In the American system, the cabinet lacks any constitutional or even statutory base. In contrast to parlia-

[9]A few other officials, such as the U.S. ambassador to the United Nations, also hold cabinet rank.

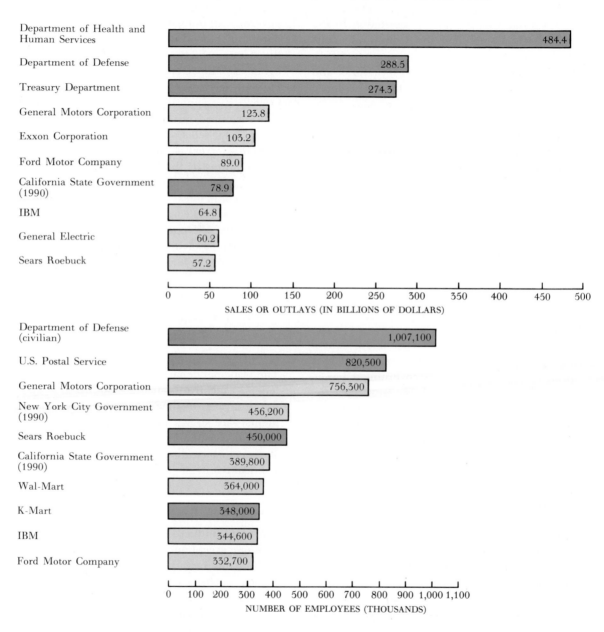

FIGURE 8.2 THE LARGEST GOVERNMENTAL AND PRIVATE BUSINESS ORGANIZATIONS (BY DOLLARS OF CORPO-
RATE SALES OR GOVERNMENTAL OUTLAYS, AND BY NUMBER OF EMPLOYEES, FOR THE YEAR 1991)

Source: Executive Office of the President, Office of Management and Budget, *Budget of the United States Government, FY 1993*, Appendix 1, pp. 46, 49, 60, 61, 92; U.S. Office of Personnel Management, *Federal Civilian Workforce Statistics: Employment and Trends as of January 1992*, pp. 17, 20; U.S. Bureau of the Census, *State Government Finance in 1990*, p. 5; idem, *Public Employment in 1990*, p. 11; idem, *City Employment in 1990*, p. 12; *Fortune*, April 20 and June 1, 1992.

FIGURE 8.3 THE EXECUTIVE BRANCH

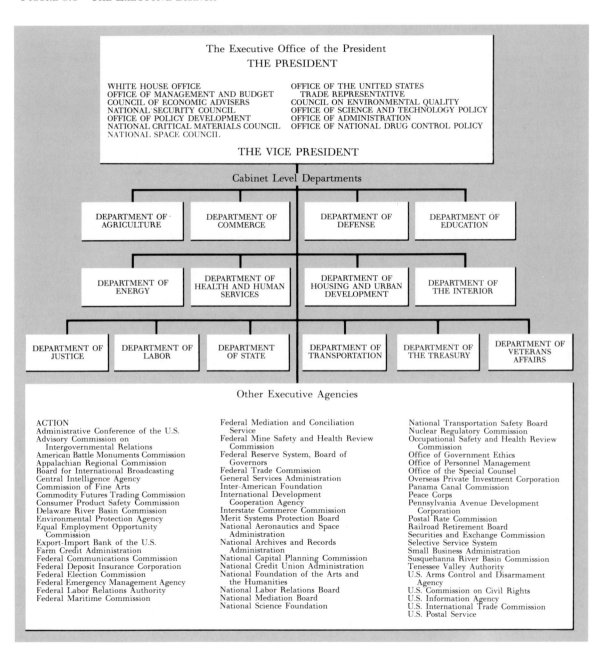

The Executive Office of the President

THE PRESIDENT

WHITE HOUSE OFFICE
OFFICE OF MANAGEMENT AND BUDGET
COUNCIL OF ECONOMIC ADVISERS
NATIONAL SECURITY COUNCIL
OFFICE OF POLICY DEVELOPMENT
NATIONAL CRITICAL MATERIALS COUNCIL
NATIONAL SPACE COUNCIL

OFFICE OF THE UNITED STATES
  TRADE REPRESENTATIVE
COUNCIL ON ENVIRONMENTAL QUALITY
OFFICE OF SCIENCE AND TECHNOLOGY POLICY
OFFICE OF ADMINISTRATION
OFFICE OF NATIONAL DRUG CONTROL POLICY

THE VICE PRESIDENT

Cabinet Level Departments

- DEPARTMENT OF AGRICULTURE
- DEPARTMENT OF COMMERCE
- DEPARTMENT OF DEFENSE
- DEPARTMENT OF EDUCATION
- DEPARTMENT OF ENERGY
- DEPARTMENT OF HEALTH AND HUMAN SERVICES
- DEPARTMENT OF HOUSING AND URBAN DEVELOPMENT
- DEPARTMENT OF THE INTERIOR
- DEPARTMENT OF JUSTICE
- DEPARTMENT OF LABOR
- DEPARTMENT OF STATE
- DEPARTMENT OF TRANSPORTATION
- DEPARTMENT OF THE TREASURY
- DEPARTMENT OF VETERANS AFFAIRS

Other Executive Agencies

ACTION
Administrative Conference of the U.S.
Advisory Commission on
  Intergovernmental Relations
American Battle Monuments Commission
Appalachian Regional Commission
Board for International Broadcasting
Central Intelligence Agency
Commission of Fine Arts
Commodity Futures Trading Commission
Consumer Product Safety Commission
Delaware River Basin Commission
Environmental Protection Agency
Equal Employment Opportunity
  Commission
Export-Import Bank of the U.S.
Farm Credit Administration
Federal Communications Commission
Federal Deposit Insurance Corporation
Federal Election Commission
Federal Emergency Management Agency
Federal Labor Relations Authority
Federal Maritime Commission

Federal Mediation and Conciliation
  Service
Federal Mine Safety and Health Review
  Commission
Federal Reserve System, Board of
  Governors
Federal Trade Commission
General Services Administration
Inter-American Foundation
International Development
  Cooperation Agency
Interstate Commerce Commission
Merit Systems Protection Board
National Aeronautics and Space
  Administration
National Archives and Records
  Administration
National Capital Planning Commission
National Credit Union Administration
National Foundation of the Arts and
  the Humanities
National Labor Relations Board
National Mediation Board
National Science Foundation

National Transportation Safety Board
Nuclear Regulatory Commission
Occupational Safety and Health Review
  Commission
Office of Government Ethics
Office of Personnel Management
Office of the Special Counsel
Overseas Private Investment Corporation
Panama Canal Commission
Peace Corps
Pennsylvania Avenue Development
  Corporation
Postal Rate Commission
Railroad Retirement Board
Securities and Exchange Commission
Selective Service System
Small Business Administration
Susquehanna River Basin Commission
Tenessee Valley Authority
U.S. Arms Control and Disarmament
  Agency
U.S. Commission on Civil Rights
U.S. Information Agency
U.S. International Trade Commission
U.S. Postal Service

Source: U.S. Senate, *Organization of Federal Executive Departments and Agencies,* January 1991.

mentary systems, where the cabinet collectively exercises governmental authority, in the United States it has no clear governing role. Presidents work closely with individual cabinet officers, of course, but rarely with the cabinet collectively. Cabinet rank is simply a symbolic affirmation of importance within the executive hierarchy.

From where does this importance stem? As the director of the then Bureau of the Budget stated in 1961 when he testified on a bill that would establish a new executive department, "Departmental status is reserved for those agencies which (1) administer a wide range of programs directed toward a common purpose of national importance; and (2) are concerned with policies and programs requiring frequent and positive presidential direction and repre-

sentation at the highest levels of Government."[10]

Table 8.2 shows the size of the fourteen cabinet-rank departments—in terms of their respective budgets as of fiscal year 1992, as well as by their number of employees.

Departmental status and cabinet rank symbolize basic national commitments and a breadth of policy responsibilities beyond what obtains in the case of other agencies. It was to reflect the growing importance of environmental issues that President Bush proposed, on January 24, 1990, that the Environmental Protection Agency be elevated to the rank of Department of Environmental Affairs.

INDEPENDENT AGENCIES

When agencies such as the Central Intelligence Agency (CIA) and the Environmental Protection Agency (EPA) are referred to as "independent," it means simply "outside the executive departments." Many of them are in no sense independent of presidential direction. The director of the CIA and the administrator of the EPA are subordinate to the president in the same way as the secretaries of State and Transportation.

Some of the **independent agencies,** however, really have been removed from presidential direction. The U.S. Postal Service (USPS) is a case in point. In urging that the Post Office Department be reorganized as an independent, noncabinet Postal Service, President Richard Nixon argued that efficiency would be served by freeing the agency "from direct control by the president, the Bureau of the Budget, and the Congress," and relatedly from partisan

TABLE 8.2 CABINET DEPARTMENTS' BUDGETS AND NUMBER OF EMPLOYEES

Departments	FY '93 budget (in billions)	Number of employees
Agriculture	59.4	110,209
Commerce	2.9	52,075
Defense	302.0	1,022,463
Education	30.4	4,848
Energy	16.3	17,724
Health and Human Services	295.8	123,238
Housing and Urban Development	28.1	13,242
Interior	6.5	73.407
Justice	10.4	84,169
Labor	38.4	18,169
State	5.2	26,474
Transportation	34.5	66,136
Treasury	312.1	177,168
Veterans Affairs	34.1	248,496

* as of 1991

Source: U.S. Department of Management and Budget, *Budget of the United States Government, FY 1993;* U.S. Senate Committee on Governmental Affairs, *Organization of Federal Executive Departments,* 1991.

[10] Statement of David E. Bell in congressional testimony, June 21, 1961.

political pressure. Under the Postal Reorganization Act of 1970, the Postal Service got much of the independence Nixon recommended. It is headed by an eleven-person board of governors, appointed by the president with Senate confirmation. The governors serve nine-year overlapping terms. The administrative head of the Postal Service, the postmaster general, is appointed by and responsible to this board of governors—not the president. The Postal Service is largely self-financing, and it can borrow money and sell bonds as it sees fit, as long as its total indebtedness does not exceed $10 billion. Only about 3 percent of its current operating budget comes from congressional appropriations—principally subsidies for mailings by some nonprofit groups and pension payments for postal workers who were employed prior to 1970.

Still, the USPS remains a federal agency, and it sometimes is required by Congress and the Office of Management and Budget to do things that it doesn't want to do. For example, in a budget agreement between the administration and Congress reached in December 1987, the Postal Service was required to help the federal government save $1.2 billion over fiscal years 1988 and 1989. The legislation mandated that money had to come from savings in the USPS operating budget and not from increased borrowing or higher postal rates. In response, the agency cut retail window hours, curbed weekend mail sorting, and suspended about 700 capital improvement projects. Predictably, the reductions in service brought howls of protest from postal patrons.

Arguments over the Postal Service's status are continuing. Some conservatives favor "privatization," turning mail delivery over to private enterprise and ending the federal monopoly on first-class mail. Others, including Representative Mickey Leland (D-Texas), who chairs the House Post Office and Civil Service Subcommittee on Postal Operations, think the 1970 reorganization went too far in removing Congressional oversight of the USPS.[11]

FOUNDATIONS AND INSTITUTES

A number of **foundations** and **institutes** have been established in the executive branch to promote science and scholarship. The first to be established, the Smithsonian Institution, is now a century and a half old. James Smithson of England bequeathed his entire estate to the United States to establish in Washington an institution "for the increase and diffusion of knowledge. . . ." Federal subsidies followed. But only after World War II did the federal government's investment in science and the arts become massive, with the establishment of the National Science Foundation, the National Institutes of Health (and its many components such as the National Cancer Institute and the National Heart Institute), and most recently, the National Endowment for the Arts and the National Endowment for the Humanities.

In all of these cases it was felt that a degree of agency insulation from regular political direction was in order. The oldest of the federal scientific establishments, the Smithsonian has the greatest autonomy. Its business is conducted by a board of regents that consists of the vice president, the chief justice of the Supreme Court, three members of the Senate, three members of the House of Representatives, and six others appointed by joint resolution of the Congress. The chief executive officer of the institution is chosen by this highly independent board. When the National Science Foundation was established in 1947 to provide federal funding for scientific research, espe-

[11] Richard Cowan, "Postal Service Faces Era of 'Power Sharing,'" *Congressional Quarterly*, February 27, 1988, pp. 507–11.

cially at the nation's colleges and universities, the scientific community worked hard to achieve for the new facility a high measure of independence from political interference. The aim was to create a kind of university structure within the executive branch, and this was substantially realized. Policy-making authority resides in a twenty-four-person National Science Board, appointed for six-year terms by the president, with the advice and consent of the Senate.

INDEPENDENT REGULATORY COMMISSIONS

Another large group of federal agencies, the **independent regulatory commissions,** were set up with the idea that they should be insulated from regular presidential leadership and political direction. We described one of these organizations, the Board of Governors of the Federal Reserve System, earlier in the chapter. The first of the independent commissions was the Interstate Commerce Commission, established in 1887 to regulate such carriers as railroads and shipping lines engaged in interstate commerce. A number of others were subsequently created, including the Securities and Exchange Commission (SEC), the Federal Trade Commission (FTC), and the Federal Communications Commission (FCC). Economic regulation is not the exclusive province of the independent commissions—various bureaus in the regular departments, such as the Food and Drug Administration (FDA) within Health and

A "camel" truck designed by government committee

Many complain about governmental regulation.

One view of getting through the bureaucracy.

Human Services, and the Occupational Safety and Health Administration (OSHA) in the Labor Department, play prominent regulatory roles—but the commissions are key regulatory bodies.

In contrast to most of the important executive departments and agencies, the regulatory commissions are headed by boards rather than single executives. By law these boards must be bipartisan. The commissioners' terms are long (five years or more) and overlapping, and commissioners may be dismissed by the president only for "inefficiency, neglect of duty, or malfeasance in office." Commissioners cannot be fired simply because the president doesn't like their views. The president still has influence over regulatory commission policies. He appoints commissioners. Even with their long overlapping terms, he usually gets to see his appointees established as a majority on each regulatory body; he is certain to do so if he serves a second term. The requirement of bipartisanship in commission membership is of little consequence; a Republican president can always pick conservative Democrats, and a Democratic president liberal Republicans.

THE BUREAU

The **bureau** is the basic unit of federal administration. The word *bureaucracy* was coined in eighteenth-century France, a neologism formed from the French word for a place where officials worked (the bureau) and a suffix derived from the Greek word for *rule*. The root meaning of bureaucracy connotes *rule by officialdom*. The *Dictionary of the French Academy* defined *bureaucratie* in 1798 as "power, influence of the heads and staff of governmental bureaus."[12] In subsequent usage, *bureaucracy*

[12] Martin Albrow, *Bureaucracy* (New York: Praeger, 1970), p. 17.

has lost some of its original stress on *rule*, but the idea of appointed officials organized around an administrative office is still central to most modern conceptions of bureaucracy.

Today, bureaus are the administrative organizations set up actually to operate the various programs of the executive departments—as in the Bureau of the Census of the Department of Commerce. The same type of administrative structure is sometimes called an *office* (the Office of Surface Mining Reclamation and Enforcement of the Department of Interior), an *administration* (the Food and Drug Administration of the Department of Health and Human Services), or a *service* (the Internal Revenue Service of the Department of the Treasury). James Fesler notes that "these operating units are so important in federal administration that one could regard the executive branch as literally a 'bureaucracy'—that is, a government by bureaus—and could treat the departmental and presidential levels merely as superstructure."[13] Most of the executive departments are really collections of bureaus. Some bureaus are older than the departments in which they are now located. The Bureau of Land Management was established in 1812, thirteen years before the Interior Department, of which it is now a part, was formed. And five bureaus are actually larger (in number of employees) than the Department of State, Labor, Energy, Housing and Urban Development, and Education. (These are the Social Security Administration, the Internal Revenue Service, the Public Health Service, the Forest Service, and the Army Corps of Engineers—for civil functions.)

To understand the scope of federal government activities and the kinds of programs and services the government provides, we must look beneath the "umbrella" departments to the constituent bureaus, offices, administrations,

and services. Figure 8.4 shows the operating structure of the Department of Agriculture—a middle-sized executive department. More than twenty services (bureaus) run the department's wide-ranging programs. A number of these services are huge governmental agencies. For example, the Farmers Home Administration, established to provide credit for people in rural areas unable to obtain credit at reasonable rates elsewhere, makes loans to low-income people to buy houses in the open country, to farm owners and operators for land conservation, to those wanting to repair farm homes and service buildings, to young people (ages 10–21) who want "to establish and operate income-producing enterprises of modest size," and many others. In 1991 the Farmers Home Administration employed almost 15,000 people and expended roughly $6.4 billion.

The main federal bureaus, with their large, ongoing programs, have naturally become focal points for interest groups and, in turn, look to interest groups to help protect and maintain themselves. And members of Congress serving on the committees and subcommittees with jurisdiction over the programs that bureaus manage have come to take a close interest in bureau affairs. A complex and important set of policies has gradually emerged in the federal executive, with the bureau typically at the center.

THE BUREAU: HUB OF FEDERAL POLICY

A president is elected, and upon taking office he appoints a group of political executives to give direction to his administration's programs. The formal authority of these executives, and their political influence deriving from the mandate the voters give the president, are substantial. But many observers stress the limits rather than the extent of their power. For the president and his cabinet secretaries often have less

---

[13] James W. Fesler, *Public Administration, Theory and Practice* (Englewood Cliffs, N.J.: Prentice-Hall, 1980), p. 45.

FIGURE 8.4 UNITED STATES DEPARTMENT OF AGRICULTURE (THE BUREAUS ARE SHOWN IN CAPITAL LETTERS)

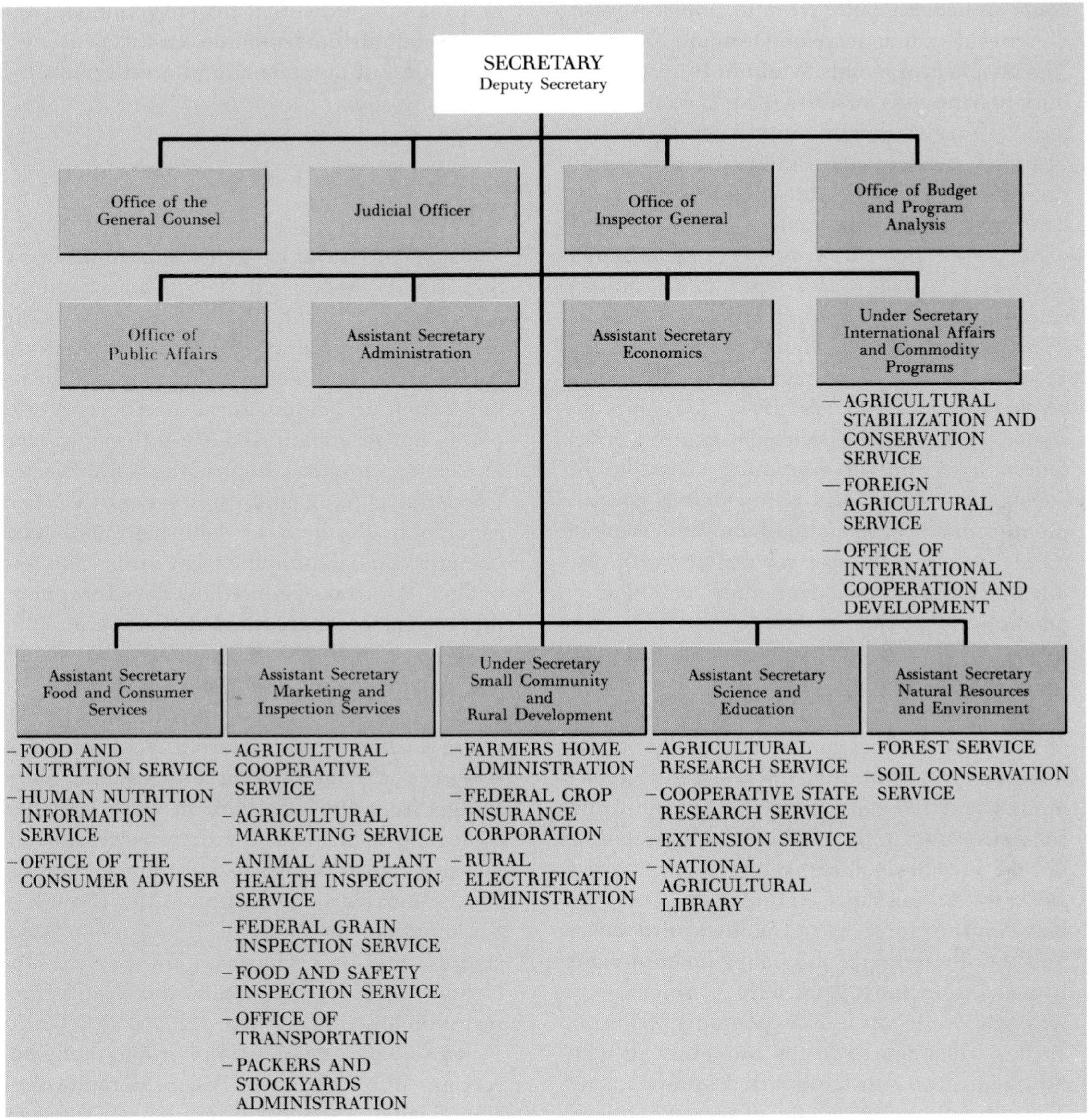

Source: *The United States Government Manual, 1990–91, p. 105.*

enduring roles in federal programs than do the heads of governmental bureaus. The former come and go; the latter seem to go on forever.

A president may serve one term, two at most. The people he appoints to administer the executive departments on average have even shorter terms. For example, a 1987 study by the National Academy of Public Administration noted the brief and declining tenure of Senate-confirmed political appointees. Average length of service dropped from nearly 3 years under Lyndon Johnson, to 2.5 years under Jimmy Carter, to just 2 years under Ronald Reagan. "The single most obvious characteristic of Washington's political appointees," political scientist Hugh Heclo observes, "is their transience."[14] Among the political executives of the federal government, everything seems to be constantly in flux. They have come to government from all corners of national life. Many of them have had little or no contact with one another prior to receiving their presidential appointments. They must try to master exceedingly complex jobs in short periods of time and in the context of almost entirely new executive teams.

The political direction coming to the bureau from the president, and the cabinet secretary or assistant secretary, is short-term and episodic. In contrast, the relationship between the bureau and the political interests that have a stake in its programs endures. This contrast between the transience of political executives and the durability of the policy environments in which they must work tells us much about why practical control over programs resides to such a large degree in the bureaus and with the political interests organized around them. The strength and durability of bureaus' role in federal policy results, too, from the mutually supporting nature of their ties to interest groups. When two different organisms are associated in a manner of mutual benefit, biologists call their relationship symbiotic. In this sense, the association of bureaus and interest groups is a symbiotic one.

INTEREST GROUPS AND BUREAUS

Consider the Rural Electrification Administration (REA) within the U.S. Department of Agriculture (USDA). It delivers important services to rural dwellers—organized through the National Rural Electric Cooperative Association—such as helping rural electric and telephone utilities obtain financing through loans and loan guarantees. In turn, the Rural Electric Cooperative Association has served as a personal lobby for the REA, lobbying members of Congress on behalf of the REA's programs and budget. Political scientist Theodore Lowi notes that a principal agricultural interest group, the American Farm Bureau Federation, has had a similar connection with the Extension Service of the Agriculture Department throughout its entire history.[15] And Harold Seidman, who served as assistant director of the Bureau of the Budget from 1964 to 1968, observes, "Each of the agencies dispensing federal largess has its personal lobby: the Corps of Engineers has the Rivers and Harbors Congress; the Bureau of Reclamation, the National Reclamation Association; the Soil Conservation Service, the National Association of Soil and Water Conservation Districts."[16]

Some depict these ties as grubby and self-serving. But the matter is considerably more complicated. A federal program like rural elec-

[14] Hugh Heclo, *A Government of Strangers* (Washington, D.C.: Brookings Institution, 1977). p. 103.

[15] Theodore J. Lowi, *The End of Liberalism* (New York: Norton, 1979), p. 72.
[16] Harold Seidman, *Politics, Position, and Power*, 3rd ed. (New York: Oxford University Press, 1980), p. 164.

trification began with a clear and respectable need: It cost much more to extend electric and telephone service to remote rural areas than to cities and towns, because wires had to be strung across miles of isolated and sparsely settled territory to reach a few paying customers. The REA stepped into the breach by providing the funding. It is neither surprising nor troubling that the bureau and the interests it served established a firm and mutually supporting association. Once enough of these ties have been established, however, the position of the cabinet secretary and assistant secretaries becomes very weak, because they find it hard to control the bureau's commitments. Furthermore, the line between legitimate interest in extending needed services and the narrow interest of group/agency self-advancement is both blurred and easily crossed.

The symbiotic nature of the ties between bureaus and interest groups has led some to question conventional descriptions of group power. In many of the cases we have been describing, it would be misleading to suggest that a powerful interest group has muscled its way in and forced government to do its bidding. Rather, the agency and the interest group have compatible objectives and need each other.

CONGRESS AND BUREAUS

Just as the associations of interest groups and bureaus are often enduring, so are those of congressional leadership and bureaus. As we saw in chapter 6, power in the U.S. Congress is highly fragmented, distributed across an elaborate system of nearly 300 committees and subcommittees. Each executive-agency bureau falls within the jurisdiction of one or several subcommittees that develop legislation defining bureau programs and provide funding for them. Subcommittee chairpeople usually pay close attention to the work of "their bureau" because they may care deeply about it, because

it matters to their constituents, and because they thereby gain power. Here again the symbiosis: Members of Congress and bureau administrators need and use each other. And the permanence of their ties, coupled with the transience of cabinet secretaries and other senior political executives, further encourages the remarkable fragmentation of executive authority.

Members of Congress do not have formal grants of administrative responsibility, but they often play large roles in guiding agency programs. In fact, a legislator's reach over executive-branch programs sometimes far exceeds that of cabinet secretaries. For example, Representative Jami Whitten of Mississippi, chairman of the House Appropriations Committee and, as well, chairman of the Appropriations Subcommittee on Rural Development, Agriculture, and Related Agencies, has been called the "permanent secretary of Agriculture." Over the last quarter-century, a time when the Democrats have continuously controlled the House of Representatives, Whitten's say in agricultural programs has been immense.

THE LIFE OF THE BUREAU CHIEF

The administrators who head federal bureaus are responsible not just to their executive superiors—the cabinet secretaries and the president. In a very real sense they are also responsible unofficially to congressional committee leaders and to influential interest groups. This means that bureau chiefs have a confusing mix of "masters"—but also that they can attain a striking degree of political autonomy. If astute and inclined to play one master against another, a bureau chief can achieve a measure of longevity and program control that does not exist in the administration of other democratic governments. Within our pluralistic government, bureaus are not merely administrative units, but also the focal points of a system of dispersed power. Bureau chiefs are typically policy makers, not merely administrators of policies others make.

Once in place, the bureau–subcommittee–interest group triangle becomes a familiar and comfortable policy environment for its participants. And they will resist attempts at reorganization. Committee leaders often don't like change because it might disrupt their established channels of oversight and influence. Interest groups fear that new arrangements might weaken their claims. And bureau chiefs find their own autonomy and influence enhanced by established and enduring congressional and group ties. Many efforts at change initiated by presidents and cabinet secretaries have crashed against these "iron triangles."

Change is made especially difficult by the fact that the triangular interactions often involve intensely held inside interests and weak or diffuse outside concerns. For example, a program of agricultural price supports—maintaining farm prices at levels deemed fair to farmers—may benefit only a small group of farmers at the expense of a large group of consumers. But the interests of the former are intense while those of the latter are by comparison weak and disjointed. It isn't always this way. Sometimes outside interests can become strong enough to overturn established policy systems. One recent example has to do with the public's concern over the environment. By 1970 environmental interests had gained enough political muscle to get Congress to establish the Environmental Protection Agency (EPA). The EPA assumed authority in a variety of areas that had been under the jurisdiction of old-line departments. For instance, it took over the regulation of pesticides that had formerly been lodged with a bureau in the Department of Agriculture. Firms manufacturing pesticides felt more comfortable with their ties to the USDA and resisted the shift. But the environmental lobby succeeded in severing the old interest group–bureau bond. Today environmental groups look upon the various offices or bureaus of the EPA as their own, much as agricultural interest groups have for a long time viewed the USDA as their own.

THE PUBLIC INTEREST

This description of interest-group ties to bureaus does not give us much help in determining whether the resultant programs are legitimate ones, as judged by the standard of the public interest. Interest groups invariably claim that the programs they favor serve larger national ends, not just their own interests, and often they sincerely believe they do. Different groups will inevitably construe the public interest in different ways. The fact that an interest group strongly backs a program does not mean that the program is bad. What is clear is that American public-policy formation, built as it is around a multiplicity of interest group, bureau, and congressional committee interrelations, is remarkably fragmented.

As Figure 8.5 suggests, the federal bureau is frequently the hub of a set of interactions involving 1) administration leadership, 2) congressional leadership (usually defined at the committee or subcommittee levels, 3) inside group interests, and 4) outside group interests. The strength of any one part will vary from one program area to another and may shift over time. For example, a politically popular president and an effective cabinet secretary may well be able to build upon public support for change to override the preferences of inside interests and established congressional committee preferences. Conversely, a strong subcommittee chairperson, especially if he or she is operating in conjunction with well-organized inside interests and in the absence of sustained opposing efforts by the president, may be able

FIGURE 8.5 THE POLICY WHEEL IN EXECUTIVE
ORGANIZATION

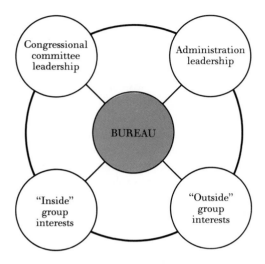

to push bureau activities decisively in a direction that he or she favors. Inside interests—such as those of farm groups in USDA programs—are often highly influential, but they may be overridden by the growth of outside interests. While their relative strength varies from case to case, the component parts of the policy wheel seem to be constants. And viewed from the perspective of executive-branch organization and operation, the bureau is typically the focal point of the policy wheel.

THE PRESIDENT AND
THE BUREAUCRACY

Neither the president nor his chief appointees—such as cabinet secretaries—are involved in matters of hiring or dismissing most of the 3 million executive-branch employees. The bulk of these workers are covered by provisions of one or another civil service system, the largest of which is administered by the government's

central personnel agency, the Office of Personnel Management (OPM), discussed later in this chapter. When George Bush took office on January 20, 1989, the government's official listing of political appointments for the new president—known as the "plum book"—showed about 4,500 such posts, out of the more than 3 million executive-branch jobs.

Filling even this number is an enormous chore. No president or small group of presidential assistants knows 4,500 people prepared to leave their present jobs and serve ably in diverse posts throughout the executive branch. Recent presidents have set up quite elaborate recruitment efforts, but the results have still often been disappointing. For certain positions the problem is not choosing among a number of worthy candidates but rather encouraging able people to leave jobs in the private sector—where they receive higher salaries and much greater security and privacy—and come to Washington.

Of the 4,500 "plum book" positions, perhaps 500–700 are key managers. They include heads of the cabinet departments and other agencies, and such second-tier political executives as deputy secretaries and assistant secretaries. Attention focuses on the cabinet secretaries, especially those who direct such prestigious and influential departments as State, Defense, and Treasury. But the next rung of positions, if mostly invisible to the public at large, often carry with them great responsibilities.

For example, within the Office of Management and Budget, under the budget director, are four associate directors for programs: (1) natural resources, environment, energy, and science; (2) labor, health and human services, education, veterans affairs, and programs that fall within twenty-two other smaller agencies; (3) transportation, justice, commerce, Treasury Department matters, drug policy, and the postal service; and (4) the entire array of defense matters. One of these associate directors in the early Bush administration, Thomas Scully, was almost completely unknown outside Washington circles. But, as the *Washington Post* pointed out, in March 1990 alone Scully worked out a compromise on food stamps with key Senate aides, killed a move to forgive delinquent graduate school loans, and worked to limit food subsidies. In addition, "he tried to negotiate a compromise child-care bill that would placate top congressional Democrats as well as conservatives in the Republican party. In between, he squeezed in time to review testimony to be given by Veterans Affairs officials and he mediated a dispute between the Agriculture Department and the Food and Drug Administration over who would regulate seafood inspection."[17]

Such influence and responsibilities reflect in part the fact that OMB has become the key agency through which presidents try to exert control over the far-flung executive branch. Associate directors of OMB are bound to wield great power. But the story of Thomas Scully's role also reminds us just how much the executive branch does and how important are a number of second-tier posts within it that are out of the public eye but in the middle of policy making.

PRESIDENTIAL CONTROL

Presidents and their political executives often complain that they lack sufficient control over the executive-branch bureaucracy. But here they in fact are referring to only a very small segment of all federal workers. As we have seen, the president appoints the top political administrators and can fire them if they fail to do his bidding. The bulk of federal workers, of course, do not play policy roles at all. They issue Social Security checks, deliver the mail, process tax

returns, and more. These jobs are vital to government, but they involve routine operations that presidents have no interest in "controlling." Most of these positions are handled through civil service systems.

Presidents' concern over bureaucratic unresponsiveness revolves around a relatively small group of career officials—perhaps numbering not more than 20,000—who are involved in policy but who are not subject to presidential appointment or dismissal. At the bureau level, virtually all key staff, the bureau chief included, are career officials. Presidents and cabinet secretaries come and go; senior career personnel usually stay much longer. Their relative longevity and dominant place in the bureaus— which have large policy-making responsibilities—give them great influence.

Any administration, anxious to implement its programs and encountering all kinds of obstacles in the American system of divided power, is bound to feel some frustration when it encounters bureaucratic resistance. Presidents and the political appointees have often expressed the concern that career officials don't fully support administration policies and indeed resist them. Many experienced government officials think, however, that the problem of bureaucratic unresponsiveness is overstated. They maintain that most career officials will respond to effective leadership from political appointees and that, most of the time, it is only the inept political executives who encounter disabling resistance. Even when an administration takes office determined to change policy substantially, it can usually gain the sufficient assistance—rather than the determined resistance—of career civil servants.

The recent record offers much support for this view. An occasional political official in a sensitive post gets embroiled in bitter internal battles with agency staff, but most skilled appointees seem to have little difficulty directing their career staffs, even when major program changes are the order of the day.

[17] Steven Mufson, "The Anonymous Face," *Washington Post, National Weekly Edition*, May 7–13, 1990, p. 6.

"POLITICAL" VERSUS "CAREER" APPOINTMENTS

Recent presidents have enlarged the number of executive-branch posts subject to presidential appointment, at the expense of senior career service positions. Under Jimmy Carter, a number of career posts were reclassified as so-called "Schedule C" jobs, subject to political appointment. Under Ronald Reagan, the share of the executive branch's **Senior Executive Service** (SES) positions held by career administrators declined substantially, while the proportion filled by non-career executives rose.

The Senior Executive Service was established in 1978. It now includes about 7,100 government managers in the three highest General Schedule (GS) grades of federal employment and in the lower two grades (levels IV and V) of the Executive Schedule. (There are eighteen grades in all in the General Schedule; the Executive Schedule covers top government executives not under the General Schedule.) The civil service reformers who pushed for the SES wanted a corps of senior career administrators not locked into particular bureaus and programs. Rather than being tied to specific positions, members of the SES are supposed to constitute a mobile pool of top managerial talent, available for assignment where needed in the executive branch. (The Foreign Service Act of 1980 created a Senior Foreign Service that parallels the Senior Executive Service in most regards.)

A second, related goal was to provide the executive branch with a staff of skilled career managers who see themselves and, in turn, are seen by presidents and political appointees as sources of neutral competence rather than program advocacy. It should be possible, civil service reformers have long thought, to create in the United States a cadre of skilled, experienced career officials able and willing to serve any properly constituted administration, and in turn trusted and relied upon by administrations with contrasting political goals. The SES should not be merely skilled administrative "hired guns." "Just tell us what to do, boss" is not the desired end. Civil servants take an oath to uphold the Constitution, and out of this commitment grows a defensible basis for making judgments independent from those of the political executives of the day. Beyond this, senior administrators have a responsibility to argue with their political superiors (even if they ultimately acquiesce), for their experience and understanding must be brought into play: "SES personnel should embody the 'institutional memory' that has so often rescued political leadership from disastrous adventures."[18]

Students of American public administration have long felt that some nations—among them, Great Britain—have done a better job than the United States in producing cadres of senior career officials with a high esprit de corps and a reputation for neutral competence in the service of shifting political executives. In Britain, the civil service's "administrative class" of about 7,500 officials assists cabinet ministers in all facets of governing: providing them with information about what is happening within their departments, identifying alternate courses of action, and translating the policy goals of the party in power into concrete programs and legislation. The ideal of neutral competence figures prominently in the work of the senior British civil service, for once a policy is determined by a minister or by the cabinet, career administrators are supposed to execute it loyally even when they personally disagree with it. As one British administrator put it: "The soul of the service is the loyalty with which we execute ordained error."[19]

The efforts of civil service reformers to build a Senior Executive Service along a European,

[18]John A. Rohr, "Ethics for the Senior Executive Service," *Administration and Society* 12 (August 1980), p. 211.
[19]As quoted in Ian Gilmour, *The Body Politic* (London: Hutchinson, 1969), p. 198.

especially British, model have met with mixed results. Some observers believe that the number of non-career SES jobs needs to be cut sharply, as part of a general reduction of political appointees in the executive branch. Paul Volcker, the former chairman of the Federal Reserve Board, who between 1987 and 1989 chaired the National Commission on Public Service (discussed below), has argued strongly that half the government's political appointments could and should be filled by career civil servants. He and others on the commission maintained that the excessive use of political appointees in top government management posts has led to a serious morale problem among the career staff and prevented the ideal behind the Senior Executive Service from being realized.

A QUIET CRISIS?

The intermittent skirmishing that goes on between presidents—popularly elected and trying to advance their goals in the American system of divided government—and the senior levels of the career bureaucracy is hardly inconsequential. But it appears to many experts as relatively unimportant today, set against what increasingly seems to be the real problem in governmental service—attracting (and keeping) able people who can give government the management talent it needs. Paul Volcker has argued that "government in general, and the federal government in particular, is increasingly unable to attract, retain, and motivate the kinds of people it will need to do the essential work of the republic in the years and decades ahead."[20] This perspective led him and other

prominent Americans—including former president Gerald Ford, former vice president Walter Mondale, former U.S. senator and secretary of state Edmund Muskie, and Harvard University president Derek Bok—to form in 1987 the National Commission on Public Service. Supported by private funds, the commission issued its report on the problem, and remedies, in March 1989.

The Volcker Commission proposed a number of remedies for what it considered the serious deterioration in the quality and morale of the senior federal service. One needed response, the commission maintained, was for the president and Congress to "articulate early and often the necessary and honorable role that public servants play in the democratic process." There had been too much "bureaucrat bashing" in recent years. Careers in government deserve more recognition than they now receive, the commission maintained, and from more recognition would come better recruits. Derek Bok had noted earlier that only 2 percent of Harvard Law School graduates have been taking government jobs in recent years.

The commission recommended establishing a Presidential Public Service Scholarship program targeted to 1,000 college students each year to encourage them to enter governmental service. It called on giving cabinet officers and agency heads more flexibility in managing their departments—including more freedom to hire and fire personnel—on the grounds that improved management practices, along the lines found in the best of the private sector, would produce a managerial environment that worked better and thus was more attractive to able people.

The commission recommendation that received the most attention was its call for an immediate 25 percent increase in executive, judicial, and legislative branch salaries for senior executive employees, with a second comparable increase after the 1990 elections. An earlier

[20] Quoted in John Schachter, "Volcker's Target: A Flagging Federal Service," *Congressional Quarterly*, November 26, 1988, p. 3404.

provision, linked to a large pay increase for senators and representatives, had been rejected in February 1989, when Congress yielded to public protests largely directed against the increases that would have resulted for members of Congress themselves. Many experts felt that, whatever was appropriate for Congress's pay, big increases were needed for judges and the senior executive service, where pay had been dropping in real terms for twenty years, to the point where it had become uncompetitive with compensation in comparable private sector jobs. The linking of salaries in the executive and judiciary to those in Congress had meant that the former suffered from public opposition to increases of the latter.

Even before the Volcker Commission's pay recommendations, President Bush, like President Reagan before him, had endorsed the argument that big increases were needed to make senior government positions more competitive in terms of salary. A presidential advisory commission told Reagan in August 1988 that there was a more than 25 percent disparity between federal pay and pay in private business. Paul Volcker said that senior civil servants were getting 40 percent less pay in real, inflation-controlled terms than they had in 1969. As a result, it was getting harder to recruit able people, and job turnover was rising.

Responding to all these considerations, President Bush proposed in July 1989 legislation that would provide much higher salaries for a small number of executive employees in positions requiring specialized and critical skills, and increases of 8 to 25 percent for senior executive branch officials generally. He had made comparable recommendations for the judiciary in April 1989. "The pay of senior Government officials has eroded significantly in relation to the pay of executives in comparable jobs in the private and not-for-profit sectors of the economy," the president said. "This pay gap is affecting the Federal Government's ability to attract and retain the skilled and motivated senior executives necessary to direct the complex, wide-ranging, and critical functions of the Federal Government."

In November 1989, Congress finally approved a pay package that included all three branches. For the executive, it provided for a 7.9 percent pay increase for senior managers and top officials effective in February 1990, a 25 percent increase effective July 1, 1991, and annual cost-of-living increases (not to exceed 5 percent per year). Linked effectively to other actions, the pay hike should help strengthen the senior federal civil service.

ORGANIZATION OF THE FEDERAL CIVIL SERVICE

Over 90 percent of all federal civilian workers are now covered under some kind of **merit system.** What is meant by a merit system? Basically, the term has been closely linked in the United States with civil service, referring to procedures for the appointment of civil servants on the basis of competitive examinations rather than political sponsorship. Civil service merit systems came into being in the late nineteenth century to replace the so-called spoils system, under which each administration had a free hand to hire and fire virtually all federal workers: "To the victor, the spoils." The initial idea of a merit-system alternative was largely negative, focusing on the importance of keeping political influence out of appointments and promotions.

The Pendleton Civil Service Act of 1883 was the first important piece of reform legislation at the federal level in the United States. Borrowing heavily from the practices of the British civil service of the time, the Pendleton Act required competitive examinations for federal appointments, guaranteed tenure of office (assuming competent performance), and required civil service workers to be politically neutral (not to use their posts to advance party goals or to discriminate on a partisan basis). Initially only about 10 percent of the federal workforce was covered by Pendleton Act provisions, but the proportion grew steadily. Today, more than nine out of ten federal workers are covered by a merit system.

The largest merit system today, encompassing 1.8 million workers, is administered by the Office of Personnel Management (OPM). The OPM was established in 1978 as one of two successor agencies to the old Civil Service Commission. By law, a number of agencies are outside the OPM-run civil service, including the U.S. Postal Service and its 820,000 full-time employees. Other "excepted" agencies are the Federal Bureau of Investigation, the intelligence agencies, the Foreign Service of the State Department, and the Tennessee Valley Authority. All of these operate their own independent merit systems.

GETTING A CIVIL SERVICE JOB

Staffing the federal bureaucracy first involves calculating the personnel requirements of the departments and agencies. With passage of the Civil Service Reform Act of 1978, such planning became the responsibility of the OPM. The OPM announces examinations designed to measure applicants' qualifications for various openings, processes applications, and administers the tests. Some exams are narrowly fitted to specific positions; others are of the "broad-band" variety—that is, designed to certify applicants for a range of different posts in government.

Actually, many candidates for civil service jobs never take a written test. Middle-level and upper-level positions in the civil service (GS grade levels 9–18) require the "unassembled"

examination, which isn't an examination at all. Each candidate submits a statement that describes his or her relevant educational background and other pertinent training or experience, and lists persons, such as previous employers and teachers, who could be contacted for informed evaluations. What the candidate submits for these senior professional and managerial jobs in the government is exactly what he or she would for a comparable position in a university or a private business corporation.

Why call it an "examination"? The elusive goal is a type of objective certification that removes any opportunity for bias on the part of those doing the hiring. But no one has been able to devise satisfactory written examinations for many complex professional and managerial positions. Those who know what such posts require must assess candidates in terms of training and experience and arrive at the best judgment as to who are most qualified. Yet the greater the need for judgment, the greater the opportunity for bias or favoritism. One interesting indication of the quest for objectivity is that the curriculum vitae submitted by candidates for upper-level civil service positions are actually "graded" with numeric scores.

VETERANS IN THE CIVIL SERVICE

Probably the most substantial denial of the merit principle in the federal civil service system is extraneous to the examination process. All veterans of the armed services who sustained a service-related disability get 10-point bonuses added to their examination scores; all other veterans get 5 points (except for those who entered the military after 1976 and served only in peacetime). In addition to their 10-point bonuses, disabled veterans are placed at the head of the eligible register for all openings except scientific and professional positions at

GS-9 and above. This means that they must be put on the list for hiring ahead of nonveterans, even those with much higher examination scores. Veterans receive a number of other advantages in federal hiring as well.

DISMISSING CIVIL SERVICE WORKERS

Another dilemma presents itself when questions of dismissing workers arise. Civil service arrangements were implemented in large part to preclude the political favoritism of the spoils system. One way to make it hard to fire people was by requiring that a "preponderance of evidence" establish an employee's unacceptable performance before he or she could be dismissed. Anything less than that, it was felt, would make it too easy for supervisors to continue political favoritism by simply claiming that work was deficient. Strong federal employees' unions now add their weight as well to the side of protecting employees' rights.

But the same civil service regulations and union pressure that make it hard to dismiss employees for such illegitimate reasons as political preference also make it hard to fire lazy, unreliable, or insufficiently competent workers. Leonard Reed argues that "for many fine and capable civil servants, the acceptance of the incompetent and the slacker affects their own attitudes and performance. For federal executives the invulnerability of the unproductive worker makes a mockery of the whole concept of efficient management."[21]

To try to correct this problem, the 1978 Civil Service Reform Act gave greater authority to agency heads in matters of dismissals, and streamlined discharge and demotion procedures. Now when an employee is dismissed for unacceptable performance and appeals to the

[21] Leonard Reed, "Firing a Federal Employee: The Impossible Dream," in Charles Peters and Michael Nelson, eds., *The Culture of Bureaucracy* (New York: Holt, Rinehart and Winston, 1979), p. 208.

Merit Systems Protection Board, the dismissal will be upheld if supported by "substantial evidence" rather than "a preponderance of evidence." The Volcker Commission proposed in 1989 giving agency heads greater authority to dismiss malperforming employees.

ETHICS AND THE EXECUTIVE BRANCH

Ethical violations by governmental officials—high, middle, and low—are very much in the public's eye these days. It's hard to say whether there has been a general decline in moral and ethical standards in the United States generally. It's easy to see that when government gets as big as ours has and does as much, many interests will try to shape it—some improperly. We saw in chapter 6 that Congress has had an enormous problem coping with the efforts of

interests to achieve (through campaign contributions, other financial favors, etc.) undue influence and with the inclination of too many of its members to go along. On the executive side, despite much more stringent rules bearing on acceptance of money and favors from outside groups, abuses continue to occur.

THE SAVINGS AND LOAN SCANDALS

In costs, complexity, and duration no other current government-related scandals approach those involving the savings and loan industry. Savings and loans are a type of bank set up initially to provide loans to home buyers. The main culprits in the savings and loan debacle were not government officials, but a combination of circumstances and the dishonesty and incompetence of officers of hundreds of "thrifts." These officers, through mismanagement and fraud, brought their institutions to financial

CHARLES WERNER
Courtesy Indianapolis Star

ruin. Because the federal government insures accounts up to $100,000 per depositor, per bank, the bad judgment and thievery of all-too-many thrift officials will cost countless billions. By the spring of 1992, about $90 billion had already been expended on the S & L bailout, and an estimated $40 billion would also be required over the next year alone. This financial debacle was one more factor fueling voter anger in 1992.

Within government, there is more than enough blame to go around. State agencies charged with supervising thrifts were often irresponsibly lax. In Congress, some members developed too-cozy ties with S & Ls from whom they received campaign contributions and on whose behalf they intervened with regulators. As for the executive branch, the main criticism is that officials permitted thrifts to expand into new lines of business—outside their historic area of mortgage loans to home buyers—without adequate supervision and that when problems developed, regulators often moved too slowly to correct them.

The federal regulatory apparatus is complex. Until 1989, the main agency in thrift supervision was the Federal Home Loan Bank Board. When the S & L mess deepened, the Bank Board was terminated; its responsibilities were assigned to other agencies, the most important share going to the Federal Deposit Insurance Corporation (FDIC). The Office of Thrift Supervision, within the Treasury Department, also examines the operations of S & Ls.

SUMMARY

Over the last two centuries, a vast governmental system has evolved to administer the American federal government. The executive branch now includes over one hundred cabinet departments, independent agencies, regulatory commissions, foundations, boards, and related organizations and employs about 3 million men and women in civilian service.

The executive agencies with the broadest policy mandates and the greatest prestige are the fourteen departments with cabinet rank. Four of them trace their lineage back to the start of George Washington's administration: State, Treasury, Defense (originally the War Department), and Justice (originally the office of the Attorney General). The other ten departments are, in the order in which they were established: Interior, Agriculture, Commerce, Labor, Health and Human Services, Housing and Urban Development, Transportation, Energy, Education, and Veterans Affairs.

The Constitution vests executive authority in the president, but effective presidential direction of the sprawling executive branch is not easily achieved. While the president appoints the heads of the various executive agencies and their principal deputies (with the Senate's advice and consent), and may remove most of these officials without congressional action, Congress plays an active role in executive-branch management. One reason why congressional influence is so great involves the strength and independence of the bureaus, the main units of program responsibility and administration. Headed typically by senior career civil servants, bureaus are tied not just to the departments and agencies of which they are a part, but also to the congressional committees that legislate the substance of their programs and appropriate their budgets.

Sometimes battles have broken out between presidents and their political appointees on one hand, and senior career administrators in the various executive agency bureaus on the other hand, as presidents and their political appointees have sought to exercise greater policy control over the bureaucracy. In an effort to break the cycle of conflict and recrimination, the Carter administration proposed, and Congress enacted, the 1978 Civil Service Reform Act. One portion of this act establishes the Senior Executive Service, comprised of about 7,000 high career administrators. These officials of the permanent government would be less tied to specific bureaus and programs and more a source of much-needed neutral competence in executive-branch administration. The SES has thus far gotten mixed reviews. Some experts think that the number of political appointees needs to be reduced further, perhaps cut in half, to increase the responsibilities and attractiveness of the senior career service.

By the end of the 1980s, most observers also believed that senior government salaries, by dropping well below the levels of the private sector, had contributed to a loss of good employees and difficulties in attracting new ones. In late 1989, a pay-increase bill was passed to address this problem.

Apart from the issue of political direction and responsiveness, personnel management for the civil service involves classic public administration problems. How can one preclude civil servants being fired because of political favoritism, while permitting them to be dismissed for such proper reasons as incompetent performance? Federal employment has acquired the reputation for erring excessively on the side of job security—a reputation it seems to have earned.

Ethics violations are a continuing problem on the executive-branch side as they are in Congress. The mismanagement and fraud in the S & L industry—which is supervised in part by federal agencies—and the enormous costs of the resultant bailout were a main source of voter discontent in the 1992 election.

FOR FURTHER STUDY

Dodd, Lawrence C., and Richard L. Schott. *Congress and the Administrative State.* New York: Wiley, 1979. A most useful account of the complex relationships of Congress with the agencies of the executive branch.

Fesler, James W. *Public Administration, Theory and Practice.* Englewood Cliffs, N.J.: Prentice-Hall, 1980. A penetrating description of public bureaucracies, their organization, and their operations.

Heclo, Hugh. *A Government of Strangers.* Washington, D.C.: Brookings Institution, 1977. A major treatment of the relationship between political appointees to the executive branch and career civil servants.

Mosher, Frederick C. *Democracy and the Public Service,* 2nd ed. New York: Oxford University Press, 1982. Provides a useful description and analysis of recent developments affecting career civil service—including the unionization of governmental employees, the operation of merit systems, professionalization, etc.

Office of the Federal Register, National Archives and Records Administration. *The United States Government Manual 1991–92.* (Washington, D.C.: Government Printing Office, 1991). Published annually as the official handbook of the federal government, the manual is a comprehensive source of information on all agencies, including all units of the executive branch.

Peters, Charles, and Michael Nelson, eds. *The Culture of Bureaucracy.* New York: Holt, Rinehart and Winston, 1979. A thoughtful, sometimes satiric account of the values and culture of bureaucratic Washington.

Seidman, Harold, and Robert Gilmour. *Politics, Position, and Power: From the Positive to the Regulatory State.* New York: Oxford University Press, 1986. A brilliant description of how government agencies operate and an important critique of proposals for bureaucratic reform, by Seidman, a former deputy director of the Bureau of the Budget (now Office of Management and Budget).

Wildavsky, Aaron. *The New Politics of the Budgetary Process,* revised ed. Glenn View, Ill.: Scott Foresman, 1988. The best account of the nature of the federal budgetary process and its implications for American public policy.

Chapter 9

THE JUDICIARY

We have little difficulty seeing the executive and legislative branches in explicitly *political terms*. After all, the president and members of both houses of Congress are chosen through partisan elections, and the contending Democratic and Republican stands are evident throughout the many programs and policies they develop, debate, compromise upon, and ultimately implement. The judicial branch may often seem quite different. The corridors of the Supreme Court building on Capitol Hill, the home of the nation's highest court, are quiet and subdued, reflecting little of the political energy and bustle so evident in the halls of Congress, across the street. Judges wear black robes and usually speak in measured and judicious tones—citing earlier cases, as they interpret statutes that legislatures have enacted and executives implemented, and even, most magisterially, expounding upon the basic rights of all Americans set forth in the Constitution. Though the way they work is distinct and their role and responsibilities different from those of the other branches, the federal courts are prominently involved in making public policy and thus very much in the American political arena.

THE COURTS AND POLICY MAKING

The framers of the Constitution intended that the federal courts—especially the Supreme Court—would be a major political institution, one of the three branches of national government that would check and balance the other two. Yet if judges were to be politicians, they would be politicians of a special sort, and the courts a special type of political institution, bound by norms and practices distinct from those of other governmental units. They make policy within a structure and tradition that exerts great influence over the results.

The best way to get a sense of the special properties of judicial policy making is to examine decisions rendered by the U.S. Supreme Court. The Supreme Court makes policy by reviewing points of law in cases brought before it and handing down binding decisions on these points of law. The Court's authority and procedures, including the basic mechanism of *judicial review*, are discussed below (pp. 256–58). As the highest court in the land, the Supreme Court usually hears only cases of substantial importance to national policy.

Whenever a legislature enacts a law, it makes policy, but the scope of these policy initiatives varies widely. There is a vast difference between the implications for public policy of a new parking ordinance and of sweeping Social Security legislation. Similarly, a court's policy role is much more limited when it applies a specific drunk-driving law than when it interprets an act setting complex new environmental goals and requirements. As a general rule, the narrower the scope of a law and the more precisely and unambiguously its terms are pre-

Inscription on the Supreme Court building, Washington, D.C.

scribed, the less policy discretion courts have. The wider the substantive reach of a law, and the more expansive the goals it proclaims, the greater are the court's policy powers stemming from interpretation of the law.

Decisions of the Supreme Court are an unusual blend of practical political action and political philosophy. The latter comes into play prominently because the Court's influence depends in significant part upon its success in convincing other actors—the president, members of Congress, lower-court judges, lawyers, and, to some extent, the public at large—of the intellectual soundness of its legal interpretations. When the law in question is the Constitution itself, the Court expounds on the most fundamental values of the American polity. Through Court decisions, concrete disputes get resolved but, at the same time, large philosophic questions are consciously explored. Because the Court is often divided, and one or more judges in the minority issue dissenting opinions, the argument gets joined directly and, on occasion, with great force.

A CASE STUDY IN JUDICIAL POLICY MAKING: THE ABORTION QUESTION

The Supreme Court sets policy by deciding cases and from time to time enters subjects on which Americans are deeply divided. The political implications of some cases are such that early in the twentieth century Justice Oliver Wendell Holmes deemed the Court a "storm centre" of political controversy.[1] To see this judicial policy making in action, we need only look at a subject of bitter controversy in the United States: abortion.

In 1973, abortion became an important national issue with the Supreme Court's land-

mark ruling in **Roe v. Wade.** In *Roe*, a 7–2 majority declared unconstitutional all legislation—on the books in a large majority of the fifty states—banning abortion in the first six months of pregnancy (or the first and second "trimesters," as the Court put it). The majority held that a *right of privacy*—perhaps defined in the Fourteenth Amendment's "concept of personal liberty and restrictions upon state action," perhaps in the Ninth Amendment's "reservations of rights to the people"—*includes the abortion decision.* States could intrude regulatorily into this area of privacy and personal choice in the first six months of a pregnancy for no purpose other than safeguarding the pregnant woman's health. Only after a fetus reaches *viability*—when life outside the mother's body becomes possible, a stage of development reached early in the third trimester—does the state's interest in "the potentiality of human life" become sufficient to permit it to ban abortion altogether.

When the decision in *Roe* was rendered, many observers believed that, after initial protests by church groups and others opposed to the decision, the issue would gradually lose intensity. They felt that the idea of a substantial constitutional right to abortion would with time become ever more widely accepted and firmly established. We know now, of course, that nothing of the kind was to occur. Many Americans do indeed endorse the expansive definition of abortion rights that *Roe* set forth, but many others strongly oppose it. The political debate over abortion certainly isn't lessening. Leaders and activists on both sides of the issue are arguing more, not less, heatedly for the rightness of their respective positions and working even harder to push waivering politicians to support their stands.

The Supreme Court has continued in recent years to grapple with the abortion issue. In 1989, attention focused on a case reaching the Court on appeal from the state of Missouri—

[1] David O'Brien, *Storm Center: The Supreme Court in American Politics*, 2nd ed. (New York: Norton, 1990).

The right to an abortion remains a divisive issue.

Webster v. Reproductive Health Services. Like a number of other states, Missouri had imposed new regulations and restrictions on abortions, though it had not challenged the central thrust of *Roe.* The Court decided *Webster* on July 3, 1989, upholding key sections of the Missouri statute. (We discuss its ruling below.) Though relatively limited, the decision added to the sense that big changes might be forthcoming in abortion policy. Defenders of *Roe*—known as the "pro-choice" camp, as opposed to the anti-abortion activists, known as "pro-life"—became alarmed and fought back politically, bringing the abortion issue to new heights of intensity.

The most recent of the high court's major rulings on abortion policy was handed down in June 1992 in *Planned Parenthood of Southeastern Pennsylvania, et al. v. Robert Casey, et al.,* hereafter referred to simply as *Planned Parenthood v. Casey.* At issue was the constitutionality of Pennsylvania legislation imposing a series of restrictions on abortion, including the requirement that physicians provide women seeking abortions with information that argues against it and the reqirement that women under eighteen obtain the written consent of one parent or, in lieu of that, a court order through a "judicial bypass" procedure. In *Planned Parenhood v. Casey,* the Supreme Court upheld the Pennsylvania law and, going further, for the first time explicitly modified *Roe.* But, by a 5–4 majority, the Court left in force some central elements of *Roe,* most important the ruling that a state may not ban abortions to be performed prior to the time the fetus reaches viability.

HISTORY AND CONTEXT

Because the Court's ruling in *Roe v. Wade* is the centerpiece of the contemporary debate over abortion policy, we need to look at it from several different angles: what public policy was before the decision, the ruling's intellectual antecedents, the country's practical experience with abortion over the past seventeen years, what has happened to the Court's philosophic make-up since *Roe,* and abortion law as it now stands in the wake of *Planned Parenthood v. Casey.*

Abortion Policy before Roe. Like many matters of American public policy, abortion was historically a state issue. The states gradually developed bodies of legislation on abortion and the conditions under which it might be legally performed. (See chapter 5 for discussions of the

U.S. federal system and the states' large role in shaping public policy.)

In his majority opinion in *Roe* Justice Harry Blackmun reviewed this diverse state legislative experience. In 1821, Connecticut was the first state to enact abortion legislation. In 1828, New York passed a statute that was to serve as a model for action in other states. New York barred abortion before and after "quickening"—the point at which the mother first recognizes movement of the fetus in the uterus, usually around the sixteenth week of pregnancy—but it treated the two cases differently. The law made the induced abortion of an unquickened fetus a misdemeanor, but it made abortion of the fetus after quickening second-degree manslaughter. In the late nineteenth century, most states dropped the distinction between abortion done before and after quickening. And by this time most had banned abortions except when performed to preserve the mother's life.

Much later, in the 1960s and early 1970s but before the *Roe* decision, many states liberalized their abortion legislation. Four states repealed altogether criminal penalties for abortions performed in early pregnancy: Alaska, Hawaii, Washington, and New York.

Justice Blackmun argued that this review of state legislative experience buttressed the new ruling that the Court was handing down in *Roe*. That is, abortion had not been uniformly opposed in state law and had been treated very differently over time. *Roe* might be seen, then, as but the latest chapter in evolving norms and standards on this issue. Of course, the vast and diverse state experience historically could just as easily be taken as an argument against *Roe*. In all the years until 1973, abortion policy had remained essentially *state policy*. The Court broke with this in *Roe* by finding a *national* right, contained in the Constitution, that barred states from curbing abortion, whatever their

political majorities wanted done, until viability was attained.

The Griswold *Precedent.* Eight years before *Roe* the Supreme Court had signaled an important shift of interpretation that was to provide the intellectual base for the *Roe* decision. In *Griswold v. Connecticut* (1965), the Court ruled that Connecticut's birth control law, which banned the sale and use of contraceptives and barred physicians and clinics from counseling on birth control, was unconstitutional. At issue here was not whether this legislation was wise but whether by enacting it the state legislature had strayed into an area where the Constitution did not allow it to go. The majority in *Griswold* thought that it had. The Court held that the Constitution defines fundamental rights, not expressly enumerated, that create "zones of privacy" where government shall not pass. In *Roe*, the Court applied this basic right-of-privacy construction even further, arguing that the Constitution provides a right to privacy "broad enough to encompass a woman's decision whether or not to terminate her pregnancy."

*The Post-*Roe *Experience.* Prior to *Roe*, many abortions were being performed legally in states around the country. Nearly 600,000 legal abortions were reported in 1972, immediately preceding *Roe* (Figure 9.1). Nonetheless, *Roe* produced an immediate, dramatic increase in legal abortions. By 1975 the number was nearly double what it had been three years earlier, having crossed the 1 million mark, and by 1980 the annual total stood at between 1.5 and 1.6 million—where it has since remained constant. In the United States in the 1980s, the data show, roughly 30 percent of all pregnancies were ended by induced abortion. This high abortion rate clearly heightened the controversy surrounding the issue.

Figure 9.1   Legal Abortions Performed, 1972–88

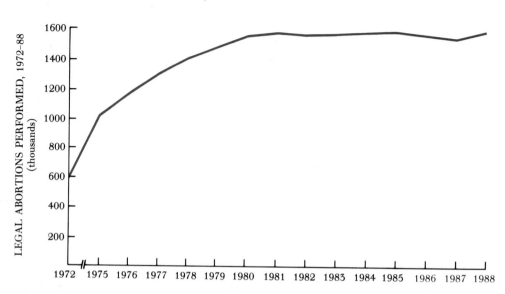

Source: *Statistical Abstract of the United States*, 1991, p. 71, 72.

Changes on the Court. The Supreme Court decided *Roe* by 7 votes to 2. It's likely that the persistence of such a decisive Court majority would have dampened subsequent political hopes of abortion opponents. If the Court were going to continue to uphold *Roe*'s substantial abortion guarantees, pro-life groups would have only one recourse short of civil disobedience: secure a constitutional amendment banning abortion (in most instances). And the U.S. Constitution is exceedingly hard to amend.

In fact though, the Court's philosophic center shifted steadily over the 1980s and early 1990s, due to Ronald Reagan's and George Bush's appointment of more conservative justices (see Table 9.1). The two dissenters from *Roe*—William Rehnquist and Byron White—have remained on the Court, and one of them, Rehnquist, was elevated in 1986 by President Reagan to the position of chief justice. Five justices who helped comprise the *Roe* majority have retired since 1981 and been replaced by

conservatives: Potter Stewart, who was replaced in 1981 by Sandra Day O'Connor; Warren Burger, himself a conservative, though in the *Roe* majority, whose seat on the Court (though not his position as chief justice) was taken by Antonin Scalia in 1986; Lewis Powell, who retired in 1987 and was replaced in 1988 by Anthony M. Kennedy; William Brennan, who retired in 1990 and was replaced by David H. Souter; and Thurgood Marshall, who stepped down in 1991 and whose seat was taken by Clarence Thomas.

The importance of the changes in the Court's makeup was signaled as early as 1986, in *Thornburgh v. American College of Obstetricians and Gynecologists.* The Court struck down by only the narrowest of margins, 5 to 4, provisions of a 1982 Pennsylvania statute that required doctors to provide women seeking abortion with detailed information about its risks and the alternatives to it. The Pennsylvania legislation also provided that women must

TABLE 9.1 MEMBERS OF THE U.S. SUPREME COURT, AS OF JULY 1992

Name	Place of birth	Age as of 1/1/92	Law school from which graduated	President who appointed
White, Byron Raymond	Fort Collins, CO	74	Yale	Kennedy (1962)
Blackmun, Harry A.	Nashville, IL	83	Harvard	Nixon (1970)
Rehnquist, William Hubbs*	Milwaukee, WI	67	Stanford	Nixon (1971) Reagan (1986)
Stevens, John Paul	Chicago, IL	71	Chicago	Ford (1975)
O'Connor, Sandra Day	El Paso, TX	61	Stanford	Reagan (1981)
Scalia, Antonin	Trenton, NJ	55	Harvard	Reagan (1986)
Kennedy, Anthony McLeod	Sacramento, CA	55	Harvard	Reagan (1988)
Souter, David H.	Melrose, MA	52	Harvard	Bush (1990)
Thomas, Clarence	Savannah, GA	43	Yale	Bush (1991)

*Rehnquist was nominated to the U.S. Supreme Court in 1971 by Richard Nixon; he was nominated as chief justice by Ronald Reagan in 1986.

The Supreme Court of the United States, seated left to right: Associate Justices John Paul Stevens, Byron R. White, Chief Justice William H. Rehnquist, Associate Justices Harry A. Blackmun and Sandra Day O'Connor. Standing left to right: Associate Justices David H. Souter, Antonin Scalia, Anthony M. Kennedy, and Clarence Thomas.

be given materials describing the "probable anatomical and physiological characteristics of the unborn child at two-week intervals during its gestation." "The printed materials . . . seem to us nothing less than an outright attempt to drive the Commonwealth's [that is, Pennsylvania's] message discouraging abortion into the privacy of the informed-consent dialogue between the woman and her physician," Justice Blackmun wrote for the majority. Four justices—Rehnquist, White, O'Connor, and Burger—had disagreed and were prepared to uphold the Pennsylvania law.

Against this backdrop, President Reagan's 1988 appointment of Anthony M. Kennedy to a seat on the Court was seen by many observers as likely to produce a new conservative majority in general and in particular a majority prepared in some way to amend *Roe*. The first major test of what the new Court might do on the issue came, as noted, in 1989 in a Missouri case involving legislation similar to the Pennsylvania statute that the Court had declared unconstitutional in 1982.

The Webster *Ruling.* The *Webster* decision showed that the Court had shifted significantly but that there was not as yet a new majority prepared to reverse *Roe*. Four justices—Rehnquist, White, Scalia, and Kennedy—would have in effect reversed *Roe*, though three of them only indirectly. Antonin Scalia's opinion, which, along with portions of the rest of the *Webster* opinions, is reprinted in Ladd Report #8, displayed evident exasperation with three generally like-minded colleagues for not confronting directly the substance of *Roe*. "It thus appears that the mansion of constitutionalized abortion law, constructed overnight in *Roe v. Wade*, must be disassembled door jam by door jam, and never entirely brought down, no matter how wrong it may be. . . ."

At the same time, four other justices—Blackmun, who had written the majority opinion in

Roe; William Brennan; Thurgood Marshall; and John Paul Stevens—were prepared to uphold *Roe*. This left Sandra Day O'Connor the swing vote. Even before the ruling she had been recognized by most as being undecided on *Roe* and hence as being a swing vote, and she had thus been subjected to an extraordinary lobbying campaign, which included her being deluged with letters from supporters of abortion rights. The mail was so heavy that for a time she could not get much important professional correspondence, which was lost within the thousands upon thousands of missives on abortion. Mail clerks simply couldn't keep up.

In *Webster* Justice O'Connor concurred with Chief Justice Rehnquist and Justices White, Kennedy, and Scalia in upholding the main provisions of the Missouri statute, but she wasn't prepared to join them in a more expansive rejection of *Roe*. As a result, states were told only that limited abortion regulations and restrictions, beyond what the Court had countenanced since 1973, could now be constitutionally enacted.

The provisions of the Missouri statute that the majority in *Webster* sustained are:

1. A preamble that contains "findings" by the state legislature that "the life of each human being begins at conception" and that "unborn children have protectable interests in life, health, and well-being." The majority held that there was nothing preventing the state from expressing "that sort of value judgment" if it so chose.

2. A provision that "it shall be unlawful for any public employee within the scope of his employment to perform or assist in an abortion not necessary to save the life of the mother." The Court of Appeals for the Eighth Circuit, which had heard the case prior to its reaching the Supreme Court, had struck down this provision as contravening the Court's abortion decisions. Here, as on the other main elements of the statute, the majority in *Webster* reversed the Court of Appeals and upheld the state law.

3. A section that makes it "unlawful for any public facility to be used for the purpose of performing or assisting an abortion not necessary to save the life of the mother."

4. A provision barring the use of public funds to counsel a woman to have an abortion not necessary to save her life.

5. A section stipulating that "before a physician performs an abortion on a woman he has reason to believe is carrying an unborn child of twenty or more weeks gestational age, the physician shall first determine if the unborn child is viable by using or exercising that degree of care, skill, and proficiency commonly exercised by the ordinarily skillful, careful, and prudent physician. . . ." Here, too, the Court of Appeals for the Eighth Circuit had found the Missouri law unconstitutional, on the grounds that it put a barrier between the woman and the right to abortion beyond what the court had countenanced in *Roe*. But the majority in *Webster* let stand this provision of the Missouri law, though they disagreed in their reasons for doing so.

In a part of the *Webster* opinion that did not have majority support, Chief Justice Rehnquist strongly criticized "the rigid *Roe* framework." He wrote that

> the key elements of the *Roe* framework—trimester and viability—are not found in the text of the Constitution or in any place else one would expect to find a constitutional principle. . . . In the second place, we do not see why the states' interests in protecting potential human life should come into existence only at the point of viability, and that there should therefore be a rigid line allowing state regulation after viability but prohibiting it before viability. . . .

While she upheld the Missouri statute, Justice O'Connor was unwilling to join her colleagues in the Court's conservative bloc in so far-reaching a rejection of *Roe*. All of the provisions of the Missouri legislation that were before the Court in the *Webster* case could be upheld, she argued, as consistent with *Roe*. "Only when the constitutional invalidity of a state abortion statute actually turns on the constitutional validity of *Roe* will it be necessary, and timely, to re-examine *Roe* itself." Thus Justice O'Connor solidified her "swing vote" standing.

Beyond Webster. Just before it adjourned in June 1990, the high court issued a ruling in *Hodgson v. Minnesota* that attested both to the continuing erosion of earlier precedents and the justices' uncertainty over how far state regulations should be allowed to extend. A 5–4 majority upheld a state statute prohibiting teenage girls from obtaining abortions without

Kathryn Kolbert, the attorney who delivered the oral argument before the Supreme Court for Planned Parenthood in Planned Parenthood of Southeastern Pennsylvania v. Casey.

first notifying their parents. But with Justice O'Connor casting the deciding vote, the Court held that the require-ment that *both parents* be notified even if a teenager lives with only one was constitutional only because the state provided for a "judicial bypass." That is, a girl could get a judge's permission to bypass consulting the second parent from whom she might be estranged.

Planned Parenthood v. Casey. The Court's next major ruling on abortion was to come in 1992 in *Planned Parenthood v. Casey.* At issue here was the constitutionality of Pennsylvania legislation similar in reach to what the Court had upheld by a narrow 5–4 majority in *Webster* three years earlier. Three provisions of the Pennsylvania statute were the immediate focus of the challenge in this case: the requirement that a woman seeking an abortion give her informed consent prior to the procedure, which means that she be provided with certain information about it at least twenty-four hours before it is performed; the requirement that a minor seeking an abortion have the informed consent of at least one parent or be granted a bypass of this by a court; the provision that a married woman seeking an abortion sign a statement indicating that she has notified her husband.

Like *Webster, Planned Parenthood v. Casey* did not simply present the Court with a choice of whether to overturn *Roe.* There were three main alternatives: First, the Court could substantially reaffirm *Roe,* which would mean striking down the above provisions of the Pennsylvania law because *Roe* allowed no such regulation of abortions performed in the first two trimesters. This is the position advocated by Planned Parenthood and other abortion rights groups. Second, it could not only uphold the Pennsylvania regulations, but it could also indicate that states had even more expansive regulatory authority. This is what most pro-life groups wanted the Court to decide. Or, third, it could largely uphold the Pennsylvania stat-

ute but indicate that there were sharp limits on the extent of permissible state regulation.

What Planned Parenthood v. Casey *decided.* In a complicated set of judgments not unlike those rendered in *Webster,* the Court in effect took the middle course. By a 7–2 majority, with only Justices Blackmun and Stevens dissenting, the Court did, as expected, uphold most of Pennsylvania's abortion law. The one provision overturned was that requiring notification of the husband. A majority found this requirement an undue burden: In any healthy marriage the woman would naturally inform her husband, whether or not the law said she must do so. Were she to fear abuse from her spouse, she should not be forced to notify him. This provision aside, Pennsylvania's regulation of abortion was found to be constitutional.

Only four justices—Rehnquist, White, Scalia, and Thomas—contended that the Court erred in *Roe* when it held the right to abortion to be "fundamental." Because abortion involves "the purposeful termination of potential life," these four justices reasoned, the abortion decision is different in kind from the rights protected in earlier cases under the rubric of personal or family privacy. Hence, they argued, state statutes abridging the right need not be subject to strict judicial scrutiny; states have great leeway in deciding what curbs are to be imposed.

Five justices—Blackmun and Stevens, who would have stricken the Pennsylvania statute, together with O'Connor, Souter, and Kennedy, who had upheld the Pennsylvania law—were not prepared to abandon *Roe.* Blackmun and Stevens would not grant states the regulatory reach that O'Connor, Souter, and Kennedy give them, but they stand with the latter three in denying the degree of state restriction that Rehnquist et al. find constitutionally permissible. Thus, while just three of the nine justices took the position that Sandra Day O'Connor had taken the lead in crafting, this position became the law of the land.

The O'Connor-Souter-Kennedy position has three main components: (1) Respecting the fact that *Roe* has been the law of the land for twenty years, and has come to be seen as settled law by many people, a woman's basic right to choose to have an abortion prior to fetal viability must receive continuing constitutional recognition. (2) At the same time, state governments have a "profound interest in potential life," and they may impose certain regulations on abortion pursuant to that interest. Which regulations? Those that do not impose an "undue burden" on women seeking abortion before fetal viability. Making sure that a woman's choice is informed, requiring short waiting periods, requiring minors in most cases to receive parental consent prior to having an abortion— such measures do not impose an undue burden. (3) *Roe*'s "rigid trimester framework" is rejected. The key factor is now fetal viability. Before viability, states may regulate abortion, but only in ways that do not impose an undue burden or curb the basic right; after viability, states can impose whatever curbs they believe proper, including a categoric ban on abortions except in cases where the life of the mother is at stake.

The political scene after the *Planned Parenthood* decision remains tense and uncertain. Abortion rights groups argue that, while much of *Roe* remains law, abortion rights have been limited, and four justices—just one short of a majority—would limit them further. Pro-life groups, on the other hand, argue that the Court did not go nearly far enough in dismantling *Roe*. They are especially critical of Justice Kennedy, who appeared to be of the same position as Chief Justice Rehnquist in *Webster*, but who left that position and joined Justices O'Connor and Souter in *Planned Parenthood v. Casey*.

We can't know how much Justices O'Connor, Souter, and Kennedy were influenced by their reading of public opinion on the abortion issue. We can say, however, that their position conforms broadly to majority public opinion. That is, most Americans would not bar abortions categorically prior to fetal viability, but they do support certain curbs or limits, like those the Court has upheld in *Webster* and *Planned Parenthood*.

BROWN V. BOARD OF EDUCATION OF TOPEKA (1954)

The Supreme Court has been at the storm center many times over its history. In the 1950s, for example, it was at the center of a great political battle over racial segregation, and its rulings helped set the country on a new course toward desegregation. One of its rulings in this area, **Brown v. Board of Education of Topeka** (1954), is probably the single most important Court decision of modern times. *Brown* and its companion cases came to the Supreme Court as specific challenges to what was then the general southern and border states' practice of maintaining two separate public school systems: one for whites and one for blacks. At issue was the requirement of section 1 of the Fourteenth Amendment: "No state shall . . . deny to any person within its jurisdiction the equal protection of the laws." Did the prevailing segregation of black students deny them equal protection mandated by the Fourteenth Amendment?

Chief Justice Earl Warren, speaking for a unanimous Court, concluded, "We have now announced that such segregation is a denial of equal protection of the laws." (See Box 9.1, p. 251.) With this decided, the nation was launched on a new policy course that would entail major changes in educational programs by local, state, and national government. Narrowly construed, separation of powers and checks and balances envision a situation where the excesses of one branch are curbed by another. In a more general sense, this constitutional doctrine allows for the failure of one part of government in discharging its constitu-

*Segregated classroom in Atlanta, Georgia, May 21, 1954, four days after Chief Justice
Earl Warren delivered the unanimous opinion in* Brown v. Board of Education of
Topeka.

tional duties to be corrected by another part of government not subject to the same political constraints. The work of the Supreme Court in *Brown* shows this process at its best. By the 1950s, many Americans believed that the presence of segregated schools throughout the South grossly denied the constitutional claim to equal rights for all citizens. But opinion among the white majority in southern states was such that local government would not act to end segregation. Congress had ample legislative authority to act, but the near-unanimous opposition of southern congressmen, many of whom held positions of great authority in the congressional committee system, was sufficient to block legislation. Of all the branches of government in a position to act, only the Supreme Court was sufficiently insulated from such political pressures to take corrective steps.

When Congress passes a statute treating a central question of national policy, the objective set forth in the statute is not always promptly and harmoniously achieved. So it is with Supreme Court decisions. *Brown* was immediately engulfed in intense controversy. At once hailed by some for signaling the demise of the "separate but equal" doctrine instituted in 1896, it was vigorously denounced by others as a usurpation of state prerogatives. In March 1956, 101 of the 128 members of Congress from eleven southern and border states issued a tract that labeled the *Brown* decision "a clear abuse of judicial power" and applauded states intending to "resist enforced integration by any means."[2]

[2]U.S. Congress, Senate, "Declaration of Constitutional Principles," *Congressional Record* 102 (March 12, 1956), p. 4460.

Box 9.1
Brown v. Board of Education of Topeka (1954)

Facts. Five cases originating in the states of Kansas, South Carolina, Virginia, and Delaware, and in the District of Columbia, came to the Supreme Court for re-argument on June 8, 1953. All involved challenges to the constitutionality of racial segregation in public schools. In each, black school children through counsel sought admission to community schools to which they had been denied access. The lead case involved a suit by Oliver Brown to require the Board of Education of Topeka, Kansas, to admit his eight-year-old daughter Linda to a then all-white public school only five blocks from her home.

Decision. In a unanimous opinion the court held that the segregation that the plaintiffs complained of violated the guarantee of equal protection of the laws under the Fourteenth Amendment to the U.S. Constitution. Chief Justice Warren, delivering the opinion of the Court, said in part:

> . . . Today, education is perhaps the most important function of state and local governments. In these days, it is doubtful that any child may reasonably be expected to succeed in life if he is denied the opportunity of an education. Such an opportunity, where the state has undertaken to provide it, is a right which must be made available to all on equal terms.
>
> We come then to the question presented: Does segregation of children in public schools solely on the basis of race, even though the physical facilities and other "tangible" factors may be equal, deprive the children of the minority group of equal educational opportunities? We believe that it does. . . . To separate them [children in grade and high schools] from others of similar age and qualifications solely because of their race generates a feeling of inferiority as to their status in the community that may affect their hearts and minds in a way unlikely ever to be undone. The effect of this separation on their educational opportunities was well stated by a finding in the Kansas case by a court which nevertheless felt compelled to rule against the Negro plaintiffs: "Segregation of white and colored children in public schools has a detrimental effect upon the colored children. The impact is greater when it has the sanction of the law; for the policy of separating the races is usually interpreted as denoting the inferiority of the Negro group. A sense of inferiority affects the motivation of a child to learn. Segregation with the sanction of law, therefore, has a tendency to [retard] the educational and mental development of Negro children and to deprive them of some of the benefits they would receive in a racial[ly] integrated school system." We conclude that in the field of public education the doctrine of "separate but equal" has no place. Separate educational facilities are inherently unequal. Therefore, we hold that the plaintiffs and others similarly situated for whom the actions have been brought are, by reason of the segregation complained of, deprived of the equal protection of the laws guaranteed by the Fourteenth Amendment. . . .

Massive resistance in many southern states followed for years after.

DEVELOPMENTS IN JUDICIAL INTERVENTION

The *Roe*, *Webster*, and *Brown* decisions show how the Supreme Court becomes involved in political controversy and policy making. In their constitutional role of saying what the law is, other courts, at the federal and state level, have also been heavily involved in policy formation throughout the country's history. But over the last two decades there has been a significant broadening of judicial intervention—and this has generated intense controversy. "Today no action of government seems complete without litigation," judicial scholar Martin Shapiro writes.

> Our newspapers tell us of judges who forbid the transfer of air-force squadrons from one base to another, delay multi-million construction projects, intervene in complex negotiations between public employers and their employees, oversee the operation of railroads, and decide the location of schools. . . . Judges now joyously try their hand at everything from the engineering of atomic reactors to the validation of I.Q. tests. They run school districts, do regional land use planning, redesign welfare programs, and calculate energy needs. . . . Today there seems to be no public policy issue, no matter how massive, complex, or technical that some judge somewhere has not felt fully capable of deciding, aided only by the standard processes of litigation.[3]

[3] Martin Shapiro, "Judicial Activism," in Seymour Martin Lipset, ed., *The Third Century: America as a Post-Industrial Society* (Chicago: University of Chicago Press, 1979), p. 125.

Departing from past practice, many federal district courts and some state courts became directly involved in the daily management of major public agencies: prisons, mental hospitals, facilities for the elderly, local school systems. In *Wyatt v. Stickney* (1972), federal district judge Frank M. Johnson found "intolerable and deplorable" conditions prevailing in Alabama's largest state mental health facility. The court held that, as a matter of due process under the Fourteenth Amendment, hospital inmates "unquestionably have a constitutional right to receive such individual treatment as will give each of them a realistic opportunity to be cured or to improve his or her mental condition. . . ." In support of this finding, the court set forth detailed constitutional standards of care and treatment. Similarly, in *Hamilton v. Schiro* (1970), federal district judge Herbert W. Christenberry ordered that the mayor of New Orleans "immediately implement" directives for the reform of New Orleans prisons: providing specified medical and dental services, constructing a new hospital, guaranteeing "adequate security for medical personnel to facilitate the needs of the medical program," maintaining a year-round recreational program, building an indoor recreation area, and limiting the number of prisoners in the main facility.

JUDICIAL INTERVENTION: A JUDGE RAISES TAXES

A striking recent example of the new style of judicial intervention involves federal district judge Russell G. Clark of Kansas City, Missouri. In September 1987, Judge Clark, frustrated by the inability of the Kansas City school board to pay its share of the costs of a major desegregation plan he had approved and by the refusal of the school district's voters to raise taxes to finance the plan, issued sweeping orders. He ordered property taxes (on residences, business property, cars, etc.) in the Kansas City school district doubled. He also imposed a surcharge on the Missouri income tax, raising the levy for those who lived in the school district 25 percent. The desegregation plan Judge Clark ordered was enormously costly, which is why the tax increases he mandated to pay for it were so high. The plan included major capital improvements for existing schools and the building of numerous new "magnet" schools—with the total price tag, as estimated in 1989, surpassing $700 million.[4]

Did Judge Clark overreach? Certainly many Kansas City residents think so. Some of them even tore up their voter registration cards and mailed them to the judge. "With the decision of one man to go ahead and impose this tax, why vote?" said one resident. The state of Missouri, which took the case to the Supreme Court on appeal, argued that Judge Clark should have scaled back his desegregation plan to affordable levels. "This is an egregious example of a judge absolutely consumed with the ability of the bench to enforce its orders at whatever cost to society," said Gary McDowell of the National Legal Center for the Public Interest, a conservative "think tank" in legal policy.[5]

Civil liberties and civil rights groups defended the judge's actions. John Powell, legal director of the American Civil Liberties Union, argued that the Supreme Court's overturning Judge Clark's orders "would essentially cripple the Judiciary from executing its role protecting constitutional rights."[6]

In *Missouri v. Jenkins* (1990), the Supreme Court decided the issue. It was sharply split, however, and the majority ruling itself displayed an underlying discomfort with the way the case posed the issue of the courts' proper role. For a five-justice majority, Byron White wrote that the district court—that is, Judge Clark—had indeed abused its discretion in imposing the tax. White held, however, that a court *can* constitutionally direct a local government to increase its taxes, when necessary to "vindicate constitutional guarantees."

The problem with Clark's approach, White wrote, was that "the tax increase controvened the principles of comity" among the branches of government. The district court thought it had no alternative but to impose a tax increase, given the requirements of its desegregation plan. "But there was an alternative. . . . It could have authorized or required the [Kansas City school district] to levy property taxes at a rate adequate to fund the desegregation remedy. . . ." Judge Clark should not have gone so far into the specific workings of another branch; he should simply have required that branch itself to do what was needed.

The other four justices agreed that Clark had exceeded his authority, but disagreed with what Anthony Kennedy—writing for them in dissent—called a "casual embrace of taxation imposed by the un-elected, life-tenured federal judiciary. . . ." If a judge can order a tax increase whenever he sees an important objective to be promoted, Kennedy argued, the basic design of separation of powers is violated.

PROBLEMS WITH INCREASED JUDICIAL INTERVENTION

The development of a more activist judicial branch is a natural response to changes in American society and politics. But it is not problem free. One problem, as we have seen, is that the courts are not responsible, as legislators or executives are, for the costs of their actions. A related problem involves the increased difficulty in adjusting priorities and finding compromises when interests get expressed as

[4] Stephen Wermiel, "Test of Power: Can a Federal Judge Raise Property Taxes?" *Wall Street Journal*, October 2, 1989, pp. 1, 9.

[5] Ibid., p. 9.

[6] Ibid.

basic legal rights. When, for example, a question of providing a particular service is brought before the executive and legislative branches, decision makers can argue about whether expending millions of dollars on it is merited, considering the benefits that would accrue from alternate uses of the same funds. However, when a court declares that individuals have a *right* to it, the service must be provided—even if the costs appear to most people to be prohibitively high, set against the benefits gained.

THE COURT SYSTEM OF THE UNITED STATES

American federalism posits two distinct levels of government: national and state (with local government a subdivision of state). This federal structure extends into the judiciary. Two distinct sets of courts operate in the United States: federal courts exist side by side with courts established by the fifty states. In the pages that follow, we will examine the important question of **jurisdiction:** which cases originate in the federal courts and which in the state courts? The country's highest judicial authority, the Supreme Court of the United States, is at the apex of the dual court system; by deciding appeals from both the highest state courts and lower federal courts, it establishes necessary uniformity in national law and legal practices.

The basic national court structure includes the **U.S. district courts,** which function as trial courts or courts of original jurisdiction (where a case is first tried); the **U.S. courts of appeal,** which are the lower federal appellate courts (hearing appeals of decisions rendered in lower courts); and the **U.S. Supreme Court.** In 1988, there were 94 district courts and 12 U.S. courts of appeal. (See Figure 9.2.)

JURISDICTION

What determines which cases are heard in this federal court system and which by state courts? Part of the answer may be found in Article IV, section 2, of the U.S. Constitution, which permits federal court jurisdiction in "all cases, in law and equity" that meet one of two sets of standards—involving either the subject matter of the case or the character of the parties to the suit. Under the first standard, federal courts have jurisdiction in

1. cases arising under the U.S. Constitution, a federal law, or a treaty;

2. cases involving admiralty and maritime laws.

Under the second standard, federal jurisdiction is granted when

3. the U.S. government is a party to the suit;

4. one or more state governments is a party;

5. the controversy is between citizens of different states;

6. a case involves an ambassador or some other official representative of a foreign country;

7. a case arises between citizens of the same state because of a dispute involving land grants claimed under titles of two or more states.

When the federal courts have jurisdiction, cases typically originate in the U.S. district courts. Congress has given the district courts original jurisdiction only; they are the "workhorse' trial courts where the cases and controversies are first heard. The U.S. courts of appeal and the Supreme Court have only limited original jurisdiction; most of the cases reaching them do so on appeal.

Article III, section 2, sets the outer limits of federal court jurisdiction, but nothing in the Constitution prevents Congress from assigning

FIGURE 9.2   ORGANIZATION OF THE FEDERAL COURTS

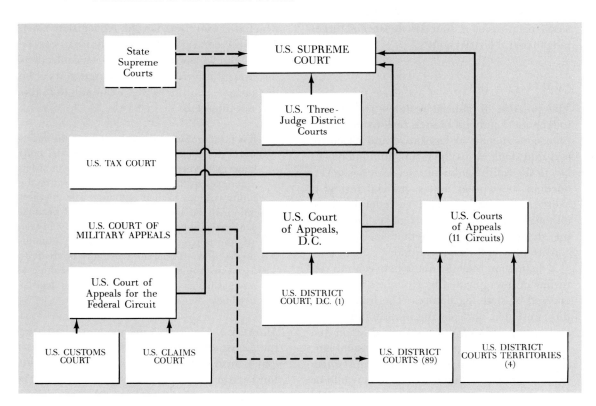

Source: Adapted from Howard Ball, *Courts and Politics: The Federal Judicial System* (Englewood Cliffs, N.J.: Prentice-Hall, 1980), p. 74. The arrows show the direction of appeals through the system.

certain portions of this jurisdiction to state courts, on a concurrent or even on an exclusive basis. Concurrent jurisdiction means that a case may originate in either a state or a federal court; exclusive jurisdiction means it is assigned only to one or the other. For example, Congress has provided that if the dollar amount in civil suits involving citizens of different states exceeds a certain amount—set at $50,000 in 1989—the case may be tried in either a federal district court or a state court. Otherwise, exclusive jurisdiction is granted to the state courts. This provision was enacted to reduce the federal court workload. U.S. district courts have the sole power to hear all proceedings in bankruptcy. This exclusive federal jurisdiction accounts for a substantial portion of the district courts' workload: There were 880,399 bankruptcy filings in 1991 alone. In addition, Congress has granted exclusive original jurisdiction to the federal courts in all prosecutions for violation of federal criminal laws.

In most instances where a case arises under a state law, exclusive original jurisdiction is held by the trial courts of that state. Appeals may be brought, though, from the highest state courts to the U.S. Supreme Court when a substantial federal question is raised. And challenges to state laws on the grounds they violate the U.S. Constitution or federal statutes may in some instances be initiated in the special three-judge federal district courts.

JUDICIAL REVIEW

The practice of **judicial review**—whereby an independent judicial branch reviews and gives final construction to legislative and executive acts and determines their constitutionality—is key to the courts' political role. As it has developed in the United States, judicial review is exercised by state as well as federal courts, although the Supreme Court makes final binding determination of whether legislation is consistent with the Constitution.

A distinction must be made between judicial review of laws enacted by Congress and those enacted by state legislatures. The framers saw the Supreme Court playing umpire in the federal system, striking down state legislation that clashed with the requirements of national law. Alexander Hamilton argued in *Federalist Paper* No. 22 that true national government would be impossible if each state court system could separately decide what the Constitution and federal legislation require. It is essential "to establish one court paramount to the rest, possessing a general superintendence and authorized to settle and declare in the last resort a uniform rule of civil justice." Section 25 of the Judiciary Act of 1789 (enacted by a Congress of which many of the framers were members) explicitly conferred upon the Supreme Court authority to review state court decisions involving state actions in which a federal claim was raised.

On the issue of the Court's striking down acts of Congress, however, the historical record is more ambiguous. Some framers argued strongly for this power, as Hamilton did forcefully in *Federalist Paper* No. 78: "There is no position which depends on clearer principles than that every act of a delegated authority, contrary to the tenor of the commission under which it is exercised, is void. No legislative act, therefore, contrary to the Constitution, can be valid." But who is to decide if an act contradicts the Constitution? Shouldn't Congress itself be the judge? Hamilton was adamant that this was not intended.

> It is far more rational to suppose that the courts were designed to be an intermediate body between the people and the legislature in order, among other things, to keep the latter within the limits assigned to their authority. The interpretation of the laws is the proper and peculiar province of the courts. A constitution is, in fact, and must be regarded by the judges as a fundamental law. It therefore belongs to them to ascertain its meaning as well as the meaning of any particular act proceeding from the legislative body.

Marbury v. Madison. A decade and a half after the Constitution was ratified, Supreme Court Chief Justice John Marshall echoed Hamilton's argument. "The Constitution is either a superior paramount law, unchangeable by ordinary means, or it is on a level with ordinary legislative acts. . . . If the former part of the alternative be true, then a legislative act contrary to the Constitution is not law. . . . It is, emphatically, the province and duty of the judicial department, to say what the law is." Marshall concluded that "a law repugnant to the Constitution is void; and that courts, as well as other departments, are bound by that instrument."

The case in which Marshall delivered this momentous ruling was *Marbury v. Madison,* decided in 1803. William Marbury had been an official in the administration of President John Adams. Along with more than fifty others in the Federalist party, he was nominated and confirmed for a federal judgeship just before Adams left office in March 1801. Final work

John Marshall, chief justice of the Supreme Court for thirty-four years, 1801–35.

on Marbury's commission was completed so late, however, that it did not get delivered before Thomas Jefferson and his new administration took office. Angered by Adams's attempt to stack the federal judiciary with so many Federalist party members, Jefferson ordered that Marbury's commission (and others similarly not delivered) be held back. Marbury took his case to the Supreme Court, seeking an order requiring the Jefferson administration to give him his appointment.

John Marshall had been secretary of state in Adams's administration, and it was actually his oversight that had led to Marbury's commission not being delivered. By the time the Supreme Court heard Marbury's appeal, Marshall was chief justice. The case seemed to

present him with a no-win dilemma. If the Court issued the order Marbury wanted, Jefferson and his secretary of state, James Madison, would certainly ignore it. The Court had no means to enforce compliance. And, as a new institution trying to establish itself, the Court might suffer permanent damage from such a precedent. But if it did not issue the order, the Court would be seen to be caving in to Jefferson's point of view.

In the ruling for a unanimous Court, the chief justice found a way to escape this dilemma and expand upon the Court's authority. Since the president had signed the commissions and the secretary of state had recorded them, the appointments were in order, Marshall wrote. The Jefferson administration was wrong in not releasing them to Marbury and his colleagues. Having thus rebuked Jefferson and Madison, Marshall turned to the question of whether the Supreme Court had the authority to issue the order Marbury wanted—and he concluded that it did not. Marshall found that a minor provision in the Judiciary Act of 1789 under which Marbury had sought remedy gave the Court original jurisdiction beyond what the Constitution allowed and had to be struck down. Thus was the Court's power to declare an act of Congress unconstitutional first formally enunciated.

In subsequent years, the Hamilton-Marshall position on judicial review triumphed. But it was by no means generally accepted at the time. Insofar as judicial review of congressional acts was considered at all by most framers, it was endorsed only in a narrow form: as a means whereby flagrant violations of the Constitution by Congress or the president could be declared void.[7] It would be a weapon in reserve,

[7] Sheldon Goldman, *Constitutional Law and Supreme Court Decision-Making* (New York: Harper and Row, 1982), p. 12.

to be used rarely as a check in extreme cases, not the expansive power it has in fact become.

Since its beginnings, the Supreme Court has held over 900 state acts to be unconstitutional, and has voided more than 120 federal statutes in whole or in part.[8] Up until the Civil War, only two congressional acts had been held unconstitutional; the rate of such findings increased substantially in the late nineteenth century and has increased even more in the twentieth century. Four-fifths of all federal statutes (or portions thereof) struck down by the Court have been voided since 1900.

Judicial Review Abroad. Comparable powers of judicial review are by no means commonly held by courts in other democracies. In Great Britain the constitutional doctrine of the supremacy of Parliament means that the courts may not strike down any law that the legislature has enacted. In France, only a circumscribed power resembling judicial review exists, and it resides not in the courts but in the Constitutional Council (which includes a number of ranking political officials, among them all living past presidents of France). Private individuals cannot challenge a law's constitutionality; only the president, the premier, the heads of the two houses of the legislature, or a group of at least 60 members of the legislature by petition may do so.

Other countries have developed certain aspects of judicial review, but not the full-blown form one sees in the United States. In Germany no ordinary court is permitted to decide constitutional questions in the course of litigation. A Federal Constitution Court has wide-reaching powers to decide all controversies involving the meaning of the German Basic Law (the country's constitution). In Canada and a handful of other countries, most of which have federal systems of government, the ordinary courts exercise judicial review much as in the United States. For example, in Canada authority to declare acts of Parliament void clearly does not flow from English common law—Canada's legal heritage—which recognizes the principle of parliamentary supremacy, and the Canadian Constitution says nothing at all about judicial review power. Nonetheless, through continuing use, judicial review has developed into an unwritten rule, "a binding convention of our [Canadian] Constitution."[9] The roots of judicial review in Canada can be "traced to pragmatic considerations flowing implicitly from the principle of federalism. . . ." With their separate state or provincial governments, federal systems need some central body able to decide when state actions contradict national legislation. The regular courts have assumed this role in a number of former British colonies, including Canada and Australia.

HOW CASES REACH THE U.S. SUPREME COURT

The original jurisdiction of the U.S. Supreme Court—where it is the first court to hear a case—is very limited. Cases taken up by the Court under its original jurisdiction have averaged less than one a year. The vast majority of cases reaching the Supreme Court come on appeal from other courts, specifically from the highest state courts, the three-judge federal district courts, and the U.S. courts of appeal. The Constitution gives Congress broad power to determine the Supreme Court's appellate

[8] Congressional Research Service, *Constitution of the United States of America, Analysis and Interpretation* (1980 supplement), Senate Document 96-64, 1982; and Henry J. Abraham, *The Judicial Process* (New York: Oxford University Press, 1980), pp. 304–10.

[9] Richard J. Van Loon and Michael S. Whittington, *The Canadian Political System* (Toronto: McGraw-Hill Ryerson, 1981), p. 179.

jurisdiction; Congress has in turn given the Supreme Court great discretion to decide which cases it will devote its scarcest resource—time— to hearing.

Certiorari. Most cases that the Court reviews come to it through one of two procedures. The first involves the **writ of certiorari**: an order to a court whose decision is under challenge to send the records of the case to a higher court so that the latter may review the decision. One of the parties to a lower-court decision petitions the higher court to issue the writ. Legislation enacted by Congress in 1925 gave the Supreme Court power to grant or deny writs of certiorari at its own discretion. As Howard Ball notes, through this authority "the justices of the Supreme Court carefully select a very small percentage of petitions to the Court for review on the merits. In order for the Court to take the case, it must—in the estimation of the sitting justices—be a controversy of major proportions."[10] At least four of the nine justices must agree to hear the case in order for a writ of certiorari to be issued. This does not mean that these four justices will vote to decide the case in the same way. Rather, they simply agree that the case merits a Supreme Court hearing.

Appeal. The second main avenue to Supreme Court review is by the legal **right of appeal.** The Supreme Court must accept cases on appeal when:

1. the highest court of a state declares a federal law or a portion of it to be unconstitutional;

2. the highest court of a state upholds state law when it is challenged on the grounds that it violates the U.S. Constitution or an act of Congress;

3. a U.S. court of appeal holds a section of a state constitution or a state statute unconstitutional; and

4. a lower federal court declares an act of Congress unconstitutional and the U.S. government is a party to the suit.

Appeals may also be brought directly to the Supreme Court from the three-judge district courts—but the Court in practice rejects many of these cases "for lack of a substantial federal question."

SPECIAL PROCEDURES IN SUPREME COURT ACTION

The Supreme Court has evolved a number of rules and procedures bearing on what sorts of cases it will hear. One of the most important is the insistence that the Court will intervene only when there is a definite case of controversy involving bona fide adversaries. The Court will not issue advisory opinions. It will not hear contrived cases developed merely to test a law. This limits, of course, the Court's control over the timing and the form of various issues brought to it.

Standing. For a party to bring a suit he or she must have **standing.** This means that the party must show that he or she has sustained or is threatened with real injury.[11] A famous example of lack of standing involved Dr. Wilder Tileston, a physician who wanted to challenge Connecticut's legislation preventing "the use of drugs or instruments to prevent conception, and the giving of assistance or counsel in their use." The U.S. Supreme Court held that "no question is raised in the record with respect to the definition of [Dr. Tileston's] liberty or prop-

---

[10] Howard Ball, *Courts and Politics: The Federal Judicial System* (Englewood Cliffs, N.J.: Prentice-Hall, 1980), p. 108.

[11] See Caren Orren, "Standing to Sue: Interest Group Influence in the Federal Courts," *American Political Science Review* 70 (1976), p. 723.

erty in contravention of the Fourteenth Amendment. . . . [Hence] the appeal must be dismissed on the ground that appellant has no standing to litigate the constitutional question which the record presents."[12] In short, Dr. Tileston suffered no real injury.

In a subsequent case (discussed earlier in this chapter), Estelle Griswold, executive director of the Planned Parenthood League of Connecticut, and Dr. C. Lee Buxton, medical director of a center that the league operated, were *convicted* of violating the same Connecticut statute and fined $100 each. Unlike Dr. Tileston, Griswold and Boxton were personally affected or injured: they now had standing. The Court granted their appeal, made on the grounds that the law violated their Fourteenth Amendment rights. In *Griswold v. Connecticut* (1965) the Court declared Connecticut's statute banning contraception unconstitutional.

Class-Action Suits. A **class-action suit** is one filed by an individual on behalf of himself or herself and perhaps many hundreds or thousands of others allegedly wronged in the same fashion. The petitioner in a class-action suit must show membership in the affected class and not simply sympathy with it. Among the well-known instances of successful class-action suits are the school desegregation cases of 1954, which were initiated on behalf of all pupils affected by the prevailing educational segregation in the school districts under challenge. In a number of cases in the 1970s, the Supreme Court narrowed the availability of the class-action challenge by stipulating that a person bringing such a suit must notify all the members of the "class" potentially benefiting and must bear the costs of notification.[13] Personal injury and more than nominal involvement with others for whom a legal challenge is mounted have been significant facets of the rule of standing.

Justiciability. Another important limitation that the courts have imposed on their intervention in policy disputes involves **justiciability.** At issue here is not whether an individual has standing to sue, but whether courts are institutionally suited to provide remedies in the particular type of case. Political scientist Sheldon Goldman identified several central questions that bear upon justiciability:

1. Is there something that a court can do for a plaintiff assuming that the plaintiff is in the legal right?

2. Is the dispute moot (no longer a dispute)?

3. Is the subject matter of the dispute one that is essentially a political question best resolved by the political branches of government?

4. Is the subject amenable to judicial resolution?[14]

At first glance, arguing whether a litigant has standing to sue, or whether a particular controversy is justiciable, may seem simply an abstract preoccupation of the legal profession. In fact, these judicial standards are important factors defining the special kind of political role American courts play. If every significant political issue were considered justiciable, and if every interested person could bring suit, the federal courts would be handling the entire range of political controversies dealt with by the executive and legislative branches. Judicial rules such as those involving standing and judiciability are an expression of judicial respect for separation of powers.

[12] *Tileston v. Ullman*, 318 U.S. 44 (1943).
[13] See, for example, *Eisan v. Karlyle and Jacqueline*, 416 U.S. 979 (1974).
[14] Goldman, *Constitutional Law*, p. 8.

ADMINISTRATION OF THE FEDERAL COURTS

We have come to expect that those who direct government agencies will favor developments that increase their agencies' workload and responsibilities. More work can mean more staff and bigger budgets, and the opportunity for greater influence. Interestingly enough, the judicial branch takes the opposite position. During his tenure as chief justice, Warren Burger argued forcefully that courts in general—but especially federal courts—now perform tasks they need not. The answer is not primarily more staff—although Burger thought additional judges were needed—but going outside traditional judge-directed proceedings altogether (more informal conciliation efforts now being tried in many states) and delegating functions to lower courts.

Looking to state courts, Justice Burger questioned whether judges are needed initially to preside over probate matters (involving wills and estates), to resolve child custody cases, or to handle divorces. Regarding federal courts, he expressed doubts that judges are required at the outset to administer bankrupt estates "when only a small proportion of these cases involve contested issues requiring judicial decision. . . ." He strongly urged getting the federal courts out of "diversity of citizenship" cases.[15] Asked Chief Justice Burger, "How long must we wait to keep out of federal courts an automobile intersection collision which reaches federal courts simply because one driver lives in Newark and the other in New York? Or one in Virginia and one across the Potomac in Washington?"[16]

A Litigation Explosion. These efforts to trim the courts' workload must be seen against the vast increase in recent years in the number of disputes brought to courts for resolution. Justice Burger noted that in the first year his predecessor, Earl Warren, was chief justice (1953), the Supreme Court had 1,312 case filings and issued 65 signed opinions. During the 1989–90 term, the Court had 6,316 cases on its docket and issued 121 signed opinions.

The entire legal system has been challenged by extraordinary increases in cases. In 1990–91, 253,477 new cases were filed in federal district courts. Of these, 207,742 were civil cases, nearly double the number filed in 1975. And 42,033 appeals were brought to the U.S. courts of appeal, up from less than 17,000 in 1975 and just 7,000 in 1965.

Federal court organization has changed slowly in response to these heightened demands. District court judges are now provided with a variety of assistants; along with stenographers, court reporters, bailiffs, and law clerks, they are assigned administrators and magistrates. The professional court administrators take from the judges much of the burden of overseeing the courts' increasingly complex administrative machinery. Under the Federal Magistrates Act of 1968, judges are permitted to appoint magistrates (for eight- and four-year terms of office) to assist in processing court case loads. In 1987 magistrates handled over 392,010 court proceedings—including trial jurisdiction in 76,691 misdemeanor cases and over 148,439 preliminary proceedings in arrest warrants, search warrants, bail reviews, detention hearings, arraignments, and other areas. Even with these improvements, the workload of federal judges spirals upward. Richard Posner projects a possible caseload for the year 2000 of almost 845,000.[17]

---

[15] See also Erwin N. Griswold, "Helping the Supreme Court by Reducing the Flow of Cases into the Courts of Appeals," *Judicature* 67, 2 (August 1983), p. 60.

[16] Warren E. Burger, *1982 Year-End Report on the Judiciary*, p. 3.

[17] Richard A. Posner, *The Federal Courts: Crisis and Reform* (Cambridge, Mass.: Harvard University Press, 1985), p. 93.

SELECTION OF
FEDERAL JUDGES

Just as the courts are a special type of political institution, so judges are a special type of politician. The political side of judgeships extends throughout the process by which they are selected for the bench. As Joseph C. Goulden observed, "judges are of political, not divine, origin. . . ."[18] What is the political process through which judges reach the bench?

Article III of the U.S. Constitution says little about judicial selection. It provides only that judges of the Supreme Court and of the lower courts "shall hold their offices during good behavior"—that is, for life terms. Article II, section 2, stipulates that the president shall have the power to nominate, and with the "advice and consent of the Senate" to appoint "ambassadors, other public ministers and consuls, judges of the Supreme Court, and all other officers of the United States. . . ."

The formal process for selecting federal judges seems straightforward. The president proposes candidates and submits their names to the Senate; if the Senate concurs by majority vote, the president's nominees are confirmed and take office. But as it has evolved over two centuries, the process is considerably more complicated than the constitutional form might suggest. Different practices apply in selecting federal district judges, judges of the courts of appeal, and justices of the Supreme Court.

District Court Appointments. The constitutional requirement that the Senate approve judicial nominees, coupled with the fact that district judges serve jurisdictions within individual states, has led to the informal but powerful practice of senatorial courtesy in district

court appointments. Once a nomination has been sent to the Senate, it is given to the Senate Judiciary Committee. The chairperson routinely sends out what are known as "blue slips." These are forms that alert the senators from the nominee's home state and ask for their opinions and information concerning the nomination.

In effect, through the blue slip the Judiciary Committee asks the senators whether the president's nominee is acceptable. If a senator receiving the blue slip is of the same party as the president, his or her failure to return it with a statement of endorsement is taken under senatorial courtesy as a veto of the nominee. The willingness of the Senate to grant de facto veto power to senators of the president's party from the nominee's state is a form of mutual back scratching. By following the practice, senators know that when a nominee from their own state is submitted, their brethren will grant them this same courtesy—more precisely, this same power. When the senators from the nominee's state are not of the president's party, this right of veto does not apply. This reflects political realism, for to require a president to consult senators of the other party with the same care and diligence with which he consults senators of his own party would upset the normal sense of political fairness.

The Senate's willingness to veto a nominee who does not receive proper home-state clearance is rarely tested, because a system of prior consultation has developed. Before the nomination is ever submitted, negotiations take place between the senators from a prospective nominee's state and the attorney general or deputy attorney general representing the administration. The extent to which Justice Department officials will defer to the home-state senators' wishes depends upon instructions from the president. Presidents Eisenhower and Kennedy made it clear that their Justice Department subordinates were authorized to negotiate

[18]Joseph C. Goulden, *The Bench Warmers* (New York: Weybright and Talley, 1974), p. 23.

for the best possible nominees. Lyndon Johnson was willing to defer to the preferences of the home-state senators as long as the individuals they recommended were not clearly unacceptable to him. The only absolute in this process is that a nomination will surely fail if the home-state senator or senators of the president's party strongly oppose it.

Independently of the above process, candidates for district court appointments are informally investigated by the Justice Department; their names are then given to the Standing Committee on Federal Judiciary of the American Bar Association. The committee ranks these nominees on a scale: "exceptionally well qualified," "well qualified," "qualified," or "not qualified." At early stages in the review process, the ABA committee provides the Justice Department with information on what is likely to be the rating of the leading contenders; poor preliminary ratings may be the basis for eliminating candidates from further consideration.[19] Nominees are sometimes approved, however, even when they receive "not qualified" ABA ratings. This may reflect the clout of the nominee's home-state senators. Or it may reflect doubts about the ABA's standards in particular cases. For example, the ABA committee will not approve anyone who has reached the age of sixty-four—a standard many senators do not generally accept.

Supreme Court Appointments. Since the Supreme Court has national jurisdiction, the tradition of senatorial courtesy has never applied to nominations to it. The president makes nominations with broad national policy consid-erations in mind, and traditionally the Senate has granted him considerable leeway. This does not mean that the president's nominations always have smooth sailing in the Senate. In the nineteenth century, about one out of every three nominations failed; in the twentieth, about one in nine.[20] The last four presidential nominees to be rejected were Clement Haynsworth and Harrold Carswell, Richard Nixon nominees in 1969 and 1970; and Robert Bork and Douglas Ginsburg, Reagan nominees in 1987.

ROUTES TO THE JUDICIARY:
BACKGROUNDS OF FEDERAL
COURT APPOINTEES

Federal court appointments throughout U.S. history, including those to the Supreme Court, have typically gone to members of the president's party. Even when presidents reach across party lines for nominations—as Richard Nixon did when he chose Lewis F. Powell, Jr., of Virginia for a Supreme Court opening in 1971—they usually pick individuals of a philosophic bent similar to their own. While nominally a Democrat, Powell's conservatism was compatible with the views of the president who picked him. In this century, only three presidents have given more than 10 percent of their judicial appointments to individuals outside their own parties, none more than 20 percent.

Presidents appoint to the bench fellow partisans and people who, as best they can determine, hold compatible policy perspectives. They also frequently send other political signals in making their appointments. Jimmy Carter appointed women and ethnic minorities to the federal judiciary in greater numbers than any other president. He had pledged to make the federal judiciary more diverse and pluralistic

---

[19] See Sheldon Goldman and Thomas P. Jahnige, *The Federal Courts as a Political System*, 2nd ed. (New York: Harper and Row, 1976), pp. 49–50. For a review of Reagan administration practices in selecting federal judges, see Goldman "Reagan's Judicial Appointments at Mid-term," *Judicature* 66 (March 1983), p. 342.

[20] Goulden, *Constitutional Law*, p. 19.

with regard to ethnicity and sex. As Table 9.2 shows, he succeeded. About 14 percent of Carter's appointees to U.S. district courts were women, compared to just 1.6 percent of Johnson's, 0.6 of Nixon's, 1.9 percent of Ford's, and 8 percent of Reagan's. In all, Carter appointed 40 women, 38 blacks, and 16 Hispanics to the federal bench; and Reagan, 31 women, 8 blacks, and 13 Hispanics. By January 1992, Bush had put 124 judges on the federal bench, and there were over 100 vacancies. Of his 124 appointees, 15 percent are women, 7 percent blacks, and 3 percent Hispanics.

Informal political criteria also guide presidents in their Supreme Court appointments. For example, nominations have at times served to recognize social groups that had been excluded from full participation in American social and political life. President Lyndon Johnson finally broke the color barrier when he appointed Thurgood Marshall to the Supreme Court in 1967; President Ronald Reagan broke the gender barrier in 1981 when he appointed Sandra Day O'Connor the first female Supreme Court justice. The current Supreme Court is composed of eight justices whose party background prior to appointment was at least nominally Republican, and just one—Byron White—who was a Democrat.

POLITICAL SHIFT IN SELECTING JUDGES

Over the last quarter-century a shift has occurred in the selection of federal judges. A surge of new legislation in the 1960s and 1970s established expansive performance standards and entitlements in many areas, from education to the environment. As court cases arose under these new laws, federal judges were pushed more extensively into the policy-making process. What is more, as a result of court decisions they often found themselves involved in much the same fashion as political executives and legislators—for example, overseeing the operations of public school systems and prisons and settling the detailed requirements of environmental legislation.

From this experience a new view of the courts took shape—a view of their role as more explicitly political and necessarily involved in the regular policy process. Inevitably, groups with a wide array of interests began examining prospective court appointees, lobbying and even campaigning for and against them much as has been done traditionally for executive and legislative seats. Jimmy Carter was not notably partisan or ideological, but studies show his appointees to the federal courts of general jurisdiction to be a distinctively liberal group.

TABLE 9.2   JUDICIAL APPOINTMENTS OF RECENT PRESIDENTS BY SEX AND ETHNICITY (IN PERCENT)

	Women	Blacks	Hispanics
U.S. Courts of Appeals			
Johnson	3	5	*
Nixon	0	0	*
Ford	0	0	*
Carter	20	16	4
Reagan	7	1	1
Bush	15	4	7
U.S. District Courts			
Johnson	2	4	3
Nixon	1	3	1
Ford	2	6	2
Carter	14	14	7
Reagan	8	2	5
Bush	15	7	2

*Data not available.

Source: Johnson, Nixon, and Ford: Sheldon Goldman, "Carter's Judicial Appointments: A Lasting Legacy," *Judicature* 64, 8 (March 1981), pp. 344–55. Carter appointments: *Congressional Quarterly*, December 8, 1984, p. 3075. Reagan appointments: *Congressional Quarterly*, January 6, 1990. Bush appointments: *Congressional Quarterly*, January 18, 1992, p. 112.

In turn, Reagan's and Bush's appointees have proven distinctively conservative.[21]

THE SHIFTING PHILOSOPHIC CENTER OF THE COURTS

The fact that Carter and Reagan were in a position to make an unusually large number of federal court appointments has further heightened political sensitivity. Jimmy Carter did not have a chance to appoint anyone to the Supreme Court, but in his one term he appointed more district and appeals judges than any previous president—including Franklin Roosevelt, who was in office over twelve years—because a 1978 act greatly expanded the number of judges. By the end of his second term, Ronald Reagan had been able to make even greater changes proportionately than Jimmy Carter in the makeup of the federal judiciary. He made 385 confirmed appointments to the federal bench, nearly half of all sitting judges.[22] (See Table 9.3.) Both supporters and opponents of Reagan's views have come to see his political legacy in court appointment as especially large and consequential.

As noted, by January 1992 George Bush had appointed 124 federal judges—2 to the Supreme Court, 27 to the circuit courts of appeal, and 95 to the district courts. Together this vast number of Reagan-Bush appointees, many of them judicial conservatives of one sort or another, has shifted the philosophic center of gravity of the federal judiciary.

[21] The results of a number of empirical studies of the voting and opinions of district and appeals judges have been summarized by Sheldon Goldman in "The Bush Imprint on the Judiciary: Carrying on a Tradition," *Judicature*, April–May 1991, pp. 294–306.

[22] In addition to the more than 700 federal judges with full-time status, about 290 others have "senior" status—meaning they are semi-retired with reduced case loads. The vast majority of these senior judges were appointed by Reagan's predecessors.

TABLE 9.3   NUMBERS OF FEDERAL JUDGES APPOINTED BY PRESIDENTS ROOSEVELT THROUGH BUSH

President	Number of judges	In approximate number of years
Franklin Roosevelt	194	12
Harry Truman	136	8
Dwight Eisenhower	170	8
John Kennedy	129	3
Lyndon Johnson	156	5
Richard Nixon	226	5.5
Gerald Ford	60	2.5
Jimmy Carter	258	4
Ronald Reagan	385	8
George Bush	124	3

Source: Congressional Quarterly Weekly Reports, selected issues, latest that of January 18, 1992.

In his presidency, Bill Clinton will apply sharply different political criteria than did Presidents Reagan and Bush in selecting Supreme Court and other federal judges. Now Republicans will be dissenting. But the bitter partisan battles over nominees, described below, appear certain to continue.

THE NOMINATION OF ROBERT BORK

The first in what has become a string of bitter nomination battles, in which the Democratic and Republican parties were aligned sharply against each other, came in 1987 on Reagan's nomination of Robert Bork to the seat that had been held by Justice Lewis Powell. The confirmation hearings on Bork were dominated by a major argument over judicial philosophy. Bork, who had been a law school professor and (under Nixon) solicitor general of the United States and was, at the time Reagan nominated him to the Court, a judge on the Court of Appeals for the Washington, D.C. circuit, maintained that in deciding constitutional issues judges should

Judge Robert Bork answering questions during the Senate Judiciary Committee confirmation hearings.

stick closely to the intentions of those who framed and ratified the Constitution. Once he "abandons the lawyer's task of interpretation" of these stated or clearly implied intentions underlying the various constitutional provisions, the judge finds himself with no guidelines other than his own preferences and values.[23] If he chooses to assert these, Bork maintains, the courts lose legitimacy.[24]

Bork believed that in a constitutional democracy like the United States,

> the moral content of law [in the sense of larger ends it is to serve] must be given by the morality of the framer or the legislator, never by the morality of the judge. The sole task of the latter—and it is a task quite large enough for anyone's wisdom, skill, and virtue—is to translate the framer's or the legislator's morality into a rule to govern unforeseen circumstances.[25]

"The original Constitution," Bork observed, "was devoted primarily to the mechanisms of democratic choice."[26] It did not prescribe a set of answers to the many substantive questions coming before the polity, but rather a governmental structure and practice for arriving at those answers. At its core is the principle of majority rule, with its stipulations that popular majorities, through the legislators, governors, presidents, and other officials they elect, should decide policy on most issues, both large and small.

The U.S. Constitution is not completely majoritarian. It modified majoritarianism with the principle that some rights are so important that they must not be infringed by any group, however large. The Supreme Court draws its legitimacy from the need—in a democratic system predicated not just on majority rule but also on minority rights—for a nonelective branch, insulated from majoritarianism, to patrol the boundaries and determine the areas in which majority preferences may not determine policy. But, in Bork's view, for this to work the Court must limit itself to implementing the minority rights that those who framed the original Constitution and its later amendments

[23] Robert Bork, "The Struggle Over the Role of the Court," *National Review*, September 17, 1982, pp. 1137–38.
[24] Ibid., p. 1138.

[25] Robert Bork, "Tradition and Morality in Constitutional Law," in Mark W. Cannon and David M. O'Brien, eds., *Views from the Bench* (Chatham, N.J.: Chatham House Publishers, 1958), pp. 171–72.
[26] Ibid., p. 170.

intended to guarantee.[27] Judges must not simply substitute their own values.[28]

In testifying against Judge Bork's confirmation at the Senate hearings, Laurence Tribe, a prominent constitutional scholar, argued that the judge's position is

> a uniquely narrow and constricted view of "liberty" and of the Supreme Court's place in protecting it. It sets Judge Bork apart from the entire 200-year-old tradition of thought about rights that underlies the American Constitution. And it suggests an incapacity to address in any meaningful way a whole spectrum of cases that we can expect will be vital in our national life during the next quarter-century.[29]

The core of the problem, as Tribe and other critics saw it, was Bork's radical view of the U.S. Constitution: that the people of the United States in ratifying the Constitution surrendered to government all the natural rights they had believed themselves to have possessed except for those specifically enumerated in the Bill of Rights. "Despite Judge Bork's espousal of a theory of 'original intent,' " Tribe argued,

> no understanding of the Constitution could be further from the clear purpose of those who wrote and ratified the Constitution and its first ten amendments. The principal aim of the original Constitution—and the impetus for the insistence as a condition of ratification, upon a Bill of Rights to preserve natural rights that had been recognized for centuries—was to create a national government that, although sufficiently powerful to bind together states of great diversity, would not threaten the individual liberty

that the people retained and did not cede to any level of government.[30]

The U.S. Supreme Court from the beginning of the republic, Tribe maintained, has recognized that the people of the United States retained various "unenumerated rights." The American nation is bound together by a broad and vital conception of individual liberty. This conception has evolved and enlarged with the passage of time. "Judge Bork's rejection of the Supreme Court's historic role in articulating an evolving concept of 'liberty' protected by the Constitution—not simply protecting a fixed set of 'liberties' from an evolving set of threats," Tribe insisted, challenges deeply held American expectations and values.[31] The Judiciary Committee majority took this same stand.

After an unusually spirited battle, the Senate tide flowed strongly against Bork's nomination. He lost the support of virtually all the senators who had been cross-pressured and undecided. The full Senate rejected his nomination by a margin of 16—42 in favor, 58 against.

KENNEDY TO THE COURT

After Bork's defeat, the president named a second nominee, Douglas H. Ginsburg, age 41, since 1986 a judge on the U.S. Court of Appeals for the District of Columbia. Almost immediately, Ginsburg's nomination ran into trouble, and he soon withdrew his nomination.

Judge Anthony Kennedy of the Ninth Circuit Court had been a finalist in the previous round of nominee selection, and he got the president's backing this time. While the president of the National Organization for Women strongly opposed Kennedy, most of the interest groups that had jumped so actively into the fray against Bork stayed on the sidelines this time.

---

[27] Robert Bork, "Neutral Principles and Some First Amendment Problems," *Indiana Law Journal*, Fall 1971, pp. 1–35.

[28] Ibid., p. 6.

[29] From the typescript of Laurence H. Tribe's prepared testimony before the Senate Judiciary Committee, September 22, 1987, p. 9.

[30] Ibid., pp. 10–11.

[31] Ibid., p. 16.

Everyone had been worn out by the bruising battle that had just been waged. Anthony Kennedy was unanimously confirmed by the Senate, 97–0.

THE SOUTER NOMINATION

Shortly after the high court concluded its 1989–90 term, Justice William J. Brennan, Jr., who had been appointed by Dwight Eisenhower thirty-four years earlier in 1956 and was thus the longest-serving justice, announced his retirement. Brennan's decision was something of a political bombshell. He had been one of the most influential justices in Supreme Court history and was the clear, if informal, leader of the current Court's declining liberal wing. It was, of course, immediately evident to every-

one that the retirement gave the president an opportunity to shift the balance of the high court further toward the conservative end of the spectrum.

To fill the seat Bush nominated David H. Souter. Souter had been New Hampshire's attorney general and had served on that state's supreme court. He was currently a judge on the U.S. Court of Appeals for the first circuit. A graduate of Harvard College and Harvard Law School and a former Rhodes scholar, David Souter was evidently a man of intellect and ability. But, everyone wanted to know, where would he fit on the spectrum of judicial philosophy?

It wasn't easy to tell. No one who had followed his previous service doubted that he was in some sense a conservative. But he had said

Federal Appeals Court Judge David Souter speaking after being nominated by President Bush to replace Justice William Brennan on the Supreme Court.

and written little indicating precisely where he stood on the most divisive judicial questions of the day, such as abortion. Whereas Robert Bork had championed controversial positions in an ongoing string of judicial battles, David Souter was a decidedly nonconfrontational personality. It had been said of Reagan's last appointee to the Court, Anthony Kennedy, that he was "Bork without a paper trail"—without, that is, a record of stands on contentious court issues on which an opposing group could seize. Souter had left even less of a "paper trail." Was this, some critics wondered, a disturbing feature of the new judicial politics—that outspoken advocates were excluded; quieter, perhaps more cautious candidates rewarded?

Testifying before the Senate Judiciary Committee, Souter got generally high marks for his open-mindedness, intelligence, and sophisticated grasp of the law. But he took pains to conceal his personal views and did not comment, even indirectly, on divisive issues. Many women's groups opposed Souter's nomination because he refused to say whether he believed the Constitution establishes a fundamental right to abortion. In the end, the committee endorsed the nomination by 13 to 1; only Edward Kennedy of Massachusetts voted no. The full Senate confirmed Souter, 90 votes to 9. Those in opposition were all Democrats.

In his relatively brief tenure on the Court to date, Souter has shown himself to be a moderate conservative. On a number of important votes, including cases involving the rights of the accused and the big abortion ruling in *Planned Parenthood v. Casey*, he has struck a position between that of the Court's core conservative bloc—William Rehnquist, Antonin Scalia, and now Clarence Thomas—and that of the two most liberal justices, John Paul Stevens and Harry Blackmun. Though no two justices see eye-to-eye on all judicial issues, Souter is fairly close to Sandra Day O'Connor in outlook and judicial temperament. In the

1992 term, Anthony Kennedy also appeared to move toward this moderate-conservative stance. O'Connor, Souter, and Kennedy voted together in a number of key cases, including those involving school prayer *(Lee v. Weisman)* and abortion *(Planned Parenthood v. Casey)*.

THE NASTY FIGHT OVER THE NOMINATION OF CLARENCE THOMAS

The decision in 1991 of Justice Thurgood Marshall to retire from the Court, and President Bush's choice of Judge Clarence Thomas as Marshall's replacement, set the stage for the most bruising and painful confirmation hearing in U.S. history. Thurgood Marshall was the first black American to hold a seat on the High Court; Thomas would become the second. But their common racial ancestry aside, the two men had little in common. In his twenty-four years as a Supreme Court justice, Thurgood Marshall had been unswervingly a member of the Court's liberal wing. Thomas, in marked contrast, was a forceful young black conservative. As chairman of the Equal Employment Opportunity Commission (1982–90), he was a strong critic of racially based affirmative action programs, arguing that, far from aiding blacks' advancement, they often encouraged a culture of dependency. In a number of articles and public speeches, and in decisions he wrote during his brief tenure (1990–91) as a judge on the U.S. Court of Appeals for the District of Columbia, Thomas had made it clear that he espoused a judicial philosophy broadly similar to that of Robert Bork (described above), one which would place him squarely in the Court's conservative bloc.

Clarence Thomas's life story was an inspiring one of rapid advancement through determined effort, from a beginning in grinding poverty and racial discrimination. But from a standpoint of political philosophy, Thomas was

Appearing in front of the Senate Judiciary Committee before his appointment to the Supreme Court, Justice Clarence Thomas denies charges that he sexually harrassed Anita Hill.

ings did not hinge directly on judicial philosophy, however, but rather on the charge that Thomas had sexually harassed an employee who had worked for him first at the Department of Education and subsequently at the Equal Employment Opportunity Commission. Anita F. Hill, at the time of the hearings a law school professor, and like Thomas a black conservative, made her accusations in dramatic testimony before the Judiciary Committee. Thomas categorically denied the charges, calling the testimony "high-tech lynching for an uppity black. . . ." Many women's groups sided strongly with Professor Hill.

In the end, the Senate narrowly confirmed Clarence Thomas, by a vote of 52–48. Among Republican senators, 41 voted to confirm, just 2 to reject the nomination. Forty-six Senate Democrats voted no, but 11 backed him—7 of them Southerners. Thomas's high measure of support among blacks, a very large component of Democratic support in the South, probably tipped the scales in his favor.

unacceptable to many Senate Democrats. Judiciary Committee Chairman Joseph Biden (D-Del.) spoke for many of his Senate Democratic colleagues when he criticized the president, in nominating Thomas, of continuing to "pack" the Supreme Court with "ultra-conservatives." "A fervent minority within the President's party," Biden argued, "is engaging in an open campaign . . . to shift the Court dramatically to the right. And the President has not been willing to engage in the kind of consultation with the Senate that would give this body more assurance that his nominees are not paricipants in that campaign."[32]

The angriest part of the confirmation hear-

[32] Quoted in Joan Biskupic, "With a Split Vote over Thomas, Panel Sends Bush a Message," *Congressional Quarterly,* September 28, 1991, p. 2787.

Law school professor Anita Hill testifiying at Clarence Thomas's confirmation hearing.

SUMMARY

The Supreme Court has often found itself a "storm center" in debates over American public policy. At present the Court is at the center of the fierce national debate over abortion. Its decision in *Roe v. Wade* (1973) held that a broad constitutional right to privacy barred states from curbing a woman's decision on whether to have an abortion in the first or second "trimesters" of her pregnancy. Sixteen years later, in *Webster v. Reproductive Health Services* (1989) and again in *Planned Parenthood v. Casey* (1992), the Court modified its *Roe* ruling, enlarging the scope of permissible state regulation of abortion. Pro-choice and pro-life forces continue to press their respective stands.

The framers of the U.S. Constitution provided for a system of federal courts as a third separate branch of the national government. Together with a set of lower federal courts, the Supreme Court was made the repository of "the judicial power of the United States." The courts are in many ways weak institutions, compared to legislatures and executives. In Alexander Hamilton's words, they are without the powers of the purse and the sword. But the authority to say what the law is has proved a formidable one. One fact of it is judicial review, the power to review acts of legislatures and actions of executive officials to determine whether they are in conformity with the Constitution, and to declare them void if they are held not to be.

The framers believed that American federalism required federal courts to exercise judicial review over state legislative actions; otherwise there could be no uniform and respected national law. The Supreme Court would be the umpire of the federal system. Whether the framers believed that judicial review should extend to declaring unconstitutional acts of a co-equal branch of national government is less clear. Hamilton asserted strongly that judicial review of acts of Congress was essential. Most of those who drafted the Constitution apparently gave little thought to this question and expected that if the courts were to invalidate congressional acts they would do so only when there was the clearest violation of constitutional requirements.

In interpreting constitutional provisions or statutes, courts make law as surely as legislatures do. Furthermore, federal courts are now often heavily involved in administrative matters. This growing intervention has prompted criticism, including the charge of "judicial legislation"—that judges are too inclined to discover constitutional or statutory provisions mandating what are in fact their own political views and values. Of course, in one sense every branch of government is now activist compared to times past, partly in response to increased public demands for governmental efforts to redress all manner of problems.

The fact that courts are political institutions that make policy does not mean that there is nothing special about how they enter the policy process. Courts operate within a context defined by a limiting set of judicial rules and standards. Real cases or controversies in law, involving appellants who have suffered injury that is appropriately redressed through judicial action, are the prime vehicle for judicial action. Separation of powers requires that the courts follow procedures distinct from those governing political executives and legislatures.

The United States has a dual court system, with federal and state courts existing side by side and sometimes sharing jurisdiction. Concurrent jurisdiction means that a case may originate in either a state or a federal court; exclusive jurisdiction means it is assigned exclusively to one or the other. When a case arises under a state law, exclusive original jurisdiction usually belongs to the trial courts of the state. However, appeals may be brought from the highest state courts to the U.S. Supreme Court when a substantial federal question is raised.

All federal justices are appointed by the president, with the Senate's advice and consent. For appointments to the federal district courts, the practice of senatorial courtesy is followed: The Senate will not confirm the president's choice unless that individual is acceptable to the senators of the president's party from the state in which the judge would sit. Presidential appointments to the Supreme Court are scrutinized, instead, in terms of broad national policy and whether the requisite level of judicial competence has been met.

FOR FURTHER STUDY

Goldman, Sheldon. *Constitutional Law and Supreme Court Decision-Making.* New York: Harper and Row, 1982. A careful, systematic description of the principal Supreme Court rulings and developments in American constitutional interpretation. Idem., *Constitutional Law: Cases and Essays,* New York: Harper and Row, 1987.

Goldman, Sheldon, and Thomas P. Jahnige. *The Federal Courts as a Political System,* 3rd ed. New York: Harper and Row, 1985. Interprets the federal courts as a set of political institutions, bound by their own unique versions of political interests and dynamics.

O'Brien, David M. *Storm Center: The Supreme Court in American Politics,* 3rd ed. New York: Norton, 1993. A major interpretation of the high court, including such elements of the court's internal operations as the role of law clerks and administrative staff. Idem. *Supreme Court Watch.* New York: Norton, annual. A yearly review of major Court cases and decisions.

Posner, Richard A. *The Federal Courts: Crisis and Reform.* Cambridge, Mass.: Harvard University Press, 1985. A valuable description of problems confronting the federal court system, including the explosive growth in the number of court cases, written by a former law school professor now on the U.S. Circuit Court of Appeals.

Shapiro, Martin. *Courts: A Comparative and Political Analysis.* Chicago, Ill. University of Chicago Press, 1981; paperback, 1986. A major interpretation that examines court systems cross-nationally.

OPTIONAL COMPUTER EXERCISES

for *The Ladd Election ANALYZER*

THE ABORTION QUESTION

Over the past two decades the courts have ruled on various aspects of the abortion question (see pp. 240–49). But what do the voters think? Look at the responses to the one question on this complex subject included in the 1992 exit poll of voters done by the TV networks and included in the *ANALYZER*. You can assess the impact of the abortion issue on the 1992 election by asking: How did Republican men and women who believed abortion should be legal vote? Were they significantly more likely to defect from their party than Republican men and women who believed abortion should be illegal? What about Democratic men and women? Were those who believed abortion should be illegal more likely to defect from their party than those who backed Clinton's position that it should be legal? Overall, how much did the abortion issue influence the 1992 presidential outcome? Select "Usual party affiliation" from the "Vote questions" menu to identify Republicans and Democrats before going up to the abortion question on the "Policy views" menu to find out.

Part 4

PARTICIPATION

Chapter *10*

PUBLIC OPINION

Democracy endows public opinion with a moral or ethical status: Democratic government simply does not exist if citizens' preferences on the many questions of public policy are not respected—even if the majority's wishes must sometimes be subordinated to basic minority rights. As we will see in this chapter, however, the task of understanding what the public wants policy to be is not easy or straightforward. This is especially true because the public often wants a number of different things, each worthy, that come into conflict in complex policy decisions. This ambivalence is a dominant characteristic of public opinion.

Questions of government's performance and proper role are a good case in point. In remarks that he made after becoming chairman of the National Commission on Public Service in 1987, Paul Volcker observed that

> we Americans have always been ambivalent about government. For that matter, we started out that way. Instinctively, we still have a lot of feeling that that government is best that governs least; nonetheless we are quick and caustic with our complaints and our rhetoric when government doesn't produce what we expect of it. And as we've grown in size and in the complexity of our society, for better or worse we've asked and expected more of government.[1]

[1] Volcker is best known for his work as chairman of the board of governors of the Federal Reserve system, a position he held from 1979 through 1987.

GOVERNMENT'S ROLE: COLLIDING VALUES AND ASSESSMENTS

Volcker is right that large numbers of Americans see government at once as problem and solution. Solid majorities told Gallup interviewers in the spring of 1988 that they thought the federal government controlled too much of their lives. In the same survey, over 80 percent said that the federal government should run only those things that cannot be run at the local level. Sixty-eight percent in 1989 agreed that "when something is run by government, it is usually inefficient and wasteful." (See Figure 10.1.) In another survey, done by Gallup in

FIGURE 10.1 GOVERNMENT IS TOO BIG ... BUT SHOULD BE BIGGER

Agree   Disagree

1. The federal government should run only those things that cannot be run at the local level

81%
19%

2. When something is run by the government, it is usually inefficient and wasteful

68%
32%

3. The federal government controls too much of our daily lives

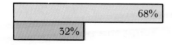
57%
43%

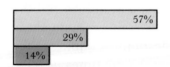
Yes   No
No opinion

The federal government has a responsibility ...

4. ... to provide health insurance coverage for those people who don't have it?

57%
29%
14%

5. ... to help people pay for nursing homes and other long-term medical care?

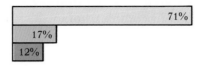
71%
17%
12%

6. Some working people don't earn enough to pay for services like health care, day care, or college tuitions without difficulty. Should the government provide services or programs to help people who are employed, or isn't this the responsibility of the federal government?

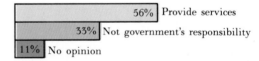
56% Provide services
33% Not government's responsibility
11% No opinion

Source: Question 1: Survey by the Gallup Organization, May 13–22, 1988. *Questions 2, 3:* Ibid., January 27–February 5, 1989. *Questions 4–6:* Survey by CBS News / *New York Times,* February 2–5, 1989.

January 1989, respondents were asked their sense of the proportion "of every tax dollar that goes to the federal government" that is wasted. The *median* response given—meaning that half said more and half less—was that 50 cents of every tax dollar is wasted.

At the same time, though, over 70 percent of those polled by CBS News in 1989 on what they thought the federal government should do for them said they thought the government had a responsibility to help people pay for nursing homes or other long-term medical care. Fifty-six percent felt that the government should help even those who are employed pay for such services as day-care and college tuition. The public appetite for government services and assistance remains robust.

Similar tensions are evident on the issue of government regulation. A May 1988 survey conducted by Gallup showed considerable skepticism about governmental regulation, with 57 percent agreeing that "government regulation of business usually does more harm than good." In an NBC News / *Wall Street Journal* survey taken in January 1990, 55 percent said too much government poses greater dangers to the economy than not enough regulation. But the same survey found majorities favoring more regulation with regard to the environment and consumer product safety (Figure 10.2). In general, the public endorses government regulation in many specific areas—in part to check another big institution, business. Americans simply don't believe that business will do the job by itself.

The mix of answers cited above becomes a lot less confusing if one keeps in mind that most Americans approach questions of the government's role and performance on a case-by-case basis, without any overall organizing notion

FIGURE 10.2 REGULATION IS OFTEN HARMFUL . . . AND WE NEED MORE OF IT

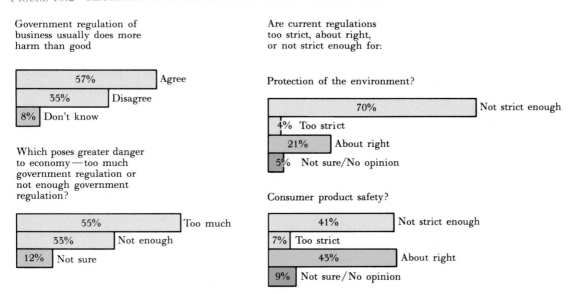

Source: First question: Survey of the Gallup Organization for Times Mirror Company, May 13–22, 1988. *Other questions:* Surveys by NBC News / *Wall Street Journal*, January 13–16, 1990.

of the state as inherently helpful or harmful. A good sense of this emerges from a survey done in the spring of 1989 by the University of Chicago's National Opinion Research Center (NORC). Respondents were asked to locate themselves on a scale: Choosing one end affirmed that the national government should do everything possible to improve the living standards of all poor Americans; selecting the other end was to insist that this is not the government's responsibility and that each individual should take care of himself or herself. Thirty-two percent put themselves in the first camp, 24 percent in the latter. Forty-four percent, however, put themselves at a mid-point on this scale, which was labeled "agree with both positions."

The lesson isn't that people always want to have their cake and eat it too. As we will see, public opinion displays both form and coherence. People do make choices—and stick to them. The lesson is that public opinion is not a unidimensional thing, like the temperature of a sample of water. It isn't "47 percent believe that. . . ." It is rich and variegated, full of shades and gradations. Measuring public opinion is a challenge; responding to it is an even greater one.

THE ENVIRONMENT: STRONG SUPPORT YET A COMPLEX JUDGMENT

Environmental issues strongly show the public holding conflicting values and objectives, and prepared to make distinctions—sometimes subtle ones.

Americans are strongly supportive of actions to achieve an attractive and healthy environment. As the United States has grown wealthier, Americans have come to expect more in virtually all areas of their material existence.

Calls for cleaner air and water, more parklands, the preservation of wildlife, and other services are part of a general progression that has been going on for a long time. Environmentalism was, for example, much stronger at the time of Theodore Roosevelt early in this century than it had been fifty or seventy years earlier. In many regards, environmental devastation reached its most severe levels in the mid-nineteenth century—with massive deforestation and the destruction of wildlife—but the poorer farming society of that era couldn't see any alternative. Later industrialization produced its own environmental problems, but it also created the resources that encouraged demands for conservation. Today, of course, we have much greater resources than were available in Teddy Roosevelt's time—and we in turn expect better performance in many areas, including the environment. (See Table 10.1.)

Despite this experience, contemporary polling on environmental matters often pushes the public to choose between economic well-being and an attractive environment. In December 1989, for instance, the *Los Angeles Times* poll asked respondents whether they favored protecting the environment "even if that means some people will lose their jobs and government will have to spend a great deal of money," or favored jobs and an expanding economy "even if that means some destruction of the environment." (See Table 10.2.) In fact, every time it has been given a chance the public says that with proper effort the United States can avoid so unpalatable a choice. In December 1989, Opinion Dynamics put the matter this way: "Some people say that . . . to protect the environment we are going to have to make sacrifices and accept a lower standard of living, [while others say] that we can have both continued economic growth and a cleaner environment." About two-thirds associated themselves with the latter view.

TABLE 10.1   PUBLIC OPINION ON THE STATE OF THE ENVIRONMENT

Pollution is worse . . .		but	. . . Some progress	
For the country as a whole—is pollution a serious problem that's getting worse, or a problem but one that is not so serious, or not much of a problem?			How much progress have we made in dealing with environmental problems in this country over the last twenty years—a great deal . . . only some . . . or hardly any?	
Getting worse	86%		Great deal	14%
Not so serious	11%		Only some	64%
Not much of a problem	3%		Hardly any	21%

Source: Survey by CBS News/*New York Times*, March 30–April 2, 1990.

Source: Survey by the Gallup Organization, April 5–8, 1990.

TABLE 10.2   PUBLIC OPINION ON THE ENVIRONMENT VS. GROWTH

Jobs vs. environment . . .		or	. . . Do both	
Are you in favor of protecting the environment even if that means some people will lose their jobs and the government will have to spend a great deal of money . . . or are you in favor of providing more jobs and expanding the economy even if that means some destruction of the environment?			Some people say that in order to protect the environment we are going to have to make sacrifices and accept a lower standard of living. Other people say that we can have both continued economic growth and a cleaner environment. . . . Which do you think is more likely to be true?	
Environment	65%		Have both	64%
Both (vol.)	5%		Accept slower economic growth	36%
Economy	29%			

Source: Survey of the *Los Angeles Times*, December 16–20, 1989.

Source: Survey by Opinion Dynamics Corporation, December 12–18, 1989.

Americans' commitment to the environment is genuine and substantial. And just as we expect to pay for good housing and medical care, so we're prepared to pay for clean air and water. Yet polls continue to "discover" the latter, as though it's somehow surprising.

The public is not prepared, however, to pay any price for greater environmental protection. *The New York Times* reported in 1989 that its poll found that 78 percent said that "protecting the environment is so important that requirements and standards cannot be too high and continuing environmental improvements must be made *regardless* of cost." The *Times* failed to report other data that make clear that this response must be understood not literally but as a symbolic commitment to a goal. (See Figure 10.3.)

When, in October 1989, Gallup asked, "Would you be willing to pay $200 more in taxes each year to increase federal spending for . . . reducing air pollution?" 71 percent said no. In December 1989, Opinion Dynamics found a majority opposed to a 25-cent-per-gallon gas tax that would be used to control pollution. On the other hand, the latter survey found 76 percent saying they might be willing to pay an extra $50 in taxes to solve air pollution.

Poll reporting often errs by suggesting that public opinion on environmental matters is

FIGURE 10.3   SPENDING FOR THE ENVIRONMENT: A MORE COMPLEX STORY

Affirming the goal

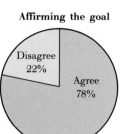

1. Do you agree or disagree with the following statement: Protecting the environment is so important that requirements and standards cannot be too high and continuing environmental improvements must be regardless of cost.

Balancing contending needs

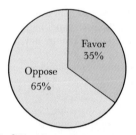

2. Would you be willing to pay $200 more in taxes each year to increase federal spending for... reducing air pollution?

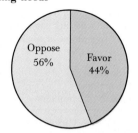

3. [Would you] strongly favor, somewhat favor, somewhat oppose, or strongly oppose each of these measures....A 25 cent per gallon gasoline tax that would be used control pollution?

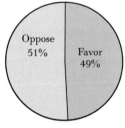

4a. Everyone wants a clean environment...but...at what cost or inconvenience....[Would you] favor or oppose...a 20-cent-per-gallon increase in the price of gasoline for cleaner-burning alternative fuels?

4b. [Would you favor or oppose...] closing pollution producing factories which would result in the loss of jobs?

Source: Question 1: Survey by CBS News/*New York Times*, March 30–April 2, 1990. *Question 2:* Survey by the Gallup Organization, October 5–8, 1989. *Question 3:* Survey by Opinion Dynamics Corporation, December 12–18, 1989. *Question 4:* Survey by NBC News/*Wall Street Journal*, April 1990.

one-dimensional or that poll findings on each dimension of what is in fact a complex mix of perceptions and values should be read as though it stood alone. A 1990 release of a Connecticut Poll (conducted, I should acknowledge, by an organization I direct) reported that the Connecticut public is deeply troubled because it sees environmental problems actually worsening. *The New York Times* offered the same assessment in a 1990 Earth Day poll story:

"Eighty-four percent of Americans say pollution is a serious national problem that is getting worse. . . ." If, in fact, the public believes the country is still going downhill environmentally, after twenty years of major effort and heavy expenditures, that's political dynamite. But all sorts of other poll data make clear that the above answers reflect more a general anxiety Americans seem always to feel about important institutions and values—including, along with

Earth Day celebration.

the environment, work, religion, and the family—than the literal judgment that things are sliding. For example, a Gallup survey done in the spring of 1990 found 77 percent saying the United States has made some progress on environmental problems over the last twenty years, only 21 percent that it has made hardly any progress at all.

Two such contradictory findings—84 percent opining that pollution is getting worse and 77 percent believing that at least some progress is being made—should have set off loud alarms: Both can't be literally true.

Many Americans are now doing things individually to improve the environment, such as recycling newspapers and bottles. They will support more governmental spending for this end. They want further progress on environmental matters and firmly reject counsels of complacency. But a careful reading of available research shows that the public's commitments to environmentalism are hardly unlimited or made without regard to competing values or based on the mistaken notion that the substantial efforts of the past two decades have been a sham.

PUBLIC OPINION AND DEMOCRATIC GOVERNMENT

Political scientist V. O. Key defined public opinion as "those opinions held by private persons which governments find it prudent to heed."[2] Government acts on an issue when it is understood to be of public rather than purely private consequence—and public opinion involves preferences and perspectives on public issues. We amend Key's definition slightly: **Public opinion** is the aggregate of citizens' opinions on questions considered part of public as opposed to private life. All of the preferences, hopes, fears, aspirations that people hold do not necessarily comprise public opinion, because many of them involve strictly private choice. The color a person prefers in a house, the type of music one likes best, the college one wants one's children to attend are not public issues; there isn't public opinion on Beethoven and Madonna, although there are certainly musical tastes that can be measured.

Distinctions are often made among opinions, attitudes, and values. Opinions connote less deeply rooted judgments on current policies, leaders, and events. "What is your opinion on

[2]V. O. Key, Jr., *Public Opinion and American Democracy* (New York: Knopf, 1961), p. 14.

the president's trip to China?" Political attitudes suggest more fundamental perspectives on enduring social and political questions, such as attitudes toward race relations. Values are people's ideals and the commitments they make, involving religious beliefs, standards for interpersonal relations, moral and ethical judgments. All three comprise public opinion in the term's broadest sense.

THE DEBATE OVER ROLE

In *The American Commonwealth*, English theorist James Bryce saw the role of public opinion gradually advancing through a series of stages, "from its unconscious and passive into its conscious and active condition." He foresaw the possibility of a new stage, not then realized,

> if the will of the majority of the citizens were to become ascertainable at all times, and without the need of its passing through a body of representatives, possibly even without the need of voting machinery at all.... [When this happens] popular government would have been pushed so far as almost to dispense with, or at any rate to anticipate, the legal modes in which the majority speaks its will at the polling booths. ... To such a condition of things the phrase, "Rule of public opinion," might be most properly applied, for public opinion would not only reign but govern.[3]

The advent of scientific public opinion polling in the 1930s was seen by some observers to make possible the ultimate evolution of public opinion's role envisioned by Bryce. Did not the polls permit "the will of the majority of citizens ... to become ascertainable at all times"? The most important figure in the founding and early development of public opinion polling,

George H. Gallup, clearly thought so. The polls, he argued, "can make this a truer democracy."[4] Anything that enlarges the sway of public opinion over governmental decision making is desirable.

Others rejected the direct democrats' expectations for public opinion as simplistic and unattainable. The distinguished journalist Walter Lippmann, in *The Phantom Public*, offered one of the strongest rebuttals over a half-century ago. The populace is poorly equipped in its level of information and interest for what "rule by public opinion" suggests. Mass publics just don't involve themselves in the details of policies and legislation, only in broad questions of ends and means. They are perfectly capable of passing judgment on the general objectives and approach of a governmental program, and they are competent to decide which party or candidate is best able to carry out the program. But this is where their role stops. As Lippmann saw it, democratic theory had created much confusion through its overstated definition of the proper role of the public and public opinion. Thus democracy

> has never developed an education for the public. ... It has, in fact, aimed not at making good citizens but at making a mass of amateur executives. It has not taught the child how to act as a member of the public. It has merely given him a hasty, incomplete taste of what he might have to know if he meddled in everything. The result is a bewildered public and a mass of insufficiently trained officials.[5]

[3]James Bryce, *The American Commonwealth* (New York: Macmillan, 1916), vol. II, pp. 261–62.

[4]George H. Gallup, "Polls and the Political Process—Past, Present, and Future," *Public Opinion Quarterly* (Winter 1965), p. 549. See, too, George Gallup and Saul Forbes Rae, *The Pulse of Democracy: The Public Opinion Poll and How It Works* (Westport, Conn.: Greenwood Press, 1968; first published, 1940).

[5]Walter Lippmann, *The Phantom Public* (New York: Harcourt, Brace, 1925), pp. 61–109 *passim*, pp. 144–45, 147–49.

CAN PUBLIC OPINION BE MANIPULATED?

Other issues enter the debate over the proper role of public opinion: Are people's political opinions basically their own, reflective of their true inner values and interests, or are they in some sense manufactured for them by powerful interests?

The Helpless Public. Many theorists have insisted that mass publics are all too easily manipulated, and the image of an ill-informed and emotional populace, preyed upon by demagogues, has often been invoked. The success that dictators Benito Mussolini and Adolf Hitler had in the 1920s and 1930s in rallying many of their countrymen behind antidemocratic, expansionist, and racist appeals added to such fears. European theorists of that time, such as Gustave Le Bon and Robert Michels, argued that the "common man" was just too susceptible to demagoguery for democracy to work well, if at all.[6] In Europe in the early days of democratic experience, conservative theorists were the most likely to express foreboding about the ease with which the masses could be persuaded to support bad leaders and bad policies—not surprising since traditional conservatism had been uncomfortable with the idea of democracy in all of its forms. But in our own day, the Left as well as the Right expresses fears about manufactured public opinion.

False Consciousness. Some theorists invoke the idea of "false consciousness," in which the public is seen as manipulated into views that are not really its own. Marxist theorist Herbert Marcuse argued, for example, that the great wealth of the contemporary United States has enabled it to smother discontent in a blanket of affluence and in effect buy consent to policies that elites favor. The "establishment" has succeeded in imposing on the public an outlook that serves its own needs.

> We are again confronted with one of the most vexing aspects of advanced industrial civilization: the rational character of its irrationality. Its productivity and efficiency, its capacity to increase and spread comforts, to turn waste into need, and destruction into construction, the extent to which this civilization transforms the object world into an extension of man's mind and body makes the very notion of alienation questionable. The people recognize themselves in their commodities; they find their soul in their automobile, hi-fi set, split-level home, kitchen equipment. The very mechanism which ties the individual to his society has changed, and social control is anchored in the new needs which it has produced.[7]

Of course, if one wants to belittle a democratic society, it is convenient to argue that the public opinion to which it professes such respect and obedience is basically a farce, the product of elitist manipulations. But many commentators in many different settings have raised questions about how authentic public opinion really is. In present-day America it isn't just critics of democracy who portray the public as easily manipulated. This assessment underlies the perspectives of many in the advertising and public relations professions (although they profess no unease about it). Advertising theorists insist that improvements in their techniques, together with new communications technology and vast commitments of financial resources, permit the engineering of public acceptance of products, institutions, and ideas.

---

[6] See Gustave Le Bon, *The Crowd* (New York: Penguin, 1977; first published, 1919); and Robert Michels, *Political Parties* (New York: Dover, 1959; first published in English, 1915).

[7] Herbert Marcuse, *One Dimensional Man* (Boston: Beacon Press, 1964), pp. xii–xiii, 7–9 *passim.*

Selling the Candidate. From the claim that consumer tastes and product preferences can be induced, it was not a very great step to the conclusion that political tastes can also be shaped by advertising. Over the last two decades, a small army of advertising people, media specialists, and other campaign consultants have assumed a dramatically enlarged role in American electioneering, around the basic premise that techniques that sell soap can sell candidates and causes. V. O. Key observed:

> Propagandists and advertising men encouraged the acceptance of the most exaggerated estimates of their powers. Given enough money, they could sell soap, cigarettes, policies, presidential candidates. . . . Eventually the image of public opinion as an irresistible giant yielded to the image of the all-powerful opinion manipulators, engineers of consent and molders of mass opinion.[8]

The idea that "selling is selling" is now commonly expressed. A veteran political consultant, who had been "selling" candidates for many years, decided he would like a change and secured a senior post in a large advertising agency specializing in consumer products.

> When I first spoke to them, they were a little concerned that perhaps my background in marketing candidates was not just right for the new post selling . . . [a well-known consumer product]. But as we talked, they saw that I was right, that there really isn't any difference. If you are good at selling, what difference does it make if you are promoting a candidate or a soft drink?[9]

Many consultants insist that public consent to candidates can quite easily be engineered, assuming that the "product" (i.e., the candidate) cooperates. When his candidate loses a race, the consultant often complains that "he

The film, The Candidate, *portrayed the "selling" of a candidate who, after his election, asks his campaign manager, "What do I do now?"*

just wouldn't do what we told him to do." Political consultants also argue that manipulating political opinion is no less reputable than manipulating consumer tastes. Media consultant Michael Kaye makes the latter claim unashamedly: "If I sell a car, I am not a bad guy. The minute you add one ingredient, the politician, all of a sudden it becomes distasteful or wrong. I am still waiting for someone to say why it is wrong. Why is it wrong to sell politicians?"[10]

[8]Key, *Public Opinion,* p. 6.
[9]Personal communication to the author, July 1, 1983.

[10]Michael Kaye, quoted in Larry J. Sabato, *The Rise of Political Consultants* (New York: Basic Books, 1981), p. 321.

This increasingly manipulative tone, so evident in recent campaigns, troubles many observers. Of course a candidate should be presented in his best light. But democracy assumes—more, requires—the presence of public opinion that reflects the people's needs and interests, not those of advertising hucksters. Does public opinion live up to its democratic billing?

We do not ask whether public opinion can ever be fooled or manipulated; of course it can be. Over a century ago Abraham Lincoln told a visitor to the White House that "you may fool all the people some of the time; you can even fool some of the people all the time. [But] you can't fool all the people all the time." Lincoln's whimsically put but serious point is the same one that occupies us here. In the pages that follow, we explore what is known about American public opinion to learn whether it still meets Lincoln's expectation. We will see how general properties and overall patterns bear on the argument whether public opinion is authentic and autonomous or the plaything of those who would manipulate it for their own ends.

PROPERTIES OF PUBLIC OPINION

Public opinion undoubtedly has certain common characteristics in all or most countries, but its patterns are also shaped by the specific social, economic, and political experience of individual nations. What we see in the United States reflects the country's two hundred years under one set of democratic institutions, the absence of sharp class polarization, the levels of public education and communication, and other formative elements.

AN INFORMED PUBLIC?

On first review, survey research seems to raise serious doubts about whether Americans know enough about the various questions of public affairs to play the part democratic theory assigns them. A cursory examination of poll data reveals extraordinary lack of interest and a high measure of unawareness, even on basic facts of political life. This finding lends support to those who argue that mass publics can readily be manipulated because they know so little about issues they are supposed to decide.

Americans are entitled to elect the members of the U.S. House of Representatives every two years. But, polls show, they typically know little about individual representatives. For example, an ABC News / *Washington Post* poll of May 1989 found that only 28 percent of respondents could even *name* the member from their local district. Looking at levels of factual information about complex policies, we see even more unawareness. We need to be cautious about claims like "82 percent of Americans favor" this or that program. Often the public just does not have enough information and awareness to justify them.

BIG SWINGS IN MOOD

Polls of late have been showing extremely large swings in a series of measures of political sentiment, economic concern, and confidence in overall national direction. For example, George Bush's presidential approval rating reached an all-time high of 89 percent in the Gallup poll taken as the Gulf War ended in March 1991. But that autumn it dropped off sharply: Just 50 percent expressed approval at the end of November. In September 1992, Bush's approval rating was down to 35 percent.

Similarly, the proportion of Americans saying "things in the nation are generally headed in the right direction," as opposed to being "on

the wrong track," shifted dramatically, moving from 41 percent saying "right direction" versus 38 percent saying "wrong track" at the end of August 1991 to 19 percent saying "right direction" versus 64 percent saying "wrong track" in late November of that year. The Conference Board's Index of Consumer Confidence, which measures the economic mood, fell 22 points from August to November 1991 and continued to show great volatility throughout 1992.

These shifts appear even more dramatic when viewed against past performance. The fall 1991 drop in the Consumer Confidence Index took that measure to one of the lowest readings recorded in its twenty-two-year existence. (The lowest mark, 43, came in December 1974, shortly after Richard Nixon resigned the presidency.) Just 14 percent of Americans surveyed in May 1992 by NBC News and the *Wall Street Journal* said that the United States was moving in the right direction—the lowest rating ever

recorded for this question in all the scores of times it has been asked.

Why, Then, Such Sharp Changes? Though ostensibly very different in their focus, the various measures of consumer confidence, presidential approval, and so on all tap a diffuse amalgam we can simply call the "national mood." In our age of pervasive electronic communication, the rapid dissemination of information in brief—both positive and negative—makes this mood, at least at the surface, behave like an express elevator, rushing willy-nilly from cellar to penthouse and back. What's more, it doesn't take major shifts in the country's foundations to bring about a dramatic mood swing. In the fall of 1990, for example, the spectacle of president and Congress locked in endless budget wrangling and the president backing off on his "no new taxes" pledge were enough to sour public sentiment.

In the case of the Gulf War, it was the president's leadership and the military's performance, widely applauded, that dramatically raised the national mood and, in turn, led people to proclaim greater economic confidence. Of course, Americans were bound to feel better about the nation's well-being when they were hearing nightly of victories in the Persian Gulf than when they were being told nightly that the economy was in shambles, as was the case in the fall of 1991 and winter of 1992.

When asked generally "how it is all going," in a world where so much is going on and so much is being transported into their living rooms in full color each night, Americans evince big, if fairly superficial, swings of mood. This is one more novel feature of the media centered, information laden "post-industustrial" politics.

The Anchor of Personal Experience. On the other hand, when people are asked about their own economic position—about which they have full personal knowledge—their responses show great stability. Most Americans' economic fortunes stay fairly constant, and their assessments reflect this. Each year since 1972, the NORC has asked its respondents whether they are "pretty well satisfied," "more or less satisfied," or "not at all satisifed" with their personal financial situation. Not once over these two decades has the porportion saying they are dissatisfied dropped lower than 23 percent or risen higher than 30 percent. In the survey taken in 1991, it was 27 percent. In the summer and fall of 1991, when measures of consumer confidence were showing such a steep decline, surveys by NBC News and the *Wall Street Journal* found Americans' assessments of their own economic situations changing not at all.

Similarly, when asked about their family life, or their social and religious values, people's responses vary little, whatever the headlines of the day. They are firmly anchored by concrete experience.

HOW STABLE AND STRUCTURED IS PUBLIC OPINION?

Consider two hypothetical individuals. The first eats, sleeps, and breathes politics. She devours *The New York Times* and other leading newspapers and closely follows virtually every major political issue. When asked her views on a particular program, she answers confidently, because she has reached her conclusions through a pains-taking accumulation of pertinent facts. Her opinions have a bedrock firmness. The second individual, in contrast, pays little attention to the intricacies of governmental programs and political arguments. She gives the daily newspapers, except the sports page, only a cursory glance. When asked her views on a program, her answers are more a spur-of-the-moment reaction than a considered judgment. If individuals of the latter type predominate, public opinion on many governmental questions may be highly unstable.

Political scientist Philip E. Converse addressed this subject and concluded that the amount of political information people have goes far toward determining the structure, constraint, and stability of their beliefs. Without much factual information, the beliefs of large segments of the populace bounce around wildly over time. Between 1956 and 1960, the Institute for Social Research at the University of Michigan posed the same questions to the same people on three separate occasions, asking their views on issues such as school desegregation, federal aid to education, foreign aid, and federal housing. Many respondents moved from one side to the other on these questions in successive interviews. Examining this pattern, Converse concluded that most of the move-

*"Glad you brought that up, Jim. The latest research on polls has turned up
some interesting variables. It turns out, for example, that people will tell you
any old thing that pops into their heads."*

Drawing by Saxon; © 1984 The New Yorker Magazine, Inc.

ment was not true opinion change but rather the result of respondents answering in essentially a random fashion. Only a distinct minority had something close to hard-core opinions. "For the remainder of the population, response sequences over time are statistically random."[11]

If this is true, it carries substantial implications for the role of public opinion in democratic government. Giving great weight to the clear, considered preferences of the people is supported by everyone sympathetic to democracy. But should views that are virtually "statis-tically random" be accorded such weight? If the public really knows little about most policy disputes—even those that have been extensively discussed—and if the opinions it expresses are very lightly held, why should politicians or anyone else pay attention to them?

Converse's work stimulated further research on the subject. Several investigations concluded that his findings held up only for a particular period of time: the 1950s. During the mid- to late 1960s, these studies concluded, the relatively issueless politics of the Eisenhower years gave way to heated divisions over civil rights, Vietnam, and social issues. When the political parties and their nominees began taking distinct positions on such divisive issues, they imparted to voters ideological cues that had been lacking in the previous decade. This

[11]Philip E. Converse, "The Nature of Belief Systems in Mass Publics," in David Apter, ed., *Ideology and Discontent* (New York: Free Press, 1964), p. 242.

led to more structured and stable public responses.[12]

GENERAL VALUES VERSUS PROGRAM SPECIFICS

Another type of public opinion research yields conclusions very different from Converse's or even those of his critics. It focuses on the overall patterns of responses Americans give. These turn out to be remarkably stable and predictable. The Gallup Organization has polled American opinion continuously since the mid-1930s, asking questions on foreign policy, the role of government, many different domestic programs, a wide range of social issues from abortion to race relations, and more. The findings in each of these areas at all times show a clear, persisting structure in what people are saying. Through all the changes in political events and circumstances, Americans make basic distinctions and express general preferences that in the aggregate don't look random or uninformed.

The basic source of this contradiction in assessments of public opinion can be traced to a central distinction that democratic theory has long made: Mass publics can hold underlying values and express broad preferences coherently, even while they are inattentive to much of the detail of governmental programs and policies. As we have seen, Walter Lippmann took it as evident that the public is unlikely to initiate specific programs or immerse itself in their detailed specifications. But it can choose perfectly well between contrasting approaches presented to it by political leaders.

Elmo Roper was one of the founders of modern public opinion research. In 1942 he reviewed what he had learned from his first decade of survey investigations:

> I believe that a great many of us make two mistakes in our judgment of the common man. *We overestimate the amount of information he has; we underestimate his intelligence.* I know that during my eight years of asking the common man questions about what he thinks and what he wants I have often been surprised and disappointed to discover that he has less information than we think he should have about some question we consider vital. But I have more often been surprised and elated to discover that, despite his lack of information, the common man's native intelligence generally brings him to a sound conclusion.[13]

Roper's commentary states the wisdom of the distinction orthodox democratic theory has made between the public's role and that of leaders and activists in the process of democratic government. Most people do not have responsibility for writing laws or determining the specific shape of programs, and they clearly do not pay much attention to programs at such a level. While we might wish that schools would do a better job of giving students information on government or that more people would spend more time deepening their knowledge, this is a different matter than whether the public can play the role specified by democratic theory: determining "the basic ends of public policy." A populace may be quite attentive to those ends, and notably clear and consistent in its specifications on them, without having much

[12] For studies concluding that Converse's findings were time-bound and not reflective of the pattern that appeared in the 1960s, see Norman Nie and Kristi Andersen, "Mass Belief Systems Revisited: Political Change and Attitude Structure," *Journal of Politics*, August 1974, pp. 541–91; John C. Pierce and Douglas D. Rose, "Non-Attitudes and American Public Opinion: The Examination of a Thesis," *American Political Science Review*, June 1974, pp. 626–49; and Norman H. Nie, Sidney Verba, and John R. Petrocik, *The Changing American Voter* (Cambridge, Mass.: Harvard University Press, 1976), especially chap. 7.

[13] Elmo Roper, "So the Blind Shall Not Lead," *Fortune*, February 1942, p. 102. Emphasis added.

factual knowledge of program details. Recent empirical research on public opinion, including an important study by political scientists Benjamin Page and Robert Shapiro, has further demonstrated that the U.S. public does indeed fit these specifications.[14]

AMBIVALENCE OF OPINIONS

We noted at the outset of this chapter that on a great many policy questions the public is highly ambivalent—pulled this way and that by conflicting values. Public opinion seems a poor guide to policy action because it is so often on both sides of the fence. Americans do have mixed minds about many things—including the proper role and scope of contemporary government. Those who are flatly pro-government or anti-government are rare; most people make conflicting assessments. These responses, though, do not seem to reflect an immature desire to have one's cake and eat it too.

Instead, this ambivalence follows naturally from the joining of legacies from America's ideological past with some contemporary developments. It is often assumed that the American tradition is anti-state, but this isn't so. The founders of the American republic were an unusual breed philosophically: strongly committed to the state and architects of a new national union under the Constitution, but also certain that a government unchecked would usurp and tyrannize. This mix of pro- and anti-government perspectives taught the public to revere coherent and active national government, and at the same time to be vigilant against governmental abuse. Americans began

their modern political experience without an ideological tradition wholeheartedly for or against the state. Recent experience has enlarged the scope and meaning of this legacy.

ABORTION: A CASE STUDY IN AMBIVALENCE

As the abortion debate proceeded in the late 1980s and early 1990s, many commentators badly misinterpreted public opinion on this issue, in part because they assumed that most people who have thought about the issue and who have strong feelings on it must ultimately come down either "for" or "against." Millions *are* wholly supportive of the right to abortion, of course, or strongly opposed to abortion in most if not all circumstances—but the vast majority of Americans aren't in either camp.

Often when a large segment of the public is somewhere in the middle on an issue, it means simply that they haven't thought much about it and lack a clear view. That's not the case with abortion, however. The public is informed and interested—and has in fact reached a judgment.

Part of the judgment reached by many Americans in the middle is that on abortion as on so many other questions the idea of letting individuals choose deserves great respect. When, for example, pollsters ask "if a woman wants to have an abortion, and her doctor agrees to it," should she be permitted to have it, large majorities consistently say yes. The other part of the judgment, however, is that abortions have been performed too often and too casually since the *Roe v. Wade* decision in 1973 (discussed in chapter 9, pp. 241–49). (See Figure 10.4.)

The impact of these two sets of views is shown clearly by a number of comprehensive studies—including polls taken in March 1989 by the *Los Angeles Times*, in September 1989 by CBS News and the *New York Times*, and in

---

[14]Benjamin Page and Robert Shapiro, *The Rational Public: Fifty Years of Trends in Americans' Policy Preferences* (Chicago: University of Chicago Press, 1992).

FIGURE 10.4   ABORTION: OVERVIEW OF A COMPLEX QUESTION

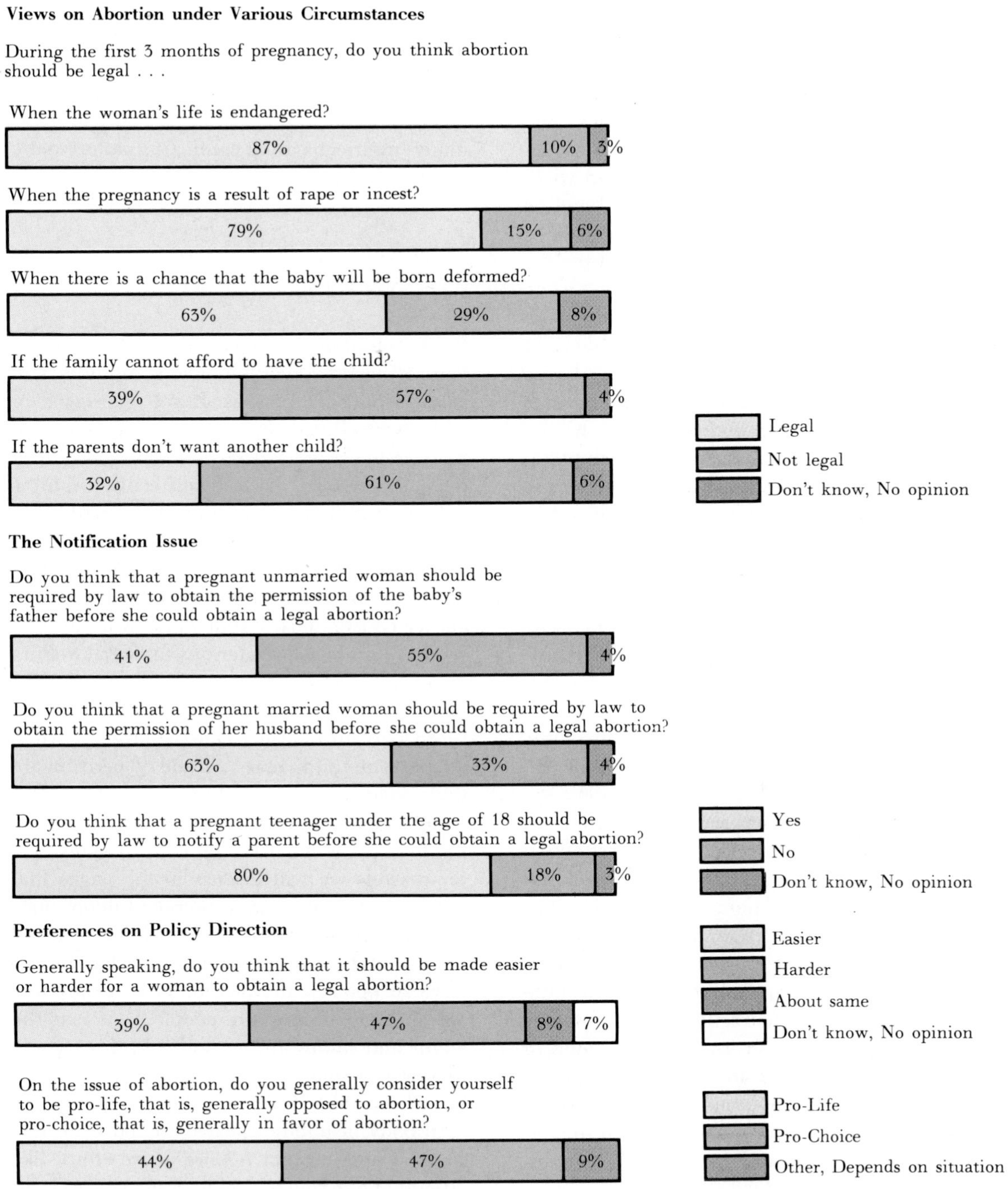

Views on Abortion under Various Circumstances

During the first 3 months of pregnancy, do you think abortion
should be legal . . .

When the woman's life is endangered?

| 87% | 10% | 3% |

When the pregnancy is a result of rape or incest?

| 79% | 15% | 6% |

When there is a chance that the baby will be born deformed?

| 63% | 29% | 8% |

If the family cannot afford to have the child?

| 39% | 57% | 4% |

If the parents don't want another child?

| 32% | 61% | 6% |

Legend:
- Legal
- Not legal
- Don't know, No opinion

The Notification Issue

Do you think that a pregnant unmarried woman should be
required by law to obtain the permission of the baby's
father before she could obtain a legal abortion?

| 41% | 55% | 4% |

Do you think that a pregnant married woman should be required by law to
obtain the permission of her husband before she could obtain a legal abortion?

| 63% | 33% | 4% |

Do you think that a pregnant teenager under the age of 18 should be
required by law to notify a parent before she could obtain a legal abortion?

| 80% | 18% | 3% |

Legend:
- Yes
- No
- Don't know, No opinion

Preferences on Policy Direction

Generally speaking, do you think that it should be made easier
or harder for a woman to obtain a legal abortion?

| 39% | 47% | 8% | 7% |

Legend:
- Easier
- Harder
- About same
- Don't know, No opinion

On the issue of abortion, do you generally consider yourself
to be pro-life, that is, generally opposed to abortion, or
pro-choice, that is, generally in favor of abortion?

| 44% | 47% | 9% |

Legend:
- Pro-Life
- Pro-Choice
- Other, Depends on situation

Source: Survey by *The Washington Post*, March 27–31, 1992.

March 1992 by the *Washington Post*—each of which asked batteries of questions. These studies show that a large majority rejects a constitutional amendment that would categorically prohibit abortion. A woman so choosing should be able to get a legal abortion when the pregnancy results from rape or incest, and when there is a significant chance the child will be genetically deformed. Almost consensually, Americans would permit abortion to save the mother's life.

But while the mother should be able to choose to have an abortion in some instances, her right of choice should not be unlimited. Large majorities would make abortion illegal in cases where the claim for an abortion is that having a child would force the woman to interrupt her career, that the father is unwilling to help raise the child, or that the pregnancy would cause financial strain. Almost consensually, Americans oppose abortion as a means of birth control.

Polls have regularly shown a clear majority opposed to having abortion legal in all circumstances and about half the public willing to have its legality limited to very restricted circumstances. For example, the CBS News / *New York Times* poll of September 17–20, 1989, found 43 percent saying abortion should be "legal as it is now," 40 percent wanting it legal "only in such cases as rape, incest, or to save the life of the mother," and 13 percent not permitting it at all. There is substantial support, the March 1992 *Washington Post* survey found, for making it "harder for a woman to obtain a legal abortion," although there is little support for sweeping curbs. A majority opposes legislation requiring an unmarried women to obtain the permission of the baby's father before obtaining an abortion, but an even larger (two-thirds) majority would require a married woman to obtain the husband's consent before an abortion could be performed.

Some Americans would reverse the 1973 *Roe v. Wade* ruling altogether, while others would let it stand entirely unmodified. But *majority opinion* has long been otherwise—and remains so today. It stipulates that abortion should not be banned, but also should not be established as an absolute right. More generally, a great many Americans bring conflicting values to the abortion issue.

POLLING AND ITS INFLUENCE

Public opinion, we have said, is the sum of citizens' personal views—opinions, attitudes, and values—on public issues. It gets expressed in many ways. People write letters to newspapers, hold rallies, cast votes on election day. But increasingly over the last half-century, public opinion has been expressed through polls conducted among representative samples of the populace. The idea that public opinion is what polls say it is represents quite a leap from earlier conceptions. Public opinion used to be seen as an almost mysterious force, a swelling up of popular feelings on this issue or that. Now it is practically a statistical exercise: "Sixty-seven percent of Americans believe . . . while 24 percent think that . . . and 9 percent are undecided."

Polls can be wrong. They can yield misleading pictures of what the public's thinking is—for reasons we will discuss in the pages that follow. But they came to be relied upon, once their techniques were perfected, because all other outlets or expressions of public opinion were so open to the possibility that they had left out large numbers of people. Letters to the editor and rallies are notorious in this regard; they reflect some people's opinions, of course, but whose? How faithful a slice are they of the total body of public thinking? Even if expressions of opinion that require active effort, like attending a march to protest some governmental action, should receive more weight because the effort suggests greater commitment, the fact is that such expressions are partial rather than complete. The views of more activist segments of the population may not accord with majority sentiment.

Opinion polling can claim to be truly democratic. Samples are drawn so as to represent all groups and classes in proportion to their actual size in the entire population. Questions can be framed more or less neutrally and precisely, and everyone's answers fairly recorded. Polling offers a more objective means of gauging public opinion. As a result, systematic polling has become the dominant tool for opinion measurement. An assortment of groups and institutions, including the communications media, politicians, business corporations, and other interest groups have concluded that opinion polling is useful enough to them to justify spending large sums of money on it. The polling industry has become a big one, and it plays a large part in contemporary politics. Polls have become a staple of political assessment and commentary in every advanced industrial democracy.

Today it is rare when a candidate for major office does not commission polls to assess what voters want and how well his campaign is registering. Presidential candidates routinely set up large polling operations that conduct surveys almost daily during the campaign. Pollsters have become important campaign strategists, working hand in hand with media experts and other consultants in planning all aspects of campaigns. Candidates are not the only political actors using polls. Interest groups sponsor surveys on subjects of political importance to them and then introduce results into political debate, often to demonstrate that the people really endorse what the group is urging. The American Medical Association (AMA) is one interest group that makes heavy use of polls in its lobbying efforts. Polls have become widely used political weapons. In recent lobbying on environmental issues, for example, both sides have emphasized poll findings in

Drawing by Dana Fradon; © 1980 The New Yorker Magazine, Inc.

their efforts to set the terms of the debate favorable to what they want done.

HOW POLLING DEVELOPED

"Must I drink the whole bottle," Belgian mathematician Adolphe Quetelet once asked, "in order to judge the quality of the wine?" If the answer were yes, wine tasting would be a quite different art. A small sample is sufficient to judge, providing it has all of the important characteristics of the larger unit. This principle of sampling is today employed by researchers in many fields. When marine biologists chart the chemical properties of a bay, they cannot submit all of it to laboratory analysis, nor do they collect samples wherever they feel like it. They draw portions of the water from different spots throughout the area, at different depths, using procedures so that their samples reflect the range of properties of the entire bay. Sam-

Box 10.1
How Polls Are Taken

Of a number of books and manuals available on public opinion polling, among the best is Charles W. Roll and Albert H. Cantril, *Polls: Their Use and Misuse* (Cabin John, Md.: Seven Locks Press, 1980). Here, very briefly, are some of the "nuts and bolts."

Polling by Mail, Telephone, and in Person. The least expensive type of polling is the mail questionnaire. And in some instances, especially where one needs to pose a lengthy and complex set of questions to a very interested group within the population, data gathering by mail can be very effective. But most of the time this approach yields unacceptably low returns of completed questionnaires, and it is very slow.

The pioneering survey research organizations in the United States began their work almost exclusively with in-person interviewing; Gallup and Roper still do much of their interviewing in respondents' homes. The advantage of this form is the opportunity it presents a skillful interviewer to establish rapport with respondents. Many people seem to be more willing to explore controversial subjects in a thoughtfully conducted in-person interview than over the telephone.

But telephone interviewing is taking over the industry. It is faster and cheaper than in-person interviewing. Over 97 percent of all households in America now have telephones, so the old argument that telephone interviewing leaves out large numbers of less affluent people no longer applies. Survey organizations are finding that, especially in the high-crime sections of cities, refusal rates are lower when interviewing is done by telephone rather than in person. The ABC News / *Washington Post*, CBS News / *New York Times*, NBC News, and *Los Angeles Times* polls are all conducted by telephone.

Drawing a Sample. In the early years of U.S. polling, samples of the population were drawn largely through the *quota* method. (Quota sampling is still common outside the United States.) In this type of sampling, census information is utilized to find the distribution of the population by such relevant attributes as age, education, income, and region. A frame is then designed so that the makeup of the interviews conducted matches the overall population distributions. Interviewers are instructed as to how many respondents they are to get in the various specified

pling in public opinion research follows this same general idea. (See Box 10.1, "How Polls Are Taken.")

THE *LITERARY DIGEST* AND THE BIRTH OF SYSTEMATIC POLLING

One event a half-century ago dramatized the basic premises of sampling applied to the study of public opinion and helped change the course of opinion research: the famous "*Literary Digest* fiasco" of 1936. The *Literary Digest* was a large circulation magazine with articles on topics of general interest: economic, cultural, political. As early as 1895, it began collecting the names of prospective subscribers as part of its general efforts to increase circulation, and its mailing list rapidly grew to include millions of names. In 1920 the magazine's editors first hit upon the categories: so many men and women, so many people 18 to 29 years of age, etc. This approach is quite efficient, but it has major drawbacks and has largely been abandoned in the United States. Chief among the drawbacks is the fact that the interviewer makes the decision as to which individuals are to be interviewed. The element of randomness is lost. And various forms of bias creep in. Anyone who has ever been out with interviewers working on quota samples has heard such statements as "Oh, I'm not going to interview *him*, he looks so grouchy."

Probability Sampling. U.S. survey firms now rely on sampling procedures that make use of probability principles. The idea behind them is to give every individual an equal or known chance of falling into the sample. One common approach is to divide the population into categories on the basis of the size and location of the places people live. Particular areas (such as city blocks) are then chosen on a systematic or random basis. So many interviews are assigned for each block, selecting every *n*th household. People are interviewed solely because the place they live is within an area included in the sample.

Random-Digit Dialing (RDD). This approach applies the theory of probability sampling to telephone interviewing. A survey firm obtains from the telephone company a tape of information on the working three-digit prefixes (called COCs, for central office codes) in telephone numbers and the assigned banks of the latter four digits. COCs are then selected at random, and a number of interviews to be completed is assigned to each COC—depending on how many working residential numbers there are within it. Random-digit numbers are then generated for each COC or prefix. Calls are continued until the desired number of interview completions is achieved.

Sampling Error. Statisticians know how to calculate what the chances are that a sample will be representative of the population. "Sampling error" refers to the extent to which the results in a sample can be expected to differ from the results that would have been obtained if everyone in a population had been interviewed. *Sampling error* encompasses only a small fraction of possible *survey error*. Inaccurate poll results can stem from bad question wording, poor interviewing, sloppy sampling, and many other sources. Sampling error per se is exclusively statistical. The laws of probability can result in samples that are unrepresentative of the total population.

idea of using these lists as a base from which to test political sentiment. By 1928 the *Digest* was conducting a presidential poll in which 18 million ballots were distributed through their mailing lists. Those receiving ballots were asked to check off their choice for president and return their "vote" to the magazine. The *Digest* tabulated them and printed the results at intervals during the campaign, showing the grand total in the last issue before the election.

Over several elections, the *Literary Digest* poll results corresponded remarkably closely to actual election results—and its prestige naturally rose. In 1928, for example, the poll predicted a victory for Republican Herbert Hoover with 63 percent of the popular vote: Hoover won the election with 59 percent. Four years later, the *Digest* poll indicated that the Democratic candidate, Franklin Roosevelt, would win handily, and he did. The final poll results in

1932 were within 1.5 percent of the actual vote distribution. In 1936, however, the poll fell on its face—and in such a dramatic fashion that the magazine itself was discredited. All during the 1936 campaign, the *Digest* issued reports on the return of its mailed ballots showing Republican Alfred Landon well ahead of incumbent Franklin Roosevelt. The *Digest*'s final report, based on nearly 2.4 million ballots, pointed to a resounding Landon victory. Republicans were shown carrying 32 states with a total of 370 electoral votes and winning 54 percent of the popular vote. In the actual balloting on November 5, however, Roosevelt won 61 percent of the popular vote and 523 of the 531 electoral votes. Landon was buried under the biggest landslide in American political history. Why the *Digest* poll failed became a topic of intense discussion.

In fact, the *Literary Digest*'s failure was predicted well in advance of the election, and its source was explained by George Gallup and a

The cover of the Literary Digest *announcing the "final returns of the mammoth nationwide presidential poll."*

number of others who were founding public opinion research in the United States on the basis of new sampling procedures. As Gallup pointed out, while the 2.4 million returned ballots seemed an impressive number, they could be no more reliable than the sampling frame from which they were drawn: the magazine's mailing list. And that list was skewed toward the middle and upper middle class. In the 1936 election, where class lines were relatively sharp, and lower- and working-class voters much more supportive of Roosevelt than those in the middle class, the bias of the *Digest*'s sample was immense. Another problem was that the magazine mailed out over 20 million ballots but received back just over 10 percent of them; it had no way of determining whether those taking the trouble to "vote" were even a cross-section of those receiving the ballots, much less of the entire American electorate. And the *Digest*'s method of polling was insensitive to opinion shifts occurring at later stages of the race, because it provided for only one mailing during the campaign.

For many who followed the *Literary Digest* fiasco, perhaps the most striking thing was the contrast between the immense, cumbersome efforts of the magazine and the lean, efficient new scientific surveys pioneered by Gallup, Elmo Roper, and Archibald Crossley. Whereas the *Digest* "surveyed" millions, the new polling methods sampled only a few thousand. But because the latter could achieve samples that corresponded at least roughly to the makeup of the entire population, they were dramatically more successful. That "little" Gallup poll was largely right while the huge *Literary Digest* effort was embarrassingly wrong—this juxtaposition brought the new age of polling in with a bang. As George Gallup and Saul Forbes Rae were to observe later, "One fundamental lesson became clear in the 1936 election: the heart of the problem of obtaining an accurate measure of public opinion lay in the cross-

section, and no mere accumulation of ballots could hope to eliminate the error that sprang from a biased sample."[15]

POLLING AND THE PRESS

The major breakthrough in sampling made by Gallup and Roper in 1936 forever changed the way public opinion is measured. Later work by statisticians improved upon the sampling techniques, but the underlying principles had been sound. Today, the problem with polls generally has little to do with the way samples of respondents are drawn from the total population. But the polls' performance is not problem-free. Poll findings should not be accepted uncritically.

One set of problems arises from the incompatibility of survey research methods with some of the needs of the media. The press, meaning all mass communications media, must work quickly in order to do its mandated job, to bring the story promptly to the audience. From this basic requirement, speed and timeliness have become highly regarded values. But to do its job, properly and reasonably, polling must move slowly; time is required to frame questions unambiguously, pretest and refine them, do the field work, transform the resulting data to computer-readable form, and perform careful analysis of them. (See Box 10.2.) The results of opinion polling on issues of consequence also typically require extensive, time-consuming explanation and exposition.

But news media must often move quickly in their canvass of political events, and a great variety of developments vie for press attention. Given this competition for media time and space, public opinion on, for example, a complex health policy issue can rarely expect to receive as much as 60 seconds of television

---

[15] Gallup and Rae, *The Pulse of Democracy*, pp. 54–55.

Box 10.2
The Difficult Task of Question Wording

All survey research, to the extent it tries to understand the public's thinking rather than provide ammunition to advance a cause, confronts a perplexing set of challenges in the area of question wording. When misleading results accrue from surveys, deficiencies in question form and language are the principal source of the problem.

Technical Problems. Some survey items inadvertently pose two separate questions within one, making it impossible to know what respondents are actually answering: "Please tell me whether you agree or disagree with the following statement: It is important that the federal deficit be substantially reduced and that spending for national defense be cut below the president's proposal." This is called a "double-barreled" question. Even if the first part of this statement were separated to stand by itself, there would still be an easily recognizable problem: "It is important that the federal deficit be substantially reduced" poses a variation of the old "motherhood and apple pie" factor. Who is going to declare himself against it? Everyone wants to reduce the federal deficit; the problem comes in finding a way to accomplish the objective with the least harm to other values. A great many different types of problems in question design have been detected. The polling literature has given helpful guidance in avoiding these pitfalls.

Ambivalence and Low Levels of Information. Other problems are trickier to handle. It is especially difficult to frame questions on subjects where the level of relevant information among the general public is low. "One very real difficulty with interpreting opinion data from surveys is that since many people are responding to questions to which they have not given much previous thought, their replies can vary with even subtle differences in the way the questions are worded."*

On abstract policy issues, as we have seen, the public's opinions often haven't taken clear form. How questions are worded helps determine the apparent major-

*Robert S. Erikson, Norman R. Luttbeg, and Kent L. Tedin, *American Public Opinion* (New York: Wiley, 1980). p. 29.

newscast or 500 words in a newspaper article. An obvious problem arises when such accounts cannot begin to explicate the subject properly. In such cases—which are common, not exceptional—"tight editing" equals "gross oversimplification."

Good news reporting has focus and arrives at relatively clear and unambiguous conclu-

sions. In contrast, good opinion research typically reveals such characteristics of public thinking as tentativeness, ambivalence, and lack of information or awareness. The journalist wants crisp answers to such questions as: Is the United States public becoming more conservative? Do Americans favor or oppose economic assistance to Russia? Frequently, though, results

ity position. That problem is compounded when the public has mixed feelings on the issue being investigated.

Question wording presents only minimal challenges for the experienced survey research specialist when:

1) the level of relevant information among respondents is high;
2) the public has focused on the issue in the context of an actual decision;
3) the choice presented is not complex;
4) the issue is not distinguished by high levels of public ambivalence.

A common instance where the above conditions apply is asking respondents how they plan to vote late in a campaign, when the candidates of both parties are well known and the decision is a real one for most respondents because they will actually be making it shortly in the voting booth.

When the opposite of all of these elements apply, however—when the information level is low, opinions have not crystallized, the question is complex, and many people are ambivalent—even the most sensitive approach to question wording can yield unreliable results. Any version of the question is likely to produce findings significantly different from other equally valid and informed questions. The latter conditions can be found in varying degrees in polling on virtually every complicated policy issue. The deeper one probes, the tougher the problem appears. The very design of the structured public-opinion survey may be incapable of dealing with the complexity of opinion, given the mix of contrasting values and expectations that vie for priority in our thinking on issues.

The conclusion that Leo Bogart, a leading public-opinion researcher, draws is not that opinion research is incapable of yielding useful knowledge. Instead, he gives greater force to the caution that "the mechanics of survey research, like any other human enterprise, are subject to a substantial range of error. . . ."† Survey questions are like the blind men before the elephant—each reaches out trying to grasp and comprehend something it really cannot see.

* Robert S. Erikson, Norman R. Luttbeg, and Kent L. Tedin, *American Public Opinion* (New York: Wiley, 1980). p. 29.
† Leo Bogart, *Silent Politics: Polls and the Awareness of Public Opinion* (New York: Wiley-Interscience, 1972), p. 17.

of the best survey research aren't consistent with journalists' needs. Conclusions emerging from polling on the various issues often fail to sustain the focused conclusion that is the staple of news reporting. Today, with the press so heavily involved in the financial sponsorship and even the actual management of polls, there are powerful incentives to act as though poll findings are newsworthy. Law professor Michael Wheeler maintains that "the most flagrant error of the press is the common practice of reporting polls as if each American holds a firm opinion on every topic."[16]

[16] Michael Wheeler, "Reining in Horse-Race Journalism," *Public Opinion*, February/March 1980, p. 42.

Drawing by M. Stevens; © 1989 The New Yorker Magazine, Inc.

A RECENT RUSH OF POLLING PROBLEMS

The pollsters really fell on their faces in the April 1992 British general election. The picture provided by the five major national polls conducted and published just prior to the balloting showed the Labour party narrowly ahead. In fact Conservatives won by a margin of nearly 8 percent over Labour. Systematically conducted surveys may never have missed the mark so badly in a major national election. Drawing on their findings, most British analysts had predicted a "hung Parliament"—no party winning a majority of seats—with Labour putting together a coalition government. Instead, the Conservatives not only won a comfortable majority in the House of Commons, but they did so by getting a plurality of the popular vote that stands on the high side in modern British

experience: their fourth lowest margin over their principal opposition in the fourteen British general elections since World War II. It was surpassed only in the Labour victory of 1945 and in the landslides won by Margaret Thatcher and the Conservatives in 1983 and 1987.

Were the big failure of polls in Great Britain's election a one-of-a-kind occurrence, it should prompt curiosity, perhaps some amusement, but little more. But while it was more spectacular than most, the 1992 British miss was only the latest in a stream of election polling "errors." In Februry 1992, the exit polls taken during the New Hampshire Republican primary badly underestimated George Bush's vote and suggested that he and Patrick Buchanan would closely split the vote when in fact Bush won comfortably. Warren Mitofsky, executive director of Voter Research & Surveys, the four-network consortium that is the leading exit poller, described the New Hampshire performance as, in the history of election-day surveys, unusually wide of the mark.[17]

In 1990, the polls taken in the New York City mayoral race and the Virginia gubernatorial contest—both the late pre-election surveys and the exit polls—misread the vote. They showed Democrat David Dinkins winning handily in New York; he actually bested Republican Rudolph Giuliani by just 2 percentage points. Similarly, late polls put Democrat Douglas Wilder well ahead of Republican Marshall Coleman in Virginia. In fact, the race ended in a virtual dead heat.

For all the improvements in methods, the general environment for election polling now makes the enterprise far more difficult and

[17] Warren J. Mitofsky, "What Went Wrong With Exit Polling in New Hampshire," *The Public Perspective* 3,3 (March/April 1992), p. 17.

demanding than it was in 1948. The polling failure that year has entered popular mythology as the greatest ever. It wasn't, in fact, and what went wrong that year was easy to correct. Present problems are vastly more challenging. It is true, of course, that all the polls taken in 1948 put Republican Thomas Dewey ahead of the Democratic incumbent, Harry Truman. But their findings never justified proclamations of a Dewey victory. Two of the polling organizations, Gallup's and Crossley's, both underestimated Truman's percentage of the popular vote by about 5 points. But Crossley did this final interviewing in mid-October. Gallup concluded just a bit later—two weeks before the election. Had Gallup stopped polling in 1968 at the same point he did in 1948, his 1968 "predictions" would have been far off.

In 1948 Gallup found Dewey's margin declining—from 12 points to just 5—from August to October. Any reasonable interpreta-

tion would have considered the possibility that the Democrats—who had controlled the White House since the depths of the Great Depression—might have gained further strength as election day approached and the vote became a real "priced" choice, one that really counted. Surely some voters, while dissatisfied with Truman and ready for a change after sixteen years of Democratic rule, must have wondered whether they dared take a chance on "those Republicans." Surveys available before the election made abundantly clear that the country was still in an era favorable to the Democrats.

The "polling error" in 1948 was one of judgment and interpretation: a failure to take into account what should have seemed obvious even without 20-20 hindsight, that a Dewey victory in the balloting could not be projected from a 5 point or so lead in mid-October in a poll trial heat. Today, much more than naive misinterpretation of poll findings lies at the root of the election polls' problems.

One important factor involves the large and growing proportion of Americans who refuse to participate in surveys of any sort. Polling is now seen in countries such as Russia as an exciting new means of popular expression. But in the United States where we have had free expression for more than two centuries and polls for roughly sixty years, and where the number of surveys and pseudo-surveys has grown exponentially, many people are saying "Enough already." As refusal rates soar, it gets harder to figure out whether or not those who agree to participate are a reasonable microcosm of the actual electorate. Ironically, despite improvements in methodology, it's becoming harder these days, not easier, to get reliable electoral estimates from polls.

SOLUTIONS TO POLLING PROBLEMS

As polls become more widely used, those of us who "consume" them need to become "smarter shoppers." Governmental legislation restricting polling doesn't seem to offer a satisfactory solution, because polling appears to fall well within the bounds of free inquiry, which the U.S. Constitution mandates, and because much useful information is gathered from polls. The answers, then, must involve more knowledge about polls and wiser use of them.

Journalists need to learn more about polls. Courses on public-opinion research that are specially tailored to the needs of the press are already being developed. Journalists also need ready access to larger bodies of polling information. Is a particular question biased or otherwise defective? It is becoming possible for journalists to plug into data banks that contain large numbers of related questions, and this should stimulate more informed press coverage.

Citizens who read poll results also need to be more sensitive to the distortions that can arise from polling. The cautions contained in this chapter are a starting point. Groups of responsible polling organizations try to set higher standards for their profession, and these efforts need to be supplemented. The National Council on Public Polls (NCPP) and the American Association for Public Opinion Research (AAPOR) already do important "self-policing" with regard to professional standards. They need to do more, especially to publicize problems inherent in question form and wording, the area in opinion research that presents the greatest difficulties.

SUMMARY

Public opinion is assigned a critical role in a democracy. Government by the people, democracy, must mean government responsive to the public's preferences for leaders and policies, or it is a sham.

Questions have been raised from a variety of perspectives as to whether public opinion can meet democracy's requirements. Many observers have argued that the public is insufficiently informed about and attentive to the issues on which its judgment is supposed to exercise control. Critics have portrayed the public as too easily manipulated by demagogic leaders. In the United States, some charge, the "establishment" has succeeded in imposing on the people outlooks that serve its, not their, needs. Arguments made by advertising and public relations theorists in a way back up the critics, through their stress on how easily consent to candidates and causes can be engineered.

Opinion research in the United States does reveal a public strikingly inattentive to the details of even the most consequential and controversial policies. This suggests a potential for manipulation. But the research also indicates great stability and coherence in the public's underlying attitudes and values. Americans show themselves perfectly capable of making the distinctions needed to determine the basic ends of public policy and of pursuing these logically and clearly. There is a persisting structure to American opinion that belies the picture of a populace helpless before the "engineers of consent."

To observe that the public holds strongly to basic values is not to assert that its preferences are always clear or readily followed. People are frequently ambivalent—committed at the same time to opposing or competing goals. They think that contemporary government is too big, too powerful, and too costly, and they would like to see it reined in. But they also look to government for help in solving a great variety of problems and don't think there is any alternative to an expansive role for the state. Such pushes and pulls of contending values dominate American public opinion.

The public's ambivalent responses pose some tricky measurement problems for opinion research. It is no easy task to frame questions so as to give proper weight to the contending objectives people so often bring to complex policy issues. In general, problems related to question design contribute more to deficiencies in opinion research than any other factor.

Pioneered a half-century ago by George Gallup and Elmo Roper, systematic polling has become the dominant tool for opinion measurement. A wide assortment of groups and institutions—including academic social scientists, the press, politicians, business, and other interest groups—all find polling valuable in their work. But each makes its own special use of poll information, very different from those of the others. Journalists look to polls as sources of news, whereas political interest groups want poll findings that buttress their positions or help them chart strategies. Given the varied uses, the maxim *caveat emptor* is very much in order: The buyer or consumer of poll reports should be wary.

FOR FURTHER STUDY

Bogart, Leo. *Silent Politics: Polls and the Awareness of Public Opinion*. New York: Wiley-Interscience, 1972. A brilliant analysis of what public opinion is and isn't, and how polls can be used in the study of public opinion.

Erikson, Robert S., et al. *American Public Opinion*, 3rd ed. New York: Macmillan, 1988. A good review of polling information on American public opinion in various policy areas.

Gallup, George, and Saul Forbes Rae. *The Pulse of Democracy*. Westport, Conn.: Greenwood Press, 1968; first published, 1940. One of the founders of modern public opinion polling, George Gallup, defends the enterprise as one that can enlarge and strengthen democracy itself.

Gilboa, Eytau. *American Public Opinion Toward Israel and the Arab-Israeli Conflict*. Boston: D. C. Heath, 1987. A careful, systematic review of American opinion in an area of great importance in U.S. foreign policy.

Ginsberg, Benjamin. *The Captive Public: How Mass Opinion Promotes State Power*. New York: Basic Books, 1986. A forceful argument that increased instantaneous access to mass public opinion has enabled governments to manage it for their own purposes.

Key, V. O., Jr. *Public Opinion and American Democracy*. New York: Knopf, 1961. A systematic examination by a leading political scientist of the properties of public opinion and its role in American government and politics.

Lane, Robert E. *Political Ideology*. New York: Free Press, 1962. A classic examination of how people think about political life, based on lengthy interviews with fifteen citizens in one American city, New Haven, Connecticut.

Lippmann, Walter. *Public Opinion*. New York: Macmillan, 1960; first published, 1922. A classic account of public opinion—how it is formed and how it helps shape politics.

Page, Benjamin, and Robert Shapiro. *The Rational Public: Fifty Years of Trends in Americans' Policy Preferences*. Chicago: University of Chicago Press, 1992. An extensive review of survey findings, demonstrating stability and structure in the public's stands on policy questions.

The Public Perspective. A bimonthly publication of the Roper Center for Public Opinion Research charts trends in public opinion on various issues and examines problems in public opinion research.

OPTIONAL COMPUTER EXERCISES

for *The Ladd Election ANALYZER*

THE PROPER ROLE OF GOVERNMENT

How far did voters in 1992 feel that government should go in providing services and levying taxes? Should the government provide more services at a higher cost or fewer services at a lower cost? Select "Government taxes/services" from the "Policy views" menu to find out. How did those identifying themselves as Democrats differ from those identifying themselves as Republicans? How did the young differ from the old and those with higher incomes from those with lower incomes? How did different ethnic/racial groups (blacks, whites, Hispanics) vary on this issue?

Chapter *11*

INTEREST GROUPS

J ames Madison's assessment of interest groups—which he called "factions"—in *Federalist* No. 10 is an American classic. (See the Appendix, pp. A21–A25 for *Federalist* No. 10.) Any society will inevitably have many contending interests, he argued, because "the latent causes of faction are . . . sown in the nature of man. . . . " People will hold different opinions and interests on such matters as power, religion, and, especially, economics. If by chance we couldn't think of a good reason to divide up into contending interests we would invent one. Madison observed: "So strong is this propensity of mankind to fall into mutual animosities that where no substantial occasion presents itself the most frivolous and fanciful distinctions have been sufficient to kindle their unfriendly passions and excite their most violent conflicts."

In Madison's view, interest groups are in many regards undesirable. They are invariably narrow and self-serving. Indeed, he defined a faction as "a number of citizens . . . who are united and actuated by some common impulse or passion, or of interest, *adverse to the rights of other citizens, or to the permanent and aggregate interests of the community*" (emphasis added).

This should not mean that Madison thought the new American nation should strive to throttle interest groups. It could never eliminate the diversity of interests. And if it ever sought to prevent the organized expression of those interests, it would lose the most precious thing it was striving to obtain—freedom. "Liberty," he insisted "is to faction what air is to fire, an aliment without which it instantly expires. But it could not be a less folly to abolish liberty, which is essential to political life, because it nourishes faction than it would be to wish the annihilation of air, which is essential to animal life, because it imparts to fire its destructive agency."

The only way to proceed, then, is try to organize society and especially government so as to force groups into situations where they must compete and none can get too strong. We explored this approach in general terms in chapters 3 and 4. Arguments have gone on throughout U.S. history as to whether certain groups—large business corporations, for example—have not in fact gotten too strong. Various proposals have been made to regulate interest-group behavior. In recent years, for example, a lively argument has proceeded on whether some groups have undue electoral influence because they contribute so much money to political campaigns; we will discuss debate over political action committees (PACs) later in this chapter. In chapter 12 we review legislation that has been enacted to regulate private interest money in campaigns and proposals to curb these contributions further. Whatever one thinks about the need for more regulation of groups, though, the core of Madison's arguments is impressive. Efforts by organized interests to advance their objectives are part and parcel of a free society.

A NATION OF JOINERS

After visiting the United States in the 1830s, Alexis de Tocqueville wrote that "in no country in the world has the principle of association

been more successfully used or applied to a greater multitude of objects than in America." Americans were a nation of joiners. Tocqueville explained this propensity, interestingly, in terms of individualism: "The citizen of the United States is taught from infancy to rely upon his own exertions in order to resist the evils and the difficulties of life; he looks upon the social authority with an eye of mistrust and anxiety, and he claims its assistance only when he is unable to do without it. . . ."

Joining together with other like-minded people to attack common problems expresses a sense of individual responsibility and self-confidence:

> If a stoppage occurs in a thoroughfare and the circulation of vehicles is hindered, the neighbors immediately form themselves into a deliberative body; and this extemporaneous assembly gives rise to an executive power which remedies the inconvenience before anybody has thought of recurring to a pre-existing authority superior to that of the persons immediately concerned. . . . In the United States associations are established to promote the public safety, commerce, industry, morality, and religion. There is no end which the human will despairs of attaining through the combined power of individuals united into a society.[1]

A NATION OF INTEREST GROUPS

Tocqueville's observation still applies. This general proclivity for forming private associations to meet public needs extends to the pursuit of political interests. The variety of interest groups in the United States ranges from strictly local associations, such as small-town chambers of commerce (which try among other things to influence town councils on off-street parking or zoning regulations) to massive national asso-

[1]Tocqueville, *Democracy in America*, vol. 1, p. 198.

The classic American interest-group predicament.

ciations like the American Federation of Labor and Congress of Industrial Organizations (AFL-CIO), the principal U.S. labor union federation, and the National Association of Manufacturers (NAM), a huge industry association comprising over 12,500 companies. Every conceivable issue before the American polity at the national, state, and local levels has a distinct set of interest groups and associations trying to shape policy on it.

How many interest groups are there in the United States? No one can say precisely. While some groups are exclusively political and required by law to register as lobbyists (see below) and hence can be counted, many other groups intervene only sporadically in political affairs and never register. They often don't think of themselves as interest groups, even though they sometimes work actively for political goals. For example, the roughly 350,000 individuals churches and parishes in the United States, with a total membership of about 145,000,000, exist primarily for religious and social purposes. But on occasion, these churches and their national denominational organizations try to influence public policy, often on social questions such as abortion, school prayer, and the death penalty. Churches are also at times outspoken on questions of foreign policy and national defense, such as the development of nuclear weapons.

Virtually every large business corporation in the United States and many small businesses have strong legislative interests. General Motors and Boeing Aircraft are affected by governmental actions in many ways: Each gets government contracts, is subjected to a welter of federal and state regulations, pays taxes, has a big stake in international trade policy. Are most businesses interest groups? Sometimes, and to some extent. Business firms exist for many purposes and objectives other than those political, but at times they function as interest groups as they try to influence what government does.

THE INTEREST-GROUP ARENA

As the federal government has come to play an ever-larger role over the last fifty years, more and more groups have come to be actively concerned with influencing federal action. Lobbying has burgeoned.[2] The most comprehensive accounting of Washington lobbyists is the volume *Washington Representatives*, a privately published listing of "persons working to influence government policies and actions to advance their own interests." In 1977, 4,000 names were listed; just fourteen years later, in 1991, *Washington Representatives* listed about 14,400 who fitted its definition of national lobbyists.

INTEREST-GROUP ETHICS: A CASE STUDY

Inevitably, people with good connections to Congress and the executive branch—and this includes, in particular, former members of those branches—have come to be in high demand as interest-group representatives. Ethical issues abound. Sometimes the law is broken. The case of Michael K. Deaver is instructive.

After he left his post as White House deputy chief of staff in 1985, Deaver set up a public relations firm, Michael K. Deaver and Associates. There is no doubt that the firm's primary assets were the many contacts and ties Deaver himself had established over his twenty years as an aide to Ronald Reagan—and especially during his four-plus years as a White House official. Many of the interests Deaver began to represent were foreign governments concerned

with and affected by various U.S. actions. His clients (and their annual fees) included the embassy of the government of Canada ($100,000), the government of Singapore ($250,000), the Ministry of Commerce and Industrial Development of the government of Mexico ($250,000), the government of Korea and the International Cultural Society of Korea ($475,000), and the Royal Embassy of Saudi Arabia ($500,000). In reports that he filed with the Justice Department (as required by the Foreign Agents Act), Deaver reported contacts with U.S. cabinet officers and other administration officials on behalf of his foreign government clients—including meetings with the then Treasury Secretary James Baker III, Secretary of State George Shultz, and Commerce Secretary Malcolm Baldrige.

The principal charge that was brought against Michael Deaver was that he violated conflict-of-interest laws by representing Canada on acid rain shortly after helping to determine administration policy on the issue as a White House official. Deputy Counsel of the General Accounting Office James Hinchman stated in May 1986 that there was "enough basis" for believing that the law governing permissible

HY ROSEN
Courtesy Albany Times-Union

" LEAVE IT TO DEAVER "

---

[2]The term *lobby* came into use in seventeenth-century England, when a large anteroom near the House of Commons was referred to as the "lobby." Those who approached members of Parliament, trying to persuade them to vote a certain way, were lobbying.

lobbying activity following federal service had been violated to warrant referring the case to the Justice Department. The end results were the appointment of an independent counsel to determine whether Deaver had broken the Ethics in Government Act or any other federal statute and Deaver's subsequent indictment and conviction on perjury charges.

A long line of former presidential assistants have gone on to successful careers as Washington lobbyists, in part trading off old ties to public officials. Most have not run afoul of the law. Still, ethical problems are always present in situations where former high officials lobby past colleagues. And the problem hardly stops with White House aides. Retired members of Congress often stay on in Washington as lobbyists. Retired generals become representatives for defense contractors. A similar situation occurs in state and city government, where former officials take jobs in the private sector that involve trying to shape the programs of the agencies they once served.

TYPES OF INTEREST GROUPS

The Federal Regulation of Lobbying Act, passed in 1946, requires that groups attempting to influence legislation before Congress register and report the amount they expend in lobbying efforts. This legislation is full of loopholes and it contains almost no enforcement provisions. Any organization that really prefers not to register finds it easy to avoid doing so. As a result, the number of formally registered groups is certainly smaller at any given time than the number of organizations actively engaged in lobbying. But the law states an obligation that many groups heed. More than 8,100 groups were registered in the spring of 1992, according to the Senate Public Records Office.

The roster of those registered gives a sense of the extent and diversity of interest groups nationally. Among them are major business associations, such as the Business Roundtable and National Association of Manufacturers; individual corporations, from American Express to Phillips Petroleum to the Kellogg Company; trade and professional associations, including the American Petroleum Institute, the American Meat Institute, the Electronic Industries Association, the National Education Association, and the American Medical Association; trade unions such as the American Federation of State, County, and Municipal Employees AFL-CIO, and the Amalgamated Clothing and Textile Workers' Union AFL-CIO; and a wide variety of organizations known as citizens' groups, among them the National Rifle Association, the National Clean Air Coalition, the Sierra Club, and the Religious Coalition for Abortion Rights.

These registered interest groups are only the tip of the iceberg. There are, for example, some 6,200 national trade and professional associations alone, and virtually every one of them has policy interests. The asbestos industry has five trade associations. Nine associations represent brewers. There are four trade associations for china tableware and four for chocolate. The trucking industry has approximately sixty trade associations. About fifteen associations promote the interests of businesses that produce and sell wine. More than 4,000 individual business corporations retain representatives in Washington, D.C. By the beginning of the 1980s, Washington had also become the leading headquarters city, with about 30 percent of all national nonprofit associations headquartered there.[3]

---

[3] Robert H. Salisbury, with John P. Heinz, Edward O. Laumann, and Robert L. Nelson, "Soaking and Poking Among the Movers and Shakers: Quantitative Ethnography Along the K Street Corridor," paper presented at the annual meeting of the American Political Science Association, Washington, D.C., August 30–September 2, 1984. See also *National Trade and Professional Associations of the United States*, 23rd ed. (Washington, D.C.: Columbia Books, 1988).

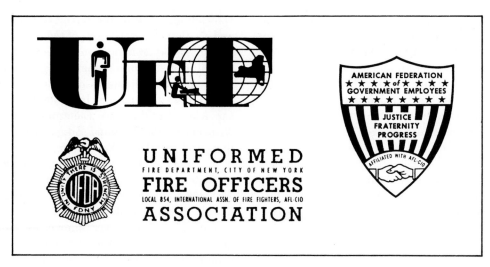

Government employees: a growing economic interest group.

All in all, the interest-group world in the United States is massive. Tens of thousands of individuals and groups expend hundreds of millions of dollars each year in efforts to shape public policy. Little wonder that Thomas P. O'Neill, House of Representatives speaker from 1977 through 1986, remarked with exasperation that "everybody in America has a lobby."

ECONOMIC INTERESTS

The sheer volume of interest groups does not mean that all the different kinds of interests in the country are more or less equally engaged in interest-group activity. Some interests are disproportionately represented. Madison saw the pattern two centuries ago. He wrote in *Federalist* No. 10 that, while every type of political interest gets mobilized in a democracy,

> the most common and durable source of factions has been the various and unequal distribution of property. Those who hold and those who are without property have ever formed distinct interests in society. Those who are creditors, and those who are debtors, fall under a like

discrimination. A landed interest, a manufacturing interest, a mercantile interest, a monied interest, with many lesser interests, grow up of necessity in civilized nations, and divide them into different classes, actuated by different sentiments and views.

The prime source of organized interests, then, is economic status. Interest groups spring up to represent claims of different sectors in the economy (Madison listed farming, manufacturing, trade, and banking as the most important) and the interests of economic "haves" and "have nots." The consuming conflict of America in the 1780s was not between rich and poor. It was among farm interests in different parts of the country, and between farm interests and the mercantile and monied interests concentrated along the northeastern seaboard.

Is this interpretation of interest-group organization and conflict valid today? The answer must be a qualified yes. The lion's share of interest-group activity has involved economic interests, with the horizontal or sector split far more prominent than the vertical or haves-versus-have-nots split. We see this today when

TABLE 11.1 LOBBY REGISTRATIONS FILED WITH U.S. HOUSE OF REPRESENTATIVES BY TYPE OF GROUP, JANUARY 1, 1991–JANUARY 1, 1992 (IN PERCENT)

Business corporations	44%
Trade associations	24
Labor unions	1
State and local governments	7
Citizens' groups (misc.)	14
Foreign governments	1
Miscellaneous	9
Total number	2,732

Source: Data compiled from *Congressional Quarterly*, weekly reports of March 30, May 25, June 29, August 24, 31, December 14,1991; January 11, 25, April 18, May 9, 1992.

we look at interest-group activity in Washington. In 1991 over 2,700 separate interest groups were involved in new registrations with the clerk of the U.S. House of Representatives and the secretary of the Senate, under the terms of the Federal Regulation of Lobbying Act. Their overwhelmingly economic bias is evident. As Table 11.1 indicates, 44 percent of all new registrants were business corporations and another 24 percent trade associations. About 70 percent of all groups registering or reregistering as lobbyists in 1991 had predominantly economic objectives. They cover the widest range of economic pursuits. The many different sectors of economic life, represented by the variety of business corporations and trade associations, distinguish this interest-group world.

GOVERNMENT LOBBYING GOVERNMENT

These economic interests in what government does extend beyond business and labor to government itself. We described in chapter 5 the expansion during the 1960s and 1970s in federal programs providing aid for states and municipalities. Responding to these new programs and the billions of dollars distributed

through them each year, state and local governments dramatically extended their Washington lobbying. In this period, for instance, the state of Louisiana, the Kansas Corporation Commission, the city of New Orleans, Los Angeles county, and the state of Maryland all registered as congressional lobbyists. Thirty states and more than 100 cities and counties have established offices or hired agents in Washington. The National Governors' Association has been especially active. Its marble building, called the Hall of the States, is just a stone's throw from the U.S. Capitol. Near the Hall of the States is the new headquarters of the National Association of Counties (NACO). A mile away, the National League of Cities has a new office complex, housing lobbyists for many individual municipalities. The headquarters of the U.S. Conference of Mayors is also nearby. These state and local government lobbies are now a major part of Washington interest representation.

Government lobbying government is not confined to the states and municipalities; the federal government lobbies itself. Various agencies that have a great stake in congressional appropriations and other legislative provisions actively lobby Congress. Every cabinet department has a top congressional liaison person of assistant-secretary rank and several subordinates to assist in these efforts.

PUBLIC-INTEREST GROUPS

One of the most widely discussed developments in interest-group activity in recent years is the prominent role of public-interest groups. A **public-interest group** is "one that seeks a collective good, the achievement of which will not selectively or materially benefit the membership or activists of the organization."[4] The

[4] Jeffrey M. Berry, *Lobbying for the People* (Princeton, N.J.: Princeton University Press, 1977), p. 7.

Sometimes, public-interest groups run head on into a congressman's interest-group preference. Compare the American Heart Association's poster (below) with this cartoon aligning Senator Jesse Helms (R-North Carolina) with the tobacco industry in his state.

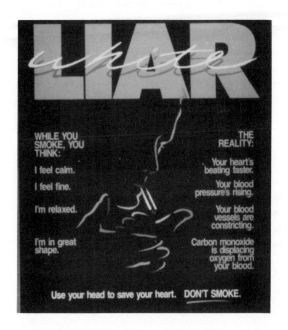

roster of public-interest groups includes environmentalists, such as Friends of the Earth, the National Wildlife Federation, and the Sierra Club. Others seek to reform the organization and conduct of American political life, the most prominent being Common Cause. Consumers Union tries to mobilize the diffuse interests of purchasers rather than producers. Foreign-policy goals such as arms control have been the focus of the Arms Control Association and the World Federalists.

Do these groups really speak for the public interest? While the concept of public interest is not simple or unambiguous, it calls attention to the general claims and needs of the whole population as opposed to those of special and private interests. Groups are rarely organized around the broadest and most unselfish aspirations of a society. Rather they grow to advance narrower objectives. Indeed, it is typically the special nature of their claims that spurs their organization. Many public-interest groups, including those that take stands on environmental questions, consumer affairs, and governmental reform, argue that there are general public interests in their respective areas that are sometimes denied by the actions of special interests like private business corporations. Yet when public-interest groups make their own proposals, they very often articulate another set of special interests and perspectives. Nonetheless, they encourage a competition of ideas and claims, and the values they pursue do not lead to the narrow economic benefit of their members.

The growth of public-interest groups is a product of larger changes in the composition of American society. As noted in chapter 2, there has been a recent and huge increase in the number of college-educated men and women employed in professional occupations. With this expansion has come the vast growth of a relatively new stratum of political actors: people who are well-educated, highly skilled, and attentive to issues rather than political patronage.[5] One of the ways the expanding stratum of middle-class activists has expressed itself is through public-interest groups. There are now many thousands of public-interest organizations operating at the local, state, and national level in the United States.[6] And this development has not been confined to the United States. Groups protesting the use of nuclear power for the generation of electricity have been active throughout Western Europe and Japan. The "green movement," expressing environmental concerns, is similarly influential

in other industrialized nations. The largest environmental group in France, for example, Les Amis de la Terre (Friends of the Earth) advances environmental programs and policies similar to those of Friends of the Earth and the Sierra Club in the United States.

EXPANDING SECTOR
COVERAGE BY INTEREST
GROUPS

In numerical terms economic interest groups still predominate. But extensive group organization now exists in many sectors outside the traditional ones of business and labor. For example, the interests of women are represented by scores of organizations nationally and by thousands of group affiliates at the state and local levels. Education is a major activity in the United States and almost every conceivable dimension of it has formal representation.

Some groups, it should be noted, are not as heavily represented by organized interest groups; the poor and minorities are the most prominent of these. For example, while the National Association for the Advancement of Colored People (NAACP) and the National Urban League are well-established and have long been active in advancing the goals of black Americans, interest-group involvement in this area is less substantial than in other sectors such as environmental and educational concerns, to say nothing of business.

Women's Groups. This expression of interests is not limited to widely publicized organizations associated with the women's movement, such as the National Organization for Women (NOW). Women who work for the national government are represented by Federally Employed Women (FEW). The widows of army, navy, air force, and marine veterans have interests in survivor benefit programs, represented by the National Association of Mil-

[5] For an early account of the expansion of one part of this new group of political activists, see James Q. Wilson, *The Amateur Democrat* (Chicago: University of Chicago Press, 1962).

[6] See Jeffrey M. Berry, *The Interest Group Society* (Boston: Little, Brown, 1984).

TABLE 11.2 A SAMPLING OF WOMEN'S INTEREST GROUPS

Interest Group	Who Belongs
American Association of University Women	Women graduates of regionally accredited colleges, universities, and recognized foreign institutions.
Federally Employed Women (FEW)	Women and men who work for the federal government.
Federation of Organizations for Professional Women	Women's caucuses and committees in professional associations and organizations, and people interested in equal educational and employment opportunities for women.
General Federation of Women's Clubs	Volunteer women, interested in conservation, education, home life, public affairs, and the arts.
League of Women Voters of the United States	Women and men interested in nonpartisan political action and study.
National Association of Military Widows	Military widows on matters related to survivor benefit programs.
National Association of Women Business Owners	Women who own their own businesses.
National Federation of Republican Women	Volunteers for support of Republican candidates for national, state, and local offices.
National Organization for Women (NOW)	Individuals interested in advancing women's rights.
National Women's Political Caucus	Persons interested in greater involvement of women in politics.
Women's Equity Action League	Individuals working for economic advances and equality for women.

itary Widows. For women in education there are such groups as the National Council of Administrative Women in Education and the American Association of University Women. To advance athletic programs, there is the National Association for Girls and Women in Sports. Few areas where women's interests are found in the contemporary United States now lack formal organization (see Table 11.2).

Educational Groups. School teachers work through the American Federation of Teachers, AFL-CIO, and the National Education Association. Private schools are represented by such groups as the Lutheran Educational Confer-

ence of North America, the National Association of Independent Schools, the National Catholic Education Association, and the Christian College Coalition. College and university interests get expressed through varied groups, among them the Association of American Colleges, the Association of American Universities, the American Council on Education, the American Association of University Professors, the Council of Graduate Schools in the United States, the Council for the Advancement of Small Colleges, the Women's College Coalition, and the National Association for Equal Opportunity in Higher Education (see Table 11.3).

TABLE 11.3   A SAMPLING OF EDUCATIONAL INTEREST GROUPS

Interest Group	Who Belongs
American Association of School Administrators	Chief school executives and other administrators at district or higher level, and teachers of school administration.
American Association of University Professors	College and university faculty and graduate students.
American Council on Education	Colleges, universities, and education associations.
American Federation of Teachers, AFL-CIO	Preschool through postsecondary level teachers
Association of American Universities	Public and private universities with emphasis on graduate and professional education and research.
Association of Catholic Colleges and Universities	Colleges, universities, and individuals interested in Catholic education.
Council for American Private Education (CAPE)	National organizations serving private elementary and secondary schools.
Council for Exceptional Children	Teachers, researchers, administrators. students, social workers, psychologists, and physicians who work with handicapped or gifted children.
Council for Graduate Schools in the United States	Degree-granting graduate schools and graduate programs at private and public colleges and universities.
National Association for Equal Opportunity in Higher Education	Predominantly black colleges and universities.
National Coalition of Public Education and Religious Liberty	Coalition of groups that oppose federal aid to nonpublic schools.
National Education Association	Teachers, from elementary through postsecondary level, and other educational professionals.
United States Student Association	College and university student government associations.

INTEREST-GROUP RESOURCES

The thousands of interest groups in the American political scene vary greatly in the impact they are able to have on public policy. Some have far greater resources than others. While it is not possible to specify exactly how much influence a group will have, given its particular mix of resources, it is possible to identify the principal types of resources that groups call upon as they try to influence policy.

SIZE OF MEMBERSHIP

In a democratic political system, the size of an interest group's following is and should be an important factor. Numbers matter. About 14 million men and women belong to the labor unions that make up the AFL-CIO, which unquestionably adds weight to the representation AFL-CIO leaders make on behalf of various programs. Through the staff and organization of their unions, labor officials have formal ties and channels of communication to many people. But a number of actors restrict the weight of numbers. For one thing, every large group is certain to have a membership with very heterogeneous interests. AFL-CIO lobbyists claim to speak for millions of trade unionists, but in fact few pieces of legislation come before Congress where this is truly persuasive. Politicians know that unionists are divided on most political matters—much like any comparably large body of Americans. One almost never encounters the situation on a controversial question where 90 percent of the union membership is on one side and just 10 percent on the other. In the 1988 presidential election, for example, when the AFL-CIO and most member unions endorsed Democrat Michael Dukakis and made a concerted effort on his behalf in the general election battle against George Bush, their efforts clearly produced results. Dukakis did much better, for instance, among workers who belonged to unions than he did among nonunionized workers in the same general economic position; part of the leadership message got across to the members. Still, Dukakis won the support of just 58 percent of trade unionists and their families, according to the CBS News / *New York Times* election-day survey (Table 11.4).

It is not surprising that splits develop between union leadership and the rank-and-file membership on various policy questions. Any large group attracts its members for limited objectives—in the case of the labor unions, to improve wages and working conditions. Sustained by this base, labor leaders then proceed to take stands on a broad range of important policy questions, such as race relations, taxing and spending, and foreign affairs. These positions are by-products of an institutional arrangement organized for another purpose. There is no reason to expect leaders to represent the rank and file's view directly outside of the objectives for which the group membership was developed. This does not mean that the 14-million-member AFL-CIO is a feeble giant. More than any other organization it is listened to when it speaks for American labor. Its membership supports an organizational structure that is often skillfully committed in election contests and policy debates. But the impact of these numbers is diluted by the great heterogeneity of interests they entail.

FINANCIAL RESOURCES

Numbers are only one element determining a group's influence. Money is another critical political resource. Some groups have a lot of it, others very little. Lobbying by business corporations and trade associations—groups that are relatively weak in number of members—is often very well financed. Groups use money in a variety of ways to advance their interests,

TABLE 11.4   PRESIDENTIAL VOTE BY UNION MEMBERSHIP, 1980, 1984, AND 1988 (in percent)

	1980			*1984*		*1988*	
	Carter	Reagan	Anderson	Mondale	Reagan	Dukakis	Bush
Members of labor households	47	44	7	54	46	58	42
Members of households where no one belongs to a union	35	55	8	37	63	42	58

Source: Election-day surveys by CBS News and the *New York Times*, November 4, 1980, November 6, 1984, and November 8, 1988.

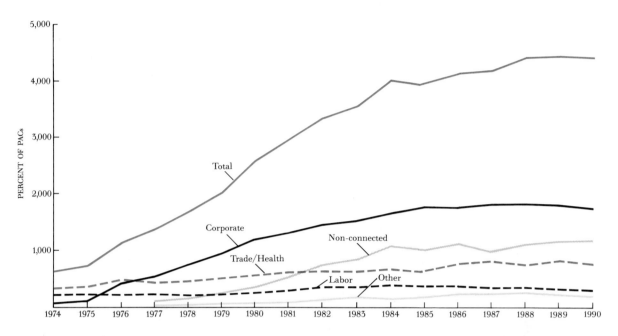

FIGURE 11.1 GROWTH OF POLITICAL ACTION COMMITTEES

Source: Federal Elections Commission Annual Report of January, 1982; FEC releases of January 20, 1986, January 18, 1988, and July 25, 1990.

most of which are straightforward and legal. Well-financed associations of business or professional people, like the National Association of Manufacturers and the American Medical Association, employ large and politically astute staffs. They mount effective public-relations campaigns, utilizing the mass media to present their positions. In general, they use their financial resources to get their messages before legislators, other political decision makers, and the public, to an extent quite beyond the reach of groups that lack such substantial funding.

Interests that can draw on large financial resources can also increase their access to officials, something that is troubling even when it is completely legal. One common means of increasing or protecting access is by making campaign contributions to candidates. Electioneering is very expensive, and it is becoming steadily more so, especially as the use of television expands. Candidates turn to well-financed groups for campaign contributions, and the groups often oblige. These groups do not think

they are buying votes and typically they are not, but they do think their contributions entitle them to get in the door and make their case the next time an issue of importance to them comes along. Or they are afraid that if they refuse an influential incumbent's request for a contribution, he or she may be unreceptive to their future appeals.

Federal campaign-finance legislation enacted in the 1970s encouraged expansion in the number of political action committees (PACs), discussed in greater detail in chapter 12. PACs are the political campaign arms of business, labor, professional, and other interest groups, legally entitled to raise funds on a voluntary basis and to make contributions to favored candidates and parties. The number of these special-interest-group organizations grew from just 600 in 1974 to nearly 4,200 in 1990, according to a report issued by the Federal Elections Commission. PACs are now a major vehicle for bringing private money into electoral campaigns (Figure 11.1).

As of March 31, 1992, House of Representatives incumbents had received roughly $61 million from PACs in the 1991–92 election cycle, compared to just $5 million for House challengers. This disproportion is one factor accounting for the extraordinary success incumbents have had—even in the 1990 campaign, when voters were plainly disgruntled—in getting reelected. That so much money flows from interest groups to members of Congress—members whom the groups are seeking to influence on various pieces of legislation—has to raise serious ethical concerns. Even if not one vote is actually "bought," should access be for sale?

The Congress has tried again and again in recent years to enact new campaign finance legislation—but each time it has failed. Partisan differences are the main reason for these failures. Many Republicans favor banning PACs, which now give disproportionately to Democratic candidates. But Republicans oppose the Democrats' call for federal funding of congressional campaigns. The bill that passed both houses in 1992 with Democratic support, and that was then vetoed by President Bush, provided $200,000 in federal matching funds for each candidate for the House of Representatives who accepted overall spending limits, and it offered taxpayer-financed vouchers for Senate candidates to use in buying advertising time on television.

Lamenting the failure to reform campaign finance, the *New York Times* argued in a January 1991 editorial that senators and representatives are now far too beholden to "the special interests that flood money into their campaigns. . . . The stench emanating from that flow of favor-seeking money cannot be ignored." What troubles observers, such as the *Times*'s editors, is not that groups have political interests that they seek to advance. Rather, it is that in an age of big government so many well-heeled interests have established such intimate ties with those who make the laws. Interest-group funding of legislative campaigns contributes to these too-cozy ties.

ORGANIZATION

Interest groups are better organized today than ever before, and thus the disadvantages of ineffectively organized groups are greater than ever before.

Organization is an even more critical resource because American government is so fragmented and awash with contending claims and interests. Getting one's case across in this noisy, cluttered, diverse, and pluralistic setting requires planning and systematic effort. The old stereotype of the effective lobbyist as one who knows the right people and meets with them periodically to cut deals is increasingly out of touch with a political environment that puts a premium on careful organization in group dealings with a big and complex government.

INTENSITY OF INTEREST

When a legislator casts a vote that a group of his or her constituents favors, he or she often hears nothing about it from them. But when the legislator goes against some deeply felt interest, even if it is one held by only a distinct minority, the complaints are loud and persisting. Constantly bombarded, even the most principled legislators take pains to limit criticism whenever they can without doing violence to their basic policy commitments. If an interest group has the capacity to hurt them politically, legislators have a vested interest in placating it, especially if they can do so relatively easily. This helps explain why groups with intensely held interests often get their way on questions where a majority of the public and a majority of the legislators themselves, in their own private judgments, hold to the other side. For example, public opinion surveys have shown

JERRY ROBINSON
© Cartoonists & Writers Syndicate

that large majorities of the American public favor stronger gun-control legislation. Yet congressional efforts to get stronger laws, opposed by groups like the National Rifle Association (NRA), have failed. This is not because the legislators doubt the polls or have been personally convinced by NRA lobbyists of the inherent wisdom of the latter's views; nor is it a result of bribery or other illicit means of persuasion. In a system where political party organization is weak and individual legislators operate largely on their own, there are strong incentives to placate interest groups. The NRA's intensity of concern, compared to the less focused involvement of most of the public, gives it a capacity to cause trouble. Members of Congress are sorely tempted to appease the group unless they are strongly committed to gun control.

Interest groups sometimes "target" senators and representatives whose stands on issues they find especially unsatisfactory; that is, they commit resources to defeating them in the next election. These efforts may at times contribute to their desired end, but at least as often, it seems, they backfire. Many voters resent it when an interest group wages electoral warfare on their members of Congress. Groups with intensively held interests gain their major successes in a different way, by convincing wavering legislators who do not have strong feelings on an issue that it just is not worth antagonizing the group on the matter.

INTEREST-GROUP TACTICS AND STRATEGIES: AN ENVIRONMENTAL CASE STUDY

On every major question of American public policy, and on many relatively minor ones, interest groups work to persuade governmental officials to take actions consistent with what the groups think should be done. This may mean passing a law, imposing or removing a regulation, funding a program, changing the tax code, committing the country to some new objective, or countless other actions within the

Interest in the quality of the environment goes way back. Here, President Theodore Roosevelt on Glacier Point above the Yosemite Valley, California, with John Muir (right) who had founded the Sierra Club in 1892.

scope of modern government. Interest-group tactics and strategies are as diverse as the objectives for which groups intervene in public life.

Some of the hottest and most interesting interest-group battles of recent years have occurred on environmental issues. In the latter part of the 1960s American public opinion began to swing rather sharply in favor of greater national efforts at making the country's environment safer and cleaner than it had been. Groups such as the Sierra Club, the National Audubon Society, the National Wildlife Federation, and the Environmental Defense Fund became active proponents of new legislation. On the other side, business corporations and related associations often took issue with the

environmentalists' proposals—claiming, for example, that the legislation would impose economic hardships on them and would harm the U.S. economy generally. One major area of environmental action, efforts to reduce air pollution, has prompted a continuing, almost classic interest-group campaign. The contending groups use many of the tactics that have become staples in contemporary lobbying. Looming in the background have been large questions of policy direction and compelling public interests.

EARLY LEGISLATION

In 1970, Congress passed the Clean Air Act, which required the Environmental Protection Agency (EPA) to determine what concentrations could be safely permitted for seven major air pollutants and then to see that these levels were not exceeded. The act was intended to gain major reductions in air pollution in order to promote the health of the general public.

These general objectives seem straightforward, but in fact the act is highly complex, and the detailed regulations issued by the EPA pursuant to its responsibilities under the law are even more complicated. Citizens who want to understand fully the controversies that have ensued around this statute must master such terms and acronyms as NAAQS (National Ambient Air Quality Standards), PSD (Prevention of Significant Deterioration) provisions, RACT (Reasonably Available Controlled Technology), BACT (Best Available Controlled Technology), LAER (Lowest Achievable Emission Rate), and SIP (State Implementation Plans), among others.

THE BATTLE OVER AMENDING THE ACT

The debate over the act has not involved its general goals but rather has centered around various standards enforced to achieve the goals, such as standards for the acceptable level of auto emissions. It has also considered various tradeoffs: How do you ensure environmental cleanliness without excessively obtrusive regulation? How do you protect the environment without setting back other important policy goals such as economic growth, creation of new jobs, and greater use of coal and other domestic energy resources? Many groups, including virtually all affected industries—auto, chemical, and oil companies, some trade unions, state agencies involved in implementation of the EPA standards, and others—had concluded by 1981 that the act unreasonably hampered some legitimate economic objectives and produced regulatory confusion. But many other groups—including virtually all environmentalist associations, some trade unions, government-reform groups like the League of Women Voters, and others—feared that business-led efforts to amend the act would go too far and set back the cause of a clean and healthful environment. The all-out battle in 1981–82 between industrial and environmental groups over renewal and amendment of the Clean Air Act is a classic interest-group campaign.

Business groups said they wanted to reform the act in certain limited ways, with a view toward boosting the economy and employment. They favored such specific changes as modification of the emissions standards and deadlines affecting the auto industry, and an end to the "off-set" rule affecting the building of new plants. Under the "off-set" rule, any company wanting to build in an area where the air did not meet pollution standards not only had to install the best possible pollution control equipment, but also had to buy "emission offsets" from companies already operating in the area. That is, the incoming business had to get other companies to reduce their emissions by at least as much as the new plant would add to the overall volume of pollutants being released in the area.

Environmental groups wanted to avoid any weakening of the clean air legislation. They wanted to retain the "off-set" policy. They wanted to keep strict deadlines for compliance. They feared that, in the words of Democratic Congressman Henry A. Waxman of California, chairman of the House subcommittees charged with environmental legislation, the industry-backed amendments were, cumulatively, "a blueprint for the destruction of our clean air laws."[7]

TACTICS: BUILDING COALITIONS

A key feature of group tactics in the clean air fight was the formation of formal coalitions. Many corporations, trade associations, labor unions, and environmental groups lobbied actively on an individual basis. But, in addition, they worked together in organized alliances for and against amending the act. On one side, various business and trade associations—including the Chamber of Commerce of the United States, the American Petroleum Institute, the National Coal Association, the Iron and Steel Institute, the Chemical Manufacturers' Association, the National Association of Manufacturers, the Business Roundtable, the Paper Institute, and the Edison Electric Institute—channeled much of their activity through the Clean Air Working Group (CAWG). Another influential coalition was the National Environmental Development Association / Clean Air Act Project (NEDA / CAAP). Many of the major businesses that banded together in this alliance had obvious and direct stakes in applications of the legislation—oil companies like Exxon, chemical companies like du Pont, and automobile manufacturers like General Motors. But special effort was made to enlist other

---

[7] Remarks by Representative Henry A. Waxman, as quoted in the *New York Times*, June 20, 1981, p. 10.

organizations that didn't have such immediate interests. International Business Machine (IBM) was brought into NEDA / CAAP, a nice addition because it was so little affected by the act: Computers are a "clean" industry. The Building and Construction Trade Unions, AFL-CIO, were also included, attesting to labor-business agreement on the need for changes in the legislation.

On the other side, many environmental groups joined together in the National Clean Air Coalition (NCAC). Represented here was the core of the environmental movement—Friends of the Earth, the Sierra Club, the National Wildlife Federation, the Wilderness Society, and others. NCAC was also at pains to diversify its coalition, and it brought in such "disinterested" groups as the League of Women Voters and a number of trade unions, including the United Steel Workers of America and the Amalgamated Clothing and Textile Workers' Union (see Table 11.5). By 1990, 35 groups belonged to the NCAC.

The establishment of coalitions of interest groups on behalf of broad policy positions is by no means unique to the battle over amending the Clean Air Act. It has become a generally important part of lobbying. Just as trade associations appeared to pool the resources of individual companies, so group coalitions have developed to integrate lobbying on behalf of broad policy goals. One prominent coalition or "working group" that has operated in Washington in recent years is the Trucking Alliance. It brought together in favor of deregulation of the trucking industry such normally contending groups as Common Cause and Ralph Nader's Congress Watch on the one hand, and the National Association of Manufacturers and the American Conservative Union on the other. Another coalition is the Longshore Action Committee, which united seventy-four different groups, from the National Association of Manufacturers to the American Farm Bureau Federation, on behalf of legislation curtailing

a federal program that compensates longshoremen, and workers in such related industries as shipbuilding and harbor construction, for on-the-job injuries. The Consumer Issues Working Group lobbied for eight years (successfully) against establishment of a federal Consumer Protection Agency. The Alaska Coalition, an alliance of environmental groups, secured passage of legislation to preserve from development large segments of the state of Alaska.

Various factors have contributed to the increasing recourse to carefully organized coalitions, in place of the more independent and loosely coordinated lobbying in the past. For example, power in Congress, once concentrated in the leadership and committee chairmen, was dispersed much more widely among the membership by the reforms of the late 1960s and 1970s. At the same time, congressional staff grew tremendously. Lobbyists found that they had to influence many more people to accomplish their goals. This suggested that they pool resources.[8] The use of coalitions, as in lobbying over Clean Air Act revisions, was also a step by interest groups to avoid speaking with a babble of conflicting voices. The coalition approach required groups to get their houses in order before going to Congress. Extensive interaction and compromise are necessary to hammer out reasonably united coalition positions. In the process, a whole new layer gets added to lobbying. Interest groups must spend much more time lobbying each other to build plausible coalitions and formulate common legislative approaches.

TACTICS: FINDING ALLIES WHERE YOU CAN

We tend to think of business and labor as opposing interest groups, and they often are.

[8]Bill Keller, "Coalitions and Associations Transformed Strategy, Methods of Lobbying in Washington," *Congressional Quarterly*, January 23, 1982, p. 119.

TABLE 11.5 CONTENDING GROUPS IN THE BATTLE OVER THE CLEAN AIR ACT

Don't Amend the Act (The National Clean Air Coalition)	Amend the Act (The National Environmental Development Association / Clean Air Act Project)
Amalgamated Clothing & Textile Workers	Allied Chemical Corporation
Americans for Democratic Action	Ashland Oil, Inc.
American Lung Association	Atlantic Richfield Company
Center for Auto Safety	Building and Construction Trades Department, AFL-CIO
Citizens for a Better Environment	Campbell Soup Company
Environmental Action	Celanese Corporation
Environmental Defense Fund	Chevron U.S.A., Inc.
Environmental Policy Center	Consolidated Coal Company
Friends of the Earth	Crown Zellerbach Corporation
International Association of Machinists & Aerospace Workers	Dow Chemical Company
Izaak Walton League of America	Dravo Corporation
League of American Bicyclists	E. I. du Pont de Nemours & Company
League of Women Voters of the United States	Exxon Company, U.S.A.
Sierra Club	Fluor Corporation
National Audubon Society	General Electric Company
National Consumer League	General Motors Corporation
National Farmers Union	Getty Oil Corporation
National Parks & Conservation Association	International Business Corporation
National Wildlife Federation	International Paper Company
Natural Resources Defense Council	Kaiser Aluminum & Chemical Corporation
Oil, Chemical & Atomic Association	Mobil Oil Corporation
United Steelworkers of America	Occidental Petroleum Corporation
Wilderness Society	Pennzoil Company
Western Organization of Resource Councils	Phillips Petroleum Company
	PPG Industries, Inc.
	Procter & Gamble Company
	Shell Oil Company
	Standard Oil Company (Indiana)
	Standard Oil Company (Ohio)
	Stauffer Chemical Company
	Sun Company, Inc.
	Tenneco Chemicals, Inc.
	Texaco Inc.
	Texas Oil & Gas Corporation
	Union Oil Company of California
	Westvaco
	Weyerhaeuser Company

But as it turned out, many businesses and labor unions shared an interest in amending the Clean Air Act. Automobile manufacturers felt that the legislation created unfair burdens for their industry; so, too, did the United Auto Workers' Union. The UAW, a liberal union, usually aligns itself against the business community. But the financial troubles of auto manufacturing have meant financial troubles for auto workers, and the UAW committed itself to working with business to modify the act.

Most important legislative battles involve bipartisan support for proposed changes and bipartisan opposition to them. This was the case with the Clean Air Act amendments. For example, the bill containing amendments strongly backed by industry was introduced by six members of the House of Representatives: three Democrats and three Republicans. Such bipartisan alliances on controversial measures are rare in the legislatures of most democratic countries, but they are the rule in the U.S. Congress, where party ranks are broken with abandon. Interest groups understand the importance of ad hoc legislative alliances, and they seek out "friends" on particular measures where they can find them. A liberal Democrat like John Dingell of Michigan would not usually be found working in tandem with a conservative Republican like James T. Broyhill of North Carolina. But in this case the UAW, whose members are a big part of Dingell's constituency, favored the same changes that industry wanted.

TACTICS: PROVIDING INFORMATION

Having to deal with many hundreds of pieces of legislation each session, members of Congress need information and technical guidance on complex issues like the Clean Air Act revisions. Interest groups are more than happy to provide them. The Business Roundtable, for example, financed a $400,000 study of various proposed changes in the clean air legislation. The Chamber of Commerce of the United States issued detailed "suggestions for improving the Act." On the other side, the National Clean Air Coalition set forth its positions and recommendations.

Congress wanted more than technical information; it wanted policy guidance. Many legislators, not just those notably friendly to industry, wanted to know what aspects of the act most troubled business. In the same way legislators wanted to know which of the proposed changes especially bothered environmental groups. "You can't have everything you want. What are your priorities?" This was an important part of the information exchanged between the contending groups and Congress.

TACTICS: GRASSROOTS LOBBYING

During the debate on amending the Clean Air Act, interest groups made countless representations to members of Congress. But they also sought to mobilize individuals and groups back home to communicate with their representatives. Environmental groups worked through their state and local networks. One very active business group, the U.S. Chamber of Commerce, devoted extensive resources to rallying municipal chambers of commerce around the country, to get them involved in trying to persuade their local representatives to support amending the act.

TACTICS: USING POLLS

Polling is an increasingly important part of lobbying efforts. Groups vie with one another in telling legislators that they should do what the group wants because it is also what the people want. We saw in chapter 10 that the way questions are worded can affect the opinions people voice on complicated policy issues. Recognizing this, interest groups sometimes sponsor or otherwise encourage polls where questions are worded so as to prompt the desired answers. Or they emphasize only part of the answers people give—the part favorable to the group's position. The object is to get a message to legislators: "Polls are showing that big majorities of Americans want this action taken. If you don't go along, you or your party are going to pay the price for defying the will of the people."

WHO WON?

The big battle over air pollution legislation in the early Reagan administration had all of the ingredients of a classic *High Noon* interest-group confrontation. The stakes were high: the requirements of a growing economy on one hand and vital health and aesthetic needs on the other. Two big coalitions of interest groups went into battle—industry versus environmentalists—each claiming to be on the side of the angels. Each used its full complement of lobbying tactics. The public was both interested and confused.

Each of the two political parties was internally divided on the question of amending the Clean Air Act. The bill that industry favored had the strong backing of the Reagan administration. President Reagan urged amendments that, "while protecting the environment, will make it possible for industry to rebuild its productive base and create more jobs." But the bill also had the support of some key House Democrats, including John Dingell, chairman of the Energy and Commerce Committee. On the other side, opposed to the bill, was Henry Waxman, the Democratic chair of the Subcommittee on Health and the Environment. Many Senate Republicans were also opposed to the position held by the Reagan administration and industry. The bill reported out by the Senate Environment and Public Works Committee made only modest changes in the Clean Air Act and was generally supported by environmentalists.

What was the outcome of this stage in the ongoing group struggle over air pollution legislation? The environmental groups won hands down. The House Energy and Commerce Committee was deadlocked, and the bill was never reported out. No amendments of any kind passed either the House or the Senate. While environmental groups would have liked to enact changes of their own to strengthen clean air standards further, their main goal was to resist industry-backed changes that they thought weakened the legislation; in this they had complete success. The effort to amend the Clean Air Act in the ninety-seventh Congress (1981–83) ended with Congress sharply divided over what to do and thus making no changes at all.

STAGE TWO: CLEAN AIR LEGISLATION IN THE BUSH ADMINISTRATION

George Bush ran for office in 1988 saying he wanted to be known as "the environmental president." There's no reason to doubt his personal commitment to a healthy and attractive physical environment—something most Americans share. But it's also evident that Bush and his advisers recognized that the environment was one area where the Reagan administration had lost most of the political battles. The Democrats had generally succeeded in gaining public support for their argument that Reagan policies were too beholden to business interests and too weak to achieve the needed environmental advances. If Bush were to be seen as a carbon copy of his predecessor in this area, his administration would suffer politically.

The Bush administration differentiated itself by proposing legislation to reauthorize the Clean Air Act and set new, tighter controls on smog, acid rain, and toxic air pollutants. Many environmental interest groups felt the Bush proposals didn't go far enough and lobbied hard in the House and Senate for more stringent standards. Nonetheless, Bush's actions in proposing new clean air legislation dramatically transformed the politics of the issue—and weakened the position of business interests, such as the auto industry, which argued that the new rules would cost too much and lead to the loss of jobs. With the public strongly committed to the goal of a clean environment, and with many in Congress favoring new legislation, the addition of White House backing was more than industry could withstand. New clean air legislation—the product of compromises struck by the Bush administration and Democratic leaders—passed the Senate 81 to 11 on April 3, 1990, and similar legislation carried easily, 401 to 21, in the House on May 23.

The environmentalists, not industry, clearly dominated the 1990 clean air debate. This does not mean, however, that industry lobbyists weren't active—they in fact made intense efforts—or entirely unsuccessful. The 1990 debate was not over a broad goal: Virtually everyone endorsed the objective of improving air quality. It was over what specific actions should be taken to advance the goal at a reasonable cost. Business interests won some of these important battles.

For example, the auto industry waged a multi-million dollar lobbying effort on the legislation. One area where it was concerned involved the imposition of stricter fuel-economy standards. Environmentalists were pushing for improved gasoline mileage as a key to slowing global warming—climate change linked to the burning of fossil fuels. Auto makers argued that a tough fuel-economy law would force them to shrink the size of their cars at a time when many buyers were indicating a preference for larger models. The industry won this skirmish when an amendment requiring much stiffer

Another view of George Bush as the "environmental president," reflecting the sentiments of some environmental groups.

President Bush signs the 1990 clean air legislation with Secretary of Energy James Watkins (left) and EPA Administrator William Reilly looking on.

fuel-economy standards was dropped from the clean air bill.[9] Auto makers also gained some of what they wanted on the issue of the stringency of tailpipe emissions controls.

Industry spent heavily in its efforts to shape the legislation. For instance, 110 political action committees from interested firms gave nearly $612,000 to the campaigns of House Energy and Commerce Committee members—the committee with jurisdiction over clean air laws—in 1989 alone. Table 11.6 (page 328) shows the largest contributors.[10] One utility-lobbying

coalition—Citizens for Sensible Control of Acid Rain—reported that it collected more than $500,000 from industry executives for its 1989 activities. But the environmental interest groups were intensely active too and very well funded. Representative Mike Synar (D-Oklahoma), who sits on the House energy committee, believed that there was so much lobbying on all sides "that it all tended to cancel each other out."[11]

Wrangling over the final shape of the new clean air legislation between Bush administration and congressional Democrats, and between House and Senate, dragged on throughout the spring and summer of 1990. The differences were finally resolved in late October, after an all-night bargaining session involving House and Senate conferees. The final package of clean air amendments passed the House by an overwhelming 401–25 margin and the Senate by 89–10. Bush signed the bill into law in mid-November, seventeen months after he had pushed the idea forward by introducing his own clean air proposals.

The final legislation was plainly not to the liking of many businesses affected by it. Industry lobbyists said the new law would add hundreds of dollars to the cost of cars, that gasoline and electricity prices would be forced up, that many manufacturers would have to spend large sums to install new pollution controls at their plants—costs that would have to be passed on to consumers—and that small businesses would have a hard time complying with expensive permit requirements. Still, the industry coalition did not oppose the final legislation. It concluded that it had gotten the best bill possible under the circumstances. "There were a lot of winners and losers," one observer remarked. "We shouldn't keep score."

[9] Neal Temlin, "Environmentalists and Auto Makers Rev Up for Battle," *Wall Street Journal*, April 4, 1990, p. A15; and Jill Abramson, "Auto Makers Lobbied Hard Against Stricter Fuel Rules," *Wall Street Journal*, April 4, 1990, p. A15.
[10] Chuck Alston, "As Clean-Air Bill Took Off, So Did PAC Contributions," *Congressional Quarterly*, March 17, 1990, pp. 811–17.
[11] Quoted by Jill Abramson, "Auto Makers Lobbied Hard," p. A15.

TABLE 11.6 PAC CONTRIBUTORS (1989) TO HOUSE COMMITTEE WITH CLEAN AIR JURISDICTION

Amount given	Type of industry	Corporation / trade association sponsoring PAC
$19,150	Auto–TA	National Automobile Dealers Association
18,600	Auto	Ford Motor Company
18,000	Auto	General Motors Corporation
13,350	Oil	British Petroleum Company
12,950	EUtil	Southern California Edison Company
12,850	EUtil	Virginia Electric and Power Company
12,700	Oil	Atlantic Richfield Company
12,450	EUtil	Alabama Power Company (parent: The Southern Company)
12,400	EUtil–TA	National Rural Electric Cooperative Association
12,275	Gas	Columbia Hydrocarbon Corporation (parent: Columbia Gas System, Inc.)
12,000	Gas	Enron Corporation
11,900	Oil	Amoco Corporation
11,900	Oil–Ret	Petroleum Marketers Association of America
11,050	Gas	Pacific Enterprises
10,950	Energy	The Coastal Corporation
10,900	Oil	Ashland Oil, Inc.
10,150	Oil–Ret	Society of Independent Gasoline Marketers of America
9,750	EUtil	American Electric Power
9,700	Oil	Texaco, Inc.
9,550	EUtil	The Southern Company
9,250	Oil	Chevron Corporation
8,950	Coal–TA	National Coal Association
8,800	Gas	Columbia Natural Resources, Inc. (parent: Columbia Gas System, Inc.)
8,600	Auto	Chrysler Corporation
8,600	Chem	CIBA-GEIGY, Ltd.
8,550	EUtil	Texas Utilities Electric Company
8,500	EUtil	Houston Industries, Inc.
8,500	Steel–TA	Institute of Scrap Recycling Industries
8,250	Oil	Mobil Corporation
7,750	Chem	W. R. Grace & Company
7,700	GasEUtil	Pacific Gas & Electric Company
7,050	Coal	Peabody Coal Company
6,600	EUtil–TA	Edison Electric Institute
6,450	EUtil	Texas Utilities Company
6,350	Coal	International Union United Mine Workers of America
6,300	Oil	Union Oil Company of California
6,100	Oil	Exxon Corporation
6,100	Coal	The Pittston Company
5,750	Oil	Shell Oil Company
5,400	EUtil	Georgia Power Company (parent: The Southern Company)
5,150	EUtil	General Public Utilities Corporation
5,000	HEQ	Deere & Company
5,000	HEQ	Navistar International Corporation
5,000	Oil	Phillips Petroleum Company

Over 100 political action committees with an interest in clean air legislation contributed more than $1000 each to members of the House committee with jurisdiction over clean air issues (House Energy and Commerce Committee) in 1989. Here we list only those that gave $5000 or more. (Consult abbreviations.)

Energy—Producers of oil, gas, coal

TA—Trade association GasEUtil—Gas and electric utility Oil-Ret—Gas, oil products retailing

EUtil—Electric utility HEQ—Maker of heavy off-road vehicles Gas—Natural gas exploration / transmission / distribution

Source: Congressional Quarterly Weekly Report, March 17, 1990.

"WELL, THAT SOLVES THE ACID RAIN PROBLEM FOR A WHILE"

1/18/85

Pitted against the formidable groups in Table 11.6 are numerous other groups, and the occasional political cartoonist.

CONTRASTING INTEREST-GROUP EFFORTS

The big interest-group battles over environmental legislation reveal many facets of interest-group activities. But no case study can illustrate the whole range; in other areas, objectives, competition, and tactics are different.

NARROWER OBJECTIVES

The clean air debate involved broad and highly visible issues. The public may not have under-stood the technical points being debated, but the basic controversies around the competing claims of environmental and economic objectives were of general public concern. In contrast, many instances of interest-group intervention involve narrower issues that, though important to specific groups, do not pose questions central to the entire polity. Independent service station operators try to get Congress to pass legislation prohibiting the major oil companies from operating service stations. Dairy farmers seek to maintain a federal price-support program for milk products they cannot sell at a set price. The domestic shipbuilding industry wants to continue to receive federal subsidies initiated to make U.S. ship building more competitive with foreign yards.

NO BATTLE OF THE GROUPS

On occasion, as with some environmental legislation, elaborate armies of contending groups organize on each side of an issue. Working with friendly members of Congress, each of these coalitions tries to bring undecided legislators to its side. But in many other cases, most of the organization and activity takes place on one side only. Interest-group conflict isn't uncommon, of course, but the elaborate mobilization of contending groups that happened in the clean air debates occurs on a limited number of issues.

LOBBYING THE EXECUTIVE BRANCH AND THE JUDICIARY

In many instances, lobbying efforts center not on Congress (or a state legislature) but on executive-branch departments and agencies. Earlier in American history, when the enterprise of government was smaller, the scope of policy initiatives by administrative agencies was tightly circumscribed. Today, however, government does so much and programs are of such complexity that program administration is often a central part of policy formation. Executive bureaucracies have become a main arena of interest-group activity.

Lobbying reaches the judiciary as well. As we saw in chapter 9, a primary means of group intervention in the judicial arena comes through test cases. The National Association for the Advancement of Colored People (NAACP) Legal Defense Fund has provided skilled attorneys and directed a long series of court challenges to racial discrimination. Similarly, the American Civil Liberties Union (ACLU) has concentrated its efforts in the courts rather than in the other branches. In recent years, many of the newer public-interest groups, including those concerned with environmental issues, have also relied heavily on litigation: for example, by seeking court rulings to restrict the construction of nuclear power plants or to extend the scope of governmental regulation under environmental statutes.

The highly technical issue of standing (as we saw in chapter 9) has a bearing on the extent to which public-interest groups can advance policy goals through litigation. In order to have standing to sue, a party must show a real or threatened injury. The more stringent the requirements the courts set, the harder it is for groups to mount judicial challenges to statutes they oppose. On the whole, federal courts have over the last decade shifted a bit toward stiffer requirements of demonstrated injury in order for standing to be granted in challenges brought by public-interest groups, a development that reflects the impact of Reagan appointees to the courts.[12]

Interest groups also pursue their objectives in the judicial arena in ways apart from initiating and supporting litigation. They "speak" to the judges and try to persuade them to adopt philosophies that the groups find attractive. Courts are a special part of the political process, and the etiquette for group attempts at persuasion is different for them than for other governmental institutions. When a group wants to convey its policy views to Congress, it sends its representatives directly to the legislators, or it may take out full-page ads in leading newspapers. Judges are not supposed to be lobbied in such ways, and for the most part they are not. To get the message through, a prime vehicle is the filing of *amicus curiae* (friend of the court) briefs. In a major case, it is not uncommon to find scores of interest groups filing *amicus* briefs on behalf of one or the other of the primary litigants. These briefs contain legal argument, but they are also a formal mechanism through which groups make known to judges their policy interpretations and preferences. Many hundreds of groups, for example, filed *amicus* briefs in the big 1992 abortion case, *Planned Parenthood v. Casey* (discussed in chapter 9, pp. 248–49).

WHY SO MUCH AMERICAN INTEREST-GROUP ACTIVITY?

As noted earlier, Tocqueville argued in the 1830s that Americans were unusually active in interest groups and voluntary associations. Contemporary studies come to this same conclusion. Gabriel Almond and Sidney Verba found a quarter-century ago that a higher proportion of citizens belonged to voluntary associations in the United States than in Britain, West Germany, Italy, or Mexico.[13] Americans

[12]See Rochelle L. Stanfield, "Out-Standing in Court," *National Journal*, February 13, 1988, pp. 388–91.

[13]Gabriel A. Almond and Sidney Verba, *The Civic Culture: Political Attitudes and Democracy in Five Nations* (Princeton, N.J.: Princeton University Press, 1963), pp. 301–2.

were much more likely, moreover, to have multiple group memberships. A later study by Sidney Verba and Norman Nye showed 32 percent of Americans as active members in community organizations, compared to 15 percent in the Netherlands, 11 percent in Japan, and 9 percent in Austria.[14] The sheer numbers of groups and the vigorous roles they play are a distinctive feature of U.S. experience. Why is this so?

One would expect relatively free and open societies to have more extensive group participation than those with authoritarian regimes. But, as we have seen, even in established democracies like Britain, the Netherlands, Germany, and Italy, interest-group activity lags behind that exhibited in the United States. A highly educated and affluent populace has the time, training, confidence, and other resources necessary for group organization, much more than the public of a poor country, where educational and communications resources are restricted. But, again, the United States is not alone in having the requisite education, sources of information, and economic position. Explanation for the unusually extensive group organization in America, compared to other industrial democracies, lies elsewhere.

One factor seems to be the heterogeneity of American society. James Madison felt in 1787 that one of the virtues of a large republic like the one provided for by the Constitution was the capacity to sustain a more diverse set of groups or factions to compete against each other. American experience has borne out Madison's expectations. The United States comprises a great variety of groups—ethnic, religious, cultural, regional, and more.

Tocqueville thought the strength of American individualism contributed importantly to the country's vigorous group life. One might think the opposite: that practitioners of rugged individualism would be social and political loners. Tocqueville saw that, in the United States, a nation of self-confident and assertive individuals would produce a welter of group action, as people banded together to accomplish various objectives. Passivity, or the absence of a sense of individual efficacy, are the true deterrents to a vigorous associational life. "I'm important—and I can do something" spurs the formation of voluntary associations.

Groups organize around units where decisions get made, and governmental arrangements are a key factor determining what these units are. The decentralization of U.S. government encourages a proliferation of interest groups at national, state, and local levels. In contrast, centralized governmental systems, like those of Britain and France, produce interest-group centralization. Britain has, for instance, just one national organization of farmers, just one major business association. There is no counterpart in France to the fifty state AFL-CIO units, for the simple reason that there is no counterpart in France to the fifty states.

INTEREST-GROUP POWER

We have seen the propensity of the populace for vigorous group participation and the central role that well-organized and well-financed interest groups play in governmental decision making. What remains is to examine the central issue of group power as it relates to democratic governance. Specifically, are groups too strong? Do the maneuverings of special interests threaten the public interest? The research on these questions support a complex conclusion: Interest groups and their active involvement in political life are 1) inevitable, 2) desirable, and 3) a continuing source of problems.

---

[14]Norman H. Nye and Sidney Verba, "Political Participation," in Fred I. Greenstein and Nelson W. Polsby, eds., *Handbook of Political Science* (Reading, Mass.: Addison-Wesley, 1975), vol. 4, pp. 24–25.

Interest groups are **inevitable** for the basic reasons Madison noted in *Federalist* No. 10. The presence of liberty, essential and desirable, ensures an abundance of self-serving groups. And it would be utopian to think that this country could have dynamic groups and associations without some of them acquiring resources that give them a competitive advantage over others. While the United States need not adopt an "anything goes" posture before the claims of organized interests, both the active presence of interest groups and the disproportionate resources of some of them are inevitable features of American democracy.

Many proponents of democracy find interest groups not only inevitable but also **desirable.** Committed to popular sovereignty, democrats must applaud conditions whereby bodies of people who share political interests can seek their expression and realization. Advocates of democracy may condemn certain forms of group activity, but they can hardly dispute that interest groups are the primary means through which popular sovereignty is realized. We might contrast this with the historic experience of totalitarian societies, where there was deep aversion to interest-group activity. Essential to the definition of totalitarianism, as that concept is applied to national socialism in Hitler's Germany or to Soviet communism under Lenin and Stalin, is the sustained effort to stamp out all forms of intermediate group life that might challenge the regime and organize people for independent political activity. The presence of strong independent interest groups imposes important limits on the power of government.

Democratic theory has long emphasized the essential place of a vigorous system of interest groups and other mediating structures through which the varied interests making up a society are organized and expressed.[15] Through groups people are given meaningful identities, and the alienation of mass society is reduced.[16] Organized groups also play important roles in articulating the demands and needs of the many diverse interests within a population.[17]

From James Madison on, the operation of organized interests has been seen as **problem causing.** In the early twentieth century, a political movement known as Progressivism grew up with a prime objective of purging excessive interest-group influence from political parties, legislatures, and governmental administration locally and nationally. The Progressives saw American democracy dominated by a struggle between "the interests" and "the people," and they sought political reforms that would shift the balance of power from the former to the latter. The Progressives were especially troubled by what they considered the excessive power of big business interests—"the trusts," as they had developed in such industries as oil, steel, and banking. In 1913, Woodrow Wilson, just elected president and with ties to the Progressive movement, issued a statement denouncing the role of special interests in current legislation.

> I think that the public ought to know the extraordinary exertions being made by the lobby in Washington to gain recognition for certain alterations of the tariff bill. Washington has seldom seen so numerous, so industrious, or so insidious a lobby. . . . It is of serious interest to the country that the people at large should have no lobby and be voiceless in these matters, while great bodies of astute men seek to create an artificial opinion and to overcome the interests

---

[15] For a thoughtful general statement of the essential place of interest groups in a democratic society, see Ernest Bar-

ker, *Reflections on Government* (New York: Oxford University Press, 1958).

[16] See, for example, William Kornhauser, *The Politics of Mass Society* (Glencoe, Ill.: Free Press, 1959); and Seymour Martin Lipset, *Political Man* (Garden City, N.Y.: Anchor Books, 1963), especially chaps. 1 and 2.

[17] David B. Truman, *The Governmental Process* (New York: Knopf, 1951).

of the public for their private profit. . . . The Government in all its branches ought to be relieved from this intolerable burden and this constant interruption to the calm progress of debate.[18]

THREE ENDURING CONCERNS ABOUT GROUP POWER

Americans still lament the role of pressure groups and pressure politics. Citizens have complained as much in recent years about the power of "Big Oil" as their counterparts seven and eight decades ago did about "the trusts." The savings and loan scandals of the present decade have rekindled concern over the wheeling and dealing of financial interests. Lobbying is considered an often unsavory activity that carries the onus of excessive influence by big private money. There is a vivid perception of too-cozy relationships between interest groups and politicians, of wheeling and dealing behind closed doors for ends antithetical to the public interest. Three different concerns are often tangled in the general indictment of excessive group influence. One is the fear that some interests may actually come to dominate American government as a coherent power elite. A second is that groups are able to take over not the entire government but rather a great number of specific policy areas where they have special interests and get their way with little general public scrutiny or control. The third concern is about the fact that some interests are much better organized and represented than others.

[18] *State Papers and Addresses by Woodrow Wilson, President of the United States* (New York: George H. Doran, 1918), pp. 9–10.

"NAH — IT WOULDN'T BE PRACTICAL"

Copyright 1989 by Herblock in The Washington Post

Madison addressed the problem of **group tyranny** directly, and he and the other framers of the Constitution thought they had found a satisfactory, long-term answer. We saw in chapter 4 that their answer was to so divide power, and check and balance it, that group tyranny would be impossible. A government of dispersed authority operating in a diverse and pluralistic society would be sufficient to maintain popular sovereignty and individual liberty.

Political scientist Grant McConnell dismissed the idea of power-elite domination, observing that the American interest-group world is highly fragmented and decentralized. Political organization in the United States, he noted, has been based persistently on "small constituencies."[19] The fragmented groups of small constituencies have "on the whole had limited ends; their tactics have been limited and often more economic than political. Where they have been openly political, they have relied upon group self-help through the exercise of well-isolated segments of public authority rather than upon action through political parties and elections."[20] Interest-group success has come, typically, in **dominating narrow policy sectors** of special interest to the group.

Madison wanted political organization based on small constituencies to serve as a check on group power, and today the United States has that arrangement to a degree that might surprise even its brilliant proponent.

The present problem grows out of the very success of the Madisonian solution. As Americans have come in recent decades to accept an enlarged mission for government, thousands of new lobbies have developed around the expansive governmental system. As the Advisory Commission on Intergovernmental Relations has noted, "Every program, every protective regulation, every tax loophole appears to have acquired its coterie of organized beneficiaries." The proliferating interest groups found the traditional dispersion of authority much to their liking. For, while the whole of government was impervious to control by any group, the many separate parts proved to be uniquely susceptible to special-interest pressures.

We saw in chapter 8 how interest groups, congressional subcommittees, and executive-agency bureaus have operated relatively closed policy systems in many discrete program areas. "Molecular government," Joseph Califano called it when he was secretary of Health, Education, and Welfare and thus unusually well placed to observe the problem. "Washing-ton has become a city of political molecules," he observed, "with fragmentation of power, and often authority and responsibility, among increasingly narrow, what's-in-it-for-me interest groups and their responsive counterparts in the executive and legislative branches."[21] National policy is too often made not for the nation but for narrow, autonomous sectors defined by special interests. The total of programs determined in each sector makes up national policy—but it is a national policy no one planned or intended. These interest-group/ executive-agency bureau/congressional sub-committee linkages have been called "iron triangles."

In solving the problem that Madison considered the primary problem of democratic governance—preventing groups from dominating the totality of government—institutional arrangements were established that have led to a different problem: Special interests do not control the nation, but their influence over discrete policy sectors makes coherent national policy that is properly responsive to the public interest difficult to achieve.

Criticizing the argument of some analysts that the great variety of organized groups contending with each other preserves a pluralistic balance, political scientist E. E. Schattschneider observed that "the flaw in the pluralist heaven is that the heavenly chorus sings with a strong upper-class accent."[22] The economically privileged enjoy greater group representation than do the poor. As Schattschneider saw it, in other words, **too much power to groups of economic privilege** has been a persistent problem.

There are a number of reasons why business people and other high-status groups have a

---

[19] Grant McConnell, *Private Power and American Democracy* (New York: Knopf, 1966), p. 342.
[20] Ibid., p. 345.

[21] Remarks by Joseph A. Califano, Jr., before the Economic Club of Chicago, April 20, 1978.
[22] E. E. Schattschneider, *The Semi-Sovereign People* (New York: Holt, 1960), p. 35.

disproportionately large place in the interest-group process. They have the financial means to sustain organized group action. This is notably the case with corporate executives, who are able to command the resources of major corporations. Also, people with large amounts of formal education have skills and training that equip them better to engage in complex political action. Economist Mancur Olson explained another facet: In certain types of small groups, an individual may find that his or her personal gain from achieving some collective good—a benefit for the entire group—is so substantial that it is in the individual's interest to support an organization set up to advance it even if he or she has to pay all the cost of the organization's effort. The high degree to which business interests are organized in the United States results, then, from the fact that the business community "is divided into a series of . . . 'industries,' each of which contains only a fairly small number of firms."[23] Each firm, operating through relatively compact units such as trade associations, has a big stake in voluntarily contributing to the organized group activity because of the large individual gain it may expect.

One can probably never attain a condition where all segments of the population are equally represented by interest-group efforts. Some segments simply have greater resources and incentives for group action. This does not mean that the economically disadvantaged cannot have their needs represented. What it does mean, as Schattschneider and McConnell have argued, is that adequate representation of the poor and the disadvantaged is unlikely to be achieved through the interest-group structure.

A free society must permit the free organization of groups and must confer on them considerable latitude in making their claims.

[23]Mancur Olson, Jr., *The Logic of Collective Action* (Cambridge, Mass.: Harvard University Press, 1965), p. 34.

But adequate attention to broad national interests, including the claims of people insufficiently spoken for by interest groups, requires the interventions of such primary representative institutions as political parties and the presidency. Only a *vox populi* expressed by elected representatives bound to do the people's business can counterbalance the "upper-class accents" coming from interest groups.

SUMMARY

The United States displays a great variety of interest groups and, in general, a high level of group participation. While organized interests can be found in every sector touched by public policy, economic policy has prompted the greatest profusion of groups. In recent years, though, other sectors such as women's affairs, education, and environmental issues have seen a proliferation of interest groups. Public-interest groups, those that pursue collective goals that are not of immediate material benefit to their members, have also expanded greatly.

Various resources determine the extent of group influence. Numbers are important, as groups speaking for large constituencies can make a special claim upon political attention. But having a large constituency often means that the group also encompasses a great heterogeneity of interests, and on many issues it cannot really speak for the bulk of its members.

Money is always a critical resource. Well-financed groups can hire skilled staff, make campaign contributions, advertise, and do other things needed to gain favorable attention for their proposals. Groups speaking for intensely held interests have an advantage over those whose memberships, though perhaps larger, are not strongly engaged. Some interests are able to find support broadly across the society, while others must largely go it alone.

The tactics used by interest groups have been evolving. The organization of formal coalitions of groups around key policy interests is now common. It has been prompted in part by the greater dispersion of power in Congress. Groups have always been concerned with public opinion, but they now devote greater resources than previously to the measurement of opinion through polls and to efforts to demonstrate through poll data that the people are on their side.

American interest groups operate in a political environment where the parties are organizationally weak and often split internally. So the groups have learned to find their allies where they can across party lines. They also operate in a governmental system of divided powers; and they must concentrate on executive agencies and the judiciary as well as Con-

gress, and on the state capitals as well as Washington.

It is always tempting to reach for a simple, focused conclusion on the role of interest groups in American democracy, like "They are too strong and threaten the public interest." But political life is too complicated for that. Groups are an inevitable part of democratic experience, reflecting the free choice of interests to express themselves. Groups are a desirable part of democratic experience, barring excessive power by government, providing people with greater representation and identification. And interest groups are a problem-causing side of democracy as they dominate specific policy sectors and give greater voice to some interests than others. Group power, speaking for small constituencies, must be balanced by recognition of the claims of the entire public through national institutions and electoral mandates.

FOR FURTHER STUDY

Berry, Jeffrey M. *The Interest Group Society*. Boston: Little, Brown, 1984. A thoughtful account of the relationship of interest-group politics to broader aspects of the American political system, including especially the relationship of interest groups to political parties.

————. *Lobbying for the People*. Princeton, N.J.: Princeton University Press, 1977. Still the best available account of public-interest groups like Common Cause and the Sierra Club, and the role they play in contemporary American politics.

Lowi, Theodore J. *The End of Liberalism: Ideology, Policy, and the Crisis of Public Authority*, 2nd ed. New York: Norton, 1979. A brilliant analysis and a trenchant criticism of interest-group politics as they have evolved in the United States over the last half-century.

McConnell, Grant. *Private Power and American Democracy*. New York: Knopf, 1966. A penetrating exami-

nation of the role and power of interest groups, which argues that specific clusters of interests dominate the various narrow areas of public policy.

Olsen, Mancur, Jr. *The Logic of Collective Action: Public Goods and the Theory of Groups*, 2nd ed. Cambridge, Mass.: Harvard University Press, 1971. Applies economic analysis to the relationships between individuals, their self-interest, and their commitments to interest groups.

Schattschneider, E. E. *The Semi-Sovereign People*. New York: Holt, 1960. An elegant study which argues that interest groups represent disproportionately a set of established, upper-class interests.

Truman, David B. *The Governmental Process*, 2nd ed. New York: Knopf, 1971. Advances a theory of interest groups and applies it in explaining how decisions get made in the American governmental process.

Chapter *12*

POLITICAL PARTIES
AND ELECTIONS

During Franklin D. Roosevelt's presidency in the 1930s, the Democrats emerged as the country's majority party. Their ascendancy was evident at all levels of government, from the cities and statehouses to Congress and the presidency. More Americans identified themselves as Democrats than as Republicans—even though the Republicans had been the majority party for more than three decades up to the Great Depression. This massive shift in party fortunes is known as the New Deal realignment.

In our own time, changes as consequential as those of the New Deal era have been occurring in the political parties and in the elections. The current transformations have taken very different forms, however. In the 1930s, for example, attention centered on the emergence of a new majority party and on where it was taking the country. Today, the United States lacks a majority party. The Democrats and Republicans are nearly equal in strength of underlying voter support, and for an extended period they have shared control of the national government—a phenomenon we discussed in chapter 5. More-over, apart from the matter of their relative strength, both of America's old, established parties find themselves organizationally weaker than they were in times past, unable to make strong claims on voters' loyalties. Independent H. Ross Perot's 1992 presidential bid, while ultimately collapsing, underscored the weakening of voter ties to the political parties. [The 1992 campaign is examined in detail in a special chapter, written at the election's end in November 1992 and included in the Appendix to this text, beginning on p. A29.]

In addition to the important shifts involving the political parties' institutional life and electoral coalitions, the form of American political campaigning has changed greatly. The mass media, especially television, are right in the center of the new order. As we will discuss in chapter 13, most voters these days get their information on the candidates largely through television. Though candidates' speeches may air in full on the cable channel C-SPAN, the television networks generally limit their direct coverage to short excerpts—the much discussed and lamented "sound bites," usually fifteen or thirty seconds long. The candidates in turn direct their campaign energies to getting on the "tube" and fashioning an attractive image. Their campaigns are, as a result, increasingly dominated by media experts, crafters of television commercials, and pollsters supposedly able to define how it is all playing with the folks back home. Traditional campaign activities—including reliance on the efforts of ward or precinct party organizations—are increasingly pushed aside in this brave new world of electronic electioneering.

But for all the changes that have taken place in political parties and elections—which we examine in detail later in this chapter—many other of their features have remained unchanged. If political parties have been weakened, they are still essential representative

Party loyalties seem more fragile than ever as witnessed by the support independent H. Ross Perot received in the 1992 presidential campaign.

institutions. The American party system today would in many regards seem familiar to those who knew our party system a century ago. Similarly, the structure of our electoral system is fundamentally unchanged, for all the innovations in campaigning. We open this chapter, then, with a review of the formal features of parties and elections in the United States that continue to distinguish our system from those of most other democracies.

PARTIES AS REPRESENTATIVE INSTITUTIONS

The American party system is the oldest in the world, fast approaching its second centennial. In the late 1790s, when parties took shape in the United States and began a struggle for control of government in popular elections, their architects had no blueprints to follow. A new political institution was being established. Less than two hundred years later, political parties are found throughout the world.

In the sweep of governmental experience, parties are very young institutions. They became necessary only after the revolutionary changes that gripped Western societies in the seventeenth and eighteenth centuries and that dominated American origins: the collapse of aristocratic society; the extension of social and political egalitarianism; and the development of political ideologies, especially classical liberalism, that assigned individuals a far more elevated position than they had ever enjoyed.

Political parties are the children of egalitarianism. They appeared as a necessary institutional response to the idea of popular sovereignty, to the belief that the rank-and-file citizen should have final authority in the business of governing. In pre-egalitarian societies small groups of citizens organized to influence the affairs of state through cabals, cliques, and factions. The egalitarian revolution of the seventeenth and eighteenth centuries gave legitimacy to the idea that the entire public should be considered and consulted.

Once the notion of popular sovereignty took hold, political parties evolved rapidly. They set up organizations among the populace and linked up local units with national leadership—for example, with party officials in the legislature. They provided common political identities for elites and the rank and file, promoting popular cohesion for and against contrasting philosophies of government. They put flesh on the skeletal idea of representation.

EDMUND BURKE AND THE EARLY ARGUMENT OVER PARTIES

Parties did not emerge without a struggle. For some time after the first stirrings of egalitarianism in the seventeenth century, philosophers and politicians had trouble conceiving a permanent and legitimate role for political parties. To those like the English leader and political theorist Henry St. John, Viscount Bolingbroke, parties were "a political evil,"[1] institutions of a dangerous and untried democracy. They would represent special interests against the national interest. They would break a nation into parts, involving it in endless squabbles, blocking the pursuit of the common good.

Prior to the nineteenth century, only one theorist raised and defended the idea of political parties as essential instruments of emerging representative government: the great British politician and philosopher Edmund Burke

---

[1] Henry Saint-John Bolingbroke, "A Dissertation Upon Parties," in *The Works of Lord Bolingbroke*, vol. 2 (Philadelphia: Carey and Hart, 1841). "Dissertation" was first published in England in 1733.

(1729–97). It is testimony to Burke's genius that he developed the case for a mature party system long before one came to exist. The proper question, as Burke saw it, was how the various interests in the country could be organized so as to determine policy. His answer was through political parties. "Party is a body of men united, for promoting by their joint endeavors the national interest, upon some particular principle in which they are all agreed."[2] He recognized that there would be different and competing ideas of how best to serve the national interest; all would inevitably prove futile unless their proponents organized for effective action. Once organized, political parties would become the necessary great connection between groups of citizens and governmental institutions.

Although parties as we know them did not yet exist, Burke was already what we would call a "strong party man." He believed that political figures should assess the various issues, decide which political group they would side with in order to advance a shared view of the public interest, and then give their party sustained support. Burke was not sympathetic to the argument that continuing support for a party requires a politician to subordinate the claims of his own conscience. What is incumbent upon a politician in a representative government, he insisted, is the thoughtful choice of a party whose "leading general principles in government" he can support. When an issue arises that is not of great moment, he should go along with his party, even if he happens to disagree with it. Only rarely, Burke thought, will a politician be required by deep conviction to separate himself from a party whose general goals he shares.

[2] Edmund Burke, "Thoughts on the Cause of the Present Discontents," in *The Works of Edmund Burke*, vol. 2 (London: Rivington, 1815), p. 335. "Thoughts" was written in 1770.

DEVELOPMENT OF PARTIES IN THE UNITED STATES

Burke's insights into the necessary place of parties in representative governments were not readily accepted. Here in the United States, where parties first matured, James Madison did not contemplate a place for them in the constitutional order. Madison did recognize the place of interest groups or factions, but he did not foresee an essential representative role for parties. And, in his farewell address in 1796, George Washington warned "in the most solemn manner against the harmful effects of the spirit of party."

Thomas Jefferson had similar views, even though he was the architect of one of the world's first full-fledged parties: the Republicans, later called Democratic-Republicans, and eventually called the Democrats. The alliance Jefferson put together is the direct ancestor of the present-day Democratic party. But he considered parties troublesome enterprises, not great instruments for extending democracy. While president in 1804, Jefferson wrote William Short that "the party division in this country is certainly not among its pleasant features. To a certain degree it will always exist: and chiefly in mercantile places. In the country and those states where the Republicans have a decided superiority, party hostility has ceased to infest society."

Jefferson lamented that, while he had been quite prepared to offer his partisan opponents a few minor places in his government if they would cease to be an opposition force, they had spurned this! Even among the most prescient of Americans of the day, there was no real picture of parties as regular, necessary instruments through which the divergent views of the public could be organized and expressed in an egalitarian polity.

Still, if Americans were uncertain as to the purpose of political parties, they nonetheless went ahead building them rapidly. The first stirrings of party were in the policy conflict between Hamilton and Jefferson in Washington's administration, a division that was part of a much broader argument over public policy in the new regime. As the dispute deepened, Hamilton turned to his friends in Congress, Jefferson to his—one result being that factional ties between executive and legislative leaders became much tighter. Hamilton's group took a name that raised memories of the successful fight for the Constitution: the Federalists. At this time the Jeffersonians called themselves the Republicans.

A CORE DEMOCRATIC FUNCTION

Political parties sprang up so quickly because they were needed to link the people to government in the first egalitarian society. They aggregated the preferences of the public for political leadership and policy choice, and converted what was incoherent and diffuse into specific, responsive public decisions. There are three distinct but closely interrelated parts to this basic function.

Representation. The potential electorate in the United States (citizens of voting age) numbers over 180 million. It is no small task to get candidates and programs that reflect the preferences of so large and diverse a public. Effective representation is achieved when government translates popular preferences into programs, and the public concludes that government is generally responsive to its wishes. Representation, then, requires a number of things that only parties can do: it needs coalitions to be built and the policies that meet the needs of coalitions to be articulated; it needs popular and effective candidates to win office and to implement those policies; it needs alternative candidates to those in power to be found and

offered, so that when popular majorities are dissatisfied with governmental performance, they have somewhere to turn.

Popular Control. Political parties are also necessary to enable citizens to control their government and ensure the responsiveness of public institutions. There are so many different elective offices in a country like the United States that citizens cannot consider their votes meaningful in controlling policy unless the many separate election contests are linked in some understandable fashion: For instance, balloting for the national legislature can be seen as a competition of one party against another, rather than as the unrelated competition of individuals.

Beyond this, only parties are in a position to so organize policy choices that mass publics can make judgments on them. Parties provide the "conduit or sluice by which the waters of social thought and discussion are brought to the wheels of political machinery and set to turn those wheels," as Ernest Barker once put it.[3] When they make elected officials in some sense collectively, rather than individually, responsible to the electorate, parties expand the level of meaningful popular control.

Integration. Today's government, with all of its far-flung activities, is incredibly complex. It has so many different parts responsive to so many different interests that the natural centrifugal pressures are sometimes almost irresistible. Party is the one acceptable counteracting, centripetal force. Governmental integration is especially demanding in the United States, because of the extreme dispersion of authority resulting from federalism and the separation of powers. In such a system, coherence in policy simply cannot be obtained unless parties are

[3] Ernest Barker, *Reflections on Government* (New York: Oxford University Press, 1958; first published, 1942). p. 39.

available for bridging governmental divisions, for example, by bringing together officials in the executive and legislative branches through common partisan ties and commitments.

CHARACTERISTICS OF THE AMERICAN PARTY SYSTEM

Even among democracies there is considerable variety in party arrangements. A distinctively American party system evolved early in the nineteenth century; to a striking degree, it has persisted.

A TWO-PARTY SYSTEM

By the time Democrats and Whigs grappled for power in the 1830s, a two-party system was securely in place. In most of the major elections, only Whigs or Democrats won. Today, Democrats and Republicans similarly dominate—this despite the attention focused for a time on H. Ross Perot's bid as an independent in the 1992 presidential race. Most democracies operate with some type of multi-party system in which at least three and often many more parties regularly draw substantial support.

One reason for America's continuing attachment to this rare type of party competition is that our electoral arrangements impose severe handicaps on third-party challengers. Especially influential is the election of most candidates by the single-member district, simple-majority system (described further below, on pp. 347–49.) In each district only one party's candidate wins a seat. The party that comes in second can argue plausibly that it is the realistic alternative for all those dissatisfied with the winner. Other parties are vulnerable to the charge that a vote for them is simply wasted.

Another important reason why two parties have dominated contests for elective office throughout U.S. history is the fact of a highly consensual society distinguished by minimal ideological disagreements. As we noted in chapter 3, classical liberalism has enjoyed preeminence in American thought from the country's inception. The absence of competing ideological traditions has prevented parties representing different perspectives, such as the socialists, from finding a firm base on which to build. There has been insufficient ideological room in which to establish third and fourth parties, especially since electoral mechanics have made it hard for such challengers to operate.

PARTIES OF ACCOMMODATION

The extraordinary continuity evident in the persistence of a two-party system is also seen in the pragmatic cast of American party competition and the weakness of exclusive ideological appeals. The major parties of a century and a half ago were not doctrinal, and neither are their counterparts today. In this regard, though, the U.S. parties now stand out much less than they did formerly in comparison to democratic parties elsewhere. All across Europe, for example, political parties are losing their once-sharp doctrinal distinctiveness.

The heterogeneous character of party coalitions in the United States has encouraged the parties to practice a politics of accommodation. American parties have been "creatures of compromise . . . vast, gaudy, friendly umbrellas under which all Americans, whoever and wherever and however minded they may be, are invited to stand for the sake of being counted in the next election."[4] Although the major American parties have not always successfully appealed to every group, our accommodationist two-party system has unquestionably

[4] Rossiter, *Parties and Politics in America* (Ithaca, N.Y.: Cornell Univeristy Press, 1960), p. 11.

"ACTUALLY, THEY REMIND ME OF THE CHOICE BETWEEN THE REPUBLICANS AND DEMOCRATS THIS YEAR."

encouraged a broadening of appeals and pun-ished failures to do so. The typical range of both Democratic and Republican support within various social groups has been between the 40 and 60 percent marks; a party's support from a given group is considered seriously weak when it falls below 40 percent.

LOOSE AND UNDEMANDING ALLIANCES

Throughout U.S. history the two major parties have not required very much of either their rank-and-file supporters or the elected officials who bear their names. A citizen's ties to an American party are rarely formal. The Demo-crats and the Republicans don't have regularly enrolled, card-carrying, and dues-paying mem-bers. There are no "official formalities" for admission, "no precise criteria of member-ship."[5] A voter becomes a Republican or a Democrat by a simple declaration, and he assumes no responsibilities when he makes

that declaration. To participáte in primary elections for selecting a party's candidates, vot-ers have at most to declare their affiliation at some specified time prior to the primary, and they may change their affiliation as they wish. "An American party," Clinton Rossiter wrote, "is not an army, not a church, not a way of life, not even a lodge. It asks nothing of one of its adherents but his vote, a few dollars, and, if he seems willing, a few hours of his time for manning the polls, licking stamps, and ringing doorbells; and it would settle willingly for a sure vote."[6] American parties are also unde-manding of the leaders who operate under their standards. The Democratic and Republi-can parties at both the national and state levels are undisciplined and lacking in internal cohe-sion by comparison to governmental parties in most other democracies.

Congressional Republicans and Democrats hold office not because of the blessings and assistance of national party leaders, but because of the work they and their supporters have

[5] Maurice Duverger, *Political Parties*, 2nd English ed. (London: Methuen, 1959), pp. 63–65.

[6] Rossiter, *Parties and Politics in America*, p. 25.

done in the districts they represent. Successful congressional candidates of both parties "did not rise through disciplined organizations," and thus "they are individualists from the beginning of their political careers. As candidates they were self-selected, self-organized, self-propelled, self-reliant. . . ."[7] In most party systems, for a member of the legislature to go against his party is to betray it. The American tradition is very different. From the earliest party experience in this country, voting independently and not being "beholden to party bosses" have been considered virtues. Few American legislators have ever lost their seats because they developed reputations for "flinty independence."

WEAK PARTY ORGANIZATIONS

In American political folklore, the activities of strong party organizations or "machines" are both celebrated and condemned. Such political figures as E. H. "Boss" Crump, who headed the Democratic machine in Memphis from 1932 to 1948, and Richard Daley, who led the strong Democratic organization in Chicago for a quarter-century until his death in 1976, are among the legendary party "bosses." They dominated the machinery of their political parties and maintained strangleholds on almost all aspects of the political life of their cities.

Strong party organizations have indeed existed at various times in different parts of the United States, especially in big cities when large numbers of immigrants were arriving. These party machines provided services to the newcomers, helping them find jobs and assisting them in bringing their problems to government agencies. In turn, the parties could count on followings that would loyally back their candidates.

[7]James Sundquist, "The Crisis of Competence in Our National Government," *Political Science Quarterly*, Summer 1980, p. 198.

But muscular party organizations have been the exception in the United States, not the rule. The strong current of political individualism throughout American culture generates resentment of strong party leadership. Our very vocabulary attests to this: Disciplined organizations are referred to as "machines" and their leaders depicted as undemocratic "bosses."

"Let the people, not the bosses, pick the candidates" seems to most Americans a natural position. But in other democracies no comparable perspective obtains. In Japan party candidates are chosen by the party hierarchy. Choosing candidates through primary elections has no appeal to most Japanese voters. In Great Britain, France, and Germany as well, control of nominations is thought by most voters to be properly a party affair. That the leadership of American party organizations does not decide on nominees—who are instead typically chosen in primaries—has meant that American parties are organizationally weaker than their counterparts in other democracies. Prospective nominees take their case directly to the voters; party officials have few sanctions over them. The Democrats and Republicans reflect durable loyalties; they have managed to hold their dominant place in electoral competition since the 1860s. Yet as organizations they are weak and undisciplined compared to most other major democratic parties.

PARTY REFORM

From time to time, campaigns have been mounted to "reform" American political parties. The goal has often been to make political parties more democratic. Early in this century direct primaries were introduced to weaken party "bosses" and give the rank and file a bigger role in the most important of all party functions: picking candidates for offices. Beginning in the late 1960s, the latest of the attempts at party reform concentrated on changing the way presidential nominees are selected. These efforts originated largely within the Democratic party.

The Democrats were deeply divided in 1968 between the wing that backed President Lyndon Johnson in his conduct of the Vietnam War and the bloc in the party that bitterly opposed him on this issue. The latter felt that nominating procedures unfairly benefited the party establishment under Johnson, who wanted Vice President Hubert Humphrey to succeed him. (Humphrey did win the 1968 Democratic nomination but was defeated by Republican Richard Nixon in the general election.)

Following their tumultuous 1968 presidential convention in Chicago, the Democrats established the McGovern-Fraser Commission to explore changes in the party's presidential nomination procedures and to recommend changes for the next nomination contest in 1972. This commission was chaired first by Senator George McGovern of South Dakota and later by Congressman Donald Fraser of Minnesota. Reporting to the Democratic National Committee (DNC) in 1971, McGovern-Fraser urged reform to advance *internal party democracy;* its achievement, the commission argued, would make the party more representative of the populace and thereby stronger and more competitive. It recommended that presidential delegates either be chosen by caucuses and conventions that are open to all party adherents, with delegates apportioned among the contending candidates through proportional representation, or that they be selected through primaries. If a state Democratic party insisted on permitting its central committee to play a role in choosing delegates to the national convention, it had to limit the number thus selected to 10 percent of the total. Forbidden was the practice whereby "certain public or party officeholders are delegates to county, state, and national conventions by virtue of their official position." That is, being a major party

official would no longer entitle anyone to a formal role in selecting the party's presidential nominee.

These new rules caused the proliferation of presidential primaries. A later party report noted in 1978 that "while the McGovern-Fraser Commission was neutral on the question of primaries, many state parties felt that a primary offered the most protection against a challenge at the next convention."[8] There were seventeen Democratic presidential primaries in 1968; the number rose to twenty-three in 1972 and to thirty in 1976. Less than half of all delegates to the 1968 Democratic convention had been chosen by primaries; nearly three-fourths of the 1976 Democratic delegates were thus selected. The new rules also weakened Democratic party organizations, as "state party organizations [took] *on more of an administrative role rather than a decision-making role in recent presidential nominations.*"[9] The Republicans showed little enthusiasm for the kinds of changes the Democrats were imposing. But the GOP nonetheless felt the impact of some of them, like the greater reliance on primaries, which were written into state law and were applied to both parties.

By the late 1970s, many Democrats were asserting that the McGovern-Fraser reforms actually weakened the party. Their concerns led to the appointment of another body to review the rules: the Commission on Presidential Nomination, chaired by Governor James B. Hunt of North Carolina. Early in 1982, the Hunt Commission reported to the DNC, which then approved new rules for 1984. One important change brought party officials back into the nomination process. About 550 seats were

[8] *Openness, Participation and Party Building: Reforms for a Strong Democratic Party*, report of the Commission on Presidential Nomination and Party Structure [the McGovern-Fraser Commission], 1978, Morley Winograd, chairman, p. 24.
[9] Ibid. Emphasis added.

allocated for *party* and *elected officials* as unpledged delegates. Some of these delegates, known as *superdelegates*, would be named by the House and Senate Democratic caucuses—with seats given to three-fifths of all congressional Democrats—and the balance would be named by state parties, giving priority to governors and big-city mayors. Unpledged delegate slots would also be reserved for each state's chair and vice-chair. Under the McGovern-Fraser rules, party leaders had been required to run for delegate seats like anyone else, something most of them would not do. It would be humiliating to lose, and winning might not be much better—since in the course of the contest they might anger an important group of constituents whose support they would need later.

The Hunt Commission designed other changes to increase the chances of a decisive outcome in the search for delegates as well. We will see later in the chapter that winner-take-all electoral systems encourage unambiguous electoral outcomes (clear winners and losers) while proportional representation—which allots seats in proportion to votes—may prevent anyone getting a majority. Hunt Commission rules led the Democrats away from the proportional representation in delegate selection introduced by the McGovern-Fraser Commission.

During convention preparations in 1988 the continuing Democratic struggle over rules for delegate selection took another turn. Candidate Jesse Jackson and his supporters sought major changes in the rules, cutting back the superdelegates—who had given him little support in 1988—and relying on a strictly proportional scheme for delegate selection—so that, for instance, 10 percent of the primary vote would yield 10 percent of the delegates. Frontrunner Michael Dukakis had the votes on the convention's Rules Committee to block Jackson's initiatives, but he decided to place harmony in 1988 over preservation of the rules that many party leaders had thought worked well. The number of superdelegates was cut by 250, and winner-take-all delegate selection arrangements were banned completely.

CHARACTERISTICS OF THE AMERICAN ELECTORAL SYSTEM

The formal structure of elections—the arrangements under which votes are cast and tallied—often exerts considerable influence over election outcomes. And no set of electoral mechanics is politically neutral. The single-member district, simple-majority electoral system used by the United States leads to results different in important regards from those encouraged by systems built around plural-member districts and proportional representation.

TRANSLATING VOTES INTO SEATS

Perhaps the most important single feature of an electoral system is the way it translates the votes people cast into the election of legislators and other office holders. Consider a hypothetical example. Votersland is a small country with 1,000,000 registered voters and three political parties. The Liberty party is backed by 40 percent of the people, the Equality party by 30 percent, and the Brotherhood party by 30 percent. Votersland held its 1986 national election under an arrangement where the country was divided into 100 districts, each with 10,000 electors. The party winning the most votes in each had its candidate chosen as the district's representative. Since the Liberty party's 40 percent was evenly distributed across the country (as were the votes of its rivals), it had a plurality in every district. Thus the results were:

Liberty   100 seats
Equality   0 seats
Brotherhood   0 seats

As would be expected, there was a storm of protest. A party with just 40 percent of the popular vote had, in a free and open election, gained all the seats. Bowing to demands for electoral change, the legislature proceeded to rewrite the law. The new statute provided that no candidate would be declared the winner unless he or she received over 50 percent of the vote. If no one did, there would be a runoff election between the two candidates with the highest totals in the first round.

The 1988 elections were conducted under these new rules. The total popular vote was exactly the same as in 1986, but this time it meant no one was elected in the first round. The Liberty party had 40 percent in each district, more than its rivals but not a majority. Before the second round, the Equality and Brotherhood parties reached an arrangement whereby the one of them coming in third (and thus disqualified for the second round) in a district would throw its support to the other. In half the districts this was Equality, in half Brotherhood. Voters followed their leaders' wishes, and when the second-round votes were tallied, the results in half the districts were Liberty 0 seats, Brotherhood 0 seats, Equality 50 seats. In the other half, the final tally read Liberty 0, Equality 0, Brotherhood 50.

With no shift in the popular vote, representation of the Liberty backers fell from 100 to 0. Naturally, protests again erupted, and once more the rules were changed. This time the districts were abolished, and representatives were elected on the basis of the distribution of the partisan vote nationally. Each party submitted a list of 100 candidates, with the understanding that a percentage of them would be declared elected exactly in proportion to the party's share of the popular vote. These new rules were tried in the 1990 elections. The popular vote was distributed as in the two previous contests. This meant that the first 40 candidates on Liberty's list were elected, the first 30 on Equality's, and the first 30 on Brotherhood's.

The Votersland example is obviously contrived, assuming such things as the popular vote being evenly distributed across an entire country and not changing from one election to the next. But the example is revealing. It shows how in perfectly free elections very different results can be obtained just by changing electoral mechanics. Variants of the three sets of rules used in the example are actually found in democratic countries around the world.

SINGLE-MEMBER DISTRICTS

The United States conducts most of its elections under a single-member district, simple-majority, single-ballot system. Elections for seats in the U.S. House of Representatives, the Senate, state legislatures, for governorships, and for many other offices fit within this general order. In a **single-member district** system the area covered by the election—the entire United States in the case of House of Representatives elections, a given state for state legislative contests—is carved into a series of districts, each of which elects a single representative. In contrast, many countries employ systems with **plural-member districts**—where a single constituency chooses more than one representative. The United States has some plural-member district elections—for example, in cities where the entire council or board of aldermen is chosen by voters at large rather than in single-member council or aldermanic districts. But single-member districts are the rule. The American arrangement is also a **simple-majority** and **single-ballot** system: The candidate who gets the most votes in his district is awarded the seat on the basis of a single casting of

Voting—a basic hallmark of democracy.

ballots. The alternative is an absolute-majority requirement, where the winner must not only get more votes than any rival but must get more than 50 percent of all ballots cast. This requires, in some instances, recourse to a second ballot or runoff election between the two highest contenders.

Some other countries operate with this single-member district, simple-majority arrangement, but they are confined largely to the English-speaking world. Britain is the political progenitor of this system. A majority of the world's democracies—including Italy, Germany, Sweden, Israel, and Japan—count votes and award seats through some form of plural-member districts with **proportional representation** (PR). In such systems representatives are chosen from districts in which more than one candidate is elected. In Norway, for example, in 1980, 155 seats in the national legislature were spread over 20 voting constituencies; in Japan, 511 seats were allocated among 130 constituencies; and in the Netherlands, all 150

seats in the lower house of the national legislature were elected from a single constituency: the entire nation. The idea of PR is to divide seats among the contending parties in proportion to the percentage of the vote won by each of the parties. In theory, if a party receives 27 percent of the vote in a given legislative election, under PR it should get about 27 percent of the seats. The particular electoral mechanics employed under PR vary; some come closer than others to an exact link of vote and seat proportion. But the underlying idea is always the same. For PR to work, you must have plural-member districts, and you must then divide the seats among the contending parties in proportion to their percentages of the votes cast.

Is the simple-majority system, as it operates in U.S. elections, basically unfair because it typically gives the winning party more seats than its share of the popular vote would suggest? Not necessarily. If an exact ratio of votes to seats is the goal, the U.S. arrangements are obviously flawed. But by another standard for assessing systems of representation, elections are vehicles for choosing a government by the principle of majority rule. Absolute proportionality in votes won and seats gained is not universally held essential to that end. In fact, sometimes proportionality makes it hard to form a coherent government. A common criticism of PR is that it fractures legislatures by producing such a mix of parties that governing is difficult. The purer the form of PR, the more likely fracturing will occur. The price of the fairness of a pure system of PR may be prolonged governmental instability.[10] If elections are seen as means for gaining "an ideological census, a declaration of the voters' fundamental position on the left-right spectrum," as British political

scientist David Butler puts it, there is much to be said for a pure PR arrangement, since the legislature should be a direct reflection of the proportional party preferences of the electorate. But if the goal is seen as one of choosing "viable governments" and giving such governments legitimacy, Butler suggests, the single-member system may be better. He argues that "a clear answer may be better for the country than a mathematically exact one. . . . A legislature that is a perfect mirror of what the electorate felt on one particular polling day may not be as satisfactory a basis for effective government as one that offers a cruder but more decisive reflection of majority trends."[11]

PRIMARY ELECTIONS

As discussed above, American electoral arrangements generally included **primary elections** for choosing party nominees. State gov-

[10] David Butler, "Electorial System," in David Butler, Howard R. Penniman, and Austin Ranny, eds. *Democracy at the Polls: A Comparative Study of Competitive National Elections* (Washington, D.C.: American Enterprise Institute for Public Policy Research, 1981), p. 19.

[11] Ibid., pp. 22–23.

One view of the 1992 presidential primary.

ernments supervise all facets of these primaries, including the printing of ballots. The direct primary in the United States developed early in the twentieth century and was effectively promoted by the Progressives (see chapter 4, pp. 85–86). They argued that leaving the choice of candidates to the party "bosses" was undemocratic and that the fullest participation of the rank and file in candidate choice was desirable. American individualism provided fertile soil for this appeal.

Primaries are now widely used to pick delegates to the national parties' presidential nominating conventions. In 1992, 37 states employed primaries, although in several of these states, they applied to only one party. Historically, presidential primaries have come in a number of varieties: primaries that actually elect delegates to the national conventions and those that merely give voters an opportunity to express their preferences (so-called beauty contests), advisory to some party committee or convention that chooses the delegates; primaries that bind the delegates to support, for at least one ballot, the nominee for whom they were pledged at the time of the primary and those that pick delegates who are then free to exercise their own preferences at the national convention. Today, most presidential primaries bind delegates for the first convention ballot.

CHANGES IN STRUCTURE OF ELECTIONS: REAPPORTIONMENT

Every ten years the United States conducts a national census, after which the boundaries of legislative districts are redrawn to take into account population shifts. Sometimes the needed overhaul of district lines is very substantial. In California, for example, the adjustment of congressional seats and districts following the 1990 census involved the state's gaining 7 additional seats: California now has

52 members in the U.S. House of Representatives, compared to 45 during the 1980s. Adding 7 new districts required, of course, major changes in the boundaries of many of the existing districts. Figure 12.1 shows the shifts in House seats for all fifty states, based on the 1990 census. Since population continues to move south and west, so, too, do House seats.

Reapportionment often entails a big political battle. Incumbent members of Congress try to make sure the political complexion of the new district in which they will run is not drawn in a way that hurts their electoral chances. Even more, the Republican and Democratic parties struggle to get district boundaries that give their candidates the best chances overall.

There are limits on what the parties can do to work reapportionment in their favor, however. The Supreme Court ruled in the landmark case of *Baker v. Carr* (1962) that the inequitability of legislative districts can be subjected to judicial standards and remedies under the equal protection clause of the Fourteenth Amendment. In the flurry of cases that fol-

Elkanah Tisdale's 1812 depiction of the redrawn districts in Massachusetts as fearsome gerrymander.

FIGURE 12.1   ALLOCATION OF SEATS IN HOUSE OF REPRESENTATIVES FOLLOWING THE 1990 CENSUS

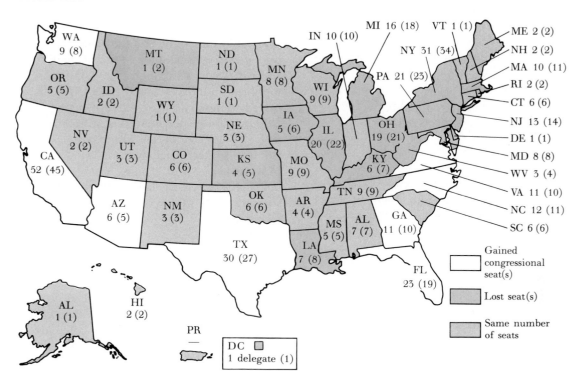

Source: U.S. Bureau of the Census, *Total Institutional Population by State, 1990 and 1980.*

lowed *Baker,* the court enlarged upon and implemented its new policy. In *Wesberry v. Sanders* (1963), Justice Hugo Black, speaking for the majority, held that "the command of Article I, section 2, that representatives be chosen 'by the people of the several states' means that as nearly as is practicable, one man's vote in a congressional election is to be worth as much as another's." And in *Reynolds v. Sims* (1964), Chief Justice Earl Warren, writing for the majority, held that

> the right of suffrage can be denied by a debasement of suffrage or dilution of the weight of a citizen's vote just as effectively as by wholly prohibiting the free exercise of the franchise. . . .

Legislators represent people, not trees or acres. Legislators are elected by voters, not farms or cities or economic interests. . . . The Equal Protection clause requires that the seats in both houses of a bicameral state legislature must be apportioned on a population basis.

Nonetheless, the **gerrymander**—which means district lines drawn for gross partisan advantage—is by no means dead.[12] Districts do have

[12] The term "gerrymander" refers to Massachusetts governor Elbridge Gerry, who in 1811 signed a reapportionment bill designed to help the Democratic Republican party and weaken the Federalists. The governor's plan included a weird-looking district that resembled some mythical dragon—today, everyone's vision of a gerrymander.

to be equal in population. But advances in computers and census technologies give party strategists all kinds of tools to rearrange districts subtly for advantages that are relatively small but possibly just enough to make the difference between winning and losing.

TRANSFORMATIONS OF THE PARTY COALITIONS

Clearly, the type of political party the United States has and the electoral system in which our parties compete show great continuity. But the shape of partisan competition has been greatly changed over the last quarter-century. Elements of such change are often referred to as **realignment.**

Let's imagine a political Rip Van Winkle who falls into a deep sleep just after Franklin Roosevelt's presidency and wakes up in the early 1990s. He finds that white southerners, who had stood so solidly behind FDR (and all preceding Democrats back to the Civil War), have moved substantially into the Republican camp—so much so that presidential strategists now start with the assumption that the South is the GOP's best region. He finds black voters now overwhelmingly Democratic and a major component of that party's national coalition. When Rip fell asleep New England was, as it had long been, the most Republican region. Now it's the least Republican. Young voters were the Democrats' best group in the New Deal years. Now the young are the Republicans' best age group.

REPUBLICAN GAINS

Group alignments have certainly shifted. So, too, has the party balance. The GOP has strengthened itself in its share of party loyalties. The last half-century shows the Republicans at first severely weakened by the experiences of the Depression decade. They reasserted themselves in the latter half of the 1940s and 1950s but, even in the Eisenhower years, they did not reverse the pattern that saw the Democrats beating them in the contest for support among new voters. The GOP fell further back in the 1960s and early 1970s, hammered by their disastrous defeat in the 1964 election, by the Vietnam War turmoil of the early 1970s, and by the Watergate scandals. From this post-Watergate nadir, the party climbed back up to achieve basic parity with the Democrats. In the late 1980s, the GOP was stronger than at any time since the Great Depression.

This chronicle of Republican ups and downs should remind us forcefully of two things: First, the partisan balance of power has been far from stable over the last half-century. It has changed significantly on several occasions. Second, while underlying group attachments to the parties evolve slowly, the mix of current events, policies, and candidates is capable of moving each party's backing well above or below its base-line support. Current political conditions matter: Republican and Democratic strength in most social groups rises and falls, as the case may be, depending on such factors as the attractiveness of presidential candidates and how things seem to be going in the country.

Party identification is the standard U.S. measure of underlying partisan strength. As they developed the profession during the 1930s, George Gallup, Elmo Roper, and other founders of polling recognized that they couldn't ask most people which party they "belonged to," because most Americans don't belong to political parties in the sense of holding formal membership and paying dues. We become Republicans and Democrats by *thinking of ourselves* as adherents of one party or the other. So Gallup began asking: "Do you *regard yourself* as a Republican, a Democrat, a Socialist, or an independent in politics?" Variations of this basic question, emphasizing *identification* rather than *membership*, have been widely used over the last half-century.

The exact proportions of Americans identifying themselves as Democrats and Republicans vary from one survey to another. In the spring of 1992, for example, some polls showed the two parties with exactly the same shares—about one-third each—of party identification, while others showed the Democrats ahead by a few points. But all polls find the Republicans having made substantial gains since the 1970s. (See, for example, the year-to-year results on party identification from the surveys conducted by CBS News and the *New York Times* in Figure 12.2).

Whatever their precise mix, party loyalties have weakened for much of the U.S. electorate—a subject we will discuss later in this chapter. More and more voters are prepared to cast their presidential ballots for the candidate and party they see most likely to advance various policies and objectives. American elections increasingly hinge on perceptions of current performance or capability rather than traditional loyalties rooted in such matters as regional and ethnic experience. On the question of which party does the better job managing the economy and keeping the country prosperous, the Democrats gained a huge advantage during the New Deal years. This advantage persisted beyond Franklin D. Roosevelt's presidency.

FIGURE 12.2   PARTY IDENTIFICATION, 1976–92 (IN PERCENT)

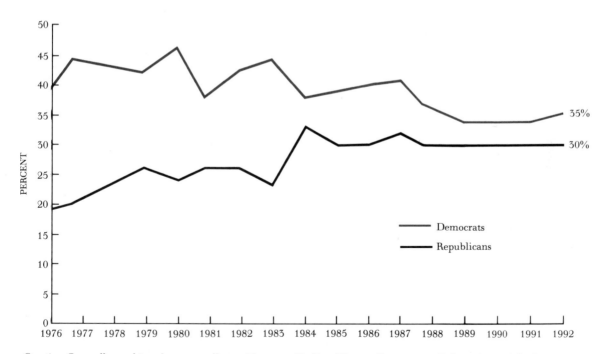

Question: Generally speaking, do you usually consider yourself a Republican, a Democrat, an Independent, or what?
Source: Combined surveys done by CBS News / *New York Times* in each year. The 1992 data are based on polls taken only in the first five months of the year, January through May.

FIGURE 12.3   WHICH PARTY IS BEST FOR PROSPERITY? (PERCENTAGE OF PUBLIC SAYING EACH PARTY)

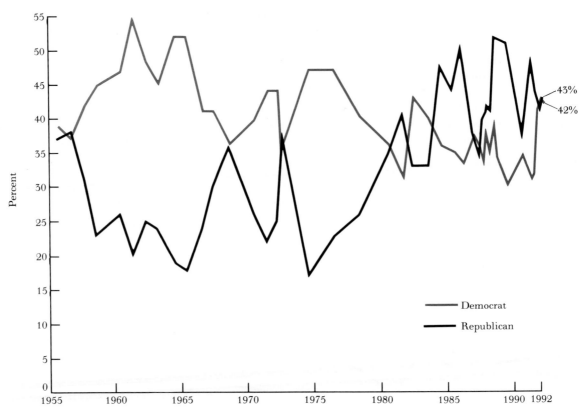

Question: Looking ahead to the next few years, which political party—the Republicans or the Democrats—do you think will do the better job of keeping the country prosperous?

Source: Gallup polls of dates shown. I have shown one set of responses in each year the question was asked from 1955 through 1986—except in 1972 when I showed two sets of responses, because the question got a very different response early in the year than it did at election time. I have shown every set of responses since January of 1987. The difference between the Democratic and Republican percentages shown and 100 percent are accounted for by respondents who said "no difference" or "no opinion."

Asked in March 1947 which party they preferred to have in office "if hard times come again," 51 percent of those interviewed by the Gallup Organization named the Democrats, just 30 percent the Republicans. Fifty-four percent in this survey credited the Democrats with being better able to keep wages high; only 22 percent credited the Republicans with superior ability in this category.

Near the end of Dwight Eisenhower's first term, the GOP had drawn even with the Democrats in terms of the proportion seeing it likely to "do better keeping the country prosperous." It couldn't hold this position, though, and by the end of Eisenhower's presidency a substantial plurality of Americans again credited the Democrats with being the party of prosperity. Figure 12.3 shows that the Democrats maintained this status through virtually all of the ensuing two decades, often by overwhelming margins. In the 1980s, however, the Republicans caught up with the Democrats on this key performance measure. Surveys asking which party is better at keeping the U.S. economy healthy have given the Republicans a clear edge. for most of the period since 1984, although the Democrats came back on this measure during the recession of the early 1990s.

Today's public makes a complex set of distinctions about partisan capabilities or performance, preferring the Republicans in some important areas and the Democrats in others. In general, pluralities credit the GOP with doing a better job handling foreign affairs, maintaining a strong defense, and curbing inflation. The Democrats are seen as stronger on controlling defense spending, addressing unemployment, extending social services, and helping those in need.

UP FOR GRABS

A shift in the partisan balance need not involve the creation of a new majority. We see this historically with the emergence of the Republican party. The GOP became a major party at the time of the Civil War, but for the next thirty years—up until the mid-1890s—it operated in rough parity with the Democrats.

Today each of the two major parties has its strongholds. The Republicans have done especially well in presidential balloting. They were victorious in five of the six presidential elections between 1968 and 1988, gaining 55 percent of the total two-party vote over this span. After winning narrowly in 1968, the GOP's victory margins have been 23 percentage points in 1972, 10 points in 1980, 18 points in 1984, and 8 points in 1988. The one election the Democrats won, 1976, is in a sense the most graphic confirmation of the GOP's ascendancy: Jimmy Carter and the Democrats managed

only the narrowest win in 1976, even though the Republican party had been decimated by the massive Watergate scandals that culminated in the forced resignation of a Republican president, Richard Nixon. The Republican presidential margins of the last quarter-century are large by any historic comparison. They are comparable to those the Democrats achieved during the New Deal elections (1932–48) and to the Republicans' own presidential ascendancy from 1896 through 1928. Still, the Democrats' overall position has remained strong. They have enjoyed a majority in the House of Representatives continuously since 1955. In the 1990 voting, they renewed their decisive legislative majorities at both the national and state levels, winning 267 of the 435 House seats, holding 56 of 100 in the Senate, and 60 percent of all seats in the state legislatures.

Some observers explain these split results in terms of Americans' liking for separation of powers and checks and balances. If the direction the Republicans propose for national policy is to be encouraged by the election of Republican presidents, isn't some check on it useful in Congress and the State houses? Besides, many people are ambivalent about the role of government and other central policy issues. What better way to express their mixed feelings than by ordaining divided party control?

Such factors have undoubtedly been at work. But they are almost certainly not the main reason why the results of congressional elections have diverged so sharply from those of presidential elections. As we saw in chapter 6, voting for the House of Representatives hinges much more on the advantages of incumbency than on decisions to back one party's programs over the other's. Members of Congress now have large staffs and other resources of incumbency useful in advancing their reelection. Gaining high levels of name recognition and emphasizing their nonpartisan service to constituents, they can often divorce their own electoral fortunes from those of their parties' presidential nominees. In addition, incumbents frequently are able to outspend their challengers by substantial margins. Congressional incumbents of both parties enjoy a big edge over their challengers in campaign finance partly because many interest groups have a proclivity for backing incumbents—with whom they deal in pressing their various policy objectives. The Democrats entered the modern period with a big edge in congressional seats, and the advantages of incumbency have been theirs more than the Republicans'.

The United States simply does not have a majority party at present, and this condition may persist. Probably never as stable as it was once thought to be, party identification has shown a great deal of movement lately. In the television age, changes in the mix of issues, events, and leadership seem to have the potential for causing more rapid shifts in party fortunes than ever before.

Even more importantly, voting along party lines has greatly declined. That is, the proportion of the electorate prepared to support one party or the other across the board, in all offices, has dropped off sharply from what it was in times past. Voting for the man or woman who is running for the office, rather than for the party, has become the rule. Ticket splitting has reached massive proportions. In this context, the traditional concept of a "majority party" has been put in doubt.

DEALIGNMENT

This weakening of voter loyalties to political parties is sometimes called **dealignment.** As we saw above, the contemporary electorate is less anchored today than throughout most of American history. A dealigned electorate is like an unanchored boat—it can be easily moved. American voters are highly volatile, moving

this way and that over the course of a campaign and from one campaign to another. This does not mean that large numbers of voters will be in a state of flux every campaign. But the weak party loyalties characteristic of the contemporary electorate leave it inherently more volatile or changeable than electorates used to be.

Discussions of the progress of electoral dealignment typically emphasize two broad sources: the *sociological* and the *political-institutional.* The sociological explanation notes that an affluent, leisured, highly educated public no longer perceives the need for political parties as intermediary institutions to the degree that less-educated and less-secure publics did in the past. The political-institutional explanation stresses the deterioration of political party organizations, producing a situation where increasingly ineffective party bodies give voters scant reason to back them strongly. It also notes that other institutions, especially the national communications media and the welfare state, have assumed functions that parties once performed.

While these factors are important, another key precipitant of dealignment has received little attention: Large segments of the American public have become so ambivalent about the proper course of public policy that they are unable to give a clear endorsement to the competing positions of the parties. Today, Democrats and Republicans offer contrasting approaches that probably are as distinct as at any time in the past, but most voters do not feel confident about either set of partisan answers. We discussed this ambivalence in chapter 10 (pp. 290–92). With regard to the role of government, many voters are of mixed minds. They do not see any alternative to government's doing a lot, but they are clearly dissatisfied with its recent performance. Not certain just what course they actually favor, many Americans have been reluctant to give strong and unequivocal support to either party.

CHANGING GROUP ALIGNMENTS

While party allegiance has weakened, most voters still identify themselves with one major party or the other. How do these attachments form? Individuals generally gain a frame of reference from the decisive events of the period when they first come to political consciousness—usually in their late teens or early twenties—which then shape their subsequent values and actions.[13] Of course, rich and poor youth, factory workers and college students, blacks and whites, men and women may experience their generational scene in different ways. Still, whatever the specific generational unit, the early political values are likely to continue to influence the group's outlook even many years in the future.

GENERATIONAL EXPERIENCES

Our discussion of the formation of partisan attachments permits us to refine the idea of political generations and apply it specifically to changes in party strength in the United States. A group comes of age politically at a time when certain political leaders are on the stage. These leaders are not viewed in the same way by everyone, of course, but some are decidedly more respected and popular than others. Sometimes these ascendant politicians are Republicans and sometimes they are Democrats. For new voters without a lot of past political experience, the impressions gained from this powerful first personal exposure to political

leaders may be very important. Similarly, a distinctive mix of issues dominates political argument as these new voters come of age politically; if the mix generally favors one party over the other—as was the case in the 1930s when the Democrats were developing new programs and initiatives—the impact on people without much previous personal political experience is apt to be substantial. As the group ages, it begins to have new and sometimes conflicting political experiences—but these are filtered through an established pattern of party loyalties that are likely to persist, unless and until the mix of new experiences produces a sustained break.

Do available data support this interpretation? Let's begin by looking at the party preferences of different age groups in the United States as shown by Gallup surveys taken in 1952 and in 1992 (Table 12.1). The first thing we see is a striking difference in the party preferences of the age groups now as compared to forty years ago. In 1952 the Democrats' best group were the young and middle-aged, while the Republicans had large leads among the more elderly voters. In 1991–92, however, the Republicans were strongest among the young, while the Democrats had their greatest strength among people in their sixties and seventies.

Let's translate these data more directly into the frame of generational experience, showing groups by the time when they came of age politically rather than by current age. "Coming of age politically" will be expressed here as reaching eighteen years of age, which seems adequate as a rough standard. Looking at Table 12.2, we see a broad array of groups, from those who reached eighteen way back in the early 1890s—who were still part of the electorate in 1952—to people who only reached voting age in the last few years. Using both the 1952 and the 1991–92 surveys extends the range of our generational examination. Some groups are represented in both the 1952 and the 1992

[13] See Karl Mannheim, *Ideology and Utopia* (New York: Harcourt, Brace, 1936); idem, "The Sociological Problem of Generations," in *Essays on the Sociology of Knowledge* (New York: Oxford University Press, 1952), pp. 276–322; Sigmund Neumann, *Permanent Revolution* (New York: Harper and Brothers, 1942); Rudolf Herbele, *Social Movements* (New York: Appleton-Century-Crofts, 1951).

TABLE 12.1 PARTY IDENTIFICATION BY AGE, 1952 AND 1991–92 (IN PERCENT)

| | 1952 | | | 1991–92 | | | Democratic minus Republican | |
Age	D	R	I	D	R	I	1952	1991–92
18–21	40	25	35	28	34	38	+15	−7
22–25	42	27	31	27	35	38	+15	−8
26–29	43	26	31	28	38	35	+17	−10
30–33	45	26	29	28	36	35	+19	−8
34–37	43	29	28	30	34	36	+14	−4
38–41	45	30	26	32	30	38	+15	−2
42–45	38	36	25	27	32	40	+2	−5
46–49	39	36	25	30	30	40	+3	0
50–53	42	32	25	35	32	33	+10	+3
54–57	39	38	24	37	31	32	+1	+6
58–61	41	37	21	36	32	32	+4	+4
62–65	39	39	22	36	36	27	0	0
66–69	37	45	18	41	32	27	−8	+9
70–73	40	43	17	42	33	25	−3	+9
74–77	36	49	14	40	35	25	−13	+5
78–81	34	50	16	42	39	19	−16	+3
82 and over	31	57	12	41	40	19	−26	+1
All ages	41	33	26	33	34	33	+8	−1

Source: Gallup polls conducted April through July 1952 (seven) and October 1991 through May 1992 (eight).

polls. Those who were just coming of political age in 1952 are now in their late fifties.

The relative standing of the major parties varies substantially across generational groups in a fashion that corresponds in rough terms to what we know of decisive political experiences. For example, both the 1952 and 1991–92 Gallup polls show the Democrats' margin over the Republicans highest among those who came of age politically at the height of the Democrats' New Deal ascendancy. Since static enters into polling and poll responses, it is especially impressive that the picture provided by the two batches of surveys separated by forty years is so consistent.

People who reached political maturity in the late 1930s and early 1940s were in 1952 unusually pro-Democratic—and so they are today. Republicans had a big edge in the 1890s, but they began to lose this among new voters coming of age in the early twentieth century— reflecting in part the impact immigration had on the makeup of the population. In the 1930s the Democrats began to achieve an overwhelming generational advantage over the Republicans, which was not interrupted until the late 1950s when various developments, among them Dwight Eisenhower's personal popularity, cut into the Democrats' edge among new voters. Over the last decade and a half the GOP has steadily pulled ahead among new voters. The new Republican margin among those who came of voting age in the late 1980s is quite large.

These data help us understand why in recent years no dramatic overall swing to the Republicans has occurred in party identification, though the Democrats' position has dimin-

TABLE 12.2 PARTY IDENTIFICATION BY YEARS OF COMING OF VOTING AGE, 1952 AND 1991–92

Years coming of voting age	1952 Data		1991–92 Data	
	% Republican	% Democratic minus % Republican	% Democratic minus % Republican	% Republican
1890–93	63	− 26		
1894–97	54	− 8		
1898–1901	51	− 2		
1902–05	54	− 8		
1906–09	49	+ 2		
1910–13	48	+ 4		
1914–17	47	+ 6		
1918–21	46	+ 8		
1922–25	48	+ 4		
1926–29	46	+ 8		
1930–33	41	+ 18	+ 12	44
1934–37	39	+ 22	+ 7	46
1938–41	37	+ 26	+ 10	45
1942–45	39	+ 22	+ 11	44
1946–49	39	+ 22	+ 5	53
1950–53			+ 11	44
1954–57			+ 9	46
1958–61			+ 1	49
1962–65			− 3	52
1966–69			− 2	51
1970–73			− 5	52
1974–77			− 7	53
1978–81			− 15	57
1982–85			− 13	56
1986–89			− 18	59
1990–92			− 5	52

Since the object of this table is to focus on the relative Republican versus Democratic strength in each generation, independents have been excluded from the calculations. To take an example of how the data should be read, among those who reached 18 years of age in the 1986–89 span, who identify with one or the other major party, 59 percent are Republican (and 41 percent Democratic). Subtracting the percentage Republican from the percentage Democratic, one gets − 18, the figure shown in the table.
Source: 1952 and 1991–92 Gallup polls.

ished. The Democrats put together a long string where they bested the Republicans among new voters, and they continue to reap the benefits: People who came of age politically from the 1930s through the 1960s remain a large part of the electorate, and the impressive Democratic base built among these age groups has by no means been obliterated. In recent years, the Republicans have reversed the trend among new entrants; should they continue to have this success, they will in time shift the underlying partisan base in their favor. Generational replacement continues to occur, with older groups dying and new ones entering the electorate. But the Democrats, while down from their once clear ascendance, still have a lot of generational capital.

GROUP CONVERSIONS

Their attachments thus set, these groups move slowly through the generational pipeline. The total of the different generational experiences among groups in the electorate at a given point is a major component of overall party strength, because party identification once formed persists. A party does best in its current share of party loyalties when it has its largest number of favorable generational groups still in the electorate. The Democrats were especially far ahead of the Republicans in the mid- to late 1970s, even though at that time they were not doing nearly as well as they had at earlier points in attracting new voters. They were living off their generational capital. Conversely, in the late 1930s and 1940s the Democrats had done very well in attracting new voters, but their lead over the Republicans among all voters was relatively modest because pre–New Deal (and more Republican) age groups were still a major part of the electorate.

Base-line strength is determined in part by the mix of generational groups in the pipeline at any time. Current political and economic experience then moves each party above or below its base line. For example, if the Republicans control the presidency and the economy is booming, their share of party loyalties across most groups will rise; conversely, their share of party loyalties will fall when the party is in power during a recession. But a party enlarges its base only slowly, by attracting disproportionate numbers of new voters entering the electorate.

There are exceptions to this process. On rare occasions, a party manages to convert quickly large numbers of people of all ages in a social group—when the policies it supports are especially and unambiguously attractive to the group or, conversely, when the other party's policies are seen as exceptionally unsatisfactory.

BLACK AMERICANS AND THE DEMOCRATIC PARTY

The shift of blacks to the Democratic party, first in the 1930s and then in the 1960s, is a case in point. This was no gradual shift in support through generational replacement. The New Deal experience had brought blacks into the Democratic party in large numbers. Through 1960, however, a substantial proportion, especially of older blacks, retained their attachments to the GOP—because of old memories of the Republicans as the party of Lincoln and because much of the Democratic party in the South was so strongly associated with policies of white supremacy.

The presidential election of 1964 was a critical one in the black community. The Johnson administration had committed itself to carrying forward the civil rights revolution, while the Republicans, through the 1964 presidential candidacy of Barry Goldwater, were seen aligning with resistance to racial change. A massive, immediate partisan swing occurred. Since 1964 Republican support in the black community has been very weak.

Moreover, party differences among blacks by age, sex, education, income, region, and so on, are small. For example, the Democrats' margin over the Republicans among those with less than high school educations in 1988 was almost exactly the same as among black college graduates. Black Americans differ substantially in many important interests, outlooks, and values; this ethnic group is far from homogeneous. When it comes to party choice, though, most blacks prefer the Democrats over the Republicans. Individual GOP candidates have managed to attract large numbers of black votes. For example, Thomas Kean, the Republican incumbent running for reelection, apparently won over half the black vote in the 1985 New Jersey gubernatorial election. But overall, black voters have since the mid-1960s backed Democratic candidates overwhelmingly.

As a result, blacks are a very large part of the Democratic coalition—especially in major cities and in the South, where they are large parts of the total population. Reflecting this strength, black Democrats are moving into more and more leadership posts in the party. The current Democratic national chairman, Ronald Brown, is black. In 1989, the Democrats nominated blacks, for the first time, for mayor of New York City and governor of Virginia. Both—David Dinkins in New York and Douglas Wilder in Virginia—won their elections. In 1990, blacks received the Democratic nominations for U.S. senator in North Carolina and governor in South Carolina—also firsts and an extraordinary shift from conditions just a few decades ago, when white segregationists dominated many southern Democratic parties.

HISPANIC AMERICANS' PARTY PREFERENCES

The story is quite different for Hispanic Americans—showing the danger in referring sweepingly to the preferences of "minority groups." Hispanics and blacks are both groups that have experienced discrimination and that are composed disproportionately of people less well-off than the national average. But they have had different historical and cultural experiences, and their party loyalties are different.

Moreover, the Hispanic communities in the United States are several rather than one. Those living in the South Atlantic states, especially Florida, are heavily represented by people who left Cuba after Fidel Castro came to power. This group is as firmly Republican as the Mex-

ican-American populations of the Southwest and Pacific Coast states are Democratic. Furthermore, among Hispanic Americans, socioeconomic status is highly correlated with party preference: The Democrats are much stronger among those with low than those with high incomes. Overall, the Democrats have a clear margin among Hispanics—15 percentage points in the 1991–92 Gallup data—but the Republicans are still very much in the running.

WHITE SOUTHERNERS AND THE REPUBLICAN PARTY

In the last half-century there have been only two cases of "critical group conversion"—where an entire social group swings decisively from one party to the other. As we have seen, the shift of blacks to the Democrats is one; the

THE RETURN TO TARA

THE ONCE SOLID SOUTH

2/11/87

move of white southerners to the Republicans is the other. As late as 1965 the Democrats had a lead of about 36 percentage points in party identification among white southerners, according to Gallup data. This margin eroded gradually from the late 1960s through the early 1980s. Since the mid-1980s, it has vanished altogether. According to Gallup surveys, southern whites were more Republican than Democratic by a margin of 6 percent in 1991–92. The shift has been especially great among young voters, who came of age politically at a time when the mix of race, economic policy, and candidates pushed so strongly in a Republican direction. During the Eisenhower years, young (18–24) whites throughout the South were

overwhelmingly Democratic. Not even the slightest erosion of the historic group attachments could be seen. Today the youngest white southerners are decisively Republican.

RELIGIOUS GROUPS AND THE PARTIES

Dramatic when they occur, sweeping conversions of the kind we have seen for blacks and southern whites are rare. Much more common are group shifts that involve the gradual erosion of once-strong party ties and the establishment of new ones, as succeeding generations of group members come of age in a social and political environment different from what group

TABLE 12.3   PARTY IDENTIFICATION BY RELIGIOUS AND ETHNOCULTURAL BACKGROUND
(PERCENT REPUBLICANS—LEFT COLUMN EACH YEAR—AND PERCENT DEMOCRAT MINUS REPUBLICAN—
RIGHT COLUMN EACH YEAR)

	1947		1952		1955		1960		1965	
Protestants	Religion		36	+ 5	35	+ 7	36	+ 8	29	+19
Catholics	not		22	+28	26	+22	20	+36	13	+54
Jews	asked		13	+39	10	+48	9	+58	8	+54
Northern white Protestants	in 1947		44	−14	44	−12	46	−13	41	− 5
Northern white Catholics			23	+25	28	+19	21	+33	14	+52
Southern white Protestants			17	+49	22	+37	20	+44	20	+32
Blacks	34	+ 9	20	+35	18	+44	25	+28	9	+70
All respondents	35	+ 7	33	+ 8	32	+12	31	+16	24	+28

	1970		1975		1979		1984		1991–92	
Protestants	34	+ 5	25	+18	28	+15	31	+10	37	− 3
Catholics	21	+31	13	+39	16	+33	24	+21	32	+ 1
Jews	5	+57	8	+50	10	+45	13	+47	23	+24
Northern white Protestants	44	−13	33	− 1	37	− 7	39	−11	42	−15
Northern white Catholics	22	+28	15	+37	16	+31	24	+19	32	+ 1
Southern white Protestants	27	+16	22	+24	25	+20	29	+15	40	− 6
Blacks	9	+67	5	+68	8	+66	5	+74	8	+51
All respondents	29	+14	21	+24	23	+21	28	+14	34	− 1

Source: Gallup polls in the years shown.

members had experienced historically. The case of Catholics and Protestants is a fairly typical one (Table 12.3).

The ethnic diversity of the United States was extended throughout the late nineteenth and early twentieth centuries by heavy immigration from eastern, central, and southern Europe. This inevitably made for continuing ethnic conflict, much of it organized around Protestant and Catholic lines. Whereas the earlier British, Irish, and other Northern European immigrants had been heavily Protestant, later immigrants were much more heavily Roman Catholic and Jewish. Tensions generated by this religious change got sorted out along partisan lines. Outside the South where a different source for party loyalties pertained, Republicans became the party of older stock Protestants, the Democrats of newer stock Catholics. Differences in style and culture, and in policy interests, often left the partisan split between Protestants and Catholics wide and deep.

In the twentieth century social, economic, and political differences between Protestants and Catholics have declined greatly. For one thing, the older / newer immigrant distinction has grown more and more irrelevant as the United States has gotten further away from the period of its heavy immigration from Catholic Europe—the four decades or so from the mid-1880s to the mid-1920s. But Protestant / Catholic differences in partisan loyalties have lessened only gradually. As late as 1979, according to Gallup data, the Democratic edge over Republicans in party identification among white, northern Catholics was 31 percentage points, while the Republicans' margin over the Democrats among white, northern Protestants was 7 points—a net gap of 38 percentage points. By 1991–92, however, Protestant / Catholic differences in party identification had shrunk to their smallest margin ever. According to Gallup surveys, northern white Protestants in 1991–92 were 15 points more Republican than Democratic, while northern white Catholics were just 1 point more Democratic than Republican—a net gap of 16 percentage points.

GENDER AND THE PARTIES

So far as we can tell—we don't have survey data prior to the 1930s—men and women almost

TABLE 12.4 PARTY IDENTIFICATION BY SEX (IN PERCENT)

Year	Women		Men	
	Republican*	Democrat– Republican†	Republican*	Democrat– Republican†
1947	35	+8	35	+6
1952	34	+8	33	+7
1955	34	+10	29	+16
1960	33	+15	29	+18
1965	25	+30	24	+26
1970	30	+14	28	+14
1975	22	+25	19	+24
1979	23	+24	22	+19
1985	34	+6	34	0
1991–92	33	+4	35	−7

*Percent describing themselves as Republicans.
†Percent describing themselves as Democrats minus the percent describing themselves as Republicans.
Source: Gallup polls in the years shown.

never differed significantly in their patterns of party support earlier in this century. In the 1930s, for example, the Democrats had large and equivalent leads over Republicans among women and men alike.

Beginning in the late 1970s, however, partisan differences by gender began to appear—not huge differences, to be sure, but persistent ones. According to Gallup surveys taken in 1991–92, for example, the Democrats had an edge of 4 points in party identification among women, while they trailed the Republicans among men by 7 points (Table 12.4). Similar differences have appeared in congressional and presidential voting, and on a number of policy questions. The growth of the women's move-

ment and its increased political activity over the past fifteen years may have contributed to the relatively small but clear "gender gap"; so, too, may the fact that some women have encountered new sets of problems in recent years attendant upon, for example, their greater entry into the labor force.

SOCIOECONOMIC GROUPS AND THE PARTIES

Throughout the New Deal years the Democrats were stronger among the "have nots" in the United States—whether measured by education, occupation, income, or some other component of socioeconomic status (SES)—than they were among the "haves."[14] These relationships persist at present in large measure, no doubt, as a straightforward response to the two parties' policies. Democrats continue to give more backing to programs designed specifically to assist low-income people; Republicans put more emphasis on restraining the growth of federal spending on domestic programs and on cutting taxes. Leaders of both parties believe, of course, that what they are proposing is really best for lower and upper SES groups alike: Republicans think that promoting vigorous economic growth with low inflation is the best way to advance the economic position of the less affluent; Democrats insist that low-income people require higher levels of governmental assistance than Republicans want to provide. Today as during the New Deal, however, the Democrats are more inclined to tax and spend for social welfare programs, and this has gained them support among lower SES groups and cost them backing among higher SES groups.

Are the differences in party support by socioeconomic position a case of the glass being half-full or half-empty? Is the extent of the differences what's remarkable, or is it the limited nature of these differences what's really striking? Consider the differences by education. In 1991–92 according to the Gallup data, the Democrats had a 15 percentage point edge among those with less than a high school education, while the Republicans led by 11 points among the college educated (Table 12.5). The story is much the same for income groups. According to these Gallup surveys, Democrats outnumber Republicans by about 20 percent-

Table 12.5 PARTY IDENTIFICATION IN 1991–92, BY SOCIOECONOMIC POSITION (IN PERCENT)

	Democrat	Republican	Independent
Education			
Less than high school	43	28	30
High school graduate	34	32	34
Some college	29	37	33
College graduate	27	38	35
Income			
Less than $10,000	45	25	30
$10,000–$14,999	40	29	31
$15,000–$19,999	36	29	35
$20,000–$29,999	33	32	35
$30,000–$49,999	31	35	34
$50,000–$75,000	27	39	34
$75,000 & over	21	46	32

Source: Combined surveys conducted by the Gallup organization, 1991–92.

age points among those with the lowest incomes (under $10,000 a year), while the Republicans outnumber Democrats by a 25 point margin among those with the highest incomes ($75,000 and up). People with family incomes in the middle ranges are evenly divided in party loyalties. A case can be made that these are fairly small differences, considering the gap between the groups in socioeconomic status.

WHAT'S WRONG—AND RIGHT—WITH U.S. ELECTIONEERING?

Most observers agree that a core element of the problem with campaigns today is *money*. That's where agreement ends, however. As we will see, there are sharp disagreements over what the "money problem" actually is and what needs to be done.

The number and length of political cam-

[14] For more detailed discussion of socioeconomic position and party ties in the New Deal years, see Everett Ladd, with Charles D. Hadley, *Transformations of the American Party System*, 2nd ed. (New York: Norton, 1978), pp. 64–74, 93–111.

paigns in the United States, and the extent to which they now require large amounts of costly resources such as television time for speeches and advertisements, make American electioneering a very expensive business. Without substantial funding, parties and candidates can't take their cases to voters. But money can become too important and can be used in ways that abuse and bias popular choice. In the United States, as in other democracies, there is a continuing argument over what arrangements need be made so that the important task of communicating with voters can proceed without certain special interests, which have disproportionate access to funding, gaining an improper advantage.

Until the 1970s, the law governing federal campaign financing in the United States was the Corrupt Practices Act of 1925. It set a statutory maximum of $25,000 for total expenditures in a U.S. Senate race and $10,000 for a House campaign. These spending limits were wholly unrealistic, and they were ignored. Finance reports were supposed to be filed with the clerk of the House or the secretary of the Senate, but enforcement of this requirement, too, was lax. In a message dealing with the campaign finance legislation, President Lyndon Johnson described it as "more loophole than law."

THE FEDERAL ELECTION CAMPAIGN ACT

Sweeping changes were made in federal campaign finance legislation in the 1970s. The Federal Election Campaign Act (FECA) of 1971, and the major amendments to this act passed in 1974, 1976, and 1979, dealt with three different dimensions of campaign finance. Let's look briefly at each one.

Disclosure. The FECA assumed that, in an age where elections require a lot of money, the

One view of the "money problem."

public should have some reasonable sense of where funds come from. Getting information out in the open as to who gives how much to whom would advance public confidence in the integrity of the electoral process. The very idea that large sums might be changing hands between contributors and candidates without any effective public scrutiny could only encourage public cynicism. While the reporting requirements of the FECA are sometimes a frustrating exercise of bureaucratic authority, these requirements, together with the creation of an agency (the Federal Elections Commission) to enforce them and make intelligible the mountains of reported data, have given Americans a more complete and reliable picture of election finance than was ever before available.

TABLE 12.6 FEDERAL CAMPAIGN CONTRIBUTION LIMITS

	To each candidate or candidate committee per election	To national party committees per calendar year	To any other political committee per calendar year	Total contributions to federal candidates per calendar year
Contributor:				
Individual	$1,000	$20,000	$5,000	$25,000
Multicandidate committee *	$5,000	$15,000	$5,000	No limit
Other political committee	$1,000	$20,000	$5,000	No limit
Republican or Democratic senatorial campaign committee or the national party committee, or a combination of both	$17,500 to U.S. Senate candidate† during the year in which candidate seeks election	Not applicable	Not applicable	Not applicable

* A multicandidate committee is any political committee with more than fifty contributors which has been registered for at least six months and, with the exception of state party committees, has made contributions to five or more federal candidates.

†Limitation applies to either candidate for nomination or candidate for election to post of U.S. senator.

Source: Federal Election Commission, *Contributions*, March 1984; idem, *Federal Election Campaign Laws*, January 1984, p. 49.

Contribution and Spending Limits. The FECA removed all spending limits on House and Senate campaigns, keeping only contribution limits. The only surviving spending limits for candidates in the new legislation apply to presidential contenders who accept federal funding. On the contributions side, the FECA imposes limits on what individuals and political action committees (PACs) can contribute to candidates for federal office and what parties can give to their candidates. (See Table 12.6.) These limits represent an obvious attempt to respond to the problem of inequality of modern-day finance. The legislation provides, for example, that no individual can contribute more than $25,000 to federal candidates each calendar year. A number of factors make this limit less restrictive than it may at first appear. For one, $25,000 can be contributed by each adult member of a family (although not by little children, deemed incapable of making such a judgment independently). For another, the limit applies only to federal candidates, not those for state and local office; many states do not impose such limits on these latter. Still, the FECA limits do have practical implications and did establish, for the first time in U.S. history, some truly enforceable standards.

The FECA permits contributions by PACs— discussed below, pp. 370–73—but puts limits on them. At present no individual can give more than $5,000 to political action committees in any calendar year, and no PAC can give more than $5,000 to any federal candidate in an election. There have not been, however, any legal limits on how much a given PAC can contribute to *all* federal candidates or on how much a candidate can receive from all PACs. In 1987–88 the Realtors Political Action Committee surpassed all others in contributions to federal candidates; it gave just over $3 million.

Public Funding. The third area where the FECA attempted to apply democratic standards to the financing of elections was the governmental funding of presidential campaigns and the imposition of spending limits on those who accept this funding. Before the conventions at which the parties pick their nominees, candidates are entitled to receive federal matching funds. To qualify, they must receive contributions of at least $5,000 from people in twenty or more states, with no single contribution exceeding $250. Once these provisions are met, federal funds are available covering 50 percent of a candidate's total expenditures up to the prescribed limits. In 1988, this meant that a candidate could receive roughly $27 million in federal funds prior to the party conventions. During the general election campaign in 1988, George Bush and Michael Dukakis each received just over $45 million in federal funding of their campaigns and had their direct spending limited to this amount. The basic idea was, first, to give each major party candidate roughly the same financial resources and, second, to curb the financial intervention of wealthy individuals and well-heeled interests. These goals have been only partly realized. Millions of dollars of interest-group money still find their way into the campaign—going ostensibly for voter registration drives and being funneled through the state parties.

ARE CAMPAIGNS TOO EXPENSIVE?

One persistent set of issues involves the sheer cost of present-day campaigning. State campaign spending data are now available in better form than ever before; from these various sources Herbert E. Alexander, director of the Citizen's Research Foundation, estimated that $525 million was expended on state and local politics in the 1983–84 election cycle, and $850 million in 1987–88. Using FEC data, Alexander further estimated that total monetary expenditures for federal elections were just under $1.3 billion in 1983–84 and just over $2.1 billion during the presidential election in 1987–88.

Is this just too much money? In one sense, this issue is a hard one to deal with because observers can decide for themselves how much is "too much." But do we have any objective standards that can help us reach a judgment?

Those inclined to argue that present campaign spending is not too high often compare current expenditures for this "vital act of democratic participation" with what we spend for fairly frivolous things—like snowmobiles, lipstick, and chewing gum. Those who think present spending levels are too high find this response unsatisfactory, and there is much to commend their position. Spending for electioneering has nothing to do with spending for chewing gum, and the comparison can have only a certain sophomoric appeal. But there is a more meaningful comparison available. Campaign spending all comes back in one way or another to efforts to persuade voters—and, disproportionately, to efforts at persuasion that involve sending messages over television and radio, by newspaper advertising, mailed flyers, and the like. The proper comparison, then, weighs the communications resources made available to candidates and parties against those available to other organizations and interests that vie for the attention of the American citizenry in communicating on politics and public issues.

Specifically, is there any evidence that campaign spending for political communication by candidates and parties has grown disproportionately, compared to the total spent on public affairs communications? Candidates and parties try to bring their views on issues and events to voters' attention, to influence voters' electoral choices. If this party/candidate role in the larger process of political communications has grown inordinately, compared to other parts, that fact would at least suggest that limits might be desirable. But if instead the party/candidate share of total spending relating to communications on public issues has steadily shrunk, it is hard to see precisely why we should want to shrink it further. Surely party / candidate communications to voters is a legitimate part of political communications in this and any other democracy.

Early on in American history, the parties exercised the decisive role in political communications. Today, however, the United States is very far from the party-dominated communications of its early years, Americans receive the bulk of their information on political issues not from the parties but from national communications media that maintain a steadfast independence of all party influence, much less direction, as the cornerstone of their professional self-definition. Network news programs command many millions of viewers. The resources committed to public affairs communications by the television networks alone dwarf those available to parties and candidates. CBS News takes in for its evening news program far more than both the Democratic and Republican parties at all levels take in for every act of political communication within their domains. It is hard, then, to see a sound basis for the argument that party spending for campaigning is in some absolute sense too high. Is it desirable for the party / candidate role to be even more subordinate to that of the national communications

media and the journalistic profession? The case has not been made convincingly. In contrast, political scientists going back to Woodrow Wilson have made the case that parties are important instruments of the democratic process and that their institutional roles need to be expanded, not weakened.

While the sheer amount of money spent on campaigning does not appear to be a vaild issue, were one party to have clear financial advantage over the other, electoral fairness might be compromised. Is one party advantaged? Substantial balance or parity between the two major parties has been achieved in several major areas of campaign finance, although some imbalances still exist. With regard to the much-discussed PAC contributions, FEC data show that in the 1989–90 election cycle PACs together contributed $92 million to Democratic congressional candidates and $57 million to Republicans—continuing the clear Democratic edge evident in preceding elections. As we saw in chapter 6, PAC money actually is not so much Democratic or Republican money as it is incumbent money. PACs give overwhelmingly to incumbents with whom they expect to have to continue to deal, and the Democrats have more ranking incumbents (Table 12.7). Democratic House and Senate candidates received about

TABLE 12.7 PAC CONTRIBUTIONS (1989–90) TO FEDERAL CANDIDATES
(IN MILLIONS OF DOLLARS)

Type of PAC	Candidate status			Party affiliation of recipient	
	Incumbent	Challenger	Open seat	Democrat	Republican
Corporation	43.7	4.9	4.8	24.8	28.7
Trade/member/health	34.7	3.2	4.6	23.4	19.1
Labor organization	23.7	5.0	4.9	31.4	2.1
Non-connected	9.8	2.1	2.4	9.1	5.2
Other	5.1	.4	.5	3.7	2.2
Total	117.0	15.6	17.2	92.4	57.3

Source: Federal Election Commission, press release of December 10, 1991.

TABLE 12.8 POLITICAL PARTY FUNDRAISING, 1989–90

Party	Net Receipts
Democratic	
National committee	$ 14,483,089
Senatorial	17,536,049
Congressional	9,088,467
Assoc. State Chair	8,829,462
State/Local	35,821,089
Total Democratic	85,758,156
Republican	
National committee	$ 68,713,896
Senatorial	65,063,462
Congressional	33,224,093
State/Local	39,349,372
Total Republican	206,350,823

Source: Federal Election Commission, press release of December 10, 1991.

$121 million in contributions from individuals, the Republicans the same. The net receipts of Democratic House and Senate candidates were about $25.3 million. Direct spending by the Democratic and Republican presidential nominees has been roughly equalized through the public finance provisions of the FECA.

The biggest imbalance in campaign resources involves "institutional" fundraising. The Republicans enjoy a large advantage over the Democrats in this area. (See Table 12.8.) FEC data for 1989–90 show the Republican National Committee, House and Senate campaign committees, and state and local committees raising roughly $206 million to the Democrats' $86 million. The GOP's fundraising achievements have made it a formidable electoral force—one admired by its friends and envied by its opponents.[15] The Democrats have had some recent success, though, in reducing the GOP's advantage.

[15] Herbert E. Alexander, "Political Parties and the Dollar," *Society,* January / February 1985, p. 56.

Are PACs the Problem? As a result of the campaign finance legislation enacted in the 1970s, the role of political action committees was greatly expanded. PACs are organizations formed by business corporations, trade associations, labor unions, and the like to raise and disburse funds to advance political objectives. The emergence of corporate and labor PACs followed a long period in which such activity was restricted by law. In 1907, the Tillman Act banned corporate gifts of money to candidates for federal elective office or to any committees that supported such candidates—which does not mean, of course, that the contributions actually stopped. The ban was incorporated into the Federal Corrupt Practices Act of 1925, which extended the prohibition to cover contributions of "anything of value." The Smith-Connally Act of 1943 and the Taft-Hartley Act of 1947 banned contributions to federal-office candidates by unions from their members' dues.

The Federal Election Campaign Act of 1971 introduced an important change in this area. It permitted the use of corporate funds and union treasury money for "the establishment, administration, and solicitation of contributions to a separate, segregated fund to be used for a political purpose." These funds have become known as PACs. Under the law, an individual can give up to $5,000 to a PAC. By July 1990, 1,782 corporate PACs were registered with the Federal Election Commission, along with 753 trade association PACs, 346 representing labor unions, and close to 1,300 more in assorted other categories. As noted, PACs contributed in 1987–88 about $160 million to candidates in federal election campaigns. Table 12.9 shows the twenty biggest PACs in 1989–90, measured in terms of the total amount of their contributions to federal candidates.

Many, perhaps most, observers see PACs at the heart of current problems involving money and politics. But PACs are only the structure that interest groups and their efforts at influ-

TABLE 12.9   TOP 20 PAC CONTRIBUTORS TO FEDERAL CANDIDATES, 1989–90

Rank	Name	Receipts
1.	Democratic Republican Independent Voter Education Committee	$10,516,473
2.	American Medical Association Political Action Committee	$5,694,970
3.	Realtors Political Action Committee	$5,305,837
4.	Voter Guide	$5,083,520
5.	National Education Association Political Action Committee	$4,505,678
6.	United Auto Workers Union (UAW) Voluntary Community Action Program	$4,013,900
7.	American Federation of State County & Municipal Employees—PEOPLE, Qualified	$3,894,670
8.	Association of Trial Lawyers of America Political Action Committee	$3,848,999
9.	National Rifle Association (NRA) Political Victory Fund	$3,697,816
10.	National Congressional Club	$3,548,765
11.	Machinists Non-Partisan Political League	$3,129,851
12.	Auto Dealers and Driver for Free Trade PAC	$3,084,823
13.	American Telephone & Telegraph Company Inc PAC (AT&T PAC)	$2,836,313
14.	American Citizens for Political Action	$2,773,896
15.	Dealers Election Action Committee of the National Automobile Dealers Association (NADA)	$2,765,629
16.	Committee on Letter Carriers Political Education (Letter Carriers Political Action Fund)	$2,650,416
17.	National Committee to Preserve Social Security and Medicare—PAC	$2,567,978
18.	Campaign America	$2,436,736
19.	National Association of Retired Federal Employees Political Action Committee (NARFE-PAC)	$2,315,393
20.	California Democratic Voter Checklist	$2,299,005

Source: Federal Election Commission, press release of December 10, 1991.

ence now assume. PACs should be abolished, some argue. But the interests—business, union, trade association, environmental, and more— would still be there, if the legal form political action committees took in the 1970s through federal legislation was removed. The "PAC problem" is in fact one of some interests having much greater resources than others and using them to advance their goals.

Many interest groups behave responsibly— but others don't. The presence of so much money surrounding a legislature that does so much that interest groups of all sorts care about provides temptations—for irresponsible lobbyists and legislators alike. The personal account of the problem given by Jim Calaway, a Texas oilman who was active in interest-group fund raising for members of Congress, is instructive.

"I was a fat cat," Calaway acknowledged in an interview with the *New York Times.* "Although I hate that term, that's what I was, a fat cat raising money for other fat cats. It was wrong, and I made a mistake."[16] Calaway said that he saw just "too much money floating around . . . and not enough public service." He saw, for example, a congressman facing no real opposition to re-election collect $500,000 in PAC contributions.

[16] Robert Suro, "Fund-Raiser Attacks the Practices He Thrived On," *New York Times,* June 5, 1989, p. A15.

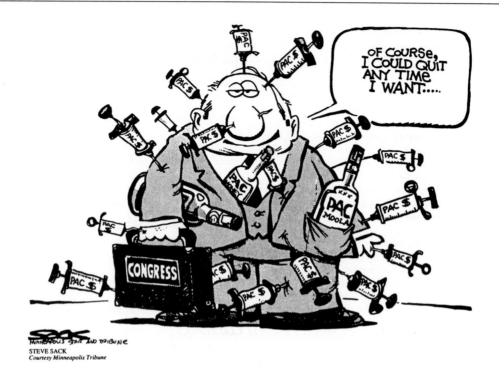

STEVE SACK
Courtesy Minneapolis Tribune

Abolish PACs? Members of Congress of both parties heard strong protests against the wash of interest-group money around congressional campaigns. Many Republicans developed an additional reason for souring on PACs. As noted, the bulk of PAC contributions go to established figures in Congress, which means the Democrats—who have controlled the House continuously since January 1955 and the Senate for all but six years since that date—have had the advantage.

In campaign reform legislation introduced in Congress in 1990, and again in 1992, both parties proposed PAC curbs. The Republicans endorsed the total elimination of federal-level PACs and their contributions. There is doubt whether a prohibition against business and union PACs—made on grounds of promoting fair elections and enhancing public confidence—could be extended to so-called ideolog-

ical PACs that form around issues like the environment or abortion. The Supreme Court has indicated a distinction between the two types of interest groups. In a Court decision involving activities in the state of Michigan, the ideological or pure-issue groups were found to have stronger claims to unrestricted participation—including campaign contributions—under the First Amendment guarantees of free speech and association. In any case, the bulk of PAC money comes from businesses, trade associations, and union groups—whose contributions can probably, though not certainly, be barred constitutionally. The Democrats' proposal would limit PAC contributions and provide for public funding in its stead.

Others are not sure that efforts at eliminating PAC contributions are a good thing. Some take the view that as long as there are interest groups with money, they will find a way, in our free society, to spend it to advance their programs. The present law allows PAC contributions—and requires that they be fully reported. At least now, defenders of the existing rules argue, we have a substantial public record of what groups are doing. Curtis Gans, who directs the Committee for the Study of the American Electorate, maintains that the real answer is to attack the costs of campaigns, not seek to limit PAC contributions or overall spending. He would cut campaign costs by granting blocs of free television time to candidates. (Many other democracies do this, as Table 12.10 indicates.) Gans would also reduce the role of PAC money by increasing the limits on individual contributions to candidates—now $1,000—and granting tax deductions for such contributions.

And he would put the spotlight on big-spending PACs by increasing full and speedy public disclosure of their actions.[17]

THE CONTEMPORARY CAMPAIGN "INDUSTRY"

The advent of PACs is not the only change to have affected campaigning recently. Over the last quarter-century, changes in the technology of mass communications have transformed American electioneering. The biggest single factor, of course, is the increasing use of tele-

[17]Quoted by Michael Oreskes and Robin Toner, "A Swamp of Political Abuses Spurs Constituents of Change," *New York Times*, March 21, 1990, pp. A1, 22.

TABLE 12.10   HOW OTHER DEMOCRACIES FUND THEIR ELECTION CAMPAIGNS

	Government grants	Limits on fund raising or spending	Television
Britain	No	Yes	Free time, allocated according to party's strength in previous election
Denmark	Allowance to parties, based on strength in previous election	No	Parties given equal and free time on public stations
France	Reimbursement to candidates, according to votes received	Yes	Free and equal time to candidates
Italy	Reimbursement to candidates, according to votes received	No	Free and equal time to candidates on state-run stations, but parties control major private stations
Israel	No	No	Parties given equal and free time on public stations
Japan	No	Yes	Candidates given some free time for speeches, no negative advertising
Germany	Reimbursement to parties, according to votes received	No	Free time to candidates on public stations

Source: Michael Oreskes with Robin Toner, "A Swamp of Political Abuses Spurs Constituents of Change," *New York Times*, March 21, 1990, p. A22.

vision: Candidates can reach far more people through television news coverage, political advertisements, and televised debates than through the most vigorous traditional campaigning. Still, most candidates are unfamiliar with television at the technical level; they don't know how to buy air time, how to schedule it most advantageously, or how to develop the most effective television appeals. The more they use television, and the more dimensions the medium offers (the spread of cable networks, for instance, has opened new possibilities), the more candidates must turn to media consultants. Technological change intrudes in other areas: The application of computers to direct-mail efforts has greatly enlarged the reach of political fundraising. Polling has become a large part of the apparatus of modern campaigns. As a result, a whole "elections industry" has grown up.

Selling Soap and Electing Presidents. A student once wrote to the great nineteenth-century British prime minister, Benjamin Disraeli, asking how he should prepare for a career in public life. Disraeli replied that there were only two things he needed to know to succeed in politics: "You must know yourself, and you must know the times." Political scientist William Schneider observes: "That is still true. Only these days, candidates have to hire political consultants to find out who they are and what's going on."[18]

Many others, we suspect, share Schneider's concern. The army of technicians surrounding candidates seems too engrossed in the manipulative side of things, and the candidates themselves often appear too inclined to listen to the new salespeople. "It's not like selling soap," we sometimes feel like shouting. "Electing a president is really serious and important. Don't

worry so much about running clever political ads or coming up with a catchy slogan. Just give us the facts as best you can on where you hope to lead the country and why you think you have the ability to get it there."

"Winning elections," Michael Oreskes of the *New York Times* has observed, "has become a business, a big business with professional associations and magazines, where volunteers have been replaced by computer-assisted polling, the pamphlet by the television spot."[19] Everything about campaigns seems more contrived than in the past—because in fact it is more contrived. The domination of technicians, argues Mickey Kantor, an attorney long active in Democratic party politics, "tends to homogenize the process. . . . It takes the ideology out of it. It stifles creativity and strong stands, all of which is not good for the country."[20]

The apparatus through which the industry presents candidates to the electorate would not allow an Aristotle to escape banality. Its current centerpiece is the celebrated thiry-second sound bite. Presumably on the assumption that the skills needed in a president are akin to those of a good quiz-show host—being able to think fast on one's feet and toss out witty retorts—the industry has made the televised presidential debates into a key test of candidates' strength. And when, through the structure it ordains, the candidates appear superficial, the industry chants, Greek-chorus-like, "Give us substance."

There is cause for concern. Still, some of the hand-wringing about contemporary campaigns appears excessive. One hears a lot about "negative campaigning" these days—and there is a lot. In the 1988 campaign, for example, much was made of such George Bush ads as one

---

[18] William Schneider, "What's Going to Sell in Next Year's Race?" *National Journal*, April 25, 1987, p. 1016.

[19] Michael Oreskes, "America's Politics Loses Way as Its Vision Changes World," *New York Times*, March 18, 1990, pp. A1, 22.

[20] Ibid.

graphically depicting pollution in Boston Harbor, which was used to suggest that Massachusetts governor Michael Dukakis couldn't even handle pollution in his own back yard. In fact, of course, this pollution had sources that the Dukakis administration could not do much about in the short run. A little nasty? Perhaps. But campaigns got pretty nasty in the past too. In free and open politics, some will take the political low road, but there are correctives. Surveys suggest, for example, that many voters are turned off by candidates who rely on low-road appeals. Voters are not helpless pawns in the campaign process.

Though turnout was lower than we would like to see it in the 1988 presidential election, roughly 91.6 million citizens went to the polls and cast their votes. It was the 51st time, in an unbroken string reaching back to George Washington's election in 1789, that Americans have participated in the peaceful, democratic choice of their chief executive. The 1990 elections were the 102d consecutive free election of the national legislature. This record of democratic longevity is unmatched in any other country. We might, without unseemly boasting, take some satisfaction in a truly remarkable accomplishment. But it's hard to detect evidence of pride and pleasure. The candidates are faulted for negative campaigning and for failing to address the "real" issues. The press is charged with hype, superficiality, and bias. The public is at once blamed for not taking more interest in voting and for allowing itself to be bamboozled by the candidates' vacuous sloganeering—and commiserated with for being treated so shabbily by a flawed system.

The campaign performance of the press and especially of television leaves much to be desired. Still, as cable coverage has been extended, viewers are being given more alternatives in what to watch. If the fifteen- and thirty-second sound bites that are the stuff of much of television's campaign coverage are terribly inadequate, through such cable channels as C-SPAN millions of voters now have an opportunity to hear and observe the candidates to an extent that dwarfs that of any previous era. The press feeds on polls and through polling encourages a narrow "horse race" view of the presidential contest. But there is more than a little irony in the fact that journalists—so often criticized for their insularity, "pack" behavior, and elitism—are now being attacked for relying too much on a medium whose essential feature is its sustained examination of the views of ordinary citizens.

American voters have their own ideas about what the country needs and assess candidates against demanding standards. As *New York Times* columnist Tom Wicker noted,

> this is a far more complex—even mysterious—process than the "selling soap" comparison so often invoked. Not even Ronald Reagan was elected for his smile or his hairdo, and no one will be in 1988 either. . . . Voters look ultimately for someone to believe in. What causes them to place their confidence in a candidate is not always clear, but it's seldom because he or she acts and talks like everyone else in the race, and even less often because of an artifice or posturing on television.[21]

Beyond the selling is the searching—and the searching should command our respect.

PARTICIPATION IN AMERICAN ELECTIONS

Millions of Americans take their job of assessing candidates very seriously. It must be acknowledged, however, that other millions stand on the sidelines, deciding not to vote.

[21] Tom Wicker, "The Seven Dwarfs," *New York Times*, July 4, 1987, p. 27.

FIGURE 12.4   PERCENT OF VOTING-AGE POPULATION VOTING FOR PRESIDENT SINCE 1920

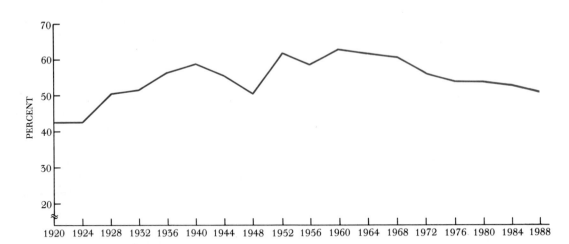

Source: 1932–88: U.S. Bureau of the Census, *Statistical Abstract of the United States, 1979*, p. 513; 1990, p. 264; 1920–28: Idem, *Historical Statistics of the United States: Colonial Times to 1970*, p. 1073.

And over the last thirty years voter turnout has declined further. According to official statistics, just over 50 percent of voting-age residents voted for president in the 1988 election, more than 12 points below the turnout in the 1960 Kennedy-Nixon contest (Figure 12.4).

Turnout is even lower in voting for the U.S. House of Representatives. In 1976 it dropped below the 50 percent mark for the first time in a presidential election year since the 1940s, and it was only 48 percent in 1984. In "off-year" voting for the House, without the added spur and visibility of the more publicized presidential contest, participation is lower still. Only 38 percent of the voting-age public participated in the 1982 House contests, 33 percent voted in 1986, and 34 percent in 1990.

A CONFOUNDING DECLINE

The country's low and somewhat declining voter participation is made more striking by its occurrence in the face of developments designed to spur voting. The drop-off in turnout of the last decade and a half has taken place at the very time the poll tax was outlawed, discrimination at polling places on the basis of race or language was prohibited, residency requirements were greatly eased, unreasonable registration dates were discarded, and many states initiated procedures to enhance participation such as mobile registrars, postcard registration, and even election-day registration.[22] Other developments associated with higher participation have also been occurring, the most notable of which is the steady increase in the electorate's level of formal education. As data presented later in this chapter show, the strongest observed link between the social characteristics of a population and the inclination to vote involves education: The more of it citizens have, the higher their participation lev-

[22] Curtis Gans, "The Cause: The Empty Voting Booths," *Washington Monthly*, October 1978, p. 28.

els in elections of all types.[23] And yet as the formal education of the populace has been growing so impressively, voter turnout has been falling.

Concern has been spurred further by comparisons of voter turnout in the United States to that in other democracies. Although, as we will see, comparisons are more difficult to make than is sometimes supposed, the mean (or average) turnout in national elections 1945–80 was 95 percent in Australia and the Netherlands, 87 percent in West Germany, 81 percent in Norway, 79 percent in France, 77 percent in Great Britain, 76 percent in Canada, and 73 percent in Japan—while in American presidential elections during this period turnout was just 59 percent.

IS VOTER TURNOUT A PROBLEM?

The United States is the world's oldest democracy and a pioneer in the extension of the vote to the entire population, but it appears to have one of the lowest voter-participation rates among the world's democracies. America has taken a number of measures to spur registration, and the population now seems better equipped to vote, given its high formal education, but still turnout is falling off. A debate is going on over the source and nature of the problem and its consequences.

Some argue that low turnout diminishes the capacity of those not participating to represent their interests and shape policy. For example, after reviewing data suggesting that the decline in turnout between 1960 and 1976 did not take place evenly across the population but was sharpest among whites of low income and education, Howard Reiter expressed concern that

this "may make federal policy-makers less responsive to their [lower-status whites'] desires than they used to be. This may be especially significant for the Democratic party, which has claimed to speak for lower and working-class interests."[24] Frances Fox Piven and Richard Cloward maintain that U.S. voter registration statutes requiring that individuals themselves come forward to get registered—rather than being registered automatically by a government agency—are in fact a greater barrier to the poor than to the affluent. As a result these statutes serve to underrepresent the poor and shift the electorate more to the right than it otherwise would be.[25]

Other experts disagree. Ruy A. Teixeira argues that "quite simply, for many Americans voting just doesn't seem worth the bother. . . . Nonvoting [is hardly] an indicator of suppressed radicalism or any other political viewpoint." While nonvoters differ from voters in some regards, such as educational background, they don't differ much in political outlook. From a partisan point of view, "the question of mobilizing nonvoters is logically inseparable from the question of mobilizing voters. A party unable to sway the existing pool of voters with its message would be unlikely to change its fortunes by mobilizing more nonvoters to vote."[26]

Voter participation is central to the democratic process, and the debate over the consequences of nonvoting is an important one. As we will see, however, the whole subject of who

[23] See Raymond E. Wolfinger and Steven J. Rosenstone, *Who Votes?* (New Haven, Conn.: Yale University Press, 1980).

[24] Howard L. Reiter, "Why Is Turnout Down?" *Public Opinion Quarterly*, Fall 1979, p. 310. See, too, Reiter, *Parties and Elections in Corporate America* (New York: St. Martin's Press, 1987), pp. 134–57.

[25] Frances Fox Piven and Richard Cloward, *Why Americans Don't Vote* (New York: Pantheon, 1988).

[26] Ruy A. Teixeira, "Will the Real Nonvoter Please Stand Up?" *Public Opinion*, July / August 1988, pp. 42, 44. See, too, Teixeira, *Why Americans Don't Vote: Turnout Decline in the United States, 1960–84* (Westport, Conn.: Greenwood Press, 1987).

votes and who doesn't, and what this means, is quite complicated. We need to try to assemble some pertinent information. One source of confusion on American voter turnout as opposed to other democracies is the lack of fully comparable statistics. The conclusion our data so obviously suggest, that voter turnout is lower here than abroad, is valid. But important qualifications on this conclusion are often overlooked. Voter turnout for the United States is regularly computed on the basis of votes as a percentage of the voting age population; in all other countries, turnout is calculated on votes cast as a percentage of registered voters. Additionally, in the United States only valid votes are counted in the total turnout, while in the other countries invalid and blank ballots are also in the total figure. These statistical dissimilarities make turnout in the United States seem lower than it actually is.

Part of the reason why data are published with one statistical convention for the United States and another elsewhere is that American registration laws result in a substantial proportion of the voting-age population not being registered in any given election. Were turnout in the United States represented as a proportion of only those actually registered, it would convey a sense of very robust participation that would be misleading. (Table 12.11 shows that in recent elections the percentage of registered voters turning out in presidential elections is in line with turnout in national elections in other democracies.)

Most democracies have registration procedures intended to register automatically virtually the entire adult citizenry; for these nations measuring turnout as a proportion of registered voters is appropriate. But as British political scientist Ivor Crewe has pointed out, "The

TABLE 12.11 REGISTRATION AND VOTING AROUND THE WORLD

Turnout as a percentage of registered voters		Penalties for not voting	Automatic registration?
1. Belgium	95	Yes	Yes
2. Australia	95	Yes	No
3. Austria	92	No	Yes
4. Sweden	91	No	Yes
5. Italy	90	Yes	Yes
6. Iceland	89	n.a.	n.a.
7. New Zealand	89	No	No
8. Luxembourg	89	n.a.	n.a.
9. W. Germany	89	No	Yes
10. Netherlands	87	No	Yes
11. United States	87	No	No
12. France	86	No	No
13. Portugal	84	n.a.	n.a.
14. Denmark	83	No	Yes
15. Norway	82	No	Yes
16. Greece	79	Yes	Yes
17. Israel	79	No	Yes
18. United Kingdom	76	No	Yes
19. Japan	75	No	Yes
20. Canada	69	No	Yes
21. Spain	68	Yes	Yes
22. Finland	64	No	Yes
23. Ireland	62	No	Yes
24. Switzerland	48	No	Yes

Source: David Glass, Peverill Squire, and Raymond Wolfinger, "Voter Turnout: An International Comparison," *Public Opinion* (December / January 1984), p. 52. The authors based this table on the most recent national election held in each country as of 1981.

accuracy of the turnout figures [for all countries except the United States] depends on the efficiency of the electoral registers on which they are all based...."[27] In those instances where "the registers omit those unlikely to exercise their right to vote (the homeless, tenants of single rooms, immigrants), turnout figures will be artificially inflated." Any situation where significant numbers of people are not counted among registered voters makes turnout appear higher than it really is; computing turnout on the basis of those registered always inflates participation rates since no registration system ever records all voting-age residents.

At the time of the 1988 U.S. presidential election, the noninstitutionalized voting-age population of the United States was about 178 million. But just 130 million Americans were registered to vote in 1988. Why were 40 million voting-age residents of the United States not registered? Certainly many of them did not register because they did not intend to vote. Registration and voting in the United States are part of one continuous act of electoral participation. The government does not assume

[27] Ivor Crewe, "Electoral Participation," in Butler et al., *Democracy at the Polls,* p. 232.

the responsibility of registering people but rather requires that citizens initiate the step; millions of people who for whatever reason do not plan to vote just do not register. But among the unregistered residents are millions who are off the rolls not because they lack interest but because by law they cannot register or vote. Perhaps as many as 9 million resident aliens of voting age in the United States don't have the citizenship required for voting. The census figures on voting-age residents also regularly include "institutional" populations. Those jailed for felonies are barred by law from registering and voting. Many other people who are institutionalized, like inmates of mental facilities, cannot vote. All of this means that millions of people in the United States who are of voting age are barred from registration by reasonable, consciously developed legal standards. By continuing to compute turnout on the basis of all those of voting age, we substantially overstate the magnitude of American nonvoting.

Most political scientists and other analysts who study the matter believe that voter turnout would not be greatly affected by any changes made in registration procedures.[28] Nonetheless, turnout would almost certainly be helped somewhat if all adult citizens were more or less automatically registered, rather than, as in most states in the past, being required to initiate registration themselves. A bill passed Congress in 1992 that would have automatically registered anyone applying for a driver's license. Voter registration would also have been made

available at several public offices. The measure was vetoed, however, and the veto was not overridden.

If provisions are made to make fraud difficult—that is, verification that registrants are eligible and reside where they say they do—easier registration is a good idea. But all who are concerned that so many Americans don't vote shouldn't let themselves be distracted by this issue. The sources of low turnout aren't in election laws. Turnout will go up only when more people *want* to vote or feel voting is a responsibility of citizenship.

VOTER PARTICIPATION ACROSS HISTORY

If turnout is low in America, it has long been that way. As we saw in Figure 12.4, participation in 1924 (as a percentage of the voting-age population) was just 43 percent, 7 percent lower than in 1988. And electoral participation in 1936 was only modestly higher than at present. Yet a very different cast has been given to participation in Roosevelt's big victory of 1936 than to such recent contests as Ford-Carter in 1976, Reagan-Mondale in 1984, and Bush-Dukakis in 1988. With the country in the midst of a great depression, which had sapped national confidence, Roosevelt came to office, told the people "the only thing we have to fear is fear itself," and proceeded to chart a bold course that rallied much of the populace to his banner. Opposition to the new initiatives was also vigorous, and the 1936 election was a spirited referendum on the New Deal. This historical account seems valid. But then why was voter participation in this buoyant referendum similar to that in recent elections in which, according to many accounts, the public has often been unenthusiastic about the candidates of both parties, dissatisfied with the quality of leadership, and uneasy about the programmatic approaches the parties were offering?

[28] For an interesting exchange on the impact of registration procedures and requirements on turnout, see four articles in the June 1990 issue of *PS: Political Science and Politics:* Stephen Earl Bennett, "The Uses and Abuses of Registration and Turnout Data: An Analysis of Piven and Cloward's Studies of Nonvoting in America," pp. 166–71; Francis Fox Piven and Richard L. Cloward, "A Reply to Bennett," pp. 172–73; Stephen Earl Bennett, "Rejoinder to Piven and Cloward," pp. 173–75; and Curtis B. Gans, "A Rejoinder to Piven and Cloward," pp. 175–78.

There is a dimension of nonvoting in the United States unrelated to dissatisfaction with democratic performance or with the parties and their leaders. As S. M. Lipset, among others, has noted, American nonvoting is "a reflection of the stability of the system" and confidence that the next election will not produce threatening or dangerous results.[29] Elections in many countries involve contenders far more dissimilar in their programs and outlooks than are the Democrats and Republicans in the United States. The two major American political parties are middle-class alliances that share many basic ideological commitments. For a Democrat, the prospect of a Republican being elected is not usually wildly threatening, and vice versa. In Britain, the division between the leadership of the Labour and Conservative parties is much greater; in France, the gap between the Communist party and the Center-Right is greater still. Less interested or involved people are more likely to participate electorally in contests where they see the stakes to be high. As a stable democracy that has operated under the same constitutional structure for two centuries, the United States has a political system that is not so stress-filled, and many people feel they can afford the luxury of not voting.

One rebuttal to this argument is that voter turnout was much higher in the United States in the late nineteenth century than at present. According to data collected by Walter Dean Burnham, voter turnout was 75 percent in the presidential election of 1892, 79 percent in 1896, and 73 percent in 1900.[30] Turnout undoubtedly was higher in the last century than in our own, but not as much higher as

these statistics would suggest. Voting fraud occurred more frequently in the nineteenth century because it could be committed so easily. Stipulations on eligibility requirements were few and easily avoided. The paper ballots were printed by the political parties, not by the government. The counting of votes was often controlled by the parties and, in areas of one-party dominance, padding of the totals was commonplace. As a result, the number of votes reported in nineteenth-century elections was probably, as a routine matter, considerably larger than the number of voting-age citizens actually casting ballots. One often-cited instance of exaggeration of turnout is that of West Virginia, where the reported turnout in 1888 was actually 12,000 votes higher than the total eligible to vote!

SOURCES OF DIMINISHED VOTER TURNOUT

When all these factors are considered, it is still clear that current voter turnout in the United States has dropped off over the last quarter-century. One reason involves the status of political parties. Parties have undergone a great variety of changes in recent decades. While it is certainly not true that all of these shifts have left them weaker than they were in earlier eras, local party organizations have on the whole been weakened. In times past, strong, local party organizations had the institutional resources needed to increase turnout. They canvassed potential voters and urged participation on behalf of party nominees. They conducted "get out the vote" drives, took people whom they expected to vote for the party's candidates to and from the polls, and in general helped maintain a sense of partisan awareness and interest in the electorate. Today, in many areas of the United States, parties do such things less vigorously than they used to.

[29] Seymour Martin Lipset, *Political Man* (Garden City, N.Y.: Doubleday, 1960), p. 181.

[30] These data have been published in *Historical Statistics of the United States: Colonial Times to 1970*, part 2 (Washington, D.C.: Government Printing Office, 1975), pp. 1071–72.

A second factor in declining voter turnout may involve the increasing scale and remoteness of the governmental process. Survey data, for example, show that large and growing segments of the population now feel that the complexity of politics and decision making have become beyond their control. Modern government is big and distant. It seems set apart from the average citizen's world, something that encourages frustration and resentment. Sixty-seven percent held that "the government is pretty much run by a few big interests looking out for themselves. . . ."[31]

The general sense of distance between the individual citizen and "big government" is likely to persist. In nineteenth-century America, most of government's work began and ended at the local level. It was easier, in such a context, for the individual voter to believe that the decision he made on election day shaped governmental action. A citizen in Bucksport, Maine, in 1840 saw a shorter and more direct link between his vote and actual governmental response than any American can today. While one may conclude that voting remains a basic check on government and recognize that collectively the millions of votes cast determine who the nation's leaders will be, the scope of modern government must detract from a sense of voter efficacy and confidence, especially among those who have little training to understand such complexity.

Yet another factor that may contribute to turnout decline is the shift in tone and content of news coverage of campaigns. Political scientist Thomas Patterson notes that the coverage of presidential candidates in 1960 was vastly more positive than in 1988. The same trend could be found in both newspapers and television. "Increasingly," Patterson observes, "the thread running through it is, 'There is something wrong with the campaign, there is something wrong with the candidate.' "[32] If elections are depicted as such a boring and debased spectacle, might not some potential voters be encouraged to say, "Why bother"?

WHO VOTES?

People of high socioeconomic status generally vote at a much higher rate than those of low status, data analysis from massive surveys conducted by the Bureau of the Census shows. Education is especially important: It "has a very substantial effect on the probability that one will vote."[33] In 1988, people with college degrees voted at a rate of 41 percentage points higher than those with eight years of schooling or less (Table 12.12). Income and occupation were independently much less important: Once education is held constant, income differences have little effect on rates of voter participation. Yet the variations in rates of voting by educational level are very large within all income groups.[34] Education

> imparts information about politics . . . and about a variety of skills, some of which facilitate political learning. . . . Schooling increases one's capacity for understanding and working with complex, abstract, and intangible subjects, that is, subjects like politics. . . . Learning about politics doubtless heightens interests; the more sense one can make of the political world, the more likely that one is to pay attention to it.[35]

Presumably, the increasingly complex and abstract character of politics makes education a bigger factor in determining the likelihood of voting.

[31] Center for Political Studies, University of Michigan, 1988 election surveys.

[32] Quoted in Oreskes, "America's Politics Loses Way . . . ," p. A22.
[33] Wolfinger and Rosenstone, *Who Votes?*
[34] Ibid., pp. 23–28.
[35] Ibid., p. 18.

TABLE 12.12 REPORTED VOTING RATES IN 1988 OF SELECTED GROUPS IN THE UNITED STATES

Characteristic	Persons of voting age	Percentage reporting they voted
Total	178,100	57
Male	84,500	56
Female	93,600	58
White	152,800	59
Black	19,700	52
18–20 years old	10,700	32
21–24 years old	14,800	38
25–34 years old	42,700	48
35–44 years old	35,200	61
45–64 years old	45,900	68
65 years old and over	28,800	69
North and West residence	117,400	59
South residence	60,700	55
Years of school completed:		
8 years or less	19,100	37
9–11 years	21,052	41
12 years	70,000	55
More than 12 years	67,900	65*
		78†
Employed	113,800	58
Unemployed	5,800	39
Not in labor force	58,500	57

* One to three years of college.
† Four years or more of college.

Source: U.S. Bureau of the Census, "Voting and Registration in the Election of November, 1988," *Current Population Reports*, Series P-20. No. 440, pp. 13, 16, 17, 23, 44, 50.

An Immediate Stake. Another factor that comes into play is whether individuals have highly concrete interests in election outcomes. Those who do are more likely to vote. For example, farm owners, who are highly dependent on governmental decisions for their livelihood, are notably active participants. So, too, are governmental employees, who are affected by what government does just as other citizens are, but who in addition have their wages and other conditions of employment determined by elected officials.[36]

Age. Voter turnout is lowest at the beginning of adult life, increases to reach a plateau in middle age, and then declines in old age.[37] Beyond this, the lower levels of voting by young adults are much more pronounced outside the ranks of the college-educated than for those with college training. "In other words, the start-up costs of voting [developing a level of understanding and interest in politics] are not borne equally by all young people. The cost of entering the political system is relatively small for the educated, but for those without such skills the costs are [as a statistical expression] nearly three times as great."[38]

Partisan Implications. How much do voters differ from nonvoters in political terms? Voters are generally of higher socioeconomic standing and have more formal education than nonvoters, but are their political interests and values different? If voters and nonvoters are very different politically, then the widespread nonvoting in contemporary American politics means that our electorates can be highly unrepresentative.

As a group, voters used to be slightly higher in Republican identification than the entire adult population by a few percentage points.[39] This may be changing, however. In 1986, voters were a bit more Democratic than the voting-age populace as a whole. The main story is that political differences between voters and nonvoters are small. "On some issues voters are a shade more liberal than the entire population; and on others they are a trifle more

[36] Ibid., pp. 30–35.
[37] Lipset, *Political Man*, p. 189.
[38] Wolfinger and Rosenstone, *Who Votes?* p. 60.
[39] Ibid., pp. 109–10.

conservative. . . . In short, on these issues voters are virtually a carbon copy of the citizen population. Those most likely to be underrepresented are people who lack opinions."[40] The tiny differences between voters and the entire citizenry on various policy issues "suggest that on these political questions people who vote are representative of the population as a whole."[41]

OTHER FORMS OF POLITICAL PARTICIPATION

Americans may turn out at the polls at a lower rate than their counterparts in other democracies, but they exercise their control over the political process through a much more extensive array of elections than any other citizenry. Over 500,000 offices are filled by election in the United States within every four-year election cycle. "No country can approach the United States in the frequency and variety of elections and thus in the amount of electoral participation in which its citizens have a right."[42] No other country chooses the lower house of its national legislature as often as every two years, as the United States does. No other country has such a broad array of offices—including judges, sheriffs, city treasurers, attorneys general— subject to election. No other country (with the exception of Switzerland) approaches the United States in the number or variety of local referenda on policy issues. The United States is almost alone in using primary elections as the vehicle for choosing party nominees; in most democratic nations party organizations pick the nominees. Ivor Crewe concludes that "the average American is entitled to do far more

electing—probably by a factor of three or four— than the citizenry of any other democracy."

This suggests a critical modification of the common observation that voter participation is low in the United States. Turnout in national elections is indeed low, but in other regards voter participation is very high. The American electorate expresses itself in more political decisions through casting ballots than the electorate of any other country. In fact, some observers suggest that the very frequency of elections in America serves to reduce the proportion turning out in any given contest: "Hohum—another election."

Besides, elections are not the only way in which people participate politically.[43] And, outside the electoral arena, Americans appear highly participatory compared to their counterparts in other countries. We noted in chapter 11 the high level of involvement in interest groups and voluntary associations in the United States. As in voting, participation in these other political activities is strongly related to socioeconomic status (Table 12.13). Only 20 percent of those with less than a high school education said in 1988 that they were "very interested" in political campaigns, compared to 24 percent of high school graduates, 38 percent of those with some college, 46 percent of college graduates, and 54 percent of those with advanced degrees. Only 1 percent of those with little education indicated that they had made a financial contribution to a candidate, compared to 14 percent of those with the highest levels of formal training.

---

[40] Ibid., p. 109.

[41] Ibid., p. 111.

[42] Crewe, "Electoral Participation," in *Democracy at the Polls*, p. 232.

[43] Ronald Mason argues that political science has placed too much stress on the narrowly electoral forms of political participation. See Ronald M. Mason, "Toward A Non-Liberal Perspective on Participation," paper presented at the Midwest Political Science Association Meeting, April 1980.

TABLE 12.13 LEVELS OF POLITICAL INTEREST AND PARTICIPATION BY
SOCIOECONOMIC POSITION (IN PERCENT)

	Very interested in political campaigns	Contributed money to a candidate during the 1984 campaign	Attended political meetings, rallies, or other political activity
Education			
College graduate plus advanced training	54	14	18
College graduate	46	11	12
Some college	38	8	10
High school graduate	24	3	4
Less than four years of high school	20	1	3
Family income			
$50,000 or more	43	14	13
35,000–49,999	31	9	10
25,000–34,999	34	6	7
20,000–24,999	30	5	8
15,000–19,999	30	1	3
10,000–14,999	30	2	4
Under $10,000	21	1	4

Source: Center for Political Studies, University of Michigan, 1988 election surveys.

SUMMARY

Political parties as we now know them first took form in the infant United States at the end of the eighteenth century. An institutional response to the new reality of political egalitarianism, they have become central institutions in all democracies and in many other countries as well. Parties form a link between the public and government. Properly organized in a democratic system, they can greatly increase voters' control over their governmental officials and public decision making.

The American party system has a number of distinctive attributes. Almost alone in the world, it is a two-party system. For over a century, the Republicans and Democrats have won the overwhelming majority of votes and offices. American parties are inclusive and heterogeneous practitioners of political compromise and accommodation. They do not have members, only adherents; they exercise remarkably little discipline over their elites. Party organization is weak in the face of strong currents of political individualism. Rank-and-file voters typically select nominees through primary elections. No other democracy gives party leaders so little control over candidate selection.

Two features of American electoral arrangements are especially distinguishing. One is the heavy use of primary elections to pick party nominees. The other is the reliance on the single-member district, single-ballot, simple-majority system for translating votes into seats. This system has done much to bolster the ascendancy of the two major parties. If the United States instituted plural-member districts with proportional representation, it is likely that third parties would proliferate.

The shape of the party coalitions has changed greatly in modern times. Many social groups manifest new party loyalties and voting behavior. The shift in the partisan attachments of white southerners and blacks has been especially dramatic. The partisan balance of power has also changed. A weak second to the Democrats through much of the New Deal era and into late 1970s, the Republicans have found their electoral position significantly strengthened. In the early 1990s, the two main parties stand in positions of rough parity.

Even as the coalitions have shifted, voter ties to both parties have weakened. *Dealignment*, the moving of voters away from strong partisan loyalties, has accelerated over the past fifteen years. The electorate is now less anchored by party identifications than it used to be, and it can be shifted more easily by the issues of the time.

Election campaigns are seen by many observers of U.S. politics as manifesting a slew of problems. The role of interest-group money is notable among them. What to do about it is a source of vigorous debate—but nothing approaching consensus has yet been arrived at.

Important federal legislation covering campaign spending was enacted in the 1970s. Limits were imposed on how much individuals and groups could contribute to federal candidates. Effective disclosure provisions were instituted, to be administered by the Federal Election Commission (FEC). Public funding was established for presidential elections, along with tight spending limits for candidates who accept governmental assistance.

The legislation also encouraged the formation of political action committees (PACs) by business corporations, trade associations, labor unions, and other groups, to collect and disseminate funds for political purposes. Though tightly supervised by the FEC, PACs became the hub of current contention over money in politics. PACs give much more support to incumbents of both parties than to challengers. Many now believe that curbs need to be placed on PAC money, though the shape of a proper system of campaign finance is hotly debated.

Today there is also concern over the low and somewhat diminished level of voter turnout in the United States. Just over 50 percent of voting-age residents cast ballots in the 1988 presidential election; this was well below the 63 percent turnout in 1960, the modern high in the United States.

But the curious way the United States expresses its rate of voter participation—as a percentage of the resident adult population, even though millions of these residents by law cannot vote—makes turnout seem lower than it really is. Still, it is lower than in most other democracies. This is partly because the United States has so many elections that it is hard for any one to seem a special event. The low turnout is also partly a response to a system where political stresses have been relatively manageable. The perceived cost of not voting, in short, has not been nearly as high in the United States as in most other democracies.

Voter turnout has been declining over the last thirty years. The weakening of local party organization and the increasing distance and complexity of government have probably been major factors accounting for the dropoff in voting. The negative, even disparaging, tone of campaign coverage in the media may also have encouraged some to "tune out."

FOR FURTHER STUDY

Butler, David, Howard R. Penniman, and Austin Ranney, eds. *Democracy at the Polls: A Comparative Study of Competitive National Elections.* Washington, D.C.:

American Enterprise Institute for Public Policy Research, 1981. A superb collection of articles comparing electoral experience in democracies around the world.

Congressional Quarterly. *Guide to U.S. Elections.* Washington, D.C.: Congressional Quarterly Press, 1985. A compendium of information on U.S. presidential elections from 1789 through 1984.

Federal Election Commission. Miscellaneous reports: campaign guides, federal election campaign laws, FEC reports on financial activity (of candidates, parties, and PACs) and numerous other documents—many provided free—by the FEC, 999 E Street and 1325 K Street, NW, Washington, D.C.

Polsby, Nelson W. *Consequences of Party Reform.* New York: Oxford University Press, 1983. Advances a strong criticism of changes made in the presidential nominating system, especially by the Democrats, in the 1960s, and 1970s.

Polsby, Nelson W. and Aaron Wildavsky. *Presidential Elections: Contemporary Strategies of American Electoral Politics*, 8th ed. New York: Free Press, 1991. The best analysis of recent presidential elections in the United States.

Ranney, Austin. *Curing the Mischiefs of Faction: Party Reform in America.* Berkeley, Calif.: University of California Press, 1975. The best available analysis of the theory and practice of party reform historically in the United States.

Rossiter, Clinton. *Parties and Politics in America.* Ithaca, N.Y.: Cornell University Press, 1960. A highly readable yet thoughtful account of what is distinctive about American political parties.

Sabato, Larry J. *The Rise of Political Consultants.* New York: Basic Books / Harper and Row, 1981. A study of the changing dynamics of campaigning in the United States, centering on the increased role of professional campaign consultants.

Sartori, Giovanni. *Parties and Party Systems: A Framework for Analysis.* Cambridge: Cambridge University Press, 1976. A comparison of party systems in countries around the world.

Scammon, Richard C. Alive V. McGillivray, eds. *America Votes: A Handbook of Contemporary American Election Statistics.* Washington, D.C.: Congressional Quarterly, latest volume, 1991. A compendium of electoral data on each biennial election, by state, since 1948.

Wolfinger, Raymond E., and Steven J. Rosenstone. *Who Votes?* New Haven, Conn.: Yale University Press, 1980. The best available study of who votes and who doesn't vote in the United States, based on analysis of surveys conducted by the U.S. Bureau of the Census.

OPTIONAL COMPUTER EXERCISES

for *The Ladd Election ANALYZER*

VOTERS AND THEIR PARTIES

In the discussion on party identification (pp. 352–60), we saw that the Republican party has gained increasing support from among the ranks of young people in recent years. Did this support show up in the 1992 electorate? Among those who went to the polls, were the young once again a good group for the Republicans? What was the best age group for the Democrats? Choose "1992 vote" from the "Vote questions" menu (under "Select question to analyze"); select "Age" from the "Demographics" menu and "Usual Party Affiliation" from the "Vote Questions" menu as your respondents' characteristics.

A few advanced analyses. Compare how various age groups among voters identified their party affiliation in the 1988 and 1992 elections. Were there any significant changes over this span? Also, compare the pattern of party identification for racial, ethnic, and religious groups—for example, whites, blacks, Hispanics, Roman Catholics, white Protestants—in the 1988 and 1992 electorates.

[Note: See Appendix 4, "The 1992 Election and the Clinton Administration" for many more vote and party related end-of-chapter computer exercises.]

Chapter *13*

THE MEDIA

Developments in the technologies of communication, especially in television, are having profound political impact. Again and again we are seeing how, in today's "global village" of pervasive electronic communication, events in one country immediately attain international currency. Television's role in China's aborted pro-democracy revolution of the spring of 1989 is a dramatic case in point.

Through the medium of broadcast satellites and television, millions of Americans in homes all across the United States—together with countless millions more in other countries—saw the Goddess of Democracy unveiled in Tiananmen Square, in the heart of the Chinese capital, on May 30, 1989. For three days and nights, their democracy movement under siege, students at the Central Academy of Fine Arts in Beijing had labored to create the ultimate expression of their yearnings—and their defiance of China's communist regime. Using styrofoam, wood, and gleaming plaster of Paris, the student sculptors fashioned a gigantic figure of a woman, hair blowing in the wind, her two arms raised and together clutching a torch of freedom. No one who has seen the Statue of Liberty in New York Harbor could fail to see the pro-

The Goddess of Democracy in Tiananmen Square, Beijing, photographed by a journalist prior to the Chinese government's suppression of the democracy demonstrations.

found resemblance. "We will dedicate this statue to the student cause," one protest leader announced to 30,000 cheering supporters. "We dedicate this to the millions of students in China, to the people of Beijing, China, and the world who support our movement. . . . We have won victory after victory because the power of the people cannot be defeated. This government does not have any humanity. They are using obscenities and cheating and lies to cover Beijing in a cloud of darkness. They want to kill the democratic movement in the cradle. But the judgment days are coming for these leaders."[1]

TELEVISION SHRINKS THE PLANET

The full, televised immediacy of this scene and other events in Tiananmen Square in May and

[1] Quoted in Scott Simmie and Bob Nixon, *Tiananmen Square* (Seattle: University of Washington Press, 1989), p. 159.

early June 1989—until Chinese authorities shut down the Western telecasts and suppressed the prodemocracy marchers—clearly gripped the American public. The Chinese government had a long record of oppressing its people; its use of force against the protesters in Tiananmen Square and their allies elsewhere in the country was not out of character. But *reading* about a government's injustice is one thing; *seeing*, in full color, brave young people articulate the highest ideals of freedom and democracy and then have their aspirations trampled is something different. Television—especially the U.S. Cable News Network (CNN)—was a major political force in China's extraordinary grasp for revolutionary change in 1989.

Television's expanded role globally extends, of course, far beyond the events in China. Through the use of equipment that permits pictures to be beamed up directly to broadcast satellites and then transmitted into homes and offices around the world, the medium has been freed from dependence on local transmission facilities and given an immediate reach beyond anything imaginable even a decade ago. While by no means alone in this latest stage of the "television revolution," Cable News Network, with its extensive facilities and 24-hour-a-day news telecasts, has become the premier player. "I said on '60 Minutes' ten years ago that we had the dream of making CNN available to the whole world," Ted Turner, CNN's founder, observed in a recent interview. "I wanted to use communications as a positive force in the world, to tie the world together. And you know something, it's working."[2] Hubert Vebrine, national security adviser to President François Mitterand of France, argues that the increased availability of CNN and other networks via satellites is "both an element of stability and an element of contagion." "No leader," he states, "can any longer keep his people hostage using Goebbels-like propaganda. It's become technically impossible."[3]

Political and business leaders around the world use CNN as a means of communicating instantaneously with one another. When U.S. troops intervened in Panama in December 1989, the Soviet Union's foreign ministry made its first call not to the American embassy but to CNN's Moscow bureau. The network's camera crew then found a Soviet spokesman eager to read on camera a statement condemning the American action—before the statement had run on the official Tass news agency. In the Gulf War in 1991, CNN was a principal source of information on developments in Baghdad, the capital of Iraq. Its coverage was widely praised. "Whenever we smell something cooking, we keep CNN on," a Japanese foreign ministry spokesman remarked recently. "It's the quick-

est way . . . of confirming events taking place unexpectedly."[4]

TRANSFORMING TECHNOLOGY

Even in its basic form television is only a half-century old. But already it has gone through a series of stages. As we saw, the latest in the past decade is an extraordinary increase in the medium's capacity to reach instantly around the world; at the same time, there has been a huge expansion in the range of television programming available to viewers. In the United States the number of independent stations—not tied to the traditional networks—doubled from 197 to 398 between 1983 and 1989. A new network, Fox, was created; in 1990 it had 129 affiliated stations in 45 states.

But cable has truly transformed the U.S. television scene. Roughly 60 percent of Amer-

[4]Ibid.

FIGURE 13.1 AVERAGE TELEVISION USAGE PER HOUSEHOLD PER DAY

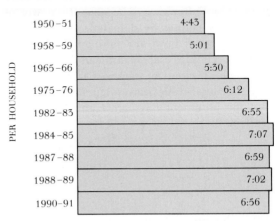

1950–51	4:43
1958–59	5:01
1965–66	5:30
1975–76	6:12
1982–83	6:55
1984–85	7:07
1987–88	6:59
1988–89	7:02
1990–91	6:56

PER HOUSEHOLD

Data reflects usage from September through August for each season.
Source: Nielsen Media Research, *Report on Television 1990,* and unpublished data from Nielsen, Communications Branch, 1992.

[2]Philip Reuzin, Peter Waldman, and Peter Gumbel, "Ted Turner's CNN Having Global Influence and Diplomatic Role," *Wall Street Journal,* February 1, 1990, pp. 1, 14.
[3]Ibid. Joseph Paul Goebbels was minister of propaganda under Adolf Hitler in Nazi Germany, 1933–45.

FIGURE 13.2   TELEVISION TECHNOLOGIES RAPIDLY UNFOLD

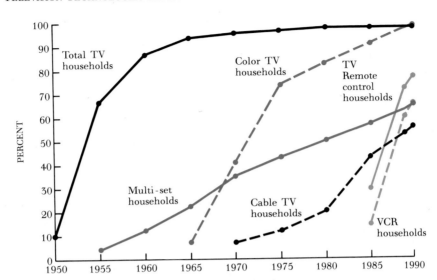

Estimated U.S. television households = 92.1 million on January 1, 1990 (Nielsen).
Source: Nielsen Media Research, *Television Audience*, 1989.

ican houses are now wired for cable. The Nielsen ratings service measures about 20 cable networks, the largest of which are CNN, ESPN, WTBS (a "superstation" widely carried by local cable outlets), USA, and HBO (a pay cable network featuring first-run movies). As a result of cable's growth, the number of channels available in households has increased dramatically as has the amount of time spent watching television. (See Figure 13.1 and 13.2)

THE PRESS: POWER AND PRESTIGE

Early in American history, much of the work of government was done locally, in the nation's then-predominant small towns and rural areas. It was "up close and personal": People could see it firsthand, talk with the decision makers, ask them to explain or defend their actions. Today things are greatly changed. The work of government is far more complex and remote. Most citizens literally never see in person the state and national government officials whose decisions have such large consequences for their lives. In today's conditions, if we are to gain the information we need about politicians, politics, and events, we will do so for the most part through mass media of communication—large-circulation national and metropolitan newspapers like the *New York Times*, the *Wall Street Journal*, and *USA Today*; popular news magazines such as *Time*, *Newsweek*, and *U.S. News & World Report*; and, especially, radio and TV.

From this basic development the media or "the press" has emerged as an ever more central social and political institution. It is relied upon—and complained about. The extent of its power and how that power is employed are much discussed. These and other matters bearing on the role of the media in modern American democracy will be discussed in this chapter.

It is not hard to detect the consequences of the use of power in certain instances, as when an authoritarian government uses its control of the police and armed forces to stifle opposition. But in many cases the effects are hard to measure: How much power does big business have in the United States? Organized labor? There is not even agreement on how to understand the concept of power in such instances, much less any precise measure of that power or what it achieves. We are on firmer ground when we talk not about power but about resources relevant to the exercise of power. The economic resources available to those who head certain

Facing the power and prestige of the press and its reporting—now a constant of the U.S. political scene and of many other areas in American society—is not always to the public's liking (see cartoon, next page).

major corporations in the United States can be described, and we can see where there is discretion in employing them and where there is not. This does not give us a definitive picture of the power or influence of American business leaders, but it does provide us with a better sense of their potential power vis-à-vis other groups. Similarly, by examining the resources available to the communications media, we gain a clearer understanding of what the debate over the power of the press involves.

Let us begin with a hypothetical question. What would be the consequences for democracy if these two conditions obtained: (1) Government scrupulously maintained a "hands off" position with regard to the press, not using its authority to limit who communicates what to whom, but (2) certain private interests held huge and disproportionate communications resources and used these to advance their own perspectives on politics? (By communications resources we mean facilities for collecting political information and presenting it to mass audiences.) What if certain private interests owned all the television stations and used them to reach mass audiences to push their own political preferences, ignoring or misrepresenting other points of view? Could democratic government function satisfactorily in this situation? Few think that it could. Press resources matter, and even scrupulous enforcement of the First Amendment cannot solve all problems regarding these resources.

MASS AUDIENCES

In the past, concerns about press resources seemed remote. The economics and technology of communications allowed new communications media, typically newspapers, to be established easily, and none of them could reach very large audiences. Resources were widely dispersed. As long as government did not intervene to throttle freedom of commu-

nication, there was little to worry about. For example, in New York, the nation's largest city, the *Morning Herald* was started in 1835 with just $500 and the *Tribune* in 1841 with $3,000.[5] Anyone with a little money and writing ability could set up a newspaper and compete effectively in the dissemination of political ideas. Newspapers reached at most a few thousand people and did not cost much to establish.

Subsequent developments in transportation and communications changed this—making possible big audiences and requiring great financial outlays. Even with greater competition from cable, on an average weekday evening, about 50 million Americans tune in to the national news broadcasts of CBS, NBC, ABC, and public television. Whereas most cit-izens can express their views to at most a few score of their fellows, a nightly network news telecast reaches 15 million people or more. The question of how much a TV anchor influences American political life has been endlessly debated with few certain conclusions. But the mere act of creating audiences of the size generated by contemporary American television news programming has encouraged the perception that vast communications power is thus imparted. Network television audiences are unusually large, but a number of print media also have huge circulations. Table 13.1 shows the ten individual newspapers with the largest circulations. At the top of the list, with a paid circulation of nearly 2 million (and hence perhaps 4 million readers daily) is the *Wall Street Journal.*

[5] For a general discussion of press resources prior to the Civil War, see Frank Luther Mott, *American Journalism: A History of 250 Years, 1690 to 1940* (New York: Macmillan, 1947), pp. 215–323.

FINANCIAL RESOURCES

The attainment of large audiences permits the great print and electronic media to generate

TABLE 13.1   PAID CIRCULATION OF THE TEN
LARGEST U.S. DAILY NEWSPAPERS

Newspaper	Circulation
Wall Street Journal	1,835,713
USA Today	1,325,507
New York Daily News	1,194,237
Los Angeles Times	1,107,623
New York Times	1,068,217
Washington Post	772,749
Chicago Tribune	720,155
New York Post	700,174
Detroit News	690,422
Detroit Free Press	626,434

Source: 1990 Editor and Publisher International Yearbook
(New York: Editor and Publisher Co., 1990). The reporting
date for circulation of above newspapers is September 30,
1989.

enormous revenues, especially through the sale
of advertising.

The financial resources generated by the
largest communications media are used for
many things, including news coverage far
beyond that of any previous period. The networks have recently experienced cutbacks,
reflecting the loss of audience noted above.
Still, CBS News has about 200 full-time staff
members in its Washington bureau, including
a score of on-the-air reporters. The Associated
Press's Washington, D.C., bureau has 100
reporters. In all, about 1,700 reporters are
assigned to the White House alone. Big special
news events attract throngs of reporters. The
national party conventions, for example, now
draw as many as 15,000 journalists—who thus
far outnumber the conventions' official participants. Such numbers make it possible for
political actions to be probed and dissected to
a detail unimaginable in the past.

The great financial resources of the major
communications media permit them to support
their staffs far more generously than in the

past. Historically, journalists were a poorly paid
professional group. At the New York Times in
1990, however, a reporter earned a minimum
of $56,000 a year, and leading columnists and
top editors received salaries several times as
great. The most dramatic salary gains have
been recorded in television news, where national
news personalities are now paid multimillion
dollar salaries. Not surprisingly, the enhanced
pay of journalists and the huge audiences now
open to those reporting for the leading media
have increased the prestige and glamour of the
profession of journalism.

ORGANIZATION OF
THE PRESS

Though it is not a part of the government in
any democracy, the press plays an essential
public-sector role, performing functions central to political life. Even when it is wholly
privately owned and operated, the press has
broad public responsibilities, chief of which is
seeing to it that citizens have access to the
information they need to decide the issues before
them.

In most democracies, a distinction is made
in practice between those segments of the press
that articulate particular group interests and
perspectives, partisan or ideological, and those
that are general-circulation vehicles of news
dissemination. There is little debate over what
public policy should be with regard to the former: Government should simply stay out of the
way, allowing the journals of opinion to speak
their mind freely. But with regard to general-
circulation news media, there is argument in
every democratic nation. How should the mass-
audience press be organized to perform its
broad public-sector responsibility of assuring
the citizenry access to needed information?

OWNERSHIP

In the United States, there has been general agreement on one part of the answer: The press should be privately owned and operated, with the fewest possible governmental regulations and restraints. Democracy requires a free press, and freedom is most securely attained when government is kept at arm's length. The natural interplay of market forces will ensure a variety of general-circulation communications media that, in competition with one another, will see to it that the news is as fully and fairly reported as is practically possible. Note that this emphasis on free markets is akin to the more general American rationale for a private business system, which emphasizes the importance of free competition in meeting consumers' needs.

American newspapers and news magazines are private corporations, owned and operated much like other private businesses. Those wishing to establish a new paper capitalize it like those wishing to set up any other business; if they cannot maintain their news business profitably, they cease to operate. Every year a number of newspapers and magazines are established while others close their doors. Newspaper births and deaths have largely balanced out in recent decades; there were 1,763 daily newspapers in the United States at the end of World War II and about 1,650 in 1990.[6]

The ownership status of the general-circulation print media in America is essentially what one finds in other democratic countries, where the print media are privately owned. The organization of radio and television in the United States differs substantially, however, from that

[6]Leo Bogart, "Newspapers in Transition," *Wilson Quarterly*, special issue (1982), p. 69; see also *1990 Gale Directory of Publications.*

"And as the campaign heats up, the latest poll shows the Dan Rather news team running slightly ahead of the Peter Jennings news team, with the Tom Brokaw team just two points back and gaining."

Drawing by Lorenz; © 1988 The New Yorker Magazine, Inc.

in other democracies. The three major television networks—the Columbia Broadcasting System (CBS), the American Broadcasting Company (ABC), and the National Broadcasting Company (NBC)—together with a preponderance of local television stations, are privately owned businesses. Throughout Europe telecommunications was seen from the beginning as a public utility to be run as a national monopoly. Government's role in managing radio and television is still greater in the European democracies than in the United States. In recent years, however, privately owned media have been given increasing scope in Europe and are expanding greatly.

REGULATION

Radio and television regulation is the one area where the U.S. government is significantly involved in the mass communications media. The Federal Communications Commission (FCC) licenses radio and television stations. A corporation wishing to establish a VHF or UHF television station cannot simply purchase the necessary equipment, hire staff, and begin broadcasting. The FCC must license it to operate on a particular frequency. The now rather detailed provisions of FCC licensing developed from the straightforward premise that some basic regulation of who could broadcast at what frequency was needed to prevent a hopeless scrambling of signals. There are no technical limits on the number of newspapers or news magazines that can be disseminated in a particular market; but the airwaves are a finite common property, defined by the laws of physics, rather than simply by laws of supply and demand.

If the basic rationale for governmental regulation of the broadcast media is unexceptionable, the result has been to establish a governmental agency—the FCC, which is an independent regulatory commission—with substantial authority. Television stations now must go before the commission every five years to renew their licenses. AM and FM radio stations must seek renewal every seven years. In practice they are rarely turned down, but there have been a few dramatic cases of denial. On what grounds can the FCC deny renewal? From the beginning of the broadcast industry, U.S. policy has stipulated that a license to broadcast, once conferred, is not permanent. Subsequent performance must be taken into account in determining whether renewal is to be granted. Stations are given access to a vital public resource, the airwaves. Do they use it responsibly? Are they attuned to the needs and interests of their broadcast areas? Few would argue that the FCC should automatically extend licenses regardless of what stations do on the air. But on the issue of what constitutes insufficient performance, confusion reigns. The sword rarely falls—but it is left hanging.

Federal regulation of news broadcasting has occurred in three related areas: (1) the fairness doctrine, (2) the equal-time provision, and (3) the right of rebuttal. Involved are so-called access rights, established initially through Section 315 of the Federal Communications Act of 1934 and its various amendments and interpretations. The **fairness doctrine** required broadcasters who aired material on controversial issues to provide reasonable time for the expression of opposing views. Critics of this provision long argued that it had the effect of discouraging the media from covering certain controversial issues, to avoid having to air opposing views in place of programs that generate revenue.[7] The broadcast industry opposed the regulation and had challenged it in the courts on the grounds that it infringed First Amendment rights. In August 1987, the FCC

---

[7] For a discussion of the effects see Doris A. Graber, *Mass Media and American Politics*, 3rd ed. (Washington, D.C.: Congressional Quarterly Press, 1989), pp. 115–18.

voted 4–0 to repeal the fairness doctrine—partly responding to the legal challenge and partly reflecting the general commitment of Reagan appointees to deregulating the broadcast industry. These appointees believed that the dramatic expansion of television-viewing options—cable systems, videotape cassettes, and more—has increased market competition and thus obviated the need for some of the traditional forms of regulation.

Similarly, since television stations are now seen as vigorously competing against other stations, as well as other types of television media (especially cable networks), the FCC proposed in May 1992 reducing curbs on the number of stations a single owner can hold. Up to now owners have been restricted to twelve stations nationwide. The proposal would raise that number to twenty or twenty-four.

The **equal-time** provision, still in force, stipulates that broadcasters who permit one candidate for public office to campaign on their stations must give equal opportunities to every other candidate for that office. For example, they cannot sell air time to a Republican candidate for a U.S. Senate seat and deny the same type of time, at the same rates, to a Democratic, Libertarian, or other party candidate. Like the fairness doctrine, the equal-time provision has been under legal challenge as violating broadcasters' First Amendment rights. In 1988, however, the Supreme Court refused to hear an appeal of a lower court decision on the constitutional issue, in effect stating that it considered the equal-time rule to be constitutionally permitted regulation.

The **right-of-rebuttal** provisions are ancillaries of the fairness doctrine that have remained in force. They involve the right of individuals to respond to personal attacks made over radio or television that might be held to damage their reputations. In the case of *Red Lion Broadcasting v. Federal Communications Commission* (1969), a liberal newsman who had written a

book critical of conservative Senator Barry Goldwater brought suit because he was denied free air time to rebut an aired attack on his book by a conservative clergyman. The clergyman headed a religious organization—known as the Christian Crusade—that bought and paid for the program on which the book was attacked. In the *Red Lion* case, the Supreme Court granted the newsman the air time he had demanded, free of charge, holding that maligned individuals deserve an opportunity to reply and that the public deserves the opportunity to hear opposing views.[8] Interestingly, the litigation that the newsman brought in the *Red Lion* case was supported and paid for by the Democratic National Committee. The DNC was seeking to generate a rush of demands for rebuttal to conservative radio and TV programs—with the hope that stations would cancel the programs to avoid having to provide free rebuttals. The DNC's plan worked. By late 1975, the Christian Crusade had been dropped by 300 of its 350 stations. In response to developments such as this, the FCC has softened somewhat its broad support of rebuttal rights at station expense—which encouraged stations to avoid controversial programming altogether.

Outside of radio and television broadcasting, the press in the United States has not felt the regulatory hand of government very heavily. In Florida, legislation was enacted in the 1960s that in effect carried the right-of-rebuttal provision over to newspapers. Candidates attacked by a newspaper editorially were given the right to reply on the pages of the paper. A case arising under this statute was decided by the U.S. Supreme Court in 1974: *Miami Herald Publishing Company v. Tornillo*. The Court struck down Florida's law. Chief Justice Warren Burger ruled that the case for rebuttal rights, which applies in radio and TV from the use of a limited public resource, the airwaves,

8 Graber, *Mass Media*, pp. 118–19.

does not extend to print media. "Even if a newspaper would face no additional costs to comply with a compulsory access law and would not be forced to forgo publication of news or opinion by the inclusion of a reply, the Florida statute fails to clear the barriers of the First Amendment because of its intrusion into the function of editors," the Chief Justice wrote. "A newspaper is more than a passive receptacle or conduit for news, comment, and advertising. The choice of material to go into a newspaper, and the decisions made as to limitations on the size and content of the paper, and treatment of public issues and public officials—whether fair or unfair—constitute the exercise of editorial control and judgment."

LIBEL LAW

The application of libel laws in Great Britain and the United States provides an illustration of the comparative freedom of the American press from regulatory controls. What if a newspaper story about a political leader states things harmful to his reputation that can be demonstrated to be untrue? If he can prove in a court of law that the accounts are false, can he collect damages from the newspaper? In Britain, the answer is generally yes. Not surprisingly, the British press is reluctant to print critical materials when it is not certain that it can establish their accuracy. "British newspapers are often forced to delay publication until their evidence is watertight or until foreign newspapers and the underground press have made an item common knowledge."[9] The author of a story, the publisher, and those selling the paper or book can all be sued in Britain for defamatory libel.

In the United States, more than defamatory inaccuracy must be proved before a conviction for libel may be sustained. In the 1964 case of *New York Times Company v. Sullivan*, the Supreme Court ruled that a "public official" seeking libel damages for a matter relating to his official conduct must prove that the false statement about him had been made with "actual malice"—that is, with conscious knowledge that the statement was false or with "reckless disregard" for whether it was false or not. The Court held that, otherwise, the press or other critics would be restrained from speaking or writing for fear they could not readily demonstrate that what they had said was true. As a practical matter, it is very hard to prove that defamatory falsehoods about a public official were made with "actual malice," and the American communications media are largely free from the threat of libel action in their reporting on public officials.[10]

The High Court strongly reaffirmed its *New York Times* standard in a 1988 case, *Hustler Magazine, Inc. v. Falwell*. The Reverend Jerry Falwell, a prominent conservative clergyman, was portrayed in the pages of this less-than-distinguished skin magazine as, among other things, having engaged in a drunken incestuous rendezvous with his mother in an outhouse. Falwell sued. Without a dissenting vote, the Court ruled that the First and Fourteenth Amendments prohibit public figures from recovering damages for distress intentionally inflicted upon them by publications such as the Hustler "parody." Chief Justice Rehnquist wrote

[9]Max Belloff and Gillian Peole, *The Government of the United Kingdom: Political Authority in a Changing Society* (New York: Norton, 1980), pp. 336–37.

[10]A. E. Dick Howard, "The Press in Court," *Wilson Quarterly*, special issue (1982), pp. 87–90; see also *New York Times Company v. Sullivan*, 376 U.S. 254 (1964). In recent years, the Supreme Court has shown no sign of backing away from the strong protection it gave the press in *New York Times Company v. Sullivan*. For example, in June 1986, in *Anderson v. Liberty Lobby*, the Court made it easier for press defendants in libel cases to win pretrial dismissal of suits against them.

that "Falwell is a 'public figure' for purposes of First Amendment law," and as such cannot enjoy the protection a private citizen might receive. "This is not merely a 'blind application' of *The New York Times* standard . . . it reflects our considered judgment that such a standard is necessary to give adequate 'breathing space' to the freedoms [here of the press] protected by the First Amendment."

Distinctions between the legal position of the American and British press can be seen in other areas. For example, the British Official Secrets Act, passed in 1911, makes the *unauthorized receipt* of official government documents, as well as their *unauthorized publication*, an offense. While the government has not used this legislation in an oppressive manner, the act is still a source of governmental restraint on the press. In contrast, in the United States, the Freedom of Information Act (1974) gives the press a strong legal base from which to force the government to release documents that they might choose to withhold. The burden is on the government to prove that some harm, as to national security, might come from release of the documents.

CONTRADICTORY TRENDS

Communications media in the United States have been experiencing contradictory developments in terms of centralization and decentralization. Historically, as noted, America did not have a national press. Its newspapers—unlike Great Britain's, for example—were predominantly local, circulating only in one urban area or state. In recent years, though, this has been changing. New communications technology has made it possible for a newspaper whose editorial staff is located in one city to transmit information via satellite to printing plants located throughout the country. The paper is then distributed from the local plants to newsstands and subscribers just like any other local paper.

The *Wall Street Journal* was the first American newspaper to take full advantage of this new technology. The *New York Times*, perhaps the most prestigious paper in the country, began following suit in the early 1980s, although the New York City base of many of its advertising clients presented serious obstacles. New York department stores usually do not want to pay for advertising in other geographic areas. In September 1982, the Gannett chain of newspapers established *USA Today*, the first daily in American history established as a nationwide, general-circulation, general-news publication. Fifteen months after its birth, "America's newspaper," as Gannett calls it, was selling about 1.2 million copies a day all across the country. No longer could it be said that the United States lacked a national press.

These recent centralizing developments have been in addition to the long-established role of the national wire services in news reporting. Local papers draw much of their coverage from the Associated Press (AP), United Press International (UPI), the *New York Times*, *Washington Post*, or *Los Angeles Times* wire services.[11] The masthead may say Bangor, Maine; Tucson, Arizona; Spokane, Washington; or Savannah, Georgia; but when it comes to news of national and international politics, a few centralized reportorial organizations, with great resources, dominate the scene.[12]

The first few decades of television were characterized by a very different condition than the one that prevailed historically with newspapers. Television-station ownership was dispersed, but both entertainment and national news reporting were highly centralized—dominated by the three big commercial networks. Now, however,

---

[11] The roots of the AP and UPI go back to 1848, when six New York newspapers banded together to share the costs of gathering foreign news. The major wire services now maintain huge staffs of reporters throughout the world.

[12] See Bogart, "Newspapers in Transition," p. 58.

Television viewers have more choice today than in the era of the big-three network dominance. Cable hookups allow viewers to pick up CNN (Cable News Network), C-SPAN, and other cable news broadcasts.

the television industry is experiencing an extraordinary fracturing, as many new players challenge the stranglehold on audience that ABC, CBS, and NBC used to have. We have seen that the extension of cable television to more and more households—and with it, the emergence of new cable networks—is the major source for change in this area. In particular, new national news programs have been established in recent years, eroding the dominant position that the "Big Three" networks long enjoyed. More pluralism and diversity, not more concentration, is television's future.

EVOLUTION OF THE PRESS

The communications media in the United States today differ greatly in size, resources, organization, and modes of operation from their counterparts in earlier periods. The press evolved in the years following ratification of the Constitution with very close ties to the infant political parties. Indeed, historians often refer to newspapers in the early years as "the party press."

NEWSPAPERS AND POLITICAL PARTIES

As the new parties took shape, politicians began starting or enlisting newspapers to help them communicate their partisan interpretations of political events to their constituents. A leading historian of American journalism, Frank Luther Mott, notes that

as party feelings grew, a new reason for the existence of newspapers came to be recognized. Whereas nearly all newspapers heretofore had been set up as auxiliaries to printing establishments and had been looked upon merely as means which enterprising printers used to make a living, now they were more and more often founded as spokesmen of political parties. This gave a new dignity and a new color to American journalism.[13]

The *Gazette of the United States* was established in 1789 as a semi-weekly newspaper, with the avowed intent of telling the Federalist side of things. It was to be an organ of the new government. Its founder was a Boston school teacher, John Fenno. Fenno intended "to hold up the people's own government, in a favorable point of light—and by every exertion, to endear the GENERAL GOVERNMENT TO THE PEOPLE."[14] As the Republican opposition to the Federalists took shape, its leaders, especially Thomas Jefferson and James Madison, felt the need for a new paper in the capital to reflect their political point of view. Madison and Jefferson enlisted the services of Philip Freneau to edit and publish their paper, and the *National Gazette* appeared in October 1791. Other party-press ties were established around the country. The political tone of the press became so harsh, so reflective of partisan emotion, that Mott calls "the whole period of 1801–1833 a kind of 'Dark Ages' of American journalism."

Another important feature of the press in the early years was its rapid assumption of a key role in American democratic life. For all their faults, early American papers succeeded in supplying common people with access to political information. The resultant growth of the press was phenomenal. At the beginning of the nineteenth century, the United States had about 200 little newspapers, few of which were published daily. By 1835, however, the country had more than 1,200 newspapers, about 65 of which were dailies. This gave the United States more papers and a larger total circulation than any other country.[15]

DEVELOPMENT OF AN INDEPENDENT POPULAR PRESS

In the years after the Civil War, new printing technology greatly reduced publishing costs. New communications technology, appearing first in the telegraph, permitted news to be transmitted electronically from one part of the country to another, or from Europe to the United States, almost instantaneously. As major cities developed, they provided the population and financial base for great mass circulation dailies. The number of newspapers increased phenomenally, from about 3,500 in 1870, to roughly 7,000 in 1880, to over 12,000 in 1890. As this occurred, the controlling audience for the American press shifted from partisan groups to a mass audience. Papers gradually emerged from domination by political parties. The press came increasingly to deal with a wide variety of subjects of popular interest in addition to politics.

A key figure in the development of the mass-circulation popular press in late-nineteenth-century America was Joseph Pulitzer (after whom the well-known journalism award, the Pulitzer Prize, has been named). Pulitzer got his start as a newspaper owner in 1878, when he bought the bankrupt *St. Louis Dispatch*. Successful with that paper (which after a merger became the *Post-Dispatch*), Pulitzer moved into New York publishing in the 1880s. In 1883 he bought the *New York World* and announced what he intended to do with it:

> There is room in this great and growing city for a journal that is not only cheap but bright, not only bright but large, not only large but truly democratic—dedicated to the cause of the peo-

---

[13] Mott, *American Journalism*, pp. 113–14.
[14] *Gazette of the United States*, April 27, 1791, as quoted in Frank L. Mott, *Jefferson and the Press* (Baton Rouge: Louisiana State University Press, 1943), p. 15.

[15] Mott, *American Journalism*, pp. 167–68.

William Randolph Hearst wielded enormous power through his publishing empire.

ple rather than to that of the purse potentates— devoted more to the news of the New than of the Old World—that will expose all fraud and sham, fight all public evils and abuses—that will battle for the people with earnest sincerity.[16]

The energy and flare of the *World*, and its catering to popular tastes, quickly made it enormously successful. From a circulation of 20,000 in 1883, the *World* reached 100,000 in September 1884, 250,000 in 1886, and 374,000 in 1892. It had become the largest and, carrying vast amounts of advertising, the most profitable newspaper ever published.

In the late nineteenth century and the early years of the twentieth, the search for ever larger audiences produced a flourishing of what has been called *yellow journalism*. Be sensational, and don't let facts slow you down—such might have been the motto of this new journalism. The battle for circulation between press lords Joseph Pulitzer and William Randolph Hearst in New York City in the 1890s displayed yellow

journalism in its most rambunctious form. Perhaps the most famous story of this press battle came in 1897, when Hearst sent a leading fiction writer, Richard Harding Davis, and a distinguished illustrator, Frederic Remington, to Cuba to investigate conditions in that Spanish colony and to send back features. James Creelman, who was also a reporter for Hearst, claims that the following telegraphic exchange took place:

HEARST, JOURNAL, NEW YORK:
EVERYTHING IS QUIET. THERE IS NO TROUBLE HERE.
THERE WILL BE NO WAR. WISH TO RETURN. REMINGTON.

REMINGTON, HAVANA:
PLEASE REMAIN. YOU FURNISH THE PICTURES AND I'LL FURNISH THE WAR. HEARST.[17]

[17] James Creelman, *On the Great Highway: The Wanderings and Adventures of a Special Correspondent* (Boston: Lothrop, 1901), pp. 177–78.

[16] Ibid., p. 434.

THE RISE OF PROFESSIONALISM

Gradually a new ethos made its way through the American press; its watchword was "professionalism." Reacting against the political distortions arising from partisan domination of the press and those resulting from the insistent sensationalism of yellow journalism, some reporters concluded that their field needed to become a profession, with its own norms and ethical standards, like law and medicine. Intellectual independence—to describe things as they are—was a key objective in this pursuit of professionalism; care, objectivity, attention to factual detail were emphasized.

Special programs were developed to teach journalists the technical tools of their profession and to instill in them professional standards. The first journalism curriculum was offered by the Wharton School of Business at the University of Pennsylvania. The first four-year program for journalism was set up in 1904 at the University of Illinois. And the first independent school of journalism was established in 1908 at the University of Missouri. In 1903 Joseph Pulitzer endowed a college of journalism at Columbia University, contributing $2 million. When the Columbia School of Journalism finally opened its doors in 1912, there were more than thirty colleges and universities offering formal training in the field. Books on the practice of journalism began to appear. And in 1910, newspaper editors in the state of Kansas adopted the first formal code of ethics for the profession.[18]

Perhaps the most important change brought about by this new professionalism was the growth of journalistic independence. The press should be independent of politicians, reporting on them and their actions as fully and fairly as possible. Journalists should be independent of

the control of publishers who should run the business side; the pressroom should operate according to journalistic cannons. Newsmen should write without fear or favor, subject only to their own standards of ethics and professional competency.

The idea of journalism as an autonomous profession dramatically altered the way the mass media reported the news. This commitment is now a key part of the idea of "freedom of the press." The national media organizations, such as the *New York Times* and CBS News, draw their resources largely from American business; but the norm of journalistic independence has greatly minimized business influence in reporting and editorial coverage.

TELEVISION

Television's share of the total news audience has risen over the last quarter-century. In one series of surveys, respondents were asked: "Where do you usually get your news about what's going on in the world today—from the newspapers, or radio, or television, or magazines, or talking to people, or where?" Figure 13.3 shows the changing mix. In 1959, just 29 percent listed television, not newspapers, as their prime news source; in 1988, however, the proportion stood at 44 percent. The proportion mentioning newspapers but not television dropped from 31 to 22 percent.

In May 1992, a survey done for the Times Mirror Company—which publishes many newspapers, including the *Los Angeles Times*—asked how respondents were getting most of their news about the presidential election campaign. They could mention more than one source if they relied heavily on more than one. Eighty-six percent mentioned television as a prime source of campaign information, compared to 51 percent mentioning newspapers, 17 percent radio, and 6 percent magazines. Clearly, television has become a vastly more

---

[18]Mott, *American Journalism*, pp. 604–5.

FIGURE 13.3   SOURCES OF NEWS INFORMATION

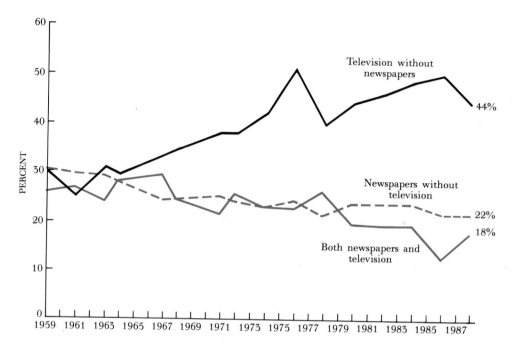

Question: Where do you usually get most of your news about what's going on in the world today—from the newspapers or radio or television or magazines?
Source: Surveys by the Roper Organization, for the Television Information Office, latest that of November 1988.

important news source over the past quarter-century.

Americans also now indicate that they are more inclined to accept the television news version of a story than that of newspapers, radio, or magazines, in cases where these media present conflicting versions. In November 1988, 49 percent said they would tend to believe television, compared to 26 percent saying newspapers, 7 percent radio, and 5 percent magazines (Figure 13.4). Is the public asserting that "the camera cannot lie"?

Figure 13.5 shows that people draw on the various media in sharply different ways depending upon the aspect of politics they are following. In the case of presidential campaigns, for instance, Americans learn about the candidates largely through television. When it comes to information on candidates for the House of Representatives—for the most part, not covered on the network news programs, of course—newspapers draw to near parity with TV as a source. And with regard to local candidates, newspapers are by a small margin the prime source of information for the general public.

FIGURE 13.4   TRUSTWORTHINESS OF NEWS SOURCES

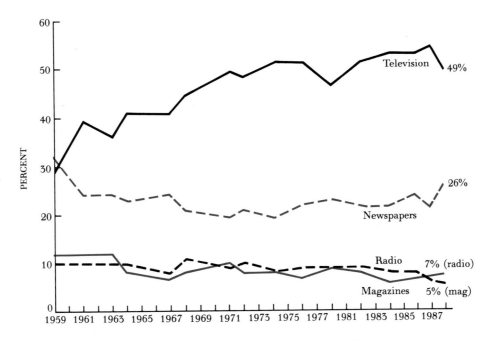

Question: If you got conflicting or different reports of the same news story from radio, television, the magazines, and the newspapers, which of the four versions would you be most inclined to believe—the one on radio or television or in magazines or newspapers?

Source: Surveys by the Roper Organization for the Television Information Office, latest that of November 1988.

FIGURE 13.5   INFORMATION SOURCES, BY LEVEL OF ELECTIVE OFFICE

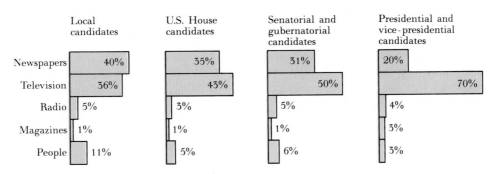

Question: During the last election campaign, from what source did you become best acquainted with the candidates (running in local elections—like mayor, members of the state legislature, etc.; for the U.S. House of Representatives from this district; running in the statewide elections—like U.S. senator and governor; in national elections for president and vice president): from the newspapers, or radio, or television, or magazines, or talking to people, or where?

Source: Surveys by the Roper Organization for the Television Information Office, November 12–19, 1988.

THE PRESS AND GOVERNMENTAL INSTITUTIONS

The press envelops the government in the United States. Independent of those who wield governmental authority, but tied to them in a complex relationship both cooperative and adversarial, journalists form a critical part of government's primary audience. The president, his key aides, cabinet members, United States legislators, and other officials interact more with the national press corps than they do with almost any other group—far more on a day-to-day basis than, say, with business and labor leaders.

The amount of contact American news reporters have with officials has long been a distinguishing feature of U.S. politics. In its openness to the press,

> American government differs markedly from European (even British) governments. All European journalists are immediately struck by this difference. The American reporter not only has access to official announcements and press releases; he also has the opportunity of becoming the confidante of the official and of enjoying limited but regular access to his personal thoughts, official secrets, internal departmental gossip, and the like.[19]

Not only does the U.S. press play the primary role of disseminating information on what government does, but its members are a numerically imposing segment of the political community, interacting closely with governmental officials as the latter do their official work.

THE PRESS AND THE POLITICAL PARTIES

The press's involvement in the political process applies with special force to party politics and electoral campaigns. The retinue of a presidential candidate typically includes a relatively small number of aides who travel with him and, if he is thought to have any likelihood of succeeding, a very large press contingent. The press's role is not confined simply to reporting what the candidate says and does. Members of the press have come to act as "talent scouts," screening the candidates, conveying the judgment that some are promising while others are without talent. Journalists act as race-callers or handicappers telling the public how the contest is going and why one candidate is ahead of another. They function at times as self-perceived public defenders, bent on exposing what they consider to be the frailties, duplicities, and sundry inadequacies of a candidate. They even sometimes slip into the role of "assistant campaign managers," informally advising a candidate and publicly, if indirectly, promoting his cause.[20]

The expanded campaign role of the national communications media is both a cause and an effect of the weakening of political parties. The extent to which the parties have introduced mechanisms for candidate selection that make voters-at-large the final judges has obviously made the press more important. The national nominating contests now center not in party committees or conventions but in mass-public-participation primaries across the country. The press has unparalleled resources for covering these contemporary campaigns; indeed, it is the only institution that can do it.

---

[19] Paul H. Weaver, "The New Journalism and the Old—Thoughts after Watergate," *The Public Interest,* Spring 1974, p. 72.

[20] David S. Broder, "Political Reporters in Presidential Politics," in Charles Peters and Timothy J. Adams, eds., *Inside the System: A Washington Monthly Reader* (New York: Praeger, 1970), pp. 3–22 *passim.*

C. S. WELLS
Courtesy Augusta Chronicle

But even if the political parties had not given up so much of their historic institutional responsibility for selecting candidates, the vast communications resources of the mass media would have severely challenged the parties. Political parties can no longer compete with the press as sources of information on candidates and the progress of electoral campaigns. Earlier in U.S. history, handbills printed by the parties and house-to-house canvassing by local party officials were the primary sources of electoral information, but today they cannot compete with the pervasiveness, visual force, immediacy, and general audience reach of television. It is the press that brings the campaign's personalities and issues into the homes and consciousness of American voters. Political parties are now ancillary structures in the whole process of communication between candidates and elected officials on one side and voters on the other.

THE PRESS AND THE PRESIDENT

The relationship between the press and the president is a particularly consequential one. Washington is, of course, the center of U.S. government and the hometown of the national political elite; it is consequently the center for the national press. The Washington press corps dwarfs that of any other American city, and Washington is the hub for national news reporting. Though the Washington press hardly confines itself to reporting on the president and his administration, it does give the White House vast attention, partly because the presidency is a very important office in the country and partly because presidential actions lend themselves to highly visible and focused news stories.

The contrast between press treatment of the president and Congress demonstrates this point. The executive and legislative branches are coequal in the American constitutional scheme and in practical political power as well. The president is 1 person, however, while Congress is 535. From a news standpoint, reporting what happens in Congress is vastly more difficult, because of the numbers and because the story is usually less focused. As a result the press gives disproportionate attention to the president.

The extensive coverage given presidential actions and utterances, from the crucial to the trivial, has helped elevate further the presidency in contemporary American government. As television news became a more important part of the overall journalistic mix, the time-sensitive and visual properties of television made the distinctive singularity of the presidential office especially attractive, compared to the disjointed multiplicity of Congress. This bright spotlight the press has put on the presidency shows off strengths and makes the president seem larger than life; but it also illumines every weakness and alleged shortcoming. The inordinate press attention the president gets is a two-edged sword. We have seen presidents both rapidly elevated and diminished by this scrutiny. Political scientist Austin Ranney reminds us that

> no television correspondent or anchorman has ever won an Emmy or Peabody or even a promotion for a series of broadcasts focusing on what a marvelous job a president is doing. Those rewards go to newspeople who expose the moral lapses, lies, and policy failures of public officials, and the president is the biggest game of all in the perennial hunt.[21]

Presidents and their aides thus have concluded that they must try to "manage" press treatment. The relationship is too important, and the consequences of negative scrutiny too great. Every modern presidency has devoted great attention—reaching well beyond the work of press secretaries—to turning the enormous powers of media coverage to the president's advantage. And still, for all the effort, no modern administration has emerged from its intricate dance with the national communications media without a sense of frustration.

Tension between president and press is inevitable because the two institutions have contrasting responsibilities. Arthur Krock, for many years head of the *New York Times* Washington bureau, notes that the job of the press is to uncover the news and then get the stories to the public. The more that is reported, the better. "But the statesman has other considerations. Is it [publication of a particular account of events or intended actions] premature? Will publication make the going more difficult? Will publication tend to confuse, rather than to clarify, the popular mind?"[22] A press is supposed to bring out "all the news that's fit to print," while a president is supposed to govern effectively. These contrasting objectives can never rest in perfect harmony. The amount of contemporary press coverage simply exaggerates the inherent tension.

THE PRESS AND GOVERNMENTAL PLURALISM

In 1959, journalist and commentator Douglass Cater sought to describe the imposing role that the press had assumed in American government with an instructive title: The Fourth Branch of Government. News reporting is such a large and central undertaking in present-day democracy that it must be seen as a formal, if extra-constitutional, "branch" of government itself.

---

[21] J. Austin Ranney, *Channels of Power: The Impact of Television on American Politics* (New York: Basic Books, 1983), p. 141.

[22] Arthur Krock, as quoted by Douglass Cater, *The Fourth Branch of Government* (New York: Vantage, 1965), p. 19.

From the standpoint of politicians, the press is both an opportunity and a problem: an opportunity, because it provides them with the coverage and publicity they need to advance their candidacies and programs; a problem because press coverage may not reflect what they want brought to the public's attention. For the press, politicians are sources of exciting stories but also authors of attempts to manipulate them. From another perspective, the key element in press-politician ties is not the tensions that result but the important complementarity of their roles in American liberal democracy. James Madison and other founding fathers believed in a government of dispersed power, where no unit was too strong. The Constitution, as we have seen, has established an elaborate institutional framework to ensure the dispersion of governmental power. If this constitutional model is still sound, as many Americans believe it to be, the press, as the fourth branch of government, enlarges pluralism by further dispersing power.

Of course, the vast communications resources in the hands of an independent press are often employed in ways that governmental officials find troubling. And many neutral observers fear that in the last twenty years or so segments of the press have become too inclined to probe for weaknesses and imperfections, thus helping to erode popular confidence in the governing process.[23] "The White House will remain in a state of siege, as the normal transactions of the political system are unearthed, magnified, and then distorted by the media."[24]

Still, the net effect of the extensive, autono-

[23] For two important survey research studies by political scientists pointing to this conclusion, see Michael J. Robinson, "Public Affairs Television and the Growth of Political Malaise," *American Political Science Review*, June 1976, pp. 409–32; and Arthur Miller et al., "Type-Set Politics: Impact of Newspapers on Public Confidence," *American Political Science Review*, March 1979, pp. 67–84.

[24] Richard Pious concludes his book *The American Presidency* with this lament. ([New York: Basic Books, 1979], p. 417).

BRUCE BEATTIE
Courtesy Daytona Beach News Journal

"Do you think we should allow presidential candidates like you more privacy?"

mous, quasi-governmental powers of the American communications media seems to be to disperse governmental power further. Those inclined to believe that Madison was basically right have reason to look with some satisfaction on the part the American communications media plays in contemporary governance. Those who have always felt that Madison erred by overemphasizing the advantages of fragmenting authority, to the point where coherence in policy making and other governmental actions is hard to achieve, have reason to be concerned about the increasingly prominent political role of the press as a kind of fourth branch. For the fourth branch does make it harder for the other three to act coherently. And the more effectively it exposes their failings, the more it diminishes them in general political terms. The autonomy and centrality of the press mean that political authority, in the broadest sense, is even more dispersed and fragmented than the Madisonian constitution itself requires.

THE MEDIA, POLITICS, AND RESPONSIBILITY

Because the press plays a substantial part in political life, many are concerned with its *political outlook*—partisan and ideological. If the press is virtually a fourth branch of government, the political preferences of those who inhabit it merit attention. Those who believe that their own political preferences are underrepresented among journalists are naturally the most likely to protest against alleged press bias. For the last twenty-five years or so, conservatives and Republicans have more often accused the national press of bias than liberals and Democrats have. Liberal politicians who assert that the press is a hotbed of conservatism are rare, while conservative politicians who find

the press a hotbed of liberalism are about as common as mosquitoes in the Everglades.

The liberal-conservative debate over the press has been a hot one at times. And it has made many members of the press defensive. We need to broaden the query into possible press biases and answer three sets of questions.

1) Do national journalists in the United States as a group reflect some distinctive political viewpoint? Are they, for example, more liberal or conservative in their own personal political preferences than Americans generally?

2) If the press has a distinctive political viewpoint, does this intrude in news reporting? Journalists might have some clear political preferences personally, but do they keep these on the sidelines in professional work?

3) Is the issue of press liberalism / conservatism the key one? Are other aspects of the outlook of journalists more important in shaping their political role and performance than the side of the ideological or partisan spectrum on which a majority of them stand? Are there professional norms and outlooks in American journalism that impose certain biases in news reporting?

PRESS LIBERALISM

Surveys leave little doubt that the tilt among national journalists in the United States is toward values and policies generally thought of as liberal (in the current meaning of that word). National journalists give more backing to liberal candidates than the American public does. Surveys show, for example, that in 1972, when Republican Richard Nixon won 61 percent of the vote in the country, only 19 percent of the journalists supported him while 81 percent backed Democrat George McGovern. In 1984, Ronald Reagan was backed by about 59 percent of the entire electorate but by just 26 percent of reporters and editors—the latter according to a national survey taken by the *Los*

THE MEDIA, POLITICS, AND RESPONSIBILITY 411

Angeles Times.[25] The *Times* poll also found that 55 percent of the journalists called themselves liberal and just 17 percent conservative. The pollsters reported that newspaper journalists were also "markedly more liberal than others of similar educational and professional standing." On a wide variety of social and cultural issues—such as affirmative-action programs for blacks and other minorities, abortion, sexual norms and conduct—journalists are notably more liberal than the general public.

Many other groups, of course, give disproportionate backing to one side or the other of the political spectrum. Thus labor union leaders are heavily liberal and Democratic, while top officials of *Fortune 500* business corporations are generally conservative and Republican. The special interest—and, in some circles, concern—that is now expressed with regard to the political outlook of the national press reflects the press's unique role at the center of the dissemination of political information to the general public.

PRESS LIBERALISM AND BIAS IN REPORTING

It does not follow that if newspeople are disproportionately liberal, their reporting of the news must reflect a liberal bias. As Michael Robinson points out, "press behavior—not opinion—is the key. Bias that counts must be in the copy, not just in the minds of those who write it."[26] Robinson conducted a research project to find out if there were signs of liberal news bias in the press during the 1980 presidential campaign. After analyzing about 6,000 news stories, in print and electronic media alike, he did not find liberal bias. Not only did the content of stories not reflect any distinctive political leaning, but even more tellingly, the selection of stories to be covered did not betray any political bias.

This latter point is important and often overlooked. A story may be treated in an objective fashion, but if only a certain type of story is selected for coverage, bias still results. As Robinson points out,

> if the press covered all business scandals objectively, but only covered business scandals, that agenda alone would support a theory of partisan bias. If the media always covered cost-overruns at the Pentagon but failed to cover any cheating in AFDC programs, that too would be political bias, regardless of how fair the reports themselves may seem.[27]

Even on this level, he found few signs of liberal bias during the 1980 campaign. Of course, the fact that political bias was not evident in press coverage of that campaign does not mean bias is always absent. Campaign '80 might have minimized liberal-conservative bias because the Democratic incumbent was widely seen by liberals as well as conservatives to be ineffective. Not many liberals anywhere rallied strongly to Jimmy Carter in 1980. Four years later, in 1984, Robinson found that network coverage *was* more inclined to include criticism of Republicans Reagan and Bush than of Democrats Mondale and Ferraro. Nonetheless, he concluded that overall the networks "did not do nearly enough to overcome real events, real conditions, and real style. In short, the network

[25] The survey findings are summarized by S. Robert Lichter, Stanley Rothman, and Linda S. Lichter, *The Media Elite* (Bethesda, Md.: Adler and Adler, 1986), pp. 38–41.

[26] Michael J. Robinson, "Just How Liberal Is the News? 1980 Revisited," *Public Opinion*, February/March 1983, p. 56; see also Michael J. Robinson and Margaret A. Sheehan, *Over the Wire and on TV* (New York: Russell Sage Foundation, 1983).

[27] Robinson, "Just How Liberal Is the News?" pp. 59–60; see also Robinson and Sheehan, *Over the Wire.*

coverage was so 'responsible' that it carried almost no weight in the campaign."[28]

Studies done during the 1988 campaign by the Center for Media and Public Affairs found that the distinguishing feature of media coverage was the amount of *bad* press *both* presidential candidates received. Both George Bush and Michael Dukakis attracted over twice as much unfavorable as favorable coverage on the networks' evening news broadcasts, the Center reported.[29] The networks did vary, however, with "CBS Evening News" giving Dukakis relatively more favorable coverage while ABC's "World News Tonight" was a bit more favorable to Bush.[30]

Early in the 1992 campaign Bush again found himself the object of heavily negative coverage. Just 18 percent of the network stories on him in April and May were positive. In contrast, 58 percent of the stories on Democrat Bill Clinton in this period were positive, and a whopping 73 percent on newcomer H. Ross Perot were positive.[31]

Others have found clearer signs of press bias on certain issues. Stanley Rothman and Robert Lichter report that the press has greatly exaggerated the amount of opposition of informed scientists to the use of nuclear power to generate electricity. Their data indicate that many scientists with knowledge about nuclear energy favor its use and do not reject it on safety grounds, but press reporting portrays the scientific community as deeply split on the issue.[32]

Some observers have concluded that the national press is especially receptive to certain kinds of issues linked to a liberal political outlook. For example, Michael Pertschuk—chairman of the Federal Trade Commission under President Carter, an ally of Ralph Nader, and a Democrat with strongly held liberal views—argues that one of the factors critical to the development of support for consumer-rights initiatives in the late 1960s and 1970s was "a newly aggressive corps of investigative and advocacy journalists, who shared the advocates' view of consumer initiatives as moral imperatives. . . ."[33] While he welcomed this development, Pertschuk himself saw the press as an ally rather than as an opponent or as what it claims to be—simply a fair-minded reporter of the news.

POLITICAL CYNICISM

A number of recent studies emphasize the issue of *political negativism* or *cynicism*, suggesting that the distinguishing bias of the press results not from its political ideology but from its professional outlook. This may encourage holding up politicians and politics as more seamy and less worthy of public support than they in fact are. Paul Weaver argues, for example, that journalists generally, and television newspeople in particular, tend to see politics as in essence "a game played by individual politicians for personal advancement, gain, or power." From this perspective, politicians are naturally inclined "to exaggerate their good qualities and to minimize their bad ones, to be deceitful, to engage in hypocrisies, to manipulate appearances." The task of the press is to expose these bad tendencies of the political world.[34] Austin

[28]Michael J. Robinson, "The Media in Campaign '84: Wingless, Toothless, and Hopeless," *Public Opinion*, February/March 1985, pp. 43–44.

[29]*Media Monitor* 2, 8 (October 1988).

[30]*Media Monitor* 2, 9 (November 1988).

[31]Content analysis of the networks' candidate coverage in 1992 was performed on an on-going basis by the Washington-based Center for Media and Public Affirs. The above data are from their *Media Monitor* for June 1992.

[32]Stanley Rothman and S. Robert Lichter, "The Nuclear Energy Debate: Scientists, the Media and the Public," *Public Opinion*, August/September 1982, pp. 47–52.

[33]Michael Pertschuk, *Revolt Against Regulation: The Rise and Pause of the Consumer Movement* (Berkeley: University of California Press, 1982), p. 23.

[34]Paul H. Weaver, "Is Television News Biased?" *Public Interest*, Winter 1972, p. 69.

Ranney makes the same argument. There is not so much "a political bias in favor of liberalism or conservatism, as a structural bias." The latter encourages a cynical and excessively manipulative view of politics.[35]

Michael Robinson's research supports the view that the press fosters a kind of political cynicism.

> Events are frequently conveyed by television news through an inferential structure that often injects a negativistic, contentious, or anti-institutional bias. These biases, frequently dramatized by film portrayals of violence and aggression, evoke images of American politics and social life which are inordinately sinister and despairing.[36]

The effect of this, Robinson finds, is most substantial on viewers who approach politics without a great deal of political information or interest. Such viewers lack the political sophistication to reject the media depiction. As a result, they are apt to become themselves more cynical about political institutions and less confident that they can deal with such a political system.

Such findings may help us understand an important set of survey results. Public-opinion researchers have noted over the last two decades that Americans have become less confident than they were previously in the leadership of central institutions in the society, more distrustful politically, and more cynical. We have seen some decline in this cynicism, as part of the general recovery of public confidence in recent years; still, professed political cynicism is much higher now than it was a decade ago. According to one interpretation, the public simply reacted logically to a string of negative events and performances, from the long Vietnam War and the domestic protests it engendered in the 1960s and 1970s, to the savings and loan debacle and the check-kiting scandal in the 1990s. These developments almost certainly were an important factor; but according to another view that work like Robinson's supports, increased public cynicism may have also resulted in part from an increasing cynicism in national news reporting, especially network television.

NEW PROFESSIONAL NORMS

Some students of the press think it has become more negative in its portrayal of politics because an earlier set of professional norms has weakened and a newer set has become more prominent. John Johnstone and his colleagues identify the competing normative models as the "neutral" and the "participant." In the former, "the primary journalistic sins are sensationalism—overstatements of the natural reality of events, and bias—a violation of the observer's neutrality vis-à-vis information."[37] In contrast, the "participant" press model insists that journalists should give readers the interpretative background they need to put events in a proper perspective. "In this sense, the primary journalistic value is relevance, and the cardinal sins, news suppression and superficiality." Journalists are supposed to play a more active and, to some degree, creative part in developing what is newsworthy. Johnstone and his associates found sections of the press, especially younger and more highly educated journalists, swinging toward the participant model, which invites a more critical posture.

Paul Weaver expanded on this distinction and came down harder in his evaluation. As Weaver sees it, there are two main traditions in American journalism. The one that has been dominant throughout most of the modern

---

[35] Ranney, *Channels of Power*, pp. 54–55.
[36] Robinson, "Public Affairs Television," p. 430.

[37] John W. C. Johnstone et al., "The Professional Values of American Newsmen," *Public Opinion Quarterly*, Winter 1972–73, p. 523.

Some "cynical" views of politicians.

American experience he calls "liberal" journalism. It resembles Johnstone's "neutral" model. Liberal journalism "is characterized by a preoccupation with facts and events as such, and by an indifference to—indeed, a systematic effort to avoid—an explicitly ideological point of view."[38] In the late 1960s and 1970s, a new approach emerged that Weaver calls "partisan" journalism. To the degree that it triumphs, the press finds it harder to operate as a source of reliable factual, "neutral" information for the general citizenry. It becomes more of an advocate and critic.

The "participant," "partisan" critical approach seems to have reached its high tide in the mid-1970s, after Watergate and Vietnam. Today, there appears to be a swing back to the "liberal" model. Charles B. Seib of the *Wash-*

[38] Weaver, "The New Journalism and the Old," p. 69.

ington Post notes that "in the old days, when a reporter let his opinions show he was quickly brought to heel by an editor," and in time was turned into "what we call an objective reporter—meaning a reporter who stuck strictly to the raw, unvarnished facts." Now, Seib maintains, while it is good that the old search for "blind objectivity" is over, "too often the new permissiveness is carried too far." The search for objectivity needs renewed emphasis.[39]

Time magazine notes that the highly critical "investigative" impulse of "participant" journalism worries many news executives. It quotes the editor of the *Oakland Tribune* as criticizing the trend of the 1960s and 1970s: "We are too hungry for blood—it sometimes seems to readers that we will not do the story unless we can do someone in." *Time* itself concludes that "the suspicious attitude among reporters leads to negativism in news coverage. The outlook of today's generation of journalists was formed during Watergate and Vietnam, when figures of authority seemed so often to be the proper adversary."[40] Work by John Immerwahr and John Doble suggests that most Americans think the press should hold to the "liberal" model. They want it to present the facts as objectively as possible. And they want it to be fair. The public believes that the general-news-dissemination segments of the press—television news and the daily papers—have an obligation not to be unduly partisan or critical, a constitutional responsibility to see to it that the populace has easy access to a balanced rendering of political happenings.[41]

[39] Charles B. Seib's observations are discussed by James Boylan, "News People," *Wilson Quarterly*, special issue (1982), pp. 82–83.
[40] "Journalism Under Fire," *Time*, December 2, 1983, p. 79.
[41] John Immerwahr and John Doble, "Freedom of the Press," *Public Opinion Quarterly*, Summer 1982, p. 185.

WHAT TO REPORT: A CASE STUDY

The debate over professional norms is not the only such issue occupying members of the press. An interesting case in 1983 that involved press handling of some missing State Department files illustrates another recurring issue in press ethics. The State Department sent a big collection of its file cabinets to the District of Columbia jail for refurbishing. Through a lapse of security at State, one drawer in one cabinet was not emptied. Prison inmates got hold of the files, which contained "telexes from embassies around the world, communications with CIA agents, sources in foreign embassies around the world." The classified files "dealt with Soviet missiles, the Druse in Lebanon, the border situation in Nicaragua [and the monitoring of a potential coup in the Third World]," among other things. The mistake was discovered, and most of the files were recovered and returned to the State Department. One set of files, however, was not found. The prisoner who had gotten hold of these called a reporter for a Washington television station and offered him the materials. The reporter picked them up, took them back to the station, and together with his editor perused them. The question was whether the station should put these classified materials on the air or return them to the State Department without reporting on them.

The reporter who got the files, James Adams, and his editor, Betty Endicott, decided to return the materials without reporting on them. They called Senator Charles Mathias (Republican of Maryland), a member of the Foreign Relations Committee who was cleared to read such classified materials. On November 8, 1983, reporter Adams and Senator Mathias together brought the files back to State.

On what basis did Adams and Endicott reach their judgment? Endicott has stated that the key issue for her was that the documents contained no evidence that the government had lied. "If you find that the government is lying to the people, then I think you have a responsibility [to publish information revealing the lie]," she indicated. Adams has stated that "I didn't want to have a role in compromising national security. I kept asking myself the question, What good would it do?" Adams merely reported on the air that the files had been given to him and that he had returned them to the State Department. He did not divulge their substance.

This incident prompted a lively debate among journalists. Adams has stated that many news organizations called him asking for copies and refused to believe that he had not made copies before returning the documents. "You're giving gold away," they said. Staff for Jack Anderson, the syndicated columnist, were particularly insistent in prodding Adams to give them copies of the files.[42]

The deans of two major schools of journalism split on the issue. James Atwater, dean of the University of Missouri School of Journalism, the oldest in the country, supported Adams's decision. Atwater carried Adams's position one step further, stating that he would not even have read the documents prior to returning them. "I would feel like I was prying in some sense in an area I should not be involved in," he stated. "It's a complicated ethical issue." By way of contrast, the dean of the Columbia University School of Journalism, Osborn Elliott, argued that "a reporter's responsibility is to report. I can conceive of instances where the materials are indeed so sensitive as to require great care in their publi-

cation. But I would feel impelled to publish them unless I found very strong reasons internally not to."

Who is right? The story has been told of Secretary of War Stimson, in the 1930s, coming into receipt of some correspondence addressed to another political figure, material that might have proved embarrassing to the latter if Stimson had read and used it. The secretary of war refused even to read the material and returned it to its rightful owner. "Gentlemen do not read other gentlemen's mail," he reportedly stated. Is such an ethic outdated or not applicable to journalists? Dean Atwater of the University of Missouri School of Journalism clearly does not think so. Or was editor Endicott right: that journalists should, in effect, read the government's mail but not report on it unless there is indication of clear governmental culpability? "Gentlemen can read other gentlemen's mail to see if the latter are lying and hence really not gentlemen." Or was Dean Elliott of Columbia University's School of Journalism on sound ground in stressing a journalistic responsibility to report everything relevant to politics, unless the gravest harm would be done? Journalists are not "gentlemen" at all, but rather "watchdogs for the people."

The debate goes on, and its importance extends far beyond one case involving State Department files. American journalists, with unparalleled access to governmental officials, and at times inadvertent access to various private communications, have to decide where their reportorial imperatives leave off and other values—such as the right of the government to private communication—begin. In many ways, this argument is too important to be left to journalists alone, because it has important implications for the way the business of government is conducted. Wouldn't the country generally be better off if both government and

[42] For a thoughtful report on the State Department files and the journalistic debate over their disposition, see Jonathan Kwitny, "Returning State Department Files," *Wall Street Journal*, November 30, 1983, p. 28.

the press consistently acted toward one another as gentlemen? The debate over journalistic ethics must become a debate over political ethics in the broadest sense, in an era when the press is indeed a fourth branch of government.

SUMMARY

Recent developments in communications technology, especially those involving television, are augmenting and otherwise changing the media's political role. Through satellite transmissions, the world is now linked far more closely than ever before. Events in one country—such as the pro-democracy protests in China in the spring of 1989—become the immediate experience of people around the globe. Technological advances in cable and direct broadcast satellite (DBS) television are giving viewers far greater choice in programming—including coverage of political events.

News reporting plays an important part in democratic governance. Without ample and reliable sources of information on political officials, policies, and events, the public cannot be in a position to determine where their interests and values should lead them.

But the press—all organizations, television and newspapers included, involved in the mass dissemination of news—can never be simply a neutral source of a vital substance, a river from which citizens drink as they see fit. It is a social, economic, and political institution that gets organized in a distinctive way, that has great resources and hence potentially great power, and that is composed of men and women whose outlooks shape how they do their jobs.

In the United States the press is composed primarily of private news businesses. Regulation of the print media is minimal, but the regulatory reach of government is substantial in the case of radio and television. The airwaves are a finite public resource. The Federal Communications Commission grants and renews licenses to broadcast, and it imposes such regulatory standards as the equal-time rule and the fairness doctrine.

To reach mass audiences, large-scale organizations and extensive physical facilities are required. We have come a long way from the situation of a century and a half ago when the largest news medium in the country's biggest city (New York) reached only a few thousand readers and was capitalized with a few thousand dollars. Inevitably, greater attention is now paid to the press's political role.

Though conservatives have often charged the national media, especially television news, with having a liberal bias in their reporting, studies do not clearly substantiate this criticism. The studies do suggest, however, that journalists are now more likely to see themselves in an adversarial relationship to other central institutions, including government, and to stress exposure of the latter's shortcomings and foibles. Some students of the press worry that its professional norms have contributed to the rise of an excessively cynical and manipulative view of political life.

The press and government are bound closely together in the United States. Journalists have unusually open access to government officials and they form an important part of the group with whom political figures have regular contact. Journalists are themselves part of the political community, not distant reporters on it. The press has come to play an especially extensive institutional role in the American electoral process. The news media, not the political parties, are for most voters the main source of information about candidates and the shape of campaigns.

FOR FURTHER STUDY

Cater, Douglass. *The Fourth Branch of Government.* New York: Vantage, 1965. Cater argues that the role of the press in contemporary government and politics has become so central that the press is appropriately seen as virtually a branch of government.

Graber, Doris A. *Mass Media and American Politics,* 3rd ed. Washington, D.C.: Congressional Quarterly Press, 1989. A useful review of the role of the contemporary mass media in American politics.

Joyce, Ed. *Prime Times, Bad Times.* New York: Doubleday, 1988. A gossipy but nonetheless valuable account of the changing culture within one large television news organization, CBS News.

Lichter, S. Robert, Stanley Rothman, and Linda S. Lichter. *The Media Elite.* Bethesda, Md.: Adler and Adler, 1986. A study that uses survey research imaginatively to assess the social and political values of journalists, editors, and others who direct America's mass media of communication.

Mott, Frank Luther. *American Journalism: A History of Newspapers in the United States through 250 Years, 1690 to 1940.* New York: Macmillan, 1947. A definitive history of the evolution of the press in the United States.

Weaver, Paul H. "The New Journalism and the Old— Thoughts after Watergate," *The Public Interest,* Spring 1974, pp. 67–84. A classic essay on changing norms and standards among American journalists.

Part 5

PUBLIC POLICY

Chapter *14*

CIVIL LIBERTIES
AND CIVIL RIGHTS

Does an American have the right—established under the First Amendment's guarantee of freedom of expression—to burn the American flag? The Supreme Court decided in June 1989 that a citizen does have that right. The first part of this chapter examines the flag controversy—partly because it is of current political interest, but even more because it illustrates many of the elements that are recurring across the range of civil liberties and civil rights issues. What is the nature and precise scope of *rights of American citizenship*, set forth in the Constitution, especially in the Bill of Rights and the Fourteenth Amendment? Where do these rights preclude any interfering action by legislatures and political executives, no matter how strong the public sentiment to which the latter are responding? The flag debate also illustrates the very large role that the courts play in setting national policies on civil liberties and civil rights.

Civil liberties and civil rights form the one major policy area where the Constitution makes detailed and explicit provisions. In other areas, it only outlines the institutional framework for decision making. For example, on foreign policy the Constitution sets important guidelines, but these reach only to how such policy is to be made, not what it is to be. The president is commander in chief of the armed forces; treaties do not take effect until they have secured the approval of at least two-thirds of the Senate. In the case of civil liberties and civil rights, however, the Constitution includes explicit policy statements.

Civil liberties and civil rights comprise the basic political tools and entitlements of the American people. When, for example, states deny some of their residents "the equal protection of the laws," they deny them a key element of their citizenship. Civil liberties and civil rights policies differ from those in other sectors in that they involve conditions without which democratic citizenship cannot exist. Because of this, we often assign civil liberties and civil rights issues to another area: where *rights* are involved rather than legitimate *policy choices*.

The idea that a right of citizenship is at issue strongly suggests that there can be only one proper course of action: that which ensures or guarantees the right. We debate what U.S. policy should be in the Middle East or what government should do about the size of the federal deficit, all the while recognizing, even though we have personal preferences, that in these areas there is more than one valid choice. But if there is only one choice—a right to be fulfilled (even if it has at times been flagrantly denied)—public policy becomes an effort to rectify present or past failings or otherwise to ensure the proper realization of this fundamental right of American citizenship. No matter how weak its claimants are numerically, a right of citizenship must be honored.

This brings us back to the basic idea of American democracy discussed in chapter 5: Democracy encompasses both majority rule and minority rights. In many areas of public policy, Americans have long believed that the preferences of the majority should be followed. But in some areas fundamental rights of individuals must take precedence over majority wishes.

Civil liberties and civil rights are often discussed in these terms.

We review the major changes that have occurred in civil rights policy over the last several decades and look at the cutting edge of civil rights arguments today, in the second section of this chapter. Race relations provide the most dramatic and pervasive instance where the proud claim of "unalienable Rights" of every person to "Life, Liberty, and the pursuit of Happiness" is at stake. Slavery flourished in the South in America's first century. And for the next century gross categorical discrimination survived as black Americans were denied the vote and access to equal education, barred from many public facilities or segregated within

The Rev. Martin Luther King, Jr., delivering his "I Have a Dream" speech during the 1963 march on Washington—one of the historic events in the securing of racial justice.

them, and abused by police and the courts. Although this was the result of conscious public policy, these policies were simply wrong, morally and constitutionally.

There are many other issues in civil liberties and civil rights, however, where policy differences are such that we should submit to majoritarian resolution, where "reasonable" men and women, all committed to the constitutional system, simply disagree as to which policy is best. In these cases, conditions similar to those in other policy sectors apply: (1) A general goal may be readily articulated, but there is great uncertainty as to how that goal is best achieved; and (2) the choice is not between accepting or rejecting a fundamental right, but rather involves the relative weight to be assigned two or more competing values, all of which are worthy and consistent with national political beliefs. This is true even in the case of First Amendment questions, where the language of the Constitution seems clear and absolute: "Congress shall make no law ... abridging the freedom of speech, or of the press. ..." Freedom of speech is, in the American system, a fundamental right of everyone, which even large majorities may not curtail—but not every policy issue or question that arises concerning First Amendment guarantees involves an absolute and unequivocal right that must be upheld without regard to competing values or majoritarian claims.

Because issues of civil liberties and civil rights often do involve fundamental considerations of citizenship, it is tempting politically for groups and individuals to insist that a fundamental right of theirs is being denied—of speech, of the press, of the accused—rather than that an arguable policy choice is being made. For if a policy can be construed as denying me a basic right, I have gone a long way toward carrying the day. Our language in this policy area is replete, sometimes misleadingly so, with references to "rights"; we need to remind ourselves that the more common conditions of public policy—where reasonable people can and should differ, and majorities should carry the day—frequently apply.

THE NATION AND THE FLAG

The television cameras panned the throng gathered on the banks of the Charles River for the concert given by the Boston Pops Esplanade Orchestra in the 1990 Independence Day celebration. A viewer might have expected at least subtle differences from observances of times past. Aren't Americans now, after all, more blasé about physical demonstrations of patriotism, and isn't "sophisticated" Boston less demonstrative than, say, a "heartland" city such as Indianapolis? But the cameras' images joined easily with those stored from Fourth observances in other places and other eras: The crowd, mostly young, awash in waving flags, sang along heartily as the orchestra played the traditional songs of national celebration.

Events and expressions like the Esplanade concert have remained a source of puzzlement and amusement, even consternation, for foreign observers. They find the emotional force that surrounds the various symbols of nation in the United States to be jarring. How can it be that the highpoint in the most important political speech given by the man who became president in 1989 was his recitation of the Pledge of Allegiance? And the flag? Is it really sensible, they ask, for the world's most powerful country, with its vast international responsibilities, to spend a full year—as the United States did following the Supreme Court's ruling in *Texas v. Johnson* in June 1989—debating whether the flag needs a constitutional amendment protecting it? Two years ago, in comparing the two countries formed from British North America, the British magazine *The Economist*

The right to burn the flag in protest—a civil liberty?

noted with more than a trace of satisfaction that, unlike Americans, "Canadians do not chant an oath of allegiance or salute the flag."[1]

Yet it was an Englishman, G. K. Chesterton, who in 1922 did perhaps the best job anyone has ever done explaining why it is that Americans chant and salute. The United States, Chesterton reminded his readers, was built not on common ethnicity but instead on a body of political ideas. "America is the only nation in the world," he wrote, "that is founded on a creed"—on a philosophy that is "set forth with dogmatic and even theological lucidity."[2]

"Now a creed is at once the broadest and the narrowest thing in the world," Chesterton continued. "America invites all men to become citizens; but it implies the dogma that there is such a thing as citizenship." We become U.S. citizens in the full, rather than narrowly legal, sense through commitment to the political ideas proclaimed in the Declaration and the Constitution, the great documents of America's republican founding. The nation and the republic are one.

Constitutional arguments in the United States have been described as "theological," which is really quite precise. They have the same moral intensity, the same sense that opposing views are more than ill-advised, that they are *wrong*, the same inclination to engage in intricate extrapolation from a text that is seen as endowed with fundamental meaning and purpose, often present in great religious arguments. The flag debate is part of this tradition. Baffling to many people who stand outside it, the debate is accepted by most Americans as part of an essential, ongoing search, in matters both large and small, for understanding what their nationhood requires.

[1] "Bleeding-Heart Conservatives," *The Economist*, October 8, 1988, p. 4.
[2] G. K. Chesterton, *What I Saw in America* (New York: De Capo Press, 1968; first published 1922), p. 7.

THE FLAG AND
THE FIRST AMENDMENT

The flag is a very special symbol of American nationhood. The First Amendment to the Constitution provides expansive guarantees of freedom of expression. When an individual burns the flag in a public display designed to express his feelings of contempt for the American system, these two values come into direct conflict and one has to give way. Either we have to remove protection for the flag as a national symbol or curb the particular form of expression that burning the flag conveys.

In 1989, 48 of the 50 states, and the federal government, had statutes protecting the flag from burning or similar displays of contempt by specifying punishment for those who did it. Though the Supreme Court had previously struck down certain state actions against specific acts of flag mutilation, it had never, prior to 1989, ruled that state legislation protecting the flag is, in general, an unconstitutional curb on First Amendment rights.

TEXAS V. JOHNSON

The state of Texas was one of the 48 states with flag protection legislation on its books. In 1984, Gregory Lee Johnson was arrested and convicted under this law for dousing an American flag with kerosene and setting it on fire in front of the Dallas city hall, as part of a political protest. While the flag burned, the protesters chanted, "America, the red, white, and blue, we spit on you." Johnson appealed his conviction, and the case finally arrived at the U.S. Supreme Court for argument in March 1989. The Court's decision was handed down three months later, on June 21.

A sharply divided (5–4) Court overturned Johnson's conviction in language so broad as to make evident that no bar to flag burning could get past its current reading of what the First Amendment requires. The key issue, Justice William Brennan argued in the majority opinion, is whether "the State's interest in preserving the flag as a symbol of nationhood and national unity justified Johnson's conviction." Texas had argued that while its interest might not allow it to prohibit words or some expressive conduct critical of the flag, it does permit it to bar the flag's outright physical destruction. Not so, wrote Brennan. Government "may not prohibit expression simply because it disagrees with its message," Brennan maintained, and this requirement "is not dependent on the particular mode in which we choose to express an idea." Johnson burned the flag to express an idea. The state's interest in preserving the flag as a special symbol cannot justify convicting Gregory Johnson or anyone else for burning it as a means of political expression.

Four justices disagreed. In a caustic dissent, Justice John Paul Stevens argued that

> the Court is . . . quite wrong in blandly asserting that respondent "was prosecuted for his expression of dissatisfaction with the policies of this country, expression situated at the core of our First Amendment values." Respondent was prosecuted because of the method he chose to express his dissatisfaction. . . . Had he chosen to spray paint . . . his message of dissatisfaction on the façade of the Lincoln Memorial, there would be no question about the power of the Government to prohibit his means of expression. . . . The creation of a federal right to post bulletin boards and graffiti on the Washington Monument might enlarge the market for free expression, but at a cost I would not pay.

Of course the flag is different from the monuments, Stevens acknowledged, in that it is an intangible asset. But "given its unique value," the same interest that permits government to limit the expression involved in painting political protest messages on the Lincoln Memorial "supports a prohibition on the desecration of the American flag."

UNITED STATES V. EICHMAN

The Court's decision prompted strong protests. Some proposed passage of an amendment to the Constitution that would permit flag-protection statutes, but others maintained that the goal could be achieved through a simple statute. The latter approach won support in Congress late in 1989, and a new flag-protection law won overwhelming approval in both houses. The expressed rationale behind it was that the Court might countenance flag-protection legislation that focused narrowly on *prohibited conduct*—burning, mutilating, or other abuse of the flag—without regard to the intent behind it. The language of the statute finally enacted provided that "whoever knowingly mutilates, defaces, burns, tramples upon, or in any way physically defiles any flag of the United States shall be fined under this title or imprisoned for not more than one year, or both." Arguing for the statute rather than a constitutional amendment, Jack Brooks (D-Texas), chair of the House Judiciary Committee, urged that the House "give this statutory solution a chance to work." It would, he said, "be irresponsible to move to amend the Constitution without first determining that that was the only option available to us." It's difficult, though, to see how members of Congress could have thought that the new legislation was sufficiently different from what had been held unconstitutional to pass muster under the precepts of *Texas v. Johnson.*

The statutory approach was especially attractive to politicians—mostly Democrats—who believed the public "wanted action," but were themselves convinced it was a bad idea to amend the Constitution to overturn a Court ruling on the First Amendment. At least the statute would buy time to let feelings cool. Most Republicans argued that only a constitutional amendment could achieve adequate flag protection and went along with the statute only reluctantly. President Bush let the bill become law without his

JOHN SHEVCHIK
Courtesy Valley Tribune (Pa.)

signature—a means by which a president can express dissatisfaction with a measure without actually vetoing it.

The new law reached the Supreme Court in the spring of 1990 under provision for expedited review—language in the statute that called for a direct referral to the Court as soon as a federal district court had ruled on a case arising under the statute. To the surprise of few observers, the Court ruled on June 11 in *United States v. Eichman, et al.* that it had meant what it said in *Texas v. Johnson.* "Punishing desecration of the flag," Justice Brennan wrote for the majority, "dilutes the very freedom that makes this emblem so revered, and worth revering." The four dissenters in the Texas case—Stevens, Rehnquist, Scalia, and O'Connor—restated their dissenting views in *Eichman.*

AMEND THE CONSTITUTION?

There was no longer room for argument over alternate approaches to the same end. Either an amendment would be added to the Constitution or it would remain the law of the land that mutilating the flag in public displays, however offensive to the large majority of Americans (Figure 14.1), is constitutionally protected political expression. A proposed amendment was quickly brought to a vote in Congress. It was, at the least, a model of brevity: "The Congress and the states shall have the power to prohibit the physical desecration of the flag of the United States." In the subsequent vote, the sharp partisan split, which had been partially masked in the earlier enactment of a statute, was evident. The House voted June 21, 1990: 254 for the amendment, 177 against it. It thus fell 34 votes shy of the two-thirds needed

FIGURE 14.1   DO WE NEED A FLAG AMENDMENT? WHAT THE U.S. PUBLIC SAID.

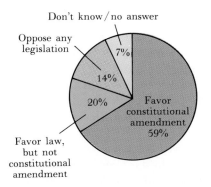

Questions: Should burning or destroying the American flag as a form of political protest be legal or should it be against the law? If "against the law" ask: If the only way to make flag destruction illegal was to change the Constitution, would you favor or oppose a constitutional amendment making it illegal to destroy the flag for political reasons?
Source: Survey by CBS News / *New York Times*, May 22–24, 1990.

for passage. Of Republicans, 159 voted for, just 17 against; among Democrats it was 95 for, 160 against. The vote in the Senate five days later was much the same: 58 in favor, 42 opposed—well short of the required two-thirds. At least for 1990, the flag-burning amendment was dead.

OVER-CONSTITUTIONALIZATION

There is a constant danger in the U.S. system of "over-constitutionalizing" routine policy disagreements—that is, of insisting that perfectly ordinary differences about which is the best way to proceed with policy are neatly settled in American higher law. This is evident in the flag cases. The whole discussion of the issue was cast in terms of unambiguous constitutional rights and requirements attending American citizenship. "The hard fact is," wrote Justice Anthony Kennedy in his concurring opinion in the Texas case, "that sometimes we must make decisions we do not like. We make them because they are right, *right in the sense that the law and the constitution . . . compel the result*" (emphasis added). But never before 1989 did the High Court decide that the Constitution compelled the overturning of all flag-protection statutes. Justices have been wildly divided as to what the Constitution requires on questions of flag protection—not only in the two most recent cases but in a number of earlier ones as well. Ardent civil libertarians such as former Chief Justice Earl Warren and former Justice Hugo Black argued forcefully that reasonably crafted prohibitions against flag burning do not violate the Constitution, while conservatives such as Justice Kennedy have insisted they do.

The only clear conclusion is that intelligent men and women, equally dedicated to the broad ideals of the American system, disagree about whether we better enhance the flag as a uniquely powerful symbol of American nationhood by providing modest sanctions against those who defile it in public displays or by leaving it physically vulnerable to represent the essential constitutional guarantee of individual dissent. But most of us—from Supreme Court justices on down to ordinary citizens—find it hard to avoid insisting that the handling of the flag issue is somehow linked to the most fundamental sense of American citizenship.

This is our philosophic inheritance as a nation founded on a creed. It invites some political showboating, and at times we sound too absolutist. Overall, though, the United States gains much from the strength of concern and feeling evident in the argument over flag protection. That we still bring so much moral energy, two centuries and more after the American experiment began, to debates over its meaning and what it requires of us is quite striking. The central political ideals on which the United States was founded remain vital.

CIVIL RIGHTS IN AMERICA

The question of whether small, unpopular political minorities have a constitutional right to express their dissatisfaction with the U.S. system by burning the flag is a **civil liberties** issue. Civil liberties problems typically involve the "rights of citizenship" of isolated individuals, such as persons accused of crimes and groups made unpopular by their beliefs—religious, cultural, or political—rather than by attributes of birth like race or sex. Problems of **civil rights** were for a long time synonymous with segregation and discrimination against black Americans, but the term is now more inclusive. Civil rights issues involve other groups in the population that have encountered categoric discrimination: for example, other ethnic minorities and women. Membership in groups

subject to this kind of discrimination is something over which one has no control.

EXTENDING RIGHTS

All across the area of civil liberties and civil rights, one sees a clear progression or pattern of change, centered around increasing expectations and demands, and policy shifts that have come in response. This is especially noticeable in the years since World War II. The timing and magnitude of change varies from one sector to another. The political movement to advance the civil rights of African-Americans was particularly strong in the 1960s; that for women's rights was more active in the late 1970s and in the 1980s. But heightened demands and important policy changes have been prominent in almost every sector of civil liberties and civil rights over the last forty years.

CURBING RACIAL DISCRIMINATION

Changes in expectations and demands with regard to rights of citizenship have been occurring since the early nineteenth century; they have been especially pronounced over the last half-century in the area of race relations. In the South, to which black GIs returned in 1945 and 1946, the black population was almost totally excluded from decision making in all institutions that served the general, as opposed to solely the black, population. Nearly all public facilities in the region, including city parks and playgrounds, theaters, hotels, and restaurants, were rigidly segregated. As one small example of the pervasiveness of segregation in public facilities, the Southern Political Science Association long held its annual meeting in the tiny mountain town of Gatlinburg, in eastern Tennessee, because it was one of the very few spots in the entire South where blacks and whites (in this case, as college teachers) could

The "Jim Crow" system of racial segregation.

meet, eat, and reside together in a resort hotel. School systems across the South were totally segregated. And African-Americans were almost completely disenfranchised: In the early 1940s, only 5 percent of voting-age black citizens in the South were registered voters.[3]

Violence Against Blacks. The most reprehensible denial of basic citizenship rights was the vulnerability of blacks throughout much of the South to assaults on their personal safety and well-being. The Swedish social scientist Gunnar Myrdal observed in the 1940s that

> in the South the Negro's person and property are practically subject to the whim of any white

person who wishes to take advantage of him or to punish him for any real or fancied wrong doing or "insult." A white man can steal from or maltreat a Negro in almost any way without fear of reprisal, because a Negro cannot claim the protection of the police or courts, and personal vengeance on the part of the offended Negro usually results in organized retaliation in the form of bodily injury (including lynching), home burning or banishment. . . . Physical violence and threats against personal security do not, of course, occur to every Negro every day. . . . But violence may occur at any time, and it is the fear of it as much as violence itself which creates the injustice and the insecurity.[4]

Myrdal was not exaggerating. At least 3,275 black Americans were lynched in the South

---

[3]For further discussion of black political participation in the South and of the changes that took place over the 1940s, 1950s, and 1960s, see Everett Ladd, *Negro Political Leadership in the South* (New York: Atheneum, 1969).

[4]Gunnar Myrdal, *An American Dilemma* (New York: McGraw-Hill, 1964; first published, 1944), p. 530.

between 1882 and 1936.[5] And, as Myrdal pointed out, even if violations, intimidations, and frauds occurred only sporadically, the threat was always present.

Racial discrimination was not exclusively southern. But the denial of equal citizenship to blacks was far more extreme in the South than elsewhere in the country. And, as late as 1950, two-thirds of all black Americans resided in the eleven states that had seceded in 1861 to form the Confederacy.

Assertion of American Values. Today, although debate goes on over the adequacy of the nation's response in the area of civil rights, there is no doubt that extraordinary changes have occurred over the last forty years, greatly extending the rights of black citizens. The sources of this transformation are complex. Gunnar Myrdal identified one source when he pointed to the "ever-raging conflict" between the general principles of the American creed and the historic reality of American race relations—a conflict that could not persist forever. The average American is "more of a believer and defender of the faith in humanity than the rest of the Occidentals. It is a relatively important matter to him to be true to his own ideals and to carry them out in actual life."[6]

The crucial question is not why the system of gross racial discrimination finally broke down in a rush in the 1950s and 1960s, but why this change was so slow in coming. The tensions between beliefs and practice were fundamental. A century earlier, Lincoln had seen clearly the extent and destructiveness of this contradiction. In his "House Divided" speech, delivered to the Republican state convention in Springfield, Illinois, on June 17, 1858, Lincoln cited the biblical passage "A house divided

against itself cannot stand." He went on: "I believe this government cannot endure, permanently half slave and half free. I do not expect the Union to be dissolved—I do not expect the house to fall—but I do expect it will cease to be divided." But America's house was to remain divided for another century before the beliefs summoned sufficient action.

Effects of Demographic Changes. Another source of change has to do with population movement. Sweeping shifts of blacks from rural to urban areas, and from the South to a more national distribution, increased the political power of black Americans. Prior to World War I, most of the black population of the United States resided in the South, largely in rural areas, and worked in agriculture. But World War I, with its increased demand for labor in war industries, provided large numbers of blacks with the economic opportunity to leave southern agriculture. "They began one of the most massive internal migrations in the history of the United States. . . . Three-quarters of a million Negroes moved North within a four-year period during World War I."[7] Migration continued after the war, and it expanded again during World War II. Between 1940 and 1970, the net migration of blacks from the South into northern states was more than 4.4 million. A dramatic reversal has occurred, however, since the mid-1970s. More blacks are now moving into the South than are leaving it—reflecting in part the improved racial climate in the region. The proportion of black Americans living in the South, 90 percent in 1900, dropped to 77 percent in 1940 and reached its historic low of 52 percent in 1975, as migration from the region continued apace. Then the reversal took place. At present, about 54 percent of all Afri-

[5] E. Franklin Frazier, *The Negro in the United States* (New York: Macmillan, 1957), p. 160.
[6] Myrdal, *An American Dilemma*, p. lxx.

[7] Thomas Sowell, *Race and Economics* (New York: McKay, 1975), p. 49.

FIGURE 14.2   BLACK POPULATION BY REGION, 1980, 1990

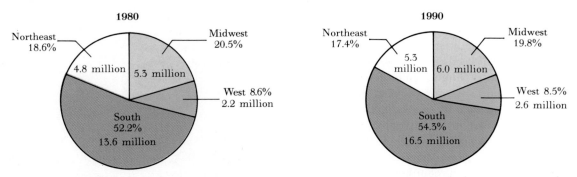

Source: U.S. Bureau of the Census, Current Population Reports, *The Black Population in the United States*, March 1988, Series P-20, No. 442, p. 3; idem, *The Black Population in the United States, March 1990 and 1989*, p. 23.

can-Americans live in the South. The proportion of the total population of African-American background is now declining moderately in the Northeast and Midwest (Figure 14.2).

The 1960 census was the first to show a majority of southern blacks residing in metropolitan areas. By 1980, a population that had been concentrated on farms and in small towns in the states of the old Confederacy was overwhelmingly urban. According to the 1980 Census, only 15 percent of blacks nationally lived in small towns and rural areas, compared to 29 percent of whites. African-Americans still are disproportionately city dwellers, but during the 1980s they became slightly less so—a development that accompanied the movement back to the South. In 1988, 18 percent of blacks lived in small towns and rural areas, up 3 percent from the 1980 figure.[8]

How did these shifts affect race relations? The system of gross discrimination and segregation (sometimes known as "Jim Crow") had been a product of the rural South. It reflected attitudes that derived from the historical expe-

rience of slavery and the extreme vulnerability of rural blacks to intimidation and violence. The movement of large numbers of blacks to the North brought them into environments where the traditions and institutions of segregation had never been firmly established. It made black votes of increasing concern to northern politicians. The movement of blacks from rural to urban areas, South as well as North, brought them into settings where political and social organization could proceed far more readily. And extralegal violence was far less pervasive among the concentrated black populations of southern cities than among the scattered populations of the rural South. Overall, the great demographic shifts of 1920–70 brought blacks into positions where political organization was easier and political influence much greater.

Against this backdrop, a concerted political effort was mounted in the first two decades after World War II. It went on simultaneously in five different arenas: (1) in the courts, especially the federal courts; (2) through direct action by the civil rights movement, in marches, boycotts, sit-ins, and elsewhere; (3) within the legislative and executive branches of government, again especially at the federal level; (4) through

[8]U.S. Bureau of the Census, *The Black Population in the United States: March 1988* (Washington, D.C.: Government Printing Office, 1989), pp. 2–4.

voting and elections; and (5) in the "court" of American public opinion.

Brown v. Board of Education of Topeka. Many of the critical early steps were taken in the courts. Years of legal effort, led by the NAACP Legal Defense Fund, culminated in the Supreme Court's historic decision in *Brown v. Board of Education of Topeka* (and a series of companion cases) in 1954. (Brown is discussed in detail in chapter 9.) For the first time, segregated schools were declared in violation of the Equal Protection requirement of the Fourteenth Amendment. "Separate educational facilities are inherently unequal," wrote Chief Justice Earl Warren on behalf of a unanimous Court. *Brown* announced the end of "Jim Crow." It removed the aura of legitimacy and constitutionality from the entire system of racial exclusion. Although the case applied only to schools, and some recalcitrant judges tried to limit it to that arena, the Supreme Court followed up by citing *Brown* as authority for treating all official segregation as unconstitutional.[9]

Direct-Action Protests. The early direct-action protests in the South, notably those led by a young black clergyman, Martin Luther King, Jr., played a key role. King, the son of a distinguished clergyman in Atlanta, first came to national attention in 1955 when he led a bus boycott in Montgomery, Alabama. A black woman, Rosa Parks, had been arrested in Montgomery for refusing to move to the "colored" section in the back of the bus. The boycott focused national attention not only on bus segregation in Montgomery, but on the whole pattern of segregation in public facilities across the South. It was followed by an expanding

Civil rights workers led by the Rev. Martin Luther King, Jr., during a 1965 march from Selma to Montgomery, Alabama.

stream of direct-action protests: against discriminatory treatment by law-enforcement officials, school segregation, laws, and practices that prevented blacks from eating with whites in restaurants and at lunch counters, and against almost all the forms of the old racial system.

Martin Luther King, Jr., was the single most influential black leader; he gave force and moral direction to the civil rights movement. Through his personal courage, eloquence as a speaker, strong commitment to nonviolence, and unflagging insistence that America honor its claim to the idea of equality, King helped shift the ground in race relations until his death at the hands of an assassin in 1968.

[9]Richard Kluger, *Simple Justice: The History of Brown v. Board of Education and Black America's Struggle for Equality* (New York: Knopf, 1976).

TABLE 14.1   MAJOR CIVIL RIGHTS LAWS AND COURT DECISIONS: TWO DECADES OF SWEEPING
CHANGE IN LAW

Year	Policy shift	Major acts, landmark cases
1948	Executive branch decrees end to discrimination against blacks in the military.	*Executive Order #9981*, issued by President Truman
1954	"Separate but equal" doctrine struck down.	*Brown* v. *Board of Education of Topeka* (347 U.S. 483) and companion cases
1957, 1960	Acts signal the federal government to enter into a law enforcement role to protect voter rights. Actions take form of court injunctions.	*Civil Rights Act of 1957* (Public Law [PL] 85-315) *Civil Rights Act of 1960* (PL 86-449)
1963	Employers required to pay equal wages to men and women for equal work.	*Equal Pay Act of 1963* (PL 88-38)
1964	Most significant policy departures in civil rights legislation since Reconstruction: guaranteeing blacks access to public accommodation and equal employment opportunity.	*Civil Rights Act* (PL 88-352)
1964	Constitutionality of 1964 Civil Rights Act sustained.	*Heart of Atlanta Motel* v. *United States* (379 U.S. 241) *Katzenbach* v. *McClung* (379 U.S. 297)
1965	Major federal effort to guarantee voting rights to blacks.	*Voting Rights Act* (PL 89-110)
1968	Racially discriminatory housing practices made illegal. Constitutionality of 1968 fair housing policies sustained. Signals end to "officially sanctioned *de jure* racial segregation in housing," public as well as private.	*Civil Rights Act of 1968* *Jones* v. *Alfred H. Meyer Co.*

Legislation and Voting. New legislation strengthened the hand of the civil rights movement (Table 14.1). Title II of the Civil Rights Act of 1964 established the substantive right not to be discriminated against in places of public accommodation. Titles III and IV authorized the Justice Department to bring suits to secure the desegregation of schools and other public facilities, upon the complaint of aggrieved parties who lacked the resources to pursue their own legal actions. The Civil Rights Acts of 1957 and 1960 were early efforts to extend the right of blacks to vote, but they had been badly watered down to get past filibusters by

southern senators. The Voting Rights Act of 1965, however, put the federal government behind the full extension and free exercise of the vote by blacks.

Public Opinion and Race Relations. Much attention has focused in recent years on black-white tensions in our major cities and on incidents of racial violence. The spring 1992 acquittal by an all-white jury of white Los Angeles police officers accused of beating Rodney King, a black motorist, and the rioting that followed this verdict are vivid reminders of the tensions that remain part of U.S. race rela-

The National Guard was brought in to stop racial violence that broke out in Los Angeles following the acquittal of white police officers accused of using excessive force against black motorist Rodney King.

tions. Nonetheless, the overall trend has clearly been toward greater racial tolerance and integration.

A review of opinion surveys reminds us that such changes, if slow, have together been substantial. The National Opinion Research Center (NORC) of the University of Chicago has asked of the white majority a number of questions on equality in the same form over the past three decades. In 1956 just half of the white public professed support for the ideal of integrated education. By 1968 the proportion had risen to almost three-fourths, and in 1985, when NORC stopped asking the question, it had climbed above 90 percent. Roughly 40 percent of whites rejected prohibitions against racial intermarriage in 1968, the year of King's death. Now, 80 percent oppose them. The idea that whites have a right to exclude blacks from their neighborhoods was opposed by only 4 in 10 white Americans in 1963, nearly 6 in 10 in 1977, and 8 in 10 in 1991.

Some of the biggest shifts have occurred in the South, where whites long responded very differently to issues of racial equality than did their counterparts elsewhere. In 1948, for example, segregation in public transportation was backed by over three-fourths of southern whites, compared to one-fifth in the Northeast, according to Gallup polls. That same year, when federal fair-employment practice legislation was endorsed by about 55 percent of

New England and the Middle Atlantic whites, it was supported by just 10 percent in the old Confederacy.

Since Martin Luther King's day, though, the South has slowly rejoined the nation. In 1972, the view that whites have a right to keep blacks from their neighborhoods was backed by a proportion 21 points higher in the South than elsewhere in the country, according to an NORC survey (53 percent to 32 percent). In 1991, though, the gap was just 5 points (23 to 18 percent). In 1972 only 52 percent of southern whites said they would vote for a black person nominated by their party for president, even if they considered him qualified; 82 percent of nonsouthern whites said they would vote for him. By 1991, however, the margin had largely disappeared: 80 percent of southern whites and 87 percent of whites outside the region accepted the standard that a person shouldn't be barred by race from the presidency.

Movement toward a fuller acceptance of the ideal of racial equality is even more evident when one looks only at people who have come of age since the civil rights revolution of the 1960s. NORC surveys show, for example, that support for prohibitions against racial intermarriage is now only one-third as high among whites in their twenties and thirties as among those in their late fifties and older. Similarly, the proportion of whites claiming a right to exclude blacks from their neighborhoods is just half as great among persons 18–29 as among those over 55.

Looking back on his forty years in survey research, Burns Roper has remarked that often the biggest attitudinal shifts are displayed not in the answers to specific questions but in the changing substance of the questions themselves. In 1940 Gallup asked respondents if they approved of proposed federal legislation against lynching, which would "fine and imprison local police officers who fail to protect a prisoner from a lynch mob, and make a county in which a lynching occurs pay a fine up to $10,000 to the victim or his family." In 1964, NORC asked whether "a restaurant owner should . . . have to serve Negroes if he doesn't want to." In the 1990s, surveys will be asking about affirmative-action programs and other proposals for eradicating the legacy of Jim Crow.

Most of the data reviewed here involve *professed adherence* to a norm. Don't some people lie about such matters, retreating to the "socially acceptable"? Of course they do. But surely Abraham Lincoln was right in insisting that a steady rise in recognition of the proper norm is the essential mark of progress.

Survey data point to behavioral consequences in Americans' personal lives of the greater recognition of the ideal. In 1966, for instance, 45 percent of whites told NORC interviewers that they had "a good friend who was a Negro." By 1981, 54 percent in an ABC News / *Washington Post* poll said that they knew at least one black person whom they considered "a close personal friend," and in a 1989 ABC / *Washington Post* poll the figure had climbed to 66 percent. The latter survey also found 80 percent of blacks saying they had at least one close personal friend among whites, up from 69 percent in 1981. Whites and blacks alike were in 1989 far more likely to live in integrated neighborhoods than they had been two decades earlier. And as they did at the end of the 1970s, both groups in 1989 looked back on the decade past and pronounced it one of racial progress (see Figure 14.3).

GAINS IN CIVIL RIGHTS

The net results of the various contributing factors are dramatic. Public accommodations throughout the country are now free of segregation. *De jure* segregation of the schools—that is, segregation based on law and enforced by

FIGURE 14.3   BLACKS AND WHITES: A SENSE OF SOME PROGRESS

Compared to ten years ago, do you think blacks in America are a lot better off, a little better off, about the same, a little worse off, or a lot worse off?

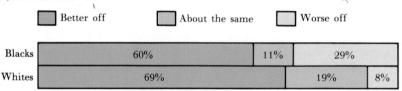

Generally speaking, has racial prejudice been a problem you encounter ...

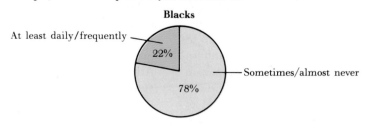

Do you yourself know any (black/white) person whom you consider a fairly close personal friend?

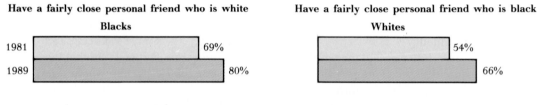

Would you say the white children in your neighborhood tend to associate with the black children ...

Source: Question 1: Survey by NBC News and the *Wall Street Journal,* July 6–10, 1990. *Question 2:* Survey of black adults by Gordon S. Black Corporation for *USA Today,* August 30–31, 1989. *Questions 3 and 4:* Survey by ABC News / *Washington Post,* latest that of September 28–October 3, 1989.

government—has been eliminated. Registration and voting by African-Americans is now similar to that for whites (Figure 14.4). Blacks now have substantial electoral power in many cities, North and South, as the success of black candidates attests. A number of major U.S. cities, including Washington, New York, Philadelphia, Chicago, Detroit, Los Angeles, and Atlanta, have black mayors. The number of blacks holding elective office climbed from just 1,500 in 1970 to over 7,300 in 1990 (Figure 14.5).

FIGURE 14.4   BLACK AND WHITE REGISTRATION AND VOTING, 1976–88

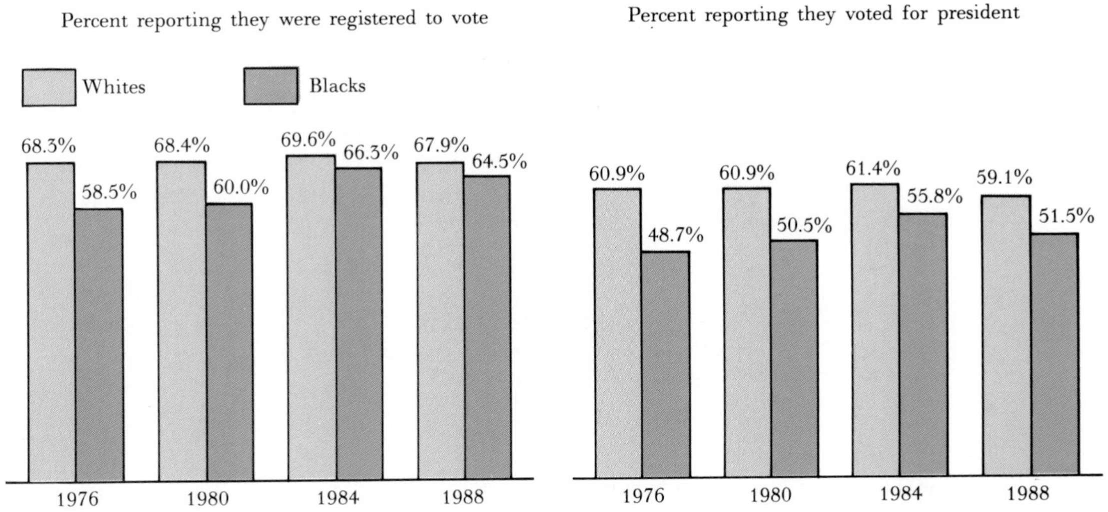

Percent reporting they were registered to vote   Percent reporting they voted for president

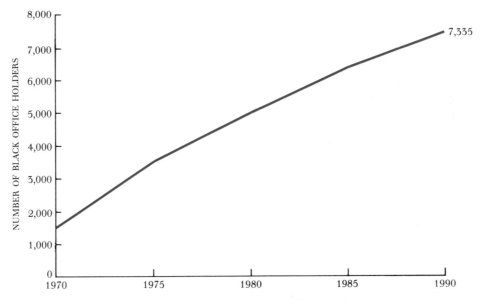

FIGURE 14.5   BLACKS HOLDING ELECTIVE OFFICE SINCE 1970

Source: U.S. Bureau of the Census, *Statistical Abstract of the United States, 1991*, p. 266.

TABLE 14.2   EDUCATIONAL ATTAINMENT BY RACE, 1940, 1990

| | Percent of persons 25 years old or over who completed | | | |
| | Four years of high school or more | | Four years of college or more | |
	1940	1990	1940	1990
White	26.1	79.1	4.9	22.0
Black	7.3	66.2	1.3	11.3
Asian or Pacific Islander	22.6	80.4	3.9	39.9
Hispanic (any race)	NA	50.8	NA	9.2
Total	24.5	77.6	4.6	21.3

Source: U.S. Bureau of the Census, *Population Profile of the United States, 1991,* Current Population Reports, Special Studies, Series P-23, No. 173, p. 4.

FIGURE 14.6   A DRAMATIC NARROWING OF THE EDUCATIONAL GAP BETWEEN YOUNG BLACK AND WHITE AMERICANS (DATA ARE FOR PERSONS 25 TO 29 YEARS OF AGE)

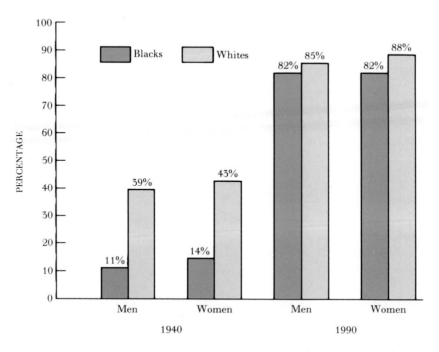

Percentages represent the proportion of the respective populations in the years shown who had completed four years of high school or more.
Source: Graphs are based on 1990 Census data printed in U.S. Bureau of the Census, *Population Profile of the United States, 1991,* Current Population Reports, Special Studies, Series P-23, No. 173, pp. 4–5.

FIGURE 14.7   BUT UNEMPLOYMENT FAR HIGHER FOR BLACK AMERICANS

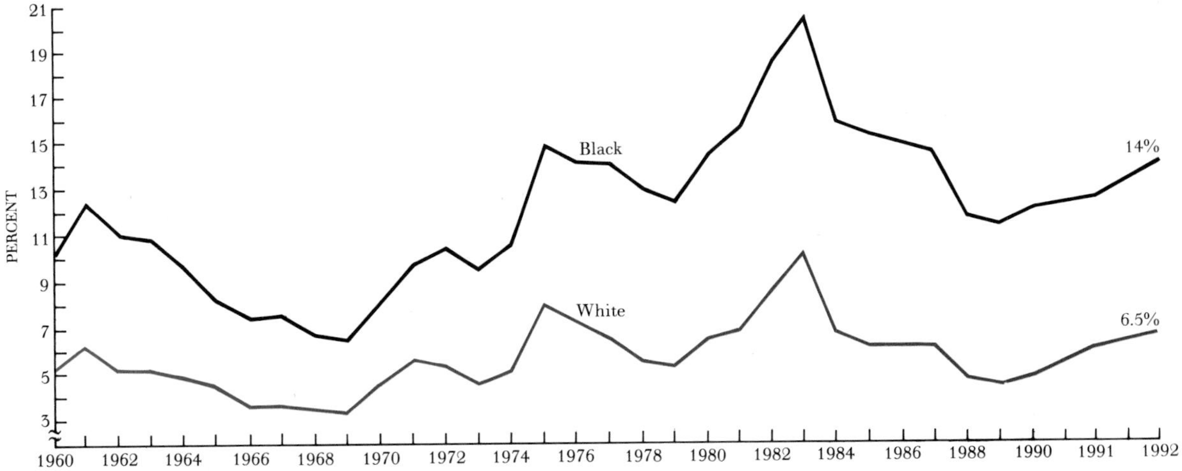

Source: Data for 1960–1970 are from *Historical Statistics of the United States*, part 1, p. 135; data for 1972–1982 are from *Statistical Abstract of the United States, 1984*, p. 422; data for 1984–1992 are from *Economic Indicators*, April 1992, p. 12; and Bureau of Labor Statistics, September 1992 data. Data on blacks for 1960–1971 are in fact for "blacks and other races."

The proportion of blacks with at least a high school education grew from just 8 percent in 1940 to 66 percent in 1990. Fifty years ago, the gap between the proportion of African-Americans ages 25–29 having attained at least a high-school education trailed that of young whites by a huge margin. Today, though, young blacks are almost as likely to have graduated from high school as are young whites, though they still lag in terms of college training (Table 14.2 and Figure 14.6). Similar advances can be seen in the occupational area, as the proportion of blacks in professional and managerial occupations has increased appreciably.

In two other critical areas, however, the experience of the last decade is far less encouraging. The income of black families continues to lag substantially behind that of white families: In 1990 the median income of black families was $21,400 compared to $36,900 for white families. The ratio of the incomes of the two groups has changed little over the last quarter-century. As Figure 14.7 indicates, unemployment has consistently been much higher among blacks than among whites. In the spring of 1992, black unemployment was 14 percent, that of whites a far lower 6.5 percent.

AFFIRMATIVE ACTION

What further action does the United States need to take to remove as quickly as possible the vestiges of racial discrimination? Part of the answer seems clear and generates little debate: Where discrimination exists in law and formal practice, it should be ended. Governmental power should be used to prevent various private groups from continuing to block participation by blacks and other minorities. But is this all that is required? If a group has been subject to a pervasive pattern of discrimination over an extended period, is it enough simply to end legal discrimination? Or are additional positive steps—**affirmative action**—needed, at least in the short run, to extend further opportunities to the deprived group and to increase its representation in various arenas of national life? President Lyndon Johnson made the case for special national responses to overcome the effects of past discrimination in a commencement address at Washington's Howard University in 1965. "You do not take a person who, for years, has been hobbled by chains and liberate him," Johnson argued, "bring him up to the starting line of a race and then say, 'You are free to compete with all the others,' and still justly believe that you have been completely fair."

Most Americans believe that the ultimate goal is a "color blind" society where individuals are recognized strictly on the basis of their own efforts and merit and where government no more aids certain groups than it discriminates against others. But aren't some special compensatory programs needed in the short run? How long is compensatory treatment justified? And what forms should it take? Arguments over these issues are sharp, and they go on within the black community itself. Many black leaders argue that affirmative action is still very much needed. For example, Randall Kennedy, a black professor at Harvard Law School, maintains that "I think we have to say to whites, 'Listen, you have benefitted in countless ways from racism. . . . We have a problem in this country—a people has been kept down for hundreds of years and we've got a lot of work to undo that. You've got to pay a cost, my friend, just like when we go to war. We all pay taxes. Think of affirmative action as a cost, part of the social overhead.' "[10]

But a growing if still relatively small group of black leaders and intellectuals argue that while racial prejudice continues to afflict American society, emphasis on it, and on racial preference policies to remedy it, is actually harmful to the black community. Some, such as San Jose State University professor Shelby Steele, maintain that affirmative action programs

> diminish our [blacks'] sense of possibility. I think this . . . is a burden for blacks, because it is built around our collective insecurity rather than a faith in our human capacity to seize opportunity as individuals. It amounts to a self-protective collectivism that focuses on black unity instead of individual initiative. . . . [M]y deepest feeling is that in a society of increasingly limited resources, there will never be enough programs to meet the need. We black Americans will never be saved or even assisted terribly much by others, never be repaid for our suffering, and never find that symmetrical, historical justice that we cannot help but long for.[11]

THE COURT AND AFFIRMATIVE ACTION

As with most important controversies involving civil liberties and civil rights, the argument over affirmative action has been thrust heavily on the courts for resolution. And, reflecting the complexity of the issue and the extent of the differences in this country on how best to end discrimination, the Supreme Court itself has been sharply divided. One important recent case that reflects the Court's divisions originated in a suit brought by the Equal Employment Opportunity Commission (EEOC), an executive-branch agency. The EEOC sued a

---

[10] Randall Kennedy quoted in Ethan Bronner, "High Court's Split on Affirmative Action Echoes Nation's Division," *Boston Globe*, June 29, 1990, p. 9.

[11] Shelby Steele, "Ghettoized by Black Unity," *Harper's*, May 1990, p. 22; idem., *The Content of Our Character: A New Vision of Race in America* (New York: St. Martin's Press, 1990).

local of the Sheet Metal Workers' International Union for discriminating against non-white candidates for membership. A federal district court judge found the union local guilty and ordered it to increase its non-white membership to 29 percent of the total by July 1, 1981 (later extended, though with fines imposed on the local, to July 31, 1987). The case was appealed to the Second Circuit Court of Appeals and finally reached the Supreme Court in 1985.

In the decision handed down in July 1986, *Sheet Metal Workers' International v. EEOC,* Justice William J. Brennan, Jr., spoke for a closely divided (5–4) Court. The majority upheld the lower court rulings requiring the union to increase its non-white membership proportion to 29 percent. Justice Brennan argued that "in most cases the Court need only order the employer or the union to cease engaging in discriminatory practices, and award make-whole relief to the individuals victimized by those practices." In some instances, however, it may be necessary to require the employer or union to take affirmative steps to end discrimination effectively. "If the company or the union has shown particularly long-standing or egregious discrimination," Brennan wrote, the requirement that it "hire and . . . admit qualified minorities roughly in proportion to the number of qualified minorities in the workforce may be the only effective way to ensure the full enjoyment of the rights protected by Title VII" of the 1964 Civil Rights Act. In a dissenting opinion, Justice Byron R. White maintained that the lower court had ordered "not just a minority membership goal but also a strict racial quota. We have not heretofore approved this kind of racially discriminatory hiring practice and I would not do so now."

The Court reached a different conclusion in *Wygant v. Jackson Board of Education* (1986). The case involved the question of whether a governmental agency—here the Board of Education of Jackson, Michigan—could in the absence of a judicial finding of discrimination adopt an affirmative action plan that protects black teachers from layoffs at the expense of whites with more seniority. Until the 1960s the schools of Jackson, Michigan, were segregated, not by law but as a result of housing patterns. The first African-American teacher was not hired in Jackson until 1953, and in 1968 only 4 percent of the system's teaching staff were black, although 15 percent of the students were black.

To create an integrated system, school officials began a concerted effort to hire black teachers; as part of this the 1972 contract with the teachers' union provided special protection for newly hired minority teachers. In the event of layoffs, white teachers would be dismissed instead of more junior black teachers if such action was needed to preserve the existing minority proportion in the teaching staff. This provision was to be continued until the percentage of minority teachers was as great as the percentage of minority pupils. Under this provision, when layoffs were required in 1981, a number of senior teachers, including Wendy Wygant, were laid off while more junior black teachers were retained. Wygant and seven other white teachers sued, attacking the relevant section of the contract as unconstitutional.

Writing for a narrow 5–4 majority, Justice Lewis Powell agreed with the assertion of the Jackson Board of Education that, as Powell put it, "as part of this nation's dedication to eradicating racial discrimination, innocent persons may be called upon to bear some of the burden of the remedy." But in this instance the remedy imposed an undue burden on the white teachers who were fired, in effect, because of their race. "In cases involving valid hiring goals," Powell wrote, "the burden to be borne by innocent individuals is diffused to a considerable extent among society generally." In contrast, "layoffs impose the entire burden of achieving racial equality on particular individuals, often resulting in serious disruption of their lives.

That burden is too intrusive. We therefore hold that, as a means of accomplishing purposes that otherwise may be legitimate, the Board's layoff plan is not sufficiently narrowly tailored."

Concurring in the judgment, Justice White would have gone further: "The layoff policy in this case—laying off whites who would otherwise be retained in order to keep blacks on the job . . . is . . . violative of the Equal Protection Clause [of the U.S. Constitution]." In one of the dissents, Justice Thurgood Marshall maintained that "remedial use of race is permissible if it serves 'important governmental objectives. . . .'" He argued that "when an elected school board and a teachers' union collectively bargain a layoff provision designed to preserve the effects of a valid recruitment plan . . . that provision should not be upset by this Court on constitutional grounds."

In these two cases, then, the Supreme Court upheld enforcement of a minority membership percentage on a labor union, as part of an effort to eradicate past discrimination, but it struck down a layoff provision designed to maintain a racial balance achieved through the implementation of hiring goals. Both judgments saw the Court split 5–4, and both produced a number of concurring and dissenting opinions.

Often dividing along liberal/conservative lines, the Supreme Court continues to struggle to define areas where affirmative action is justified and those where such programs go too far and themselves clash with the goal of a discrimination-free society. In *City of Richmond v. J. A. Croson Company* (1989), by a vote of 6 to 3 the Court struck down an affirmative action plan that set aside 30 percent of city construction contracts for minority-owned businesses. Justices Brennan, Marshall, and Blackmun dissented. Looking to the future, it's important to note that two of these dissenting justices, William Brennan and Thurgood Marshall, have since retired from the Court. Marshall's replacement, Clarence Thomas, has strongly opposed race-based hiring requirements.

AFFIRMATIVE ACTION VERSUS QUOTAS

Part of the reason for the sharp divisions is the muddied distinction between affirmative action and racial quotas. The Court has held that taking positive measures to undo the effects of past discrimination—affirmative action—is valid. But many justices draw back from measures seen as imposing racial quotas. Setting quotas means that, in order to achieve more equitable racial representation, a certain number of positions—seats in an incoming university class or new job openings—will go to applicants from groups that have endured discrimination. Where does proper affirmative action leave off and the improper fixing of racial quotas begin? The debate over this question has been going on for a long time. Clearly, it is very hard for anyone to say—and "anyone" includes Supreme Court justices.

One of the most famous Court rulings involving this debate, *Regents of University of California v. Bakke*, was handed down in 1978. The University of California at Davis Medical School, in order to increase the number of black and Hispanic graduates, had developed a two-track system for applicants, with 84 of its 100 places in each year's entering class held for open competition and the remaining 16 reserved for "disadvantaged" applicants, in practice, blacks and Mexican-Americans. This program, with its declared policy of preferential admission for ethnic minorities, was developed by personnel of the medical school without any specific outside intervention, but it was a response to general social pressure for affirmative action to hurry growth in the numbers of minority-group professionals.

Allan Bakke is a white male who applied for admission to the medical school at Davis in

1972. While employed as an engineer for a space-agency laboratory near Palo Alto, California, Bakke came in contact with physicians who had been studying the effects of space on the human body. He was stimulated and encouraged to become a doctor. And, after night courses in science and voluntary work in hospitals, he applied for medical school at the age of thirty-two. Bakke's credentials for application were generally very strong. He had impressed his medical school evaluators, receiving a score of 468 out of a possible 500 in the admissions office's summary compilation of all the measures it applied. But by the time Bakke completed his application (delayed because of family illness) most of the 84 places that had been set aside for open competition had already been filled. He was rejected—even though his scores were substantially higher than those of the minority applicants subsequently admitted.

In a July 1, 1972, letter to the medical school, Bakke stated that he was not prepared to accept his rejection as legitimate:

> Applicants chosen to be our doctors should be those representing the best qualifications, both academic and personal. . . . I am convinced a significant fraction . . . is judged by a separate criterion. I am referring to quotas, open or covert, for racial minorities. . . . I realize that the rationale for these quotas is that they attempt to atone for past discrimination. But instituting a new racial bias in favor of minorities is not a just solution.

Bakke went on to state that it was his belief "that admissions quotas based on race are illegal," and he indicated that he might challenge the Davis Medical School quota system in the courts.[12]

[12] For this and other detailed information on the Bakke case, see Allan P. Sindler, *Bakke, DeFunis, and Minority Admissions: The Quest for Equal Opportunity* (New York: Longman, 1978).

Still, Bakke's next step was not to sue, but rather to reapply for admission to the Davis Medical School, in the next year's class. But he was again rejected, and this time he did file suit. The California court of original jurisdiction upheld his claim; when the University of California appealed, Bakke's position was again sustained by the highest state court. In a ruling joined by six of the seven justices, the California Supreme Court held that since the University had never discriminated against minorities, it could not now discriminate for them. The court held that reserving sixteen places for minorities amounted to a quota based on race. The one dissenting justice attacked the decision of the court's majority: "Two centuries of slavery and racial discrimination have left our nation an awful legacy, a largely separated society in which wealth, educational resources, employment opportunities—indeed all society's benefits—remain largely the preserve of the white-Anglo majority." It was high time, the justice argued, that corrective measures like the preferential admissions program be instituted.

Having lost at the state level, the university carried its appeal to the U.S. Supreme Court. There, in a deeply divided opinion, Bakke's position was again sustained (and he was subsequently admitted to the Davis Medical School, graduating in 1982). The Supreme Court split in an unusual way: in effect, 4, 4, and 1. The one, Justice Lewis Powell, sided with one group of four in ruling that Bakke must be admitted. But he sided with the other four in rejecting the argument that the University of California could not consider race in any way in admissions. "The state certainly has a legitimate and substantial interest in ameliorating, or eliminating where feasible, the disabling effects of identified discrimination. . . . [This interest] may be served by a properly devised admissions program involving the competitive consideration of race and ethnic origin."

Justice Powell concluded that the minority-preferential admissions program of the Davis Medical School was unconstitutional, because the way it operated violated the equal-protection clause of the Fourteenth Amendment. That program, Powell held, "involves the use of an explicit racial classification never before countenanced by this Court. It tells applicants who are not Negro, Asian, or Chicano that they are totally excluded from a specific percentage of the seats in an entering class." The Constitution does not permit this. The other four judges who voted with Powell to admit Bakke wanted to strike down the Davis plan as in violation of Title VI of the Civil Rights Act of 1964. They presumably would have gone further than Powell would have in invalidating other preferential admissions programs.

"Both Sides Are Right." Especially interesting, and what in his review of the case Allan Sindler calls a "mini-amicus brief," is the editorial of the *New York Times* on June 19, 1977. Entitled "Reparation, American Style," the editorial covered a full half-page in tiny print. The *Times* thought the *Bakke* case was not only important but complex in the clash of values it presented and that "the law, without too much difficulty, could resolve this case either way." People who are equally "wise and generous," the *Times* argued, could be found on either side.

> Many grow anxious on the threshold of this case. They say we must not fight evil with evil, discrimination with "reverse discrimination." They say the entire society will suffer if it compromises standards of merit in education or employment and holds back competent people to promote the fortunes of the "less qualified." They say an America only recently liberated from official racism must require its institutions to be color-blind, to judge individuals without reference to race or ethnic origin.
>
> Others argue, with equal passion, that there can be no remedy for inherited damage without transferring some opportunity from the advantaged majority to injured minorities. They say we cannot claim equal rights and expect to achieve them without helping minorities to exercise those rights. They say the damage will endure if policy ignores the handicaps currently inherent in some racial and ethnic status—that color must be relevant today if it is to be irrelevant tomorrow.[13]

The *Times* concluded that "both sides are right. But it is in the national interest that Mr. Bakke should lose the case."

As noted, this controversy did not end with the Bakke decision. It continues to be a prominent part of the debate over civil rights policy. Supreme Court justices seem to be in much the same position as the *New York Times* editorial writer: They think both sides are right, so they try to give recognition to both positions in this clash of competing values. The goal is to be "color-blind": to assign jobs and other positions without regard to group membership. But recognizing the history of past discrimination, some forms of corrective or remedial action may be appropriate in some cases.

MEN AND WOMEN
IN THE LABOR MARKET:
"COMPARABLE WORTH"

The movement for women's rights over the last decade has produced important changes in many areas of American society and politics. Women's rights have become an important component of civil rights. The economic dimension has been especially prominent and seems certain to become more so. At issue here is ensuring nondiscrimination and equal opportunity in hiring, promoting, and compensation. With regard to the latter, especially,

---

[13] "Reparation, American Style," *New York Times*, June 19, 1977, p. E16.

women's groups and others argue that a historic pattern of discrimination against women is evident in the area of compensation and that new initiatives are needed to end it.

Some of the pertinent facts are readily determined, others not so. It is apparent that women who are full-time workers on the whole make much less than their male counterparts. As Figure 14.8 indicates, the average pay of full-time female workers has been only about 60 to 65 percent that of male workers over the last decade. As more and more women take jobs outside the home, many as the prime wage earners in their households (rather than providing supplementary earnings), and as the women's movement gives greater emphasis to the claims of equal status generally, these basic wage differences have spurred protest and action.

Several different factors contribute to the overall pay differential, and the precise weight of any one of them is not known. (1) Women have been subject to conscious, intentional wage discrimination. (2) Cultural values and norms prevailing in the past have "assigned" disproportionate numbers of higher-status jobs to male workers. (3) The recent surge of women into the labor force has produced a situation where many female workers have relatively little seniority. (4) The employment of many women has been broken by periods of child-bearing and child-rearing, which has had some cumulative impact on overall job and compensation progress. (5) Market forces deriving from the above and other factors mean that employers can in many instances hire female employees for less than they pay men. And (6) many of the occupational sectors where labor unions

FIGURE 14.8   MEDIAN MONEY INCOME OF FULL-TIME WORKERS, BY SEX

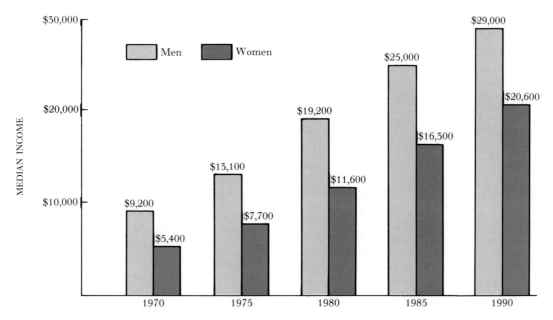

Source: U.S. Bureau of the Census, *Statistical Abstract,* 1986, p. 456; *1991,* p. 457; idem, *Current Population Reports,* Series P-60, No. 174, pp. 112, 116.

have since World War II achieved relatively high rates of compensation are occupations where women are substantially underrepresented.

The wages younger women in the labor force (those twenty to twenty-four years of age) earn lag much less significantly behind those of their male counterparts than is the case for older groups. This suggests that significant changes are occurring, such as the entry of more women into jobs that traditionally are higher paying. Still, even among full-time female workers twenty-five to thirty-four years of age, the average pay in 1988 was only 74 percent of that for male workers. Further, studies of the pay of men and women in specific occupations where similar skills and training are required suggest that the women still make less than the men. For example, female faculty members, at the rank of full professor, on average earn less than male full professors.[14]

Women employees and some labor unions are turning increasingly to the courts to find remedies for these pay differentials. One critical area in this litigation involves the distinction between "equal work" and "comparable work." While at first glance this might seem to be a minor semantic quibble, it is emerging as the hub of the controversy. In 1962, legislation was introduced into the U.S. House of Representatives to implement the Kennedy administration's commitment to equal-pay legislation. One section of the bill provided that

> no employer . . . shall discriminate . . . between employees on the basis of sex by paying wages to any employee at any rate less than the rate at which he pays wages to an employee of the opposite sex for work of comparable character on jobs the performance of which requires comparable skills, except where such payment is

made pursuant to a seniority or merit increase system which does not discriminate on the basis of sex.

In hearings on this proposed legislation, debate broke out over the "comparable character" provision. Representative Katherine St. George objected to the language and offered an amendment that limited equal pay claims to those "for equal work on jobs, the performance of which requires equal skills." She explained that her purpose was to limit wage discrimination claims to situations where men and women are paid differently for performing the same job.

> What we want to do in this bill is to make it exactly what it says. It is called equal pay for equal work in some of the committee hearings. There is a great difference between the word "comparable" and the word "equal." . . . The word "comparable" opens up great vistas. It gives tremendous latitude to whoever are the arbitrators in these disputes.

The House adopted the St. George amendment; the Senate, too, rejected the "comparable work" wording in favor of the "equal work" standard.

The matter did not end there, however, even though no subsequent congressional legislation has changed the "equal work" language. Job-classification procedures and standards have been sought, and in some instances applied, in which very different types of jobs are assessed as to their intrinsic worth or difficulty, compared to other types of jobs. Under these classifications, otherwise dissimilar jobs are grouped, with the stipulation that compensation should be equal for all of the different but comparable positions within a class.[15]

---

[14] "Average Faculty Salaries by Rank and Sex at Institutions," *Chronicle of Higher Education*, February 8, 1984, pp. 21–30.

[15] See Elaine Johansen, "From Social Doctrine to Implementation: Agenda Setting in Comparable Worth," *Policy Studies Review* 4, 1 (August 1984), pp. 71–85.

The issue of "comparable worth" burst forth front and center on the national political agenda following a December 1983 ruling by a federal district judge in Washington. In a suit brought by the American Federation of State, County, and Municipal Employees (AFSCME) against the state of Washington, the judge ruled that the state had failed to provide equal pay for jobs of comparable worth, as determined by classification studies. He ordered the state not only to "forthwith pay each and every individual plaintiff herein, the amount of compensation that they are entitled to receive as evaluated under [the] 'comparable worth' plan as adopted in May 1983," but to pay back pay, commencing from September 1979. The judge appointed a "special master" to monitor compliance. If sustained, his ruling would have raised the wages and provided back pay to thousands of state employees in female-dominated job classifications in the state of Washington. The state had argued that the burden would be too severe because of the tremendous costs involved, a severe lack of revenue given the state's depressed economy, and the serious impact on the state's work force. Besides, the state legislature was already attempting to work out a gradual long-term solution. The court found these arguments "without merit and unpersuasive."

The district court ruling was reversed by the U.S. Court of Appeals for the Ninth Circuit. Before the rehearing that the circuit court ordered could take place, however, state and union negotiations agreed on a settlement. Beginning in 1986 and continuing through 1992, the state agreed to add $10 million annually to the funding base available for eradicating wage differentials between jobs often held by women and those more highly paid and usually held by men that require comparable skill, effort, and responsibility. However, the settlement did not provide for any back pay, which had been stipulated in the original district court ruling.

THE RIGHTS OF THE ACCUSED

Since World War II and especially since 1960, the U.S. Supreme Court has issued a series of opinions that together have substantially extended constitutional guarantees to persons involved in legal proceedings. A key element in these rulings is the application to the states of the full force and specificity of the Bill of Rights, requirements that were originally intended to apply only to federal action.

SELECTIVE INCORPORATION

As we discussed in chapter 4, many Americans in the late 1780s and 1790s worried that the new national government might prove too strong and threaten individual liberty. The Bill of Rights was an important response to these concerns. It contained a set of specific prohibitions on national governmental action: "Congress shall make no law . . ." the First Amendment begins its famous stipulation of guarantees of freedom of religion, speech, press, and assembly. By the time of the Civil War, however, the context had changed greatly. Outside the South the concern was not with federal action abridging individual liberty, but rather with denials of freedom by southern state governments. Against this backdrop the Fourteenth Amendment, ratified July 9, 1868, specified that "no State shall make or enforce any law which shall abridge the privileges or immunities of citizens of the United States; nor shall any State deprive any person of life, liberty, or property, without due process of law; nor deny to any person within its jurisdiction the equal protection of the laws."

The Fourteenth Amendment was obviously intended to provide federal guarantees to black Americans against southern state denial of equality before the law. But the amendment's sweeping language has a broader reach. It does not refer just to blacks. No state government may deny any person "life, liberty, or property, without due process of law." The spirit is clear, but what specific requirements does it entail? Near the end of the nineteenth century, the Supreme Court began a process of **selective incorporation,** holding that specific limitations imposed on the national government by the Bill of Rights are similarly applied to state governments through the due-process clause of the Fourteenth Amendment. In *Chicago, Burlington, and Quincy Railroad Co. v. City of Chicago* (1897), the Court incorporated the Fifth Amendment guarantee against the taking of private property for public use without just compensation within the Fourteenth Amendment's due-process protections. Ever since that decision, as Table 14.3 shows, the Supreme Court has extended, one at a time, the range of Bill of Rights protections.

RIGHT TO COUNSEL

In a 1938 decision *(Johnson v. Zerbst)*, the Supreme Court ruled that the right to be represented by counsel is an absolute constitutional requirement in federal trials, under the

TABLE 14.3   MAJOR CASES INVOLVING SELECTIVE INCORPORATION OF THE BILL OF RIGHTS INTO THE FOURTEENTH AMENDMENT

Year	Case	Amendment incorporated
1897	*Chicago, Burlington, and Quincy Railroad Co.* v. *Chicago*	Fifth Amendment guarantee against taking of private property for public use without just compensation
1925	*Gitlow* v. *New York*	First Amendment guarantee of freedom of speech and press
1932	*Powell* v. *Alabama*	Sixth Amendment right to employ counsel
1934	*Hamilton* v. *University of California*	First Amendment guarantee of free exercise of religion
1937	*Palko* v. *Connecticut*	Concept of "selective incorporation" articulated
1942	*Betts* v. *Brady*	Sixth Amendment guarantee of appointed counsel denied
1947	*Everson* v. *Board of Education*	First Amendment prohibition of laws respecting an establishment of religion
1948	*In re Oliver*	Sixth Amendment right to a public trial
1949	*Wolf* v. *Colorado*	Fourth Amendment guarantee against unreasonable searches and seizures, but not the exclusionary rule
1961	*Mapp* v. *Ohio*	Exclusionary rule
1962	*Robinson* v. *California*	Eighth Amendment guarantee against cruel and unusual punishment
1963	*Gideon* v. *Wainwright*	Sixth Amendment guarantee of appointed counsel
1964	*Malloy* v. *Hogan*	Fifth Amendment guarantee against compulsory self-incrimination
1965	*Pointer* v. *Texas*	Sixth Amendment right to confront opposing witnesses
1966	*Parker* v. *Gladden*	Sixth Amendment right to an impartial jury
1967	*Klopfer* v. *North Carolina*	Sixth Amendment guarantee of speedy trial
1967	*Washington* v. *Texas*	Sixth Amendment guarantee of compulsory process for obtaining witnesses
1968	*Duncan* v. *Louisiana*	Sixth Amendment guarantee of trial by jury
1969	*Benton* v. *Maryland*	Fifth Amendment guarantee against double jeopardy

terms of the Sixth Amendment. It wasn't until *Gideon v. Wainwright* in 1963, however, that the Court incorporated this guarantee of appointed counsel into the Fourteenth Amendment, making it applicable to state courts, where the bulk of criminal proceedings occur. Clarence Earl Gideon had been convicted in a Florida court of breaking and entering. Since he had no funds, he asked that the court furnish him with an attorney. The Florida judge replied:

> Mr. Gideon, I am sorry, but I cannot appoint counsel to represent you in this case. Under the laws of the state of Florida, the only time the court can appoint [in effect, pay for] counsel to represent a defendant is when that person is charged with a capital offense. I am sorry, but I will have to deny your request to appoint counsel to defend you in this case.

If you want a lawyer, Mr. Gideon, you will have to find the funds to pay for him yourself. The Supreme Court disagreed. It accepted Gideon's claim that he was entitled to be represented by counsel and that Florida was required to provide him with one. The Court overturned Gideon's conviction. What had been simply a right to be represented by an attorney during a trial if the defendant wanted such counsel and could afford to pay for it, became a positive obligation upon state as well as federal courts to make certain that all individuals accused of crimes be represented by attorneys. The Court concluded that

> in our adversary system of criminal justice, any person hauled into court, who is too poor to hire a lawyer, cannot be assured a fair trial unless counsel is provided for him. . . . From the very beginning, our state and national constitutions and laws have laid great emphasis on procedural and substantive safeguards designed to assure fair trials before impartial tribunals in which every defendant stands equal before the law. This noble ideal cannot be realized if the poor man charged with crime has to face his accusers without a lawyer to assist him.[16]

THE EXCLUSIONARY RULE

In *Mapp v. Ohio* (1961), the Court enlarged the Fourth Amendment guarantee of "the right of the people to be secure in their persons, houses, papers, and effects, against unreasonable searches and seizures . . ." by requiring that the states do what the federal government had been required to do since 1914: exclude from criminal trials evidence that had been unconstitutionally obtained.

Police officers in Cleveland, Ohio, had forced their way into the residence of one Dolly Mapp, searched her dwelling, and seized "certain lewd and lascivious books, pictures, and photographs. . . ." This resulted in Mapp's conviction under an Ohio obscenity statute. The Supreme Court reversed her conviction, ruling that the Fourth Amendment guarantee is enforceable against the states "by the same sanction of exclusion as is used against the federal government." Since the evidence against Dolly Mapp had been obtained in violation of her right to privacy, it could not be used in a trial as part of the government's case against her. This is known as the exclusionary rule. In *Mapp*, the Supreme Court put the states on notice that if they convicted people on the basis of evidence unconstitutionally obtained, they could find the convictions overturned.

THE "MIRANDA RULES"

In *Miranda v. Arizona* (1966), the Supreme Court ruled that no conviction, whether in fed-

---

[16] For an interesting account of the Gideon case and its implications, see Anthony Lewis, *Gideon's Trumpet* (New York: Vintage Books, 1966).

eral or state court, could stand if evidence introduced at the trial had been obtained by law-enforcement officers in interrogations where the accused had not been specifically advised, prior to any questioning, of his constitutional rights—under the Fifth and Sixth Amendments—to remain silent and to be represented by an attorney. Ernesto A. Miranda had been convicted in a state court in Arizona of kidnapping and rape, on the basis of a confession obtained after two hours of questioning in which he was not told of his rights to counsel and to silence.

Chief Justice Earl Warren delivered the majority opinion that laid out what have come to be known as the **"Miranda Rules."** These rules have affected the way police officials all across the country handle the questioning of persons accused of crimes. A specific set of procedures must be followed, Warren wrote, in all cases of "custodial interrogation," which he defined as "questioning initiated by law-enforcement officers after a person has been taken into custody or otherwise deprived of his freedom of action in any significant way." Before any questioning,

> the person must be warned that he has a right to remain silent, that any statement he does make may be used as evidence against him, and that he has a right to the presence of an attorney, either retained or appointed. The defendant may waive effectuation of these rights, provided the waiver is made voluntarily, knowingly, and intelligently. If, however, he indicates in any manner and at any stage of the process that he wishes to consult with an attorney before speaking there can be no questioning. Likewise, if the individual is alone and indicates in any manner that he does not wish to be interrogated, the police may not question him.

Police officers are now routinely provided with a "Miranda Card," containing a statement of

the rules Warren set forth, which the officer can refer to in reading the defendant his rights.

The *Miranda* requirement is well-established but in recent years the Court has modified it significantly. In 1984, for example, the Court for the first time established a "public safety exception." A woman in Queens, New York, had hailed a police car and told the officers that a gunman had just raped her. She said that her assailant had fled into a nearby supermarket. The police entered the store, sighted a man who fitted the woman's description, chased him down an aisle and caught him. One of the officers noticed that the suspect was wearing an empty shoulder holster and asked where the gun was. The man nodded toward a pile of boxes and said, "The gun is over there." The officer had not informed the suspect of his right to remain silent before he asked about the gun, and for this reason the New York courts subsequently granted motions filed by defense attorneys to prevent the suspect's statement and the gun from being admitted as evidence. In *New York v. Quarles* (1984), a closely divided Supreme Court held that while the New York courts had been correct under the prevailing interpretation of the Miranda Rule, an exception had to be established. "We believe that this case presents a situation where concern for public safety must be paramount to adherence to the literal language of the prophylactic rules enunciated in *Miranda*," Justice William Rehnquist (now chief justice) stated for the 5–4 majority.

In its next term the Supreme Court continued its adjustments of the Miranda requirement in *Oregon v. Elstad* (1985). Eighteen-year-old Michael James Elstad, a suspect in the burglary of a neighbor's home, voluntarily and in the presence of his mother, admitted being in the neighbor's home at the time of the burglary. Taken to the sheriff's office where he was warned of his rights, Elstad waived them and confessed his involvement in the crime. Convicted of first-degree burglary, Elstad appealed, arguing that his initial admission of guilt—made before he had been formally apprised of his rights—predisposed him to make the second, and hence that it as well as the first was inadmissible. The Supreme Court disagreed. While the earlier confession was inadmissible as evidence, the latter was not thereby "tainted." Writing for a 6–3 majority, Justice Sandra O'Connor argued that the decision "in no way retreats from the bright line rule of *Miranda.*"

In a 1990 ruling the Court made clear that Miranda's "bright line"—drawn to prevent coerced confessions—would indeed be maintained. In *Minnick v. Mississippi* a 6–2 majority reaffirmed that once a defendant has invoked his right to an attorney, counsel must be present at all subsequent questioning unless the defendant specifically waives the right through a signed document.

MANDATORY DRUG TESTING: AN "UNREASONABLE SEARCH"?

The Fourth Amendment provides that "the right of the people to be secure in their persons, papers, and effects, against unreasonable searches and seizures, shall not be violated. . . ." As we have seen, cases continue to arise in which the issue of an "unreasonable search" of a person or his property is posed very much the way the framers of the Bill of Rights understood it in 1791. But we are also now seeing strikingly new issues arise regarding when a search is unreasonable. Programs requiring random drug testing of various workers are a case in point. When is such mandatory testing justified by the general national interest in reducing drug use and by specific interests in such matters as public safety, and

when does it cross the line and infringe on a person's Fourth Amendment rights? Two cases decided in 1989 required the Court to grapple with these questions.

In *Skinner v. Railway Labor Executives Association,* the Supreme Court ruled 7–2 that a policy of the Federal Railroad Administration (FRA) requiring drug and alcohol tests of railroad workers after major accidents and other safety violations is constitutional. It found the government's "compelling interests" in protecting public safety outweighed employees'

To what limits can the government extend the war on drugs? Here, federal officials unload captured marijuana in Miami. But can the government require drug testing among its own employees?

rights to privacy. Only Justices Brennan and Marshall dissented. "History teaches that grave threats to liberty often came in times of urgency," Marshall wrote, "when constitutional rights seem too extravagant to endure." He predicted that the first casualty of the war on drugs will be "the precious liberties of our citizens."

The second case saw the Court split 5–4. In *National Treasury Employees Union v. Von Raab,* it upheld mandatory drug testing as reasonable for Customs Service employees who apply for promotions to positions involving drug interdiction. Here the interest was obviously not public safety, as it was with the testing of railroad workers. Nonetheless, Justice Kennedy for the majority argued that the government's interest in law enforcement, which is sound and respected, outweighed the workers' privacy rights: How would it look to the public if it were found that drug-interdiction workers were themselves drug users and that the government wasn't actively trying to curb this? The tests could be administered, the majority held, without the agency's having reason to suspect a particular worker of being a drug user. This prompted an angry dissent from Antonin Scalia. Since there was no evidence the Customs employees were abusing drugs, Scalia wrote, such required tests were "particularly destructive of privacy and offensive to personal dignity."

Other drug-testing cases will be decided in years ahead, and in the process an important new body of Fourth Amendment jurisprudence will be developed. In general, the present majority on the Court is inclined to give government considerable leeway in its battle against drug and alcohol abuse. In a related case, the Court decided in 1990 *(Michigan v. Sitz)* by 6–3 that police may stop drivers at roadside checkpoints and examine them for signs of intoxication, without any evidence (in their driving) that justified suspicion.

COMPETING VALUES COLLIDE

One of the greatest complexities of public policy making is the frequency with which the pursuit of one value creates problems for other worthy objectives. Would it be desirable, for instance, to increase retirement benefits paid to elderly Americans under social security? Of course it would, especially for that segment of the populace that depends on social security for its sustenance. Any large increase in social security benefits requires large tax increases, however—increases that would be resented by many taxpayers. It would cause discomforts for some as great as the comforts higher benefits would confer on others. Increasing benefits is a worthy goal, but so is keeping taxes down. There does not seem to be a single, clear-cut "right" answer; rather, there is a need to compromise and adjust among competing objectives, where no one can be sure just what balance is best.

This is the situation facing the Supreme Court and the country in large areas of civil liberties and civil rights policy. A new plateau was reached in the 1960s, defined by greater attentiveness to individual rights than obtained previously. But on this new plateau the old need to strike appropriate balances among competing objectives has inevitably asserted itself.

THE EXCLUSIONARY RULE REVISITED

We noted above that the principle of the exclusionary rule's application to the states—as a deterrent to impermissible police conduct—was established in the 1960s. This does not mean that judicial policy in this area has become a consensual matter where a straightforward provision is easily followed. As it has tried to apply the exclusionary rule, the Supreme Court has run into some thorny problems and has found itself engulfed in a vigorous debate.

A highly controversial case that reached the Supreme Court in 1976 and was decided the next year involved a man, Robert Williams, who was convicted by an Iowa court for the murder on Christmas Eve, 1968, of a ten-year-old girl. While being returned by police to Des Moines, Iowa, where the crime was committed, and without his attorney present, Williams was told by a detective: "I feel that you yourself are the only person that knows where this little girl's body is. . . . And, since we will be going right past the area on the way into Des Moines, I feel we should stop and locate the body, that the parents of this little girl should be entitled to a Christian burial for the little girl. . . ." No violence or compulsion was employed. After thinking about the matter for some time, Williams directed the officers to the victim's body. He was subsequently convicted of the murder.

In *Brewer v. Williams* (1977), a deeply divided Court set aside Williams's conviction. It held that the right to the assistance of counsel, "guaranteed by the Sixth and Fourteenth Amendments, is indispensable to the fair administration of our adversary system of criminal justice." Williams's incriminating statements, made in response to police conduct that violated his constitutional right to counsel, should have been excluded, the Court ruled by a narrow 5–4 majority. Williams's attorney had been promised that no questioning would be attempted on the trip back to Des Moines. Yet the police officer had persisted. "The crime of which Williams was convicted," Justice Potter Stewart wrote for the majority,

> was senseless and brutal, calling for swift and energetic action by the police to apprehend the perpetrator and gather evidence with which he could be convicted. No mission of law enforcement is more important. Yet "disinterested zeal for the public good does not assure either wis-

dom or right in the methods it pursues." . . . The pressures on state executive and judicial officers charged with the administration of the criminal law are great, especially when the crime is murder and the victim a small child. But it is precisely the predictability of those pressures that makes imperative a resolute loyalty to the guarantees that the Constitution extends to us all.

This ruling drew strong criticism, including a bitter dissent by then Chief Justice Warren Burger.

> The result in this case ought to be intolerable in any society which purports to call itself an organized society. . . . Williams is guilty of the savage murder of a small child; no member of the Court contends he is not. While in custody, and after no fewer than five warnings of his rights to silence and to counsel, he led police to the concealed body of his victim. The Court concedes Williams was not threatened or coerced and that he spoke and acted voluntarily and with full awareness of his constitutional rights. In the face of all this, the Court now holds that because Williams was prompted by the detective's statement—not interrogation but a statement—the jury must not be told how the police found the body.

Feelings run high, even among professional jurists in the lofty setting of the U.S. Supreme Court, when key values compete for recognition in a context where something has to give. In *Brewer v. Williams*, the justices did not disagree on the high worth of both sets of contending objectives: protecting the rights of the accused and ensuring the prompt apprehension and conviction of those who commit crimes against society. But they were sharply at odds over how to balance these values in the immediate case. They disagreed on two major questions. (1) Did the police officer deny Williams his constitutional rights? The majority emphasized that the officer persisted in a kind of

One view of the exclusionary rule.

interrogation, even though a specific promise had been made that no questioning would take place in the absence of counsel. The minority stressed that a gentle appeal to the suspect's conscience is hardly equivalent to police brutality or coercion. (2) If the police did act improperly, should the evidence that resulted be excluded? Here, some justices opted for a more sweeping application of the exclusionary rule, while others felt it should not be applied to "non-egregious" police conduct—in other words, to behavior that, if technically wrong, did not threaten the "individual dignity or free will" of the suspect.

The Court has continued to search for the right balance in its use of the exclusionary rule. In *Stone v. Powell* (1976), for example, it ruled that federal courts need not require the exclusion of evidence acquired in violation of Fourth Amendment ("unreasonable searches and seizures") guarantees, unless the prisoner could show that he was denied "a full and fair" litigation of his Fourth Amendment claim in

state courts. Another exception, the inevitable discovery doctrine, was issued in a case that resulted from the retrial of Robert Williams, whose first appeal we have just discussed.

After the Court overturned Williams's conviction in *Brewer v. Williams*, the state of Iowa brought him to trial a second time in state court on the "inevitable discovery" doctrine. Williams had never been found innocent, so there was no question of double jeopardy (trying a person a second time, after he had been found not guilty). Williams's conviction had simply been set aside on the grounds that some of the evidence introduced should not have been admitted. Two hundred volunteers had been combing the area and were nearing the spot where the body was discovered when Williams led the police to it. In the second trial, the Iowa court concluded that even without Williams's statement, the body would have been discovered anyway. In *Nix v. Williams* (1984), the Supreme Court accepted the state's argument. The majority opinion—written by Chief Justice

Burger, author of the angry dissent in the Court's consideration of the case seven years earlier—held that the point of the "inevitable discovery" doctrine was to put the police "in the same, not a worse, position than they would have been if no police error or misconduct had occurred."

In another 1984 ruling, *United States v. Leon*, the Supreme Court partially adopted the "good faith" exception to the exclusionary rule. This provision follows from an argument some justices, including the chief justice, had advanced in earlier cases concerning "non-egregious" police conduct. The "good faith" exception permits the use of improperly obtained evidence as long as the police had a reasonable belief that they were acting lawfully. Writing for the majority in the *Leon* case, Justice Byron White for the present limited the application of the "good faith" exception to situations in which the police obtained a search warrant and executed a search in accord with it, only later to have the warrant found defective. The evidence obtained through such searches need not be excluded, the Court held.

THE COURT SHIFTS DIRECTION ON ISSUES OF CRIMINAL JUSTICE

Since 1975 more than 20 exceptions have been made to the Miranda Rule requirement, reducing the instances in which convictions are overturned on grounds the police failed properly to apprise the accused of his Fifth and Sixth Amendment rights. Similarly, the sweep of the exclusionary rule barring evidence from court when it was collected improperly has been limited. "This Court doesn't overturn things," argues law professor Ronald Collins. "It chips away incrementally."[17]

[17] Quoted in Marshall Ingwerson, "Bench Grows More Conservative," *Christian Science Monitor*, June 28, 1990, p. 2.

Criminal cases are more often decided subtly in favor of the state against defendants—although without overturning the basic structure of criminal justice law erected by the Court in the 1960s in such decisions as *Mapp*, *Gideon*, and *Miranda*.

The Court's complex decision in *Arizona v. Fulminante* (1991) exemplifies this approach. Oreste Fulminante had left the state of Arizona following the murder of his eleven-year-old stepdaughter. He was then convicted of an unrelated federal crime and was put in federal prison in New York. There Fulminante incriminated himself in his stepdaughter's murder in conversations with a fellow inmate who was actually an FBI informer. The latter said he would protect Fulminante from prison violence, but only if he told him the full story of the girl's death. Fulminante complied. He was subsequently convicted of the murder.

The Arizona Supreme Court held that the confession had been coerced and that its introduction in Fulminante's trial invalidated his conviction. When the case reached the U.S. Supreme Court, a 5–4 majority agreed that the confession was indeed involuntary. But another, differently constituted 5–4 majority held that the use of an involuntary confession in a criminal trial does not automatically invalidate a conviction. Chief Justice Rehnquist wrote this latter part of the Court's opinion, holding that such a confession can be excused as "harmless error" if it can be shown that other evidence, obtained independently of the confession, introduced at the trial was enough to sustain a conviction. In this instance, Fulminante, after having been given counsel, confessed to the crime a second time, providing even more detail than he had in his first confession to the FBI informer. Justice Rehnquist concluded that the use of the first confession was "a classic case of harmless error." In a dissent concurred in by Justices Marshall, Blackmun, and Stevens, Byron White argued that "the majority today abandons what until now the Court has regarded as the 'axiomatic' [proposition] that a defendant in a criminal case is deprived of due process of law if his conviction is founded, in whole or in part, upon an involuntary confession . . . even though there is ample evidence aside from the confession to support the conviction."

When conservatives David Souter and Clarence Thomas replaced liberals William Brennan and Thurgood Marshall on the Supreme Court in 1990 and 1991 respectively, the side inclined to weight the protection of the larger society more heavily than the rights of the accused was strengthened further. This means, in particular, that the Rehnquist Court of the early 1990s gives police officials more leeway in the conduct of their duties than did its immediate predecessors.

FREEDOM OF EXPRESSION

Democracy is impossible without freedom of expression—impossible if citizens are prevented from speaking and writing, meeting and organizing on behalf of their social aims. Although we draw many other satisfactions from free expression, we recognize its special importance to the operation of a democratic polity. Freedom of expression has always been given a high position in American law, from the First Amendment's insistence that Congress shall make no law curtailing the freedom of religion, speech, press, and assembly. We examined one freedom of expression argument, involving flag protection, in the first section of this chapter.

Despite the language of the First Amendment, the rights of free speech and other forms of expression have not been seen by most people or by American law as absolute. We recognize instances where uncurbed expression does violence to other worthy ends. Libelous and obscene speech have been held subject to restrictions. In his famous opinion in the case of *Schenck v. United States* (1919), Justice Oliver Wendell Holmes, Jr., offered this example of why curbs are sometimes valid: "The most stringent protection of free speech," Holmes wrote, "would not protect a man in falsely shouting fire in a theater and causing a panic." But Holmes's example is too easy. When are restrictions on political expression justified, and when do they have a "chilling effect" on a free society? This question has been debated in many different contexts, and the Supreme Court has struggled to provide coherent answers.

When the United States has faced a serious threat, notably during a war, governmental authorities have generally been more willing to enact and countenance restrictions on political speech than in less threatening times. For example, during the Civil War military officials imposed curbs on speech and press under the sanction of martial law. No question of the validity of these acts was ever brought to the Supreme Court. Curbs were also enacted during World War I. The Espionage Act of 1917 penalized any circulation of false statements made with intent to interfere with military success. The Sedition Act of 1918 made it a crime to say (or do) anything that might obstruct the sale of government bonds needed to finance the war effort, or to speak or publish words intended to bring into contempt the government of the United States, or to invite resistance to its lawful acts. The legality of these two pieces of legislation, under which almost a thousand persons were convicted, was upheld in six cases decided by the Supreme Court after the war.

In 1940, against the backdrop of the rise of fascism and communism, and the outbreak of World War II, Congress enacted the Alien Registration Act (Smith Act). It provided for

How much information the government should classify as "top secret" is another area still debated.

punishment of anyone who "knowingly or willfully advocates . . . or teaches the duty . . . or propriety of overthrowing . . . the government of the United States . . . by force or violence. . . ." It further provided for punishment of those disseminating literature advocating such overthrow, those organizing any group "to teach, advocate or encourage" such overthrow, and those who knowingly became members of any group advocating the violent overthrow of American government. In 1948 amid fear (some say hysteria) over domestic communism, eleven top leaders of the Communist Party of the United States were indicted under the Smith Act; they were convicted in federal district court in 1949, and their conviction was subsequently upheld by the Court of Appeals and by the Supreme Court (*Dennis v. United States*, 1951).

In the majority opinion, Chief Justice Frederick Vinson observed that

> the obvious purpose of the statute is to protect existing Government, not from change by peaceable, lawful constitutional means, but from change by violence, revolution and terrorism. That it is within the power of the Congress to protect the Government of the United States from armed rebellion is a proposition which requires little discussion. . . . We reject any principle of governmental helplessness in the face of preparation for revolution, which principle, carried to its logical conclusion, must lead to anarchy.

The chief justice argued that the conviction of Eugene Dennis and the other Communist leaders represented a lawful restriction of freedom of expression under a test that the courts had applied, with varying emphases, in a number of earlier cases: the "clear and present danger" rule. A highly regarded federal judge, Learned Hand (1872–1961), expressed the rule this way in his opinion for the Court of Appeals in *Dennis*: "In each case [courts] must ask whether the gravity of the 'evil,' discounted by its improbability, justifies such invasion of free speech as is necessary to avoid the danger." Is there a compelling case that political expression in a given instance might be so intertwined with action as to threaten constitutional government? The Court upheld the conviction of Dennis and his associates on the grounds that there was.

RISING STANDARDS FOR PROTECTING POLITICAL EXPRESSION

Six years later, however, in *Yates v. United States* (1957), the Supreme Court reversed the conviction of fourteen middle-level Communist party officials under the Smith Act. While the Court insisted that its *Yates* ruling was consistent with that in *Dennis*, it in fact was moving to restrict prosecution of Communist party officials. Where in 1951 a court majority had felt that the threats posed by the party were sufficient to justify the Smith Act curtailment of its political freedom, by 1957 a majority no longer felt that way.

By the 1960s, with new appointees and a changed climate of national opinion, the Supreme Court was ready to swing more fully and consistently from the perspective that had guided it in *Dennis*. It took a more expansive view of the First Amendment guarantee of the right of expression, and it was much less worried about the threat of domestic communism. In *United States v. Robel* (1967), the Court upheld the right of Eugene Frank Robel, an admitted member of the Communist party, to work in a shipyard, despite a federal statute forbidding such employment to a party member. The Court declared the statute unconstitutional. While Congress is entitled to protect sensitive activities from spies and saboteurs, the Court held that it "must achieve its goal by means which have a 'less drastic' impact on the continued vitality of First Amendment freedoms." The law, it was ruled, was much broader than nec-

essary to achieve its stated purpose, since it restricted the employment opportunities of all members of the Communist party, not merely those active in the unlawful aims of the party and thus most likely to engage in sabotage.

The Court moved in the 1960s to fashion a conception of the clear and present danger rule very different from the one it offered in *Dennis*. *Brandenburg v. Ohio* (1969) grew out of the prosecution of a Ku Klux Klan leader under Ohio's criminal syndicalism statute. A unanimous Court overturned the Klansman's conviction and declared the statute unconstitutional. Because the law purported to punish "mere advocacy" and to prevent assembly with others for such advocacy, it violated the requirement of the First and Fourteenth Amendments. The Court held that "the constitutional guarantees of free speech and free press do not permit a state to forbid or proscribe advocacy of the use of force or of law violation except *where such advocacy is directed to inciting or producing imminent lawless action and is likely to incite or produce such action*" (emphasis added). This requirement of imminency represented a fundamental shift from the Court's construction of the clear and present danger rule in *Dennis* and earlier decisions.

OBSCENITY AND COMMUNITY STANDARDS

Political speech bears a special relationship to democratic governance. Not all forms of expression can make this claim. The Supreme Court has repeatedly ruled, for instance, that obscene material is not protected by the First Amendment. Of course, even if this is accepted, it still leaves unresolved the question of what is obscene. The Court has found it hard to fashion satisfactory formulations as to when curbs are permitted and what kinds of restrictions are valid.

A few justices have dissented from the basic Court position that obscene and pornographic expression may be curbed; they have wanted to see all expression absolutely protected. Justice William O. Douglas (1898–1980) was prominent in this small camp. He argued that the First and Fourteenth Amendments absolutely protect obscene and nonobscene material alike. In one opinion, Douglas concluded that

> the First Amendment allows all ideas to be expressed—whether orthodox, popular, off-beat, or repulsive. I do not think it permissible to draw lines between the "good" and the "bad" and be true to the constitutional mandate to let all ideas alone. . . . The theory is that people are mature enough to pick and choose, to recognize trash when they see it, to be attracted to the literature that satisfies their deepest needs, and, hopefully, to move from plateau to plateau and finally reach the world of enduring ideas. I think this is the ideal of the Free Society written into our Constitution.[18]

As Douglas saw it, the constitutional claim of any one form of expression is equal to that of any other. "Some like Chopin, others like 'Rock and Roll.' . . ." Individuals choose as they see fit; the Constitution mandates governmental "hands off" from all curbs. On the 1980s Court, Justices Brennan, Marshall, and Stevens argued that the First Amendment does not permit a state to make it a crime for consenting adults to sell or buy obscene magazines, unless the transaction involves children or an "obtrusive display to unconsenting adults."

Most justices have looked for formulas that give more scope to governmental officials in regulating obscene speech. There have been efforts to give at least partial recognition to the contrasting ideas of different groups of people in different parts of the United States about what is unacceptably obscene or pornographic. When citizens, acting through duly constituted governmental bodies such as state legislatures or city councils, impose certain restrictions to uphold community sensibilities, the courts should not sweep these aside in the name of an absolute right of expression. Justice John Marshall Harlan (1899–1971) shared this perspective.

> The varying conditions across the country, the range of views on the need and reasons for curbing obscenity, and the traditions of local self-government in matters of public welfare all favor a far more flexible attitude in defining the bounds for the states. From any standpoint, the Fourteenth Amendment requires of a state only that it apply criteria rationally related to the accepted notion of obscenity and that it reach results not wholly out of step with current American standards.[19]

At the same time, Harlan and many other observers have been concerned lest narrow community standards censor even major works of literature and art in the name of obscenity. How is that balance to be struck?

In *Miller v. California* (1973), the Supreme Court issued an important obscenity ruling to which it still broadly adheres. Miller was convicted in a California court of mailing unsolicited sexually explicit material in violation of a state statute. The Supreme Court upheld his conviction, maintaining that it would be guided by three related tests in obscenity cases:

> (a) whether "the average person, applying contemporary community standards" would find that the work, taken as a whole, appeals to the prurient interest . . . ; (b) whether the work depicts or describes, in a patently offensive way, sexual

---

[18] Dissent by Justice William O. Douglas in *Ginzburg, et al., v. United States*, 383 U.S. 492 (1966).

[19] The dissenting opinion of Justice Harlan in the case *A book named "John Cleland's Memoirs of a Woman of Pleasure," et al., v. Attorney General of Massachusetts*, 383 U.S. 458 (1966).

conduct specifically defined by the applicable state law; and (c) whether the work, taken as a whole, lacks serious literary, artistic, political, or scientific value.[20]

States may curtail material that meets this obscenity test.

The Court distinguishes among various forms of expression. As noted, political expression receives the most categoric protection. Other forms, such as those at issue in questions of obscenity, are substantially but less highly protected; government curbs can be sustained more readily here than with political utterances. And when the issue involves expression that is emphatically divorced from any reasonable claim to artistic merit—such as is the case with child pornography—government curbs are still more readily sustained. In *Osborne v. Ohio* (1990), for example, the High Court by 6 to 3 ruled that states may make it a crime to possess pornographic photographs of children. Prosecution is permitted of those who own or view such material even in their own homes. Writing for the majority, Justice Byron White maintained the Ohio law was justified because it sought not to bar obscenity on grounds it would poison the minds of viewers but rather to "protect the victims of child pornography." It was, he wrote "reasonable for the state to conclude that it will decrease the production of child pornography if it penalizes those who possess and view the product, thereby decreasing

demand." Justice William Brennan dissented. "At bottom," he argued, "the Court today is so disquieted by the possible exploitation of children in the production of the pornography that it is willing to tolerate the imposition of criminal penalties for simple possession. While I share the majority's concerns, I do not believe that it has struck the proper balance between the First Amendment and the state's interests."

SUMMARY

Policy on civil liberties and civil rights differs from that in other sectors because many of its claims are presented as basic constitutional rights rather than simple group preferences. The courts try to differentiate between instances where fundamental rights of citizenship are engaged—which even large popular majorities must not infringe upon—and those where majority preferences should be respected.

The argument over whether laws against burning or otherwise mutilating the American flag violate the right of citizens to free expression, established under the First Amendment, became heated in 1989 and 1990. In *Texas v. Johnson* (1989), the Supreme Court ruled flag burning was a form of political expression that, however offensive, must receive the same high protection as other forms of political expression. Efforts to amend the Constitution to overturn this ruling were unsuccessful.

The progression of public policy in any area does not follow a straight line; it zigs and zags in response to the change of political leadership and events. But a clear direction is often evident. Since World War II, policy on civil liberties and civil rights, has moved toward more extensive recognition and guarantees of individual rights than obtained in earlier periods of American history. Characteristics of postindustrial society, including its affluence and high

[20] *Miller v. California*, 413 U.S. 24 (1973). In 1987 the Court issued another in a series of modifications of the basic rule laid down in Miller. It held by a 6–3 majority in *Pope v. Illinois* that while the contemporary standards of the local community may be employed in the first two prongs of the obscenity test, they may not be followed in deciding whether allegedly obscene materials have scientific, literary, or artistic value. A more objective national standard should be used. The value of a work does not "vary from community to community," Justice Byron White wrote for the majority, "based on the degree of local acceptance it has won."

levels of education, seem linked to generally enlarged expectations concerning individuals and their entitlements.

Since World War II the entrenched system of discrimination and segregation in the South, known as "Jim Crow," has been dismantled. This is not to say that America's racial problems have been solved. But clear and profound changes, which have promoted the principle of equality, are evident in civil rights.

In the controversy over affirmative action and quotas, the Court has recognized the importance of being "color-blind," more generally assigning jobs and other positions without regard to group identity or membership. But it has also recognized that the history of past discrimination cannot be ignored and that some form of special remedial action may be required. Policy regarding affirmative action remains divisive in American society—and the Supreme Court has itself been sharply divided over the issue.

Other components of civil liberties and civil rights policy show a similar progression. Judicial guarantees of the rights of the accused have been expanded. A prime instance is the Supreme Court's extension of the range of Bill of Rights protections incorporated within the Fourteenth Amendment's due-process clause and thus made specifically binding on the states. Fourth, Fifth, and Sixth Amendment guarantees have been enforced on state courts and law-enforcement officials, as on their federal counterparts, by excluding from criminal proceedings evidence unconstitutionally obtained.

A new plateau was reached in the first quarter-century after World War II, defined by greater attentiveness to individual rights. But on this new plateau the Court has struck a new balance. In various cases over the past decade involving issues of criminal justice, it has shifted, gradually but substantially, toward greater recognition of the needs and claims of law enforcement.

FOR FURTHER STUDY

Glendon, Mary Ann. *Rights Talk: The Impoverishment of Political Discourse.* New York: The Free Press, 1991. A cogent criticism of what the author believes is an excessive contemporary inclination in discussions of American public policy to cast every social and political *interest* in the language of immutable *rights*.

Hentoff, Nat. *The First Freedom: The Tumultuous History of Free Speech in America.* New York: Dell, 1981. A spritely, well-written review of court decisions made under the First Amendment to the U.S. Constitution.

Kluger, Richard. *Simple Justice: A History of Brown v. Board of Education and Black America's Struggle for Equality.* New York: Knopf, 1976. A superb description of the legal struggle for school integration.

Lewis, Anthony. *Gideon's Trumpet.* New York: Vintage Books, 1966. A fascinating account of a Supreme Court case that established the right of defendants in state courts to have competent legal counsel made available to them in felony cases, even when they cannot themselves pay for such counsel.

Myrdal, Gunnar. *An American Dilemma.* New York: McGraw-Hill, 1964; first published, 1944. A major study of American race relations in the 1930s and 1940s, before the civil rights revolution of the postwar years.

Sindler, Allen P. *Bakke, DeFunis, and Minority Admissions: The Quest for Equal Opportunity.* New York: Longman, 1978. A brilliant examination of a major Supreme Court decision involving remedial efforts (affirmative action) to deal with past discrimination.

Chapter *15*

THE ECONOMY AND PUBLIC WELFARE

"We the People of the United States," the preamble proclaims, "do ordain and establish this Constitution for the United States of America" to promote a number of essential ends: "a more perfect Union"; "Justice"; "domestic Tranquility"; "the common defense"; *"the general Welfare"*; and to make secure "the Blessings of Liberty." The idea of "welfare policy" seems very modern, a response to twentieth-century experience—but, in fact, using government to promote the general welfare in the United States goes back to the founding of our nation. The Constitution itself was intended to provide a governmental structure in which the welfare of the people would advance. And today vast resources are dedicated to promoting this end.

However, there are severe limits on what any official of the U.S. government can do to promote desired economic results, so dispersed is authority across the executive branch and Congress. And there are severe limits on what American government at large can accomplish, so great is the role played by individuals and groups in the private sector, by international developments such as those affecting oil supply and prices, and by foreign governments and investors. Still, the government does seek to promote a variety of economic objectives—above all, promoting prosperity and general well-being.

In order to achieve their overall economic objectives, policy-makers must deal with such present-day problems as continuing inflationary pressures. How to curb inflation without curbing growth? They must also confront the fact that the unchallenged economic ascendancy that the United States experienced for a quarter-century or so after World War II has come to an end. This is both desirable and inevitable: The postwar supremacy resulted because the U.S. economy was the only one among the world's major industrial nations not devastated by World War II. After the war the United States committed itself to programs to help its allies and former enemies rebuild. These programs did their job, and Western Europe and Japan boast thriving economies today.

Still, if we worked for the economic reconstruction that has occurred—realizing that our own long-term prosperity and security were tied to it—the European and Japanese recovery has been hard for some Americans to get used to. Business corporations—with the automobile industry a major case in point—have found themselves facing a fierce competition they largely avoided from 1945 through the late 1960s. And ordinary citizens have wondered about their own positions in an economic world of extraordinary interdependence.

THE U.S. ECONOMY TODAY

It's easy to be either complacent or alarmist—but neither is a sound response. In recent years some Americans, the press included, have tended to be alarmist. The most common manifestation has been a tendency to see Japan as an economic juggernaut, rolling across a weak-ened United States. We need to take stock briefly of what has really been happening to the U.S. economy.

ECONOMIC GROWTH

How did the U.S. economy perform over the past decade, in a world of renewed economic competition? Many key industries, including automobiles and steel, have gone through a painful adjustment involving high domestic wage rates and intense foreign competition. The economy has had to absorb "oil shocks"—large rapid price hikes—in 1973–74, 1979, and again in 1990. Despite this, GDP has risen impressively. From 1980 to 1989, for example, real GDP rose about one trillion dollars (measured in constant dollars of 1982 purchasing power)—a gain of 32 percent. This is by no means the best decade in U.S. economic history but, comparatively, the performance was good.

The 1990s began on a rocky note. Real GDP rose only slightly in the first three quarters of 1990, and then declined in the fourth, and again in the first quarter of 1991. Though the numbers turned positive in the second quarter, the U.S. economy remained very sluggish well into 1992. Controlling for inflation, GDP was essentially flat from the first quarter of 1990 through the first of 1992.

Overall, however, U.S. performance has been good compared to other industrial countries. We saw in chapter 2 that the United States, a wealthy country before World War II, enjoyed a great spurt in national wealth in the first quarter-century after the war. Since the early 1970s per capita gross domestic product has continued to rise in real terms at rates comparable to the other industrial powers. According to the Organization for Economic Cooperation and Development (OECD), per person GDP in the United States was $21,450 in 1990, that in

Japan $17,625, Germany $18,300, France $16,025, Britain $13,428, and Italy $17,425.[1]

Data on investment for the future show a mixed performance. America's savings rate has been lower than that of other industrial countries. At the same time, though, its investment in research and development has been higher. According to the OECD, the United States in 1989 was spending $580 per person on R & D. Japan, in contrast, was spending the purchasing power equivalent of $470, Germany $430, France $340, Britain $325, Canada $260, and Italy just $175. In 1989, the U.S. technological balance of payments—exports of high tech / high R & D industries, minus imports of such goods—was +$9.6 billion (in official exchange-rate terms), while Japan's was −$404 million, West Germany's −$785 million. This is a positive sign for the future; America's position in the high technology area remains strong.

CREATION OF JOBS

The idea that there has been stagnation in economic growth is contradicted even more forcefully by the national experience in job creation. The U.S. economy confronted conditions in the 1960s and 1970s that could easily have led to massively high rates of unemployment: An unprecedentedly large number of people were entering the labor force. After World War II birth rates rose dramatically and stayed high until the 1960s. By the 1970s large numbers of this "baby boom" generation were looking for jobs. Between 1946 and 1955 alone, more than 34 million people were born in the United States; by 1980 the youngest among them were twenty-five years old and most were in the labor force.

A second reason for the rise in the number of people seeking jobs was the jump in what

economists call the "labor-force participation rate" of women. In 1960 there were 61.6 million women in the United States sixteen years of age and older; 37.7 percent of them were in the labor force—employed or actively seeking paid employment outside the home. Just twenty-eight years later, in 1988, the female population sixteen years and older totaled 96.8 million, 56.6 percent of whom were in the labor force. This translates into a total increase of 31.5 million women employed or seeking work.

These statistics tell a simple story: If the United States had not created millions of new jobs in a short span of time, the unemployment rate would have gone up like a rocket. Jobs were rapidly created, however—created at a rate high even by America's historical standards. Between 1975 and 1987 the United States produced over 26 million new jobs, while the industrial nations of Western Europe produced only about 5.7 million. Figure 15.1 compares the record of the United States and Western Europe. Though Japan's "economic miracle" is often remarked upon, American job creation was at approximately twice the rate of Japan's over this span. Job creation in the United States continued strong from the 1982–83 recession up until that of 1990–92. From a low of 99.5 million in 1982, total civilian employment climbed to just under 101 million in 1983, 105 million in 1985, and over 118 million in the spring of 1990.

In the latter half of 1990, with the U.S. economy in recession, the number of persons holding jobs in the United States fell for the first time since 1982. Employment stood at 120 million in June of 1990. By November, it had dropped to 118.9 million, and in August of 1991 it bottomed out at 118.1 million.

THE RATE OF INFLATION

Handling inflation has been one of recent economic policy's most impressive successes. In-

[1] OECD in Figures (Paris: Organization for Economic Cooperation and Development, 1992), pp. 24–25.

FIGURE 15.1   HOW THE UNITED STATES STACKS UP AGAINST EUROPE IN JOB CREATION

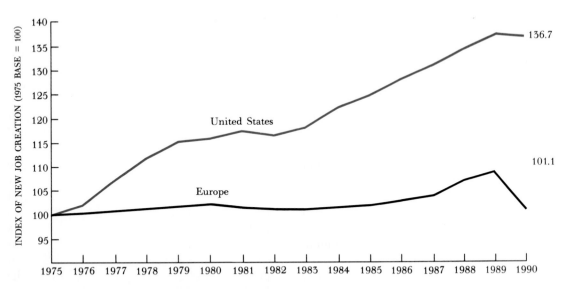

Figures for Europe are a composite of all European members of OECD, with the exception of Yugoslavia.
Source: Bureau of the Census, *Statistical Abstract of the United States, 1989*, p. 377. U.S. Bureau of Labor Statistics, Office of Current Employment Analysis, *Civilian Employment Trends in North America, Japan and Europe for Selected Years, 1970–1990*, p. 17.

flation got out of control in the 1970s in the United States and a number of other industrial countries. Over the last decade, though, it has been brought back under control. Prudent monetary management by the central banks of the leading economic powers—including the Federal Reserve in the United States (described on pp. 473–76)—has contributed importantly to this success.

Energy and food prices have been highly volatile in recent years. Outside these commodities, however, consumer prices have been quite stable. Overall, inflation bounced around in a fairly tight range from the 1982 recession through 1989. The annual rate of increase in consumer prices went below 3.8 percent only once in this span—in 1986, when it was just 1.1 percent—and never rose higher than 4.6 percent.

In 1990 inflation rose a bit, to 5.4 percent, spurred by the surge in oil prices following Iraq's invasion of Kuwait. But it fell again during the recession of the early nineties. In the first six months of 1992, for example, it was averaging just 3 percent.

DISPUTES OVER ECONOMIC THEORY

Presidents and other party leaders engage in a lot of ad hoc improvisation in their search for policies to advance such desired ends as economic growth and high employment, and to minimize such evils as inflation. But leaders are also guided by underlying economic philosophies. Although never consistently followed, these philosophies are rarely absent. The roots of the present debate over national economic policy go back more than half a century.

EVOLUTION OF U.S. ECONOMIC POLICY

Debates over economic policy often involve two entirely different questions: (1) What objectives are to be advanced through governmental intervention? (2) How does the economy really work, and how can a given economic objective best be achieved? To some extent, differences over desired ends, and over the best means to attain these ends, get scrambled together in the policy debates in every nation. But the relative weight of these two dimensions varies greatly.

In the United States, more than in most industrial countries in this century, the main disagreements have concerned how particular goals are best obtained. We want strong economic growth, high levels of employment, and low inflation—all within the general structure of a private-property–based economy. At issue are the steps the country should be taking to promote these shared objectives.

Americans turn to economists much as to medical doctors: We want them to make the patient well. This emphasis means that technical and scientific assessments offered by economists are often very important politically. While in the complex, highly pluralistic push and pull of American politics no set of economic prescriptions ever gets fully or neatly applied, politicians look to economists for general guidance on how most effectively to advance shared goals.

JOHN MAYNARD KEYNES AND KEYNESIAN ECONOMICS

The "how-to-do-it" prescriptions of a distinguished British economist, John Maynard Keynes (1883–1946), entered into the American debate over economic policy in the 1930s,

John Maynard Keynes.

against the backdrop of the Great Depression. The **Keynesian** approach came to dominate the thinking of professional economists in the United States and helped shape the policies of the Roosevelt administration and its successors.

What made Keynes so influential was the force of his argument that the ideas on which politicians had been leaning had ceased to fit actual economic conditions. Since the "old economics" no longer pointed government in the right direction, a "new economics" and new answers to problems of political economy were needed. In his celebrated *The General Theory of Employment, Interest, and Money*, Keynes provided them.[2]

---

[2]John Maynard Keynes, *The General Theory of Employment, Interest, and Money* (New York: Harcourt, Brace, 1965; first published, 1936), p. 383.

Keynes offered capitalist economies a way out of the crisis they faced in the 1930s. He maintained that full employment and high economic growth are best advanced by promoting consumption rather than savings. Savings tend to be hoarded rather than applied to productive investments. In contrast, the demand generated by increased consumption stimulates greater investment and promotes the best utilization of society's resources. The richer a society becomes—and by the late 1920s both Britain and the United States were, by any historical comparison, very rich societies—"the wider will tend to be the gap between its actual and its potential production. . . ." Such a society "will have to discover much ampler opportunities for investment if the saving propensities of its wealthier members are to be compatible with the employment of its poorer members."[3]

Rather than encouraging individual thrift, then, government should help generate consumption through such means as public-works programs. "Priming the pump" was the analogy that best conveyed the idea that government spending would lead to greater activity in the private sector. These programs would put money into the hands of poorer citizens, who would then use the money to buy goods. Furthermore, government spending should not be paid for by economizing in other areas. When demand lags, because people lack money to buy the things they need, government should run a deficit—that is, spend more than it takes in from taxes—to provide economic stimulus.

These increased expenditures need not even be productive in the usual sense. Keynes contended that unemployment could be reduced even "if the Treasury were to fill old bottles with bank notes, bury them at suitable depths in disused coal mines which are then filled up to the surface with town rubbish, and leave it to private enterprise . . . to dig the notes up

again."[4] This remark was in part facetious, but its main message was serious. Unemployment was high and production was down because many people lacked the money required to buy necessities. If only government would pump money to those who needed it, increased consumption would occur, more jobs would be created to produce goods to meet this demand, and investment in new plants would become attractive again.

It sounded almost too good to be true. Politicians who created new social programs, especially to help those in need, and who spent on these public welfare programs more than they asked people to pay in taxes, were not being profligate or crassly buying votes; they were stimulating the economy, increasing productivity, lowering unemployment, and generally making everyone more prosperous. Many politicians were understandably happy to receive this advice. But what made Keynesianism so unassailably alluring was the fact that, in the economic context in which Keynes wrote, it was right.

Unemployment. In 1900 in the United States, the rate of unemployment (the number of people unemployed as a percentage of the total civilian labor force) stood at just 5 percent. It hovered around that mark for most of the ensuing three decades: 5.9 percent in 1910, 5.2 percent in 1920, and just 3.2 percent in 1925. With the onset of the Depression, however, unemployment soared: It reached 8.7 percent in 1930 and by 1935 had climbed to 20.1 percent. Even as late as 1940 it stood at 14.6 percent. Never had so many people been out of work in America. Conditions were much the same in Europe.

Deflation. In modern times, inflationary pressures have been so prominent a feature of

[3] Ibid., p. 31.

[4] Ibid., p. 247.

American economic life that we sometimes find it hard to appreciate that throughout much of U.S. history, deflation—falling prices—was the more common problem. In the late 1920s and 1930s, because of unemployment and low consumption, prices fell dramatically. Unable to find markets for their products, manufacturers, farmers, and merchants had to cut what they were charging. According to one index, producer prices stood at 79.6 in 1920. This composite index of prices at the wholesale level fell to 50.0 in 1928, to 44.6 in 1930, and to just 33.6 in 1932. This deflationary experience was so prolonged and deep that it was not until 1948 that the composite index of wholesale prices had climbed back to its 1920 level.

Why are falling prices an economic problem? Price deflation creates a disincentive to invest in new plants, because the return that can be expected will lag behind current costs. Keynes noted:

> If, for any reason right or wrong, the business world *expects* that prices will fall, the processes of production tend to be inhibited. . . . The deflation which causes falling prices means impoverishment to labor and to enterprise by leading entrepreneurs to restrict production, in their endeavor to avoid losses to themselves; and is therefore disastrous to employment.[5]

Limited Government. Keynes's call for expanded governmental management of the economy came when government was still small, with limited responsibilities. When FDR first won election in November 1932, the total budget of the national government was just $4.7 billion, or about $37 per person. Over the 1930s, under the Roosevelt administration, expenditures rose significantly, but in 1940 they were still only

"Yes, You Remembered Me".

$9.1 billion, less than $69 a citizen. Contrast these figures to the fiscal 1992 federal budget of over 1.4 trillion dollars, or nearly $5,500 per person. Keynes's call in 1936 for a broadened governmental role appeared to many to be a measured, sensible, prudent response. And it was, then.

In the 1930s the United States and other industrial democracies found themselves with a massive economic problem. Unemployment was up, production and consumption down. The standard of living for many citizens had fallen drastically. Deflation was a prime obstacle, as it provided incentives *not* to invest in productive plants. The call for more governmental intervention, in a setting where government did relatively little, seemed excessive only to those ideologically opposed to the very idea of governmental responsibility for promoting prosperity. The triumph of Keynesianism was

[5]John Maynard Keynes, *A Tract on Monetary Reform*, in *The Collected Writings of John Maynard Keynes* (London: Macmillan, 1971), pp. 30, 33–36. The first edition of this work appeared in 1923.

fundamentally empirical or practical: It read the prevailing needs and responded to them better than any available alternative.

The Roosevelt administration did not immediately seize upon and implement Keynesian prescriptions. Many contradictory perspectives and pressures continued to be felt. The amount of stimulus given the economy in the latter half of the 1930s was modest—much too modest, most economists now agree. Only the massive government spending made necessary by America's entry into World War II finally ended the decade-long depression and brought unemployment down to stay. But the national leadership of the Democratic party was gradually converted to the "new economics," and from World War II through the 1960s, Keynesianism exerted great influence over the American approach to issues of political economy.

THE POST-KEYNESIAN ERA

The "new economics" spurred by John Maynard Keynes proved to be a generally successful response to the needs of one particular period and its economic conditions. But conditions change. The shifts were gradual, but by the 1970s enough had occurred to stimulate vast rethinking of economic issues and government's position in national economic life. First economists and then politicians joined in the search for another new economics to deal with the size of big government, an increased federal debt, and a sharp rise in inflation.

Big Government. When the New Deal expansion of government's role in the U.S. economy began, government was a modest presence. By the 1970s, it had become a major one, and it became increasingly difficult to argue that "more government" was the answer.

We are struck by how small the federal tax burden was in the early part of this century: just over $15 per person as late as 1932. After 1960, however, federal taxes rose sharply, from $512 per capita in 1960 to about $4,300 in 1990. Even when inflation is controlled for, a major increase has occurred. As a result, public opposition to tax hikes is substantial, and some economists worry about a drag on the economy from high taxation. Over the last quarter-century, the rate of growth of government spending has substantially outstripped the growth of the overall economy.

Government Debt. The federal government has run a deficit every year since 1964, regardless of whether the nation's economy was booming or in recession. According to Keynesianism, the central government should spend more than it takes in when the economy is in recession, so as to stimulate demand, but it should tax more than it spends in periods when the economy is booming, to temper inflationary pressures and sustain even growth. This adjusting of taxing and spending levels is known as **fiscal policy**. But in recent years American politicians have found fiscal policy exceedingly hard to manage. No body of economic theory justifies the federal government's running deficits each year, as it has for well over two decades now. The cuts in federal income tax rates pushed by the Reagan administration in 1981 and enacted by Congress added to the size of the deficit by reducing revenues while expenditures continued to climb. But the scope and persistence of the deficit are hardly the result of any one administration's actions or any single set of economic circumstances. They are structural problems of the contemporary political economy.

CONTROLLING THE ECONOMY: CONTENDING APPROACHES

Broad changes in the economy and in thinking about how it is best managed are now reflected in a number of competing schools of opinion among economists. In the real world, the lines separating these positions are often blurred—and, indeed, now seem increasingly blurred, as economists of all persuasions grapple with the often-confounding changes and new problems evident in the early 1990s. Still, elements of the following positions are evident in the ongoing debate over how to manage the U.S. economy through fiscal and monetary policies.

Monetarism. As a pure form of economic theory, **monetarism** puts a singular emphasis on controlling the money supply and the price of money (the interest rate) to secure a growing and inflation-free economy. While every economist recognizes that monetary policy is important, only monetarists make it their keystone. Monetarism's leading theorist is Milton Friedman, a Nobel Laureate in economics (1976) with a long and distinguished career at the University of Chicago.

Friedman and other monetarists start from the straightforward and, to a degree, unassailable proposition that inflation occurs as the result of "too much money chasing too few goods." For a variety of reasons—including the desire of politicians to "heat up the economy" so that they can go into election years with unemployment down and GDP up—the money supply in the United States over the last quarter-century has been expanded in excess of what would be justified given actual increases in productivity. The inevitable result has been a reduction in the purchasing power of the dollar—inflation.

At various times when inflation has beset the economy, there have been short-term efforts to curtail it by sharply cutting back monetary growth. Temporary monetary tightness has indeed temporarily reduced inflation, but at substantial cost: increased unemployment and diminished growth in productivity. So, after a while, expansionist policies have been resumed. What is needed, monetarists maintain, is not a

lurching between overexpansion and sharp contraction, but a stable, steady growth of the money supply corresponding to and sustaining real growth. The absence of such a policy has been the main source of the country's erratic economic performance. As a remedy, Friedman advocates legislating the monetary rule—that the money supply be expanded each year at the same annual rate as the potential growth of the country's real GDP, or at 3 to 5 percent per year. As long as this happens, any decline into recession will be modest and only temporary, and any inflationary increase in spending will burn itself out for lack of fuel.

Supply-Side Economics. Monetarists are usually catalogued as political conservatives because they stress the capacity of the competitive market system to allocate resources efficiently. Not all conservative private-market economists are monetarists, however. In the 1970s, a new emphasis took shape among some younger conservatives that was christened **supply-side economics.** In contrast to monetarists, supply-siders put great weight on fiscal policy. In particular, they argue for large across-the-board tax cuts to encourage many people (1) to work harder, since the "tax penalty" on additional earnings would be reduced, and (2) to invest more in productive enterprises, rather than trying to find economically unproductive tax shelters to escape high marginal tax rates. (The "marginal" tax rate is what taxpayers give the government on the last dollar they earn.) Growth resulting from the immediate stimulus of a large across-the-board tax cut and from long-term encouragement of greater effort at work means there will be a much larger base of national wealth to be taxed—hence, in the supply-side view, reduction of the tax rate can actually culminate in an increase in total tax revenues.

The most controversial aspect of the supply-side diagnosis was the notion that a large cut in the tax rate would not lead to big federal deficits that would accelerate the rate of inflation. In defense, proponents of the supply-side approach argue that their position here has been misstated. "The idea that supply-side economics would provide an instant, large increase in government tax revenue by reducing tax rates was simply not true to begin with. . . ."[6] What was valid, in this view, was the general idea that reducing high marginal tax rates contributes to overall economic growth—benefiting everyone, including government in its need for tax revenues.

Were supply-side prescriptions tested in the 1980s? Answers to this vary. The centerpiece of the early Reagan program was a substantial cut in income tax rates: a 23 percent cut over 3 years. But the overall mix of federal taxes under Reagan shows something quite different than a determined test of supply-side theory. While income tax rates were in fact reduced, other taxes rose—notably social security payroll taxes. In addition, much of the reduction in income tax rates merely offset the earlier effects of "bracket creep," which occurred as inflation pushed people into higher income tax brackets. Nonetheless, the Reagan administration was guided by a mix of supply-side and monetarist ideas. Supply-siders have hailed the length and strength of the recovery in the 1980s, and the relatively low rate of inflation, as at least partial confirmation of the validity of their approach.

"Mainstream" Conservative Economics. Neither monetarism nor the supply-side approach is the traditional "mainstream" economics of American conservatives—which emphasizes curbing government spending and keeping tight checks on inflation. Mainstream conservatives, whose ranks include Harvard economist Martin Feldstein and Stanford economist Michael

Boskin (both of whom advised George Bush in the 1988 campaign), have been especially unhappy with the size of federal deficits in the Reagan era. Boskin joined the Bush administration in 1989 as chairman of the Council of Economic Advisers and has been a key player in setting administration economic policy.

What is conventionally called **conservative economics** has, then, been torn three different ways in recent years: supply-siders, for whom the very idea of a tax increase is anathema; monetarists, who are primarily concerned with the failure of the Federal Reserve to follow their prescription for slow, steady monetary growth; and traditional conservatives who feel that large budget deficits carry unacceptable threats to the long-term health of the economy. Somewhat eclipsed early in the Reagan administration, the latter position made something of a comeback at the end of the 1980s. But the traditional mainstream position has been modified as its supporters have accepted significant elements of the supply-side emphasis.

Industrial Policy. The other main approaches that vie for attention have liberals as their proponents. One goes under the label of **industrial policy.** This approach blends an emphasis on stimulating economic growth—which liberals and conservatives alike can agree on—with an enlarged role for government in promoting the conditions for growth. Tensions in American society will rise, proponents of an industrial policy approach argue, unless ways are found to strengthen America's competitive position in the world economy, especially vis-à-vis Japan. Government must take the lead here, generally in finding new means of promoting growth.

How are productivity gains and more rapid growth to be achieved? The answer, according to economists such as Lester Thurow of MIT and Robert Reich of the Harvard Business School, is in part to copy those nations like

[6] Martin Anderson, "Is Supply-Side Economics Dead?" *The American Spectator*, November 1983, p. 10.

"Safe, reliable, and made right here in the good old U. S. of A."

Drawing by Lorenz; © 1992 The New Yorker Magazine, Inc.

Japan that have been doing especially well of late. The Japanese government has provided major support for the development of industries with high growth potential—sometimes called "sunrise industries." Thurow gives as an example of this encouragement Japan's great success in robotics, the use of robots to assist in manufacturing:

> The problem for the robotics industry [in Japan] was that the seller couldn't get economies of scale to sell a lot of robots so he could sell them cheaply. Buyers wanted only one or two. So JDB [the Japanese Development Bank] stepped in and financed a short-term leasing company. They didn't subsidize anyone, but they bought the robots, guaranteed producers a market of so many robots a year, and then leased the robots to industry. Now if robots had been a failure, the leasing company would have taken a bath. But they were a great success, and the Japanese conquered robots before the rest of us got started. [Today] they have 14,000; we have 4,000.[7]

[7]Interview by the author with Lester Thurow, *Public Opinion*, August/September 1983, pp. 7, 58.

In the United States, the federal government needs to step in, proponents of industrial policy insist, with new programs to encourage productivity gains and economic growth along the lines of the Japanese model.

Keynesian Economics Revisited. While having lost the intellectual and political preeminence they enjoyed from the late 1930s to the 1960s, Keynesians and the economic policies they favor still figure prominently in America's economic debates. At the core of Keynesianism are two basic elements: expansionism and the welfare state. Full employment is a central goal, one that both requires and makes possible high and rapid growth of GDP. To ensure growth, government must manage the level of demand: When demand is insufficient, government should provide economic stimulus, by spending more than it takes in; conversely, when demand is excessive, government should put the brakes on through fiscal policy.

A rapidly growing economy provides, Keynesians maintain, a "growth dividend": additional revenues that can be expended to enlarge social programs. As in earlier decades, the Keynesian emphasis now includes an expansive, growing federal responsibility for public welfare through antipoverty programs, Social Security, Medicare, and more. Keynesian economists, such as Paul Samuelson of MIT and James Tobin of Yale, remain strong advocates of an expanding welfare state.

The Bush Economic Team. The key economic policy makers who served in the Bush administration—Nicholas Brady as secretary of the Treasury, Richard Darman as director of the Office of Management and Budget (OMB), and Michael Boskin as chairman of the Council of Economic Advisers—on the whole reflected what have become mainstream conservative economic assumptions. The willingness of the Bush administration to back tax hikes in 1990 resulted in part from the fact that the supply-side approach did not find as much backing among Bush's team as it had among Reagan's. This isn't to say that the Bush administration was "less conservative" than its predecessor, but it was somewhat more influenced by an older, more traditional economic conservatism that is, for example, more worried about the effects of the federal budget deficit.

MAKING ECONOMIC POLICY: THE ROLE OF THE FEDERAL RESERVE

The U.S. Constitution confers upon Congress the power "to coin money" and to "regulate the value thereof" (Article I, section 8). But for all practical purposes, this authority has been delegated to the Federal Reserve, the central bank of the United States. Every major democracy has a central bank, because each needs a publicly controlled financial institution capable of conducting its monetary affairs.

Established in 1913, the Federal Reserve combines centralization and decentralization, and private as well as public involvement, in the U.S. central bank. The system has four main elements: (1) the Board of Governors, which has its headquarters in Washington; (2) the Federal Open-Market Committee; (3) twelve Federal Reserve banks, together with their twenty-five branches and other facilities located throughout the United States; and (4) all of the member commercial banks, including all national banks and those state-chartered banks that have elected to join the system. (See Figure 15.2 on page 474.)

THE BOARD OF GOVERNORS

The **Board of Governors** is at the apex of the system. Its seven members are appointed for staggered fourteen-year terms, to insulate them from political pressure. Terms of board members are also so arranged that one expires every two years, which means that no president, even if he served eight years in office, could appoint more than four members. These provisions prevent a president from exerting the kind of control over the Federal Reserve that he can over the cabinet departments. The chairman and vice chairman of the Federal Reserve Board are named by the president for four-year terms. The position of chairman—occupied by Paul Volcker from August 1979 through August 1987 and by Alan Greenspan since then—has become enormously influential in policy making.

The Board of Governors and its chairman have broad policy-making and supervisory authority. They establish the reserve requirements for member banks, which help determine how much money these member banks will have available for loans and thus expand or contract available credit. They also review and approve discount-rate actions of the Federal Reserve banks. The discount rate is the rate of interest charged to member banks when they borrow from the Reserve banks. The higher

FIGURE 15.2   ORGANIZATION OF THE FEDERAL RESERVE SYSTEM

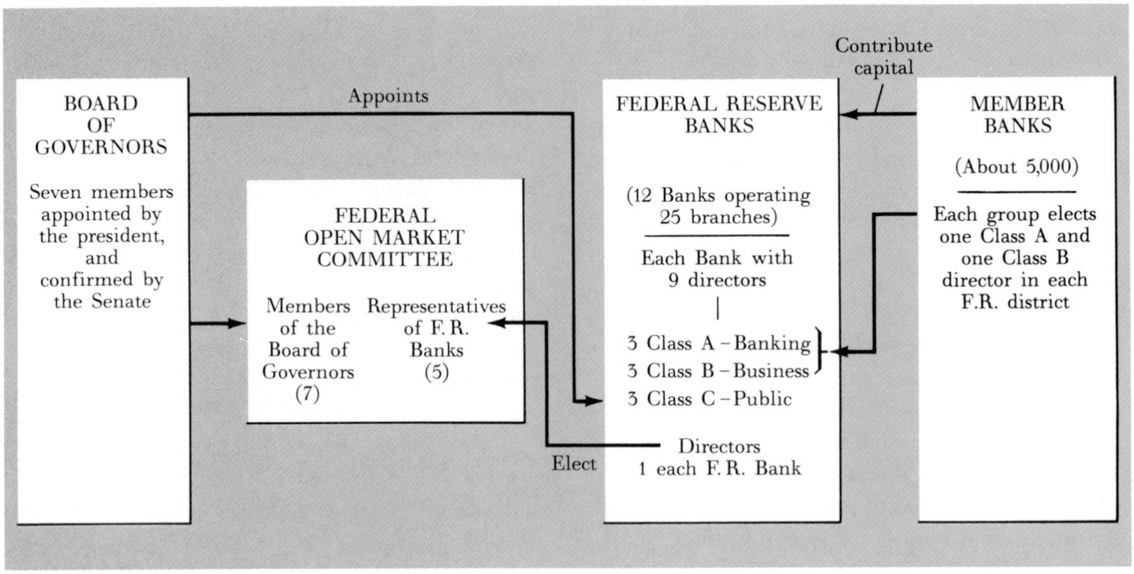

Source: Board of Governors, *The Federal Reserve System, Organizational Chart*, 1985; *United States Government Manual, 1990–91*, pp. 582–89.

the discount rate, the higher the interest rates banks will have to charge their customers for home mortgages, car loans, and the like. In addition, the Board of Governors conducts examinations of the Federal Reserve banks, requires reports from them, supervises the issue and retirement of Federal Reserve notes (the nation's paper money), and exercises jurisdiction over the admission of state banks into the Federal Reserve System. If the board finds malperformance or illegal behavior, it can issue "cease and desist orders" and suspend member banks from further use of the credit facilities of the Federal Reserve.

FEDERAL OPEN-MARKET COMMITTEE

Closely linked to the work of the Federal Reserve Board is that of the **Federal Open-Market Com-**

mittee (FOMC). Each of the seven board members is also a member of the FOMC, which includes five representatives of the Reserve banks (elected annually) as well. "Open-market operations" are the prime vehicles used by the Fed to determine the size of the nation's money supply.

The basic rules in money-supply regulation are simple enough. Too rapid an expansion of the money supply contributes to an overheating of the economy and to inflation. To take an extreme hypothetical case, if the Federal Reserve doubled the nation's money supply in the next year, the value of each dollar would be reduced, because such an expansion would not be supported by actual increases in productivity. On the other hand, if Federal Reserve restrictions on the growth of the money supply are too tight, demand is curbed and the economy is put into recession. FOMC interventions are designed to avoid these extremes.

This is easier said than done. Regulating the money supply of the United States is enormously complicated. There is no general agreement on how the money supply is understood and calculated, given current economic realities. Gone are the days when money was simply the coins or paper currency people carried in their pockets. Today, most "money" takes the form of electronic bytes of information within the computers of financial institutions: the balances of various personal and business accounts. When the Federal Reserve acts to increase the money supply, it does not literally run the printing presses and produce more pieces of paper currency. Rather, it does things such as buy back government securities—for example, bonds that the federal government issued to help finance the national debt. When the Fed buys back bonds, it pays for them by checks drawn on its accounts, and these checks are in turn deposited into various bank accounts around the country. The money supply is thus increased because these banks can lend more money.

THE FEDERAL RESERVE BANKS

The Federal Reserve Board and the FOMC are agencies of the federal government. This is not the case for the twelve **Federal Reserve banks** and their branches, often called "quasi-public" banks, for they reflect an interesting blend of private ownership and public control. Each Reserve bank is owned by the member commercial banks in its district. Upon joining the Federal Reserve System, commercial banks are required to purchase shares of stock in the Reserve bank that serves this area. Reserve banks are incorporated institutions with their own boards of directors. But despite their private ownership, Reserve banks are fundamentally public institutions. They are not motivated

by profits as private businesses must be. All of their earnings, after operating expenses have been met, are paid into the U.S. Treasury. These central banks are supposed to promote the growth and well-being of the economy as a whole.

The Reserve banks are sometimes referred to as "bankers' banks," meaning that they perform functions for commercial banks much as the latter do for the general public. Just as commercial banks receive deposits from the public and make loans to the public, so the Reserve banks receive deposits and extend loans to commercial banks. The Reserve banks also have a third main function that commercial banks no longer perform (although they once did): issuing currency. Congress has provided that the Reserve banks alone put into circulation the country's paper money. Look at a one-dollar bill; right above the portrait of Washington you will see imprinted "Federal Reserve Note."

POLITICAL PRESSURES ON THE FED

Monetary policy is critically important, and the Federal Reserve makes it. This puts the Fed in a political storm center. For example, if the Fed has been restricting the growth of the money supply in an effort to check inflation, the demand for available money is likely to be very high. This means interest rates are likely to be high. If home mortgages are at annual rates of 17 percent interest, and automobile loans are at 14 percent, large numbers of people who need such loans to make their purchases are not going to be able to afford them. The housing and automobile industries are especially vulnerable to high interest rates, so naturally they press for lower rates. There has been an effort to insulate the Fed from such pressures, but this effort has been only partly successful. No institution like the Federal Reserve can operate in a democratic nation in disregard of the policy demands made on it.

Given the pressure, the position of the president and his administration becomes critical. When the president strongly backs the Fed in its current approach to monetary policy, this usually gives it enough support to persist. Without the president's backing, however, the Fed is terribly vulnerable, given the other pressures almost certain to be placed on it. Thus, while in formal institutional terms the Fed is separate from the president and his administration, in a practical sense, it is sensitive to the suggestions for monetary policy that emanate from the White House. The president and the Federal Reserve need each other. The Fed needs the president's political backing and sustenance. And the monetary policies that the Fed conducts are extremely important to national economic performance, on which the success of any administration hinges.

Signals coming from the president in the first years of his term are much more likely to encourage the Federal Reserve to pursue a restrictive, inflation-checking approach to currency expansion than those received in the months preceding the next presidential election. No party wants to run for reelection in an economic environment where productivity is down and unemployment up. Signals sent to the Fed from the White House, when thoughts there turn to the next presidential election, have tended to encourage expansion of the money supply.[8] But this may be changing. The nation's experience with high inflation during the 1970s produced a climate of great sensitivity about anything that looks as though it might encourage a renewal of inflation.

[8] Robert J. Shapiro, "Politics and the Federal Reserve," *The Public Interest*, Winter 1982, p. 119.

TAXES, THE ECONOMY, AND THE PUBLIC GOOD

Taxes are a principal form of governmental intervention in economic affairs. Without them, various programs—assisting in health care, building roads on which people and commerce travel, providing public education—obviously can't be sustained. The relationship between what government taxes and what it spends, the existence and amount of a government budget deficit, help determine the amount of stimulus given the economy and influence the nation's rate of savings. Together taxing and spending comprise what is known as *fiscal policy*—the realm of president and Congress (as opposed to monetary policy where, as we saw above, the Federal Reserve is the principal actor).

In deciding upon fiscal policy, intricate questions and options abound. For example, analysts agree that at some point tax rates become so high as to discourage individual initiative and curb economic growth. But where is that point, and where is the balance to be struck between providing important services through government and letting people make their own economic choices? How much should tax structures be used to redistribute income—in effect, to take from one economic group and give to another? Specifically, are taxes in the United States at present progressive enough, weighted properly toward high- and upper-middle-income taxpayers and away from those with lower-middle and low incomes? Issues such as these have been much debated over the past decade, and today this debate dominates questions of political economy.

As we saw above, the federal government's role in matters involving the economy and social welfare has grown steadily through most of the last century. The sheer size of the federal budget itself attests to the extent of its current

FIGURE 15.3   FEDERAL TAXING AND SPENDING, 1992

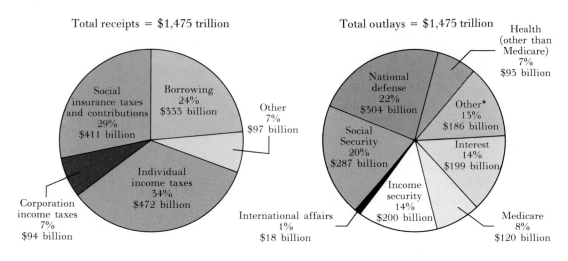

Total receipts = $1,475 trillion

Social insurance taxes and contributions 29% $411 billion

Borrowing 24% $333 billion

Other 7% $97 billion

Corporation income taxes 7% $94 billion

Individual income taxes 34% $472 billion

Where the money comes from

Total outlays = $1,475 trillion

Health (other than Medicare) 7% $93 billion

National defense 22% $304 billion

Other* 13% $186 billion

Social Security 20% $287 billion

Interest 14% $199 billion

Income security 14% $200 billion

International affairs 1% $18 billion

Medicare 8% $120 billion

Where the money goes

*Includes a great variety of programs and services, e.g., ground, air, and water transportation, health research, disaster relief and insurance, general science, space and technology.
Source: Economic Indicators, July 1992, p. 33.

reach. In fiscal year 1992 alone (which began October 1, 1991, and ended September 30, 1992), expenditures totalled 1.407 trillion dollars! This immense sum equals nearly one-quarter of the country's entire GDP, or output of goods and services.

The biggest claimants of federal spending are the health and welfare programs, notably Social Security, Medicare, and programs to assist persons in need. Together they totaled roughly $797 billion, or 13 percent of GDP (see Figure 15.3 and Table 15.1). The next biggest share went towards defense, including not only funds for the Department of Defense, but funds for other national security commitments, such as the work of the CIA, as well. The third greatest claimant was interest payments on the accumulated federal debt—about $200 billion in 1992.

TABLE 15.1   FEDERAL BUDGET FACTS FILE, 1992

Federal expenditures	As a percent of GDP
Federal defense spending	5.2
Federal health and welfare spending	13.4
Total federal spending	23.9
Federal budget deficit, 1992	5.7
Gross federal debt at end of 1992	67.9
Gross publicly-held debt	51.1
Total federal spending	$5,675 (per capita)

Source: Economic Indicators, July, 1992, pp. 1, 32, 33.

Table 15.1 gives two different figures for the size of the gross federal debt in relation to GDP at the end of 1992—67.9 percent or 51.1 percent. Some explanation is in order. At the close of fiscal 1992, investors of all sorts held $3.0 trillion in U.S. government bonds and notes—an amount equal to 51.1 percent of GDP. But the federal government borrowed another $1 trillion from the federal trust funds, principally Social Security, which has been showing large current year surpluses—that is, more Social Security tax revenue coming in than being paid out in benefits. These current surpluses will be needed to pay benefits to those now contributing. Otherwise, Social Security taxes will have to be raised, benefits will have to be reduced, or general tax revenues will have to be used to fund the program. For the time being the surpluses are being used to reduce the amount the government needs to borrow on the open market. The gross debt is 67.9 percent of GDP when you count the amount "borrowed" from the trust funds.

The national debt and the interest thereon is so high because government tax revenues have been running far below spending in recent years, requiring large-scale borrowing by the Treasury Department. In 1992, this borrowing amounted to $333.5 billion, or 5.7 percent of GDP, the largest proportion in peace time in U.S. history.

PUTTING THE FEDERAL DEBT IN PERSPECTIVE

The size of total federal borrowing is so large—more than $15,750 per person in 1992—as to leave most people breathless and more than a little concerned. It's not at all clear, however,

CLAY BENNETT
Courtesy St. Petersburg Times

just how detrimental to the public weal carrying such debt will prove. For one thing, this amount of deficit spending is seen by many analysts as a helpful economic stimulus.

Another, different factor involves the need to relate the debt to the size of the economy that sustains it. The federal debt in 1992 was the greatest it has ever been in absolute terms, but as a proportion of GDP, it was by no means the largest the United States has experienced. In 1945, for example, federal borrowing—mostly to finance our efforts in World War II—stood at roughly 120 percent of GDP: 50 to 70 percentage points greater than at present, depending on how that debt is measured.

Most economists believe that the main problem with large, persistent deficits is that they absorb savings that otherwise would be invested to spur growth in overall economic productivity. But as economist Herbert Stein, a former chairman of the President's Council of Economic Advisers under Richard Nixon, points out, when deficits were uniformly high in the 1980s, "this effect was largely matched by the inflow of capital from abroad. Investment as a fraction of GDP was only slightly lower in the 1980s than in the 1970s and higher than in the 1950s and 1960s."[9]

All this said, it would undoubtedly be good economics to get annual deficits down and at least to stop the gross debt from increasing as a percentage of GDP. Why hasn't this been achieved in recent years? Partly because politicians always find it easier, and more profitable politically, to spend for good causes than to tax people to pay for it. In addition, prolonged divided party control of the national government (discussed at length in chapter 5) has meant that neither party could impose its own budget plan. In a sense the large deficits are a by-product of the compromises both parties needed to make to come up with a budget.

GOVERNMENT SPENDING

It's a popular piece of American political mythology that federal spending rose rapidly in the 1960s and 1970s, and then was cut back sharply in the 1980s. Expenditures did in fact rise substantially in the 1960s and 1970s. But after reaching 23.7 percent of GDP in 1983, they slipped back only modestly to 21.8 percent of GDP in 1988, only to rise again in the early 1990s. They reached about 24 percent of GDP in 1992, the highest they have ever been except in times of all-out war when, of course, unusual expenditures are necessary.

In 1940 the national government of the United States spent a sum that was 10 percent of the country's gross domestic product for all purposes. Now it expends an amount that is two-and-a-half times that proportion of a vastly larger economy. Combined state and local government expenditures have climbed as well, from about 11 percent of GDP in 1940 to 15 percent in 1992. Together, government spending at all levels totals about 39 percent of the United States's output of goods and services. This growth in spending is a central fact of modern U.S. political experience.

ARE TAXES TOO HIGH OR NOT HIGH ENOUGH?

The large federal deficits of recent years can be seen in two very different lights: as the result of taxes not being high enough to pay for the level of government services and protections that Americans want or need, or as the result of excessive increases in public spending.

One thing is clear: whether enough or not, the country has been raising overall taxes for a long time. Government revenues have been rising steadily throughout the twentieth cen-

[9]Herbert Stein, "Deficits, Disaster and Ross Perot," *The Wall Street Journal*, June 17, 1992, p. A16.

tury—not just in terms of inflation-controlled dollars adjusted to a per capita base, but as a proportion of the country's gross domestic product. Today, government's share will be over one-third of total GDP, and the largest it has been in U.S. history—the World War II years included.

In 1927 all government revenues (income tax, sales tax, etc.) in the United States were roughly 13 percent of the domestic product, with the state and local share nearly twice that of the national government. The New Deal years increased the federal government's claim—remarkably modest from our vantage point. Over the 1940s, government revenues jumped enormously as a proportion of GDP, but most of the increase went into just one area of federal spending: Defense expenditures, huge during World War II of course, remained high in the postwar era. They were 11.6 percent of GDP in 1952.

In recent decades, defense spending has declined markedly as a proportion of GDP—though it increased somewhat in the Reagan years—and in 1990 totaled a bit over 5 percent. Spending in the other principal sectors has grown markedly, however, and to meet these costs government revenues have been raised even as a percentage of a growing domestic product. Much of the overall increase has come at state and local levels. The big proportional increase at the national level has come in social insurance taxes (Social Security, Medicare, etc.), which grew from just over 1 percent of GDP in 1950 to over 7 percent in 1992.

WHERE DOES THE PUBLIC STAND ON TAXES?

Are taxes too high? An extensive review of opinion on tax questions by the Roper Center for Public Opinion Research in the spring of 1990 helps clarify general public sentiment on

the tax issue.[10] The review makes clear that it's not correct to say Americans are "against taxes." We want social services and we back other costly national goals such as a strong defense—and recognize that we must be taxed for these things. But large majorities today think that taxes are *too high* in the sense of being greater than they need to be to sustain desired services (Figure 15.4). Asked "out of every dollar the federal government collects in taxes, how many cents do you think are wasted?" respondents to a May 1990 ABC News / *Washington Post* survey gave the average answer of $.46. Seventy percent of those interviewed in New Jersey in March 1990 by Rutgers' Eagleton Institute said that they pay too much for what they get from state and local taxes. A national survey taken in April 1991 by the Roper Organization found only 20 percent ready to describe federal income taxes as yielding good or excellent value. In contrast, 57 percent said they got good value for dollars spent on mail service, 49 percent on electricity, 34 percent on health insurance, and 28 percent even on auto insurance.

At the same time, as noted, the public wants services, and it considers the federal deficit a real problem—though not the most urgent problem facing the country. So the overall mood nationally is to hold the line on taxes, rather than to reduce them. Asked by Hart / Teeter Research Companies in a January 1990 survey whether the federal government should raise taxes, lower them, or keep them as they are, 58 percet opted for the current levels, only 28 percent for lowering taxes and 12 percent for raising them.

The politics of taxes show some interesting wrinkles. In May 1990, the Gallup poll asked whether President Bush should "keep his pledge

[10]The results of the examination were published in *The Public Perspective: A Roper Center Review of Public Opinion and Polling*, July/August 1990.

FIGURE 15.4   THE PUBLIC SAYS: TAXES ARE TOO HIGH

1. To reduce budget deficit...

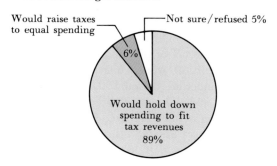

2. Since the Tax Reform Act of 1986...

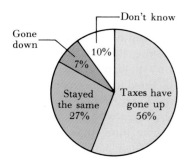

3. Connecticut:

·Level of taxes too high

4. Illinois:

1989 individual and corporate income tax increase should be...

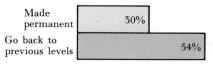

5. Massachusetts:

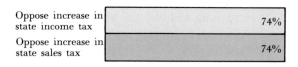

6. New Jersey:

State and local taxes are...

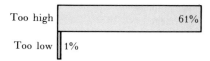

Question 1: Federal tax revenues are expected to rise by an average of 74 billion dollars a year through 1995. At the present rate, government spending will also increase about that fast, leaving the deficit above 100 billion dollars. What would you do to reduce the budget deficit—raise taxes so that they would equal spending, or hold down spending so that it fits tax revenues? *Question 2:* Since the Tax Reform Act of 1986, has the amount of taxes you now pay gone down a lot, gone down a little, gone up a little, gone up a lot, or stayed about the same. *Question 3:* Right now, do you think the level of state taxes in Connecticut is too high, too low, or just about right? *Question 4:* As you may know, this past year the Illinois state income tax was temporarily raised from 2.5% to 3% for individuals, and 4% to 4.8% for corporations. In two years both taxes are scheduled to return to lower levels. Do you think the individual and corporate income tax increases should be permanent or should they go back to their previous levels? *Question 5:* Do you support or oppose increasing (state income taxes/state sales tax)? *Question 6:* Do you think the state and local taxes you pay are too high, too low, or just about right?
Source: Question 1: Survey by the Wirthlin Group, April 16–19, 1990. *Question 2:* Survey by the Gallup Organization, March 8–11, 1990. *Question 3:* Survey by The Connecticut Poll for the *Hartford Courant,* latest that of May 15–22, 1990. *Question 4:* Survey by the Center for Governmental Studies, Northern Illinois University, November–December, 1989. *Question 5:* Survey by KRC Communications Research for the *Boston Globe* and WBZ-TV, July 5–6, 1989. *Question 6:* Survey by the Eagleton Poll for *The Star Ledger,* March 22–26, 1990.

not to raise taxes" or "consider new taxes to reduce the federal budget deficit." While a solid majority of respondents said he should keep his promise, support for the "no tax" position was strongest among the poor, the less well educated, and blacks (Table 15.2). Other polls at the time showed that higher status groups—those with high incomes, for example—were more inclined to believe that higher taxes were needed. These responses reflect in part the fact that people with low incomes would "feel" a tax hike more than those with high incomes, even if their share of the total increase were modest.

TABLE 15.2   RESISTANCE TO TAX HIKES STRONGEST AMONG GROUPS OF LOW INCOME AND SOCIOECONOMIC STATUS

	"No new taxes" Keep pledge (percent)	Consider taxes
All respondents	56	40
Education		
College graduate	44	53
Some college	54	41
High school graduate	61	36
Less than high school	62	33
Income		
$50,000 and over	44	56
$30,000–$49,999	56	41
$20,000–$29,999	53	41
Under $20,000	65	31
Race		
White	55	41
Black	67	29

Question: "George Bush said in his campaign 'read my lips: no new taxes.' As far as you are concerned, should President Bush keep his campaign pledge not to raise taxes, or should he consider new taxes to help reduce the federal budget deficit?"
Source: Survey by the Gallup Organization of 1,255 adults, May 17–20, 1990.

The income tax (whether federal or state) remains highly unpopular—with surprising uniformity across social groups. Asked in a May 1990 survey taken for the *Boston Globe* whether "in order to . . . balance the state budget [you would] rather see the state increase the income tax or broaden the sales tax," just 15 percent of Massachusetts residents with family incomes under $30,000 endorsed an income tax hike, compared to 46 percent endorsing a sales tax rise. Among those with incomes over $60,000, the respective percentages were 20 and 46.

The Social Security payroll tax is in many ways the big surprise of the tax story. Social Security taxes have risen sharply in recent years. In 1990, wage earners paid 7.65 percent of their earnings (up to $51,300) in this levy, and their employers had to pay the same proportion on their behalf. Unlike the case of income tax, there is little in the way of public demand to cut social security taxes. Asked in early 1990 by Yankelovich Clancy Shulman whether they favored reducing Social Security taxes, 65 percent with incomes under $10,000 and 59 percent earning $50,000 and higher opposed such a reduction. Seventy percent of those ages 18–29 and 67 percent in the 40–64 group rejected a Social Security tax reduction. There is a lesson here. People support Social Security taxes, even though they are high, because they think they get important value in return.

The tax issue has not played itself out. The tension generated by strong demands for public services on the one hand, and strong resistance to continuing tax hikes on the other, remains a central element in American politics. The tension at once expresses itself in, and is confounded by, the fact of large governmental deficits. At the end of the 1990 fiscal year, the total debt of the national government stood at $3.2 trillion, and the current year deficit was 4 percent of GDP. Many state governments, too,

were struggling to overcome deficits in their own budgets.

In the 1990 elections, the big losers were governors who had sought to meet service demands by raising taxes. Incumbents in both parties suffered. Republican losses in Florida, Kansas, Nebraska, Oklahoma, and Rhode Island owed much to the tax issue, as did Democratic defeats in Ohio, Michigan, Minnesota, Connecticut, and Massachusetts. U.S. Senator Bill Bradley, a Democrat, had been expected to win reelection handily in New Jersey, but he just squeaked through—even though his Republican challenger lacked the financial resources needed to run a statewide campaign. Poll data made clear that voting against Bradley became a means of protesting the tax increases pushed through earlier by New Jersey's Democratic governor, James Florio.

THE PUBLIC WELFARE

Over the years, there have been great changes in the things American government is expected to do so as to promote public welfare. In particular, since the Great Depression of the 1930s the number, reach, and costs of government welfare programs have expanded enormously. In fiscal year 1990, federal spending for all the various welfare activities totaled roughly $800 billion.

Federal welfare programs reach into virtually every sector of American life, and there are very few people who are not in one way or another beneficiaries. Farmers receive a variety of subsidy payments—the goal, to ensure that they get a fair price for their crops. They receive loans for soil and water conservation, technical

TABLE 15.3 FEDERAL WELFARE EXPENDITURES, 1992 (BILLIONS OF DOLLARS)

Agriculture	14.7*
Community and regional development	7.5
Education, training, employment, and social services	45.0
Medicare	118.6
Other health programs	94.6†
Income security	196.0**
Social Security (OASDI)	286.7
Veterans benefits and services	33.8
Total federal welfare spending	$796.9 billion

*Includes crop subsidies, technical assistance to farmers, rural housing grants, water and waste disposal grants, etc.
†Includes Medicaid.
**Includes AFDC, food stamps, low-income energy assistance, federal supplementary security income.
Source: U.S. Office of Management and Budget, Budget of The U.S. Government, FY 1993, p. A1-10–A1-13

assistance to improve crop yields, disaster relief, and more. In 1989, nearly 39 million Americans were receiving Social Security benefits, and 38 million were covered by Medicare. The Department of Housing and Urban Development (HUD) makes low-interest loans for the rehabilitation of residential property, extends mortgage insurance for housing for the elderly, awards grants for the development of decent housing in central cities, and provides rent supplement assistance for low-income families. The Department of Veterans Affairs provides hospital and nursing home care for military service veterans, educational assistance for post-Vietnam veterans and for spouses and children of disabled veterans, and a variety of pension benefits. The Education Department operates financial assistance programs for college students from low-income families, including Pell grants and guaranteed student loans. Table 15.3 gives us an overview of federal welfare programs.

As even this brief and highly selective list makes evident, a very large share of federal welfare efforts—and the same is true of state efforts as well—go not just to poor people, but to all groups and strata in American society. Assistance that is limited to people in need—such as Aid to Families with Dependent Children (AFDC), food stamps, and Medicaid, described below—are what many take *welfare* to mean, but these programs in fact account for only a minority of all welfare expenditures. Properly understood, **welfare programs** are those that use the instruments of government to advance the social and economic well-being of individuals—whether they are poor and need subsidies to buy food, have special needs such as disabled veterans, or are the large majority who want federal assistance in meeting the needs of their retirement years.

WELFARE PROGRAMS AND POLICIES

Welfare programs in which the federal government participates may be distinguished by several different dimensions: (1) whether benefits are targeted just to the poor or to the general population; (2) whether programs are run exclusively by the national government or have state participation; (3) among the latter, whether the state role extends to financing the program, administering it, or both. Table 15.4 (on pages 486–87) provides information on these dimensions for eight of the largest U.S. welfare programs. It does not include all programs; even some large ones have been omitted—such as educational assistance for needy or disadvantaged students and housing subsidies. But these eight programs are the core of American public welfare efforts and account for the preponderance of all welfare spending.

Four of these eight programs are targeted to people in financial need: federal Supplemental Security Income (SSI); Medicaid; Aid to Families with Dependent Children (AFDC); and Food Stamps. Two programs serve the general population without regard to economic status: Old Age, Survivors', and Disability Insurance (OASDI); and Medicare. The two remaining programs, Veterans' Benefits and Unemployment Compensation, are not located effectively by this distinction. Most veterans' benefits do not have means tests, but some do. One has to have served in the country's armed services (or in certain instances be a member of a veteran's family) to qualify. Unemployment Compensation does not have any means test, yet it has an obvious economic requirement: One must be out of work to qualify.

Attesting to the federalized character of American welfare programs, only three of the eight programs described in Table 15.4 are financed and operated exclusively by the national government: OASDI, Medicare, and Veterans' Benefits. The other five involve some form of joint federal-state financing or management.

The Social Security Administration administers **SSI.** Uniform national eligibility standards are imposed. But there is state financial participation. Congress requires all states to supplement the federal minimums in the SSI program to the extent necessary so that persons who had previously been receiving state-administered assistance at higher levels would not suffer a reduction of benefits in the shift to a federally administered program. These mandatory supplements are strictly transitional. But the states are also encouraged under SSI to provide optional supplements above the federal minimums. The federal government pays all costs of administering the supplements when the states opt to have the Social Security Administration handle all the paperwork.

Medicaid uses a combination of federal and state funds in providing medical assistance to the poor. About half of the program costs are borne by Washington. The states are required to provide health benefits, according to federal standards, to all who qualify for public assistance, but the states set the benefit levels and administer the program. **AFDC** involves a federal-state mix similar to that of Medicaid. The national government reimburses the states for about half of the total benefit costs. The states administer the program and set criteria for eligibility, as well as benefit levels, subject to a variety of federal requirements. The **Food Stamp** program is totally federally funded, and uniform eligibility standards are required of all states. At the same time, state welfare agencies actually administer the program.

Under **Unemployment Compensation** the states collect from employers (all those employing eight or more workers) according to a federally determined wage base, but they must place these tax receipts in the federally administered Unemployment Trust Fund (where separate accounts are maintained for each state). The federal government shares in the costs of extended benefits. When a state is overdrawn, as happens quite often in periods of high unemployment, it can borrow from the federal government to ensure a continuation of prescribed benefits. Unemployment Compensation is managed by the states subject to federal standards.

FEDERAL ROLE VS. STATE ROLE

The extent to which states and municipalities participate in financing and managing welfare programs is a feature of the American approach to welfare policy. Prior to the Great Depression, the national government had a modest role in public welfare; veterans' benefits were the one big program. But when the nationwide depression brought Washington into the welfare picture in a big way, nationally inspired and funded programs were frequently grafted onto an existing system of state-centered man-

TABLE 15.4 MAJOR PUBLIC-WELFARE PROGRAMS

Program and total costs 1992 (national and state shares)	Key legislation	Tax source	Funding	Administration	Function
1. Old Age, Survivors, and Disability Insurance (OASDI); $286.7 billion	Social Security Act of 1935, extensively amended	Payroll tax with shares paid by employers and employees.	Federal; trust funds set up in U.S. Treasury.	Federal: HHS/Social Security Adm.	National pension system for the retired, the bereaved, the orphaned, and the disabled.
2. Federal Supplemental Security Income (SSI); $19.8 billion	Social Security Amendments of 1972	General revenue	Federal; states are "encouraged to provide optional supplements."	Federal: Social Security Adm.	Assistance to the aged poor. Need, the sole criterion, is established by a means test.
3. Medicare; $118.6 billion	Social Security Amendments of 1965	For part A of program, basic health insurance: payroll tax, shares paid by employers and employees. For part B, supplementary medical care, general revenue and premiums paid by beneficiaries.	(Part A) Federal; Hospital insurance trust fund is repository for payroll tax revenues. (Part B) Federal and client funded.	Federal: HHS/Health Care Financing Adm.	Health insurance for the aged. (Part A) Basic inpatient hospital services and post-hospital care for persons 65 and older. (Part B) Payments of 80% of patient's costs for physicians and various medical specialists, regardless of where services are performed.
4. Medicaid; $140.0 billion	Social Security Amendments of 1965	General revenue	Federal matching grants provided to states according to state per capita income.	Federal and state. *Federal:* HHS/Health Care Financing Adm. *State:* basic provider of health care—according to federal standards—to those who qualify. State may set ceiling on benefits and may exercise options on choice of physicians and facilities.	Health care to the poor through payments to health-care providers—hospitals, doctors, nursing facilities, rural health clinics.
5. Aid to Families with Dependent Children (AFDC); $14.5 billion	Social Security Act of 1935, amended over 100 times, and other legislation, including the Family Support Act of 1988	General revenue	Federal government reimburses states for about half of benefit costs.	State: Set criteria for eligibility and benefit level "within broad federal rules."	Financial assistance for poor families, pegged to the care of dependent children.

Program and total costs 1992 (national and state shares)	Key legislation	Tax source	Funding	Administration	Function
6. Food Stamp Program; $22.7 billion	Food Stamp Act of 1964	General revenue	Federal, except for state share of administrative expenses.	Jointly federal, state, and local. *Federal:* USDA/Consumer Services, Family Nutrition program. *State and local:* welfare agencies	"Help lower-income Americans maintain a nutritious diet."
7. Unemployment Compensation; $31.4 billion	Social Security Act of 1935; extensively amended	Payroll tax on employers	State tax on employers funds regular benefits; state and federal taxes (in equal portions) on employers funds extended benefits.	Federal and state. *Federal:* U.S. Employment and Training Adm. (Dept. of Labor). *State:* employment security agency of each state. Each state administers its Unemployment Compensation program according to a "certified state plan." States provide benefits schedule (benefit ceilings, duration, etc.), following federal guidelines; States collect employer taxes and disburse benefits "payable under the laws of individual states."	Unemployment insurance for persons temporarily unable to find a job.
8. Veterans' Benefits; $35.8 billion	Many statutes, including Serviceman's Readjustment Act of 1944—GI Bill of Rights	General revenue	Federal	*Federal:* Veterans Administration	Benefits for U.S. war veterans and dependents, including: compensation for loss due to disabilities or death resulting from military service; pensions for the disabled; education benefits, home loan guarantees; burial expenses; medical services and care.

Source: Expenditure data from the *Budget of the U.S. Government FY 1993*, pp. A1-10—A1-13.

ROBERT DORNFRIED
© Rothco Cartoons

The states are carrying more and more of the welfare load.

agement. A few key public-welfare programs are funded and administered exclusively through national agencies—notably, OASDI and Medicare—but many of the most important programs are federal-state partnerships: Medicaid, AFDC, Food Stamps, and Unemployment Compensation. Federalism is enormously important in the American welfare system. Public-welfare programs throughout much of Europe are run by national agencies with centralized standards and uniform benefits, but the American programs are often decentralized and vary substantially from state to state.

Aid to Families with Dependent Children is a case in point. AFDC is a means-tested program developed to provide assistance for children whose parents are unable to provide properly for them. In 1950 it was expanded to give support to adults in such families, as well as to their dependent children. Today, a large proportion of AFDC recipient families are headed by single mothers: The father either is not present or is not providing support. AFDC is administered at the state level, subject to some federal regulations, with funding provided jointly by Washington and the states.

Benefits vary greatly from one state to another. Individual states have the authority to set benefit levels, and they have made different choices.

ADMINISTERING FEDERAL WELFARE PROGRAMS

The largest federal welfare agency is the **Department of Health and Human Services** (HHS). It was created in 1953 as the Department of Health, Education, and Welfare (HEW) but was redesignated in 1979. At that time Education was made a separate department. HHS describes itself as "the Cabinet-level department of the federal Executive Branch most concerned with people and most involved with the nation's human concerns." It doesn't exaggerate when it asserts that "in one way or another—whether it is mailing out Social Security checks or making health services more widely available—HHS touches the lives of more Americans than any other Federal agency."[11] HHS is the principal welfare agency of the national government (Figure 15.5).

THE SCOPE OF HHS PROGRAMS

Budget data alone give a good indication of the scope of HHS-administered programs. In 1973, the department (then HEW) became the largest in the federal government, surpassing Defense in total expenditures. Its 1990 budget of $436 billion was easily the largest, even with its education component now separate.

Within HHS the biggest unit is the Social Security Administration (SSA), created in 1946 as a successor to the original Social Security

---

[11] This description of HHS is taken from its description in the *United States Government Manual, 1989/90*, p. 299.

FIGURE 15.5 DEPARTMENT OF HEALTH AND HUMAN SERVICES

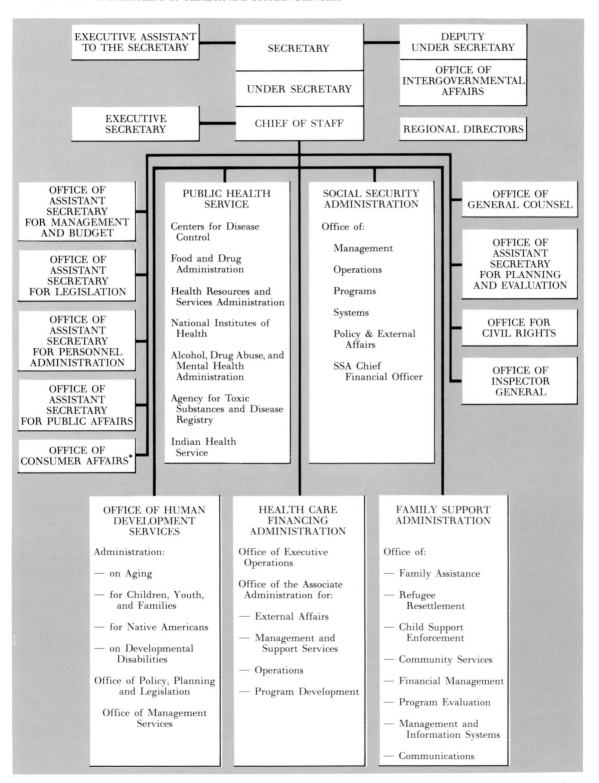

* Located administratively in HHS but reports to the president. Source: The United States Government Manual, 1990–91, p. 297.

Board. SSA's 1992 outlays of just under $287 billion would make it the second largest department in the U.S. government (exceeded only by Defense) were it free-standing. Under the direction of a commissioner, the Social Security Administration is responsible for managing the contributory social-insurance program covering pensions for retired workers, benefits for those disabled, and cash payments made to surviving members of workers' families. By one measure, it is among the most efficient of all federal agencies: It takes a relatively small staff to dispose of a very large amount of money. SSA is a medium-size federal agency, with only about 75,000 employees. Its tasks are highly routinized: dispensing social security checks and resolving questions of eligibility.

The budget of the Social Security Administration would be even more imposing if SSA had financial and management responsibilities for all of the basic social security programs. Medicare and Medicaid have been transferred, however, to another unit of HHS, the Health Care Financing Administration (HCFA). HCFA was created in 1977. Wholly a program of the federal government, Medicare is directly administered by HCFA. Medicaid, in contrast, is a joint federal- and state-financed program administered by state welfare agencies, so HCFA merely processes federal grants to the states for this program.

Another important agency within the Department of Health and Human Services is the Public Health Service (PHS). It began a long time ago, through an act of Congress of July 1798 that authorized hospitals to provide care for American merchant seamen. The Public Health Service Act of 1944 gave the PHS its present institutional form, although its responsibilities have since been substantially expanded. Among its principal units are the Alcohol, Drug Abuse, and Mental Health Administration; the Centers for Disease Control; the Food and Drug Administration; the Health Resources and Services Administration; and the National Institutes of Health. The latter conduct and support biomedical research into various diseases, including cancer, heart and lung diseases, arthritis, allergies, and infectious diseases.

OTHER AGENCIES INVOLVED IN WELFARE PROGRAMS

As mentioned above, the **Department of Agriculture** (USDA) operates a number of programs, including crop subsidies, of direct benefit to the farm community. In addition, the USDA operates food-related welfare programs—the largest of which is Food Stamps. The Food Stamps program provides needy persons with food coupons to increase their resources for food purchases. Entirely funded through the Food and Nutrition Service (FNS), and with uniform eligibility standards required of all states, food stamps are actually administered by state and local welfare agencies. Other FNS programs are the National School Lunch Program, the Child Care Food Program, the Special Milk Program for Children, and the Special Supplemental Food Program for Women, Infants and Children.

With a 1992 budget of about $24 billion, the **Department of Housing and Urban Development** (HUD) has a number of housing-related responsibilities; the biggest involves housing assistance for the needy. Together with state agencies, HUD provides partial financing for low-rent public housing projects owned, managed, and administered by local housing authorities. Income standards for occupancy are set by the local agencies, subject to HUD guidelines. Rental charges cannot exceed 25 percent of the net monthly money income of recipients. HUD funding also subsidizes rentals by low-income families in the private sector. Under rent-supplement plans, the difference between the "fair market rent" of a dwelling and the rent charged to the tenant is paid to the owner by the government. Under interest-reduction programs, the amount of interest paid on a mortgage by the owner of a property is reduced, with the requirement that the subsequent savings be passed along to low-income tenants through lower rent charges.

The **Department of Education** administers two large programs of educational assistance for low-income persons. The first, aimed at the primary and secondary school population, supports compensatory education for the disadvantaged. Its 1992 budget was about $27 billion. The second also assists needy students in higher education. Key programs here are the Basic and Supplemental Educational Opportunity Grants (Pell grants), which are restricted to students from low-income families attending institutions of higher education. As grants, these funds need not be repaid. The department also administers a program of guaranteed loans for students from lower-middle-income as well as low-income families. These loans are interest-free while the student is enrolled in undergraduate or graduate education and need not be repaid during this period; the loans must be repaid over a ten-year span after graduation. While the goal of this program is generally lauded, the rate of default on student loans has become a subject of concern.

The **Department of Veterans Affairs** (prior to March 1989, the Veterans Administration) is the last of the principal federal agencies administering welfare programs. It was established in its present form as an independent executive-branch agency in 1930, with the consolidation of several federal bureaus then handling veterans' affairs. Operating with fiscal year 1992 outlays of about $34 billion, the Veterans Department is a major federal welfare agency. Its beneficiaries are, of course, veterans of U.S. military service: for some programs, all veterans; for others, veterans of particular wars, needy veterans, those who suffered disabilities as a result of their military service, and surviving family members of veterans who lost their lives while performing military duties. The largest veterans programs are those covering disability compensation and pensions based on financial need. The next largest group provides medical benefits for veterans.

THE AMERICAN APPROACH TO WELFARE

As nations become wealthier and thus better able to finance welfare programs, these programs increase. In every Western democracy in this century, government's role in welfare has steadily expanded (as indicated by major real increases in public-welfare spending). Expenditures for welfare programs were low when the absolute need for such programs was greatest—and have reached their highest historic levels precisely when absolute need is the least severe. This does not diminish the importance of current efforts or the need for spending; but welfare spending is in significant measure "the art of the possible."

To take just one example, total expenditures on public welfare by local, state, and federal governments in the United States were $6.5 billion in 1935, in the face of overwhelming need resulting from the Great Depression. This averaged about $50 per person. In contrast, total public-welfare spending—again here for all levels of government—in 1992 was roughly $1.35 trillion, or nearly $5,400 per person. Even when the effects of inflation are taken into account, the increase is enormous. It has resulted not so much from the efforts of individual political leaders and parties as from the changing capacities and expectations made possible by modern industrial development. Other countries show the same progression, starting from different bases.

TWO APPROACHES TO WELFARE

As we will see, Americans have some ideas about government's role in the welfare area that differ quite substantially from those held by citizens of other industrial democracies. Despite similarities, each country approaches welfare issues in its own distinctive manner, reflecting its history and values. Two hypothetical contrasting national philosophies on welfare policy help us see the range and importance of these variations.

Country A has long shown a strong preference for a collectivist rather than individualistic approach. The majority of its citizens concluded from their country's historical experience that individual efforts were insufficient in the absence of major governmental efforts to extend economic security and well-being. Centralized governmental welfare programs in health, unemployment insurance, and pensions for the aged were developed in the late nineteenth century and, with strong public backing, were expanded in the twentieth century. The public sees governmental intervention as a desirable response to community needs. National values also strongly support governmental efforts to reduce economic inequality: redistributing wealth through progressive taxation and public-benefits programs.

Country B prefers an individualistic approach. Its public has concluded from national experience that great opportunities for advancement are present if individual effort is made to realize them. The public strongly backs equality of opportunity. But it rejects equality of result—where government redistributes income and other values to minimize differences in socioeconomic status. It finds that governmental intervention often causes more problems than it solves. It wants to see individual citizens given the widest freedom to make their own way and to enjoy what they earn.

Few observers would confuse the United States with the model of Country A. As we noted elsewhere (especially chapter 3), American political ideology enshrined many of the central assumptions of classical liberalism, and it is notably attentive to assertions of individual rights and interests. Political philosophies representing collectivist goals have foundered on America's singular individualism. Citizens believe that their society gives unusual opportunities to the individual and have been less inclined than their counterparts in many other countries to back collective action through the state. The American idea of equality aims at equal opportunity, not equal results.

Still, it would be a mistake to see the United States as a pure embodiment of Country B. Americans have not been hostile to government. Two types of governmental action in the welfare area have found fertile soil in the United States: (1) to provide a general climate where individual interests and pursuits can be more fully realized, and (2) to help people who through no lack of effort find themselves in need. Modern U.S. welfare policies have been shaped by the public's insistence that the policies extend social and political individualism rather than restrict it.

"HELPING THE POOR" VERSUS "WELFARE"

Opinion polls show what appears to be a basic confusion in public attitudes—that Americans back governmental efforts to help the needy but are uncomfortable with "welfare." For example, the University of Chicago's National Opinion Research Center (NORC) has periodically asked some of its respondents whether they think we are spending too much, too little, or about the right amount on "welfare," and asked other respondents with the same general characteristics the same question about "assistance to the poor." See on the next page how

	"Welfare"	"Assistance to the poor"
Too much	40%	10%
Too little	23%	67%
About right	37%	23%

differently people answered, depending on which of these two wordings were used.[12]

The reason for these divergent responses is that American egalitarianism stresses giving individuals *an equal opportunity to compete.* We back the claims of deserving individuals who find themselves in need: the ill, the elderly, those unable to find work, children whose families cannot provide for them. Our brand of egalitarianism lends support to job-training programs, programs that extend access to college education through government grants and loans, and more. But it responds quite differently with regard to individuals who are able-bodied but unwilling to make the effort to support themselves and their families. An ideology that emphasizes individual responsibility, and insists that American society offers unusual opportunities to those who try, here is much less sympathetic. Many Americans believe, in effect, "the opportunity is there; I make the effort; you should too if you are not too old, too young, or too infirm." Sympathetic to programs that extend opportunity to those whom they see as the deserving poor, many are unhappy about "welfare." In the informal shorthand of American politics, "welfare" has come to connote the avoidance of individual responsibility and effort.

The United States stands out among industrial nations in the extent to which its citizens stress individual effort over government assis-

tance. In 1987 an international social science project asked a series of questions on this subject in the United States, Australia, and a number of European countries. On the issue of whether "government should provide everyone with a guaranteed basic income," only 21 percent of Americans said it should, compared to 56 percent of West Germans, 61 percent of the British, and 67 percent of Italians.

Americans believe that government should help the deserving poor, but that able individuals should help themselves. They also believe that existing welfare programs reach large numbers who really need them but are, at the same time, exploited by those unwilling to do what they can for themselves. This mix of values and assessments generates ambivalence about the practical operations of welfare programs. Eighty-five percent of those interviewed in the NORC's *General Social Survey* in 1986 agreed with the criticism of welfare that it encourages people to work less, but 84 percent agreed with the defense of welfare that it helps people overcome difficult times. In a question posed by NORC interviewers in the spring of 1991, respondents were asked to locate themselves on a five-point scale. By picking point 1, a respondent was indicating strong agreement that "the government in Washington should do everything possible to improve the standard of living of all poor Americans"; by selecting point 5, he or she was agreeing strongly that "it is not the government's responsibility and each person should take care of himself." The midpoint on the scale was identified as "I agree with both answers." By far the largest proportion—44 percent of all respondents—put themselves at the midpoint. The contradiction here results from the pull of contending social and political values. (See Figure 15.6.)

Americans have tried to reconcile these contrasting perspectives. One result is the judgment that welfare programs should require those

---

[12]These data are from the 1991 *General Social Survey*, conducted by the National Opinion Research Center, University of Chicago.

FIGURE 15.6   AMBIVALENCE ABOUT GOVERNMENT'S ROLE IN WELFARE POLICY

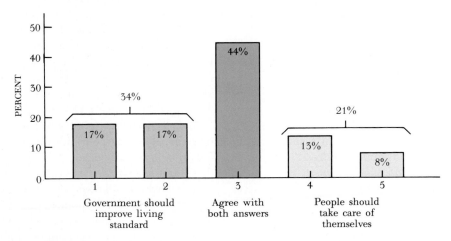

Question: "I'd like to talk with you about issues some people tell us are important. Some people think that the government in Washington should do everything possible to improve the standard of living of all poor Americans; they are at Point 1. Other people think it is not the government's responsibility and that each person should take care of himself; they are at Point 5. Where would you place yourself on this scale, or haven't you made up your mind on this?"
Source: National Opinion Research Center, *General Social Survey*, Spring 1991.

able to work to do so, as a condition for receiving public assistance; this is sometimes called "workfare." Whenever administrators have sought to implement such a rule, they have encountered serious practical difficulties. Jobs that able-bodied welfare recipients are trained to perform may not be available in significant numbers, in the right geographic areas. But Americans continue to endorse this requirement. Another response is to provide in-kind benefits rather than cash payments. People in need are given government-supported medical care, subsidized housing, and food stamps rather than simply bigger welfare checks. The idea is that need will be more directly targeted, and recipients will be less likely to be discouraged from learning to help themselves. Of all the "means-tested" welfare benefits[13] provided by

---

[13]"Means-tested" benefits are those given only to persons meeting certain standards of financial need.

local, state, and national governments in the United States, more than two-thirds are in-kind.

EXTENDING INDIVIDUAL SECURITY AND OPPORTUNITY

The strong commitments in American ideology to individual responsibility and equality of opportunity rather than results have slowed the development of the "welfare state" here. When the U.S. Congress first passed comprehensive social security legislation in 1935, most European countries had long since enacted similar programs: Germany in 1889, England in 1908, and Sweden in 1913. And throughout the twentieth century, U.S. governmental expenditures for public-welfare programs have been a significantly smaller proportion of the country's GDP than comparable programs have been of the GDPs of the European democracies. Despite this overall experience, in a few areas American spending for public welfare is proportionally greater than in Europe. Education is a case in point.

Education. In the latter half of the nineteenth century, primary and secondary education became free, public, and virtually universal in the United States—long before it was thus extended in any other country. Government-assisted mass higher education also came sooner to the United States; today a higher proportion of Americans are enrolled in colleges and universities, many with substantial government assistance, than in other wealthy nations such as West Germany, France, Britain, or Japan. America's educational expenditures, on a per capita basis, have consistently surpassed those of other industrial nations.

Is education a welfare program? Surely, it is closely linked to the idea of public welfare. Through public schools the authority and resources of government are used to make generally available a resource considered essential to personal opportunity and national well-being. Why are Americans less inclined than citizens of other industrial nations to support many governmental welfare initiatives, yet so supportive of programs in education? Public education historically has been an attractive value in the United States because of its close link to individual opportunity. Through access to education, people obtain the means of developing their talents and moving ahead socially and economically. Public spending for education extends the opportunity for individual initiative.

Social Security. During the 1930s, partly as a result of the Great Depression and partly as a more gradual response to new needs attendant upon industrialization and urbanization, many

As the society becomes more and more technological, the financial needs of its educational system increase.
Terrence McCarthy/NYT Pictures

Americans came to feel that expanded governmental welfare efforts were needed and would complement individual efforts. Passage of the Social Security Act in 1935, with such key provisions as Old Age and Survivors Insurance, and Unemployment Compensation, became possible as a result of this shift in public thinking. When Gallup asked a cross-section of Americans nationally in November 1936 whether they favored "the compulsory Old Age Insurance plan, starting in January, which requires employers and workers to make equal contributions to worker's pensions," 68 percent said they did.[14] From this high base, support grew rapidly.

In recent years, Social Security taxes have risen dramatically, because benefit levels have been raised and the proportion of currently employed workers paying into the system has declined relative to the proportion currently drawing benefits. In light of this, questions have been raised as to whether public support might erode. But it has not. The increases in Social Security benefits have been substantial, but few Americans describe them as too high. What is even more striking, given the sharp rise in employee payroll taxes for the program, is that most people do not claim that Social Security taxes are too high. During the debate in the early 1980s over what changes should be made to solve the growing financial problems of the Social Security system, polls repeatedly asked the public which way they wanted to go to bring receipts and expenditures into balance: raising taxes or reducing benefits. The response was always the same: If a choice must be made, raise taxes rather than cut benefits (Figure 15.7).

These responses attest to the prophetic character of President Franklin Roosevelt's observations at the time Social Security was enacted. Responding to the argument that the Social Security tax was relatively regressive compared to the graduated income tax, because many working-class families paid in the same amount as those in high-income brackets, the president observed:

> I guess you're right on the economics, but those taxes [payroll deductions] were never a problem of economics. They are politics all the way through. We put those payroll contributions there

so as to give the contributors a legal, moral, and political right to collect their pensions and their unemployment benefits. With those taxes in there, no damn politician can ever scrap my social security program.[15]

Social Security was not "welfare." Its benefits were to be bought and paid for by individuals to provide for their economic security and well-being. Social Security has never operated like a private annuity or pension program, where the benefits derived are a direct function of contributions made, but Roosevelt's initial idea of setting the system up on the theme of individuals' earning future benefits through regular payroll deductions was a shrewd reading of American values. Workers wanted to "pay their share." In 1938 Gallup asked whether the Social Security law should be changed so that employers pay the whole amount. The idea might have seemed attractive; the prestige of American business was low after the Great Depression, and what worker would not want to be freed from having to make payments and instead have employers foot the whole bill? But only 15 percent of those surveyed favored changing the law to eliminate the tax on individual workers.

The same sense among Americans that Social Security benefits are not "the dole" or "welfare," but something they "own" through their payroll tax deductions, persists today. This accounts for, among other things, the public's willingness to pay high Social Security taxes and the lack of any demand that these taxes be cut. When, for example, in early 1990 the polling firm of Yankelovich Clancy Shulman asked a national sample whether, among various tax proposals, they favored "reducing Social Secu-

[14] Michael E. Schiltz, "Public Attitudes toward Social Security, 1935–1965," *Research Report 33* of the Social Security Administration (Washington, D.C.: Government Printing Office, 1970), p. 18.

[15] Luther Gulick, "Memorandum on Conference with Franklin D. Roosevelt . . . Summer 1941," quoted in Arthur M. Schlesinger, Jr., *The Coming of the New Deal* (Boston: Houghton Mifflin, 1958), pp. 308–9.

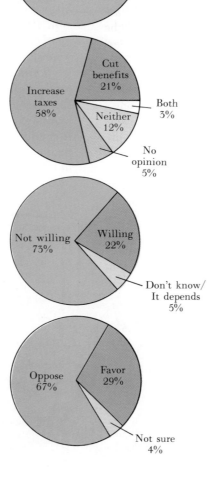

1936

Do you favor the compulsory old age insurance plan, starting in January, which requires employers and workers to make equal contributions to workers' pensions?

Yes 68%
No 32%

1938

Do you think the social security law should be changed to make the employer pay the whole amount of the security tax?

No 85%
Yes 15%

1983

Generally speaking, which would you most like to see the government do in attempting to solve the financial problems of the social security system—increase social security payroll taxes or cut social security benefits?

Increase taxes 58%
Cut benefits 21%
Both 3%
Neither 12%
No opinion 5%

1987

In order to lower the federal budget deficit, would you be willing or not willing to have the government reduce scheduled cost-of-living adjustments for people who receive social security?

Not willing 73%
Willing 22%
Don't know/ It depends 5%

1990

Please tell me if you favor or oppose reducing social security payroll taxes.

Oppose 67%
Favor 29%
Not sure 4%

Source: 1936: Survey by the Gallup Organization, November 6–11, 1936. *1938:* Survey by the Gallup Organization, December 30, 1937–January 4, 1938. *1983:* Survey by ABC News/*Washington Post,* January 18–22, 1983. *1987:* Survey by CBS News/*New York Times,* November 20–24, 1987. *1990:* Survey by Yankelovich Clancy Shulman, January 31–February 1, 1990.

rity payroll taxes," only 29 percent said they did. Cutting the Social Security tax was endorsed by just 28 percent of the youngest group—those 18 to 24—who will be paying large sums for years to come before they begin receiving benefits. Cuts were opposed by every income group.

Social Security is now a broadly supported program for which most Americans are prepared to make sacrifices (in the form of higher payroll taxes) so that a rise in benefits can be sustained. It is seen as essential in providing a measure of security for individuals, such that they can look forward to a retirement income at least sufficient for a basic standard of living. The health-care components of Social Security, added in the 1960s as medical benefits for the elderly (Medicare) and the needy (Medicaid), have found the same high public backing that the Old Age Pension and Assistance programs attained earlier. The possibility of being denied adequate health care because one lacked the money to pay for it, or of finding one's retirement savings wiped out through catastrophic illness, seems incompatible with the sense most Americans now have of their needs and entitlements.

BIG JUMPS IN WELFARE SPENDING

We noted at the outset of this chapter that a lively debate has been going on as to the level of spending on welfare programs—and especially the rapid increase in costs in the big entitlement programs of Social Security and Medicare. Whether the United States is spending more or less than it should for social-welfare programs is a matter on which party and interest-group leaders, social scientists, and others disagree. Differing political values determine "How much is enough?" But it's clear that outlays are now very high by any historic comparison.

In 1950 OASDI disbursed about $1 billion; nearly five decades later, in 1990, expenditures were almost $250 billion. Obviously, the increase is enormous. But how much of it is simply a product of inflation, and how much is real? If spending is expressed in 1980 purchasing power (constant 1980 dollars), all social-welfare expenditures by government—local, state, and national—climbed from just under $74 billion in 1950 to just over $492 billion in 1980.

Box 15.1
The Health Care Crisis

One of the biggest problems facing the nation is escalating health costs. Federal spending for health benefits is rising faster than that for any other major program. And the increases reflect developments that run the entire health care gamut— nongovernmental spending as much as governmental. Commenting on these developments, Katherine Levit and her associates noted recently that

> each year, expenditures for health in the United States consume larger and larger shares of the nation's output. In 1988, health spending totaled nearly $540 billion. . . . In 1988, health spending increased 10.4 percent from the previous year. Spending for health amounted to 11.1 percent of the gross national product (GNP) in 1988, up from 10.8 percent in 1987 and more than twice the share that it occupied in 1960. . . . Despite government and private-sector initiatives in the 1980s to hold down the rate of growth in health spending, real national health expenditures continued to exhibit strong growth, increasing 5.3 percent per year [in real terms, over and above inflation] during the decade.[*]

Getting control of costs in federal health programs is inextricably linked, then, to finding ways to reduce increases all across health care in the United States.

Many Republicans and Democrats agree that mechanisms must be found to restrict the escalating growth of medical costs, without denying people the medical care they need. Increases in expenditures under Medicare and Medicaid are so substantial that liberals and conservatives alike worry they will crowd out other programs. Since there are political limits on how much taxes can be raised, the rapid escalation of medical costs will be borne by relative reductions in other areas of welfare spending. David Swoap, who served as undersecretary in the Department of Health and Human Services in the Reagan administration, has argued that

> any real solution [to the problem of Medicare and Medicaid] must affect our entire health-care delivery system and must attack the primary reason costs are out of control: a health-care industry in this country immune from the forces of the marketplace. Government and insurance coverage insulates consumers and providers from the true cost of care; an open-ended reimbursement system rewards excessive admissions, excessive services and inefficient use of high technology; and a mass of regulations stifles the entrepreneurship and innovation the industry so badly needs to cut waste and create efficiency.[†]

[*] Katherine R. Levit, et al., "National Health Care Spending Trends: 1988," *Health Affairs*, Spring 1990, p. 171.
[†] David B. Swoap, "Medicare Crisis Is Only a Symptom," *Wall Street Journal*, January 3, 1984, p. 30.

FIGURE 15.8   FEDERAL SPENDING UNDER FOUR PRESIDENTS: FORD TO BUSH

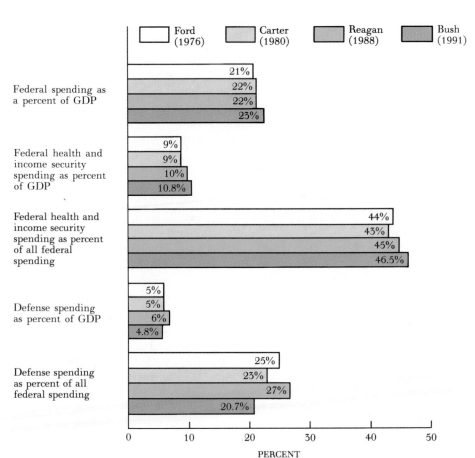

Source: Economic Indicators, November 1985 and February 1992, p. 33. The data are based on the president's last year in office, except in the case of George Bush.

Included in these totals are expenditures for Social Security, education, help for the poor, medical care, and veterans' benefits. Real per capita welfare spending increased by more than 400 percent over this thirty-year span.

Real growth in welfare spending has continued over the last decade, and it has been especially pronounced in the early 1990s. For example, expenditures under federal health programs that assist low-income people (excluding those covered by Medicare) were

$57.8 billion in 1990; two years later, in 1992, they stood at $94.6 billion. These programs, notably Medicaid, have seen their coverage greatly expanded to compensate for the absence of a comprehensive national health-insurance program. Similarly, income security programs, such as AFDC, grew from $146.6 billion in 1990 to $196.0 billion in 1992. (See Figure 15.8). In the 1950s the government was spending far more for defense than for these welfare programs; now, they are claiming more than two-and-a-half times the share defense is—and the latter's share will likely fall further over the next several years, in response to developments in Eastern Europe and the former Soviet Union.

BEYOND "HOW MUCH?" TO "HOW?"

Over the last half-century, Democrats have given stronger backing than Republicans to the expansion of government welfare programs. They can be credited with, or blamed for, the overall design and levels of American public welfare. Today, the parties remain divided philosophically over how much the government should be doing in the welfare area—with the Democrats still inclined to turn more to governmental and the Republicans more to private-sector solutions. While important, however, this partisan split is increasingly overshadowed by complex questions of how the kind of poverty we confront today can be remedied. Analysts on all sides agree that the sources of deprivation today are in many regards quite different from those of the past and require new solutions. "How much should we spend?" is still an issue, of course, but "How can we get results?" is an even bigger one.

ASSISTING THE NEEDY WITHOUT DISCOURAGING WORK

How does one go about setting benefits for the poor that are sufficiently generous but at the same time will not encourage people to stop work and "go on welfare"? Over the last quarter-century, this question has been endlessly debated, and various reforms have been proposed—with results that are to almost no one's satisfaction.

One of the most comprehensive and innovative reform proposals was made during the Nixon administration, under the initiative of Daniel P. Moynihan, then a presidential adviser. Known as the Family Assistance Plan (FAP), it was designed to replace AFDC and provide a basic income for all families—families where the head of the household was working as well as families where that individual was unemployed, and for both single-parent and two-parent families. It would have established a national minimum income below which no family would fall. All FAP recipients who were able to work would be required to do so or to enter job-training programs. Their earnings would be offset against their FAP benefits, but in such a way that, as their job income rose, they would be better off overall than if they were receiving FAP benefits only. Family Assistance was supposed to help reduce the "notch" problem, which involves families with incomes just over the level qualifying them for aid. A family whose income falls below a specific level qualifies for certain cash welfare benefits and for a great variety of in-kind assistance, such as subsidized housing, free medical care, and food stamps. Families with incomes just above the qualifying levels are sometimes worse off than many families who are on welfare and who receive the full mix of cash and in-kind assistance. FAP would help these families just above the "notch" (the working poor) by giving them additional assistance.

But Family Assistance had its own deficiencies, as Moynihan himself subsequently acknowledged.

> The Administration might seriously have hoped that Family Assistance would, subtly but powerfully, so alter incentive structures that the incidence of female-dependent families would decline, but conservatives could point out that under FAP, no less than under AFDC, any low-income family with an employed head could substantially increase the "cash flow" through

its various pockets and pocketbooks by the simple expedient of breaking up and putting the women and children on welfare. Reform indeed![16]

THE FAMILY SUPPORT ACT OF 1988

The House and Senate reached agreement in 1988 on legislation overhauling important elements of the nation's welfare system. It was signed by the president on October 13 of that year. With the goal of getting people off government assistance and into jobs that pay enough so that they can support themselves and their children, the Family Support Act requires states to establish an education, training, and employment program. By 1995 they must enroll at least 20 percent of their AFDC recipients in this program, named JOBS ("Job Opportunities and Basic Skills"). They must also guarantee child care, transportation, and other services to allow welfare recipients to participate. The legislation mandates stricter enforcement of child-support orders: At present, many single-parent, female-headed families are poor and receiving government assistance because the father isn't providing the support the law requires of him.[17]

The costs of the program are borne jointly by the federal government and the states, and a number of state officials have complained that they could find their share only by taking money from other needed programs.

The 1988 legislation is still being phased in and its results considered. In a report assessing progress under JOBS released in March 1992, Jan L. Hager and Irene Lurie concluded that so far the program's promise remains unfulfilled. "For the most part," they wrote, "the hope that states would use JOBS implementation as an opportunity to signal a change in the

[16] Daniel P. Moynihan, *The Politics of a Guaranteed Income: The Nixon Administration and the Family Assistance Plan* (New York: Random House, 1973), p. 446.

[17] For a full description of this complex legislation, see Julie Rovner, "Congress Approves Overhaul of Welfare System," *Congressional Quarterly*, October 8, 1988, pp. 2825–31.

mission of welfare systems or to redefine the social contract has not been realized."[18] On the other hand, a principal architect of the 1988 legislation, Moynihan, now a senator from New York, has pronounced himself generally satisfied by early developments under it. Don't expect too much too fast, the senator urged, noting the complexity of reducing welfare dependency.[19]

NEW WELFARE PROBLEMS OF THE POSTINDUSTRIAL ERA

Senator Moynihan, for a quarter-century a leading figure in trying to amend U.S. programs for the needy, argues, along with a growing number of social scientists, that American welfare policy was developed "to eliminate the particular kinds of poverty and distress associated with industrialism. . . ."[20] For example, many workers, brought from farms into cities and factories, found themselves with no means of support when illness prevented them from working and when advancing age forced them to stop. Programs such as Social Security and Medicare were devised to deal with these industrial-era problems—and they have been hugely successful in doing so. The proportion of the elderly in poverty has been dramatically lowered over the past forty years. Some battles in the war on poverty have been won.

But others have become larger and, if anything, are being lost today. Moynihan notes that, in the postindustrial era, "along with this new form of society has come a new form of

social distress, associated with the 'post-marital' family. As yet we have no explanation for this development, nor any great ground for thinking that we ever will. We do know, however, just how sharp and sudden the change was. It began at mid-century and has not yet stopped."[21]

Moynihan observes that the disintegration of the traditional two-parent family has created a whole new form of poverty—which encompasses many single mothers with young children, whose numbers have increased so dramatically over the past quarter-century. Family structure has become the principal determinant, overall, of how well off, or deprived, people are. Moynihan writes:

> As demographers repeat, children in single-parent families are poor, and there are more and more of them. Thus Sandra Hofferth projects that relatively few children born in 1980 will live to age seventeen with both natural parents. For white children the likelihood of living with both parents fell from 81 percent for those born in the early 1950s to 30 percent for those born in 1980. For black children it dropped from 52 to 6 percent over the same period. . . . A growing number of children—now almost one in four—are born to unmarried women. The increase in illegitimacy has been striking. In 1951 the illegitimacy rate among whites was 1.6 percent; by 1986 it had reached 15.7 percent. More extensive historical series are for some reason still hard to come by, but there can be little doubt of the trend. In 1909 W. E. B. DuBois recorded the percentage of illegitimate births among blacks in Washington, DC, for the years 1870 through 1907; it began at 19 and ended at 21. In 1986 it was 68 percent; in Baltimore it has reached 80 percent. Among blacks nationwide the rate is 61.2 percent. Family structure need not be a principal correlate of child poverty. Wealth and income can accrue in other ways than they now do, but *as* they now do, single-parent families

[18] Jan L. Hagen and Irene Lurie, *Implementing JOBS: Initial State Choices* (State University of New York: The Nelson A. Rockefeller Institute of Government, 1992), p. 22.

[19] Daniel P. Moynihan, interviewed by Jason De Parle, "'88 Welfare Act Is Falling Short, Researchers Say," *The New York Times*, March 30, 1992, pp. A2, A11.

[20] Daniel Patrick Moynihan, "Toward a Post-Industrial Social Policy," *The Public Interest*, Summer 1989, No. 96, p. 17.

[21] Ibid.

FIGURE 15.9   PERCENTAGE OF THE U.S. POPULATION BELOW THE POVERTY LINE, 1978–90

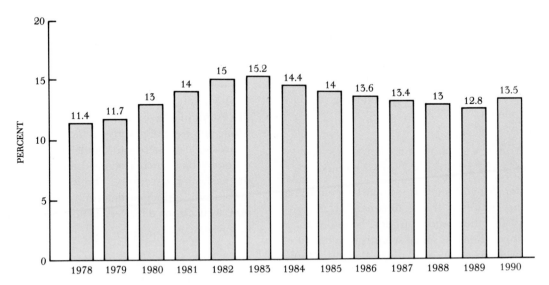

Based on money income only, and adjusted annually for changes in the Consumer Price Index.
Source: U.S. Bureau of the Census, *Money Income and Poverty Status in the United States: 1990,* p. 16.

suffer. Children in female-headed households have a poverty rate of 55 percent. This is five times the poverty rate of children in families that are not headed by single mothers.[22]

Figure 15.9 shows that the overall poverty rate in the United States has been fairly stable since the 1970s. It rose some in the late 1970s, peaked during the recession of 1982–83, fell again through the 1980s, and rose in the early 1990s. But, as Figure 15.10 indicates, the location of the poor has become wildly skewed. As Moynihan pointed out, family structure is the main correlate of poverty. Social scientists and policy makers are struggling to find some answers to these unprecedented problems. One thing is clear, however: There will not be a solution without addressing the massive degree

of family dislocation in the contemporary United States.

As significant as are the statistics on the demographics of poverty, they may not tell the whole story. Poverty and income statistics in the United States are for the most part based on money income only: cash received from employment, Social Security, public assistance and welfare, interest, property. Computing income exclusively in terms of money income mattered little prior to the 1960s because for most people, and the poor in particular, in-kind transfers were not substantial. But as in-kind transfers have expanded greatly in the last quarter-century, methods of computing economic positions that limit themselves to money income have become increasingly inadequate. With regard to the poverty issue, the Census Bureau is now using various calculations that value noncash or in-kind benefits that provide food, housing, and medical assis-

[22] Ibid., p. 22.

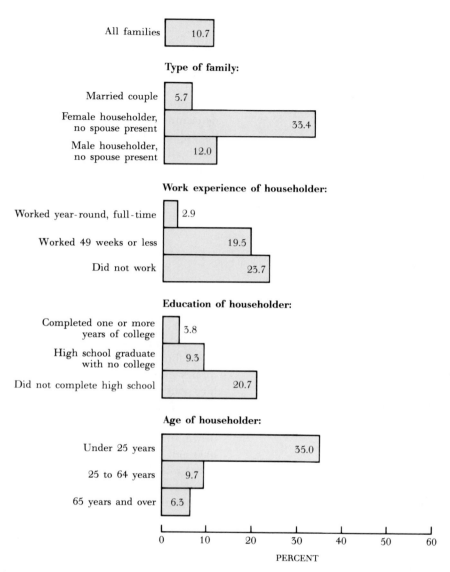

Figure 15.10 Poverty Rates for Families with Selected Characteristics, 1990

All families   10.7

Type of family:
Married couple   5.7
Female householder, no spouse present   33.4
Male householder, no spouse present   12.0

Work experience of householder:
Worked year-round, full-time   2.9
Worked 49 weeks or less   19.5
Did not work   23.7

Education of householder:
Completed one or more years of college   3.8
High school graduate with no college   9.3
Did not complete high school   20.7

Age of householder:
Under 25 years   35.0
25 to 64 years   9.7
65 years and over   6.3

0   10   20   30   40   50   60
PERCENT

Source: U.S. Bureau of the Census, Income Statistics Branch and Poverty and Wealth Statistics Branch, 1992, unpublished data.

tance. These data are still rarely cited in the press.[23] Table 15.5 shows all benefits provided by the federal government for low-income persons—cash and in-kind combined.

[23] U.S. Bureau of the Census, *Estimates of Poverty Including the Value of Noncash Benefits, Technical Paper II,* p. 57.

It should be noted that the distortion resulting from omitting in-kind transfers is not limited to income data on the poor. Census Bureau studies have not attempted to quantify all of the in-kind benefits received by middle- and upper-income families, but they have documented that these are enormous. For example,

TABLE 15.5 BENEFITS (CASH AND IN-KIND) FOR
LOW-INCOME PERSONS, BY PROGRAM AREA, 1980–
88 (IN MILLIONS OF DOLLARS)

	1980	1985	1988
Medical care	19,214	27,737	38,466
Cash aid	19,621	24,969	32,181
Food benefits	12,899	19,362	20,247
Housing benefits	8,389	14,113	14,701
Education aid	4,412	9,516	9,966
Jobs and training	8,625	3,895	3,748
Services	3,178	3,551	4,492
Energy assistance	1,738	2,261	1,764
Total	78,075	105,404	125,565

Source: Library of Congress, Congressional Research Service, "Cash and Non-Cash Benefits for Persons with Limited Income," reports issued in 1982, 1988, and 1989.

many companies pay all or part of the health insurance premiums of their employees, thus conferring substantial in-kind medical benefits. By excluding in-kind transfers, income statistics for all groups of Americans are made seriously incomplete.

GROWTH AND WELFARE: THE LINKAGE AND THE CHALLENGE

Politicians in both parties like to say these days that the best way to improve the welfare of Americans, including the neediest of our population, is to expand economic growth. And here they are unquestionably right. Growth means higher real incomes, more jobs, and more resources to be devoted to various social needs.

But if an expanding economy is ultimately the best welfare policy, achieving it is, as we have seen, no easy matter. Economists are any-

thing but agreed as to the best approach. Partisan conflict over fiscal policy often leads to results—such as the huge federal deficits of recent years—that are both unintended and unwanted. And then, of course, much of what determines economic performance lies outside the sphere of government influence together. Given all this, getting the economic policy best suited to promoting growth, and thus enhancing the public welfare, is always a most demanding challenge.

SUMMARY

Political economy involves the uses of governmental power to affect economic goals. The areas of economic policies attempted by American government include regulation of private-sector businesses; controls over the supply of money and credit, which is the field of monetary policy; and efforts to adjust levels of taxation and expenditures, which is fiscal policy.

Committed to the general ideal of a growing private-property–based economy, Americans have not engaged much in debates over basic ends; rather, questions of what are the best means, of "how to do it," have predominated. Prompted by the conditions of the Great Depression, leaders and citizens alike swung to a new view of what arrangements of the political economy would best effectuate growing prosperity. A much-expanded role for government figured prominently in the new perspective. John Maynard Keynes, a distinguished English economist, offered prescriptions that proved enormously influential and that, in the incomplete and imperfect way of democratic politics, came to underlie the claim of the Democrats as the "party of prosperity."

By the late 1960s, however, a new set of economic conditions had begun to disrupt the Keynesian view of the world. Inflation had replaced deflation as the predominant challenge to sustained economic prosperity. Major growth of government taxing, spending, and regulation appeared to require new responses. The mainstream of economic thinking shifted. This shift is evident in the work of professional economists and, as well, in the outlook and expectations of the general public.

Shifts in the economy and in thinking about how it is best managed are now reflected in the debates among the various schools of professional economic judgment. Monetarists put a singular emphasis on controlling the money supply and the price of money (interest rates) to secure a growing, inflation-free economy. Supply-siders emphasize the importance of fiscal policy, especially the stimulation of work incentives and economic growth through large cuts in the marginal tax rates: what proportion taxpayers give the government of the last dollars they earn. "Mainstream" conservatives stress balanced budgets and restraints on federal spending.

Advocates of industrial policy share the traditional liberal view that a large measure of governmental intervention in the economy is desirable, but they want government to pursue new means of stimulating economic growth, borrowing on the successes Japan has had. Keynesians continue to emphasize using fiscal policy to achieve the economic expansion that can sustain an enlargement of social-welfare programs.

Among the governmental agencies that play key roles in formulating and executing economic policy, the Federal Reserve System is especially important. The Fed is the central bank of the United States. Its Federal Open-Market Committee is charged with taking actions that determine the size and rate of expansion of the nation's money supply.

Over the last half-century, the economy of the United States and of other industrial nations has expanded. The increased capacities of modern economies mean that most people expect more consumer goods than preceding generations; they also lead people to expect more help from government, such as the assurance through Social Security and Medicare of basic retirement income and health care. Welfare is sometimes taken to include only governmental efforts to help the needy. But the majority of public-welfare programs, including Social Security and Medicare, are directed to all economic groups, not just the poor.

American ideology puts special emphasis on individual responsibility and insists that American society offers unusual opportunities to those who apply themselves. Because of this, the United States has been less inclined than other industrial democracies to back collective governmental efforts at promoting public welfare. But government action to create a climate where individual opportunity is expanded and individual interests are more fully realized, and to help people who through no lack of individual effort find themselves in need, has received strong public support.

Federalism exerts a major influence on American welfare programs. Though some of the big programs are funded and administered exclusively through national agencies—veterans' benefits, Social Security, and Medicare— many others involve partnership of the federal and state governments. This is true of Medicaid, AFDC, food stamps, and unemployment compensation. In most other democracies public-welfare programs are run by national agencies that impose uniform standards and benefits, but in the United States their administration is often decentralized and their provisions vary from state to state.

Since the New Deal, the rate of welfare spending has risen rapidly in the United States, far faster than the overall economy has expanded. Thus welfare expenditures have accounted for a steadily expanding share of the nation's GDP.

Increasingly, the key question with regard to programs for the poor is how to accomplish goals that leaders of both parties want but do not know how to achieve. New forms of poverty, accruing in large measure from what Senator Daniel Patrick Moynihan calls the "postmarital family," are not effectively addressed by welfare programs developed to meet the problems of the earlier industrial era.

FOR FURTHER STUDY

Council of Economic Advisers, for the Joint Economic Committee of Congress. *Economic Indicators.* Washington, D.C.: Government Printing Office, published monthly. Contains the latest monthly statistics on the gross domestic product, national income, personal consumption, and corporate profits; employment and wages, industrial production, and business activities; prices; money, credit, and security markets; federal finance, international finance, and business transactions.

Harrington, Michael. *The Other America.* Baltimore, Md.: Penguin Books, 1981; first published, 1962. An important and influential analysis of the nature of poverty in the United States in the early 1960s.

Keynes, John Maynard. *The General Theory of Employment, Interest, and Money.* New York: Harcourt, Brace, 1965; first published, 1936. The enormously influential study that provided the intellectual underpinnings for an expanded governmental role in economic life in the United States and other democracies in the years following the Great Depression.

Moynihan, Daniel P. *The Politics of a Guaranteed Income: The Nixon Administration and the Family Assistance Plan.* New York: Random House, 1973. A brilliant account of efforts at welfare reform in the Nixon administration, in which the author played a leading role. Also by Moynihan, "Toward a Post-Industrial Social Policy," *The Public Interest*, No. 96 (Summer 1989), pp. 16–27.

Office of Management and Budget (OMB). *Budget of the United States Government.* Washington, D.C.: Government Printing Office, each fiscal year. These basic documents contain the yearly budget message of the president to Congress and extensive tables setting forth the administration's proposal for the entire federal government for the next fiscal year.

OPTIONAL COMPUTER EXERCISES

for *The Ladd Election ANALYZER*

HOW VOTERS ASSESS THE ECONOMY

What did American voters have to say about the condition of the nation's economy at the time of the 1992 election? Choose "Condition of the nation's economy" from the "Policy views" menu as the question to analyze. Did the young and old differ in their assessments? Did high-income and low-income voters differ? How great were the differences by race. What proportion of Republicans who thought that the economy was not doing very well or was doing badly voted for Clinton? For Perot? What proportion of independents with similar views about the economy voted for Clinton? For Perot?

Chapter *16*

AMERICA IN THE WORLD

Who could have dreamed that there would no longer be a superpower called the Soviet Union? Americans who have lived through the tensions of the cold war, from the end of World War II into the 1980s, continue to ask this question in wonder. The changes in the international order of the last few years are among the most sweeping in modern history. Still, those who believed that the world would become a peaceful place following the dissolution of the USSR and the warming of relations between the United States and the countries that once made up our great rival will find their hopes disappointed. The Persian Gulf War and the continuing ethnic violence in Eastern Europe are powerful reminders that the sources of international conflict are manifold.

The revolutionary shifts have come so rapidly that the conditions obtaining just four years ago now seem like ancient history. We need to remind ourselves forcibly that New Year's Day 1989 saw the Communist party of the Soviet Union firmly entrenched, as it had been since it came to power in the October 1917 revolution, as the sole, unchallenged repository of political power in the country. Across Eastern Europe, Communist regimes established by Soviet military power after World War II and maintained by that power subsequently, continued in seemingly firm control. Close observers saw developments—notably the commitment of Mikhail Gorbachev's regime to greater political openness (*glasnost*) and a restructuring of Soviet institutions—indicating that the region's future would not be a mere continuation of the recent past. Things were changing at last. Nonetheless, no one expected the shifts to occur with such reach, force, and rapidity.

In the winter and spring of 1989, confronting an escalating economic crisis and with Soviet consent, Poland's Communist leadership engaged in negotiations with the Solidarity labor movement, led by Lech Walesa, that culminated in a power-sharing agreement: The Communists for the first time gave up their monopoly of power. On June 4, 1989, Poland held parliamentary elections in which the Communist candidates were routed. On August 24, Tadeusz Mazowiecki, a leader of the Solidarity movement, was approved by the new parliament as prime minister, the first non-Communist ever to head a Soviet-bloc nation. On October 18, with the East German Communist regime tottering, with tens of thousands of its citizens fleeing to the West, Erich Honecker, the long-time East German dictator, was pushed out as head of his country's Communist party. On November 9, East Germany allowed free travel between East and West Berlin. This opening of the Berlin Wall has come to emblematize the revolution that swept Eastern Europe. In November and December 1989 it was the turn of the Czechoslovac regime to topple; on December 29, Vaclav Havel, a dissident playwright and leading opposition figure, was sworn in as president of Czechoslovakia. Also in December, the hardline regime of Nicolae Ceausescu was overthrown in Romania, and Ceausescu and his wife were executed.

In March 1990, free elections were held in East Germany: Again, the Communists were routed and conservative parties allied to the party of West German Chancellor Helmut Kohl were victorious. In late March, in Hungary's first free election in forty-five years, anti-Communist parties dominated. On July 1, the economic merger of the two Germanys became effective, as East Germany adopted the West German mark as its currency and moved toward a free market economy. And on October 3, 1990, just one year after the Honecker regime collapsed, the full political reunification of Germany was achieved.

The Soviet Union itself became the next center of revolutionary change. On June 13, 1991, Boris Yeltsin won a presidential election in the Russian republic, becoming the first popularly elected leader in Russian history. On August 18, seeing control slipping away from them and the Soviet Union disintegrating, hard-

President of the Russian Republic Boris Yeltsin, now the most powerful leader in the former Soviet Union, meeting with President George Bush in Washington, D.C., in June of 1992.

liners attempted to seize power. Yeltsin's Russian government, much of the public, and key sectors of the army rallied in opposition to this coup attempt, however, and by August 21, it had collapsed. Though he, too, had opposed the coup, Mikhail Gorbachev found his remaining powers as Soviet leader greatly weakened. Ministers in Yeltsin's Russian Federation were appointed to run key Soviet ministries in the aftermath of the failed coup attempt.

On August 31 the Communist apparatus, deeply implicated in the attempted coup, was declared illegal. And with its collapse went the one major instrument of Soviet identity. One republic after another proclaimed its independence, and on December 21, 1991, leaders of eleven of the twelve republics signed an agreement proclaiming a new loose confederation—the Commonwealth of Independent States (CIS). Russia, the largest and most powerful republic in the Soviet system, inherited much of the old Union's military might. On December 21, 1991, Mikhail Gorbachev, the last leader of the USSR, resigned. Thus did the Soviet Union meet its end.

UNDERSTANDING THE REVOLUTIONS OF THE LATE EIGHTIES AND EARLY NINETIES

Virtually all Americans take great satisfaction in these developments. People across much of Eastern Europe are enjoying greater freedoms than at any time since their Communist regimes came to power, and cold war tensions have greatly eased. But apart from taking satisfaction, we need to try to understand why these revolutions occurred when and as they did—

and to understand their implications for American foreign and defense policy.

THE DECLINE OF THE SOVIET UNION

While events moved quickly in the breakup of the Soviet state, the conditions under which these events transpired were a long time in the making. As the 1980s proceeded, recognition grew among the Soviet leadership that their system was failing. They saw their economy falling further and further behind the economies of all the advanced industrial nations and losing ground as well to such newly industrializing countries as South Korea and Taiwan. Many in the West had long argued that only modern societies based on individual choice and freedom could manage themselves satisfactorily. But this sense that, quite apart from its intrinsic value, only freedom provides the individual motivation and creativity necessary to a modern economy, had not found acceptance within the Soviet Union prior to the 1980s. Since 1917 the USSR has stood as an exemplar of the chief alternative to liberal individualism, adhering to a philosophy that extolled extreme concentration of authority in the state. As recently as the 1950s and the 1960s, the idea that the Soviet system was a great success, and that it provided the proper model for much of the developing world, found considerable acceptance. The system's problems were often explained as the result of turbulence during the early revolutionary era, for example, or the devastation wrought by World War II and the immense tasks of recovery countries faced in the decades after the war.

By the 1980s, however, such explanations had become increasingly unsatisfactory. The magnitude of the failure of the Soviet economic system in comparison with industrial democracies and other market-centered economies had become evident. By the late 1980s neither

Shoppers line up outside a Moscow grocery store hoping to purchase products that have been in short supply.

the Soviet economic failure nor its sources were doubted by Soviet planners any more than by capitalism's prime proponents. On economic grounds alone critical sections of Soviet leadership decided that the system needed a drastic overhaul. For this, Western help was essential.

The growing sense of collapse within the Soviet Union was not based exclusively on economic analysis. Some of the most striking conclusions emerged from assessments of the country's social fabric. Tatyana Zaslavskaya, who directed a major polling center in the old Soviet Union and now does so in the Russian Republic, has been called the world's most influential sociologist, given her access to the political leadership of her country and the apparent use the country has made of her center's studies. At a spring 1990 meeting of experts in public opinion and survey research, Zaslavskaya argued that the core problem of the Soviet Union wasn't its economy, but the basic organization and ethos of its social order. "The

five years of *perestroika* [that is, from 1985 when Gorbachev assumed power, to 1990 when Zaslavskaya delivered her paper] have already demonstrated," she stated, "that not only the command-administrative system of economic control but the entire social system should be dismantled."[1]

When large segments of the populace lose faith not only in a system's performance but in its essential values as well, a legitimacy crisis occurs. The Soviet Union depicted by Zaslavskaya's studies was in the midst of a full-blown legitimacy crisis. Only 20 to 25 percent of Soviet citizens, she found in an early 1990 Soviet survey, were "consistent supporters" of the Communist party, while "principled critics" comprised 35 to 40 percent. The Soviet system

---

[1] T. I. Zaslavskaya, "Perestroika and Public Opinion," unpublished paper presented to the annual meeting of the American Association for Public Opinion Research, Lancaster, Pennsylvania, May 17–20, 1990.

of income distribution was called fair or just by only 3 percent of all respondents countrywide and basically unjust by 53 percent, with the other 45 percent criticizing it less severely. One question that Zaslavskaya's center posed in that same survey illustrates strikingly how much public confidence in the regime's institutions and values had eroded. "Of interest," she noted, "are people's ideas of for whom and in what relations our country can serve as an example. Over half (55 percent) replied that 'for no one and in nothing,' which testifies to an extreme degree of alienation from the social system."

Zaslavskaya argued that the corruptions of the Soviet system had done far more than anger the public. "One of the important barriers on the road to revitalization of our society (and the one hardest to surmount) is the loss by a large proportion of the population of the most elementary moral criteria. This manifests itself not only in that theft, swindling, and violence have become so widespread, but also in that people . . . so easily justify and forgive such acts." Here the state has played a big part as teacher. The "typical features" of its behavior toward its citizens, Zaslavskaya argued, have long been "unreliability in keeping promises, cruelty, treachery, callousness, mendacity, and other 'qualities' which, taken as a whole, mean immorality." With the old order delegitimized, without a new one fully established, public opinion in the old Soviet Union is enormously volatile and unpredictable. Zaslavskaya characterized this public sentiment in terms of its "transient character, its instability, morbid sensibility and explosiveness."[2]

THE POWER OF EXAMPLE

Gaining currency in the 1950s and the 1960s, the "domino theory" asserted that if one key country falls to Communist control, others might then topple. In the 1960s, advocates of this theory argued that a Communist triumph in Vietnam would destroy the credibility of U.S. alliance guarantees for other small nations, emboldening Communist challenges and setting in motion a string of collapses. This reasoning underlay the U.S. decision to commit large-scale military forces in Vietnam in 1965.

The notion of a domino theory became wholly caught up in the debate over the rightness or wrongness of American policy in Indochina. Critics ridiculed it as a propaganda effort to justify U.S. intervention. But however misstated and misapplied the theory may have been with regard to Vietnam, under some circumstances there is a domino effect. Let's try to recast the idea in terms of what we have learned from developments in the period from 1989 to 1991.

The domino effect that we have been witnessing involves expectations and example. In today's "global village" of pervasive electronic communication, the events in one country immediately attain international currency. Thus developments in Poland and Hungary in the spring of 1989 instantly altered expectations in East Germany and Czechoslovakia and encouraged the revolutions there in the fall. Romanians were similarly influenced by other Communist-bloc examples, as were the various national groups in the USSR. Once the revolutionary surge began, then, it created much of its own momentum. It altered expectations, encouraging people in the affected countries to take action that they previously would have deemed futile.

THE GORBACHEV FACTOR

The leadership team assembled by Mikhail Gorbachev after he came to power in 1985 committed itself to major changes in the Soviet Union. No account of the revolutions of 1989–91 can fail to recognize the independent role of

[2] Ibid.

Mikhail Gorbachev, the last leader of the Soviet Union, was instrumental in bringing about the dramatic changes that have taken place in Eastern Europe and the Soviet Union. Here, in May 1992, Gorbachev speaks at Westminster College in Fulton, Missouri. This is where British Prime Minister Winston Churchill delivered his "Iron Curtain" speech, a speech in which he brilliantly assessed the international behavior the Soviet Union would exhibit in the post–World War II years.

Gorbachev's leadership. Broad structural developments—such as those affecting the Soviet economy, and the cumulative impact of Western foreign and defense policies—surely played essential roles in promoting change. But especially with regard to its timing and the remarkably peaceful way in which the end of the Soviet empire was achieved, Gorbachev's policies were certainly critical. The Soviet decision, clearly communicated in 1989, not to use the Red Army to maintain its East European empire set in motion a wave of demands for freedom and autonomy across Eastern Europe and in the constituent republics of the Soviet Union itself.

U.S. FOREIGN POLICY SINCE WORLD WAR II

Our study of the American party system and other political institutions has revealed long periods of continuity, interrupted on occasion by some fundamental change that initiates a new course. Foreign policy can be similarly marked off into a few periods. What some are beginning to call this post–cold war period in foreign policy may prove to be such a watershed. World War II was another great watershed; U.S. policy after the war was significantly different than it had been before.

EMERGENCE AS A WORLD POWER

The most important factors changing the course of U.S. foreign policy after World War II involve national power—specifically, the major increases in U.S. power and the sharp decline in the position of the three principal international powers of the prewar era: Germany, France, and Great Britain. The bases of American influence in international affairs were not all suddenly erected in the 1940s. After the Civil War, the United States industrialized rapidly; by 1900 its industrial economy was the world's largest. These productive capabilities did not automatically mandate an expanded international role, but they were an important resource for it. For one thing, American productivity could be harnessed for military production.

In 1946, the major European states were grappling with political problems resulting from their having been ravaged by two major wars in just three decades. Quite apart from their economic capacity, their resolve to sustain world leadership had weakened. All of the European nations needed desperately to turn inward and reconstruct their own societies. While large, the American losses in World War II did not begin to approach those of the European powers. With its economy now dominant and its political will sustained, the United States was thrust into the power vacuum left by the European collapse.

The guiding approach to U.S. foreign policy prior to World War II has often been called **isolationist.** The term is misleading, however. America was never truly isolated from world affairs. **Unilateralist** is a more accurate description. George Washington thought we could and should avoid getting drawn into the European system of alliances, and for a long time American foreign policy adhered to this plan. Given the technology of the nineteenth and early twentieth centuries, the physical distance

of the United States from Europe permitted it to "go it alone." But more than anything else, American unilateralism was sustained by the vast commitment Great Britain made to maintaining a world balance of power.[3] After World War II, however, Britain was no longer able to play this role. Among the Western democracies, only the United States could sustain a new balance in the postwar world.

The new course of American foreign policy after World War II, then, was not simply a position taken by leaders who happened to be in power at the time. It reflected the structural position the United States had assumed in the international community.

CONTAINMENT

The words "balance of power" have a ring of nineteenth-century Europe, conjuring up a picture of nations forming elaborate alliances to prevent their opponents from getting too strong and threatening their interests. The words also suggest a kind of international amorality: "power politics" rather than a commitment to moral purposes. Yet early efforts to maintain a balance of power were by no means without large moral objectives. When Great Britain maintained the European balance for a century after Napoleon's defeat at Waterloo in 1815, it provided the basis for an extended period of peace.

After World War II, the United States set about performing, in its own way, the balance-of-power role that had been Britain's. America's effort was called *containment*. The United States committed itself to "containing" the Soviet Union and Communist expansion. If one had to pick a date for the inauguration of U.S. containment policy, February 21, 1947,

---

[3] John Spanier, *American Foreign Policy since World War II*, 11th ed. (Washington, D.C.: Congressional Quarterly Press, 1988), p. 3.

Box 16.1
The President: Chief Foreign Policy Maker

In no other area of U.S. public policy does the scope of the president's formal authority or the extent of his day-to-day influence approach what it is in the foreign and defense sphere. When a foreign crisis occurs or negotiations proceed on an arms limitation treaty, a president can and often does plausibly claim to articulate transcending national interests. Critics of his approach usually grant him greater room to maneuver than they would on any domestic issue.

The contemporary importance of the American military establishment in the country's foreign relations has made the president's constitutional position as commander in chief unusually influential. The president alone has a mandate to act with the dispatch and force that national security requires. President Kennedy acted forcefully, imposing a military blockade during the missile crisis of 1962, when the Soviet Union placed offensive missiles in Cuba, just 90 miles from the U.S. mainland. President Reagan sent U.S. troops to the Caribbean island of Grenada in October 1983 to prevent the establishment of a Soviet-bloc military base on the island and to protect 1,000 Americans, mostly students, who were in residence there. And Bush sent U.S. forces into Panama in December 1989 against the Noriega government and into the Middle East in 1990 following Iraq's invasion of Kuwait.

Much less stands between the president and decisive action in foreign policy than elsewhere. Executive agencies and Congress play key roles, but they typically lack the capacity to block determined presidential initiatives as they can in domestic policy spheres. Interest groups try to shape foreign policy, but they are far less numerous or muscular than their counterparts in the fields of social welfare or economic management. In part the idea of a "national interest," as distinct from contending group interests, is in reality more imposing in foreign policy than anywhere else.

[This and subsequent boxes—on the Department of State (p. 517), NATO (p. 519), the National Security Council (p. 523), the Intelligence Services (p. 524–25), and the Department of Defense (p. 530)—describe the major post–World War II foreign-policy institutions.]

would be a good choice. On that date the first secretary of the British embassy in Washington handed U.S. officials two notes from his government concerning Greece and Turkey. They both stated that Britain could no longer meet its traditional responsibilities in those two countries. Since Greece and Turkey were on the verge of collapse, Britain's decision meant that a Soviet breakthrough in the area could be stopped only by a major American commitment.

American leaders felt that they had to act. President Harry Truman appeared before a

Box 16.2
The Department of State

Among the many departments and agencies of the "foreign affairs government" of the United States, the Department of State bears the broadest formal responsibilities. Its work includes representing the United States in roughly fifty different international organizations, conducting bilateral negotiations on matters large and small with other countries, and formulating policy recommendations in virtually every facet of U.S. foreign relations. To discharge these responsibilities, the department operated (as of January 1990) a network of 275 posts throughout the world including 144 embassies, 9 missions, 71 consulates general, and 26 consulates. Extensive though this seems, the State Department is actually quite small compared to most of the other departmental bureaucracies of the executive branch. It has a staff of roughly 25,500 worldwide, which makes it a small cabinet department. The State Department's budget in 1991 was 4.4 billion.

Three other agencies involved in foreign affairs are loosely attached to the State Department: the Arms Control and Disarmament Agency (ACDA), which conducts research on arms control and disarmament policy and negotiates on these subjects with other countries: the United States Information Agency (USIA), which handles cultural and informational activities directed at overseas audiences; and the International Development Cooperation Agency (IDCA), which is responsible for coordinating U.S. economic assistance to developing countries. The Agency for International Development (AID) is the principal operating arm of the IDCA, administering the country's major bilateral aid programs.

joint session of Congress on March 12, 1947, to announce a major departure from historic American foreign policy. Setting forth what came to be known as the Truman Doctrine, the president argued that the United States must be "willing to help free peoples to maintain their institutions and their national integrity against aggressive movements that seek to impose upon them totalitarian regimes." To meet the immediate need, he urged Congress to appropriate $400 million for economic and military assistance to Greece and Turkey. He also asked authorization to send both American civilian and military personnel to help those

two countries rebuild their domestic economies and strengthen their armies.

In July 1947, a young U.S. State Department official, George Kennan, set forth the broad rationale for the general approach to the USSR that the United States and its allies were beginning to implement. The main element of that policy, Kennan wrote, must be "a long-term, patient but firm and vigilant containment of Russian expansive tendencies. . . . The Soviet pressure against the free institutions of the western world is something that can be contained by the adroit and vigilant application of counter-force at a series of constantly shifting geographical and political points. . . ."[4] The object here was more than protecting democratic governments in Western Europe. It was to convince the Soviets, ultimately, that a change in policy direction was in their interest.

> The Soviet thesis not only implies complete lack of control by the west over its own economic destiny, it likewise assumes Russian unity, discipline, and patience over an infinite period. Let us bring this apocalyptic vision down to earth, and suppose that the western world finds the strength and resourcefulness to contain Soviet power for a period of ten to fifteen years. What does that spell for Russia itself?[5]

Expansion frustrated and hopes for continuing international successes thwarted, the Soviet Union would gradually submit, as Kennan and his colleagues saw it, to internally induced changes, as its population sought greater freedom and opportunity.

> Thus the future of Soviet power may not be by any means as secure as Russian capacity for self-delusion would make it appear to the men in the Kremlin. That they can keep power themselves, they have demonstrated. That they can quietly and easily turn it over to others remains to be proved. Meanwhile the hardships of their rule and the vicissitudes of international life have taken a heavy toll on the strength and hopes of the great people on whom their power rests. . . . *The possibility remains (and in the opinion of this writer it is a strong one) that Soviet power, like the capitalist world of its conception, bears within it the seeds of its own decay, and that the sprouting of these seeds is well advanced.*[6]

We are often told of the failures of public policy. But policies sometimes succeed. Against the backdrop of the extraordinary changes that have swept Eastern Europe and the former Soviet Union, we need to remind ourselves that the "containment" policy Kennan expounded as a State Department official—and which the generation of American foreign policy makers to which he belonged managed to achieve— has been a spectacular success. Rarely has any piece of writing so captured the intellectual basis of a successful policy as did George Kennan's famous 1947 article.

THE MARSHALL PLAN AND NATO

In the wake of World War II, misery was widespread throughout devastated Europe. On humanitarian grounds alone, there was a strong case for a program of American assistance. But America's preference for a democratic Europe, and its security needs in the area, also demanded action. The most important response of the United States was the initiation of a recovery program commonly known as the Marshall Plan. It was first set forth in 1947 and named for the man who announced it, Secretary of State George C. Marshall. Through the Marshall Plan, the United States gave Western European nations over $12 billion dollars— more than half of which went to Britain, France, and West Germany. This effort was extraordinarily successful; by 1950, Western Europe was already exceeding its prewar levels of production.

As the economic program proceeded, so did the promotion of a military alliance, spurred by Soviet actions. In February 1948, the Soviets engineered the overthrow of an independent democratic government in Czechoslovakia, putting that country under Communist domination. In July 1948, the Soviets imposed a

---

[4]George F. Kennan, "The Sources of Soviet Conduct," *Foreign Affairs*, 25 (July 1947), p. 576.
[5]Ibid.
[6]Ibid., p. 580. Emphasis added.

Box 16.3
North Atlantic Treaty Organization (NATO)

FOUNDING: On April 4, 1949, the North Atlantic Treaty was signed in Washington, D.C. On July 21, 1949, the treaty was ratified by the U.S. Senate. Article 5 of the treaty provided that "an armed attack against one or more . . . shall be considered an attack against them all."

ORIGINAL MEMBERS: Belgium, Canada, Denmark, France, Great Britain, Iceland, Italy, Luxembourg, the Netherlands, Norway, Portugal, and the United States.

MEMBERSHIP CHANGES: Greece and Turkey joined in 1952, West Germany in 1954, Spain in 1982. In 1966, France pulled out of the integrated NATO military structure, although it stayed on as an alliance member.

HEADQUARTERS: Paris 1952–67; Brussels 1967 to the present.

NATO STRUCTURE: The senior decision-making organ of the alliance is the Atlantic Council, comprising representatives of all 16 member nations. The chairman of the council is the secretary general of NATO. That post is currently held by Manfred Woerner of Germany. The secretary general oversees the NATO Secretariat, which is in Brussels, and such other NATO bodies as the Defense Planning Committee and the Nuclear Planning Group. The senior military organ is its Military Committee, which is made up of senior officers of 15 member nations. France is not included. This committee has three commands—Allied Command Europe, Allied Command Atlantic, and Allied Command Channel.

U.S. FORCES: In the wake of the Soviet collapse, U.S. troop deployment to NATO forces in Europe is being sharply reduced but not, at least in the immediate future, eliminated. President Bush in early 1992 called for 150,000 military personnel to be stationed in Europe through the mid-1900s, although some members of Congress were pushing for a contingent of only 75,000 to 100,000.

blockade on Berlin, seeking to drive the Western powers out of that city. In response to such military acts, the United States and the democracies of Western Europe established a military alliance, the North Atlantic Treaty Organization (NATO). The North Atlantic Treaty was signed in April 1949, and ratified by the U.S. Senate three months later.

STRONG RHETORIC, CAUTIOUS POLICY

At times in the late 1940s and 1950s, some American political leaders sounded a call for something more than simply "containing" Soviet expansion. In the 1952 presidential campaign, the out-of-power Republicans attacked the

Democrats on the issue of containment, arguing that it conceded the initiative to the Soviet Union. As John Foster Dulles—then the leading Republican foreign policy spokesman—saw it, containment aimed only at preserving the status quo and thus was "negative, futile, and immoral." The objective of American foreign policy, Dulles argued, should be not to coexist indefinitely with a Communist threat but rather to eliminate the threat. American power should be committed to a rollback of Soviet power.

In fact, however, the Republican administration of Dwight Eisenhower, elected in 1952, continued for the most part the basic approach developed in 1947–49. The Korean War was concluded with a peace agreement that left in place the situation that prevailed before North Korea's 1950 attack on South Korea: a Communist regime allied with the Soviet Union in power north of the 38th parallel and a non-Communist regime allied to the United States in the south. More importantly, the Eisenhower administration did almost nothing to challenge Soviet control in Eastern Europe, not even in the face of the brutal use of Soviet military power in crushing the October–November 1956 revolt in Hungary against that country's Soviet-dominated regime. The United States stuck to a cautious policy of containment even though its rhetoric at times suggested an anti-Communist crusade.

One reason for this was that the American people never wanted a crusade. The public was frustrated by the Soviet Union's behavior, as in stifling national independence in Eastern Europe, but it resisted measures that would lead to war.[7] This approach seems to have

[7] See William Schneider, "Conservatism, Not Interventionism: Trends in Foreign Policy Opinion, 1974–1982," in Kenneth Dye, et al., *Eagle Defiant: United States Foreign Policy in the 1980s* (Boston: Little Brown, 1983), p. 34.

characterized American opinion since the Second World War.

VIETNAM: THE MISAPPLICATION OF CONTAINMENT

Given this attitude on the part of the American people, to win wide public support American power had to be carefully and selectively applied, distinguishing between cases vital to national security and cases not so, and taking into account the human and material costs that would be incurred in any intervention. These strictures on costs were observed fairly carefully until the mid-1960s, when the administration of Lyndon Johnson committed a half-million American soldiers to a land war 9,000 miles from the continental United States, in an area (Indochina) that was undeveloped economically, without resources that mattered to the industrial world, and that lacked strategic location. Lasting longer than any other military conflict in U.S. history, the Vietnam War claimed the lives of some 50,000 American soldiers, as well as hundreds of thousands of Vietnamese, and it drained billions of dollars in economic and military resources.

The question of costs had not been carefully considered. The United States did not start this war; it sought, not to subjugate anyone, but rather to prevent the regime in North Vietnam from toppling the regime in South Vietnam. Even with the best motives, however, democracies cannot fight ten-year wars in which they are party to great destruction in areas remote from their immediate national interests, without facing serious repercussions. In the United States, the Vietnam War sparked bitter domestic divisions, including massive protests on American college and university campuses. It created a domestic political situation that preoccupied and crippled two presidencies,

Vietnam.

Lyndon Johnson's and Richard Nixon's. Begun to attest to the strength of American resolve in containing Communist aggression, the Vietnam War shook that resolve more fundamentally than any other event.

Even now, more than a decade and a half after the United States withdrew from Indochina, the debate continues over why we intervened and what the lessons of the war for future American policy actually are. Two separate questions were at issue: first, whether the objectives and view of the world that led American officials to bring the country into the war were sound; and second, whether the immediate action and strategy were appropriate.

The position defended by Lyndon Johnson's administration held that the long-standing policy of containment was correct and that the U.S. military intervention in Vietnam was a necessary application of it. A second position objected both to the general vision and to the specific action. For those who held this view, containment was a flawed idea. It relied too much on the use of American military power, and it was too inclined to fix responsibility for international tensions on the Soviet Union and to overlook the responsibility of the United States. To those who held this second view, the American engagement in Vietnam represented a bad application of a bad general policy. But from the beginning of heavy U.S. involvement in Vietnam, some held a third position: The containment policy was generally sound, but it was misapplied in Vietnam because the human and material costs were excessive. It was just such a calculation that had led the United States not to intervene in Hungary in 1956 and Czechoslovakia in 1968, when Soviet troops crushed popular independence movements in those countries. The numbers holding to this third position grew as the Vietnam War continued.

During his grappling with the Vietnam War, President Richard Nixon made an historic trip to China to meet with its leaders.

REASSERTION

Deemphasizing the military aspects of containment fitted the American mood after the disappointment and disillusionment of Vietnam. But it did not lead to the results that the new administration of President Jimmy Carter had hoped for. The Soviet Union asserted itself aggressively in a number of areas. The invasion of Afghanistan by Soviet soldiers in late 1979 indicated to many Americans that a deemphasis by this country on the application of its military power would not encourage comparable restraint on the Soviets' part. The invasion of Afghanistan followed closely on the heels of the seizure by Iranians of the U.S. embassy and staff in Teheran, Iran, which added to a sense of frustration over national weakness. American public opinion soon reflected a new assertiveness. By the spring of 1980, the National Opinion Research Center found in its national survey of American attitudes that 60 percent of

the public believed the United States was spending too little for defense.[8]

The Carter administration shifted its emphasis. In a speech at the U.S. Naval Academy in June 1978, the president reaffirmed the country's long-standing commitment to containment, charging that the Soviet Union had exploited détente to cover "a continuing aggressive struggle for political advantage and increased influence in a variety of ways." More importantly, the Carter administration took such concrete steps as urging substantial increases in defense spending and a modernization of nuclear forces based in Western Europe for that region's defense. In his January 1980 State of the Union Address, the president announced an extension of American military commitments, in what came to be known as the Carter

---

[8] National Opinion Research Center, *General Social Survey,* Spring 1980.

Box 16.4
The National Security Council

The most important institutional change made since World War II to provide the president with more assistance in discharging his foreign policy responsibilities was the creation of the National Security Council (NSC). Established by the National Security Act of 1947, the NSC is charged with advising the president "with respect to the integration of domestic, foreign, and military policies relating to the national security." Its membership includes the president as chairman, the vice president, and the secretaries of state and defense. The director of the Central Intelligence Agency and the chairman of the Joint Chiefs of Staff are statutory advisers to the NSC. Heads of other international agencies, such as the United States Information Agency and the Agency for International Development, also participate at times in council activities. So does the president's personal staff; one of these staff positions—the assistant for national security affairs—has become exceptionally prominent.

How its members participate, and how the council operates generally, are strictly at the president's discretion. The NSC's deliberations and decisions are only advisory to him. Every president since Truman, however, has chosen to make the NSC an important instrument of presidential foreign policy management. Under John Kennedy, the NSC staff moved to fill what the president believed was a persisting deficiency of the State Department: its built-in inertia. Under Richard Nixon and his national security adviser, Henry Kissinger, the NSC staff was enlarged and its day-to-day managerial authority increased. But when Kissinger became secretary of state and gave up the post of national security adviser, influence shifted back to the State Department. Zbigniew Brzezinski, NSC chief under Jimmy Carter, also played a decisive role in managing foreign policy.

The belief of modern presidents that they need personal staff machinery for managing America's far-flung foreign commitments has proved to be enduring. Controversy over the role of the NSC has also persisted. Ronald Reagan's use of the NSC to manage delicate negotiations with Iran involving future relations and U.S. hostages held in Lebanon by pro-Iranian forces—bypassing the State Department—led to errors that shook his administration in late 1986 and 1987. Under George Bush, the NSC staff has played the relatively limited role of gathering information and presenting options to the president.

Doctrine: "An attempt by any outside force to gain control of the Persian Gulf region [important in the flow of petroleum to the United States, Europe, and Japan] will be regarded as an assault on the vital interests of the United States of America, and such an assault will be repelled by any means necessary, including military force."

The post-Vietnam reaction in U.S. foreign policy had been greatly tempered. When the Reagan administration took office in January 1981, it placed even more emphasis on

Box 16.5
Intelligence Services

The beginnings of a major U.S. effort in foreign intelligence may be traced to the Japanese bombing of Pearl Harbor. The success of that attack revealed the gross deficiencies in the country's intelligence gathering and spurred a new emphasis. Today, the United States has a vast and complex network of intelligence agencies that play a large part in foreign affairs.

The Department of Defense (DOD) does more in the intelligence-gathering area than any other executive agency. Units of the DOD expend over 80 percent of the total intelligence budget, with Air Force Intelligence the biggest single unit. Including the National Reconnaissance Office, Air Force Intelligence is responsible for the extremely costly and effective surveillance carried out through orbiting satellites.

The National Security Agency (NSA), also in DOD, is the second largest in the U.S. intelligence community in total budget. It handles "signal intelligence" and "cryptology": code breaking and code making. It does technical work for codes used by the CIA, the FBI, the military services, the State Department, and other federal agencies.

When the CIA was established in 1947, it was intended to integrate many separate pieces of national intelligence gathering. Over the ensuing years, its coordinating function has diminished, although the director of the CIA still has the general responsibility for coordinating the entire U.S. intelligence community. His considerable authority over all intelligence expenditures adds muscle to this role. He is responsible to the National Security Council and through the NSC to the president.

Only about 10 percent of the staff involved in U.S. intelligence is in the employ of the CIA. The CIA carries on its major activities within three operating units: the directorates of Intelligence, Science and Technology, and Operations. The first two are devoted principally to intelligence processing and assessment, and the third to clandestine activities.

strengthening American military forces and containing the Soviet Union. As Robert Osgood noted, "The dominant theme of President Reagan's foreign policy, to which all major policies were subordinated, was revitalizing the containment of Soviet expansion."[9] To this end,

the Reagan administration pushed hard for and won congressional approval for substantial real increases in defense spending. It worked to strengthen the Central Intelligence Agency, rebuilding its capacity to conduct covert operations abroad. It supported groups fighting against Soviet-backed regimes in Central America and Africa, and against Soviet forces in Afghanistan.

[9]Robert E. Osgood, "The Revitalization of Containment," Foreign Affairs 60, 3 (1982), p. 472.

Experts have questioned the quality of the CIA's foreign evaluations. In 1976, for example, it dramatically reversed its assessment of the rate of the Soviet Union's military build-up, saying, in effect, that it had been wrong in its calculations of the preceding years and that the USSR was in fact strengthening its military capabilities much faster than had been thought. Recently, leading Soviet economists have argued that the CIA estimates in the 1980s substantively overstated the performance of the Soviet economy.

Many Americans are ambivalent about foreign intelligence gathering. Too much of such activity seems undemocratic, but too little seems dangerous, imperiling the country's defenses against foreign adversaries. So support for the intelligence services waxes and wanes. In the mid-1970s support was waning: Congress enacted the Hughes-Ryan Amendment to the 1974 Foreign Assistance Act; this amendment required the president, in effect, to notify House and Senate committees on foreign affairs and foreign relations, appropriations, armed services, and intelligence of any covert operations he had approved. As many as 200 members of Congress and their staffs could be knowledgeable about impending secret operations in foreign countries. By 1980, however, support for intelligence gathering was waxing strong: The Hughes-Ryan Amendment had been repealed; congressional oversight in intelligence was restricted in response to the feeling that in the previous six years the United States had put a "strait jacket" on its covert operations. Under the Reagan administration and CIA Director William Casey, the CIA resumed covert operations.

U.S. intelligence gathering activities are certain to be substantially altered in the wake of the Soviet Union's collapse and the establishment, at least for the present, of far less adversarial relations between the United States and Russia. Still, there are plenty of challenges. Testifying before Congress early in 1992, CIA Director Robert M. Gates argued that while the end of the cold war meant change for the intelligence agencies, such change "must also conform to the reality of an unstable, unpredictable, dangerously over-armed and still-transforming world."

HOW MUCH OUR BROTHER'S KEEPER?

America's place in the world community extends further than national security. One important set of these nonmilitary foreign policy issues involves the level to which the United States (and other advanced industrial democracies) should assist the many nations facing grinding poverty. The planet's population is now roughly 5.5 billion, up more than two billion since 1960. While the more developed countries have curbed rapid population growth, less developed regions have not. Mexico's population alone has increased by over 30 million since 1970, India's by more than 250 million. The implications of this population growth—political, economic, environmental—are enormous.

About 45 percent of all U.S. foreign aid in 1993—funds administered by the Agency for International Development, food aid, multilateral assistance (administered through such international development agencies as the World Bank), and "other" (see Table 16.1)—goes largely for humanitarian objectives and to foster economic growth. Thirty percent of our total foreign aid goes to direct military assistance, with much of this defense assistance going to just two countries—Egypt and Israel.

Many experts believe that the present level of U.S. assistance to developing nations is insufficient given the need. And in fact total U.S. foreign assistance—13.4 billion in 1993—has actually been dropping in inflation-controlled terms. As Table 16.1 shows, the FY 1993 total is, in constant dollars, the smallest amount since 1980. The economic slowdown of the 1990s has left many in Congress increasingly unwilling to back foreign aid, reasoning that dealing with "our own problems" should come first. Many question this logic, however, pointing out that the United States has vital interests in developments around the world.

INTERNATIONAL TRADE ISSUES

Nowhere is the reach of our interests in international developments more dramatically evident today than in trade and commerce. The global economy has become ever more interconnected and interdependent. For the United States this means that managing trade policy has become an increasingly important part of the country's foreign policy. One key facet of current American trade policy involves creation of a North American free trade union. A free trade agreement with Canada under which no tariffs are imposed on imported Canadian goods or U.S. goods exported to Canada went into effect in 1989. As this is written, U.S., Mexi-

TABLE 16.1   AMOUNT AND DISTRIBUTION OF U.S. FOREIGN AID

	1991	1992	1993
Total outlays (current dollars—in billions)	$15.0	$13.9	$13.4
Percent distribution			
Agency for International Development	18	16	22
Food aid	5	9	6
Multilateral aid	8	11	11
Economic support funds	29	25	24
Military aid	37	31	31
Other*	3	8	6

*Includes refugee programs, narcotics assistance, Peace Corps, voluntary contributions to international organizations.
Source: Executive Office of the President, Office of Management and Budget, *Budget of the United States Government, FY 1993*, p. A1-6.

can, and Canadian officials have just reached agreement on a North American Free Trade Agreement (NAFTA). There is opposition to it in all three countries: U.S. opposition hinges primarily on the argument that jobs would be lost as American companies build plants in our trading partners' countries, especially south of the border. But the forces of economic integration driving the agreement are very powerful. In 1991, for example, the United States imported about $90 billion worth of goods from Canada and exported more than $80 billion worth to that country. U.S. trade with Mexico totalled more than $60 billion in both directions.

The NAFTA is just one part of a growing international movement to drop trade barriers. For years the United States has been engaged in complex international negotiations on behalf of freer trade under the General Agreement on Tariffs and Trade (GATT). The latest of the continuing GATT negotiations, known as the "Uruguay round," will, if successful—and the resistance from local interests in many countries seeking protection from cheaper imports is enormous—bring farm trade within GATT rules for the first time. Service industries would also be brought into the GATT, beginning with liberalizing trade in financial and other services.

NEW ERA, NEW DEMANDS

The collapse of the Soviet Union and the marked dampening of U.S.-Russian competition has set in motion a vast series of international changes and imposes new demands on American foreign policy.

MORE U.S.-RUSSIAN COOPERATION

One of the most dramatic examples of the new U.S. relationship with its former adversary came in early August 1990 in the wake of Iraq's invasion of its tiny, oil-rich neighbor, Kuwait. The United States and the (then still) Soviet Union stood togther in the United Nations Security Council, along with eleven other nations, in support of a resolution imposing sweeping sanctions on Iraq. Acting under chapter 7 of the UN charter, the Security Council indicated its determination "to bring the invasion and occupation of Kuwait by Iraq to an end and to restore the sovereignty, independence, and territorial integrity of Kuwait. . . ." To this end it decided that all governments should prevent "the import into their territories of all commodities and products originating in Iraq or Kuwait exported therefrom after the date of this resolution"—which means, of course, preventing Iraq from selling its oil. The resolution further required all countries to bar "the sale or supply by their nationals or from their territories . . . of any commodities or products, including weapons or other military equipment . . . but not including supplies intended strictly for medical purposes, and in humanitarian circumstances, food stuffs, to any

The United Nations, meeting here on the Iraqi crisis, has taken on greater importance as the United States and the former Soviet Union have found themselves voting together on sanctions against Iraq. DeLucia/NYT Pictures

Ethnic conflict in Eastern Europe and the former Soviet Union pose new diplomatic challenges to the international community. Here, two soldiers are taking cover on a roof in Bosnia-Herzegovina, a former Yugoslav republic that became a battleground between Serbs, Croats, and Moslem Slavs.

person or body in Kuwait or Iraq. . . ." It also stipulated "that all states shall not make available to the government of Iraq or to any commercial, industrial, or public utility undertaking in Iraq or Kuwait, any funds or other financial or economic resources. . . ."[10]

This condemnation of the Iraqi invasion and the imposition of strong sanctions were possible only because the United States and the then Soviet Union stood together on the matter. Each permanent member of the Security Council—the United States, the then Soviet Union (now Russia), China, France, and Great Britain—has a veto. Any one of these nations

by casting a vote against a resolution kills it, no matter what the majority decides. Iraq was long supported by the Soviet Union, but in the new environment of East-West relations, the Soviets endorsed the Western position on sanctions. "In the five days since Iraq occupied Kuwait," the *New York Times* observed early in the crisis, "the Soviet Union and the United States have begun testing a new working relationship that is without precedent since the onset of the cold war."[11]

All around the world in the 1990s, struggles between groups formerly backed by the USSR and those supported by the United States—like those in Central America, Angola, and

[10] Text of the resolution calling for sanctions against Iraq, adpted by the UN Security Council by a vote of 13–0, with two abstentions, August 6, 1990.

[11] Bill Keller, "U.S. and the Soviets as Allies? It's the First Time since 1945," *New York Times*, August 8, 1990, p. 15.

Afghanistan—have faded. Now, instead of pitting their third-world proxies against each other, the United States and Russia are exploring new forms of cooperation. We shouldn't get starry-eyed about this, however. Clearly, this arrangement is *quid pro quo:* Russia and the other former Soviet states badly need extensive Western financial assistance to reorganize and rebuild their devastated economies; the United States wants a major reduction in the formidable nuclear arsenal of the former Soviet Union, now controlled largely by Russia, and wants to make sure that steps are taken to prevent some of these nuclear weapons from slipping into the hands of other countries, like Iran. Pursuing these respective ends, Presidents Bush and Yeltsin reached agreement in June 1992 on a treaty that would reduce each country's nuclear

forces to between 3,000 and 3,500 warheads from a previous total of about 22,500 warheads (Figure 16.1) At the same time, and in response, Bush extended support for major American and international economic assistance for Russia, including granting it "most favored nation" trade status.

WHAT CHANGES IN NATIONAL DEFENSE?

Some of the most dramatic implications of the revolutionary changes we have been examining come with regard to U.S. defense policy. As noted, the North Atlantic Treaty Organization (NATO) was created to oppose and thus discourage Soviet military expansion in Europe. For four decades NATO and the Soviet-led

FIGURE 16.1 THE NUCLEAR ARSENALS: HOW THEY SHRINK (ESTIMATED NUMBER OF WARHEADS ON LONG-RANGE NUCLEAR WEAPONS IN THOUSANDS)

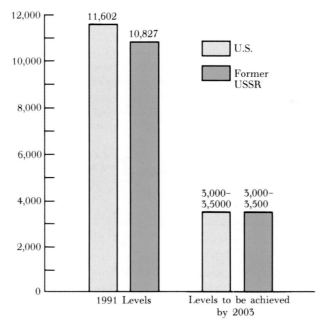

Source: Arms Control Association; Associated Press

Box 16.6
The Department of Defense

The Department of Defense (DOD) has the biggest payroll in the United States, with more than two million men and women on active duty in the armed forces and about one million civilian employees.

The foreign affairs role of the DOD results from the fact that American military power is a primary instrument of the country's foreign policy and international leadership. Adam Yarmolinsky, who served as deputy assistant secretary of defense for international security affairs under Kennedy and Johnson, argued that the central place of military calculations in U.S. foreign policy extends well beyond the intervention of military officials themselves.

> Civilians like [secretaries of state] Dean Acheson, John Foster Dulles, and Dean Rusk did not speak lines written for them by the Joint Chiefs or by secretaries of defense. They spoke their convictions in the language most likely to persuade Congress and the public. They framed their proposals in such a way as to justify open support by military men. It is fair to say that if American foreign policy became partially militarized, the blame should not be laid primarily on the military establishment, but on presidents, civilian policymakers, the Congress, and the American people—and on the situation in which they found themselves.*

Within each military service, the senior officer is responsible for advising his civilian secretary (the secretaries of the army, navy, and air force) on military issues and for maintaining the effectiveness of the armed forces under his authority. These military officials—the chiefs of staff of the army and the air force, the chief of naval operations, and the commandant of the marine corps—constitute collectively the Joint Chiefs of Staff (JCS). The chairman of the JCS is appointed by the president, subject to Senate confirmation, from among the officers of one of the military departments. Drawing on its own staff of some 400 officers, and the ideas and recommendations developed by each branch of the armed services, the JCS advises the secretary of defense and the president on all military matters relating to national security, such as what weapons systems, military assistance to countries allied to the United States, and plans for industrial mobilization, are needed. The service chiefs have not been reluctant to take their views on national security directly to influential members of Congress.

*Adam Yarmolinsky, *The Military Establishment: Its Impact on American Society* (New York: Harper and Row, 1971), p. 37.

Warsaw Pact alliance confronted each other militarily. By the start of the 1990s, as a result of the independence movements and the establishment of democratic governments in much of Eastern Europe, and the disappearance of East Germany altogether as a separate state, the Warsaw Pact for all intents and purposes had ceased to exist. The Red Army was still present in Eastern Europe, but there was no longer a military alliance. Senator Sam Nunn

(D-Georgia), chairman of the Senate Armed Services Committee, noted that "because more than half of our defense budget has traditionally been spent on European security . . . these developments have enormous consequences for the size of defense budgets in our conventional force structure."[12]

How Much, and What to Cut? Everyone agrees that real reductions in defense spending can and should occur. Such reductions have already begun. In 1989 U.S. defense spending was $256 billion, when calculated in dollars of constant (1982) purchasing power. In 1990 spending was $241 billion, $15 billion lower in real, inflation-adjusted terms. In fiscal year 1993, defense spending will drop in current-dollar terms as well—that is, even without an adjustment for inflation. This will bring military expenditures to less than 5 percent of GDP, the lowest proportion since the Korean War (Table 16.2).

But how much can be cut without affecting vital U.S. security interests? For all of the changes in the former Soviet Union, Russia retains a huge military, and the future of U.S. relations with our erstwhile adversary are hard to predict. Nor are those longstanding animosities our only worry. As the events in Iraq and Kuwait reminded us in mid-1990, the United States has vital interests—in that case, in Persian Gulf oil—that can be threatened by developments having nothing to do with Russia's policies.

The issue of *where* reductions should be made—in many ways the more difficult question—has prompted a political debate that is dividing American policy makers sharply and that will certainly continue in the years ahead.

[12]Sam Nunn, *A New Military Strategy* (Washington, D.C.: Center for Strategic and International Studies, 1990), p. 17. This volume is a collection of speeches by Senator Nunn; the one cited here was delivered March 29, 1990.

TABLE 16.2   U.S. DEFENSE SPENDING, 1940–93

Year	Defense spending in billions of dollars	Defense spending as percent of GDP
1940	1.5	1.5
1945	81.6	38.5
1950	13.1	4.6
1955	40.3	10.1
1960	48.1	9.5
1965	50.6	7.5
1970	81.7	8.3
1975	86.5	5.7
1980	134.0	5.0
1985	252.7	6.4
1990	299.3	5.4
1993 (est.)	291.2	4.8

Source: 1990–1993: Council of Economic Advisers, *Economic Indicators,* July 1992, p. 33; *1960–85:* U.S. Bureau of the Census, *Statistical Abstract of the United States, 1990,* p. 330; *1940–55:* idem, *Historical Statistics of the United States, Colonial Times to 1970,* pp. 116, 224.

Defense analysts point out that large cuts in weapons programs produce little savings in outlays in the short run, but often large savings over the long haul. If Congress decides not to go ahead with a particular weapons program, actual spending in the next year is likely to be little affected, but spending over the next five to ten years could be substantially lower.

The administration and Congress must decide, then, which weapons programs should be cut in the interest of long-term savings. But the very reason spending for weapons procurement is spread out over so many years—because these programs take a long time from initial design to actual production—explains why these decisions are often tough ones. If the country guesses wrong and terminates a program that in the future it finds it needs, it may not be able to recover for many years. Major arguments of this sort have developed over the B-2 stealth bomber and the Seawolf nuclear submarine.

Many defense analysts argue that the best way to achieve significant defense savings is to reduce the size of the U.S. *force structure*—that is, the number of men and women in the armed forces and the operating units into which military personnel are organized. Calculations by the Congressional Budget Office, made available by Senator Nunn, showed, for example, that phasing in a reduction of 411,000 army and air force personnel over five years would result in a net savings of about $33 billion in fiscal years 1991–95. In 1992 the Pentagon's plan called for reducing the active-duty Army from 725,000 (its then-current level) to 536,000 by 1997. National Guard and Army Reserve troop strength would be reduced from 741,000 to 567,000 over this period. Navy and air force personnel would be similarly reduced.

POLITICAL PRESSURES

Closing old military bases makes sense militarily, but politicians in both parties are quick to shout: "Don't cut the base in my district." Similarly, some weapons systems can be terminated, or never developed in the first place, without posing any risk to U.S. security. But politicians are bound to argue: "Don't end the weapons system produced by plants that employ my constituents." These political pressures are a natural part of the life of American democracy (and for that matter of any democratic country). Nonetheless, these pressures make it harder to achieve sensible defense reductions. How well will American democracy resolve these political pushes and pulls in the years ahead? The answer we give to that question by the end of the 1990s will be the most important verdict of all on the U.S. military transition following the revolutionary shifts in the old Soviet republics and Eastern Europe.

A NEW WORLD ORDER

Over and over in this chapter we have come back to the break up of the Soviet bloc as the decisive change driving current U.S. foreign policy. We read earlier the words George Kennan penned in 1947: "Soviet power . . . bears within it the seeds of its own decay, and . . . the sprouting of these seeds is well advanced."

Kennan's words can be seen as a response to the question posed at the beginning of this chapter—who could have dreamed that there would no longer be a superpower called the Soviet Union? Kennan could not have had a calendar telling him that the sprouting seeds of that system's decay would—forty-four years after he wrote—see such surging growth. But he understood the conditions that would, given prudent policy by the West, make such growth likely.

No irony of modern politics is greater than that communism—whose leading figures, from the nineteenth-century German philosopher Karl Marx on, saw their system's triumph as historically inevitable and "scientifically" ordained—has itself suffered a collapse that was perhaps inevitable. The ideas of liberal individualism (discussed in chapter 3), which include emphasis on personal rights and opportunities, and the choosing of political leaders through free elections, strengthen their hold as the twentieth century proceeds.

Alexis de Tocqueville came to America in the 1830s because he believed that developments here, involving the flourishing of individualism, would eventually extend everywhere. "It appears to me beyond a doubt," the young Frenchman wrote, "that, sooner or later, we [Europeans, he meant primarily] shall arrive like the Americans, at an almost complete equality of condition"—one where ordinary individuals would by their choices guide the destinies of their respective states. In part, the revolution of 1989–91 in the USSR, which brought about its demise, represents the belated assertion there of the forces of liberal individualism that Tocqueville saw in the America of the early nineteenth century.

SUMMARY

The basic approach of the United States to foreign affairs shifted after World War II. The major European powers of the prewar world—Britain, France, and Germany—had been devastated, and they needed to turn inward to reconstruct their own societies. No Western nation besides the United States had the resources to maintain an international balance of power, counterbalancing the Soviet Union, which emerged in 1945 as the dominant power on the Eurasian land mass.

The name attached to the American balance-of-power effort is containment: containing the Soviet Union and Communist expansion. Pursuing this policy, the United States assisted in the rapid postwar reconstruction of the European democracies, assumed leadership of various military alliances including NATO, maintained a large defense establishment, and committed U.S. troops in response to Communist-bloc expansion, as in the invasion of South Korea.

The one major exception in a record of generally cautious and prudent balance-of-power politics came in Vietnam, when the United States committed a half-million troops to a prolonged military effort to block the Communist takeover of South Vietnam. As the war proceeded, growing proportions of the American public concluded that the human and material costs of the conflict were excessive. Domestic divisions resulting from the war dominated U.S. politics from the mid-1960s through the mid-1970s.

The developments in the Soviet Union and Eastern Europe at the end of the 1980s ushered in a new era in East-West relations and produced dramatic changes in the nature of the problems with which U.S. defense policy has to grapple. Communist regimes that had been under Soviet direction since their establishment after World War II collapsed; in Hungary, Poland, Czechoslovakia, and East Germany, free elections were held in 1989 and 1990, and non-Communist governments were established. The Germanys were reunited. The Warsaw Pact ceased to exist as an active Soviet-led military alliance. And in December 1991, the Soviet Union itself ceased to exist, as national movements achieved independence for the various republics. The highly centralized USSR was replaced by a loose confederation known as the Commonwealth of Independent States (CIS).

Amerian foreign and defense policy in the 1990s was thus left with a different mix of demands: U.S.-Russian relations are far less conflict-ridden—in June 1992, the two countries reached agreement on massive reductions of their nuclear arsenals—but now the United States is faced with managing substantial reductions in military spending without jeopardizing continuing national security requirements.

Faced with economic problems at home, U.S. policy makers have reduced the level of assistance given to developing countries; reestablishing a political base for foreign aid is an important domestic political challenge facing American foreign policy. International trade issues also loom large in this economically interdependent post–cold war world.

FOR FURTHER STUDY

Brock, William, and Robert Hormats, eds. *The Global Economy: America's Role in the Decade Ahead.* New York: W. W. Norton, 1990. Discusses new challenges to the U.S. economy and the measures the United States needs to take in response.

Gwertzman, Bernard, and Michael T. Kaufman, eds. *The Collapse of Communism.* New York: Times Books, 1990. Reports by correspondents of the *New York Times* on the changes that swept the USSR and Eastern Europe in 1989 and early 1990.

Kegley, Charles W., Jr., and Eugene R. Wittkopf. *American Foreign Policy: Pattern and Process,* 3rd ed. New York: St. Martin's Press, 1987. A comprehensive, balanced account of contemporary decision making in American foreign policy.

Kennan, George. "The Sources of Soviet Conduct," *Foreign Affairs*, 25 (July 1947), pp. 567–82. This article, published anonymously by Kennan, set forth the rationale for a U.S. containment policy toward the Soviet Union.

Moodie, Michael. *Defense Implications of Europe 92.* Washington, D.C.: Center for Strategic and International Studies, 1990; Nunn, Sam. *A New Military Strategy.* Washington D.C.: Center for Strategic and International Studies, 1990; Nunn, Sam. *Conventional Combat Priorities: An Approach for the New Strategic Era* (Final Report of the CSIS Conventional Combat 2002 Project). Washington D.C.: Center for Strategic and International Studies, 1990. Three useful publications that examine the new defense environment and its implications for U.S. policy.

Appendix *1*

THE DECLARATION OF INDEPENDENCE

When in the course of human events, it becomes necessary for one people to dissolve the political bands which have connected them with another, and to assume among the Powers of the earth, the separate and equal station to which the Laws of Nature and of Nature's God entitle them, a decent respect to the opinions of mankind requires that they should declare the causes which impel them to the separation.

We hold these truths to be self-evident, that all men are created equal, that they are endowed by their Creator with certain unalienable rights, that among these are Life, Liberty, and the pursuit of Happiness. That to secure these rights, Governments are instituted among Men, deriving their just powers from the consent of the governed. That whenever any Form of Government becomes destructive of these ends, it is the Right of the People to alter or to abolish it, and to institute new Government, laying its foundation on such principles and organizing its powers in such form, as to them shall seem most likely to effect their Safety and Happiness. Prudence, indeed, will dictate that Governments long established should not be changed for light and transient causes; and accordingly all experience hath shown, that mankind are more disposed to suffer, while evils are sufferable, than to right themselves by abolishing the forms to which they are accustomed. But when a long train of abuses and usurpations, pursuing invariably the same Object evinces a design to reduce them under absolute Despotism, it is their right, it is their duty, to throw off such Government, and to provide new Guards for their future security.—Such has been the patient sufferance of these Colonies; and such is now the necessity which constrains them to alter their former Systems of Government. The history of the present King of Great Britain is a history of repeated injuries and usurpations, all having in direct object the establishment of an absolute Tyranny over these States. To prove this, let Facts be submitted to a candid world.

He has refused his Assent to Laws, the most wholesome and necessary for the public good.

He has forbidden his Governors to pass Laws of immediate and pressing importance, unless suspended in their operation till his Assent should be obtained; and when so suspended, he has utterly neglected to attend to them.

He has refused to pass other Laws for the accommodation of large districts of people, unless those people would relinquish the right of Representation in the Legislature, a right inestimable to them and formidable to tyrants only.

He has called together legislative bodies at places unusual, uncomfortable, and distant from the depository of their public Records, for the sole purpose of fatiguing them into compliance with his measures.

He has dissolved Representative Houses repeatedly, for opposing with manly firmness his invasions on the rights of the people.

He has refused for a long time, after such dissolutions, to cause others to be elected; whereby the Legislative powers, incapable of Annihilation, have returned to the People at large for their exercise; the State remaining in the mean time exposed to all dangers of invasion from without, and convulsions within.

He has endeavoured to prevent the population of these States; for that purpose obstructing the Laws of Naturalization of Foreigners; refusing to pass others to encourage their migrations hither, and raising the conditions of new Appropriations of Lands.

He has obstructed the Administration of Justice, by refusing his Assent to Laws for establishing Judiciative powers.

He has made Judges dependent on his Will alone, for the tenure of their offices, and the amount and payment of their salaries.

He has erected a multitude of New Offices, and sent hither swarms of Officers to harass our People, and eat out their substance.

He has kept among us, in times of peace, Standing Armies without the Consent of our legislature.

He has affected to render the Military independent of and superior to the Civil Power.

He has combined with others to subject us to a jurisdiction foreign to our constitution, and unacknowledged by our laws; giving his Assent to their Acts of pretended Legislation:

For quartering large bodies of armed troops among us:

For protecting them, by a mock Trial, from Punishment for any Murders which they should commit on the Inhabitants of these States:

For cutting off our Trade with all parts of the world:

For imposing taxes on us without our Consent:

For depriving us of many cases, of the benefits of Trial by jury:

For transporting us beyond Seas to be tried for pretended offences:

For abolishing the free System of English Laws in a neighbouring Province, establishing therein an Arbitrary government, and enlarging its Boundaries so as to render it at once an example and fit instrument for introducing the same absolute rule into these Colonies:

For taking away our Charters, abolishing our most valuable Laws, and altering fundamentally the Forms of our Governments:

For suspending our own Legislatures, and declaring themselves invested with Power to legislate for us in all cases whatsoever.

He has abdicated Government here, by declaring us out of his Protection and waging War against us.

He has plundered our seas, ravaged our Coasts, burnt our towns, and destroyed the lives of our people.

He is at this time transporting large armies of foreign mercenaries to compleat the works of death, desolation, and tyranny, already begun with circumstances of Cruelty & perfidy scarcely paralleled in the most barbarous ages, and totally unworthy the Head of a civilized nation.

He has constrained our fellow Citizens taken Captive on the high Seas to bear Arms against their Country, to become the executioners of their friends and Brethren, or to fall themselves by their Hands.

He has excited domestic insurrections amongst us, and has endeavoured to bring on the inhabitants of our frontiers, the merciless Indian Savages, whose known rule of warfare, is an undistinguished destruction of all ages, sexes, and conditions.

In every stage of these Oppressions We have Petitioned for Redress in the most humble terms: Our repeated Petitions have been answered only by repeated injury. A Prince, whose character is thus marked by every act which may define a Tyrant, is unfit to be the ruler of a free people.

Nor have We been wanting in attention to our British brethren. We have warned them from time to time of attempts by their legislature to extend an unwarrantable jurisdiction over us. We have reminded them of the circumstances of our emigration and settlement here. We have appealed to their native justice and magnanimity, and we have conjured them by the ties of our common kindred to disavow these usurpations, which, would inevitably interrupt our connections and correspondence. They too must have been deaf to the voice of justice and of consanguinity. We must, therefore, acquiesce in the necessity, which denounces our Separation, and hold them, as we hold the rest of mankind, Enemies in War, in Peace Friends.

WE, THEREFORE, the Representatives of the UNITED STATES OF AMERICA, in General Congress, Assembled, appealing to the Supreme Judge of the world for the rectitude of our intentions, do, in the Name, and by Authority of the good People of these Colonies, solemnly publish and declare, That these United Colonies are, and of Right ought to be FREE AND INDEPENDENT STATES; that they are Absolved from all Allegiance to the British Crown, and that all political connection between them and the State of Great Britain, is and ought to be totally dissolved; and that as Free and Independent States, they have full Power to levy War, conclude Peace, contract Alliances, establish Commerce, and to do all other Acts and Things which Independent States may of right do. And for the support of this Declaration, with a firm reliance on the Protection of Divine Providence, we mutually pledge to each other our Lives, our Fortunes, and our sacred Honor.

The foregoing Declaration was, by order of Congress, engrossed, and signed by the following members:

John Hancock

NEW HAMPSHIRE
Josiah Bartlett
William Whipple
Matthew Thornton

MASSACHUSETTS BAY
Samuel Adams
John Adams
Robert Treat Paine
Elbridge Gerry

RHODE ISLAND
Stephen Hopkins
William Ellery

CONNECTICUT
Roger Sherman
Samuel Huntington
William Williams
Oliver Wolcott

NEW YORK
William Floyd
Philip Livingston
Francis Lewis
Lewis Morris

NEW JERSEY
Richard Stockton
John Witherspoon
Francis Hopkinson
John Hart
Abraham Clark

PENNSYLVANIA
Robert Morris
Benjamin Rush
Benjamin Franklin
John Morton
George Clymer
James Smith
George Taylor
James Wilson
George Ross

DELAWARE
Caesar Rodney
George Read
Thomas M'Kean

MARYLAND
Samuel Chase
William Paca
Thomas Stone
Charles Carroll,
  of Carrollton

VIRGINIA
George Wythe
Richard Henry Lee
Thomas Jefferson
Benjamin Harrison
Thomas Nelson, Jr.
Francis Lightfoot Lee
Carter Braxton

NORTH CAROLINA
William Hooper
Joseph Hewes
John Penn

SOUTH CAROLINA
Edward Rutledge
Thomas Heyward, Jr.
Thomas Lynch, Jr.
Arthur Middleton

GEORGIA
Button Gwinnett
Lyman Hall
George Walton

Resolved, That copies of the Declaration be sent to the several assemblies, conventions, and committees, or councils of safety, and to the several commanding officers of the continental troops; that it be proclaimed in each of the United States, at the head of the army.

Appendix 2

THE CONSTITUTION OF
THE UNITED STATES

We the People of the United States, in order to form a more perfect Union, establish Justice, insure domestic Tranquility, provide for the common defence, promote the general Welfare, and secure the Blessings of Liberty to ourselves and our Posterity, do ordain and establish this Constitution for the United States of America.

ARTICLE I.

Section 1. All legislative Powers herein granted shall be vested in a Congress of the United States, which shall consist of a Senate and House of Representatives.

Section 2. The House of Representatives shall be composed of Members chosen every second Year by the People of the several States, and the Electors in each State shall have the Qualifications requisite for Electors of the most numerous Branch of the State Legislature.

No Person shall be a Representative who shall not have attained to the Age of twenty five Years, and been seven Years a Citizen of the United States, and who shall not, when elected, be an Inhabitant of that State in which he shall be chosen.

Representatives and direct Taxes shall be apportioned among the several States which may be included within this Union, according to their respective Numbers, which shall be determined by adding to the whole Number of free Persons, including those bound to Service for a Term of Years, and excluding Indians not taxed, three fifths of all other Persons. The actual Enumeration shall be made within three Years after the first Meeting of the Congress of the United States, and within every subsequent Term of ten Years, in such Manner as they shall by Law direct. The Number of Representatives shall not exceed one for every thirty Thousand, but each State shall have at Least one Representative; and until such enumeration shall be made, the State of New Hampshire shall be entitled to chuse three, Massachusetts eight, Rhode-Island and Providence Plantations one, Connecticut five, New-York six, New Jersey four, Pennsylvania eight, Delaware one, Maryland six, Virginia ten, North Carolina five, South Carolina five, and Georgia three.

When vacancies happen in the Representation from any State, the Executive Authority thereof shall issue Writs of Election to fill such Vacancies.

The House of Representatives shall chuse their Speaker and other Officers; and shall have the sole Power of Impeachment.

Section 3. The Senate of the United States shall be composed of two Senators from each State, chosen by the Legislature thereof, for six Years; and each Senator shall have one Vote.

Immediately after they shall be assembled in Consequence of the first Election, they shall be divided as equally as may be into three Classes. The Seats of the Senators of the first Class shall be vacated at the Expiration of the second Year, of the second Class at the Expiration of the fourth Year, and of the third Class at the Expiration of the sixth Year, so that one third may be chosen every second Year; and if Vacancies happen by Resignation, or otherwise, during the Recess of the Legislature of any State, the Executive thereof may make temporary Appointments until the next Meeting of the Legislature, which shall then fill such Vacancies.

Nor Person shall be a Senator who shall not have attained to the Age of thirty Years, and been nine Years a Citizen of the United States, and who shall not, when elected, be an Inhabitant of that State for which he shall be chosen.

The Vice President of the United States shall be President of the Senate, but shall have no Vote, unless they be equally divided.

The Senate shall chuse their other Officers, and also a President pro tempore, in the Absence of the Vice President, or when he shall exercise the Office of President of the United States.

The Senate shall have the sole Power to try all Impeachments. When sitting for that Purpose, they shall be on Oath or Affirmation. When the President of the United States is tried, the Chief Justice shall preside: And no Person shall be convicted without the Concurrence of two thirds of the Members present.

Judgment in Cases of Impeachment shall not extend further than to removal from Office, and disqualification to hold and enjoy any Office of honor, Trust or Profit under the United States: but the Party convicted shall nevertheless be liable and subject to Indictment, Trial, Judgment and Punishment, according to Law.

Section 4. The Times, Places and Manner of holding Elections for Senators and Representatives, shall be prescribed in each State by the Legislature thereof, but the Congress may at any time by Law make or alter such Regulations, except as to the Places of chusing Senators.

The Congress shall assemble at least once in every Year, and such Meeting shall be on the first Monday in December, unless they shall by Law appoint a different Day.

Section 5. Each House shall be the Judge of the Elections, Returns and Qualifications of its own Members, and a Majority of each shall constitute a Quorum to do Business; but a smaller Number may adjourn from day to day, and may be authorized to compel the Attendance of absent Members, in such Manner, and under such Penalties as each House may provide.

Each House may determine the Rules of its Proceedings, punish its Members for disorderly Behaviour, and, with the Concurrence of two thirds, expel a Member.

Each House shall keep a Journal of its Proceedings, and from time to time publish the same, excepting such Parts as may in their Judgment require Secrecy; and the Yeas and Nays of the Members of either House on any question shall, at the Desire of one fifth of those Present, be entered on the Journal.

Neither House, during the Session of Congress, shall, without the Consent of the other, adjourn for more than three days, nor to any other Place than that in which the two Houses shall be sitting.

Section 6. The Senators and Representatives shall receive a Compensation for their Services, to be ascertained by Law, and paid out of the Treasury of the United States. They shall in all Cases, except Treason, Felony and Breach of the Peace, be privileged from Arrest during their Attendance at the Session of their respective Houses, and in going to and returning from the same; and for any Speech or Debate in either House, they shall not be questioned in any other Place.

No Senator or Representative shall, during the Time for which he was elected, be appointed to any civil Office under the Authority of the United States, which shall have been created, or the Emoluments whereof shall have been encreased during such time; and no Person holding any Office under the United States, shall be a Member of either House during his Continuance in Office.

Section 7. All Bills for raising Revenue shall originate in the House of Representatives; but the Senate may propose or concur with Amendments as on other Bills.

Every Bill which shall have passed the House of Representatives and the Senate shall, before it becomes a Law, be presented to the President of the United States; If he approve he shall sign it, but if not he shall return it, with his Objections to that House in which it shall have originated, who shall enter the Objections at large on their Journal, and proceed to reconsider it. If after such Reconsideration two thirds of that House shall agree to pass the Bill, it shall be sent, together with the Objections, to the other House, by which it shall likewise be reconsidered, and if approved by two thirds of that House, it shall become a Law. But in all such Cases the Votes of both Houses shall be determined by yeas and Nays, and the Names of the Persons voting for and against the Bill shall be entered on the Journal of each House respectively. If any Bill shall not be returned by the President within ten Days (Sundays excepted) after it shall have been presented to him, the Same shall be a Law, in like Manner as if he had signed it, unless the Congress by their Adjournment prevent its Return, in which Case it shall not be a Law.

Every Order, Resolution, or Vote to which the Concurrence of the Senate and House of Representatives may be necessary (except on a question of Adjournment) shall be presented to the President of the United States; and before the Same shall take Effect, shall be approved by him, or being disapproved by him, shall be repassed by two thirds of the Senate and House of Representatives, according to the Rules and Limitations prescribed in the Case of a Bill.

Section 8. The Congress shall have Power To lay and collect Taxes, Duties, Imposts and Excises, to pay the Debts and provide for the common Defence and general Welfare of the

United States; but all Duties, Imposts and Excises shall be uniform throughout the United States.

To borrow Money on the credit of the United States;

To regulate Commerce with foreign Nations, and among the several States, and with the Indian Tribes;

To establish an uniform Rule of Naturalization, and uniform Laws on the subject of Bankruptcies throughout the United States;

To coin Money, regulate the Value thereof, and of foreign Coin, and fix the Standard of Weights and Measures;

To provide for the Punishment of counterfeiting the Securities and current Coin of the United States;

To establish Post Offices and Post Roads;

To promote the Progress of Science and useful Arts, by securing for limited Times to Authors and Inventors the exclusive Right to their respective Writings and Discoveries;

To constitute Tribunals inferior to the supreme Court;

To define and punish Piracies and Felonies committed on the high Seas, and Offences against the Law of Nations;

To declare War, grant Letters of Marque and Reprisal, and make Rules concerning Captures on Land and Water;

To raise and support Armies, but no Appropriation of Money to that Use shall be for a longer Term than two Years;

To provide and maintain a Navy;

To make Rules for the Government and Regulation of the land and naval Forces;

To provide for calling forth the Militia to execute the Laws of the Union, suppress Insurrections and repel Invasions;

To provide for organizing, arming, and disciplining, the Militia, and for governing such Part of them as may be employed in the Service of the United States, reserving to the States respectively, the Appointment of the Officers, and the Authority of training the Militia according to the discipline prescribed by Congress;

To exercise exclusive Legislation in all Cases whatsoever, over such District (not exceeding ten Miles square) as may, by Cession of particular States, and the Acceptance of Congress, become the Seat of the Government of the United States, and to exercise like Authority over all Places purchased by the Consent of the Legislature of the State in which the Same shall be, for the Erection of Forts, Magazines, Arsenals, dock-Yards, and other needful Buildings;—And

To make all Laws which shall be necessary and proper for carrying into Execution the foregoing Powers, and all other Powers vested by this Constitution in the Government of the United States, or in any Department or Officer thereof.

Section 9. The Migration or Importation of such Persons as any of the States now existing shall think proper to admit, shall not be prohibited by the Congress prior to the Year one thousand eight hundred and eight, but a Tax or duty may be imposed on such Importation, not exceeding ten dollars for each Person.

The Privilege of the Writ of Habeas Corpus shall not be suspended, unless when in Cases of Rebellion or Invasion the public Safety may require it.

No Bill of Attainder or ex post facto Law shall be passed.

No Capitation, or other direct, Tax shall be laid, unless in Proportion to the Census or Enumeration herein before directed to be taken.

No Tax or Duty shall be laid on Articles exported from any State.

No Preference shall be given by any Regulation of Commerce or Revenue to the Ports of one State over those of another; nor shall Vessels bound to, or from, one State, be obliged to enter, clear, or pay Duties in another.

No Money shall be drawn from the Treasury, but in Consequence of Appropriations made by Law, and a regular Statement and Account of the Receipts and Expenditures of all public Money shall be published from time to time.

No Title of Nobility shall be granted by the United States: And no Person holding any Office of Profit or trust under them, shall, without the Consent of the Congress, accept of any present, Emolument, Office, or Title, of any kind whatever, from any King, Prince, or foreign State.

Section 10. No State shall enter into any Treaty, Alliance, or Confederation; grant Letters of Marque and Reprisal; coin Money; emit Bills of Credit; make any Thing but gold and silver Coin a Tender in Payment of Debts; pass any Bill of Attainder, ex post facto Law, or Law impairing the Obligation of Contracts, or grant any Title of Nobility.

No State shall, without the Consent of the Congress, lay any Imposts or Duties on Imports or Exports, except what may be absolutely necessary for executing its inspection Laws: and the net Produce of all Duties and Imposts, laid by any State on Imports or Exports, shall be for the Use of the Treasury of the United States; and all such Laws shall be subject to the Revision and Controul of the Congress.

No State shall, without the Consent of Congress, lay any Duty of Tonnage, keep Troops, or Ships of War in time of Peace, enter into any Agreement or Compact with another State, or with a foreign Power, or engage in War, unless actually invaded, or in such imminent Danger as will not admit of delay.

ARTICLE II.

Section 1. The executive Power shall be vested in a President of the United States of America. He shall hold his Office during the term of four Years, and, together with the Vice President, chosen for the same Term, be elected, as follows

Each State shall appoint, in such Manner as the Legislature thereof may direct, a Number of Electors, equal to the whole Number of Senators and Representatives to which the State may be entitled in the Congress: but no Senator or Representative, or Person holding an Office of Trust or Profit under the United States, shall be appointed an Elector.

The Electors shall meet in their respective States, and vote by Ballot for two Persons, of whom one at least shall not be an Inhabitant of the same State with themselves, and they shall make a List of all the Persons voted for, and of the Number of Votes for each; which List they shall sign and certify, and transmit sealed to the Seat of the Government of the United States, directed to the President of the Senate. The President of the Senate shall, in the Presence of the Senate and House of Representatives, open all the Certificates, and the Votes shall then be counted. The Person having the greatest Number of Votes shall be the President, if such Number be a Majority of the whole Number of electors appointed; and if there be more than one who have such Majority, and have an equal Number of Votes, then the House of Representatives shall immediately chuse by Ballot one of them for President; and if no Person have a Majority, then for the five highest on the List the said House shall in like Manner chuse the President. But in chusing the President, the Votes shall be taken by States, the Representation from each State having one Vote; A quorum for this Purpose shall consist of a Member or Members from two thirds of the States, and a Majority of all the States shall be necessary to a Choice. In every Case, after the Choice of the President, the Person having the greatest Number of Votes of the Electors shall be the Vice President. But if there should remain two or more who have equal Votes, the

Senate shall chuse from them by Ballot the Vice President.

The Congress may determine the Time of chusing the Electors, and the Day on which they shall give their Votes; which Day shall be the same throughout the United States.

No Person except a natural born Citizen, or a Citizen of the United States, at the time of the Adoption of this Constitution, shall be eligible to the Office of President, neither shall any Person be eligible to that Office who shall not have attained to the Age of thirty five Years, and been fourteen Years a Resident within the United States.

In Case of the Removal of the President from Office, or of his Death, Resignation, or Inability to discharge the Powers and Duties of the said Office, the Same shall devolve on the Vice President, and the Congress may by Law provide for the Case of Removal, Death, Resignation or Inability, both of the President and Vice President, declaring what Officer shall then act as President, and such Officer shall act accordingly, until the Disibility be removed, or a President shall be elected.

The President shall, at stated Times, receive for his Services, a Compensation, which shall neither be encreased or diminished during the Period for which he shall have been elected, and he shall not receive within that Period any other Emolument from the United States, or any of them.

Before he enters on the Execution of his Office, he shall take the following Oath or Affirmation:—"I do solemnly swear (or affirm) that I will faithfully execute the Office of President of the United States, and will to the best of my Ability, preserve, protect and defend the Constitution of the United States."

Section 2. The President shall be Commander in Chief of the Army and Navy of the United States, and of the Militia of the several States, when called into the actual Service of the United States; he may require the Opinion, in writing, of the principal Officer in each of the executive Departments, upon any Subject relating to the Duties of their respective Offices, and he shall have Power to grant Reprieves and Pardons for Offences against the United States, except in Cases of Impeachment.

He shall have Power, by and with the Advice and Consent of the Senate, to make Treaties, provided two thirds of the Senators present concur; and he shall nominate, and by and with the Advice and Consent of the Senate, shall appoint Ambassadors, other public Ministers and Consuls, Judges of the supreme Court, and all other officers of the United States, whose Appointments are not herein otherwise provided for, and which shall be established by Law; but the Congress may by Law vest the Appointment of such inferior Officers, as they think proper, in the President alone, in the Courts of Law, or in the Heads of Departments.

The President shall have Power to fill up all Vacancies that may happen during the Recess of the Senate, by granting Commissions which shall expire at the End of their next Session.

Section 3. He shall from time to time give to the Congress Information of the State of the Union, and recommend to their Consideration such Measures as he shall judge necessary and expedient; he may, on extraordinary Occasions, convene both Houses, or either of them, and in Case of Disagreement between them, with Respect to the Time of Adjournment, he may adjourn them to such Time as he shall think proper; he shall receive Ambassadors and other public Ministers; he shall take Care that the Laws be faithfully executed, and shall Commission all the Officers of the United States.

Section 4. The President, Vice President and all civil Officers of the United States, shall be removed from Office on Impeachment for, and Conviction of, Treason, Bribery, or other high Crimes and Misdemeanors.

ARTICLE III.

Section 1. The judicial Power of the United States, shall be vested in one supreme Court, and in such inferior Courts as the Congress may from time to time ordain and establish. The Judges, both of the supreme and inferior Courts, shall hold their Offices during good Behaviour, and shall, at stated Times, receive for their Services, a Compensation, which shall not be diminished during their Continuance in Office.

Section 2. The judicial Power shall extend to all Cases, in Law and Equity, arising under this Constitution, the Laws of the United States, and Treaties made, or which shall be made, under their Authority;—to all Cases affecting Ambassadors, other public Ministers and Consuls;—to all Cases of admiralty and maritime Jurisdiction;—to Controversies to which the United States shall be a Party;—to Controversies between two or more States;—between a State and Citizens of another State;—between Citizens of different States,—between Citizens of the same State claiming Lands under Grants of different States, and between a State, or the Citizens thereof, and foreign States, Citizens or Subjects.

In all cases affecting Ambassadors, other public Ministers and Consuls, and those in which a State shall be Party, the supreme Court shall have original Jurisdiction. In all the other Cases before mentioned, the supreme Court shall have appellate Jurisdiction, both as to Law and Fact, with such Exceptions, and under such Regulations as the Congress shall make.

The Trial of all Crimes, except in Cases of Impeachment, shall be by Jury; and such Trial shall be held in the State where the said Crimes shall have been committed; but when not committed within any State, the Trial shall be at such Place or Places as the Congress may by Law have directed.

Section 3. Treason against the United States, shall consist only in levying War against them, or in adhering to their Enemies, giving them Aid and Comfort. No Person shall be convicted of Treason unless on the Testimony of two Witnesses to the same overt Act, or on Confession in open Court.

The Congress shall have Power to declare the Punishment of Treason, but no Attainder of Treason shall work Corruption of Blood, or Forfeiture except during the Life of the Person attainted.

ARTICLE IV.

Section 1. Full Faith and Credit shall be given in each State to the public Acts, Records, and judicial Proceedings of every other State. And the Congress may by general Laws prescribe the Manner in which such Acts, Records and Proceedings shall be proved, and the Effect thereof.

Section 2. The Citizens of each State shall be entitled to all Privileges and Immunities of Citizens in the several States.

A Person charged in any State with Treason, Felony, or other Crime, who shall flee from Justice, and be found in another State, shall on Demand of the executive Authority of the State from which he fled, be delivered up, to be removed to the State having Jurisdiction of the Crime.

No Person held to Service or Labour in one State, under the Laws thereof, escaping into another, shall, in Consequence of any Law or Regulation therein, be discharged from such Service or Labour, but shall be delivered up on Claim of the Party to whom such Service or Labour may be due.

Section 3. New States may be admitted by the Congress into this Union; but no new State shall be formed or erected within the Jurisdiction of any other State; nor any State be formed by the Junction of two or more States, or Parts of States, without the consent of the Legislatures of the States concerned as well as of the Congress.

The Congress shall have Power to dispose of an make all needful Rules and Regulations respecting the Territory or other Property belonging to the United States; and nothing in this Constitution shall be so construed as to Prejudice any Claims of the United States, or of any particular States.

Section 4. The United States shall guarantee to every State in this Union a Republican Form of Government, and shall protect each of them against Invasion; and on Application of the Legislature, or of the Executive (when the Legislature cannot be convened) against domestic Violence.

ARTICLE V.

The Congress, whenever two thirds of both Houses shall deem it necessary, shall propose Amendments to this Constitution, or, on the Application of the Legislatures of two thirds of the several States shall call a Convention for proposing Amendments, which, in either Case, shall be valid to all Intents and Purposes, as Part of this Constitution, when ratified by the Legislatures of three fourths of the several States, or by Conventions in three fourths thereof, as the one or the other Mode of Ratification may be proposed by the Congress; Provided that no Amendment which may be made prior to the Year One thousand eight hundred and eight shall in any Manner affect the first and fourth Clauses in the Ninth Section of the first Article; and that no State, without its Con-

sent, shall be deprived of its equal Suffrage in the Senate.

ARTICLE VI.

All Debts contracted and Engagements entered into, before the Adoption of this Constitution, shall be as valid against the United States under this Constitution, as under the Confederation.

This Constitution, and the Laws of the United States which shall be made in Pursuance thereof; and all Treaties made, or which shall be made, under the Authority of the United States, shall be the supreme Law of the Land; and the Judges in every State shall be bound thereby, any Thing in the Constitution or Laws of any State to the Contrary notwithstanding.

The Senators and Representatives before mentioned, and the Members of the several State Legislatures, and all executive and judicial Officers, both of the United States and of the several States, shall be bound by Oath or Affirmation, to support this Constitution; but no religious Test shall ever be required as a Qualification to any Office or public Trust under the United States.

ARTICLE VII.

The Ratification of the Conventions of nine States, shall be sufficient for the Establishment of this Constitution between the States so ratifying the Same.

Done in Convention by the Unanimous Consent of the States present the Seventeenth Day of September in the Year of our Lord one thousand seven hundred and Eighty seven and of the Independence of the United States of America the Twelfth. In witness thereof We have hereunto subscribed our Names,

Gº: WASHINGTON—President and deputy from Virginia

New Hampshire	John Langdon Nicholas Gilman	Delaware	Geo: Read Cunning Bedford jun John Dickinson Richard Bassett Jaco: Broom
Massachusetts	Nathaniel Gorham Rufus King		
Connecticut	Wᵐ Samˡ Johnson Roger Sherman	Maryland	James McHenry Dan of Sᵗ Thoˢ Jenifer Danˡ Carroll
New York	Alexander Hamilton	Virginia	John Blair— James Madison Jr.
New Jersey	Wil: Livingston David A. Brearley. Wᵐ Paterson. Jona: Dayton	North Carolina	Wᵐ. Blount Richᵈ Dobbs Spaight. Hu Williamson
Pennsylvania	B. Franklin Thomas Mifflin Robᵗ Morris Geo. Clymer Thoˢ. FitzSimons Jared Ingersoll James Wilson Gouv Morris	South Carolina	J. Rutledge Charles Cotesworth Pinckney Charles Pinckney Pierce Butler.
		Georgia	William Few Abr Baldwin

AMENDMENTS TO THE CONSTITUTION

Articles in addition to, and Amendment of the Constitution of the United States of America, proposed by Congress, and ratified by the Legislatures of the several States, pursuant to the fifth Article of the original Constitution.

AMENDMENT 1.

Congress shall make no law respecting an establishment of religion, or prohibiting the free exercise thereof; or abridging the freedom of speech, or of the press; or the right of the people peaceably to assemble, and to petition the Government for a redress of grievances.

AMENDMENT 2.

A well regulated Militia, being necessary to the security of a free State, the right of the people to keep and bear Arms, shall not be infringed.

AMENDMENT 3.

No Soldier shall, in time of peace be quartered in any house, without the consent of the Owner, nor in time of war, but in a manner to be prescribed by law.

AMENDMENT 4.

The right of the people to be secure in their persons, houses, papers, and effects, against unreasonable searches and seizures, shall not be violated, and no Warrants shall issue, but upon probable cause, supported by Oath or affirmation, and particularly describing the place to be searched, and the persons or things to be seized.

AMENDMENT 5.

No person shall be held to answer for a capital, or otherwise infamous crime, unless on a presentment or indictment of a Grand Jury, except in cases arising in the land or naval forces, or in the Militia, when in actual service in time of War or public danger; nor shall any person be subject for the same offence to be twice put in jeopardy of life or limb; nor shall be compelled in any criminal case to be a witness against himself, nor be deprived of life, liberty, or property, without due process of law; nor shall private property be taken for public use, without just compensation.

AMENDMENT 6.

In all criminal prosecutions, the accused shall enjoy the right to a speedy and public trial, by an impartial jury of the State and district wherein the crime shall have been committed, which district shall have been previously ascertained by law, and to be informed of the nature and cause of the accusation; to be confronted with the witnesses against him; to have compulsory process for obtaining witnesses in his favor, and to have the Assistance of Counsel for his defence.

AMENDMENT 7.

In Suits at common law, where the value in controversy shall exceed twenty dollars, the right of trial by jury shall be preserved, and no fact tried by a jury, shall be otherwise re-examined in any Court of the United States, than according to the rules of the common law.

AMENDMENT 8.

Excessive bail shall not be required, nor excessive fines imposed, nor cruel and unusual punishments inflicted.

AMENDMENT 9.

The enumeration in the Constitution, of certain rights, shall not be construed to deny or disparage others retained by the people.

AMENDMENT 10.

The powers not delegated to the United States by the Constitution, nor prohibited by it to the

States, are reserved to the States respectively, or to the people. [Amendments 1–10 **(The Bill of Rights)** ratified, 1791]

AMENDMENT 11.

The Judicial power of the United States shall not be construed to extend to any suit in law or equity, commenced or prosecuted against one of the United States by Citizens of another State, or by Citizens or Subjects of any Foreign State. [ratified, 1795]

AMENDMENT 12.

The Electors shall meet in their respective states, and vote by ballot for President and Vice-President, one of whom, at least, shall not be an inhabitant of the same state with themselves; they shall name in their ballots the person voted for as President, and in distinct ballots the person voted for as Vice-President, and they shall make distinct lists of all persons voted for as President, and of all persons voted for as Vice-President, and of the number of votes for each, which lists they shall sign and certify, and transmit sealed to the seat of the government of the United States, directed to the President of the Senate;—The President of the Senate shall, in the presence of the Senate and House of Representatives, open all the certificates and the votes shall then be counted;—The person having the greatest number of votes for President, shall be the President, if such number be a majority of the whole number of Electors appointed; and if no person have such majority, then from the persons having the highest numbers not exceeding three on the list of those voted for as President, the House of Representatives shall choose immediately, by ballot, the President. But in choosing the President, the votes shall be taken by states, the representation from each state having one vote: a quorum for this purpose shall consist of a member or members from two-thirds of the states, and a majority of all the states shall be necessary to a choice. And if the House of of Representatives shall not choose a President whenever the right of choice shall devolve upon them, before the fourth day of March next following, then the Vice-President shall act as President, as in the case of the death or other constitutional disability of the President.—The person having the greatest number of votes as Vice-President, shall be the Vice-President, if such number be a majority of the whole number of Electors appointed, and if no person have a majority, then from the two highest numbers on the list, the Senate shall choose the Vice-President; a quorum for the purpose shall consist of two-thirds of the whole number of Senators, and a majority of the whole number shall be necessary to a choice. But no person constitutionally ineligible to the office of President shall be eligible to that of Vice-President of the United States. [ratified, 1804]

AMENDMENT 13.

Section 1. Neither slavery nor involuntary servitude, except as a punishment for crime whereof the party shall have been duly convicted, shall exist within the United States, or any place subject to their jurisdiction.

Section 2. Congress shall have power to enforce this article by appropriate legislation. [ratified, 1865]

AMENDMENT 14.

Section 1. All persons born or naturalized in the United States, and subject to the jurisdiction thereof, are citizens of the United States and of the State wherein they reside. No State shall make or enforce any law which shall abridge the privileges or immunities of citizens of the United States; nor shall any State deprive any person of life, liberty, or property, without due process of law; not deny to any person within its jurisdiction the equal protection of the laws.

Section 2. Representatives shall be apportioned among the several States according to their respective numbers, counting the whole number of persons in each State, excluding Indians not taxed. But when the right to vote at any election for the choice of electors for President and Vice President of the United States, Representatives in Congress, the Executive and Judicial officers of a State, or the members of the Legislature thereof, is denied to any of the male inhabitants of such State, being twenty-one years of age, and citizens of the United States, or in any way abridged, except for participation in rebellion, or other crime, the basis of representation therein shall be reduced in the proportion which the number of such male citizens shall bear to the whole number of male citizens twenty-one years of age in such State.

Section 3. No person shall be a Senator or Representative in Congress, or elector of President and Vice President, or hold any office, civil or military, under the United States, or under any State, who, having previously taken an oath, as a member of Congress, or as an officer of the United States, or as a member of any State legislature, or as an executive or judicial officer of any State, to support the Constitution of the United States, shall have engaged in insurrection or rebellion against the same, or given aid or comfort to the enemies thereof. But Congress may by a vote of two-thirds of each House, remove such disability.

Section 4. The validity of the public debt of the United States, authorized by law, including debts incurred for payment of pensions and bounties for services in suppressing insurrec-

tion or rebellion, shall not be questioned. But neither the United States nor any State shall assume or pay any debt or obligation incurred in aid of insurrection or rebellion against the United States, or any claim for the loss or emancipation of any slave; but all such debts, obligations and claims shall be held illegal and void.

Section 5. The Congress shall have power to enforce, by appropriate legislation, the provisions of this article. [ratified, 1868]

AMENDMENT 15.

Section 1. The right of citizens of the United States to vote shall not be denied or abridged by the United States or by any State on account of race, color, or previous condition of servitude.

Section 2. The Congress shall have power to enforce this article by appropriate legislation. [ratified, 1870]

AMENDMENT 16.

The Congress shall have power to lay and collect taxes on incomes, from whatever source derived, without apportionment among the several States, and without regard to any census or enumeration. [ratified, 1913]

AMENDMENT 17.

The Senate of the United States shall be composed of two senators from each State, elected by the people thereof, for six years; and each Senator shall have one vote. The electors in each State shall have the qualifications requisite for electors of the most numerous branch of the State legislature.

When vacancies happen in the representation of any State in the Senate, the executive authority of such State shall issue writs of election to fill such vacancies: *Provided,* That the legislature of any State may empower the executive thereof to make temporary appointments until the people fill the vacancies by election as the legislature may direct.

This amendment shall not be so construed as to affect the election or term of any senator chosen before it becomes valid as part of the Constitution. [ratified, 1913]

AMENDMENT 18.

After one year from the ratification of this article, the manufacture, sale, or transportation of intoxicating liquors within, the importation thereof into, or the exportation thereof from the United States and all territory subject to the jurisdiction thereof for beverage purposes is hereby prohibited.

The Congress and the several States shall have concurrent power to enforce this article by appropriate legislation.

This article shall be inoperative unless it shall have been ratified as an amendment to the Constitution by the legislatures of the several States, as provided in the Constitution, within seven years from the date of the submission thereof to the States by Congress. [ratified, 1919]

AMENDMENT 19.

The right of citizens of the United States to vote shall not be denied or abridged by the United States or by any State on account of sex.

The Congress shall have power by appropriate legislation to enforce the provisions of this article. [ratified, 1920]

AMENDMENT 20.

Section 1. The terms of the President and Vice-President shall end at noon on the twentieth day of January, and the terms of Senators and Representatives at noon on the third day of January, of the years in which such terms would have ended if this article had not been ratified; and the terms of their successors shall then begin.

Section 2. The Congress shall assemble at least once in every year, and such meeting shall begin at noon on the third day of January, unless they shall by law appoint a different day.

Section 3. If, at the time fixed for the beginning of the term of the President, the President-elect shall have died, the Vice-President-elect shall become President. If a President shall not have been chosen before the time fixed for the beginning of his term, or if the President-elect shall have failed to qualify, then the Vice-President-elect shall act as President until a President shall have qualified; and the Congress may by law provide for the case wherein neither a President-elect nor a Vice-President-elect shall have qualified, declaring who shall then act as President, or the manner in which one who is to act shall be selected, and such person shall act accordingly until a President or Vice-President shall have qualified.

Section 4. The Congress may by law provide for the case of the death of any of the persons from whom the House of Representatives may choose a President whenever the right of choice shall have devolved upon them, and for the case of the death of any of the persons from whom the Senate may choose a Vice-President whenever the right of choice shall have devolved upon them.

Section 5. Sections 1 and 2 shall take effect on the 15th day of October following the ratification of this article.

Section 6. This article shall be inoperative unless it shall have been ratified as an amendment to the Constitution by the legislatures of three-fourths of the several States within seven years from the date of its submission. [ratified, 1933]

AMENDMENT 21.

Section 1. The eighteenth article of amendment to the Constitution of the United States is hereby repealed.

Section 2. The transportation or importation into any State, Territory or possession of the United States for delivery or use therein of intoxicating liquors, in violation of the laws thereof, is hereby prohibited.

Section 3. This article shall be inoperative unless it shall have been ratified as an amendment to the Constitution by convention in the several States, as provided in the Constitution, within seven years from the date of the submission thereof to the States by the Congress. [ratified, 1933]

AMENDMENT 22.

Section 1. No person shall be elected to the office of the President more than twice, and no person who has held the office of President, or acted as President, for more than two years of a term to which some other person was elected President shall be elected to the office of the President more than once. But this Article shall not apply to any person holding the office of President when this Article was proposed by the Congress, and shall not prevent any person who may be holding the office of President, or acting as President, during the term within which this Article becomes operative from holding the office of President or acting as President during the remainder of such term.

Section 2. This article shall be inoperative unless it shall have been ratified as an amendment to the Constitution by the legislatures of three-fourths of the several States within seven years from the date of its submission to the States by the Congress. [ratified, 1951]

AMENDMENT 23.

Section 1. The District constituting the seat of government of the United States shall appoint in such manner as the Congress may direct:

A number of electors of President and Vice-President equal to the whole number of Senators and Representatives in Congress to which the District would be entitled if it were a State, but in no event more than the least populous State; they shall be in addition to those appointed by the States, but they shall be considered, for the purposes of the election of President and Vice-President, to be electors appointed by a State; and they shall meet in the District and perform such duties as provided by the twelfth article of amendment.

Section 2. The Congress shall have the power to enforce this article by appropriate legislation. [ratified, 1961]

AMENDMENT 24.

Section 1. The right of citizens of the United States to vote in any primary or other election for President or Vice President, for electors for President or Vice President, or for Senator or Representative in Congress, shall not be denied or abridged by the United States or any State by reason of failure to pay any poll tax or other tax.

Section 2. The Congress shall have power to enforce this article by appropriate legislation. [ratified, 1964]

AMENDMENT 25.

Section 1. In case of the removal of the President from office or of his death or resignation, the Vice President shall become President.

Section 2. Whenever there is a vacancy in the office of Vice President, the President shall nominate a Vice President who shall take office upon confirmation by a majority vote of both Houses of Congress.

Section 3. Whenever the President transmits to the President pro tempore of the Senate and the Speaker of the House of Representatives his written declaration that he is unable to discharge the powers and duties of his office, and until he transmits to them a written declaration to the contrary, such powers and duties shall be discharged by the Vice President as Acting President.

Section 4. Whenever the Vice President and a majority of either the principal officers of the executive departments or of such other body as Congress may by law provide, transmit to the President pro tempore of the Senate and the Speaker of the House of Representatives their written declaration that the President is unable to discharge the powers and duties of his office, the Vice President shall immediately assume the powers and duties of the office as Acting President.

Thereafter, when the President transmits to the President pro tempore of the Senate and the Speaker of the House of Representatives his written declaration that no inability exists, he shall resume the powers and duties of his office unless the Vice President and a majority of either the principal officers of the executive departments or of such other body as Congress may by law provide, transmit within four days to the President pro tempore of the Senate and the Speaker of the House of Representatives their written declaration that the President is unable to discharge the powers and duties of his office. Thereupon Congress shall decide the issue, assembling within forty-eight hours for that purpose if not in session. If the Congress, within twenty-one days after receipt of the latter written declaration, or, if Congress is not in session, within twenty-one days after Congress is required to assemble, determines by two-thirds vote of both Houses that the President is unable to discharge the powers and duties of his office, the Vice President shall continue to discharge the same as Acting President; otherwise, the President shall resume the powers and duties of his office. [ratified, 1967]

AMENDMENT 26.

Section 1. The right of citizens of the United States, who are eighteen years of age or older, to vote shall not be denied or abridged by the United States or by any State on account of age.

Section 2. The Congress shall have power to enforce this article by appropriate legislation. [ratified, 1971]

AMENDMENT 27.

No law varying the compensation for the services of the Senators and Representatives shall take effect until an election of Representatives shall have intervened. [ratified, 1992]

Appendix 3

THE FEDERALIST PAPERS
NO. 10 AND NO. 51

NO. 10: MADISON

Among the numerous advantages promised by a well-constructed Union, none deserves to be more accurately developed than its tendency to break and control the violence of faction. The friend of popular governments never finds himself so much alarmed for their character and fate as when he contemplates their propensity to this dangerous vice. He will not fail, therefore, to set a due value on any plan which, without violating the principles to which he is attached, provides a proper cure for it. The instability, injustice, and confusion introduced into the public councils have, in truth, been the mortal diseases under which popular governments have everywhere perished, as they continue to be the favorite and fruitful topics from which the adversaries to liberty derive their most specious declamations. The valuable improvements made by the American constitutions on the popular models, both ancient and modern, cannot certainly be too much admired; but it would be an unwarrantable partiality to contend that they have as effectually obviated the danger on this side, as was wished and expected. Complaints are everywhere heard from our most considerate and virtuous citizens, equally the friends of public and private faith and of public and personal liberty, that our governments are too unstable, that the public good is disregarded in the conflicts of rival parties, and that measures are too often decided, not according to the rules of justice and the rights of the minor party, but by the superior force of an interested and over-bearing majority. However anxiously we may wish that these complaints had no foundation, the evidence of known facts will not permit us to deny that they are in some degree true. It will be found, indeed, on a candid review of our situation, that some of the distresses under which we labor have been erroneously charged on the operation of our governments; but it will be found, at the same time, that other causes will not alone account for many of our heaviest misfortunes; and, particularly, for that prevailing and increasing distrust of public engagements and alarm for private rights which are echoed from one end of the continent to the other. These must be chiefly, if not wholly, effects of the unsteadiness and injustice with which a factious spirit has tainted our public administration.

By a faction I understand a number of citizens, whether amounting to a majority or minority of the whole, who are united and actuated by some common impulse of passion, or of interest, adverse to the rights of other citizens, or to the permanent and aggregate interests of the community.

There are two methods of curing the mischiefs of faction: the one, by removing its causes; the other, by controlling its effects.

There are again two methods of removing the causes of faction: the one, by destroying the liberty which is essential to its existence; the other, by giving to every citizen the same opinions, the same passions, and the same interests.

It could never be more truly said than of the first remedy that it was worse than the disease. Liberty is to faction what air is to fire, an aliment without which it instantly expires. But it could not be a less folly to abolish liberty, which is essential to political life, because it nourishes faction than it would be to wish the annihilation of air, which is essential to animal life, because it imparts to fire its destructive agency.

The second expedient is as impracticable as the first would be unwise. As long as the reason of man continues fallible, and he is at liberty to exercise it, different opinions will be formed. As long as the connection subsists between his reason and his self-love, his opinions and his passions will have a reciprocal influence on each other; and the former will be objects to which the latter will attach themselves. The diversity in the faculties of men, from which the rights of property originate, is not less an insuperable obstacle to a uniformity of interests. The protection of these faculties is the first object of government. From the protection of different and unequal faculties of acquiring property, the possession of different degrees and kinds of property immediately results; and from the influence of these on the sentiments and views of the respective proprietors ensues a division of the society into different interests and parties.

The latent causes of faction are thus sown in the nature of man; and we see them everywhere brought into different degrees of activity, according to the different circumstances of civil society. A zeal for different opinions concerning religion, concerning government, and many other points, as well of speculation as of practice; an attachment to different leaders ambitiously contending for pre-eminence and power; or to persons of other descriptions whose fortunes have been interesting to the human passions, have, in turn, divided mankind into parties, inflamed them with mutual animosity, and rendered them much more disposed to vex and oppress each other than to co-operate for their common good. So strong is this propensity of mankind to fall into mutual animosities that where no substantial occasion presents itself the most frivolous and fanciful distinctions have been sufficient to kindle their unfriendly passions and excite their most violent conflicts. But the most common and durable source of factions has been the various and unequal distribution of property. Those who hold and those who are without property have ever formed distinct interests in society. Those who are creditors, and those who are debtors, fall under a like discrimination. A landed interest, a manufacturing interest, a mercantile interest, a moneyed interest, with many lesser interests, grow up of necessity in civilized nations, and divide them into different classes, actuated by different sentiments and views. The regulation of these various and interfering interests forms the principal task of modern legislation and involves the spirit of party and faction in the necessary and ordinary operations of government.

No man is allowed to be a judge in his own cause, because his interest would certainly bias his judgment, and, not improbably, corrupt his integrity. With equal, nay with greater reason, a body of men are unfit to be both judges and parties at the same time; yet what are many of the most important acts of legislation but so many judicial determinations, not indeed concerning the rights of single persons, but concerning the rights of large bodies of citizens? And what are the different classes of legislators but advocates and parties to the causes which they determine? Is a law proposed concerning private debts? It is a question to which the creditors are parties on one side and the debtors on the other. Justice ought to hold the balance between them. Yet the parties are, and must be, themselves the judges; and the most numerous party, or in other words, the most powerful faction must be expected to prevail. Shall domestic manufacturers be encouraged, and in what degree, by restictions on foreign manufacturers? are questions which would be differently decided by the landed and the manufacturing classes, and probably by neither with

a whole regard to justice and the public good. The apportionment of taxes on the various descriptions of property is an act which seems to require the most exact impartiality; yet there is, perhaps, no legislative act in which greater opportunity and temptation are given to a predominant party to trample on the rules of justice. Every shilling with which they overburden the inferior number is a shilling saved to their own pockets.

It is in vain to say that enlightened statesmen will be able to adjust these clashing interests and render them all subservient to the public good. Enlightened statesmen will not always be at the helm. Nor, in many cases, can such an adjustment be made at all without taking into view indirect and remote considerations, which will rarely prevail over the immediate interest which one party may find in disregarding the rights of another or the good of the whole.

The inference to which we are brought is that the *causes* of faction cannot be removed and that relief is only to be sought in the means of controlling its *effects*.

If a faction consists of less than a majority, relief is supplied by the republican principle, which enables the majority to defeat its sinister views by regular vote. It may clog the administration, it may convulse the society; but it will be unable to execute and mask its violence under the forms of the Constitution. When a majority is included in a faction, the form of popular government, on the other hand, enables it to sacrifice to its ruling passion or interest both the public good and the rights of other citizens. To secure the public good and private rights against the danger of such a faction, and at the same time to preserve the spirit and the form of popular government, is then the great object to which our inquiries are directed. Let me add that it is the great desideratum by which alone this form of government can be rescued from the opprobrium under which it has so long labored and be recommended to the esteem and adoption of mankind.

By what means is this object attainable? Evidently by one of two only. Either the existence of the same passion or interest in a majority at the same time must be prevented, or the majority, having such coexistent passion or interest, must be rendered, by their number and local situation, unable to concert and carry into effect schemes of oppression. If the impulse and the opportunity be suffered to coincide, we well know that neither moral nor religious motives can be relied on as an adequate control. They are not found to be such on the injustice and violence of individuals, and lose their efficacy in proportion to the number combined together, that is, in proportion as their efficacy becomes needful.

From this view of the subject it may be concluded that a pure democracy, by which I mean a society consisting of a small number of citizens, who assemble and administer the government in person, can admit of no cure for the mischiefs of faction. A common passion or interest will, in almost every case, be felt by a majority of the whole; a communication and concert results from the form of government itself; and there is nothing to check the inducements to sacrifice the weaker party or an obnoxious individual. Hence it is that such democracies have ever been spectacles of turbulence and contention; have ever been found incompatible with personal security or the rights of property; and have in general been as short in their lives as they have been violent in their deaths. Theoretic politicians, who have patronized their species of government, have erroneously supposed that by reducing mankind to a perfect equality in their poltical rights, they would at the same time be perfectly equalized and assimilated in their possessions, their opinions, and their passions.

A republic, by which I mean a government in which the scheme of representation takes place, opens a different prospect and promises the cure for which we are seeking. Let us examine the points in which it varies from pure democracy, and we shall comprehend both the nature of the cure and the efficacy which it must derive from the Union.

The two great points of difference between a democracy and a republic are: first the delegation of the government, in the latter, to a small number of citizens elected by the rest; secondly, the great number of citizens and greater sphere of country over which the latter may be extended.

The effect of the first difference is, on the one hand, to refine and enlarge the public views by passing them through the medium of a chosen body of citizens, whose wisdom may best discern the true interest of their country and whose patriotism and love of justice will be least likely to sacrifice it to temporary or partial considerations. Under such a regulation it may well happen that the public voice, pronounced by the representatives of the people, will be more consonant to the public good than if pronounced by the people themselves, convened for the purpose. On the other hand, the effect may be inverted. Men of factious tempers, of local prejudices, or of sinister designs, may, by intrigue, by corruption, or by other means, first obtain the suffrages, and then betray the interests of the people. The question resulting is, whether small or extensive republics are the most favorable to the election of proper guardians of the public weal; and it is clearly decided in favor of the latter by two obvious considerations.

In the first place it is to be remarked that however small the republic may be the representatives must be raised to a certain number in order to guard against the cabals of a few; and that however large it may be they must be limited to a certain number in order to guard against the confusion of a multitude. Hence, the number of representatives in the two cases not being in proportion to that of the constituents, and being proportionally greatest in the small republic, it follows that if the proportion of fit characters be not less in the large than in the small republic, the former will present a greater option, and consequently a greater probability of a fit choice.

In the next place, as each representative will be chosen by a greater number of citizens in the large than in the small republic, it will be more difficult for unworthy candidates to practise with success the vicious arts by which elections are too often carried; and the suffrages of the people being more free, will be more likely to center on men who possess the most attractice merit and the most diffusive and established characters.

It must be confessed that in this, as in most other cases, there is a mean, on both sides of which inconveniences will be found to lie. By enlarging too much the number of electors, you render the representative too little acquainted with all their local circumstances and lesser interests; as by reducing it too much, you render him unduly attached to these, and too little fit to comprehend and pursue great and national objects. The federal Constitution forms a happy combination in this respect; the great and aggregate interests being referred to the national, the local and particular to the State legislatures.

The other point of difference is the greater number of citizens and extent of territory which may be brought within the compass of republican than of democratic government; and it is this circumstance principally which renders factious combinations less to be dreaded in the former than in the latter. The smaller the society, the fewer probably will be the distinct parties and interests composing it; the fewer the distinct parties and interests, the more frequently will a majority be found of the same party; and the smaller the number of individuals composing a majority, and the smaller the

compass within which they are placed, the more easily will they concert and execute their plans of oppression. Extend the sphere and you take in a greater variety of parties and interests; you make it less probable that a majority of the whole will have a common motive to invade the rights of other citizens; or if such a common motive exists, it will be more difficult for all who feel it to discover their own strength and to act in unison with each other. Besides other impediments, it may be remarked that, where there is a consciousness of unjust or dishonorable purposes, communication is always checked by distrust in proportion to the number whose concurrence is necessary.

Hence, it clearly appears that the same advantage which a republic has over a democracy in controlling the effects of faction is enjoyed by a large over a small republic—is enjoyed by the Union over the States composing it. Does this advantage consist in the substitution of representatives whose enlightened views and virtuous sentiments render them superior to local prejudices and to schemes of injustice? It will not be denied that the representation of the Union will be most likely to possess these requisite endowments. Does it consist in the greater security afforded by a greater variety of parties, against the event of any one party being able to outnumber and oppress the rest? In an equal degree does the increased variety of parties comprised within the Union increase this security? Does it, in fine, consist in the greater obstacles opposed to the concert and accomplishment of the secret wishes of an unjust and interested majority? Here again the extent of the Union gives it the most palpable advantage.

The influence of factious leaders may kindle a flame within their particular States but will be unable to spread a general conflagration through the other States. A religious sect may degenerate into a political faction in a part of the Confederacy; but the variety of sects dispersed over the entire face of it must secure the national councils against any danger from that source. A rage for paper money, for an abolition of debts, for an equal division of property, or for any other improper or wicked project, will be less apt to pervade the whole body of the Union than a particular member of it, in the same proportion as such a malady is more likely to taint a particular county or district than an entire State.

In the extent and proper structure of the Union, therefore, we behold a republican remedy for the diseases most incident to republican government. And according to the degree of pleasure and pride we feel in being republicans ought to be our zeal in cherishing the spirit and supporting the character of federalists. PUBLIUS

NO. 51: MADISON

To what expedient, then, shall we finally resort, for maintaining in practice the necessary partition of power among the several departments as laid down in the Constitution? The only answer that can be given is that as all these exterior provisions are found to be inadequate the defect must be supplied, by so contriving the interior structure of the government as that its several constituent parts may, by their mutual relations, be the means of keeping each other in their proper places. Without presuming to undertake a full development of this important idea I will hazard a few general observations which may perhaps place it in a clear light, and enable us to form a more correct judgment of the principles and structure of the government planned by the convention.

In order to lay a due foundation for that separate and distinct exercise of the different powers of government, which to a certain extent is admitted on all hands to be essential to the preservation of liberty, it is evident that each department should have a will of its own; and consequently should be so constituted that the members of each should have as little agency as possible in the appointment of the members of the others. Were this principle rigorously adhered to, it would require that all the appointments for the supreme executive, legislative, and judiciary magistracies should be drawn from the same fountain of authority, the people, through channels having no communication whatever with one another. Perhaps such a plan of constructing the several departments would be less difficult in practice than it may in contemplation appear. Some difficulties, however, and some additional expense would attend the execution of it. Some deviations, therefore, from the principle must be admitted. In the constitution of the judiciary department in particular, it might be inexpedient to insist rigorously on the principle; first, because peculiar qualifications being essential in the members, the primary consideration ought to be to select that mode of choice which best secures these qualifications; second, because the permanent tenure by which the appointments are held in that department must soon destroy all sense of dependence on the authority conferring them.

It is equally evident that the members of each department should be as little dependent as possible on those of the others for the emoluments annexed to their offices. Were the executive magistrate, or the judges, not independent of the legislature in this particular, their independence in every other would be merely nominal.

But the great security against a gradual concentration of the several powers in the same department consists in giving to those who administer each department the necessary constitutional means and personal motives to resist encroachments of the others. The provision for defense must in this, as in all other cases, be made commensurate to the danger of attack.

Ambition must be made to counteract ambition. The interest of the man must be connected with the constitutional rights of the place. It may be a reflection on human nature that such devices should be necessary to control the abuses of government. But what is government itself but the greatest of all reflections on human nature? If men were angels, no government would be necessary. If angels were to govern men, neither external nor internal controls on government would be necessary. In framing a government which is to be administered by men over men, the great difficulty lies in this: you must first enable the government to control the governed; and in the next place oblige it to control itself. A dependence on the people is, no doubt, the primary control on the government; but experience has taught mankind the necessity of auxiliary precautions.

This policy of supplying, by opposite and rival interests, the defect of better motives, might be traced through the whole system of human affairs, private as well as public. We see it particularly displayed in all the subordinate distributions of power, where the constant aim is to divide and arrange the several offices in such a manner as that each may be a check on the other—that the private interest of every individual may be a sentinel over the public rights. These inventions of prudence cannot be less requisite in the distribution of the supreme powers of the State.

But it is not possible to give to each department an equal power of self-defense. In republican government, the legislative authority necessarily predominates. The remedy for this inconveniency is to divide the legislature into different branches; and to render them, by different modes of election and different principles of action, as little connected with each other as the nature of their common functions and their common dependence on the society will admit. It may even be necessary to guard against dangerous encroachments by still fur-

ther precautions. As the weight of the legislative authority requires that it should be thus divided, the weakness of the executive may require, on the other hand, that it should be fortified. An absolute negative on the legislature appears, at first view, to be the natural defense with which the executive magistrate should be armed. But perhaps it would be neither altogether safe nor alone sufficient. On ordinary occasions it might not be exerted with the requisite firmness, and on extraordinary occasions it might be perfidiously abused. May not this defect of an absolute negative be supplied by some qualified connection between this weaker department and the weaker branch of the stronger department, by which the latter may be led to support the constitutional rights of the former, without being too much detached from the rights of its own department?

If the principles on which these observations are founded be just, as I persuade myself they are, and they be applied as a criterion to the several State constitutions, and to the federal Constitution, it will be found that if the latter does not perfectly correspond with them, the former are infinitely less able to bear such a test.

There are, moreover, two considerations particularly applicable to the federal system of America, which place that system in a very interesting point of view.

First. In a single republic, all the power surrendered by the people is submitted to the administration of a single government; and the usurpations are guarded against by a division of the government into distinct and separate departments. In the compound republic of America, the power surrendered by the people is first divided between two distinct governments, and then the portion allotted to each subdivided among distinct and separate departments. Hence a double security arises to the rights of the people. The different governments will control each other, at the same time that each will be controlled by itself.

Second. It is of great importance in a republic not only to guard the society against the oppression of its rulers, but to guard one part of the society against the injustice of the other part. Different interests necessarily exist in different classes of citizens. If a majority be united by a common interest, the rights of the minority will be insecure. There are but two methods of providing against this evil: the one by creating a will in the community independent of the majority—that is, of the society itself; the other, by comprehending in the society so many separate descriptions of citizens as will render an unjust combination of a majority of the whole very improbable, if not impracticable. The first method prevails in all governments possessing an hereditary or self-appointed authority. This, at best, is but a precarious security; because a power independent of the society may as well espouse the unjust views of the major as the rightful interests of the minor party, and may possibly be turned against both parties. The second method will be exemplified in the federal republic of the United States. Whilst all authority in it will be derived from and dependent on the society, the society itself will be broken into so many parts, interests and classes of citizens, that the rights of individuals, or of the minority, will be in little danger from interested combinations of the majority. In a free government the security for civil rights must be the same as that for religious rights. It consists in the one case in the multiplicity of interests, and in the other in the multiplicity of sects. The degree of security in both cases will depend on the number of interests and sects; and this may be presumed to depend on the extent of country and number of people comprehended under the same government. This view of the subject must particularly recommend a proper federal system to all the sincere and considerate friends of republican government, since it shows that in exact proportion as the territory of the Union may be formed into more circumscribed Confederacies, of States, oppressive combinations of a majority will be facilitated; the best security, under the republican forms, for the rights of every class of citizen, will be diminished; and consequently the stability and independence of some member of the government, the only other security, must be proportionally increased. Justice is the end of government. It is the end of civil society. It ever has been and ever will be pursued until it be obtained, or until liberty be lost in the pursuit. In a society under the forms of which the stronger faction can readily unite and oppress the weaker, anarchy may as truly be said to reign as in a state of nature, where the weaker individual is not secured against the violence of the stronger; and as, in the latter state, even the stronger individuals are prompted, by the uncertainty of their condition, to submit to a government which may protect the weak as well as themselves; so, in the former state, will the more powerful factions or parties be gradually induced, by a like motive, to wish for a government which will protect all parties, the weaker as well as the more powerful. It can be little doubted that if the State of Rhode Island was separated from the Confederacy and left to itself, the insecurity of rights under the popular form of government within such narrow limits would be displayed by such reiterated oppressions of factious majorities that some power altogether independent of the people would soon be called for by the voice of the very factions whose misrule had proved the necessity of it. In the extended republic of the United States, and among the great variety of interests, parties, and sects which it embraces, a coalition of a majority of the whole society could seldom take place on any other principles than those of justice and the general good; whilst there being thus less danger to a minor from the will of a majority party, there must be less pretext, also, to provide for the security of the former, by introducing into the government a will not dependent on the latter, or, in other words, a will independent of the society itself. It is no less certain than it is important, notwithstanding the contrary opinions which have been entertained, that the larger the society, provided it lie within a practicable sphere, the more duly capable it will be of self-government. And happily for the *republican cause*, the practicable sphere may be carried to a very great extent by a judicious modification and mixture of the *federal principle*.

PUBLIUS

Appendix *4*

THE 1992 ELECTION AND THE CLINTON ADMINISTRATION

The 1992 U.S. election held surprises. Outside the presidential contest the Republicans managed to hold their own: They retained their 43 seats in the U.S. Senate and picked up a net of 9 seats in the House of Representatives, but the Democrats retained substantial majorities in both chambers (see Table A.1). At the state level Democrats picked up a net of 2 governorships, but lost a net of 147 seats in state legislatures.

In the presidential contest, though, George Bush, who had looked well-nigh unbeatable throughout much of 1991, especially in the immediate aftermath of his highly successful leadership of an international coalition in the Gulf War with Iraq, lost the presidency to his principal challenger, Governor Bill Clinton of Arkansas, by 5.5 percentage points in the popular vote. Clinton won 32 states, including the District of Columbia, with 370 electoral votes, a comfortable margin over the 270 electoral votes required for election. The map on page A32 (Figure A.1) illustrates the Democratic sweep of the Northeast, the industrial Midwest, and the Pacific coast. Bush's 18 states and 168 electoral votes were confined largely to the South, the West Central region, and the Rocky Mountain area. With this victory Clinton became the forty-second president of the United States.

On January 20, 1993, crowds gathered on Capitol Hill to watch as Chief Justice William Rehnquist administered the presidential oath to William Jefferson Clinton, thus making him the forty-second president of the United States.

TABLE A.1   THE 1992 ELECTION BOXSCORE

	1980		1984		1988		1990			1992		
House of Representatives												
	Dem.	Rep.	Dem.	Rep.	Dem.	Rep.	Dem.	Rep.	Ind.	Dem.	Rep.	Ind.
Total	243	192	252	182	260	175	267	167	1	258	176	1
Women	10	9	11	11	14	11	20	9	—	35	12	—
Blacks	17	0	20	0	24	0	25	1	—	38	1	—

	1980		1984		1988		1990		1992	
Senate										
	Dem.	Rep.	Dem.	Rep.	Dem.	Rep.	Dem.	Rep.	Dem.	Rep.
Total	46	53	47	53	55	45	56	44	57	43
Women	0	2	0	2	1	1	1	1	5	1
Blacks	0	0	0	0	0	0	0	0	1	0

	1980		1984		1988		1990			1992		
Governors												
	Dem.	Rep.	Dem.	Rep.	Dem.	Rep.	Dem.	Rep.	Ind.	Dem.	Rep.	Ind.
Total	27	23	34	16	28	22	28	20	2	30	18	2

	1980		1984		1988		1990		1992	
Members of state legislatures[a]										
	Dem.	Rep.	Dem.	Rep.	Dem.	Rep.	Dem.	Rep.	Dem.	Rep.
Total	4,483	2,918	4,404	3,057	4,480	2,922	4,489	2,906	4,342	3,005
Proportion by party	60	39	59	41	60	39	60	39	59	41
Women	887		1,087		1,260		1,368		1,503	
Blacks	318		384		416		440		513	

	1980		1984		1988		1990		1992	
Control of state legislative chambers by party[b]										
	Dem.	Rep.	Dem.	Rep.	Dem.	Rep.	Dem.	Rep.	Dem.	Rep.
National	63	35	65	31	68	29	71	23	66	29
Northeast	10	8	11	7	12	6	12	5	11	6
South	31	1	31	1	31	1	31	1	30	1
N. Central	10	12	11	11	13	8	14	7	13	8
West	12	14	12	12	12	14	14	10	12	14

	1980		1984		1988		1990		1992	
With both legislative houses and governor of the same party										
	Dem.	Rep.	Dem.	Rep.	Dem.	Rep.	Dem.	Rep.	Dem.	Rep.
	17	7	18	4	14	5	16	3	16	3

[a] Nebraska excluded from legislative house calculation because it has a unicameral nonpartisan legislative system. [b] The 1992 totals exclude Pennsylvania's upper house, which split 25–25, Michigan's lower house, which split 55–55, and Florida's upper house, which split 20–20.

Source: The American Enterprise, January/February 1991, for 1976–1990 figures; *Congressional Quarterly Weekly Report,* December 12, 1992, for members of the U.S. Congress; National Conference of State Legislatures and the Center for the American Woman and Politics, Eagleton Institute of Politics, Rutgers University, for state legislatures.

Another surprise in the 1992 presidential election was the splash made by a political newcomer who changed the face of the campaign and, to a certain extent, campaigning itself. Texas billionaire H. Ross Perot acquired vast wealth in the computer services business and spent liberally from his fortune to finance his independent campaign for the presidency. Running without any party or much formal organization, Perot relied on television—from his own paid political broadcasts to talk shows like "Larry King Live"—to get his message across. And he got results: 19 percent of the electorate voted for Perot. This was the highest proportion won by any third-party or independent candidate since former president Theodore Roosevelt garnered 27.4 percent on the Progressive party line in 1912.

FIGURE A.1 THE 1992 ELECTORAL VOTE BY STATE

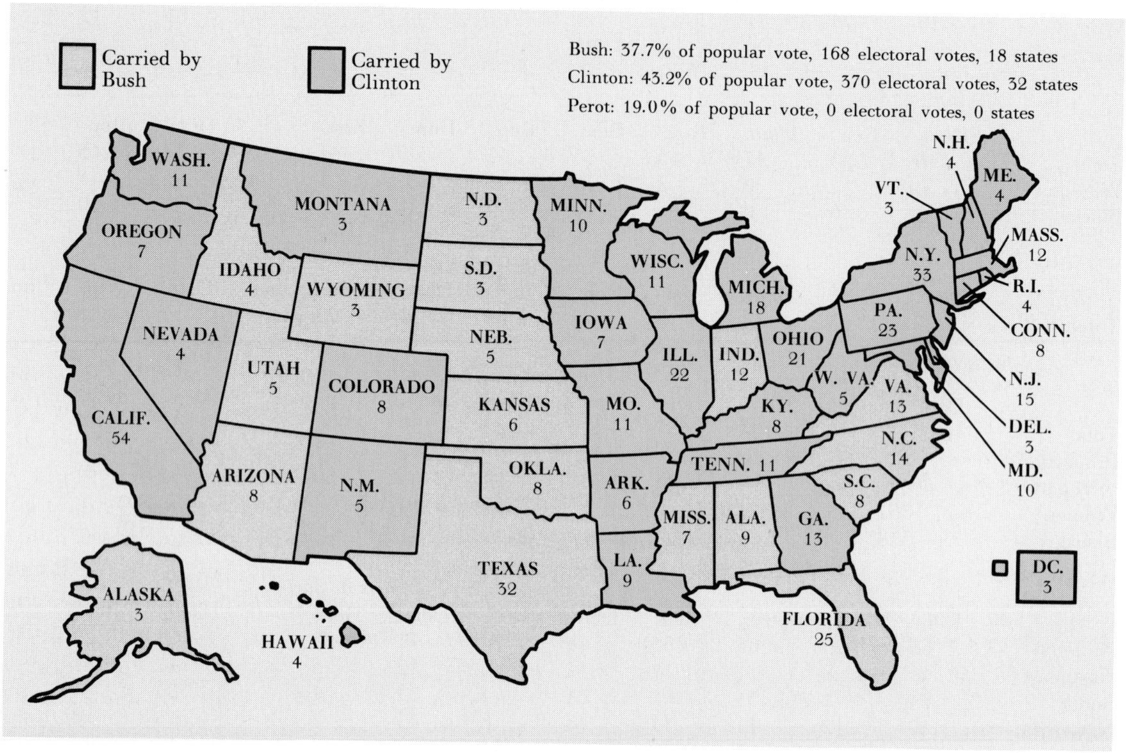

Source: *Congressional Quarterly Weekly Reports*, November 7, 1992, p. 3549.

THE EXPECTED BUSH VICTORY

The 1992 presidential results were obviously a sharp departure from those of the three preceding presidential contests, all of which were won handily by Republicans: Ronald Reagan in 1980 and 1984, and George Bush in 1988. What short-term factors produced the 1992 deviation? The campaign's colloquial answer was: "It's the economy, stupid!" And the economy was widely implicated. Still, the dynamic that took over the 1992 campaign and pushed it in a direction opposite from what most observers

had expected a year or more before the balloting was much more interesting and complicated than simply that the economy had turned sour. Most voters felt that it was "time for a change." Before exploring this dynamic, however, let's review what the election looked like in the latter part of 1991, when the long campaign was just getting underway.

Most election analysts believed that a Bush victory was highly likely. Why? First, as president, he had the resources of incumbency. The most important of these stems from the fact that an American president is more than a head of government; he is the chief of state, a primary symbol of the nation, and the embodiment of its many shared political aspirations as well. Second, over most of the first three years of his presidency Bush enjoyed high ratings by the public. The proportion saying they approved his handling of the office in those first three years averaged much higher, for example, than had the proportion backing Ronald Reagan, his popular predecessor, in any three years of his tenure. To the generally good marks that Bush earned in his first two years was added the great credit he was given for his handling of the crisis of the Persian Gulf. Following Iraqi leader Saddam Hussein's August 1990 invasion of Kuwait, George Bush led a decisive allied military campaign against Iraq, culminating in victory in March 1991. At war's end 85 to 90 percent of adult Americans said they approved the president's conduct of his office: The Gallup poll of February 28– March 3 put those approving at 89 percent; the CBS / *New York Times* poll of March 4–6 got virtually identical findings—88 percent approving, 8 percent disapproving. While everyone knew at the time that these ratings were going to fall, and fall substantially, they also knew that the ratings had a long way to drop before Bush would be in any political difficulty. Through his handling of this major foreign-policy challenge, as well as his leadership at the close of the cold war, much of the public judged that George Bush was "up to the presidency."

A third factor leading most analysts in 1991 to expect a Bush reelection evolved from the Democrats themselves. The party's most prominent and established figures—New York governor Mario Cuomo, Texas senator and 1988 vice-presidential nominee Lloyd Bentsen, Tennessee senator and 1988 contender Al Gore, and House majority leader and 1988 candidate Richard Gephardt—without exception decided not to enter the race. With only one exception—former California governor Jerry Brown—none of those who had established themselves

at the level of presidential politics chose to challenge a president who looked unbeatable. And Jerry Brown had gotten bad marks from his previous national exposure, which included a run for the Democratic nomination in 1976. The other candidates—former Massachusetts senator Paul Tsongas, Nebraska senator Bob Kerrey, Iowa senator Tom Harkin, and the eventual winner, Arkansas governor Bill Clinton—began the campaign largely unknown to the electorate.

Why Bush was not challenged by any member of the Democrats' "first team" also has to do with how presidential candidates get nominated by their political party. In the earlier days formal political party organizations would play a major role in presidential electioneering, culminating in national conventions where the parties' candidates were actually nominated. But presidential nominations are no longer conferred by party organizations; rather, a long, drawn-out string of primary elections decides the nominees. The national conventions continue to operate, but rather than choose nominees, they merely ratify the choices already made and use the convention to publicize the parties' platforms. As a result, candidates can no longer count on party organization for much assistance; the fabled "machines" of yesteryear have long-since disappeared. Instead, candidates must put together their entire campaign apparatus themselves. This means candidacies must begin early. Most decisions bearing on who the field will include are made by the summer or early fall of the year preceding the election itself—and at that point in 1991 the consensus among Democratic politicians was that Bush would be very hard to beat. The 1996 election seemed more promising.

The Democrats were right to be worried. Besides the president's high public ratings, the Republicans entered the 1992 campaign with most of the political currency the party had accrued over the Reagan years still undispersed. In the 1980s the party climbed out of the decidedly second-place status in party identification that it had occupied for most of the preceding half-century, reaching parity in underlying partisanship. And the GOP retained this position going into the 1992 campaign, so that it didn't have a gap in party loyalties to overcome. The party was also seen as better able than the Democrats to manage the country's affairs. Even in mid-1992, when economic worries were high, the GOP still often got better ratings on economic management than did the Democrats.

In the area of political philosophy, too, the GOP's assets had held up well. The government's size and performance continued to be widely criticized. Though they elected a Democrat to the presidency, voters still indicated on election day, November 3, 1992, that they favored restraint on government growth. When the Voter, Research, and Surveys (VRS) exit poll asked voters whether they wanted a government that provided more services while costing more in taxes, or that cost less while providing fewer services, only 36 percent of voters chose the former—55 percent opted for less government. When a CBS News / New York Times poll of January 12–14, 1993, asked voters whether they thought "that, in general, the federal government creates more problems than it solves . . . [or] solves more problems than it creates," respondents said the former, by 69 to 22 percent.

Lastly, when the campaign began in the latter half of 1991, most economic indicators showed trends at least modestly favorable to the incumbent party. These indicators, including changes in gross domestic product (GDP), suggested that the U.S. economy had bottomed out in the second quarter of 1991. The three quarters in which real GDP fell were the last one in 1990 and the first two in 1991. Nearly eighteen months prior to the 1992 balloting, economic decline had ended and recovery, even

if sluggish, had begun. It appeared that George Bush would not have to run for reelection in the midst of recession.

THE CLINTON CANDIDACY

Bill Clinton may yet achieve great things as president, but his candidacy for the office was often troubled. At no point in the 1992 campaign did he succeed in dispelling the doubts, among a majority of the electorate, about his suitability for the office (see chapter 7, pp. 178–80). These doubts showed up regularly in poll findings. For example, in a survey taken October 12 and 13, CBS News and *The New York Times* asked respondents whether they thought Clinton could be "trusted to deal with all the problems a president has to deal with," or whether they were "concerned that he might make serious mistakes." It's hardly newsworthy that 80 percent of Republicans polled said they were worried about him in this regard, but it is striking indeed that 57 percent of independents and 32 percent of Democrats even said so. The incumbent president was shown trailing by 13 percentage points in this survey, but nonetheless Bush got better marks on the "trust" issue than did Clinton.[1]

The election-day poll taken by VRS provided further information on the Democrat's inability to overcome widespread doubts about him. For example, VRS asked: "If Bill Clinton wins today, what best describes your feelings about what he will do as president?" The alternatives given

[1]Even just before his inauguration, in a survey done for *Time* and CNN by Yankelovich Partners, respondents were asked: "Do you think Bill Clinton is a leader you can trust, or do you have some doubts and reservations?" Only 41 percent said he was a leader they could trust; 50 percent that they still had doubts. Some honeymoon!

respondents as they left the voting stations were "excited," "optimistic, but not excited," "concerned, but not scared," and "scared." Only 41 percent picked one of the two positive assessments: 15 percent said they would be excited, 26 percent optimistic. Against these 41 percent, 57 percent said they would be concerned (27 percent) or scared (30 percent). And it wasn't just those who voted for Bush that offered a negative review. Twenty-eight percent of VRS respondents who described themselves as Democrats said a Clinton victory would worry them. Sixty percent of independents were thus negative about him.

Bill Clinton seemed at times his own worst enemy. His inability to shake questions of a personal sort—questions about his alleged affair with Gennifer Flowers, about his position regarding the draft during the Vietnam War, about whether he had ever smoked marijuana—was an important factor that a Democratic strategist scripting his party's 1992 campaign would have written differently. In other important regards, however, the Clinton campaign had things break its way. Some of these elements stemmed from the real strengths that Clinton himself brought to the race. He proved, for one, to be an impressively disciplined and determined candidate. His personal resilience, physical and emotional, was remarkable. In other regards, too, he was a good candidate: He projected affability, with

Bill Clinton appealing to voters along his often bumpy trail to the White House.

few traces of rancor. While Clinton had never before been tried in a national race, he proved able to meet the test.

Besides his personal attributes as a campaigner, Clinton had carefully studied the major lessons for his party of recent presidential elections. Prior to 1992, his work on the national stage had largely involved his leading role in the Democratic Leadership Council (DLC), an organization of Democratic moderates and conservatives that included Clinton's vice-president, Al Gore. At home, Clinton showed he could maintain his popularity and win repeated reelection in a conservative state. He talked often about the importance of individuals' taking responsibility for things—avoiding unbroken emphasis on the government's responsibility. His positions in favor of a strong national defense and a vigorous U.S. foreign policy, and his general inclination to celebrate the American idea rather than concentrate on deficiencies within it, also served to separate him from stands that have plagued his party over the last quarter-century.

The "new" Democratic party that Clinton champions resembles one that many Democratic strategists and intellectuals of the party's center-right have long been advocating. One of this company, David Kusnet—now on the White House speech-writing staff—argued in a book published in early 1992 that the Democrats could regain the presidency only if they again began "speaking American."[2] "You don't have to be a social historian—you just have to watch TV, go to the movies, talk to your neighbors, or simply search your soul—to get a sense of some of the ideas that have helped shape our nation," Kusnet wrote. "Perhaps most important is the idea that America is special, and Americans are special people. A country that doesn't define itself by language or lineage has to set other standards for citizenship, and the classic definition of American nationality includes a dedication to democratic values and a commitment to building a virtuous community—the great American experiment. . . . Far from being academic or archaic, these have echoed throughout two centuries of political debate."[3]

The problem for the Democrats, Kusnet maintained, was that "for the past decade, Republicans have been more at home with (and more adept at) the rhetoric of American exceptionalism. . . . During the Reagan-Bush years, Democrats remained reluctant to espouse a similar belief in America's place in the world. Of course, many Democratic party activists . . . were shaped by the protest movements of the 1960s, which ended up concentrating more on America's problems than its promise. Yet Jimmy Carter and Walter Mondale, whose politics weren't formed in the sixties, seemed tone deaf to the music of American specialness."[4]

The "music" of Clinton's campaign reflected perspectives like those Kusnet articulated. The campaign was a determined effort to steal the Republicans' clothes by "speaking American" better than they did.

PERCEPTIONS OF THE ECONOMY IN THE 1992 CAMPAIGN

An incumbent president, not plagued by scandal, is likely to win reelection in the United States if the economy is strong or at least recovering. As we have seen, the U.S. econ-

---

[2]David Kusnet, *Speaking American: How the Democrats Can Win in the Nineties* (New York: Thunder's Mouth Press, 1992).

[3]Ibid, p. 40.
[4]Ibid, p. 41.

omy, while growing sluggishly in late 1991, was picking up steam as 1992 proceeded. In addition, George Bush had just succeeded in the Persian Gulf War and received high marks for his handling of foreign affairs in general. In this setting a Bush defeat was unlikely—unless a large majority of the public somehow became convinced that the U.S. economy was being badly managed, threatening the nation's future and the well-being of individual Americans. In late 1991 and throughout 1992, a large majority did become convinced of such economic malperformance.

For example, in fourteen national surveys conducted throughout 1992 up to the election, CBS News and *The New York Times* asked respondents how they would rate "the conditions of the national economy these days." At no time did as many as one in four rate it very good or fairly good. More than three-fourths called the economy fairly bad or very bad throughout the election year. On election eve (a survey of October 29–November 1), 77 percent said the national economy was in bad shape, even though it was in fact growing—in real terms, at an annualized rate of roughly 3.5 to 4 percent.

Americans' concern about the economy was obviously front and center throughout the 1992 campaign. Three separate sources repeatedly told voters that the economic sky was falling. One of these, the Democratic campaign, is unremarkable. The out-of-power party often charges the "ins" with economic mismanagement as part of its case to voters that it be given a chance to govern. In 1992 the Democrats did their job more or less in the standard fashion. But the other two sources were unusual, and together they convinced Americans that, though objective data showed the economy growing, in fact the United States was in desperate straits. One of these sources was the self-financed, television-centered, independent campaign of H. Ross Perot. The other was the media.

BAD PRESS ON THE ECONOMY

The striking fact about the press's reporting on economic developments is the sustained, unremitting emphasis on problems and failure. Content analysis of ABC, CBS, and NBC evening television news, done by Robert Lichter and his colleagues at the Center for Media and Public Affairs, indicates that coverage of the economy became increasingly intense in the latter part of 1991—more than twice as heavy in October 1991–September 1992 than it had been in the preceding twelve months when the recession was underway.[5] This much might be explained largely by the fact that the Gulf War and the breakup of the Soviet Empire had commanded so much attention in the latter half of 1990 and the first half of 1991 that news of the domestic economy was largely crowded out.

This cannot account, however, for the extreme pessimism and negativism of the expanded coverage of the economy by national TV news in late 1991 and 1992, after recovery had begun. The Center for Media and Public Affairs reported that "during the most recent quarter [July–September 1992], 96 percent of the sources [cited on the evening news broadcasts] have focused on economic weakness and shortcomings."[6] Though recovery was underway, the U.S. economy still had problems aplenty during the closing months of the 1992 campaign. Television news coverage would certainly not have come down 96 percent positive or optimistic on economic performance during this span had it faithfully reflected reality. But its 96 percent negative coverage distorted what was in fact a complex picture with many posi-

[5] The results of the content analysis of news coverage of the U.S. economy may be found in "The Boom in Gloom: TV News Coverage of the American Economy, 1990–1992," *Media Monitor* 6, 8 (October 1992): 2–4.
[6] Ibid, p. 3.

tive as well as negative features. So why was economic coverage thus skewed? The press had no master plan to elect Clinton by exaggerating the economy's problems as some conspiracy theorists might have it. Rather, something far more prosaic was occurring. First, a majority of journalists simply felt closer to the Democrats' stands than to those of the Republicans. This identification is, of course, a staple of modern American politics (see chapter 13, pp. 410–16). To this, in 1992, was added the fact that after a dozen years in power the Republicans and their economic policies had become an old and tired story. Many journalists, it seems, were in a mood for something new. Finally, "the economy in shambles" is inherently a more dramatic story than "some problems and some strengths." The coming together of these three distinct elements contributed to the most important political "event" of the 1992 campaign—an uninterrupted stream of negative press reports and commentary on the nation's economy that left much of the public in a state of bewilderment and frustration.[7]

[7]A variety of other explanations have been offered for the public's foul mood with regard to the state of the economy. In one of its *Roper Reports* series, for example, the Roper Organization—a New York–based survey research organization that is not connected to the Roper Center—concluded that "consumer confidence and the public mood in 1992 were far more depressed than many observers believed warranted. Interest rates and inflation were very low, while unemployment rose only modestly by historic standards. Nonetheless, a twenty-year low of only 14 percent of Americans in this *[Roper Reports]* study said the nation is headed in the 'right direction.' [*Roper Reports*, 92-8, December 1992, p. 2.] Seeking to reconcile the apparent discrepancy, the analysts suggested: "One explanation dates back to the 1980s when Roper Reports observed signs of 'aspiration inflation,' meaning material expectations were growing much faster than achievement. In May 1989, we said: 'Given much higher material expectations, public opinion would react sharply—and extremely negatively—to any future downturn in the economy.' And so it did."

THE EFFECT OF THE PEROT CANDIDACY

Throughout the 1992 campaign, analysts pondered the impact that Ross Perot's candidacy was having and tried to divine just how much, in the final analysis, the support he drew would tip the balance between Bush and Clinton. There was never agreement on these matters, and even in the wake of the election there is unlikely to be any. Available data, especially those from the VRS exit poll, can help us understand the makeup of Perot's backers and, thus, to get a better idea where on the political spectrum they came from. But the larger question of just what the 1992 contest would have

Independent candidate H. Ross Perot at the second presidential debate. This Texas billionaire brought the economy and the deficit to the forefront during the 1992 campaign. Gaining 19 percent of the popular vote, he proved to be a factor in the election.

been like had Perot not entered it can never finally be settled by data derived from a race in which Perot's candidacy was in fact a major element.

We do know that from his first entry into the race—via the novel instrument of television talk shows—in March of 1992 on through to his television blitz down the campaign's stretch, Perot concentrated his fire on what he depicted as the profound failure of the Bush administration to comprehend the severity of the economic problems facing the country and to chart a course toward their solution. He argued that a once-great U.S. economy was in a perilous decline that threatened the historic American promise of growing abundance, not just, as he would say, for us, but especially for our grandchildren. Perot's call was a powerful one because it seemed to many so disinterested—what did the plain-speaking Texas billionaire have to gain other than the knowledge that he had helped the country he loved?—and also because it was so quintessentially American. Perot was no radical bashing the private business system. Instead, he was a man calling for a restoration of American economic greatness, based on such tried and true bourgeois principles as living within one's means and paying one's debts. Political insiders knew that Perot was intensely averse to Bush personally. But Perot, effectively, rarely revealed any personal animosity in his public presentations, and all that most voters saw was a businessman saying that the economic sky had fallen on the watch of George Bush (and, while not emphasized, on that of his Republican predecessor, Ronald Reagan). It is unlikely that the sense of an American economy in grave difficulty would have taken hold as it did, against considerable evidence to the contrary, had Perot not added his seemingly disinterested voice to the argument and campaigned so effectively to advance it.

The makeup of the 19 percent of the electorate who voted for Ross Perot indicates still further the heavy impact that this economic-sky-is-falling account had on George Bush's candidacy. Perot's voters came disproportionately from groups—defined both in terms of social status and political outlook—that had strongly supported the Republicans in recent presidential elections. They hadn't changed their stance on most major political issues in 1992, and in general they differed sharply from Clinton backers. But like the latter, Perot's voters believed the economy in deep trouble, and that its—to them apparent—weaknesses signified the failure of Bush's leadership.

These conclusions emerge clearly from analysis of the VRS exit poll data: Perot's backers were overwhelmingly non-Hispanic whites (94 percent), disproportionately male (52 percent, while the entire electorate was just 46 percent male), and western (24 percent, compared to the 19 percent of all voters coming from the western states). In terms of age and gender, Perot did best among young (18–29) men, among whom he got 26 percent of the vote, while he was supported by only 10 percent of women age 60 and older.

The Texas independent cut most deeply into what have been Republican demographic bases. But these characteristics of his backers seem relatively unimportant when compared to those of a political and attitudinal nature. Republican dominance of the presidency in recent decades has been based on the GOP's doing better among self-described Republicans than the Democratic party has done among Democrats, and vastly better than the Democrats among independents. In 1992, for the first time since 1964, the Democratic nominee got a higher proportion of the ballots of Democratic identifiers than the Republican candidate did of his party's adherents—thanks in large measure to Perot's appeal. Self-described independents favored the Republicans over the Democrats in every election since FDR up to this one, except for the 1964 Lyndon Johnson landslide. In 1976, for example, when Democrat Jimmy Carter gained the presidency, independents backed Republican Gerald Ford by a margin of 52–48 percent. In 1984, when Ronald Reagan beat Walter Mondale by 18 percentage points among all voters, he won by 28 points among independents.[8] This year, however, Clinton edged Bush out among independents, by 38 to 32 percent, in large part, it appears, because Perot got the backing of 30 percent of self-described independent voters.

Philosophically, those who voted for Perot resembled those who voted for Bush though with a more libertarian bent. Bush and Perot voters, asked in the VRS exit poll whether they would rather have "government provide more services but cost more in taxes" or "government cost less but provide fewer services," responded similarly, both saying, by margins of roughly two to one, that they wanted smaller government. In sharp contrast, a clear majority of Clinton voters—55 to 36 percent—opted for the "more government" response. Voters were also asked which should be "the highest priority for the next president": "cutting taxes," "reducing the budget deficit," or "expanding domestic programs." Again, Bush and Perot supporters had similar profiles on this question. In contrast, Clinton's backers were far more likely than either of the other groups to urge the expansion of domestic programs (see Table A.2).

Given their libertarian inclinations, Perot supporters weren't secured on the Republican side by Bush's "values" emphasis. Only 5 percent of them, for example, checked "abortion" as the one issue (or one of two issues) that "mattered most in deciding how you voted," compared to 19 percent of Bush voters. Just 28 percent of Perot's supporters said they wanted abortion illegal in most or all cases, as against

50 percent of Bush voters. Thirty-three percent of the Perot electorate indicated that they attended "religious services at least once a week"—about the same as that for Clinton voters (35 percent), but far below the 55 percent of Bush backers.

But it's not that Perot's supporters were yearning for a shift in social values either. Asked in the VRS survey whether it was more important for government to "encourage traditional family values" or "encourage tolerance of non-traditional families," 75 percent of Perot voters and 87 percent of Bush voters said the former, as against 53 percent of those who voted for Clinton. The Perot electorate weren't looking for "new values"; they just weren't much occupied by social issues, which left them more open to suasion on the economic dimension.

The VRS exit poll found that 89 percent of Perot backers, who by large margins favored less government, had concluded that the national economy was either "not good" or "poor." This was the view of 94 percent of Clinton supporters but of only 57 percent of Bush backers. Clearly, Perot voters simply wanted a restored economy: 79 percent of them checked off either the "federal budget deficit" or "economy/jobs" as the one or two issues that most determined their vote, compared to 61 percent of Clinton and 40 percent of Bush voters.

When asked how they would have voted had Perot not been on the ballot, 38 percent of his supporters said they would have backed Clinton, 37 percent Bush, and 6 percent someone else, while 14 percent said they would not have voted. Some analysts argue from these numbers that Perot had no impact on the final point spread between the two main contenders. But since Perot *was* on the ballot and had been campaigning very actively down the stretch, strongly criticizing the incumbent administration, the hypothetical question of what Perot

---

[8] The 1976 and 1984 data are from the CBS News exit polls of those years.

TABLE A.2   PEROT, BUSH, AND CLINTON VOTERS COMPARED ON GENERAL POLITICAL OUTLOOK

	Perot voters	Bush voters	Clinton voters
Question: Would you rather have (a) government provide more services, but cost more in taxes; (b) government cost less in taxes but provide fewer services?			
Cost Less/Do Less	66%	72%	36%
Cost More/Do More	26	20	55
Question: Which is more important for government to do: (a) encourage traditional family values; (b) encourage tolerance of non-traditional families?			
Encourage Traditional Values	75	87	53
Encourage Tolerance	19	9	42
Question: Which should be the highest priority for the next president: (a) cutting taxes; (b) reducing the budget deficit; (c) expanding domestic programs?			
Cutting Taxes	11	16	14
Reducing Deficit	65	59	44
Expanding Programs	14	15	33

Source: VRS Exit Poll, November 3, 1992.

voters would have done had he not been on the ballot is bereft of utility. Perot voters also indicated on the VRS survey their deep misgivings about the Democratic nominee. To the question, "If Bill Clinton wins today, what best describes your feelings about what he will do as president?" 78 percent of Perot's backers took one or the other of two negative assessments: 43 percent saying they would be "concerned," 35 percent "scared." As a challenger, without responsibility for the 'economic mess' that most Perot voters perceived, Clinton nonetheless got a poor review among them.

But the main evidence bearing on Perot's impact is elsewhere. The data show that his voters were disproportionately libertarian-inclined independents and Republicans who were angered by government excesses and wanted a more restricted governmental role, but who accepted Perot's argument that the growth of the U.S. deficit exemplified the failure of the political class and precipitated the U.S. economic decline. Fifty-six percent of Perot voters said they had backed Bush in 1988; only 17 percent of them had been for Dukakis. They were, disproportionately, demographic and attitudinal Republican voters who left Bush, not for a Democrat, but for a man they perceived as a no-nonsense billionaire interested only in restoring America's greatness.

THE BUSH CANDIDACY

Together with the boost his candidacy received from Ross Perot, Clinton also received considerable, unintended, help from the president himself. No president has seen a sharper reversal in his fortunes than George Bush did. At the conclusion of the Gulf War in early March 1991, Gallup recorded Bush's public approval at an extraordinarily high 89 percent. Twenty months later it stood at about 35 percent. According to all the Gallup surveys conducted during his tenure in office, Bush had an average of 64 percent of the public saying they approved his performance during his first year as president (1989), 66 percent approving on average the second year, an unprecedented 72 percent approving the third year—and then just 40 percent approving (and 52 percent disapproving) for all of politically decisive 1992.[9] Part of this reversal was George Bush's own doing.

As we saw in chapter 7 (pp. 175–78), Bush hurt his own reelection chances by sounding an uncertain trumpet on broad questions of domestic policy. In the foreign-policy sphere, President Bush knew exactly where he wanted to go, acted decisively most of the time, and got high marks for his work from both the general public and other political leaders. But he brought conflicting values and impulses—"individualist" on the one hand, "inclusionist" on the other, as we saw in chapter 7—to domestic policy making, and this sometimes led to waffling. After the strongly conservative bent of Reagan administration domestic policy, Bush's softer, more middle-of-the-road stance at first got good marks from much of the public. But in late 1991 and in 1992, when worries over the economy and national direction became dominant, much of the public expected the president to articulate a forceful and coherent

response. He offered none, and his standing and candidacy suffered as a result.

The Bush campaign was also widely criticized in the press and even by Republican politicians for lacking direction, never being sure of the grounds on which to base its claim that the president deserved reelection. But Bush was taking a terrible pounding from the Democrats, from Perot's supporters, and from the conservative bloc in his own party, and much of the public had become convinced the economy was in desperate straits. Under these circumstances it is understandable that the Bush campaign would find it hard to set a clear, confident, direction.

EXPLAINING THE 1992 VOTE

The 1992 presidential election broke the Republicans twelve-year hold on the presidency, but did so without altering the basic makeup of partisan preferences in the electorate. The contest was dominated by short-term demands for change strong enough to give the out-of-power Democrats occupancy of the White House for the first time since Jimmy Carter's tenure (1977–1981). But for all of the scope of the reversal that brought Bush down electorally just twenty months after he had appeared so dominant, the 1992 election was a quiet one in terms of the underlying electoral alignment. The Democrats did relatively better in presidential voting, of course, than they had in the three previous elections, but not because they had found a key to electoral realignment. As Clinton strategist James Carville acknowledged, "We didn't break the GOP electoral lock on the White House—we just picked it."[10]

[9]It should be noted that Bush's popular standing for his four years in office remained quite high, despite the plunge in 1992 which cost him reelection. For his entire term, Bush received an average approval figure of 61 percent in Gallup surveys—third, behind only John Kennedy and Dwight Eisenhower, among all modern presidents. The last Gallup poll to check Bush's approval ratings (taken January 8–11, 1993) found 56 percent saying they approved his performance, 37 percent that they disapproved.

[10]James Carville, quoted in *The Wall Street Journal*, November 27, 1992, p. A8.

FAMILIAR PATTERNS IN ETHNIC- AND RELIGIOUS-GROUP VOTING

We saw in chapter 12 (pp. 357–65) that a host of new social-group attachments to the parties developed in the two decades from the mid-1960s to the mid-1980s, transforming the system that had prevailed over the three preceding decades. For the most part, the 1992 vote saw these patterns persist. For example, the ethnocultural make-up of the 1992 vote followed the outline of recent elections, with only a few slight shifts. Since 1964 blacks have voted overwhelmingly Democratic, and they are a key element in the contemporary Democratic alliance. What success Bill Clinton had in the South—winning Arkansas, Georgia, Louisi-ana, and Tennessee—was due largely to his high support among black voters. He was swamped in the southern white electorate. Southern white Protestants, a key part of every preceding Democratic alliance, are now solidly Republican—more solidly so, even, than northern white Protestants, the GOP's historic base (see Table A.3). The realignment of the South seems to have been completed in 1992, when southern white Protestants voted Republican in House of Representatives races—not just the presidency—by a margin of roughly 3 to 2.

The familiar connection in the contemporary era between frequency of church attendance and partisan choice also continued in evidence in 1992. All groups of black Americans, including church-goers, are heavily Democratic. Among whites, though, Republicans now do

TABLE A.3   ETHNOCULTURAL AND RELIGIOUS GROUPS: THE 1992 PRESIDENTIAL VOTE AND PARTY IDENTIFICATION

	Vote for president				Party identification of voters		
	% of the 1992 electorate	% for Clinton	% for Bush	% for Perot	% Dem.	% Rep.	% Ind.
Whites, attend religious services weekly	33	31	53	16	31	44	25
Whites, "born-again Christians/ Fundamentalists"	15	23	62	15	23	52	24
All whites	85	39	40	20	34	38	28
Blacks, attend religious services weekly	4	85	9	6	79	7	13
Blacks, "born-again Christians/ Fundamentalists"	3	86	11	3	79	8	13
All blacks	10	83	10	7	75	8	17
Jews	3	80	11	9	65	13	21
Hispanics	3	61	25	14	49	28	23
Asians	1	31	55	15	26	42	32
White Catholics	22	42	37	22	41	32	26
Wh. northern Prot.	21	36	44	20	29	47	24
Wh. southern Prot.	12	30	53	17	32	44	24

Source: VRS exit poll, November 3, 1992.

far better with the church-going part of the electorate than with the non–church-going. According to the VRS election day exit poll, whites who attend religious services (a third of the national electorate) voted for Bush over Clinton by 53 to 31 percent, with 16 percent going for Perot. In contrast, all white voters gave the president just 40 percent support, 39 percent backed Clinton, and 20 percent Perot. Fifteen percent of voters interviewed by VRS in 1992 checked off the questionnaire category "born-again Christian/Fundamentalist" as applying to them. Of this group, nearly two-thirds voted for Bush. On the other hand, the president was supported by fewer than 1 in 5 of those who said they had no religious ties (7 percent of voters).

During the campaign there was considerable speculation about the impact the "religious right" was having on Republican fortunes, as in its thus-far successful efforts to keep a strong antiabortion plank in the GOP platform. In the wake of its presidential defeat, the Republican party is now often depicted in press accounts as likely to be engulfed in a battle "for its soul"—pitting conservative Christians against those more "pragmatically" inclined. It's true, of course, that any party that wants to win a

national majority must seek to be inclusive, must offer a big "tent." Still, it needs to be noted that in 1992—when by all accounts economic, not social issues were doing them in—the Republicans were kept in the presidential race in large part by the strength of the support Bush retained among religious whites in general and religious conservatives in particular. With regard to abortion, of the 12 percent of voters who told the VRS survey that it was one of the most important issues for them in deciding how to vote, 53 percent backed Bush, only 36 percent Clinton and 9 percent Perot. Their backing among large segments of the church-going public is a resource for Republicans, even as it also carries the potential for making the party too narrow in its appeal.

Hispanic Americans, the fastest growing ethnic group (although still markedly underrepresented among voters), gave the Democrats a clear margin this year, as they have been doing, but again their ranks included a substantial Republican base of 25–30 percent. Given present size and, even more importantly, potential for future growth, Hispanics are an absolutely critical group in the current battle for supremacy. Asian-Americans, a still-small, but fast-growing group, gave Bush one of his best show-

TABLE A.4   WHITE CATHOLICS AND SOUTHERN WHITE PROTESTANTS: PARTY IDENTIFICATION BY AGE

	Democratic	Republican	Independent
White Catholics			
Under 30 yrs. of age	34	42	25
30–44	36	32	32
45–59	40	32	28
60 yrs. +	57	24	19
So. white Protestants			
Under 30 yrs. of age	26	52	22
30–44	22	54	25
45–59	34	38	28
60 yrs. +	45	35	20

Source: VRS exit poll, November 3, 1992.

TABLE A.5   GENDER AND EDUCATIONAL DIFFERENCES IN THE 1992 VOTING

	High-school grad		College grad		Graduate training	
	Women	Men	Women	Men	Women	Men
Vote in the 1992 presidential race						
Percent for Clinton	43	43	44	34	55	47
Percent for Bush	38	33	40	43	30	40
Percent for Perot	18	24	16	23	15	13
Dems. margin	5	10	4	−9	25	7
Gender gap		−5		13		18
Vote in the two California senate races						
Percent for Feinstein (D)	55	55	67	51	82	56
Percent for Seymour (R)	44	39	30	43	17	44
Dems. margin	11	16	37	8	65	12
Gender gap		−5		29		53
Percent for Boxer (D)	41	45	59	46	76	51
Percent for Herschenshon (R)	55	48	36	48	21	48
Dems. margin	−14	−3	23	−2	55	3
Gender gap		−11		25		52

Gender gap is arrived at by taking percentage-point margin (plus or minus) the Democratic or female candidate has among men and subtracting it from that candidate's margin among women.
Source: VRS exit poll, November 3, 1992.

ings in 1992: 55 percent for Bush, 31 percent for Clinton. Democratic in every presidential election since the New Deal, Jews swung further from the Republicans in the 1992 balloting than any other ethnocultural group. In 1988 (according to the CBS News / *New York Times* exit poll) Jewish voters gave Bush 35 percent of their ballots; in the 1992 election, though, only 11 percent of Jews backed him, as national conditions and the Clinton campaign brought many in the group back into the Democratic camp.

Catholics, along with southern white Protestants a mainstay of earlier Democratic coalitions, continued in 1992 their long drift away from Democratic loyalties. White Catholics were just 6 percentage points more for Clinton than were northern white Protestants. The VRS exit poll showed 42 percent of white Catholic voters under age 30 identifying themselves as Republicans, as against just 34 percent calling them-

selves Democrats, and 25 percent independents. Among older Catholic voters, however, the Democrats still have a large margin in party loyalties. The age progression is essentially the same for southern white Protestants (see Table A.4).

THE GENDER GAP PERSISTS

In other areas, too, the pattern of social-group alignments that has become familiar in the contemporary era was maintained in 1992 (see chapter 12, pp. 363–64). For example, gender was again an important factor in candidate choice (see Table A.5). According to the VRS survey, women gave Clinton a 9 percentage point margin, while men favored him over Bush by just 3 points. There was no gender split in Bush-Clinton preference between men and women of high-school training. For those with graduate training, though, Clinton led Bush by a whopping 25 points, 55 to 30 percent among women, while he led the president by just 7 points, 47 to 40 percent, among men.

Continuing a now-familiar pattern of partisan support, Democratic Clinton did far better in general this year among people with postgraduate training than among all college grads. And the VRS survey found no gender gap in party identification among voters with a high-school education or less. But for those with more than four years of college, the gap was 18 percentage points.

In the eleven U.S. Senate races where a woman faced a man, the gender gap was typically large. If one takes the percentage point margin (plus or minus) the female candidate had among men and subtracts it from her margin among women, one finds gaps ranging from lows of just 3 points in Arizona, 11 points in South Dakota, and 14 in Kansas and Illinois, to highs of 27 and 28 points in the two California contests. In every case women voters gave larger shares of their votes to the female candidate than did male voters. All of the women who ran for the Senate in 1992 are Democrats, with the one exception of Republican Charlene Haar in South Dakota. In a number of U.S. Senate races—including those in California, Illinois, and Pennsylvania—Democratic women candidates got much bigger margins among highly schooled women than those with high-school training or among highly schooled males.

It's not by chance, of course, that gender differences have become an established feature of contemporary parties and elections. Since the 1960s, many women have encountered new sets of problems, attendant upon their greatly expanded participation in the workforce over this span and as a result of the sharp rise in the proportion of single-parent, female-headed households. Relatedly, family status was again an important variable in 1992. According the VRS study, married voters gave Bush a slight margin. But those single, divorced or sepa-

rated, and widowed all backed Clinton strongly—by roughly 20 percentage points in each case. Variables like gender and family status never figured prominently in the New Deal vote pattern, but they are staples of the current order.

CONTINUITIES IN PARTY IDENTIFICATION

Table A.6 brings together data on patterns in party identification among voters in the last six presidential elections. Looking at this table, we can see how closely the partisan preferences of the various social groups in the 1992 electorate resemble those in the immediately preceding elections and how much they differ in certain cases from the ones still evident in the electorates of the 1970s. In 1972 and 1976, for example, the Democrats' best age group was the youngest voters, their worst, the oldest cohort. In 1988 and 1992, however, things were almost exactly reversed; the Democrats had their best margin in party identification among voters 60 years of age and older. If one looks at all adult Americans, rather than just at voters, one sees the same shift in party ties by age.

In the 1970s, southern white Protestants hadn't yet swung over to the GOP in professed party loyalties. The 1984 presidential election was the first in U.S. history in which a plurality of this group identified with the party of Lincoln. In 1972 and 1976, the Democrats' margin in party identification was exactly the same among men and women voters. In recent contests, however, there has been a clear though not overwhelming "gender gap" in party support. The Democrats have had an edge in party identification among women, but trail narrowly among men.

Over the course of the 1992 campaign, then, little was happening with regard to the partisan

TABLE A.6 PARTY IDENTIFICATION BY SOCIAL GROUP, 1972–1992 (PERCENT DEMOCRATIC—LEFT COLUMN EACH YEAR—AND PERCENT DEMOCRATIC MINUS PERCENT REPUBLICAN)

	1972		1976		1980		1984		1988		1992	
All voters	47	11	41	16	45	15	38	3	38	3	38	3
Male	46	11	39	16	42	11	35	−1	33	−6	34	−2
Female	48	12	43	16	48	20	41	5	42	9	41	7
White	43	5	38	11	42	10	34	−5	33	−6	34	−4
Black	80	68	74	67	73	3	77	−7	77	68	75	67
Hispanic	75	59	73	65	67	52	56	29	64	48	50	26
Asian			NA								32	−1
18–24[a] years old	49	24	41	23	44	12	34	−6				
25–29[a] years old	48	18	40	22	44	18	39	4	38	0	36	−1
30–44 years old	47	13	39	15	41	13	38	6	37	3	36	1
45–59 years old	49	12	42	14	47	17	39	5	36	1	37	4
60 and older	42	−8	45	13	46	10	40	−1	42	7	45	11
Protestant	40	−5	37	7	38	0	32	−12	33	−10	33	−11
Catholic	57	33	45	28	49	27	45	18	40	8	43	12
Jewish	68	59	55	47	63	48	60	44	55	37	65	42
None	42	21	41	26	37	17	46	24	41	16	43	26
Northern wh. Prot.	31	−24	31	−4	31	−14	26	−23	28	−19	29	−18
Southern wh. Prot.	49	16	46	23	44	12	31	−10	30	−14	32	−12
Northern wh. Cath.	55	29	41	22	49	27	44	17	37	5	41	10
Southern wh. Cath.	64	43	57	42	46	16	38	1	30	−13	39	3
Union affiliation	58	32	49	31	53	31	49	24	50	25	49	24
No union affiliation	42	2	37	9	40	7	34	−6	34	−5	36	−2
Less than high school					55	28	53	23	55	29	55	27
High school grad					50	23	41	7	45	13	43	11
Some college			NA		40	9	36	−1	35	−1	36	0
College grad					37	4	34	−3	31	−9	35	−3
Blue collar worker	56	28	48	30	51	28	44	17	46	19		
White collar worker/ prof./mgr.	43	7	33	5	38	5	36	0	32	−7		
Unemployed	52	22	53	37	50	23	54	35	56	34	NA	
Homemaker	47	8					37	−4	37	0		
Student	46	19	NA				41	6	39	2		
Retired	41	−7					39	−1	42	7		

[a]The distributions in 1988 and 1992 are for persons 18–29 years of age.

The second column for each election year shows the gap between percentage Democratic and percentage Republican; a minus sign indicates a gap favorable to the Republicans.

Source: Election day surveys of voters (exit polls), 1972–88: CBS/*New York Times;* 1992: Voter Research and Surveys.

After over a quarter-century of government service, George Bush returns to private life following the 1992 election.

makeup and outlook of the American electorate, after the intense partisan ferment of the late 1960s on through the early 1980s. Having settled into a new partisan era, the electorate showed no inclination to realign its voting pattern in 1992. It did, however, opt for change in presidential leadership—and a new approach to some very stiff challenges.

CHALLENGES TO THE NEW CLINTON ADMINISTRATION

William Jefferson Clinton took the oath of office on January 20, 1993, as the nation's forty-second president. In his inaugural speech, he issued a strong call for American renewal. In his most eloquent moment, the new president observed that "our Founders saw themselves in the light of posterity. We can do no less. Anyone who has ever watched a child's eyes wander into sleep knows what posterity is. Posterity is the world to come—the world for whom we hold our ideals, from whom we have borrowed our planet, and to whom we bear sacred responsibility."

Though he won office with only 43 percent of the popular vote, Bill Clinton assumed the presidency with large majorities of Americans expressing at least cautious optimism that he would be able to make headway in many areas of policy and governance. For example, an ABC News / *Washington Post* poll of January 14–17, 1993, found 62 percent of those interviewed expecting the Clinton administration to make "substantial progress" in reducing unemployment, 70 percent in improving education, and 68 percent in dealing with environmental problems.

Nonetheless, the new administration quickly found itself off to an unusually shaky start. Its first days in office were dominated by a struggle between the president and Pentagon officials over his stated intention to remove the ban on homosexuals serving in the country's armed forces. Clinton found himself in open conflict not only with military leaders—including Colin Powell, chairman of the joint chiefs of staff—but with influential Democrats in Congress as well—among them Senate Armed Services Committee chairman, Sam Nunn of Georgia. Immediately on the heels of this dispute came the embarrassment of withdrawing two candidates for the key cabinet slot of attorney general: Clinton's first choice, former Aetna Insurance Company vice-president and general counsel Zoë Baird, when it became known she had violated federal immigration and tax law by employing an undocumented alien as a nanny and then not paying the required Social

Security taxes; and his second choice, federal district court judge Kimba Wood, when the administration feared she would bring it further embarrassment over her own version of what came to be known as "the Zoë Baird problem" (though in fact, Judge Wood's case was different as she had broken no law). In all this, Clinton and his new government were left looking clumsy politically. Women's groups charged the new administration with imposing different, higher standards on women who would assume high posts in it than on its male members; others faulted Clinton with starting the problem in the first place by deciding that a factor other than merit and political philosophy—in this case, gender—should figure prominently in the choice. The administration had decided that the new attorney general would be a women. It finally succeeded in this effort when its third selection, Janet Reno, won con-

firmation as attorney general, without opposition. Reno had been state's attorney, an elective position in Dade County, Florida, since 1978.

Part of the problem in this unsettling beginning wasn't of Bill Clinton's doing. It used to be that presidents were given "honey months"—but no more. Problems come winging thick and fast, before incoming staff have even learned their way around the West Wing of the White House. Pervasive electronic communications bring every presidential move under intense, instantaneous national scrutiny. And elements of the press now seem to think they have a solemn constitutional responsibility to pounce upon those in positions of authority. Reflecting the latter mindset, *New York Times* columnist Anthony Lewis noted that during the 1992 campaign many Republicans had charged the press with bias against George Bush. "Well, ladies and gentlemen," Lewis crowed, "look at

Shortly after assuming office, President Clinton met with congressional leaders in hopes of getting his programs enacted.

the press now and think again. Reporters and commentators are savaging Bill Clinton."[11] Such behavior, he concluded, "comes naturally to a free press." Any free press will, of course, air criticism of presidents and other political leaders. But in our time, for a variety of reasons including the spread of new professional norms, American journalism has become increasingly enveloped in a "adversary culture" (see chapter 13, especially pp. 408–10, 412–15).

And how an administration is seen handling itself politically is important: If other elements in the Washington political community conclude that a president and his team lack sufficient political savvy, they will be more likely to challenge the administration. Still, it may fairly be objected that too much attention gets focused on the cosmetics of political strategy and not enough on the substantial problems facing the United States and on how successfully, or unsuccessfully, the administration deals with this substance. The Clinton administration will ultimately be judged in large measure on how ably it responds to the great foreign and domestic challenges before it.

FOREIGN POLICY

For a brief while, in the wake of the collapse of the Soviet empire in eastern Europe, and then of the Soviet Union itself, some observers felt the United States might be entering a period in which foreign-policy matters would loom less large than they had in the past. Any such notion has, of course, quickly been vanquished. The world is a very different place now in the early 1990s than it was a decade ago, and in some important way involving vital American interests it is a less dangerous place. Nuclear proliferation is a terrible problem, and one cannot rule out the possibility that some country will launch nuclear weapons against another, but still, the threat of all-out nuclear war has been greatly diminished.

In most regards, though, the foreign-policy challenges facing the new administration are at least as demanding and perplexing as those faced by any previous presidency. For one thing, the collapse of the communist systems in eastern Europe and the former USSR has unleashed a new round of ethnic conflict of which the brutal fighting in Bosnia-Herzegovina is only the most dramatic and tragic example. Foreign-affairs writers at the *New York Times* recently identified forty-nine countries in which violence is occurring as a result of contending demands of various ethnic groups.[12] Not all of these cases impose major demands on American foreign policy, but many do. What was once a united Yugoslavia is now in ethnic conflagration, and there will be continuing insistence that the United States play a big part in dousing those flames. American troops were sent to Somalia in December of 1992 to help end clan fighting that had escalated into a full-fledged civil war, claiming hundreds of thousands of lives and leaving many more facing starvation. The old ethnic and religious divisions of the Middle East are as threatening and as dangerous as ever.

In these and other cases, Clinton administration foreign-policy makers will have to decide on the form and terms of U.S. involvement. And they will have to do so in an environment in which there are strong pressures—encouraged by the administration itself—to scale back U.S. military spending. In the field of foreign affairs, President Clinton will indeed be asked to do more (in ending conflicts abroad, reducing suffering, helping to nurture democracy in Russia and other countries caught up in politi-

---

[11] Anthony Lewis, "Not a Rose Garden," *The New York Times*, February 1, 1993, p. A19.

[12] David Binder and Barbara Crossette, "As Ethnic Wars Multiply, U.S. Strives for a Policy," *The New York Times*, February 7, 1993, pp. 1, 14.

cal change, and protecting vital American interests) with less by way of military resources.

DOMESTIC POLICY

Domestically, the Clinton administration has said that its principal objectives are (1) reforming the health care system, including curbing costs and extending coverage; (2) reducing the deficit, which stood at nearly $300 billion for fiscal 1992 alone; and (3) stimulating economic growth, especially increasing the rate at which the U.S. economy generates jobs. In the latter quest, the administration will seemingly be aided in its first year by the general economic recovery already proceeding. In the other two areas, however, health care reform and deficit reduction, Clinton and his advisors confront a daunting political challenge. The, sharp disagreements between entrenched opposing interests make coming to coherent and sustained policy extremely difficult.

Health Care Concerns. Health care issues are extraordinarily complex and demanding. Costs have been soaring for two decades now. In 1965 the United States spent slightly less than 6 percent of its gross domestic product (GDP) on health; by 1991, however, the proportion of GDP going to health had risen to 13 percent— with no end to the increases in sight. (See chapter 15, pp. 498–500, for further discussion of this problem.) Controlling for the effects of inflation, we are today spending three times as much per person on health care as we spent just three decades ago (see Figure A.2, next page). These developments have plainly shaken the confidence of much of the public that they will not be overwhelmed by future health expenses, even if at present their insurance coverage is adequate (see Figure A.3, next page). And they are asking questions like: "What if I lose my insurance through a change or loss of job?" At one level, then, the challenge to Clin-

ton administration policy makers is clear: They must restore a sense of security in the health care arena that has been shaken badly by a cost surge that is truly out of control. But what are the best mechanisms by which to get costs under control?

During the campaign, candidate Clinton showed a great deal of interest in an approach known as managed competition. At the center of all managed competition plans is the establishment of new, quasi-public organizations called health-insurance purchasing cooperatives (HIPCs). These regional or statewide cooperatives would act as purchasing agents for health-insurance buyers—employers and individuals alike. Representing hundreds of thousands of potential patients, each would have great economic clout. The federal government would set a minimum package of benefits each HIPC would have to offer, assuring at least basic coverage for all and facilitating price comparisons between cooperatives. Each HIPC would also be required to accept all applicants

Hilary Rodham Clinton, who heads up the task force on health care reform, talks to reporters with Senate majority leader George Mitchell.

FIGURE A.2 SOARING HEALTH CARE COSTS

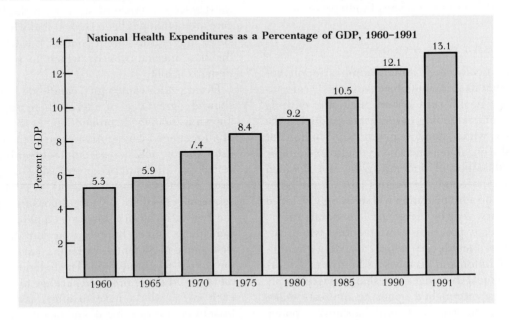

National Health Expenditures as a Percentage of GDP, 1960–1991

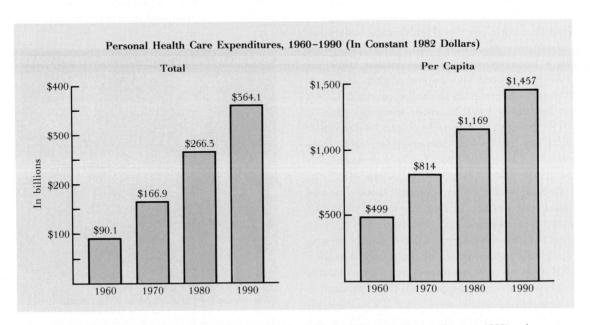

Personal Health Care Expenditures, 1960–1990 (In Constant 1982 Dollars)

Source: U.S. Health Care Financing Administration (HCFA), *Health Care Financing Review* (Summer 1992) and unpublished HCFA data; U.S. Bureau of the Census, *Statistical Abstract of the United States, 1992,* p. 8.

FIGURE A.3 THE PUBLIC'S ASSESSMENT OF THE PROBLEM: "IT'S THE COST, STUPID!"

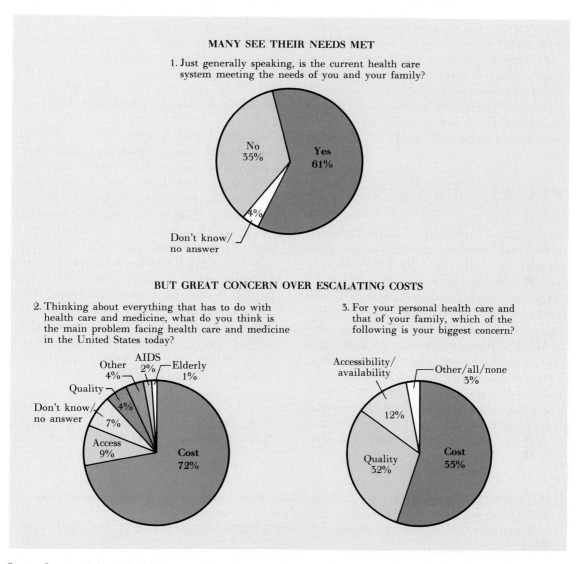

Source: Question 1: Survey by Mellman and Lazarus / Public Opinion Strategies, January 4–5, 1992; *Question 2:* Survey by Gallup Organization, January 23–February 17, 1992; *Question 3:* Survey by the Gallup Organization, June 1992.

for insurance, regardless of their health. Finally, in a number of the managed-competition proposals, employers would be allowed to subsidize no more than the price of the least expensive coverage. If an individual wanted more extensive coverage than that, he or she would have to pay the difference.

The Clinton task force on health care reform,

chaired by Hillary Rodham Clinton, was fever-ishly at work in the winter and spring of 1993, charged with bringing a set of comprehensive proposals to Congress and the country by May 1. Other ideas considered last March included limits on the fees physicians could charge for various treatments and curbs on doctors' liabil-ity lawsuits. The cost of malpractice insurance has increased so much in recent years that it has become a significant item in overall health costs.

TAXES, SPENDING, AND THE DEFICIT

On February 17, 1993, Bill Clinton presented his first budget message to the Congress. His sweeping proposals called for $267 billion in new taxes over the next four fiscal years (1994–1997). He also proposed about $100 billion in new spending over this span—for transporta-tion, environment, housing, food stamps, and the Head Start program in education, among a wide range of programs—as well as $60 billion in tax incentives. The latter would include tax credits to encourage the development of certain businesses. Finally, the president proposed various "spending changes" designed to save money. The amount of the latter is hard to estimate because, as *Congressional Quarterly* (a leading independent Washington magazine) noted in a special report on the proposed pro-gram, Clinton relied "heavily on accounting gimmicks and cost transfers to states to bring federal expenditures down and reduce the def-icit."[13] In only one area—defense—did the president propose significant reductions.

Reducing Defense Spending. With the U.S.S.R. no more and Russia a diminished military force, everyone agrees that defense expenditures can and should be reduced (see chapter 16, pp. 531–32). But by how much? President Clinton has proposed bigger cuts than those his prede-cessor, George Bush, had recommended. In particular, the Clinton plan calls for an active-duty military of 1.4 million members; Bush had recommended 1.6 million. Just 100,000 U.S. personnel would be stationed in Europe, versus the 150,000 projected by Bush. Clinton also called for additional reductions in various weapons systems. Table A.7 compares the costs of the earlier Bush plan to those advanced by President Clinton. By 1997, under the Clinton

[13]"More Money Comes in Under Plan for 'Savings' in Budget, *Congressional Quarterly*, February 20, 1993, p. 370.

TABLE A.7   THE DEFENSE BUDGETS OF CLINTON AND BUSH, 1993–1997 PROJECTIONS (IN BILLIONS OF CONSTANT DOLLARS OF NEW BUDGET AUTHORITY FOR NATIONAL DEFENSE)

	1993	1994	1995	1996	1997
Bush projections submitted January 1992	280.9	281.7	284.4	285.7	290.6
Clinton projections submitted January 1993	274.3	263.7	262.8	253.8	248.4
Clinton cuts from Bush 1992 base	−6.6	−18.0	−21.6	−31.9	−42.2

Total Clinton reductions over 1993–1997: $120.3 billion

Source: National Journal, February 27, 1993, p. 517.

FIGURE A.4   PROPOSED MILITARY BASE CLOSINGS UNDER PENTAGON PROPOSALS OF MARCH 1993

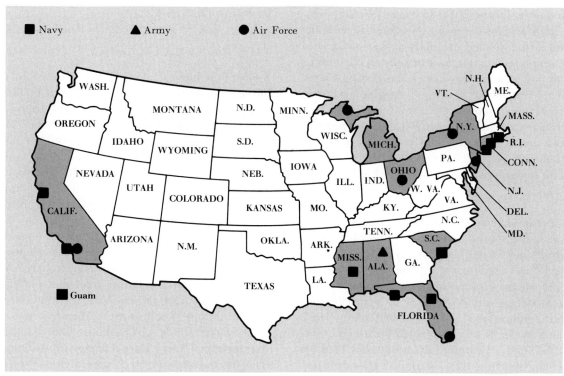

Base closings by state: Navy—Calif. 8, Fla. 3, S.C. 3, Conn. 1, Miss. 1, N.Y. 1, R.I. 1. (One base in Guam is also marked for closure.) Army—Ala. 1. Air Force—Calif. 1, Fla. 1, Mich. 1, N.J. 1, N.Y. 1, Ohio 1. About 100 other naval installations and depots will also be closed or realigned; about 30 army and 30 air force bases will be affected as well.
Source: The New York Times, March 7, 1993, pp. 1, 22.

plan, defense outlays will drop substantially from what they are now and drop some $40 billion more than they would have under Bush's proposals. Many military bases will have to be closed, which will have a serious impact on local economies around the country. Figure A.4 shows the base closings that Pentagon officers recommended to Secretary of Defense Les Aspin in March 1993. Because the downscaling of defense will be painful for many Americans employed in defense industries, as well as the many communities that have grown up around bases, President Clinton has proposed various measures, including funds for retraining displaced workers, to ease the transition.

Raising Taxes. The tax increases the president proposed to help curb the deficit would affect a large proportion of taxpayers. There would be a new top income tax rate of 36 percent for taxable incomes above $140,000 for couples ($115,000 for individuals). People with taxable incomes above $250,000 would pay an additional 10 percent income tax surcharge. Retired persons earning over $32,000 (for couples) or $25,000 (for individuals) would pay tax on a higher proportion of their Social Security benefits than previously. A new comprehensive tax would be applied on many different forms of energy, including gasoline and oil, coal, natural gas, and nuclear power. Corporation taxes would be hiked, and the deductions business can claim, limited. (In thinking about these proposals made by President Clinton, remember that when this was written they were just that—proposals. There will be a lot of pulling and tugging in Congress before final action is taken.)

Controlling the Federal Deficit. In his budget address the president made proposals that, he said, would "[reduce] the federal deficit, honestly and credibly. . . ." If all the Clinton tax and spending proposals were enacted, the federal deficit would still rise by approximately $262 billion for 1994, by $242 billion for 1995, and by $916 billion for 1994 through 1997 combined. So where is the reduction? Without changes netting the amount the president recommended, the annual deficits for 1994–1997 would be $1,241 billion or $325 billion larger than the $916 billion projected with the changes enacted.

According to analysis made by the staff of *Congressional Quarterly*, the deficit control plan set, forth by President Clinton on February 17 relied much more heavily on tax increases than on spending cuts.[14] This disproportionate reliance on new taxes drew criticism—from Republicans, from independent Ross Perot, and from many Democrats, especially those in the more conservative wing of the party. So early on, a strong effort got underway in Congress to

---

[14]George Hager, "President Throws Down Gauntlet," *Congressional Quarterly*, February 20, 1993, p. 358.

shift deficit reduction toward greater spending cuts, and Clinton signaled a readiness to compromise on this matter.

THE FEDERAL COURTS

Some of the biggest changes made by the Clinton administration are likely to come in the composition of the federal courts. The Democratically controlled Senate dragged its feet in approving Bush administration choices to fill vacant court seats, and Clinton took office with about 115 positions unfilled. In addition, retirements and resignations from the federal judiciary are now running at about 10 a month. All in all, President Clinton may be able to appoint 400 district court and courts of appeal judges over the next four years (see Figure A.5). He has pledged that he will appoint greater numbers of women and minorities than did his predecessors. And, together, his nominees are almost certain to reflect more liberal perspectives on various legal questions than did the nominees of George Bush and Ronald Reagan. The announcement by Justice Byron White that he would retire at the end of the Supreme Court's term in the summer of 1993 gave Clinton his first opportunity to reshape the philosophical makeup of the nation's highest judicial body. The battle to shape judicial policy thus shifts in the Democrats' favor, after twelve years of Republican advantage.

THE CLINTON TEAM

He promised that his cabinet and other key appointees together would "look like America," and both women and blacks are more heavily represented in the top echelons of the Clinton administration than in any of its predecessors.

FIGURE A.5   SHAPING THE FEDERAL BENCH: THE TOTAL NUMBER OF FEDERAL JUDGES APPOINTED SINCE FRANKLIN D. ROOSEVELT

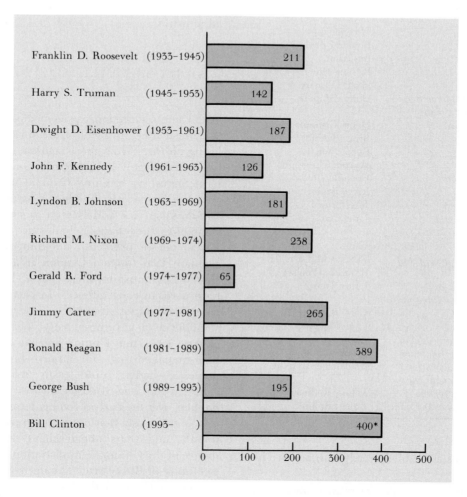

*Estimate.
Federal Judges include Supreme Court justices, court of appeals judges, and district court judges.
Source: Administrative Office of the United States Courts and *The New York Times*, March 8, 1993, pp. 1, B9.

Not surprisingly, many Clinton appointees are veterans of the Carter administration—the last time the Democrats controlled the executive branch. This is especially true of the State Department: Secretary of State Warren Chris-topher was the principal deputy to Jimmy Carter's first secretary of state, Cyrus Vance, and many of Christopher's key aides also held State Department posts under Carter. Table A.8 lists the principal officials and advisers that Bill

TABLE A.8 THE CLINTON CABINET AND OTHER KEY APPOINTMENTS (AS OF MARCH 1993)

Cabinet appointments

Agriculture	Michael Espy
Commerce	Ronald Brown
Defense	Les Aspin
Education	Richard Riley
Energy	Hazel O'Leary
Health and Human Services	Donna Shalala
Housing and Urban Development	Henry Cisneros
Interior	Bruce Babbitt
Labor	Robert Reich
State	Warren Christopher
Transportation	Frederico Peña
Treasury	Lloyd Bentsen
Veterans Affairs	Jesse Brown
Attorney General	Janet Reno

Other key positions

White House chief of staff	Thomas McLarty III
CIA director	R. James Woolsey
Economic adviser	Laura Tyson
Environmental Protection Agency	Carol Browner
OMB director	Leon Panetta
National security adviser	Anthony Lake
U.S. trade representative	Mickey Kantor
U.N. Ambassador	Madeleine Albright
Task force on national health care reform	Hillary Rodham Clinton
National Economic Council	Robert Rubin

Clinton has assembled to help him achieve his goals.

The most striking administrative change made early on by the Clinton administration involves the establishment of a National Economic Council—chaired by senior White House aide, Robert Rubin—to coordinate administration policies in the varied areas of economic activity. All of the departments and agencies involved in economic policy making are represented on the new council. In another change, as noted, Hillary Rodham Clinton, the president's wife, has assumed formal policy responsibilities as chair of a new interagency task force on national health care reform. It's a huge assignment, critically important to the economic health of the country and the political health of the new administration.

GRADING THE CLINTON ADMINISTRATION

With Clinton's election, the Democrats regained the presidency in 1992, after three straight losing efforts. While the electorate seemed to be moved largely by a combination of short-term forces, by bringing Clinton to power it gave the Democrats the chance again to have an administration widely seen as successful—something they haven't had since the mid-1960s, before problems stemming from the Vietnam War toppled Lyndon Johnson. And should this transpire, there may well be long-term partisan consequences. In particular, the Democrats might strengthen their image and standing as a governing party. Conversely, a general sense that Clinton and his colleagues had managed national affairs—foreign and domestic—badly, could easily rekindle the concerns that bedeviled Democratic presidential bids over the two preceding decades.

It is also likely that public judgments in the months and years ahead about the performance of the Clinton administration will affect the future of Ross Perot. The decisive impetus to support Perot in the last election was the sense that economic management was being botched. Any pronounced sense of political failure under Clinton is likely to stimulate efforts at institutionalizing some political "third force."

How all of this will play out during 1993 and beyond is anyone's guess. Students of American government might well want to chart the early moves of the Clinton administration and offer a scorecard of its successes and failures. How do you evaluate the start of the new administration?

President Clinton with most of his new administration (from left to right): Albert Gore, Donna Shalala, Leon Panetta, Robert Reich, Carol Browner, Jesse Brown, Richard Riley, Michael Espy, Hazel O'Leary, Bruce Babbitt, Frederico Peña, Les Aspin, Henry Cisneros, Lloyd Bentsen, and Warren Christopher. (See Table A.8, p. A58, for the post each fills.)

OPTIONAL COMPUTER EXERCISES

for *The Ladd Election ANALYZER*

THE 1992 PRESIDENTIAL VOTE

Choose "1992 vote" from the "Vote variables" menu as the topic to analyze and look separately at the data on the various respondent characteristics from the "Demographics" menu. Overall, did men favor one candidate more than women did? How did black and white Americans vote? Were there vote differences by age? Look at differences by marital status, education, and religion, too. How did those variables affect voter perference? Was a candidate favored in any particular region? Combine two or more important variables (income, age, region) that describe your parents. How did their group vote overall in 1992? In 1988? [Remember to clear your previously selected group of choosing "Include All Variables" or by hitting [Enter] again with that choice highlighted before selecting a new variable.]

Which political party had the biggest defection rate in the 1992 balloting? Find out how people who identify themselves as Republicans voted? What proportion voted for the Republican nominee, George Bush? Similarly, what proportion of Democrats voted for their party's nominee, Bill Clinton? Looking to independents, what proportion of their vote did independent candidate H. Ross Perot get in the voting?

How did liberals, moderates, and conservatives vote for president in 1992? Did Ross Perot do better among liberals or among conservatives? Was George Bush able to keep most conservatives in the Republican court, or did many of them give their votes to either Clinton or Perot? How big a proportion of the vote of liberals did Bill Clinton get?

GENDER GAP

You saw data in this chapter (pp. A45–A46) showing that women gave a higher proportion of their vote for president to the Democratic nominee than did men and that this gender gap was especially large for men and women with advanced graduate education ("Postgraduate study"). Did this gender gap extend to contests further down the ticket? Examine the 1992 vote for House of Representatives. Was there a significant difference or "gap" in the House voting between women and men with advanced graduate educations?

COMPARING THE 1988 AND 1992 VOTE FOR CONGRESS

You have in the *ANALYZER* data from the 1988 election, as well as from the 1992 contest. We know that the Democrats did relatively better in the presidential balloting in 1992, winning the contest for the first time since 1976. But did they do better in voting for the House of Representatives in 1992 than they did in 1988? Compare the 1988 and 1992 House votes for two key groups: low-income northeasterners, and southern white Protestants and other Christians. ("Low income" may be taken as incomes under $12,500 in the 1988 data and under $15,000 in the 1992 data.) To locate southern white Protestants, you need to pick "South" under the "Region" menu, "White" under the "Race" menu, and "Protestant and Other Christian" under the "Religion" menu— all of which are first found by selecting "Demographics."

VOTE RECALL AND VOTER MEMORY

How accurately do people remember how they voted in an election four years earlier? Using the *ANALYZER*, you can get some actual data bearing on this question. From the 1988 data, you can determine how the different educational groups and age groups voted for president that year. These data are the responses people gave just as they left the polls on election day in 1988. The 1992 data asks people to recall how they voted in 1988. Are the recollections of voters from various educational groups and various age groups significantly different from what those groups of voters said back in 1988?

THE VOTERS AND H. ROSS PEROT

How did those who voted for Perot feel about more government / higher taxes vs. less government / lower taxes. How did they feel about the economy? Did Republicans who voted for Perot differ from Democrats who voted for Perot? Select the appropriate variables and analyze the data to find out.

GLOSSARY

This glossary is intended to serve as a learning aid. Short definitions are given for all **boldface terms** in the text and other terms common to discussions of American government and politics. These may help you focus on particular terms, but for a full explanation, it is best to consult the text discussion. Some listings in the glossary reflect ideas in the text, though are not necessarily named as such. Text chapter and page references accompany each entry in the glossary.

activists Persons highly involved in politics, for example, by running for public office, working in campaigns, contributing time and money to political causes, etc. *[Ch. 11, pp. 311–12; Ch. 14, p. 432]*

Advice and Consent Article II, section 2, of the Constitution gives the president the power to make treaties, and to appoint various executive officials and federal judges, subject to the "Advice and Consent" of the Senate. Treaties require two-thirds approval of senators voting; executive and judicial appointments require only a simple majority. *[Ch. 4, p. 71]*

affirmative action A plan or program involving active efforts to overcome past discrimination based on race, ethnicity, or sex, through recruiting more students from the groups that have been discriminated against in the past or by extending employment opportunities to members of these groups. *[Ch. 14, pp. 439–44]*

affluent society A society where national wealth is such that most people are decisively removed from concerns over having enough food, or adequate clothing and shelter. The economic advances in the United States after World War II left much of the country's population clearly beyond subsistence concerns. *[Ch. 2, pp. 25–26]*

amendment Formal changes made in the language of a constitution, or a piece of legislation. The Constitution of the United States has been amended 27 times since the basic document was ratified in 1789. *[Ch. 4, pp. 82–83; Ch. 5, p. 115–16]*

American creed The American political philosophy or ideology. A body of ideas derived from classical liberalism that has dominated the nation's political outlook and behavior since the eighteenth century. *[Ch. 3, p. 50]* *amicus curiae* **(briefs)**   This Latin term means literally "friend of the court." Individuals or groups, not direct parties to a law suit, sometimes seek to influence the court's judgment by filing a brief—a written argument—setting forth the issues in the case as the group sees them. *[Ch. 11, p. 330]*

anti-Federalists   Americans who were against adoption of the new Constitution in 1787 and 1788, on the grounds that it established too strong a central government, one which would threaten individual and states' rights. Among the leading anti-Federalists were George Mason, Richard Henry Lee, and Patrick Henry of Virginia, and George Clinton and Robert Yates of New York. *[Ch. 4, p. 72]*

appeal   A formal legal proceeding in which a party losing a case in a lower court requests a higher court to review aspects of the decision. More specifically, the term refers to cases that may be brought to the U.S. Supreme Court—the country's highest court of appeals—as a matter of right; this includes cases where legislation is declared unconstitutional. Such cases must be heard by the Supreme Court "on appeal." *[Ch. 9, p. 259]*

appellate jurisdiction   Judicial authority to review lower court decisions. The Supreme Court and the federal circuit courts of appeal have appellate jurisdiction, and all states have appeals courts to review decisions of lower state courts. *[Ch. 9, pp. 258–59]*

appropriations bills   Measures enacted by legislatures granting funds for governmental programs and agencies. Appropriations committees of the House and Senate of the U.S. Congress have the responsibility of drafting appropriations bills for the federal government. *[Ch. 6, p. 167]*

aristocracy   The hereditary ruling class in societies built on the premise of ascribing or determining social position by birth. *[Ch. 3, pp. 47–48]*

Articles of Confederation   The first constitution of the United States, agreed to by the thirteen original states as the basis for their joint government. Drafted in 1776, the Articles were not ratified by all the states until 1781; they were replaced in 1789 by the United States Constitution. *[Ch. 4, pp. 65–66]*

balance of power   In international relations, a relationship where opposing alliances of countries are sufficiently equal that no nation or bloc is able to impose itself on the others. Countries have sometimes sought to maintain an international balance or equilibrium—as Great Britain did in the nineteenth and early twentieth centuries. *[Ch. 16, p. 515]*

bicameralism   Refers to a two-house legislature, in contrast to unicameralism, where there is only one house to a legislature. The United States Congress is bicameral, composed of the Senate and House of Representatives, and every American state legislature is bicameral with the exception of Nebraska, which is unicameral. *[Ch. 4, p. 70; Ch. 6, p. 140]*

bill of attainder   An act of a legislature declaring the guilt of an individual or a group and prescribing punishment without judicial proceeding. Sections 9 and 10 of Article I of the U.S. Constitution forbid Congress and the state legislatures from enacting bills of attainder. *[Ch. 5, p. 117]*

Bill of Rights   The first ten amendments to the U.S. Constitution, ratified in 1791, guaranteeing freedom of speech, assembly, religion, and specifying rights of persons accused of crimes. *[Ch. 4, pp. 82–83]*

boycott   An organized effort to achieve a social, economic, or political objective by refusing to deal with a person, organization, or nation seen as the offending party. Civil rights groups have urged their supporters to boycott products of corporations they consider unsupportive of civil rights objectives, such as equal employment opportunity. *[Ch. 14, p. 432]*

bureaucracy   Literally, rule by bureaus or by groups of appointed officials. The term now connotes an administrative system—governmental or private—that carries out policy through standardized procedures and is based on a specialization of duties. This term also sometimes connotes excessive growth and red tape in administrative agencies. *[Ch. 2, p. 25; Ch. 8, pp. 229–30]*

bureaus   The major working units of governmental departments or agencies. Bureaus like the Public Health Service of the federal Department of Health and Human Services and the Bureau of Indian Affairs of the Department of the Interior have primary program responsibilities in their respective areas. *[Ch. 8, pp. 223–24]*

cabinet   The heads (secretaries) of the thirteen executive departments granted senior status for the breadth and importance of their program responsibilities form an informal group known as the president's cabinet. In parliamentary systems, cabinets have formal statutory responsibilities: the cabinet is collectively the government. *[Ch. 5, pp. 109–10; Ch. 8, pp. 217–20]*

calendar   In a legislature, a schedule containing all bills to be considered. In the House of Representatives, when a committee reports out a bill, it is placed on one of five calendars: *union,* for appropriations and revenue legislation; *House,* for nonfiscal public bills; *consent,* for noncontroversial measures; *private,* for legislative measures dealing with specific individuals or groups; and *discharge,* for petitions to remove committees from their jurisdiction over a legislative measure. *[Ch. 6, pp. 143–44]*

capitalism   An economic philosophy or type of economy based on private property, in which prices are set in the market place on the basis of supply and demand. *[Ch. 3, p. 50]*

caucus   A legislative caucus is the meeting of all members of a political party in a legislature to pick party leaders or decide the party's position on proposed legislation. A nominating caucus, on the other hand, is a meeting of party officials or members to select candidates for an upcoming election. *[Ch. 6, pp. 159–60]*

certiorari, writ of   An order issued by an appeals court to a lower court to transmit the records of a case for review. Most of the cases heard by the U.S. Supreme Court reach it through *writs of certiorari,* authorized by the Judiciary Act of 1925. When at least four of the nine justices conclude a case should be reviewed, *certiorari* is granted. *[Ch. 9, p. 259]*

checks and balances   In the American system, the constitutional grant of authority to the executive, legislative, and judicial branches such that each can limit actions of the others. Examples include the president's authority to veto legislation passed by Congress and the Supreme Court's power to invalidate acts of both the executive and legislative branches on grounds of their unconstitutionality. *[Ch. 4, p. 70]*

civil liberties   The rights of individuals to the freedoms of expression specified in the First Amendment, and to protection when they are accused of crimes. Civil liberties problems typically involve persons made unpopular by their individual beliefs or actions—rather than by attributes of birth like race or sex. *[Ch. 14, pp. 421–23]*

civil rights   For a long time synonymous with the claims of black Americans for nondiscrimination and equal treatment under the laws, civil rights is now seen to encompass all groups in the population that have encountered categoric discrimination, such as other ethinic minorities and women. Membership in groups subject to this kind of discrimination is something over which individuals have no control. *[Ch. 14, pp. 421–23]*

civil service   Civilian employees of government who gain their employment through the nonpolitical standards and tests of a merit system. A civil service took shape in the United States following legislative reforms of the late nineteenth century that were designed to end the "spoils system" under which most government workers were political appointees. *[Ch. 8, pp. 233–36]*

class-action suits   A lawsuit brought by an individual or group on behalf of all individuals who share a similar grievance. The famous school desegregation case, *Brown v. Board of Education of Topeka, Kansas* (1954), is an example; it was brought not just on behalf of Linda Brown but for all black students in the Topeka public schools. *[Ch. 9, p. 259]*

class conflict   Political conflict organized around the contending interests of social classes—such as "capitalists," or business class, and "proletariats," or working class. The term connotes strong tensions or fundamental disagreements among the main economic groups making up the society. *[Ch. 2, pp. 28–32]*

classical liberalism   A broad political ideology that developed in Europe in the seventeenth and eighteenth centuries, brought to the United States by the early settlers, and still the dominant cluster of underlying American political beliefs. A strong individualism is central to classical liberalism, including an emphasis on individual rights, political liberty, private property, and a minimum of restraint by government. *[Ch. 3, pp. 46–50]*

"clear and present danger"   First propounded by Supreme Court Justice Oliver Wendell Holmes, Jr. in *Schenck v. United States* (1919), this test has been variously applied by the Court to determine the permissible boundaries under which speech may be restricted: "The question in every case is whether the words used are used in such circumstances and are of such a nature as to create a clear and present danger that they bring about the substantive evils that Congress has a right to prevent." *[Ch. 14, pp. 457–58]*

cloture A parliamentary procedure used to end debate in a legislative body which, like the U.S. Senate, provides in its general rules for unlimited debate. Senate Rule 22 provides that if a petition to end debate on a measure is approved by three-fifths of the Senate (60 senators), no senator may thereafter speak on it for more than one hour. Cloture is necessary because the right to extended debate is sometimes used by legislative minorities to "talk a bill to death." See filibuster. *[Ch. 6, p. 143]*

coalition The coming together of various parties, groups, or political interests to advance shared political objectives. Each of the two major political parties in the United States is a heterogeneous coalition of political interests united to win governmental power. *[Ch. 11, pp. 321–24]*

comparable worth A doctrine or policy perspective advanced with the support of women's groups and some trade unions to remedy inequities in the compensation levels for jobs held disproportionately by women. The doctrine of comparable worth holds that employers should be forbidden from paying employees of one sex at a rate less than that paid employees of the opposite sex for work of "comparable character" on jobs which require "comparable skills." It thus differs significantly from the idea of "*equal* pay for *equal* work," which holds only that men and women must not be paid differently for performing the same job. *[Ch. 14, pp. 444–47]*

concurrent jurisdiction Authority granted to two or more courts to adjudicate cases involving the same subject matter. The term commonly refers to areas where federal and state courts may hear the same kind of case. *[Ch. 9, p. 255]*

confederation An association of independent states, in which the latter agree to confer certain limited authority upon a central government while retaining their full individual sovereignty. The first Constitution of the United States, the Articles of Confederation, provided for such a system; the thirteen states possessed virtually all governmental power, having simply joined together in what the Articles called a "firm league of friendship." *[Ch. 4, pp. 65–67]*

conference committees Special joint committees of the U.S. Congress formed to resolve conflicts in the form of legislation passed by the House and Senate. Since a bill must be passed by both houses in exactly the same form for it to become law, conference committees are essential elements in the legislative process. *[Ch. 6, p. 146]*

conservative As used in the contemporary United States, a political philosophy that seeks to limit the role of government in domestic affairs and/or to encourage traditional social values and relationships. The term also connotes a greater inclination to project U.S. power in world affairs. *[Ch. 15, p. 470]*

constant dollars The price of goods and services expressed in dollars adjusted to account for the effects of inflation—that is, dollars of constant purchasing power. Unless constant dollar adjustments are made, comparisons of expenditures at one point in time to those at another may be very deceiving. *[Ch. 16, p. 531]*

Constitution A fundamental law that prescribes the framework of government and the nature and extent of governmental authority. The American Constitution treats only the most basic institutional arrangements and powers, and the basic rights of citizenship, leaving it to simple legislation to specify the program details. *[Ch. 4, pp. 64, 78–80]*

containment policy American foreign policy since World War II aimed at maintaining an international balance of power and curbing the Soviet or Communist expansion. *[Ch. 16, pp. 515–18]*

Court-packing plan The famous attempt by President Franklin Roosevelt in 1937 to secure congressional approval of legislation permitting the president to nominate a new Supreme Court justice for every sitting justice on the Court who, upon reaching 70 years of age, did not retire. Congress rejected Roosevelt's proposal. *[Ch. 5, p. 110]*

dealignment The weakening of voter's loyalties to the political parties, expressed in larger proportions of the electorate calling themselves independents and alternating in their support of one party's candidates and the other's. *[Ch. 12, p. 356]*

decennial census The Constitution provides (Article I, section 2) that the number of seats in the House of

Representatives "shall be apportioned among the several states . . ." according to an "enumeration" of the country's population to be made every "term of ten years." The first of these decennial censuses was conducted in 1790, and the 21st census was completed in 1990. *[Ch. 2, pp. 15–16]*

deficit   The amount by which governmental expenditures exceed revenues. *[Ch. 15, pp. 479–82]*

deflation   An economic condition in which the price of goods and services falls—as opposed to *inflation,* which is a rise in the price level. In the 1920s and the 1930s in the United States, there was a dramatic decline in prices, which discouraged investment in new factories and other productive facilities, as businessmen saw the prospect of falling returns on their investment. *[Ch. 15, pp. 467–68]*

***de jure* segregation**   Racial segregation based on the law or the formal policies of governmental agencies. Up until the school desegregation decisions of the 1950s, laws throughout the South provided for separate school systems for black and white pupils. *[Ch. 14, pp. 435–36]*

democracy   Derived from the Greek word *demos* (the people) and *kratos* (authority), democracy is a system of government in which ultimate political power rests with the public at large. The American idea of democracy blends rule by the people with an emphasis on the recognition of basic rights of minorities, which even strong popular majorities may not infringe. *[Ch. 4, pp. 78–80]*

depression   A severe economic slump including high unemployment, a reduced production of goods and services, and a falling national income. The worst of these economic crises in the United States, known as the Great Depression, began with the stock market crash in 1929 and persisted throughout the 1930s. *[Ch. 15, p. 466]*

détente   A description of efforts to reduce tensions between countries whose contending interests and philosophies leave them antagonistic; specifically, the emphasis on limited cooperation between the United States and the Soviet Union in an effort to reduce the likelihood of overt conflict between the superpowers. *[Ch. 16, p. 522]*

direct-action protests   Civil rights marches, sit-ins, boycotts, and other nonviolent actions aimed at overturning segregation and gross discrimination, especially in the American South in the 1950s and 1960s. *[Ch. 14, p. 432]*

direct democracy   Forms of decision making in which the public at large makes the decision directly—such as choosing a party's nominees through primary elections, or enacting legislation through referenda. *[Ch. 4, pp. 85–86]*

direct primary   An election in which rank-and-file members of a political party vote to determine who the party's nominees will be. Direct primaries were advanced by the Progressives in the early nineteenth century to weaken the hold of party "bosses" on nominee selection. *[Ch. 4, pp. 85–86]*

discharge petition   A legislative procedure, used in the House of Representatives, whereby a committee with jurisdiction over a bill may be relieved of its jurisdiction by majority vote of the entire House. The procedure is used when a committee is seeking to kill a bill by holding on to it and not reporting it out for House action. *[Ch. 6, p. 144]*

discount rate   The rate of interest Federal Reserve Banks charge commercial banks for the money the latter borrow from the Fed; the higher the discount rate, the higher the rate of interest commercial banks must in turn charge their customers. *[Ch. 15, pp. 473–74]*

dissenting opinion   When judges of appeals courts disagree with a decision of their court's majority, they may express their formal written disagreement. Strong, cogent dissenting opinions by Supreme Court justices have often had lasting influence in helping to reshape thinking on an issue. *[Ch. 9, p. 241]*

district courts (federal)   The courts where most cases originating in the federal system are first tried. Federal district courts have "original jurisdiction," as the workhorse trial courts. *[Ch. 9, p. 257]*

domino theory   The argument, often advanced in the 1950s and 1960s, that if one key country falls to communist control others might then follow, much as a string of dominoes topple when one of them is shoved over. The most dramatic instance of a domino effect, however, was the *collapse* of one communist regime after another in Eastern Europe from 1989 through 1991, when democratic developments in one country encouraged similar movements in neighboring states. *[Ch. 16, p. 513]*

double jeopardy The Fifth Amendment to the U.S. Constitution provides that no person shall be "subject for the same offense to be twice put in jeopardy of life or limb"; that is, a person tried for a crime and found innocent shall not be again put on trial for that same offense. The Fifth Amendment originally applied just to cases in federal court, but in 1969 the Supreme Court held the protection against double jeopardy binding on the states through the due process clause of the Fourteenth Amendment. *[Ch. 4, p. 83]*

due process The Fifth and Fourteenth Amendments to the Constitution provide that the national and state governments, respectively, shall not arbitrarily deny any person his life, liberty, or property. The idea of due process has always connoted adherence to proper procedures of action established in law, and at times the Supreme Court has additionally interpreted the term as requiring both the reasonableness of governmental actions and limits on the scope of those actions. *[Ch. 5, p. 117]*

egalitarianism A political-philosophic position that stresses the value of social equality. The "egalitarian revolution" which began in the West in the seventeenth and eighteenth centuries rejected the rigid social hierarchy and inequality inherent in the then-existing aristocratic societies. *[Ch. 3, p. 56]*

electoral college Americans do not vote directly for the candidates for president and vice-president, but rather for slates of electors in each state pledged to one candidate or the other. Each state has a number of electoral votes equal to the number of representatives it has in Congress—its two senators plus however many members of the House of Representatives it has. The candidates receiving a majority of the electoral votes (at least 270) are declared elected president and vice-president. *[Ch. 7, p. 182]*

elites Groups of persons who possess disproportionately large amounts of some scarce value—money, social prestige, political power, etc. Political elites exert extensive influence over political decision-making. *[Ch. 4, pp. 88–89]*

entitlement programs Government programs requiring the payment of benefits to all individuals who meet the established eligibility requirements set forth in the legislation. Thus expenditures for an entitlement program such as Social Security are determined not by annual appropriations limits established by Congress, but rather by what is required to give all those eligible for benefits the level of monetary payments the law prescribes. *[Ch. 15, p. 498]*

equal employment opportunity The policy that racial, religious, sex, and age discrimination must be barred in hiring and firing employees and setting other conditions of their employment. At the federal level, the Equal Employment Opportunity Commission is charged with enforcing relevant federal statutes. *[Ch. 14, pp. 440–41]*

equal protection of the laws Section 1 of the Fourteenth Amendment provides that "no State shall . . . deny to any person within its jurisdiction the equal protection of the laws." This clause has been the basis of many important court rulings in the area of civil rights. *[Ch. 5, p. 117]*

equal time rule A provision of Section 315 of the Federal Communications Act of 1934 that requires that broadcasters who permit one candidate for public office to campaign on their stations must give equal opportunity to every other candidate for that office. They cannot sell airtime to a Democratic candidate for the House of Representatives, for example, and deny the same type of time at the same rates to a Republican candidate. *[Ch. 13, p. 397]*

equality of opportunity The political-philosophic position that insists a society should take all reasonable steps to assure its citizens an equal chance to pursue successfully life, liberty, and happiness, but that it should recognize the legitimacy of different levels of actual attainment. *[Ch. 15, p. 492]*

equality of result The position that a society should seek to achieve a condition where each citizen has approximately equal resources—where, for example, salaries are relatively equal. The varieties of socialism seek some measure of equality of result. *[Ch. 15, p. 492]*

establishment clause The First Amendment to the U.S. Constitution provides that "Congress shall make no law respecting an establishment of religion. . . ."

It was enacted initially to prevent the creation of an official church or religion in the United States. *[Ch. 4, p. 81]*

exclusionary rule   A legal position developed by the Supreme Court requiring that evidence or statements unlawfully obtained may not be used in court proceedings against individuals accused of crimes. *[Ch. 14, p. 449]*

exclusive jurisdiction   The assignment to one court only of jurisdiction over a certain category of cases. For example, cases arising from alleged violation of state criminal statutes originate exclusively in the designated trial courts of the state. *[Ch. 9, p. 255]*

ex post facto law   Article I, sections 9 and 10 of the Constitution forbid the national and state governments from enacting any subsequent legislation that makes illegal an act that was legal at the time it was committed or that changes the penalty for a crime after its commission. The Latin words mean simply "after the fact." *[Ch. 5, p. 117]*

factions   A term used variously in the eighteenth century to refer to what we would now call interest groups, or loosely organized cliques of like-minded political leaders—in the sense of a "faction" in a state legislature. *[Ch. 4, p. 71; Ch. 11, p. 305]*

fairness doctrine   Section 315 of the Federal Communications Act of 1934 requires radio and television broadcasters who air material on controversial issues to provide reasonable time for the expression of opposing viewpoints. *[Ch. 13, p. 396]*

Federal Reserve System   The central bank of the United States, including the Board of Governors and the Federal Reserve Banks located throughout the United States, with broad powers to regulate the money supply and interest rates. *[Ch. 15, pp. 473–76]*

federalism   A system of government, found in the United States and a number of other countries including Canada, Switzerland, and India, in which power is constitutionally divided between a central government and governments of the constituent states or provinces. *[Ch. 5, pp. 114–28]*

Federalist Papers   Eighty-five essays authored by John Jay, James Madison, and Alexander Hamilton, published in New York newspapers in later 1787 and early 1788, defending the newly proposed U.S. Constitution and urging its ratification. *[Ch. 4, p. 80]*

federalists   Initially, those who favored ratification of the U.S. Constitution establishing a federal system of government in place of the previous confederal form. Later, a political party whose most prominent leaders were Alexander Hamilton and John Adams, which had its principal supporters among mercantile and other business interests in the Northeast. The Federalist party disappeared early in the nineteenth century. *[Ch. 4, pp. 72–73]*

filibuster   An attempt in the U.S. Senate to defeat a bill by taking advantage of the unlimited debate provisions of Senate rules and talking indefinitely on it, preventing action on other legislative business. *[Ch. 6, pp. 142–43]*

fiscal policy   Governmental efforts to maintain a prospering economy by varying taxation and expenditure levels. For example, if government increases expenditures well beyond tax revenues, its fiscal policy is providing economic stimulus. *[Ch. 15, pp. 469, 476]*

"fourth branch of government"   Refers to the prominent position of the press in government and politics in democracies like the United States—such that the press is seen figuratively as a branch of the government itself. *[Ch. 13, pp. 408–9]*

franchise   The right to vote. *[Ch. 12, p. 351]*

Frostbelt   Refers to the older industrial states of the Northeast and Midwest that have experienced at times painful adjustments with the movement of people and jobs to more newly industrializing (and warmer) states South and West. *[Ch. 2, p. 34]*

full faith and credit   Article IV, Section 1 of the U.S. Constitution requires that "full faith and credit shall be given in each state to the public acts, records, and judicial proceedings of every other state." *[Ch. 5, p. 117]*

gender gap   A term expressing the differing outlooks and attitudes held by women and men as revealed in voting patterns and aggregate responses to public policy questions. In 1988, men gave Republican George Bush a significantly higher margin of support than did women. *[Ch. 12, pp. 364–65]*

gerrymandering Drawing legislative district lines to obtain partisan political advantage. Some legislative districts have truly bizarre shapes, reflecting a party's efforts to carve the constituency to its advantage. *[Ch. 6, p. 351]*

glasnost A Russian word meaning "openness," which in recent years has come to refer to the greater political openness and candor in public discussions of problems and events in the Soviet Union. *[Ch. 16, p. 510]*

global village A term introduced by media theorist Marshall McLuhan to refer to the extent to which the entire planet has been brought together by an awareness of developments occurring in any of its parts. The electronic media of communication, especially television, have been the prime agency of this increased awareness of physically distant events. *[Ch. 2, p. 15; Ch. 13, p. 388; Ch. 16, p. 513]*

GOP Republican; the initials for the "Grand Old Party," a term that came to be used to refer to the Republicans in the 1870s. "GOP" has stuck. *[Ch. 6, p. 156]*

grants-in-aid Funds appropriated by Congress to state and local governments for various programs administered by state agencies under federal standards: health, welfare, and highway construction programs are important ones built on federal grants-in-aid. *[Ch. 5, pp. 122–24]*

gross domestic product (GDP) A statistical measure of the total value of goods and services produced in a country in a particular period. Changes in the gross domestic product of the United States from one year to another are primary indicators of the rate of economic growth. *[Ch. 15, p. 477]*

ideology A set of political beliefs and values that are constrained or linked together. Political ideologies prescribe answers to such questions as how government should be organized, what roles it should play, how a nation's economy should be managed, the distribution of resources among groups making up the populace, etc. *[Ch. 3, p. 59]*

impeachment The bringing of formal charges of misconduct in office against a public official; the president of the United States and other federal officers may be impeached for "high crimes and misdemeanors" by the House of Representatives,

following which a trial on the impeachment charges is held in the Senate. *[Ch. 7, pp. 183–84]*

impoundment The president's holding back funds which Congress appropriated for various stated purposes. Richard Nixon's ambitious use of impoundment in the late 1960s and early 1970s provoked a major confrontation with Congress and led to the passage of important new legislation restricting the president's use of this tool. *[Ch. 5, p. 113]*

incumbency The condition of holding public office. The term has acquired particular significance in recent congressional elections where the extraordinary resources available to incumbents seeking re-election—especially in House races—have given them great advantage over challengers. *[Ch. 6, pp. 131–33]*

independent regulatory commissions Agencies charged with regulation of American economic life, including interstate commerce, banking, and financial affairs, communications, and labor relations. The independent regulatory commissions were set up with the idea that they should be insulated from regular presidential leadership and political direction; commissioners are appointed for long (five years or more), staggered terms, and may be dismissed by the president only for "inefficiency, neglect of duty, or malfeasance in office." *[Ch. 8, pp. 222–23]*

individualism A political and social philosophy that places special emphasis on the rights of individuals and on individual freedom and initiative as the basis for social action. *[Ch. 3, p. 47; Ch. 11, p. 331]*

industrial policy An approach to economic policy in the contemporary United States which blends an emphasis on stimulating economic growth with an enlarged role for government, especially in promoting the conditions for growth. Advocates of industrial policy look to Japan for ideas of a new government-business partnership to stimulate growth industries. *[Ch. 15, pp. 471–72]*

inflation Increases in the price of goods and services. Bouts of "double-digit inflation"—annual increases in consumer prices of 10 percent or more—in the United States in the 1970s prompted a strong public demand for corrective actions by government. *[Ch. 15, pp. 464–65]*

initiative An electoral procedure through which citizens may propose legislation or constitutional amendments by petitions signed by a requisite number of voters—usually in the range of 5–15 percent of the total in a state. Propositions receiving the requisite number of signatures are placed on the ballot for decision by majority vote in the next election. *[Ch. 4, p. 86]*

in-kind benefits Benefits in the form of goods and services, rather than cash. For example, welfare programs in the United States often provide beneficiaries with hospital and doctor's care, subsidized housing, food stamps, and other noncash assistance. *[Ch. 15, pp. 504–6]*

interest group A body of people acting in an organized fashion to advance shared political interests. *[Ch. 11]*

iron triangle Refers to the close interaction that often occurs in policy formation in the United States among the executive-branch bureau with immediate responsibility for a policy area, the legislative subcommittee that supervises the agency and policy, and the interest groups with immediate stakes in the area. It is the relatively closed nature of these bureau-subcommittee-interest group relationships that led to their depiction as iron-hard. *[Ch. 8, pp. 226–29; Ch. 11, p. 334]*

isolationism A description often given, somewhat erroneously, to American foreign policy prior to World War II, suggesting that the U.S. somehow sought to isolate itself from the rest of the world. In fact, American foreign policy was typically based on the premise that the country should intervene in world affairs as its interests dictate, but that its intervention should *not* be through an established system of alliances. *[Ch. 16, p. 515]*

"Jim Crow" laws The name applied to a body of laws enacted in southern states for a century after the Civil War providing for the segregation of blacks and their exclusion from full participation in social, economic, and political life. *[Ch. 14, pp. 429, 431]*

joint committees Legislative committees composed of members of both houses in bicameral legislatures. *[Ch. 6, p. 146]*

joint resolution A resolution voted by both houses of Congress that expresses the sense of Congress but that does not carry the force of law. *[Ch. 6, p. 170]*

judicial activism The broadening intervention of higher courts, especially the federal courts, in policy formation and execution. Advocates of judicial activism endorse this expanded role, arguing that greater juridical protection of individual rights is needed. *[Ch. 9, pp. 252–54]*

judicial review The power of courts, such as the U.S. Supreme Court, to review acts of the legislative and executive branches and, ultimately, to invalidate them if they are held to be in violation of constitutional requirements. *[Ch. 9, pp. 256–58]*

jurisdiction The authority of a court to hear and decide a category of cases. *[Ch. 9, pp. 258–59]*

justiciability The issue of whether courts are institutionally suited to providing remedies in a particular type of case. Is there something that a court can do for a plaintiff if the plaintiff is in the legal right? Does the subject lend itself to resolution by a court of law? *[Ch. 9, p. 260]*

Keynesian economics Economic perspectives and understanding that owe an intellectual debt to the pioneering work of British economist John Maynard Keynes (1883–1946). Present-day Keynesians remain committed to the use of fiscal policy to promote economic growth and to an expanding welfare state. *[Ch. 15, pp. 466–69]*

laboratories of federalism An allusion to the states as desirable places to test different approaches to solving public policy problems. The concept was elaborated by Justice Brandeis in a famous dissent in *New State Ice Co.* v. *Liebmann* (1932). *[Ch. 5, pp. 127–28]*

"lame duck" Reference to the supposedly weakened political position of a president in his second term, who is barred by the 22nd Amendment from running again. *[Ch. 7, p. 201]*

legislative oversight The attempt by Congress (or by a state legislature) to supervise the executive branch as it administers the laws the legislature has enacted. *[Ch. 6, pp. 168–69]*

legislative veto The president or some executive branch agency is granted authority to act in a given policy or administrative area, but with the stipulation that the subsequent resolution of one or both houses of Congress may overturn the executive action. The constitutionality of the legislative veto under the

American system of separation of powers is now under challenge. [Ch. 6, pp. 169–70]

libel   Publication of a story harmful to the reputation of an individual that can be demonstrated to be untrue. In the United States, before libel may be established in the case of a public official against some news medium, not only defamatory inaccuracy but also malicious intent must be demonstrated. [Ch. 13, pp. 398–99]

liberal   In contemporary American usage, a position which favors a more expansive use of government in economic management and the promotion of public welfare. Historically, the term refers to classical liberalism—a doctrine developed in Europe in the seventeenth and eighteenth centuries and brought to the United States by early settlers, emphasizing individual rights, private property, and limited government. [Ch. 3, pp. 46–47]

line-item veto   The authority exercised by governors in most states to veto sections (or items) of an appropriations bill while signing into law the remainder of the bill. The president does not have line-item veto authority. Recent Republican presidents, especially Ronald Reagan, have argued that they need it. [Ch. 5, pp. 113–14]

lobbying   Refers to the various efforts by interest-group officials to influence governmental decisions, especially legislative votes. The term "lobby" was first used in seventeenth-century England, when a large anteroom near the House of Commons was referred to as "the lobby," and those who approached members of Parliament trying to influence them were lobbying. [Ch. 11, p. 308]

machine   The American aversion to strong party organizations has led to the use of a number of pejorative terms to refer to them. Strong organizations are "machines," and their efforts at political influence are "machine politics." The nefarious chaps who head these political machines are the party "bosses." [Ch. 12, p. 344]

majority leader   Usually, the chief spokesman and ranking official of the majority party in a legislature. In the American House of Representatives, however, the Speaker is in fact the leader of the majority party, and the person designated majority leader is in fact his principal deputy and floor lieutenant. [Ch. 6, pp. 153–55]

manifest destiny   The idea, widely shared by eighteenth- and nineteenth-century Americans, that the country was justified in expanding territorially, because of a special virtue and mission of the American people different from anything known previously. [Ch. 4, pp. 48–52]

Marxism   An economic and political philosophy derived from the writings of the nineteenth-century German theorist Karl Marx, proclaimed by modern-day Communist countries and movements as their theoretical underpinnings. [Ch. 4, p. 89]

means-tested benefits   Welfare benefits that are available only to low-income or needy persons. [Ch. 15, p. 494]

the melting pot   The idea of America as a land where people of diverse backgrounds come together to form one nation; the achievement of strong American national unity out of diverse backgrounds. [Ch. 3, p. 50]

merit system   Often used interchangeably with "civil service," a merit system is, specifically, a set of procedures for hiring, promoting, and dismissing government employees on the basis of their professional or technical performance, rather than political preference. [Ch. 8, pp. 233–34]

military-industrial complex   A term first used by President Dwight Eisenhower, referring to the growth in post-World War II America of a big permanent defense establishment and a large array of business corporations heavily dependent upon defense contracts. [Ch. 4, pp. 88–89]

minority leader   The leader of the minority party in a legislative body. [Ch. 6, pp. 154–55]

"Miranda Rules"   A specific set of procedures that the Supreme Court has required law enforcement officials to follow in questioning persons accused of crimes—including the explicit warning to the accused that he has a right to remain silent, that any statement he may make may be used as evidence against him, and that he has the right to the presence of an attorney during any interrogation. [Ch. 14, pp. 449–51]

"molecular government"   A description of the policy process in the United States as one broken down into a series of relatively small, separate and distinct environments where policies affecting a particular collection of groups or interests are worked out. *[Ch. 11, p. 334]*

monetarism A school in economic thought which places strong emphasis on controlling the money supply and the price of money (the interest rate) to secure a growing and inflation-free economy. *[Ch. 15, p. 470]*

monetary policy Encompasses issues of management of the country's money supply: decisions on how much it should be expanded at any time, and such related matters as interest rates and the ease of borrowing capital. *[Ch. 15, pp. 469–70]*

national interest A concern of paramount importance to a nation's security or well-being. *[Ch. 16, p. 516]*

"necessary and proper" clause The final clause of Article I, Section 8 of the U.S. Constitution gives Congress the authority to enact all laws "necessary and proper" to the carrying out of the specific powers and responsibilities previously enumerated. Because it is so expansive a grant of authority, it is sometimes known as the "elastic" clause. *[Ch. 5, pp. 119–20]*

neutral competence The ideal that civil servants would be seen by their political superiors, and would so see their roles, as sources of policy expertise and administrative skills serving any lawfully constituted government, whatever its political leanings. *[Ch. 8, p. 231]*

the New Deal The administration in the 1930s of Democratic president Franklin D. Roosevelt and the new programs of economic management and public welfare that his administration developed. *[Ch. 12, p. 337]*

New Deal realignment The pronounced shift in the standing of the political parties, in which the Democrats replaced the Republicans as the new majority party, on the basis of new policy commitments that secured broad approval. *[Ch. 12, p. 337]*

North Atlantic Treaty Organization (NATO) An alliance of the United States, Canada, and a number of European nations, established under the North Atlantic Treaty of 1949, as a collective defense to balance the Soviet Union and its East European satellites. *[Ch. 16, pp. 518–19]*

nullification The extreme States Rights doctrine, espoused by various political leaders including John C. Calhoun, holding that the states retain the right to review actions and laws of the central government and, if need be, to declare them "null and void." *[Ch. 5, p. 118]*

oligarchy A system of government in which political power is held and exercised by a small elite group, whose position is based on military power, wealth, and / or social position. *[Ch. 4, pp. 78–79]*

opinion of the court The majority opinion handed down by a court of law in a particular case. *[Ch. 5, p. 119; Ch. 9, p. 241]*

original jurisdiction Authority to adjudicate a case at its inception. The federal district courts are the primary courts of original jurisdiction in the federal system; trial courts in every state have this same responsibility. *[Ch. 9, p. 254]*

parliamentary government A system of government where authority is vested in the legislature and in a cabinet elected by and responsible to that legislature. At present, the British, Canadian, German, and Italian governments are examples of the parliamentary form. *[Ch. 6, p. 140]*

party identification Voters' feelings of attachment to or loyalty for a political party. In the United States, where few people hold any formal party membership, the Republican and Democratic parties are seen to be composed of people who simply think of themselves as Republicans or Democrats. *[Ch. 12, pp. 352–53]*

party press Early in American history, most newspapers had avowed ties to one political party or the other and, indeed, depended on subsidies from the parties—printing contracts and the like. Far from espousing the ideal of objectivity or neutrality, newspapers saw themselves as spokesmen for the contending parties. *[Ch. 13, pp. 400–401]*

party unity vote A measure of congressional voting, used by the magazine *Congressional Quarterly*, in which a majority of Democrats are found voting on one side of a legislative issue, a majority of Republicans on the other side. *[Ch. 6, p. 154]*

per capita GDP The total dollar value of the country's production of goods and services in a given period of time, divided by the number of people in the country; that is, the level of domestic economic output expressed on a per-person basis. *[Ch. 15, p. 463]*

perestroika A Russian word meaning "restructuring." The term was first used by Soviet leader Mikhail Gorbachev in the late 1980s to announce a fundamental shift in Soviet economic policy—away from centralized state planning and control toward a market-oriented economy. The term has come to be associated also with the entire sweep of political changes that have occurred in the Soviet Union since the late 1980s. *[Ch. 16, p. 512]*

plaintiff The person who initiates a lawsuit in civil law; in criminal law, it is the government that formally brings charges and is known as the prosecution. *[Ch. 9, p. 251]*

pluralism The concept referring to a society as composed of diverse interests and groups which compete to achieve their social and political objectives and share in the exercise of political power—as opposed to a condition of society where one group or set of interests possesses disproportionate political power, to the exclusion of other groups' interests. *[Ch. 4, pp. 90–91]*

plural-member district A legislative district from which two or more representatives are elected; in the United States, the preponderance of legislative districts are of the *single-member* variety. *[Ch. 12, p. 347]*

political action committees (PACs) Organizations formed by business corporations, labor unions, trade associations, ideological groups, and the like to raise and disperse funds for political objectives—including making contributions to candidates for electoral office. The activities of PACs are formally sanctioned and tightly regulated in federal campaign finance legislation. *[Ch. 11, p. 317; Ch. 12, pp. 369–73]*

political socialization The introduction of young people to a country's political norms and values—through the family, the press, the schools, etc. *[Ch. 3, p. 59]*

polity Generally, a term meaning "political system"; specifically, a term meaning a type of democratic government with constitutional protection of minority rights. *[Preface; Ch. 4, p. 78]*

popular sovereignty The concept which holds that ultimate political authority resides with the general public; synonymous with "government by the people," the idea of popular sovereignty is at the core of democracy. *[Ch. 4, p. 80]*

postindustrial Term referring to socioeconomic conditions which have recently appeared in the United States and a few other economically advanced countries, where the dominant occupational center has moved from manufacturing to the service sector, and where high levels of education and advanced technology contribute to new clusters of political interests as well as to a new dynamic for further economic development. *[Ch. 1, p. 13; Ch. 2, pp. 17–18]*

power elite A group or cluster of political interests held to exercise disproportionate power; a term introduced by sociologist C. Wright Mills. *[Ch. 4, pp. 88–89]*

power of the purse The historic authority of democratic legislatures to control governmental finance by the requirement that no monies may be expended without explicit legislative appropriation; Article I, Section 9 of the U.S. Constitution grants the Congress the power of the purse. *[Ch. 6, p. 167]*

presidential primary Election held for choosing delegates to the Republican or Democratic party's national presidential nominating convention; developed early in the nineteenth century to open up delegate selection to the rank and file of party adherents. *[Ch. 12, pp. 345–46, 350]*

primary election An election held before the general election, in which rank-and-file voters select candidates for the Democratic and Republican party slates; primaries began replacing party organizational bodies—such as state central committees and state conventions—as the instruments of nominee selection early in the twentieth century. *[Ch. 12, pp. 345–46; 349–50]*

probability sampling Public opinion polls now rely on select respondents through statistical approaches designed to give every individual an equal or known chance of being included in the sample. *[Ch. 10, p. 295]*

progressivism A political movement that developed in the United States early in the twentieth century, especially strong in the urban, professional middle classes, which sought governmental reforms to weaken "party bosses" and special interests and to reduce corruption. [Ch. 4, pp. 85–86; Ch. 11, p. 332]

proportional representation (PR) Electoral systems based on multi-member districts, where seats are divided among the contending parties in proportion to their percentages of the votes cast. [Ch. 12, pp. 348–49]

public-interest group An interest group that seeks collective goods, the achievement of which will not materially benefit the group's members or activists; contrasts with more conventional interest groups based on immediate economic interests; includes groups with environmental objectives, civil liberties goals, etc. [Ch. 11, pp. 311–13]

quota sampling A means of selecting respondents in public opinion polls in which quotas of respondents are drawn to match known group distributions in the population—so many men and women, so many young people, so many manual workers, etc. In the United States, quota sampling has largely been replaced by probability sampling. [Ch. 10, p. 294]

quotas The setting of numerical targets for admitting minority-group students or hiring minority employees, with the intent of increasing the representation of groups historically subject to discrimination. [Ch. 14, pp. 442–44]

random-digit dialing A means of selecting respondents in telephone surveys that applies the theory of probability sampling. [Ch. 10, p. 295]

ratification The formal approval of a constitution or compact or amendments thereto. Amendments to the U.S. Constitution require ratification by extraordinary majorities, including three-fourths of all the states. [Ch. 4, pp. 71–73]

realignment A major shift in the partisan support of the social groups making up a society and in the lines of conflict over public policy. [Ch. 13, pp. 352–56]

reapportionment The redrawing of legislative district lines to reflect changed conditions, typically, in the United States, to reflect population shifts following each decennial census. [Ch. 12, pp. 350–51]

reconciliation A legislative procedure in the U.S. Congress through which a resolution passed by both houses reconciles the specific appropriations for individual programs and agencies with an overall budget ceiling that Congress has set. [Ch. 6, p. 165]

referendum An electoral procedure widely used in American state and local governments where rank-and-file voters may approve or disapprove a legislative act; the legislature refers a policy matter or constitutional amendment to the electorate for final action. [Ch. 4, p. 86]

representative democracy A democratic system in which the public chooses representatives, including legislators, who are charged with working out the details of legislation and policy—as opposed to direct democracy in which the public expresses itself directly on specific policy questions. [Ch. 4, p. 85]

republicanism A philosophy of government which holds that institutions and policies should reflect popular wishes, rather than being the province of some elite such as a hereditary aristocracy. [Ch. 4, p. 80]

research and development (R&D) Expenditures for scientific research and technological development required for the development of new products, weaponry, medical advances, etc. [Ch. 2, pp. 17, 19–20]

revenue-sharing A form of federal grants-in-aid in which federal funds are made available to state and local governments to be used largely at the latter's discretion—subject only to the requirement that they may not be used for programs which discriminate on the basis of race, national origin, sex, age, religion, or physical handicap. [Ch. 5, pp. 123–24]

right of rebuttal A provision of Section 315 of the Federal Communications Act of 1934 which involves the right of individuals to respond to personal attacks made on them over radio or television which might be held to damage their reputations. [Ch. 13, p. 397]

roll-call vote (or record vote) The vote by a legislature in which the roll of all members of the body is called, or now in which the vote of each member is recorded electronically. [Ch. 6, p. 154]

rule A set of provisions issued by the Rules Committee of the House of Representatives which stipulate the conditions under which a bill is debated on the House floor—whether and how subsequent amendments may be introduced, the time limit for debate, etc. *[Ch. 6, pp. 143–44]*

sampling error   Refers to the extent to which the results in a sample of respondents in a public opinion survey can be expected to differ from the results that would be obtained if everyone in the population had been interviewed. *[Ch. 10, p. 295]*

secession   The extreme states' rights position which argued that the American states retained sovereignty and could leave the government established by the Constitution if they so chose; finally rejected at Appomattox Court House in 1865. *[Ch. 5, p. 118]*

segregation   The separation of whites and blacks in public facilities; established by law throughout the states of the American South after the Civil War and survived largely intact up until the 1950s and 1960s. *[Ch. 14, pp. 431–39]*

select and special committees   In Congress, committees established to investigate special problems and to report on them to the parent chamber—e.g., the House Select Committee on Aging—and those established to perform special functions for one party or the other in Congress, such as the Republican Senatorial Campaign Committee. *[Ch. 6, pp. 145–46]*

selective incorporation   A series of rulings by the U.S. Supreme Court that the various specific guarantees of the first ten amendments to the Constitution, which applied initially only to the federal government, be applied as well against state infringement through the due process clause of the Fourteenth Amendment—that no state may deny any person "life, liberty, or property, without due process of law." *[Ch. 14, pp. 447–48]*

senatorial courtesy   The unwritten agreement among senators whereby they will not agree to a president's appointment of various officials, especially federal district court judges, if these nominations are not acceptable to the senator or senators of the president's party from the state where the office is located. *[Ch. 9, p. 262]*

senior executive service (SES)   Established by the 1978 Civil Service Reform Act, the SES includes about 7,100 executives in the three highest General Service

(GS) grades of federal employment and in the top levels of the Executive Schedule; an effort to develop in the United States a cadre of skilled, experienced career officials trusted and relied upon by succeeding administrations with contrasting political goals. *[Ch. 8, pp. 231–32]*

seniority   Custom long observed in the U.S. Congress whereby many leadership positions, especially committee and subcommittee chairmanships, are assigned on the basis of length of service in Congress or on a particular committee. *[Ch. 6, p. 148]*

separate but equal doctrine   A doctrine proclaimed by the Supreme Court in *Plessy v. Ferguson* (1896), permitting segregated facilities for blacks in various states on the pretense that these facilities are equal to those available to whites. "Separate but equal" was overturned by the Supreme Court in a series of decisions in the 1940s and 1950s, especially *Brown v. Board of Education of Topeka* (1954). *[Ch. 9, p. 250]*

separation of powers   A central principle of American government whereby governmental power is constitutionally divided among the executive, legislative, and judicial branches. *[Ch. 4, pp. 70–71; Ch. 5, pp. 103–4; Ch. 6, p. 140]*

simple majority system   An electoral system in which victory goes to the candidate who has the most votes—whether or not he or she gained an absolute majority (50 percent or more). Some states require absolute majorities for election to certain offices, which means that a "run-off" election must be held between the two leading candidates when no one gets 50 percent. Members of the U.S. Senate and House of Representatives, and the president, are chosen under a simple majority system. *[Ch. 12, pp. 347–48]*

single-member districts   Legislative districts from which only a single legislator is chosen, typically by plurality vote. Seats in the U.S. Congress, and in state legislatures, are apportioned on the single-member district basis. *[Ch. 12, p. 347]*

sociopolitical periods   Refers to the persistence of underlying social and economic relationships, and their accompanying demands on government, over a span of time. The United States had seen four great sociopolitical periods or settings over the last two centuries: the first running from the 1780s to the

1860s, characterized by rural and agricultural society; the second from the 1870s to the 1920s, distinguished by industrial development; the third from the 1930s to the 1960s, involving a mature industrial base; and the fourth from the 1960s to the present, built around advanced technology, electronic communications, high levels of education and a service economy, known as postindustrialism. *[Ch. 1, pp. 7–13]*

sound bite   The condensation of news, views, or issues into a short (e.g., 30 to 60 seconds) TV spot—a style of delivery highly valued by much of the electronic media today. *[Ch. 12, p. 374]*

Speaker   The chief presiding officer of the U.S. House of Representatives, who is also the leader of the majority party in the House and elected by that majority; second in line of presidential succession, after the vice-president. *[Ch. 6, pp. 153–55]*

split-ticket voting   Ballots cast in which voters support candidates of one party for certain offices while backing the other party's candidates in other contests on the same ballot; split-ticket voting has become increasingly common over the last quarter-century. *[Ch. 12, pp. 355–56]*

spoils system   Awarding government jobs to political supporters of the winning party; widely followed in the United States until the development of merit civil service systems in the late nineteenth and early twentieth centuries. *[Ch. 8, p. 233]*

"spreading the action"   A series of steps taken in the U.S. Congress in the late 1960s and 1970s to strengthen the position of individual representatives—increasing their staffs, enlarging the number of subcommittees, extending subcommittee independence, etc. *[Ch. 6, p. 148]*

standing   To bring suit, an individual must show that he has sustained or been threatened with real injury; merely having an interest in a matter is not sufficient to establish standing to sue. *[Ch. 9, pp. 259–60]*

standing committees   The permanently established committees responsible for legislation in various major substantive areas—such as the foreign relations, judiciary, and appropriations committees in the U.S Congress. *[Ch. 6, p. 145]*

states' rights   In the most general sense, those rights and powers reserved to the states in the American federal system; more specifically, the various arguments made historically which emphasize the claims of states against various federal actions. *[Ch. 5, pp. 118–20]*

Sunbelt   Refers to the warm-weather states of the South and West that have received substantial inmigrations and economic development over the last several decades. *[Ch. 2, pp. 34–35]*

supply-side economics   An approach to questions of political economy in the United States which emphasizes the importance of tax cuts and other measures designed to encourage greater individual initiative, investment, and overall economic growth, especially by reducing high marginal tax rates. *[Ch. 15, pp. 470–71]*

third parties   In the United States, where two parties have historically dominated electoral contests, all other minor parties. *[Ch. 12, p. 342]*

three-fifths compromise   Refers to an agreement reached by delegates to the Constitutional Convention in 1787 over how slaves should be counted in determining how many House of Representatives seats states would get. In general, southerners favored a full inclusion of slaves in the population totals on which representation would be based; northerners argued for a complete exclusion, on the grounds that the southern states had denied slaves their basic rights. In the end the convention compromised, counting toward the total for determining representation a number equal to three-fifths of the slave population. *[Ch. 4, pp. 69–70]*

unanimous consent   A time-saving procedure used in Congress and other legislative bodies in the adoption of noncontroversial legislation, motions, etc.; "without objection," regular procedures, including roll-call votes, are dispensed with when such noncontroversial measures are being considered. *[Ch. 6, p. 143]*

unemployment compensation   Benefits for unemployed workers, first established in the United States at the national level by the Social Security Act of 1936. *[Ch. 15, pp. 485]*

unilateralism   The dominant approach in U.S. foreign policy until World War II in which the United

States elected to "go it alone" in the sense of avoiding a system of regular alliances with foreign countries. *[Ch. 16, p. 515]*

veto The power of a political executive, such as the president, to kill a piece of legislation by refusing to sign it; the president's veto of bills may be overridden by Congress by a two-thirds vote. *[Ch. 4, p. 71]*

welfare state A concept referring to the role of government as a basic provider of individual economic security and well-being; the complex array of social programs developed in many modern societies, in the case of the United States beginning with the New Deal. *[Ch. 15, pp. 472, 491–501]*

whip An assistant floor leader in a legislature, whose responsibilities include trying to persuade his party's legislators to hold to the position the leadership has determined. *[Ch. 6, pp. 154–55]*

yellow journalism Refers to the sensationalism which came to flourish in the American press in the late nineteenth century as publishers such as William Randolph Hearst sought to expand greatly their readership with a stream of color and titillation. *[Ch. 13, p. 402]*

PHOTOGRAPH CREDITS

Page 2, Keith Meyers / NYT Pictures; p. 4, Bettmann Archive; p. 6, (left) NASA; p. 6, (right) Arnold / Magnum Photos; p. 10, (left) Library of Congress; p. 10, (right) Warder Collection; p. 11, (left) Henry Ford Museum, The Edison Institute; p. 11, (right) Hank Morgan / Photo Researchers, Inc.; p. 12, Bettmann Archive; p. 15, Courtesy CNN; p. 17, (left) Bethlehem Steel; p. 17, (right) David Parker / Photo Researchers, Inc.; p. 29, AP / Wide World Photos; p. 30, AP / Wide World Photos; p. 44, Bettmann Archive; p. 46, Bettmann Archive; p. 49, The Historic New Orleans Collection; p. 51, Collection of Davenport West, Jr.; p. 52, Drawing by Richter, © 1984, The New Yorker Magazine, Inc.; p. 54, Bettmann Archive; p. 55, Bettmann Archive; p. 57, Reuters / Bettmann; p. 58, Don Wright, *The Palm Beach Post*; p. 63, Clements Library / University of Michigan; p. 64, The Library of Congress; p. 65, Yale University Art Gallery; p. 68 Warder Collection; p. 70, Independence National Historic Park; p. 76, Bettmann Archive; p. 79, Museo Spado / Art Resource; p. 84, *Time* Magazine; p. 85, Bettmann Archive; p. 88, Vic de Lucia / NYT Pictures; p. 91, Mark Antman / The Image Works, Inc.; p. 96, Bettmann Archive; p. 99, V. Lefteroff / Globe Photos, Inc.; p. 102, Reuters / Bettmann; p. 106, Terrence McCarthy / NYT Pictures; p. 111, The Library of Congress; p. 119, Bettmann Archive; p. 121, AP / Wide World Photos; p. 124, Summers, The Journal Herald, © *The Washington Post* Writers Group; p. 127, (left) ADM; p. 127, (right) Warder Collection; p. 131, National Geographic Society Photographer, Courtesy U.S. Capitol Historical Society; p. 132, Don Wright, *The Palm Beach Post*; p. 138, Ed Gamble, © *Florida Times-Union*, King Features Syndicate; p. 142, Hickerson / Stanfill; p. 143, Courtesy The U.S. Senate; p. 157, Drawing by Ziegler, © 1985, The New Yorker Magazine Inc.; p. 159, (left) Culver Pictures; p. 159, (right) The Library of Congress; p. 161, Bettmann Archive; p. 162, Bettmann Newsphotos; p. 163, Bettmann Newsphotos; p. 166, Ed Gamble, *Florida Times Union*, King Features Syndicate; p. 168, *Baker Communications*; p. 174, Reuters / Bettmann; p. 174, Jose R. Lopez / NYT Pictures; p. 183, Jerome Friar; p. 185, (inset) AP / Wide World Photos; p. 185, Webb / Magnum Photos, Inc.; p. 187, Bettmann Newsphotos; p. 188, Don Wright, *The Palm Beach Post*; p. 196 AP / Wide World Photos; p. 197, Bettmann Newsphotos; p. 199, Paul Schutzer, *Life* Magazine, © Time, Inc.; p. 200, Ray Cranbourne / Black Star Photos, Inc.; p. 201, UPI / Bettmann; p. 203, UPI / Bettmann; p. 204, Ronald Reagan Presidential Library and Center for Public Affairs; p. 209, (top)AP / Wide World Photos; p. 209, (bottom left) Doug Wilson / NYT Pictures; p. 209, (bottom right) "The Far Side" © 1992 The Universal Press Syndicate; p. 222, Kysor Industrial Corporations; p. 223, Stayskal / © 1986, *Tampa Tribune*; p. 235, reprinted by permission of UFS, Inc.; p. 236, Charles Werner, Courtesy *Indianap-*

olis Star; p. 240, UPI / Bettmann; p. 242, Bettye Lane; p. 245, © The National Geographic Society, courtesy, The Supreme Court Historical Society; p. 247, AP / Wide World Photos; p. 250, UPI / Bettmann; p. 257, Bettmann Archive; p. 266, Bettmann Newsphotos; p. 268, Bettmann Newsphotos; p. 270, (left) AP / Wide World Photos; p. 270, (right) AP / Wide World Photos; p. 274, Reuters / Bettmann; p. 281, UPI / Bettmann; p. 284, The Museum of Modern Art; p. 286, Ed Fischer / Rochester Post-Bulletin (Rochester, MN); p. 288, Drawing by Saxon, © 1984 The New Yorker Magazine, Inc.; p. 293, Drawing by Dana Fradon, © 1980 The New Yorker Magazine, Inc.; p. 296, New York Public Library; p. 300, Drawing by M. Stevens, © 1989 The New Yorker Magazine, Inc.; p. 301, © 1988 *Birmingham News* / Copley News Service; p. 307, Mike Peters, reprinted by permission of UFS, Inc.; p. 308, Hy Rosen, Courtesy *Albany Times-Union*; p. 312, (top) Jimmy Margulies, *The Record* (NJ); p. 312, (bottom) *White Liar Post*, Copyright 1989 American Heart Association; p. 319, Jerry Robinson, © 1986 Cartoonists and Writers Syndicate; p. 320, Bettmann Archive; p. 326, Mike Peters, reprinted by permission of UFS, Inc.; p. 327, Bettmann Archive; p. 329, © 1985, Herblock at Large; p. 333, Copyright 1989 by Herblock in the *Washington Post*; p. 338, T. Auth, copyright 1992 *The Philadelphia Inquirer*. Reprinted with the permission of Universal Press Syndicate; p. 343, Rothco; p. 348, AP / Wide World Photos; p. 349, Reprinted courtesy of Steve Greenberg and the *Seattle Post-Intelligencer*; p. 350, Granger Collection; p. 361, © 1987 Herblock at Large; p. 364, by permission of Mike Luckovich and Creators Syndicate; p. 366, © 1987, Herblock at Large; p. 372, Steve Sack, Courtesy *Star Tribune*, Minneapolis; p. 378, Tribune Media Services; p. 389, © 1989 Erica Lansner / Black Star Photos; p. 392, Reuter / Bettmann; p. 393, Tribune Media Services; p. 395, Drawing by Lorenz, © 1988 The New Yorker Magazine, Inc.; p. 400, (left) courtesy CNN; p. 400, (right) courtesy C-SPAN; p. 402, Jones, Brackley, Rockwell; p. 407, C. S. Wells, *Augusta Chronicle*; p. 409, Beattie, © 1987 *Daytona Beach News Journal*; p. 414, (top) Powell, © 1984, Los Angeles Times Syndicate; p. 414, (bottom) © 1986 Herblock at Large; p. 420, Bob Thayer, *Providence Journal-Bulletin*; p. 422, AP / Wide World Photos; p. 424, Dennis Brack, Black Star Photos, Inc.; p. 426, John Shevchik (Ambridge, PA); p. 429, (left) Dan McCoy / Black Star Photos, Inc.; p. 429, (right) Bern Keating / Black Star Photos, Inc.; p. 432, PI / Bettmann; p. 434, Reuter / Bettmann; p. 451 © 1980 *Miami Herald*, Black Star Photos, Inc.; p. 454, United Features Syndicate; p. 457, © 1981 Stayskal, *Tampa Tribune*; p. 466, Time, Inc; p. 468, The Library of Congress; p. 472, Drawing by Lorenz, © 1992 The New Yorker Magazine, Inc.; p. 478, Clay Bennett, Courtesy *St. Petersburg Times*; p. 483, Reprinted with special permission of North American Syndicate; p. 488,

Robert Dornfried, © Rothco Cartoons; p. 495, Terrence McCarthy / NYT Pictures; p. 498, Clay Bennett, *St. Petersburg Times;* p. 502, Scott Willis, Courtesy *San Jose Mercury News;* p. 510, AP / Wide World Photos; p. 512, Vladima Pcholkin / © 1990 Black Star Photos, Inc.; p. 514, Reuters / Bettmann; p. 521, Griffiths / Magnum Photos; p. 522, Tachi / Black Star Photos, Inc.; p. 527, courtesy The National Archives; p. 528, AP / Wide World Photos; p. A30, AP / Wide World Photos; p. A35, Reuters / Bettmann; p. A38, Reuters / Bettmann; p. A48, AP / Wide World Photos; p. A49, AP / Wide World Photos; p. A51, Reuters / Bettmann; p. A59, AP / Wide World Photos.

INDEX